Contents in Brief

Contents

UNIT 8 Property 447

Preface

Today's legal world is changing at an unprecedented pace. In many ways, technology is driving this change. The increasing use of the Internet in the 1990s and 2000s for business transactions is leading to new laws to govern the ways in which business is done.

Even for those students who do not enter the business world through the Internet, legal problems will arise. Thus, a solid background in business law is essential for everyone. In *Business Law: Text and Exercises,* Third Edition, we present business law in a straightforward, practical manner. The essential aspects of every important topic are covered without overburdening the reader with numerous details and explanations of arcane exceptions.

A Practical Approach

Each of the forty short chapters in this book has a number of special features. These features are designed to help your students master the legal concepts and doctrines presented in *Business Law: Text and Exercises,* Third Edition, and to give them experience in applying basic legal principles to frequently encountered situations.

Learning Objectives

Every chapter starts out with four or five learning objectives. Within the body of the text, when the material being discussed relates to a specific learning objective, we indicate this clearly in the page margin.

Facing (and Answering) a Legal Problem

Each chapter starts with an appropriate and straightforward legal problem that will be answered later in the text. It is set off in a manner that makes it distinct from the text materials. Where appropriate, after the materials necessary to answer the chapter-opening legal problem have been presented, the problem is stated again and the answer to the problem is given.

In the Courtroom

Within each chapter, there are three to six special features called *In the Courtroom.* They are set off from the rest of the text and provide easy-to-understand examples.

Chapter Summary

Every chapter ends with a chapter summary in a special format to make it easy to understand.

Legal Terminology Defined

Legal terminology is often a major stumbling block in the study of business law. We have used an important pedagogical device—*margin definitions*—to help the student understand this terminology. Whenever an important legal term or concept is introduced, it is printed in boldfaced type. A definition for the term is given in the page margin, alongside the paragraph in which the boldfaced term appears. Additionally, all boldfaced terms are again defined in a *Glossary* at the end of the text.

At the end of each chapter, all terms that were boldfaced in the chapter text are listed in alphabetical order under the heading *Terms and Concepts for Review*. The page on which the term or concept is defined is indicated after each term. Students can briefly examine the list to make sure they understand all important terms introduced in the chapter and can immediately review terms that they do not completely understand by turning to the proper page.

ACCESS TO THE INTERNET

We have continued the feature in *Business Law: Text and Exercises,* Third Edition, called *Access to the Internet.* These features which appear in nearly every chapter, indicate how you and your students can access materials relating to the chapter topics via the Internet.

BUSINESS TIPS

This feature provides some practical advice on how to apply the law discussed in the chapter to real-world business problems. These *Business Tips* are included in every chapter.

EXHIBITS AND FORMS

When appropriate, we have illustrated important aspects of the law in graphic or summary form in exhibits. These exhibits will help your students grasp the essential concepts pertaining to a certain area of the law or a particular legal doctrine. We have also included examples of forms commonly used by businesspersons.

EXPANDED ACCESS TO THE INTERNET

Every chapter ends with a feature entitled *Expanded Access to the Internet* in which students are directed to additional, useful online resources. Also included, in a feature titled *Online Legal Research,* are Internet research activities that students can perform to explore specific legal sources on the Web.

A Study Guide Is Included

A unique feature of this text is the inclusion of a study guide within the text itself. At the end of each chapter, there is a tear-out sheet, called a "Work Set." These tear-out sheets can be handed in and graded. All of the answers to the questions in the Work Sets are included in the *Instructor's Manual* (discussed later in this Preface).

Appendices

To enhance the value of *Business Law: Text and Exercises,* Third Edition, as a reference source for your students, we have included the following appendices:

A The Constitution of the United States
B Article 2 of the Uniform Commercial Code
C Spanish Equivalents for Important Legal Terms in English

Supplements

Business Law: Text and Exercises, Third Edition, provides a comprehensive supplements package. The supplements were created with a single goal in mind: to make the task of teaching and the task of learning more enjoyable and efficient. The supplements package includes printed supplements, software, and videocassettes.

Printed Supplements

We describe here the printed supplements that are available for use in conjunction with *Business Law: Text and Exercises,* Third Edition.

Instructor's Manual The *Instructor's Manual* has been written by text authors Roger LeRoy Miller and William Eric Hollowell. Having the authors of the main text write the *Instructor's Manual* has resulted in complete agreement between what is stressed in the text and what is fully outlined in the *Instructor's Manual.* Each chapter of the manual contains the following features:

- An introductory section, which highlights the main concepts and importance of the law covered in the chapter.
- A lecture outline in outline form.
- A detailed, explanatory outline of the chapter contents, which is keyed very closely to the text.
- Additional background on significant persons, statutes, and concepts that are mentioned or referred to within the text.
- Teaching suggestions, including points to be stressed, hypothetical questions to elicit class discussion, and discussion questions keyed closely to the text and based on information contained within the text.
- Suggested activities and research assignments.

The *Instructor's Manual* also includes the answers to the questions in the Work Sets, as well as the answers to the Hypothetical Questions and Real World Case Problems.

A Comprehensive Test Bank Again, to ensure consistency between the teaching materials and the text, the authors have written the test bank. The test bank contains approximately one thousand multiple-choice questions with answers and one thousand true-false questions with answers. The test bank is available in booklet form or, as discussed below, on software.

Online Legal Research Guide With every new book, your students receive a free copy of *Online Legal Research.* This is the most complete brief guide to using the Internet that exists today. There is even an appendix on how to evaluate information obtained from the Internet.

Instructor's Manuals for Software and Video Supplements Many of the software and videos that are offered with *Business Law: Text and Exercises,* Third Edition, have instructor's manuals.

Software Supplements

The *Business Law: Text and Exercises,* Third Edition, teaching/learning package offers for adopters and students a wide variety of software supplements.

Computerized Instructor's Manual For those instructors who wish to modify the *Instructor's Manual* by adding their own notes, we provide a fully computerized version of the *Instructor's Manual*. Instructors wishing to obtain these diskettes may request them directly from their West sales representatives.

Computerized Test Bank The test bank is available on the latest version of ExamView, a highly acclaimed computerized testing system, which is offered for IBM PCs. ExamView allows instructors to tailor their exams using software compatible with Microsoft Windows, as well as administer tests online via the Internet or wide-area or local-area network.

Interactive Study Center For those students who have their own computers or who have access to computers through friends, libraries, or learning labs, we have developed unique interactive programs for learning. These programs allow for flexibility in learning the subject matter based on each user's level of understanding.

***Quicken® Business Lawyer®* 2000 CD-ROM** Your students can explore the law in a practical, interactive way if you order with each copy of the text the *Quicken® Business Lawyer®* 2000 CD-ROM. With each copy of the CD-ROM is the *Quicken® Business Lawyer® 2000 CD-ROM and Applications* prepared by Roger LeRoy Miller and William Eric Hollowell. This booklet guides the student to the multimedia part of the CD-ROM. In addition, it presents problems that relate to the topics in *Business Law: Text and Exercises*. Ask your sales representative how you can bundle this CD-ROM and booklet with each copy of the text.

Videocassette Library

We are proud of our extensive videocassette library that is available for adopters of *Business Law: Text and Exercises,* Third Edition. These instructional videos can help you in the teaching of business law in a variety of areas. Many of the videos have specially prepared instructor's manuals, which were written by Roger LeRoy Miller and others.

Additionally, you can update your coverage of legal issues, as well as spark lively classroom discussion and deeper understanding of business law, by using the *CNN Legal Issues* update video. This video is produced by Turner Learning, Inc., using resources of CNN, the world's first twenty-four-hour, all-news network.

Ask you West sales representative for further information on these video supplements.

For Users of the Second Edition

We thought that those of you who have been using the Second Edition of this book would like to know some of the major changes that have been made for the Third Edition. This new edition continues the coverage of the essential legal topics covered in the previous edition, but we think that we have improved it, thanks in part to the reviews and other comments that we have received.

New E-Contracts Chapter

New to the Third Edition of *Business Law: Text and Exercises* is **Chapter 21,** titled **E-Commerce.** This chapter examines a number of important developments in the e-commerce area, including shrink-wrap agreements, click-on agreements, e-signatures, e-agents, the Uniform Computer Information Transactions Act, and the Uniform Electronic Transactions Act.

Significantly Revised Chapters

- **Chapter 5** has been newly titled **Business Torts, Intellectual Property, and Cyberlaw** to reflect the significant revisions to the chapter. The section on cyberlaw has been thoroughly rewritten and updated, and now includes a discussion of the Digital Millennium Copyright Act of 1998, among other important developments.

- **Chapter 29 (formerly, Chapter 28)** has been retitled **Formation and Termination of a Corporation** and now integrates materials formerly included in a separate chapter on corporate mergers, consolidations, and terminations.

What Else Is New?

In addition to the changes noted above, you will find other new features and changes in *Business Law: Text and Exercises,* Third Edition, as listed below.

- **Expanded Access to the Internet** features are new.
- **Online Legal Research** activities are new.
- The answers to the **Facing a Legal Problem** questions are now incorporated into the text and identified in the margin beside the answers.
- **Applying the Law** features have been retitled **In the Courtroom** to emphasize that they are based on actual court cases and decisions.
- **Work Sets** are now included at the ends of all chapters, and the entire book is perforated so that these can be easily removed.

New Supplements

- *Online Legal Research* booklet.
- Web Tutor on WebCT.
- ExamView Testing Software.

Business Law: Text and Exercises on the Web

When you visit our Web site at http://blte.westbuslaw.com, you will find a broad array of teaching/learning resources, including the following:

- **Internet activities** for each chapter.
- **Case updates** from various legal publications.
- **Hot links** to other important legal resources available for free on the Web.
- A **"Talk to the Authors"** feature that allows you to e-mail your questions about *Business Law: Text and Exercises,* Third Edition, to the authors.

Acknowledgments

Business Law: Text and Exercises could never have been written without the extremely helpful criticisms, comments, and suggestions that we received from the following professors on the previous editions:

Helena Armour
Southwestern College of Business
Tri-County, OH

Jack R. Day
Sawyer College
Cleveland Heights, OH

Lucy Dorum
Clover Park Technical College
Tacoma, WA

Austin Emeagwai
Lemoyne Owen College

Linda Ferguson
Virginia Wesleyan College

Michael Harford
Morehead State University

Sharon J. Kingrey
City College
Ft. Lauderdale, FL

Tom Severance
Mira Costa College

Al Walczak
Linn-Benton Community College

Roger D. Westrup
Heald Business College
Rancho Cordova, CA

Tom Wilson
Remington College

Additionally, we thank the following professors, whose comments and suggestions helped us in writing the Third Edition:

Garry Grau
Northeast Technical Community College

John F. Mastriani
El Paso Community College

Thomas L. Severance
Mira Costa College

All errors are solely our own responsibility. We welcome all comments and promise to respond promptly. By incorporating your ideas, we can continue to write a business law text that is best for you and best for your students.

Dedication

To Renaud and Martine,

Someday soon, your hard work
and endless efforts will
have a well-deserved payoff.
Bon courage!

R.L.M.

Para mi esposa, Luisa,
y mi hijas, Alessandra y Mariel,
con mucho amor.

W.E.H.

UNIT ONE
THE LAW AND OUR LEGAL SYSTEM

UNIT OUTLINE

1 Introduction to the Law and Our Legal System

LEARNING OBJECTIVES

When you finish this chapter, you should be able to:

1 Answer the question "What is law?"

2 List the major sources of our legal system.

3 Identify the supreme law of the land.

4 Explain the difference between our legal system and the legal systems of other nations.

FACING A LEGAL PROBLEM

John and Elaine are involved in a lawsuit. John argues that for fifty years, in cases that involved circumstances similar to those in this case, judges have ruled in a way that indicates the judge in this case should rule in John's favor. *Is this a valid argument? If so, does the judge in John and Elaine's case have to rule as those other judges have? What argument could Elaine use to counter John's point?*

Persons entering the world of business will find themselves subject to numerous laws and government regulations. An acquaintance with these laws and regulations is beneficial—if not essential—to anyone contemplating a successful career in the business world of today.

In this introductory chapter, we look at the nature of law in general. We also examine the history and sources—both domestic and international—of American law in particular.

What Is Law?

LEARNING OBJECTIVE NO. 1
Answering the Question "What Is Law?"

There have been, and will continue to be, different definitions of law. The Greek philosopher Aristotle (384–322 B.C.E.) saw law as a "pledge that citizens of a state will do justice to one another." Aristotle's teacher, Plato (427?–347 B.C.E.), believed law was a form of social control. The Roman philosopher Cicero (106–43 B.C.E.) contended that law was the agreement of reason and nature, the distinction between the just and the unjust. The British jurist Sir William Blackstone (1723–1780) described law as "a rule of civil conduct prescribed by the supreme power in a state, commanding what is right, and prohibiting what is wrong." In America, the eminent judge Oliver Wendell Holmes, Jr. (1841–1935), contended that law was a set of rules that allowed one to predict how a court would resolve a particular dispute—"the prophecies of what the courts will do in fact, and nothing more pretentious, are what I mean by the law."

Although these definitions vary in their particulars, they all are based on the following general observation concerning the nature of **law:** *law consists of enforceable rules governing relationships among individuals and between individuals and their society.*

LAW
A body of rules of conduct with legal force and effect, prescribed by the controlling authority (the government) of a society.

Sources of American Law

LEARNING OBJECTIVE NO. 2
Listing the Major Sources of our Legal System

A major source of American law is the *common law* tradition that originated in medieval England. The U.S. Constitution is the supreme law of the United States. Unless the constitutions of the states conflict with the U.S. Constitution, the state constitutions are supreme within their respective borders. These state constitutions and the U.S. Constitution together represent an important source of American law, referred to as *constitutional law.*

Other sources of American law include *statutes*—the laws enacted by Congress and the state legislatures. This source of the law is generally referred to as *statutory law,* because it is based on federal and state statutes.

Administrative law, which consists of the numerous regulations created by administrative agencies (such as the Food and Drug Administration), is yet another source of American law. Each of these important sources of law will be described in turn in the following pages.

The Common Law Tradition

Because of our colonial heritage, much of American law is based on the English legal system. A knowledge of this tradition is necessary to understand the nature of our legal system today.

Early English Courts of Law. In 1066, the Normans conquered England. William the Conqueror and his successors began the process of unifying the country under their rule. One of the means they used to this end was the establishment of the king's courts, or *curia regis.* Before the Norman Conquest, disputes had been settled according to the local legal customs and traditions in various regions of the country. The king's courts sought to establish a uniform set of customs for the whole country. The body of rules that evolved in these courts was the beginning of the **common law**—a body of general rules that prescribed social conduct and was applied throughout the entire English realm.

COMMON LAW
That body of law developed from custom or judicial decisions in English and U.S. courts, not attributable to a legislature.

Courts developed the common law rules from the principles behind the decisions in actual legal disputes. Judges attempted to be consistent. When possible, they based their decisions on the principles suggested by earlier cases. They sought to decide similar cases in a similar way. They considered new cases with care because they knew that their decisions would make new law. Each interpretation became part of the law on the subject and served as a legal **precedent** (a guide for future decisions). Later cases that involved similar legal principles or facts could be decided with reference to that precedent. The courts were guided by traditions and customs that built up in the handling of case after case.

PRECEDENT
A court decision that furnishes an example or authority for deciding subsequent cases in which identical or similar facts are presented.

Stare Decisis. The practice of deciding new cases with reference to former decisions, or precedents, eventually became a cornerstone of the English and American judicial systems. It forms a doctrine called ***stare decisis*** (pronounced *ster*-ay dih-*si*-ses)—"to stand on decided cases." Under this doctrine, judges are obligated to follow the precedents established within their jurisdictions.

STARE DECISIS
A flexible doctrine of the courts, recognizing the value of following prior decisions (precedents) in cases similar to the one before the court; the courts' practice of being consistent with prior decisions based on similar facts.

In the legal problem set out at the beginning of this chapter, John asserts that for fifty years, in cases that involved similar circumstances, judges ruled in a way that indicates the judge in this case should rule in a certain way. *Is John's assertion valid?* Yes. Under the doctrine of *stare decisis,* judges are generally bound to follow the precedents set in their jurisdictions by the judges who have decided similar cases. *Must the judge in John's case follow such decisions?* No. A judge does not always have to rule as other judges have. A judge can depart from precedent. *What argument could Elaine use to counter the assertion of the doctrine of* stare decisis? One argument is that times have changed—the social, economic, political, and other circumstances have changed—and thus it is time to change the law.

The doctrine of *stare decisis* performs many useful functions. It helps the courts to be more efficient, because if other courts have carefully reasoned through a similar case, their legal reasoning and opinions can serve as guides. *Stare decisis* also makes the law more stable and predictable, because if the law on a given subject is well settled, someone bringing a case to court can usually rely on the court to make a decision based on what the law has been.

Sometimes a court will depart from the rule of precedent if it decides that the precedent should no longer be followed. If a court decides that a ruling precedent is simply incorrect or that technological or social changes have rendered the precedent inapplicable, the court might rule contrary to the precedent. Cases that overturn precedent often receive a great deal of publicity.

Access to the Internet

The Legal Information Institute, Cornell University School of Law, is a good place to begin researching cases, including decisions of the United States Supreme Court:

http://www.law.cornell.edu

IN THE COURTROOM

Throughout much of the history of the United States, many states required separate facilities for whites and blacks—separate public restrooms, drinking fountains, theater seats, and so on—including separate schools. The legal principle that supported this mandate (known as the "separate but equal" doctrine) had been upheld as constitutional in numerous cases. The parents of an African American girl in Topeka, Kansas, sued the board of education to permit her to attend a school closer to her home than the segregated school to which she was assigned. The case was appealed to the United States Supreme Court. *Could the Court rule contrary to the precedent?* Yes. In 1954, in *Brown v. Board of Education of Topeka,* the United States Supreme Court expressly overturned the precedent when it concluded that separate educational facilities for whites and blacks were inherently unequal. The Supreme Court's departure from precedent in the *Brown* case received a tremendous amount of publicity as people began to realize the ramifications of this change in the law.

Sometimes there is no precedent on which to base a decision, or there are conflicting precedents. In these situations, courts may consider a number of factors. They may consider legal principles and policies underlying previous court decisions. They also may take into account existing statutes, fairness, social values and customs, public policy, and data and concepts drawn from the social sciences. Which of these sources is chosen or receives the greatest emphasis will depend on the nature of the case being considered and the particular judge hearing the case.

Equity. Equity is the branch of unwritten law, founded in justice and fair dealing, that seeks to supply a more equitable and adequate remedy than **damages** (the payment of money), which is the usual remedy at law. In medieval England, when individuals could not obtain an adequate remedy in a court of law, they petitioned the king for relief. Most of these petitions were decided by an adviser to the king, called the *chancellor.* The chancellor was said to be the "keeper of the king's conscience." When the chancellor thought that the claim was a fair one,

DAMAGES
Money sought as a remedy for a harm suffered.

new and unique remedies were granted. In this way, a body of chancery rules and remedies came into being. Eventually, formal chancery courts were established. These became known as *courts of equity,* granting *remedies in equity.* Thus, two distinct court systems—courts of law and courts of equity—were created, each having a different set of judges and a different set of remedies.

A court of law could grant as a remedy only damages. A court of equity, however, could order a party to perform what was promised. A court of equity could also direct a party to do or not to do a particular act. In certain cases involving contracts, when the legal remedy of the payment of money for damages was unavailable or inadequate, a court of equity might have allowed for the cancellation of a contract so that the parties would be returned to the positions that they held prior to the contract's formation. Equitable remedies will be discussed in greater detail in Chapter 15.

Today, in most states, the courts of law and equity are merged. Thus, the distinction between the two courts has largely disappeared. A court may now grant both legal and equitable remedies in the same case. Yet the merging of law and equity does not diminish the importance of distinguishing legal remedies from equitable remedies. To request the proper remedy, one must know what remedies are available for specific kinds of harms suffered.

The Common Law Today. The body of law that was first developed in England and that is still used today in the United States consists of the rules of law announced in court decisions, including court interpretations of constitutional provisions, of statutes enacted by legislatures, and of regulations created by administrative agencies. Today, this body of law is referred to variously as the common law, judge-made law, or **case law.**

CASE LAW
Rules of law announced in court decisions. Case law includes the cases that interpret judicial precedents, statutes, regulations, and constitutional provisions.

The common law governs all areas not covered by *statutory law,* which, as will be discussed shortly, generally consists of those laws enacted by state legislatures and, at the federal level, by Congress. The body of statutory law has expanded greatly since the beginning of this nation. This expansion has resulted in a proportionate reduction in the scope and applicability of the common law. Nonetheless, the common law remains a significant source of legal authority. Even when legislation has been substituted for common law principles, courts often rely on the common law as a guide to interpreting the legislation, on the theory that the people who drafted the statute intended to codify an existing common law rule.

CONSTITUTIONAL LAW

LEARNING OBJECTIVE NO. 3
Identify the Supreme Law of the Land

The federal government and the states have separate constitutions that set forth the general organization, powers, and limits of their governments. The U.S. Constitution is the supreme law of the land. A law in violation of the Constitution, no matter what its source, will be declared unconstitutional and will not be enforced.

The Tenth Amendment to the U.S. Constitution, which defines the powers and limitations of the federal government, reserves all powers not granted to the federal government to the states. Unless they conflict with the U.S. Constitution, state constitutions are supreme within their respective borders. The complete text of the U.S. Constitution is presented in Appendix A.

IN THE COURTROOM

A state legislature enacts a law that outlaws all religions that do not derive from the Judeo-Christian tradition. Joe, who follows beliefs based on Native American religious traditions, and Samantha, whose religious beliefs derive from traditions in the Far East, file a lawsuit against the state to stop the enforcement of this new law. Joe and Samantha explain to the court that the U.S. Constitution provides protection for the free exercise of religion.

Is this state law valid? No. The U.S. Constitution is the supreme law of the land. A law in violation of the Constitution will be declared unconstitutional. *Can the judge grant Joe and Samantha the remedy that they request?* Yes. The judge can order the state to stop its enforcement of the law.

STATUTORY LAW

Statutes enacted by Congress and the various state legislative bodies make up another source of law, which, as mentioned earlier, is generally referred to as **statutory law.** The statutory law of the United States also includes the ordinances passed by cities and counties, none of which can violate the U.S. Constitution or the relevant state constitution. Today, legislative bodies and regulatory agencies assume an ever-increasing share of lawmaking. Much of the work of modern courts consists of interpreting what the rulemakers meant when a law was passed and applying the law to a present set of facts.

STATUTORY LAW
Laws enacted by a legislative body (as opposed to constitutional law, administrative law, or case law).

The Internet Law Library, sponsored by the U.S. House of Representatives, offers links to legislative and regulatory materials:

http://law.house.gov/

Uniform Laws. No two states in the United States have identical statutes, constitutions, and case law. In other words, state laws differ from state to state. The differences among state laws were even more notable in the 1800s, when conflicting state statutes frequently made the rapidly developing trade and commerce among the states very difficult. To counter these problems, a group of legal scholars and lawyers formed the National Conference of Commissioners on Uniform State Laws (NCCUSL) in 1892 to draft uniform statutes for adoption by the states. The NCCUSL still exists today and continues to issue uniform statutes.

Adoption of a uniform law is a state matter. Furthermore, a state may reject all or part of the statute or rewrite it as the state legislature wishes. Hence, even when a uniform law is said to have been adopted in many states, those states' laws may not be entirely "uniform." Once adopted by a state, a uniform act becomes a part of the statutory law of that state.

The Uniform Commercial Code (UCC). The Uniform Commercial Code (UCC), which was created through the joint efforts of the NCCUSL and the American Law Institute, was issued in 1952. The UCC has been adopted in forty-nine states, the District of Columbia, and the Virgin Islands. Louisiana has adopted Articles 1, 3, 4, 5, 7, 8, and 9. The UCC facilitates commerce among the states by providing a uniform, yet flexible, set of rules governing commercial transactions. The UCC assures businesspersons that their contracts, if validly entered into, will be enforced. Because of its importance in the area of commercial law, the UCC will be discussed in Chapters 16 through 19, which cover commercial transactions. Excerpts from the UCC are presented in Appendix B.

The best way to prevent legal liability is to anticipate problems that might arise. One method to anticipate legal problems is to learn about your legal rights and duties ahead of time.

ADMINISTRATIVE LAW

Administrative law consists of the rules, orders, and decisions of administrative agencies (government bodies, such as departments, commissions, and boards, charged by Congress or a state legislature with carrying out the terms of particular laws). Regulations issued by various administrative agencies affect virtually every aspect of a business's operation, including capital structure and financing, hiring and firing procedures, relations with employees and unions, and the way a firm manufactures and markets its products. Administrative law is discussed more fully in Chapter 39.

ADMINISTRATIVE LAW
A body of law created by administrative agencies—such as the Securities and Exchange Commission and the Federal Trade Commission—in the form of rules, regulations, orders, and decisions in order to carry out their duties and responsibilities. This law can initially be enforced by these agencies outside the judicial process.

Civil Law versus Criminal Law

The huge body of the law is broken down into several classifications. An important classification divides law into *civil law* and *criminal law.* **Civil law** spells out

CIVIL LAW
The branch of law dealing with the definition and enforcement of all private or public rights, as opposed to criminal matters.

the duties that exist either between persons or between citizens and their governments (*excluding* the duty not to commit crimes). Contract law, for example, is part of civil law.

Criminal law, in contrast to civil law, has to do with a wrong committed against the public as a whole. Criminal acts are prohibited by local, state, or federal government statutes. In a criminal case, the government seeks to impose a penalty (a monetary penalty and/or imprisonment) upon an allegedly guilty person. In a civil case, one party (sometimes the government) tries to make the other party comply with a duty or pay for the damage caused by a failure to so comply.

CRIMINAL LAW
Law that governs and defines those actions that are crimes and that subject the convicted offender to punishment imposed by the government.

Law around the World

LEARNING OBJECTIVE NO. 4
Identifying the Difference between Our Legal System and the Legal Systems of Other Nations

We have just discussed one of the major legal systems of today's world—the common law system of England and the United States. Generally, countries that were once colonies of Great Britain retained their English common law heritage after they achieved their independence. Today, common law systems exist in Ireland, Canada, Australia, New Zealand, and India.

In contrast to Great Britain and the other common law countries, most of the other European nations base their legal systems on Roman civil law, or "code law." The term *civil law,* as used here, does not refer to civil as opposed to criminal law. It refers to *codified* law—an ordered grouping of legal principles enacted into law by a legislature or governing body. In a **civil law system,** the primary source of law is a statutory code. Case precedents are not judicially binding, as they are in a common law system. This is not to say that precedents are unimportant in a civil law system. On the contrary, judges in such systems commonly refer to previous decisions as sources of legal guidance. The difference is that judges in a civil law system are not bound by precedent. The doctrine of *stare decisis* does not apply.

CIVIL LAW SYSTEM
A system of law derived from that of the Roman Empire and based on a code rather than case law; the predominant system of law in the nations of continental Europe and the nations that were once their colonies. In the United States, Louisiana is the only state that has elements of a civil law system.

Today, the civil law system is followed in most of the continental European countries, as well as in the Latin American, African, and Asian countries that were once colonies of the continental European nations. Japan and South Africa also have civil law systems. Ingredients of the civil law system are found in the Islamic courts of predominantly Muslim countries. In the United States, the state of Louisiana, because of its historical ties to France, has in part a civil law system. The legal systems of Puerto Rico, Quebec, and Scotland are similarly characterized as having elements of the civil law system.

International Law

International law can be defined as a body of written and unwritten laws observed by independent nations and governing the acts of individuals as well as governments. The key difference between *national law* (the law of a particular nation) and international law is the fact that national law can be enforced by government authorities. What government can enforce international law, however? By definition, a *nation* is a sovereign entity, which means that there is no higher authority to which that nation must submit. If a nation violates an international law, the most that other countries or international organizations can do (if persuasive tactics fail) is resort to coercive actions against the violating nation. Coercive actions range from severance of diplomatic relations and boycotts to, at the last resort, war.

INTERNATIONAL LAW
The law that governs relations among nations. International customs and treaties are generally considered to be two of the most important sources of international law.

In essence, international law is the result of centuries-old attempts to reconcile the traditional need of each nation to be the final authority over its own affairs with the desire of nations to benefit economically from trade and harmonious relations with one another. Although no sovereign nation can be compelled to obey a law external to itself, nations can and do voluntarily agree to be governed in certain respects by international law for the purpose of facilitating international trade and commerce, as well as for civilized discourse.

TERMS AND CONCEPTS FOR REVIEW

administrative law 6
case law 5
civil law 6
civil law system 7
common law 3
criminal law 7
damages 4
international law 7
law 3
precedent 3
***stare decisis* 3**
statutory law 6

CHAPTER SUMMARY • INTRODUCTION TO THE LAW AND OUR LEGAL SYSTEM

Sources of American Law	**1.** *Common law*—Originated in medieval England with the creation of the king's courts; consists of past judicial decisions and reasoning; involves the application of the doctrine of *stare decisis*—the rule of precedent—in deciding cases. Common law governs all areas not covered by statutory law. **2.** *Constitutional law*—The law as expressed in the U.S. Constitution and the various state constitutions. The U.S. Constitution is the supreme law of the land. State constitutions are supreme within state borders to the extent that they do not violate a clause of the U.S. Constitution or a federal law. **3.** *Statutory law*—Laws or ordinances created by federal, state, and local legislatures and governing bodies. None of these laws can violate the U.S. Constitution or the relevant state constitutions. Uniform statutes, when adopted by a state, become statutory law in that state. **4.** *Administrative law*—The branch of law concerned with the power and actions of administrative agencies at all levels of government.
Civil Law versus Criminal Law	**1.** *Civil law*—Law concerned with acts against a person who seeks redress in the form of compensation or other relief. **2.** *Criminal law*—Law concerned with acts against society for which society seeks redress in the form of punishment.
Law around the World	**1.** *Common law system*—See the summary of common law under "Sources of American Law" above. Originating in England, the common law tradition has been adopted by the United States and other former colonies of Great Britain, including Ireland, Canada, Australia, New Zealand, and India. **2.** *Civil law system*—A legal system in which the primary source of law is a statutory code, which is an ordered grouping of legal principles enacted into law by a legislature or governing body. Precedents are not binding in a civil law system. Most of the continental European countries have a civil law system, as do those African, Latin American, and Asian nations that were once colonies of the continental European countries. Japan and South Africa also have civil law systems.
International Law	A body of written and unwritten laws observed by independent nations and governing the acts of individuals as well as governments.

HYPOTHETICAL QUESTIONS

1–1. Legal Systems. What are the key differences between a common law system and a civil law system? Why do some countries have common law systems and others have civil law systems?

1–2. *Stare Decisis*. In the text of this chapter, we stated that the doctrine of *stare decisis* "became a cornerstone of the English and American judicial systems." What does *stare decisis* mean, and why has this doctrine been so fundamental to the development of our legal tradition?

1–3. Common Law versus Statutory Law. Courts are able to overturn precedents and thus can change the common law. Should judges have the same authority to overrule statutory law? Explain.

Today, business law professors and students can go online to access information on virtually every topic covered in this text. A good point of departure for online legal research is the Web site for *Business Law: Text and Exercises,* Third Edition, at **http://blte.westbuslaw.com.** There you will find numerous materials relevant to this text and to business law generally, including links to various legal resources on the Web. Additionally, every chapter in this text ends with an *Expanded Access to the Internet* feature that contains selected Web addresses.

You can access many of the sources of law discussed in Chapter 1 at the FindLaw Web site, which is probably the most comprehensive source of free legal information on the Internet. Go to

http://www.findlaw.com

The Legal Information Institute (LII) at Cornell Law School, which offers extensive information about U.S. law, is also a good starting point for legal research. The URL for this site is

http://www.law.cornell.edu

The Library of Congress offers extensive links to state and federal government resources at

http://www.loc.gov

Villanova University's Center for Information Law and Policy provides access to numerous legal resources, including opinions from the federal appellate courts. Go to

http://www.law.villanova.edu

The Virtual Law Library Index, created and maintained by the Indiana University School of Law, provides an index of legal sources categorized by subject at

http://www.law.indiana.edu

Online Legal Research

The text's Web site also offers online research exercises. These exercises will help you find and analyze specific types of legal information available at specific Web sites. There is at least one of these exercises for each chapter in *Business Law: Text and Exercises,* Third Edition. To access these exercises, go to this book's Web site at **http://blte.westbuslaw.com** and click on "Internet Applications." When that page opens, select the relevant chapter to find the exercise or exercises relating to topics in that chapter. The following activity will direct you to some of the important sources of law discussed in Chapter 1:

Activity 1–1: Internet Sources of Law

Chapter 1 ■ WORK SET

TRUE-FALSE QUESTIONS

_____ **1.** Law consists of enforceable rules governing relationships among individuals and between individuals and their society.

_____ **2.** *Stare decisis* refers to the practice of deciding new cases with reference to previous decisions.

_____ **3.** The doctrine of *stare decisis* illustrates how unpredictable the law can be.

_____ **4.** Common law is a term that normally refers to the body of law consisting of rules of law announced in court decisions.

_____ **5.** Statutes are a primary source of law.

_____ **6.** Administrative rules and regulations have virtually no effect on the operation of a business.

_____ **7.** Each state's constitution is supreme within each state's borders even if it conflicts with the U.S. Constitution.

_____ **8.** The Uniform Commercial Code was enacted by Congress for adoption by the states.

_____ **9.** In most states, the same courts can grant both legal and equitable remedies.

MULTIPLE-CHOICE QUESTIONS

_____ **1.** The doctrine of *stare decisis* performs many useful functions, including

a. efficiency.
b. uniformity.
c. stability.
d. all of the above.

_____ **2.** In addition to case law, when making decisions, courts sometimes consider other sources of law, including

a. the U.S. Constitution.
b. state constitutions.
c. administrative agency rules and regulations.
d. all of the above.

_____ **3.** Civil law concerns

a. duties that exist between persons or between citizens and their governments.
b. wrongs committed against the public as a whole.
c. both a and b.
d. none of the above.

_____ **4.** Which of the following is a CORRECT statement about the distinction between law and equity?

a. Equity involves different remedies from those available at law.
b. Most states maintain separate courts of law and equity.
c. Damages may be awarded only in actions in equity.
d. None of the above.

_____ **5.** Under the doctrine of *stare decisis,* a judge compares the facts in a case to facts in

a. another case.
b. a hypothetical.
c. the arguments of the parties involved in the case.
d. none of the above.

_____ **6.** To learn about the coverage of a statute and how the statute is applied, a person must

a. only read the statute.
b. only see how courts in his or her jurisdiction have interpreted the statute.
c. read the statute and see how courts in his or her jurisdiction have interpreted it.
d. none of the above.

_____ **7.** Our common law system involves the application of legal principles applied in earlier cases

a. with different facts.
b. with similar facts.
c. whether or not the facts are similar.
d. none of the above.

_____ **8.** The statutory law of the United States includes

a. the statutes enacted by Congress and state legislatures.
b. the rules, orders, and decisions of administrative agencies.
c. both the statutes enacted by Congress and state legislatures and the rules, orders, and decisions of administrative agencies.
d. none of the above.

_____ **9.** In a civil law system, the primary source of law is

a. case law.
b. the decisions of administrative agencies.
c. a statutory code.
d. none of the above.

ISSUE SPOTTERS

1. Under what circumstance might a judge rely on case law to determine the intent and purpose of a statute?

2. The First Amendment of the U.S. Constitution protects the free exercise of religion. A state legislature enacts a law that outlaws all religions that do not derive from the Judeo-Christian tradition. Is this state law valid? Why or why not?

Ethics

2

LEARNING OBJECTIVES

When you finish this chapter, you should be able to:

1. Define business ethics and its relationship to personal ethics.
2. Explain the relationship between law and ethics.
3. Compare and contrast duty-based ethics and utilitarian ethics.
4. State how businesspersons can deter unethical behavior.
5. Identify the factors that change the ethical landscape.

FACING A LEGAL PROBLEM

Pharmaceuticals International, Inc., wants to market a new drug that may have adverse side effects that may not show up for many years. The U.S. Food and Drug Administration has banned the drug. The drug has not been banned in Ecuador, however. *Would it be legal for Pharmaceuticals to sell its new drug in Ecuador? Would it be* ethical *for the firm to do so?*

In preparing for a career in business, you will find that a background in business ethics and a commitment to ethical behavior is just as important as a knowledge of the specific laws that you will read about in this text. In this chapter, we first examine the nature of business ethics and some of the sources of ethical standards that have guided others in their business decision making. We then look at some of the obstacles to ethical behavior faced by businesspersons. In the remaining pages of the chapter, we explore the following issue: How can businesspersons act in an ethically responsible manner and at the same time make profits for their firms or their firms' owners?

The Nature of Business Ethics

To understand the nature of business ethics, we need to define what is meant by ethics generally. **Ethics** can be defined as the study of what constitutes right or wrong behavior. It is the branch of philosophy that focuses on morality and the way in which moral principles are applied to daily life. Ethics has to do with questions relating to the fairness, justness, rightness, or wrongness of an action. What is fair? What is just? What is the right thing to do in this situation? These are essentially ethical questions.

ETHICS
Moral principles and values applied to social behavior.

DEFINING BUSINESS ETHICS

BUSINESS ETHICS
Ethics in a business context; a consensus of what constitutes right or wrong behavior in the world of business and the application of moral principles to situations that arise in a business setting.

Business ethics focuses on what constitutes ethical behavior in the world of business. Personal ethical standards, of course, play an important role in determining what is or is not ethical, or appropriate, business behavior. Business activities are just one part of the human enterprise, and the ethical standards that guide our behavior as, say, mothers, fathers, or students apply equally well to our activities as businesspersons. Businesspersons, though, often must address more complex ethical issues and conflicts in the workplace than they do in their personal lives.

LEARNING OBJECTIVE NO. 1
Defining Business Ethics and Its Relationship to Personal Ethics

LEARNING OBJECTIVE NO. 2
Explaining the Relationship Between Law and Ethics

BUSINESS ETHICS AND THE LAW

Because the law reflects and codifies a society's ethical values, many of our ethical decisions are made for us—by our laws. Simply obeying the law does not fulfill all ethical obligations, however. No law says, for example, that it is *illegal* to lie to one's family, but it may be *unethical* to do so. Likewise, in the business world, numerous actions might be unethical but not necessarily illegal.

In short, the law has its limits—it cannot make all our ethical decisions for us. When it does not, ethical standards must guide the decision-making process.

In the legal problem set out at the beginning of this chapter, Pharmaceuticals International, Inc., wants to sell, in Ecuador, a product that is currently legal in Ecuador but has been banned in the United States. *Is it legal for Pharmaceuticals to sell the drug in Ecuador?* Yes. It not illegal for a company with a product that has been outlawed in one country to look elsewhere for potential customers. *Is it ethical for the company to sell the drug in Ecuador?* Probably not, although this question does not have a clear-cut answer. The answer depends on which ethical standards are applied.

Sources of Ethical Standards

Ethical reasoning relating to business traditionally is characterized by two fundamental approaches. One approach defines ethical behavior in terms of *duty*. The other approach determines what is ethical in terms of the *consequences*, or *outcome*, of any given action.

DUTY-BASED ETHICS

Is it wrong to cheat on an examination, if nobody will ever know that you cheated and if it helps you get into law school so that you can eventually volunteer your legal services to the poor and needy? Is it wrong to lie to your parents if the lie harms nobody but helps to keep family relations congenial? These kinds of ethical questions implicitly weigh the "end" of an action against the "means" used to attain that end. If you believe that you have an ethical *duty* not to lie or cheat, however, then lying and cheating can never be justified by the consequences, no matter how benevolent or desirable those consequences may be. Duty-based ethics may be based on religious precepts or philosophical reasoning.

Religion. Duty-based ethical standards are often derived from moral principles rooted in religious sources. In the Judeo-Christian tradition, for example, the Ten Commandments of the Old Testament establish rules for moral action. Other religions have their own sources of revealed truth—such as the Koran in the Muslim world. Within the areas of their influence, moral principles are universal and absolute—they are not to be questioned. For example, consider one of the Ten Commandments: "Thou shalt not steal." This is an absolute mandate. Even a benevolent motive for stealing (such as Robin Hood's) cannot justify the act, because the act itself is inherently immoral and thus wrong. When an act is prohibited by religious teachings, it is unethical and should not be undertaken, regardless of its consequences.

Ethical standards based on religious teachings also involve an element of *compassion*. Therefore, even though it might be profitable for a firm to lay off a less productive employee, if that employee were to find it difficult to find employment elsewhere and his or her family were to suffer as a result, this potential suffering would be given substantial weight by the decision makers. Compassionate treatment of others is also mandated—to a certain extent, at least—by the Golden Rule of the ancients ("Do unto others as you would have them do unto you"), which has been adopted by most religions.

Philosophy. Ethical standards based on a concept of duty may also be derived solely from philosophical principles. Immanuel Kant (1724–1804), for example, identified some general guiding principles for moral behavior based on what he believed to be the fundamental nature of human beings. Kant held that it is rational to assume that human beings are qualitatively different from other physical objects occupying space. Persons are endowed with moral integrity and the capacity to reason and conduct their affairs rationally. Therefore, their thoughts and actions should be respected. When human beings are treated merely as a means to an end, they are being treated as the equivalent of objects and are being denied their basic humanity.

Kant believed that individuals should evaluate their actions in light of the consequences that would follow if *everyone* in society acted in the same way. This **categorical imperative** can be applied to any action. For example, say that you are deciding whether to cheat on an examination. If you have adopted Kant's categorical imperative, you will decide not to cheat, because if everyone cheated, the examination would be meaningless.

CATEGORICAL IMPERATIVE
An ethical guideline, according to which a person should evaluate the action in terms of what would happen if everybody else in the same situation, or category, acted the same way.

UTILITARIANISM
An approach to ethical reasoning in which a "good" decision is one that results in the greatest good for the greatest number of people affected by the decision.

OUTCOME-BASED ETHICS

LEARNING OBJECTIVE NO. 3
Comparing and Contrasting Duty-Based and Utilitarian Ethics

Utilitarianism is a philosophical theory first developed by Jeremy Bentham (1748–1832) and then advanced, with some modifications, by John Stuart Mill (1806–1873)—both British philosophers. In contrast to duty-based ethics, utilitarianism is outcome oriented. It focuses on the consequences of an action, not on the nature of the action or on a set of moral values or religious beliefs.

Those who apply utilitarian ethics believe that an action is morally correct, or "right," when, among the people it affects, it produces the greatest amount of good for the greatest number. When an action affects the majority adversely, it is morally wrong. Applying utilitarian ethics requires (1) a determination of which individuals will be affected by the action in question; (2) a **cost-benefit analysis**—an assessment of the negative and positive effects of alternative actions on these individuals; and (3) a choice among alternative actions that will produce the greatest positive benefits for the greatest number of individuals.

COST-BENEFIT ANALYSIS
A decision-making technique that involves weighing the costs of a given action against the benefits of the action.

IN THE COURTROOM

International Foods Corporation (IFC) markets baby formula in developing countries. IFC learns that mothers in those countries often mix the formula with impure water, to make the formula go further. As a result, babies are suffering from malnutrition, diarrhea, and in some instances, even death. *Is IFC in violation of the law?* No. *What is IFC's ethical responsibility in this situation?* If IFC's decision makers feel that they have an absolute duty not to harm others, then their response would be to withdraw the product from those markets. If they approach the problem from a utilitarian perspective, they would engage in a cost-benefit analysis. The cost of the action (the suffering and death of babies) would be weighed against its benefit (the availability of the formula to mothers). Having the formula available frees mothers from the task of breastfeeding and thus allows them to earn income to help raise their standards of living. The question in a utilitarian analysis focuses on whether the benefit outweighs the cost.

Two factors help to create an ethical workplace: a written code of ethics, or policy statement, and the effective communication of ethical policies to employees.

Obstacles to Ethical Business Behavior

People sometimes behave unethically in the business context, just as they do in their private lives. Some businesspersons knowingly engage in unethical behavior because they think that they can "get away with it"—that no one will ever learn of their unethical actions. Examples of this kind of unethical behavior include padding expense accounts, casting doubts on the integrity of a rival co-worker to gain a job promotion, stealing company supplies or equipment, and so on. Obviously, these acts are unethical, and many of them are illegal as well.

In other situations, businesspersons who would choose to act ethically may be deterred from doing so because of situational circumstances or external pressures. We look here at how both the corporate environment and the conduct of management can sometimes act as deterrents to ethical behavior.

Ethics and the Corporate Environment

Some persons believe that the nature of the corporate structure itself acts as a deterrent to ethically responsible behavior. We will examine the corporate structure in detail in Chapters 29 and 30. Briefly, a corporation is structured as follows: The owners of the corporation are the shareholders—those who purchase shares, or stock, in the company. The shareholders, however, do not run the corporation. Rather, they elect a board of directors and entrust those directors with the responsibility of directing and overseeing the corporate enterprise. The directors, in turn, hire officers and managers to handle the day-to-day business activities of the firm. A shareholder may also be a director, and a director may also be a corporate officer.

Collective Decision Making. The corporate setting complicates ethical decision making because (normally) no one person makes a corporate decision. If you are a manager in a large company, for example, you will find that the decision as to what is right or wrong for the company is not yours to make. Managers, of course, do make decisions that affect their corporations, and their input may weigh in decisions. The ultimate decision makers, however, are the members of the board of directors, who must make decisions as a group.

Collective decision making, because it places emphasis on consensus and unity of opinion, also tends to hinder individual ethical assertiveness. For example, suppose that a director has ethical misgivings about a planned corporate venture that promises to be highly profitable. If the other directors have no such misgivings, the director who does may be swayed by the enthusiasm of the others for the project and downplay his or her own criticisms.

A good source for information on management ethics is Academy of Management Online at

http://www.aom.pace.edu

Personal Accountability. To some extent, the corporate environment may shield corporate personnel from both personal exposure to the consequences of their decisions and personal accountability for those decisions. For example, suppose that a corporate board decides to market a new product that results in several consumers' deaths. Those who made the decision do not witness or deal directly with these consequences. Furthermore, just as (normally) no one individual is responsible for a corporate decision, so (normally) no one person is held accountable for the decision. (In recent years, however, the courts have been increasingly willing to look behind the "corporate veil" and hold individual corporate actors liable, or legally responsible, for actions resulting in harm to others.)

ETHICS AND MANAGEMENT

Much unethical business behavior occurs simply because it is not always clear what ethical standards and behaviors are appropriate or acceptable in a given context. Although most firms now issue ethical policies or codes of conduct, these policies and codes are not always effective in creating an ethical workplace. At times, this is because a firm's ethical policies are not communicated clearly to employees or do not bear on the real ethical issues confronting decision makers. Additionally, particularly in a large corporation, unethical behavior in one corporate department may escape the attention of those in control of the corporation or the corporate officials responsible for monitoring the company's ethics program.

Another deterrent to ethical behavior exists when corporate management, by its own conduct, indicates that ethical considerations take second place. If management makes no attempt to deter unethical behavior—through employment terminations, for example—it will be clear to employees that management is not all that serious about ethics. Likewise, if a company gives promotions or salary increases to those who use unethical tactics to increase the firm's profits, then employees who do not resort to such tactics will be at a disadvantage. An employee in this situation may decide that because "everyone else does it," he or she might as well do so also.

LEARNING OBJECTIVE NO. 4

Stating How Businesspersons Can Deter Unethical Behavior

Of course, an even stronger deterrent to ethical behavior occurs when employers engage in obvious unethical or illegal conduct and expect their employees to do so as well. An employee in this situation faces two options, neither of which is satisfactory: participate in the conduct or "blow the whistle" on (inform authorities of) the employer's actions—and risk being fired. (See Chapter 26 for a more detailed discussion of this ethical dilemma and its consequences for employees.)

The most important factor in creating and maintaining an ethical workplace is the attitude and conduct of management.

The Corporate Balancing Act

Today's corporate decision makers are, in a sense, caught between profitability and ethical responsibility. If they emphasize profits at the expense of perceived ethical responsibilities, they may become the target of negative media coverage, consumer boycotts, and perhaps lawsuits. If they invest too heavily in good works or social causes, however, their profits may suffer.

Striking the right balance is not always easy, and usually some profits must be sacrificed in the process. Instead of *maximum profits*, many firms today aim for *optimum profits*. Optimum profits are the maximum profits that can be realized while staying within legal and ethical limits.

Ethics in the Global Context

Given the different cultures and religions of the world's nations, one might expect frequent conflicts in ethics between foreign and U.S. businesspersons. In fact, many of the most important ethical principles are common to virtually all countries. Some important ethical differences do exist, however. In Islamic (Muslim) countries, for example, the consumption of alcohol and certain foods is forbidden by the Koran (the sayings of the prophet Mohammed, which lie at the heart of Islam and Islamic law). It would be thoughtless and unwise to invite a Saudi Arabian business contact out for a drink.

Two notable differences in regard to ethics involve the role of women and the legitimacy of certain side payments to government officials.

WOMEN IN BUSINESS

The role played by women in other countries may present some difficult ethical problems for firms doing business internationally. Equal employment opportunity is a fundamental public policy in the United States, and Title VII of the Civil Rights Act of 1964 prohibits discrimination against women in the employment context (see Chapter 27). Some other countries, however, reject any role for women professionals, which may cause difficulties for American women conducting business transactions in those countries.

For example, when the World Bank sent a delegation including women to negotiate with the Central Bank of Korea, the Koreans were surprised and offended. They thought that the presence of women meant that the Koreans were not being taken seriously. (This problem might have been cured by some advance communication.) In Islamic nations, women are expected to avoid exposing their arms, legs, or hair in public. Although American women may find it difficult to respect this custom, it may be necessary for them to do so if they wish to succeed in business transactions conducted in those nations.

THE BRIBERY OF FOREIGN OFFICIALS

In the United States, the majority of contracts are formed in the private sector. In many foreign countries, however, decisions on most construction and manufacturing contracts are made by government officials because of extensive government regulation and control over trade and industry. Side payments to government officials in exchange for favorable business contracts are not unusual in such countries, nor are they considered to be unethical. In the past, U.S. corporations doing business in developing countries largely followed the saying, "When in Rome, do as the Romans do."

In the 1970s, however, the U.S. press, and government officials as well, uncovered a number of business scandals involving large side payments by American corporations—such as Lockheed Aircraft—to foreign representatives to obtain favorable contracts. In response, Congress passed the Foreign Corrupt Practices Act (FCPA) in 1977, which prohibits American businesspersons from bribing foreign officials to secure contracts. The act has made it difficult for U.S. companies to compete as effectively as they otherwise might in the global marketplace.

The Foreign Corrupt Practices Act (FCPA) of 1977 is divided into two major parts. The first part applies to all U.S. companies and their directors, officers, shareholders, employees, and agents. This part prohibits the bribery of most officials of foreign governments if the purpose is to get the official to act in his or her official capacity to provide business opportunities.

The FCPA does not prohibit payments to private foreign companies or other third parties unless the American firm knows that the payments will be passed on to a foreign government in violation of the FCPA. The FCPA also does not prohibit payment of substantial sums to minor officials whose duties are ministerial if the payments are lawful within the foreign country. These payments are often referred to as "grease," or facilitating payments. They are meant to ensure that administrative services that might otherwise be performed at a slow pace are sped up.

IN THE COURTROOM

Joan Anderson, who is a representative for American Exports, Inc., makes a payment on American's behalf to a minor official in Nigeria to speed up an import-licensing process. *Has either Anderson or her firm violated the Foreign Corrupt Practices Act?* No, if the payment does not violate Nigerian law. Generally, the Foreign Corrupt Practices Act permits small payments to foreign officials if such payments are lawful within the foreign country.

The second part of the FCPA is directed toward accountants, because in the past bribes were often concealed in corporate financial records. All companies must keep detailed records that "accurately and fairly" reflect the company's financial activities. In addition, all companies must have an accounting system that provides "reasonable assurance" that all transactions entered into by the company are accounted for and legal. These requirements assist in detecting illegal bribes. The FCPA prohibits any person from making false statements to accountants or false entries in any record or account.

Business firms that violate the act may be fined up to $2 million. Individual officers or directors who violate the FCPA may be fined up to $100,000 (the fine cannot be paid by the company) and may be imprisoned for up to five years.

The Ever-Changing Ethical Landscape

LEARNING OBJECTIVE NO. 5
Identifying the Factors That Change the Ethical Landscape

Our sense of what is ethical—what is fair or just or right in a given situation—changes over time. Conduct that might have been considered ethical ten years ago might be considered unethical today. Indeed, most of the ethical and social issues discussed in this chapter and elsewhere in this text either did not exist or were of little public concern at the turn of the twentieth century and, in some cases, even as recently as a decade ago. Technological innovations, the communications revolution, pressing environmental problems, and social movements resulting in greater rights for minorities, women, and consumers have all dramatically changed the society in which we live and, consequently, the business and ethical landscape of America.

This changing ethical landscape is perhaps nowhere more evident than in the evolution of the concept of corporate ethical responsibility. Today's business manager must not only keep an eye on his or her firm's profit margins but also keep an "ear to the ground" to detect changing social perceptions of what constitutes ethically responsible corporate behavior.

TERMS AND CONCEPTS FOR REVIEW

business ethics 14
categorical imperative 15
cost-benefit analysis 15
ethics 13
utilitarianism 15

CHAPTER SUMMARY • ETHICS

The Nature of Business Ethics	Ethics can be defined as the study of what constitutes right or wrong behavior. Business ethics focuses on how moral and ethical principles are applied in the business context. The law reflects society's convictions on what constitutes right or wrong behavior. The law has its limits, though, and some actions may be legal yet not be ethical.
Sources of Ethical Standards	**1.** *Duty-based ethics*—Ethics based on religious beliefs and philosophical reasoning, such as that of Immanuel Kant. **2.** *Outcome-based ethics (utilitarianism)*—Ethics based on philosophical reasoning, such as that of John Stuart Mill.
Obstacles to Ethical Business Behavior	**1.** *The corporate structure*— **a.** Collective decision making tends to deter individual ethical assertiveness. **b.** The corporate structure tends to shield corporate actors from responsibility and accountability. **2.** *Management*— **a.** Uncertainty on the part of employees as to what kind of behavior is expected of them makes it difficult for them to behave ethically. **b.** Unethical conduct by management shows employees that ethical behavior is not a priority.

CHAPTER SUMMARY • *Continued*

The Corporate Balancing Act	Today's corporate decision makers must balance profitability against ethical responsibility when making their decisions. Instead of maximum profits, corporations increasingly aim for optimum profits—the maximum profits that can be realized by the firm while pursuing actions that are not only legal and profitable but also ethical.
Ethics in the Global Context	Despite the cultural and religious differences among nations, the most important ethical precepts are common to virtually all countries. Two notable differences relate to the role of women in society and the practice of giving side payments to foreign officials to secure favorable contracts. The Foreign Corrupt Practices Act (FCPA) of 1977, which prohibits the bribery of foreign officials through such side payments, put U.S. businesspersons at a relative disadvantage to businesspersons from other countries who are not subject to such laws.
The Ever-Changing Ethical Landscape	What is considered ethical in a society may change over time as social customs change and new developments alter our social and business environment.

HYPOTHETICAL QUESTIONS

2–1. Business Ethics. Korman, Inc., a toy manufacturer, has its headquarters in Minneapolis, Minnesota. It markets its toys throughout the United States as well as in overseas markets. Korman has recently placed on the market a new line of dolls with such irreverent names as "Harass Me," "Spit on Me," "Pull My Hair," "Watch Me Scream," "Cut Me Quick," and "Abuse Me, Please." The dolls are a success commercially and have netted Korman more profits than any of its other toys. Parents and teachers claim that Korman's dolls encourage children to be violent and that it is unethical of Korman to continue marketing the dolls. Parent-teacher groups are organizing boycotts against Korman and the dolls and have launched a media campaign against the company. Recently, they picketed Korman's headquarters in Minneapolis, bearing such signs as "Korman Hates Kids" and "Watch Korman Scream." If you were a Korman executive, would you recommend that the company cease manufacturing the toys? What factors would Korman's directors need to consider in making this decision?

2–2. Corporate Ethical Responsibility. Assume that you are a high-level manager for a shoe manufacturer. You know that your firm could increase its profit margin by producing shoes in Indonesia, where you could hire women for $40 a month to assemble them. You also know, however, that a competing shoe manufacturer recently was accused, by human-rights advocates, of engaging in exploitative labor practices because the manufacturer sold shoes made by Indonesian women for similarly low wages. You personally do not believe that paying $40 a month to Indonesian women is unethical, because you know that in that impoverished country, $40 a month is a better-than-average wage rate. Assuming that the decision is yours to make, should you have the shoes manufactured in Indonesia and make higher profits for your company? Should you instead avoid the risk of negative publicity and the consequences of that publicity for the firm's reputation and subsequent profits? Are there other alternatives? Discuss fully.

REAL WORLD CASE PROBLEM

2–3. Consumer Welfare. The father of an eleven-year-old child sued the manufacturer of a jungle gym because the manufacturer had failed to warn users of the equipment that they might fall off the gym and get hurt, as the boy did in this case. The father also claimed that the jungle gym was unreasonably dangerous because, as his son began to fall and reached frantically for a bar to grasp, there was no bar within reach. The father based his argument in part on a previous case involving a plaintiff who was injured as a result of somersaulting off a trampoline. In that case [*Pell v. Victor J. Andrew High School,* 123 Ill.App.3d 423, 462 N.E.2d 858, 78 Ill.Dec. 739 (1984)], the court had held that the trampoline's manufacturer was liable for the plaintiff's injuries because it had failed to warn of the trampoline's propensity to cause severe spinal cord injuries if it was used for somersaulting. Should the court be convinced by the father's arguments? Why or why not? [*Cozzi v. North Palos Elementary School District No. 117,* 232 Ill.App.3d 379, 597 N.E.2d 683, 173 Ill.Dec. 709 (1992)]

For updated links to resources available on the Web, as well as a variety of other materials, visit this text's Web site at **http://blte.westbuslaw.com**.

The Web site of DePaul University's Institute for Business and Professional Ethics includes several examples of the types of ethical issues that can arise in the business context. Go to

http://www.depaul.edu/ethics/contents.html

You can find articles on issues relating to shareholders and corporate accountability at the Corporate Governance Web site. Go to

http://www.corpgov.net

Numerous online groups focus on the activities of various corporations from an ethical perspective. A good starting point for locating these kinds of Web sites is Baobab's Corporate Power Information Center at

http://www.baobabcomputing.com/corporatepower

Online Legal Research

Go to **http://blte.westbuslaw.com**, the Web site that accompanies this text. Select "Internet Applications," and then click on "Chapter 2." There you will find the following Internet research exercises that you can perform to learn more about ethics and business decision making:

Activity 2–1: Ethics in Business

Activity 2–2: Environmental Self-Audits

Chapter 2 ■ WORK SET

TRUE-FALSE QUESTIONS

_____ **1.** Ethics is the study of what constitutes right and wrong behavior.

_____ **2.** The study of business ethics is fundamentally different from the general study of ethics.

_____ **3.** According to religious principles, certain moral standards are universal.

_____ **4.** In determining how ethical an act is according to utilitarian standards, it does not matter how many people benefit from the act.

_____ **5.** A socially responsible firm will often aim for optimum profits instead of maximum profits.

_____ **6.** Ethical problems that arise in a business context normally involve clear-cut choices between good and bad alternatives.

_____ **7.** If a corporation fails to conduct itself ethically, its profits may suffer.

_____ **8.** When the legality of an action is not clear cut, a businessperson should take an action that is at least ethically defensible.

_____ **9.** Business conduct that was considered acceptable in the past is entirely acceptable today.

MULTIPLE-CHOICE QUESTIONS

_____ **1.** Business ethics focuses on the application of

a. moral principles.
b. business philosophies.
c. law.
d. none of the above.

_____ **2.** Which ethical standards derive from religious sources?

a. Duty-based ethics.
b. Utilitarianism.
c. Outcome-based ethics.
d. None of the above.

_____ **3.** Religious ethical standards are generally viewed as absolute but may also involve an element of

a. cost-benefit analysis.
b. discretion.
c. compassion.
d. none of the above.

_____ **4.** Which ethics is premised on acting so as to do the greatest good for the greatest number of people?

a. Duty-based ethics
b. Utilitarianism.
c. Religious-based ethics.
d. None of the above.

_____ **5.** Which of the following is a criticism of utilitarianism?

a. It requires choosing among conflicting ethical principles.
b. It tends to focus on society as a whole rather than on individuals.
c. It is overly concerned with ideals of perfection.
d. It is an outdated philosophy.

_____ **6.** Ethical dilemmas in a business context can require determining

a. how much consideration to give to making a profit.
b. which law to obey.
c. whether to adhere to certain ethics.
d. all of the above.

_____ **7.** When one ethical duty conflicts with another, a decision may have to be made as to which duty should prevail. Such a decision

a. does not normally have clear-cut answers.
b. may involve choices between equally good and bad alternatives.
c. both a and b.
d. none of the above.

_____ **8.** To ensure that an action is profitable, legal, and ethical,

a. some profit may need to be sacrificed.
b. the religious implications must be considered.
c. the welfare of the people involved must be reduced to plus and minus signs on a cost-benefit worksheet.
d. none of the above.

_____ **9.** If the consequences of an act that is generally considered illegal benefit a large number of people (Robin Hood stealing from the rich to give to the poor, for example), the act is considered

a. legal.
b. ethical under a duty-based standard.
c. ethical under a utilitarian-based standard.
d. all of the above.

ISSUE SPOTTERS

1. When a manufacturer has to decide whether to close a plant, the costs of doing so may be weighed against the benefits. If the benefits are greater than the costs, can closing the plant be ethically justified, considering the effect on the employees?

2. Does a manufacturer owe an ethical duty to remove from the market a product that is capable of injuring seriously a few consumers, even if the injuries result from misuse?

The Role of Courts in Our Legal System

LEARNING OBJECTIVES

When you finish this chapter, you should be able to:

1. List the basic parts of a state court system.
2. Identify when a lawsuit can be filed in a federal court.
3. Discuss the procedure of a trial.
4. Summarize the steps in a typical lawsuit.

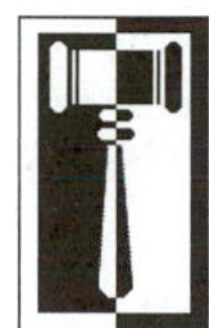

FACING A LEGAL PROBLEM

A dispute arises between Haru Koto, a resident of California, and Maria Mendez, a resident of Texas, over the ownership of the *Fairweather,* a sailboat in dry dock in San Diego, California. *Can a California state court exercise jurisdiction in the dispute?*

Nearly every businessperson faces either a potential or an actual lawsuit at some time or another in his or her career. For this reason, anyone contemplating a career in business will benefit from an understanding of American court systems.

As explained in Chapter 1, American law is based on numerous elements—the case decisions and reasoning that form the common law; federal and state constitutions; statutes passed by federal and state legislatures, including uniform laws, such as the Uniform Commercial Code, that have been adopted by the various states; administrative law; and so on. The function of the courts is to interpret and apply those laws.

Even though there are fifty-two court systems—one for each of the fifty states, one for the District of Columbia, plus a federal system—similarities abound. Keep in mind that the federal courts are not superior to the state courts. They are simply an independent system of courts. Both systems are examined in this chapter. To clarify judicial procedure, we follow a typical case through a state court system.

Jurisdiction

Jurisdiction refers either to the geographical area within which a court has the right and power to decide cases or to the right and power of a court to adjudicate (determine) matters concerning certain persons, property, or subject matter. Before any court can hear a case, it must have jurisdiction over the person against

JURISDICTION
The authority of a court to hear and decide a specific action.

whom the suit is brought or over the property involved in the suit, as well as jurisdiction over the subject matter.

Generally, a court's power is limited to the territorial boundaries of the state in which it is located. Thus, a court can exercise jurisdiction (personal jurisdiction, or *in personam* jurisdiction) over residents of the state and anyone else within its boundaries. A court can also exercise jurisdiction over property (*in rem* jurisdiction, or "jurisdiction over the thing") located within its boundaries.

In the legal problem set out at the beginning of this chapter, Haru Koto, a resident of California, and Maria Mendez, a resident of Texas, are in a dispute over the ownership of the *Fairweather,* a boat in dry dock in San Diego, California. *Can a California state court exercise jurisdiction in the dispute?* Yes. The boat is located within the boundaries of California. A California court can exercise jurisdiction.

The State Court System

One can view the typical state court system as being made up of trial courts and appellate courts. Trial courts are exactly what their name implies—courts in which trials are held and testimony is taken. Appellate courts are courts of appeal and review. They review cases decided elsewhere.

LEARNING OBJECTIVE NO. 1
Listing the Basic Parts of the State Court System

As Exhibit 3–1 indicates, there are several levels of courts within state court systems: (1) state trial courts of limited jurisdiction, (2) state trial courts of general jurisdiction, (3) appellate courts, and (4) the state supreme court. (The exhibit also shows how the federal court system is structured.) Any person who is a party to a lawsuit typically has the opportunity to plead the case before a trial court and then, if he or she loses, before at least one level of appellate courts. Finally, if a federal statute or constitutional issue is involved in the decision of the state supreme court, that decision may be further appealed to the United States Supreme Court.

EXHIBIT 3–1
Federal Courts and State Court Systems

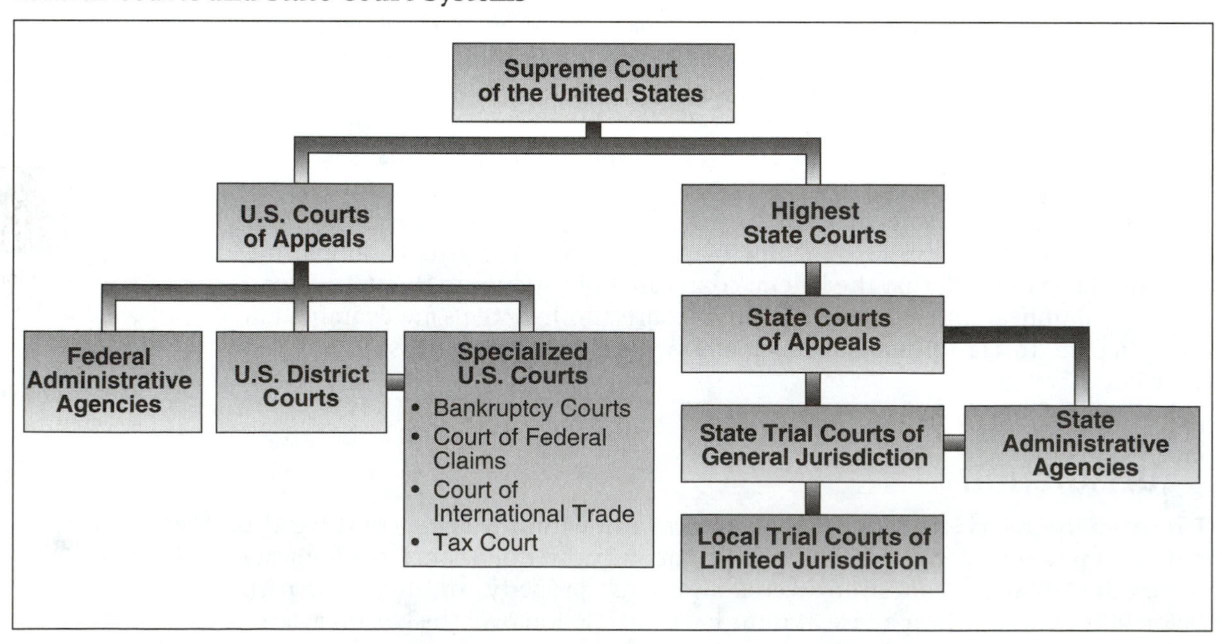

TRIAL COURTS

The state trial courts have either *general* or *limited* jurisdiction. Trial courts that have general jurisdiction as to subject matter may be called county, district, superior, or circuit courts. The jurisdiction of these courts of general and original jurisdiction is often determined by the size of the county in which the court sits. Many important cases involving businesses originate in these general trial courts.

Courts with limited jurisdiction as to subject matter are often called special inferior trial courts or minor judiciary courts. **Small claims courts** are inferior trial courts that hear only civil cases involving claims of less than a certain amount, usually $2,500. Most small claims are less than $500. Suits brought in small claims courts are generally conducted informally, and lawyers are not required. In a minority of states, lawyers are not even allowed to represent people in small claims courts for most purposes. Decisions of small claims courts may be appealed to a state trial court of general jurisdiction.

SMALL CLAIMS COURTS
Special courts in which parties may litigate small claims (usually, claims involving $2,500 or less). Attorneys are not required in small claims courts, and in many states, attorneys are not allowed to represent the parties.

Other courts of limited jurisdiction are domestic relations courts, local municipal courts, and probate courts. Domestic relations courts handle only divorce actions and child custody cases. Local municipal courts mainly handle traffic cases. Probate courts handle the administration of wills and estate settlement problems.

COURTS OF APPEALS

Every state has at least one court of appeals, or reviewing court. About half of the states have intermediate appellate courts. The subject matter jurisdiction of these courts of appeals is substantially limited to hearing appeals. Appellate courts normally examine the record of a case on appeal and determine whether the trial court committed an error. They look at questions of law and procedure, but usually not at questions of fact. An appellate court will tamper with a trial court's finding of fact, however, when the finding is clearly erroneous (that is, when it is contrary to the evidence presented at trial) or when there is no evidence to support the finding.

The highest appellate court in a state is usually called the supreme court but may be called by some other name. (For example, in both New York and Maryland, the highest state court is called the Court of Appeals.) The decisions of each state's highest court on all questions of state law are final. Only when issues of federal law are involved can a state's highest court be overruled by the United States Supreme Court.

The Federal Court System

The federal court system is similar in many ways to most state court systems. It is a three-level model consisting of (1) trial courts, (2) intermediate courts of appeals, and (3) the United States Supreme Court. Exhibit 3–1 shows the organization of the federal court system.

You can obtain information about the federal court system by accessing the Federal Court Locator at

http://vls.law.vill.edu/Locator/fedcourt.html

U.S. DISTRICT COURTS

At the federal level, the United States is divided into thirteen federal judicial "circuits" and the circuits are subdivided into districts. The equivalent of a state trial court of general jurisdiction is a federal district court. There is at least one federal district court in every state. The number of judicial districts can vary over time, primarily owing to population changes and corresponding caseloads. The law now provides for ninety-six judicial districts.

U.S. district courts have original jurisdiction in federal matters. In other words, federal cases originate in district courts. There are other trial courts with original, although special (or limited) jurisdiction, such as the U.S. Tax Court, the U.S. Bankruptcy Court, and the U.S. Court of Federal Claims.

EXHIBIT 3–2
U.S. Courts of Appeals and U.S. District Courts

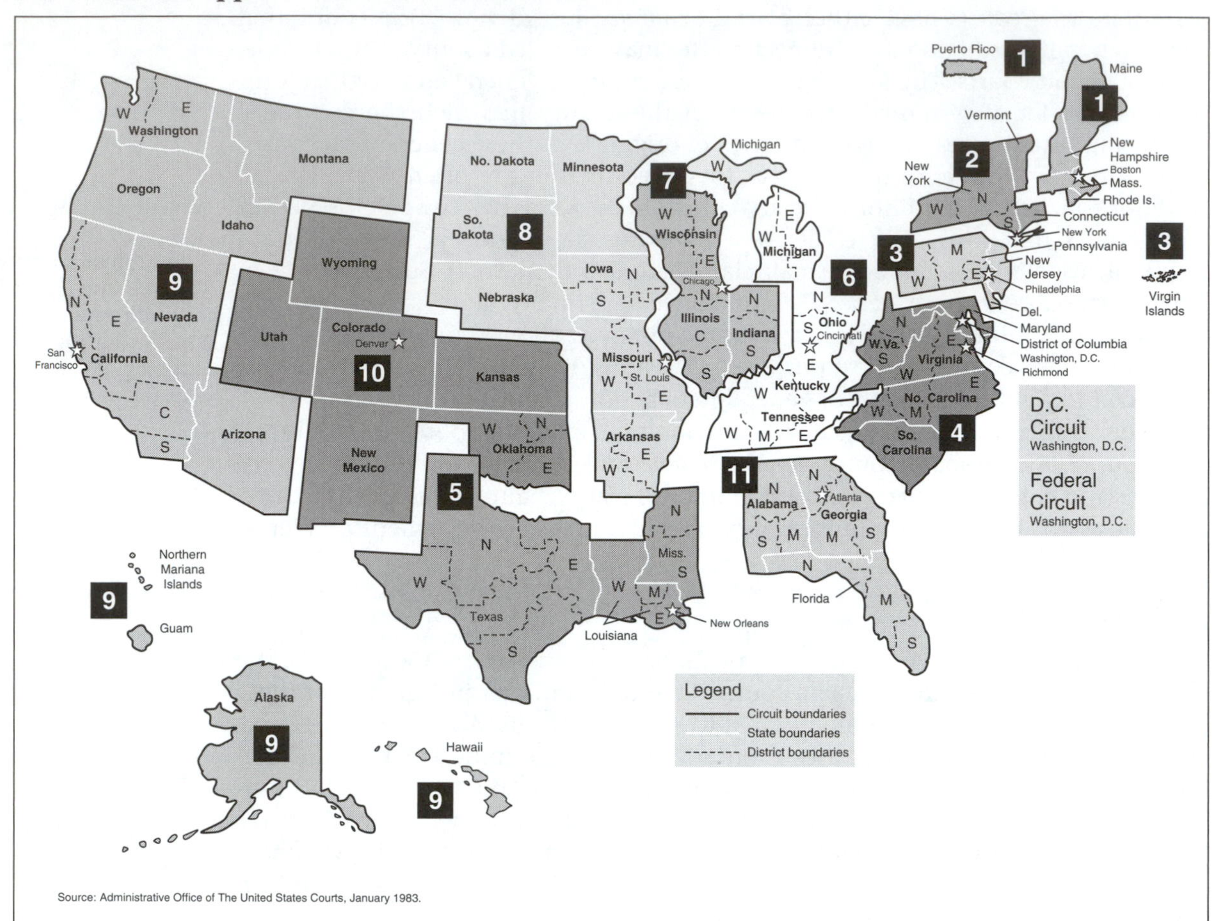

Source: Administrative Office of The United States Courts, January 1983.

U.S. Courts of Appeals

The U.S. courts of appeals for twelve of the thirteen federal judicial circuits hear appeals from the federal district courts located within their respective circuits. The court of appeals for the thirteenth circuit, called the federal circuit, has national jurisdiction over certain types of cases, such as those concerning patent law. There are currently 179 circuit court judgeships.

The decisions of the circuit courts of appeals are final in most cases. Appeal to the United States Supreme Court is possible, however. Appeals from federal administrative agencies, such as the Federal Trade Commission, are also made to the U.S. circuit courts of appeals. See Exhibit 3–2 for the geographical boundaries of U.S. district courts and U.S. courts of appeals.

The United States Supreme Court

For information on the justices of the United States Supreme Court, go to

http://oyez.nwu.edu

The highest level of the three-level model of the federal court system is the United States Supreme Court. According to the language of Article III of the U.S. Constitution, there is only one national Supreme Court. All other courts in the federal system are considered "inferior." Congress is empowered to create other inferior courts as it desires. The inferior courts that Congress has created include the second level in our model—the U.S. courts of appeals—as well as the district courts and any other courts of limited, or specialized, jurisdiction.

The United States Supreme Court consists of nine justices. These justices are nominated by the president of the United States and confirmed by the Senate. They (as do all federal district and courts of appeals judges) receive lifetime appointments (because under Article III, they "hold their offices during Good Behavior"). Although the United States Supreme Court has original, or trial, jurisdiction in rare instances (set forth in Article III, Section 2), most of its work is as an appeals court. The Supreme Court can review any case decided by any of the federal courts of appeals. It also has appellate authority over some cases decided in the state courts.

Jurisdiction of the Federal Courts

LEARNING OBJECTIVE NO. 2

Identifying When a Lawsuit Can Be Filed in a Federal Court

The Constitution gives Congress the power to control the number and kind of inferior courts in the federal system. Except in those cases in which the Constitution gives the Supreme Court original jurisdiction (including cases involving ambassadors and controversies between states), Congress can also regulate the jurisdiction of the Supreme Court.

In general, federal courts have jurisdiction over cases involving federal questions. A **federal question** is an issue of law based, at least in part, on the Constitution, a treaty, or a federal law. Any lawsuit concerning a federal question can originate in a federal court. Federal jurisdiction also extends to cases involving diversity of citizenship. **Diversity of citizenship** cases are those arising between (1) citizens of different states, (2) a foreign country and citizens of a state or of different states, or (3) citizens of a state and citizens or subjects of a foreign country. The amount in controversy in diversity cases must be more than $75,000 before a federal court can take jurisdiction.

FEDERAL QUESTION
A question that pertains to the U.S. Constitution, acts of Congress, or treaties. A federal question provides jurisdiction for federal courts. This jurisdiction arises from Article III, Section 2, of the Constitution.

DIVERSITY OF CITIZENSHIP
Under Article III, Section 2, of the Constitution, a basis for federal court jurisdiction over a lawsuit between citizens of different states.

How Cases Reach the Supreme Court

Many people are surprised to learn that there is no absolute right of appeal to the United States Supreme Court. The Supreme Court has original, or trial court, jurisdiction in a small number of situations. In all other cases, its jurisdiction is appellate. Thousands of cases are filed with the Supreme Court each year, yet it hears, on average, only about a hundred. To bring a case before the Supreme Court, a party requests the Court to issue a **writ of *certiorari*** (pronounced *sir*-she-a-*rár*-ee). A writ of *certiorari* is an order issued by the Supreme Court to a lower court requiring the latter to send it the record of a case for review. Whether the Court will issue such a writ is entirely within its discretion. In no instance is the Court required to do so.

WRIT OF *CERTIORARI*
A writ from a higher court asking the lower court for the record of a case.

Most petitions for writs of *certiorari* are denied. A denial is not a decision on the merits of a case, nor does it indicate agreement with the lower court's opinion. Denial of the writ also has no value as a precedent. The Court will not issue a writ unless at least four justices approve of such action. This is called the "rule of four." Typically, only the petitions that raise the possibility of important constitutional questions are granted.

Following a Case through the State Courts

American and English courts follow the *adversary system of justice*. The lawyer functions as the client's advocate, presenting the client's version of the facts in order to convince the judge or the jury (or both) that it is true. Judges are responsible for the appropriate application of the law. They do not have to accept the legal reasoning of the attorneys but, instead, can base a ruling and a decision on their own study of the law.

Are you prepared to pay for going to court? Make this decision only after you have consulted an attorney to get an estimate of the costs of preparing the lawsuit.

COURT PROCEDURE

Procedural law establishes the rules and standards for determining disputes in courts. The rules are very complex, and they vary from court to court. There is a set of federal rules of procedure and various sets of rules for state courts. Procedural rules differ in criminal and civil cases.

THE PLEADINGS

PLEADINGS
Statements by the plaintiff and the defendant that detail the facts, charges, and defenses.

The complaint and answer (and the counterclaim and reply)—all of which are discussed below—taken together are called the **pleadings.** The pleadings inform each party of the claims of the other and specify the issues (disputed questions) involved in the case. Pleadings remove the element of surprise from a case. They allow lawyers to gather the most persuasive evidence and to prepare better arguments, thus increasing the probability that a just and true result will be forthcoming from the trial.

COMPLAINT
The pleading made by a plaintiff or a charge made by the state alleging wrongdoing on the part of the defendant.

PLAINTIFF
One who initiates a lawsuit.

DEFENDANT
One against whom a lawsuit is brought; the accused person in a criminal proceeding.

Complaint. A lawsuit commences when a lawyer files a **complaint** (sometimes called a petition or declaration) with the clerk of the trial court with the appropriate jurisdiction. The party who files the complaint is known as the **plaintiff.** The party against whom a complaint is filed is the **defendant.** The complaint contains (1) a statement alleging the facts necessary for the court to take jurisdiction, (2) a short statement of the facts necessary to show that the plaintiff is entitled to a remedy, and (3) a statement of the remedy the plaintiff is seeking. Exhibit 3–3 shows a typical complaint (using the events described in the following *In the Courtroom* feature).

IN THE COURTROOM

Kevin Anderson, driving a Mercedes, is in an accident with Lisa Marconi, driving a Ford Taurus. The accident occurs at the intersection of Wilshire Boulevard and Rodeo Drive in Beverly Hills, California. Marconi suffers personal injuries, incurring medical and hospital expenses as well as lost wages for four months. Anderson and Marconi are unable to agree on a settlement, and Marconi wants to sue Anderson. *After obtaining a lawyer, what is Marconi's next step?* Marconi's suit commences with the filing of a complaint against Anderson. The complaint includes the facts that give rise to the suit and allegations concerning the defendant. Marconi's complaint may state that Marconi was driving her car through a green light at the specified intersection, exercising good driving habits and reasonable care, when Anderson carelessly drove his car through a red light and into the intersection from a cross street, striking Marconi and causing personal injury and property damage. The complaint should add the relief that Marconi seeks—for example, $10,000 to cover medical bills, $9,000 to cover lost wages, and $5,000 to cover damage to her car.

Summons. After the complaint has been filed, the sheriff or a deputy of the county or another person authorized by the law serves a summons and a copy of the complaint on the defendant. The *summons* notifies the defendant that he or she is required to prepare an answer to the complaint and to file a copy of the answer with both the court and the plaintiff's attorney within a specified time period (usually twenty to thirty days after the summons has been served). The summons also states that failure to answer will result in a **default judgment** for the plaintiff, meaning the plaintiff will be awarded the remedy sought in the complaint.

DEFAULT JUDGMENT
A judgment entered by a clerk or court against a party who has failed to appear in court to answer or defend against a claim that has been brought against him or her by another party.

Choices Available after Receipt of the Summons and Complaint. Once the defendant has been served with a copy of the summons and complaint, the defendant must respond by filing a *motion to dismiss* or an *answer.* If a defendant does not respond, the court may enter a default judgment against him or her.

EXHIBIT 3–3
Example of a Typical Complaint

IN THE LOS ANGELES MUNICIPAL COURT
FOR THE LOS ANGELES JUDICIAL DISTRICT

CIVIL NO. 8–1026

Lisa Marconi
Plaintiff

v.

COMPLAINT

Kevin Anderson
Defendant

Comes now the plaintiff and for her cause of action against the defendant alleges and states as follows:

1. The jurisdiction of this court is based on Section 86 of the California Civil Code

2. This action is between plaintiff, a California resident living at 1434 Palm Drive, Anaheim, California, and Defendant, a California resident living at 6950 Garrison Avenue, Los Angeles, California.

3. On September 10, 2000, plaintiff, Lisa Marconi, was exercising good driving habits and reasonable care in driving her car through the intersection of Rodeo Drive and Wilshire Boulevard when defendant, Kevin Anderson, negligently drove his vehicle through a red light at the intersection and collided with plaintiff's vehicle. Defendant was negligent in the operation of the vehicle as to:

   a. Speed,
   b. Lookout,
   c. Management and control.

4. As a result of the collision plaintiff suffered severe physical injury that prevented her from working and property damage to her car. The costs she incurred included $10,000 in medical bills, $9,000 in lost wages, and $6,000 for automobile repairs.

WHEREFORE, plaintiff demands judgment against the defendant for the sum of $25,000 plus interest at the maximum legal rate and the costs of this action.

By ______________________________
Roger Harrington
Attorney for the Plaintiff
800 Orange Avenue
Anaheim, CA 91426

Motion to Dismiss. A **motion to dismiss** is an allegation that even if the facts presented in the complaint are true, the defendant is not legally liable. For example, the defendant might allege that the plaintiff has failed to state a claim for which relief can be granted.

MOTION TO DISMISS
A pleading in which a defendant admits the facts as alleged by the plaintiff but asserts that the plaintiff's claim fails to state a cause of action (that is, has no basis in law) or that there are other grounds on which a suit should be dismissed. Also called a demurrer.

The court may deny the motion to dismiss. If so, the judge is indicating that the plaintiff has stated a recognized cause of action (that is, if the facts are true, the plaintiff has a right to judicial relief), and the defendant is given an extension of time to file an answer. If the defendant does not do so, a judgment will normally be entered for the plaintiff.

If the court grants the motion to dismiss, the judge is saying that the plaintiff has failed to state a recognized cause of action. The plaintiff generally is given time to file an amended complaint. If the plaintiff does not file an amended complaint, a judgment will be entered against the plaintiff, who will not be allowed to bring suit on the matter again.

ANSWER
Procedurally, a defendant's response to the complaint.

Answer. If the defendant has not chosen to file a motion to dismiss or has filed a motion to dismiss that has been denied, then he or she must file an **answer.** This document either admits the allegations in the complaint or denies them and outlines any defenses that the defendant may have. If the defendant admits the allegations, the court will enter a judgment for the plaintiff. If the allegations are denied, the matter will proceed to trial. The defendant can also use the answer to raise a counterclaim—any claim that he or she may have against the plaintiff, arising out of the same transaction or occurrence that gave rise to the complaint. (There are counterclaims that, in some circumstances, a defendant must bring up or they will be lost, because the defendant will not be allowed to bring them up later.) In response to a counterclaim, the plaintiff can issue a reply.

DISMISSALS AND JUDGMENTS BEFORE TRIAL

There are numerous procedural avenues for disposing of a case without a trial. Many of them involve one or the other party's attempts to get the case dismissed through the use of pretrial motions. We have already mentioned the motion to dismiss. Other important pretrial motions are the motion for a judgment on the pleadings and the motion for summary judgment.

Motion for Judgment on the Pleadings. After the pleadings are closed—after the complaint, answer, and any counterclaim and reply have been filed—either of the parties can file a *motion for judgment on the pleadings* (or *on the merits*). This motion may be used when no facts are disputed and, thus, only questions of law are at issue. On a motion for judgment on the pleadings, a court may not consider any evidence outside the pleadings.

SUMMARY JUDGMENT
A judgment entered by a trial court prior to trial that is based on the valid assertion by one of the parties that there are no disputed issues of fact that would necessitate a trial.

Motion for Summary Judgment. If there are no disagreements about the facts in a case and the only question is how the law applies to those facts, both sides can agree to the facts and ask the judge to apply the law to them. In this situation, it is appropriate for either party to move for **summary judgment.** When the court considers a motion for summary judgment, it can take into account evidence outside the pleadings. The evidence may consist of sworn statements (affidavits) by parties or witnesses and documents, such as a contract. The use of this additional evidence distinguishes this motion from the motion to dismiss and the motion for judgment on the pleadings.

IN THE COURTROOM

Mary suffers injuries in an automobile accident with Daniel, who is intoxicated and has just left the Lucky Star Bar. A state law provides that any person who "knowingly" serves an individual who is "habitually addicted" to alcohol can be held liable for injuries caused by the intoxication of that individual. On the basis of this law, Mary sues the Lucky Star. The Lucky Star files a motion for summary judgment, claiming that there is nothing to indicate that the bar knew Daniel is an alcoholic. In opposition to this claim, Mary offers Daniel's testimony of his drinking habits. Daniel testifies that in the two-year period before the accident, he went to the Lucky Star twice a week, becoming overtly intoxicated on each occasion. He says that he is well known to the bartenders, who never refused to serve him. On the night of the accident, they served him twenty shots of hard liquor. *Can the court take Daniel's testimony into consideration in ruling on the motion for summary judgment?* Yes. When a court considers a motion for summary judgment, it can take into account evidence outside the pleadings. Will the court grant the motion? Probably not.

Daniel's testimony should be enough for a finding that the Lucky Star employees knew of Daniel's addiction, based on his repeated behavior and appearance.

DISCOVERY

Before a trial begins, the parties can use a number of procedural devices to obtain information and gather evidence about the case. The process of obtaining information from the opposing party or from other witnesses is known as **discovery.** Discovery prevents surprises by giving parties access to evidence that might otherwise be hidden. This allows both parties to learn as much as they can about what to expect at a trial before they reach the courtroom. It also serves to narrow the issues so that trial time is spent on the main questions in the case.

DISCOVERY
A method by which opposing parties may obtain information from each other to prepare for trial. Generally governed by rules of procedure, but may be controlled by the court.

Depositions and Interrogatories. Discovery can involve the use of depositions, interrogatories, or both. **Depositions** are sworn testimony by the opposing party or any witness, recorded by an authorized court official. The person deposed gives sworn testimony under oath and answers questions asked by the attorneys from both sides. The questions and answers are taken down, sworn to, and signed.

DEPOSITION
A generic term that refers to any evidence verified by oath. As a legal term, it is often limited to the testimony of a witness taken under oath before a trial, with the opportunity of cross-examination.

Interrogatories are a series of written questions for which written answers are prepared and then signed under oath. The main difference between interrogatories and depositions with written questions is that interrogatories are directed to a party to the lawsuit (the plaintiff or the defendant), not to a witness, and the party can prepare answers with the aid of an attorney. The scope of interrogatories is broader, because parties are obligated to answer questions even if it means disclosing information from their records and files.

INTERROGATORY
A series of written questions for which written answers are prepared and then signed under oath by a party to a lawsuit (the plaintiff or the defendant).

Other Information. A party can serve a written request to the other party for an admission of the truth of matters relating to the trial. An admission in response to such a request is the equivalent of an admission in court. A request for admission saves time at trial, because parties will not have to spend time proving facts on which they already agree.

A party can also gain access to documents and other items not in his or her possession in order to inspect and examine them. Likewise, a party can gain "entry upon land" to inspect the premises.

When the physical or mental condition of one party is in question, the opposing party can ask the court to order a physical or mental examination. If the court is willing to make the order, the opposing party can obtain the results of the examination. It is important to note that the court will make such an order only when the need for the information outweighs the right to privacy of the person to be examined.

Compliance with Discovery Requests. If a party refuses to cooperate with requests made by the opposing party during discovery, the court may compel the party to comply with the requests by a specific date. If the party still does not comply, he or she may be held in contempt of court and, as a consequence, may be fined or imprisoned and required to pay the opposing party's resulting expenses. The court might even enter a default judgment for the opposing party.

LEARNING OBJECTIVE NO. 3
Discussing the Procedure of a Trial

AT THE TRIAL

A trial opens with the attorney for each party making an opening statement. (The plaintiff's attorney goes first.) The plaintiff's attorney then calls and questions the first witness. This questioning is called **direct examination.** The defendant's attorney then questions the witness. This is known as **cross-examination.** The plaintiff's attorney may question the witness again *(redirect examination),* and the defendant's attorney may follow again *(recross-examination).*

DIRECT EXAMINATION
The examination of a witness by the attorney who calls the witness to the stand to testify on behalf of the attorney's client.

CROSS-EXAMINATION
The questioning of an opposing witness during the trial.

REBUTTAL
The refutation of evidence introduced by an adverse party's attorney.

REJOINDER
The defendant's answer to the plaintiff's rebuttal.

CLOSING ARGUMENT
An argument made after the plaintiff and defendant have rested their cases.

MOTION FOR A DIRECTED VERDICT
A motion for the judge to direct a verdict for the moving party on the grounds that the other party has not produced sufficient evidence to support his or her claim.

After the plaintiff's attorney has called all of the witnesses and presented all of the evidence for the plaintiff's side of the case, the defendant's attorney presents the defendant's witnesses and evidence. At the conclusion of the defendant's case, the plaintiff's attorney can present a **rebuttal** (evidence and testimony refuting the defendant's case), after which the defendant can respond with a **rejoinder** (evidence and testimony refuting the plaintiff's rebuttal). Each side then presents **closing arguments** (final statements summarizing their versions of the evidence), and the court reaches a verdict.

At every stage in a trial, the parties can file various motions, including a motion to dismiss the case, a motion for summary judgment, and a **motion for a directed verdict** (known in federal courts as a *motion for judgment as a matter of law*). With a motion for a directed verdict, the defendant's attorney asks the judge to direct a verdict for the defendant on the ground that the plaintiff has presented no evidence that would justify the granting of the plaintiff's remedy. The judge looks at the evidence in the light most favorable to the plaintiff and grants the motion only if there is insufficient evidence to prove that the parties disagree about the facts.

LEARNING OBJECTIVE NO. 4
Summarizing the Steps in a Typical Lawsuit

At the end of the trial, a motion can be made to set aside the verdict and to hold a new trial. A motion for a new trial will be granted if the judge is convinced, after looking at all the evidence, that the jury was in error but does not feel it is appropriate to grant a judgment for the other side.

The events of a typical lawsuit are illustrated in Exhibit 3–4.

EXHIBIT 3–4
A Typical Lawsuit

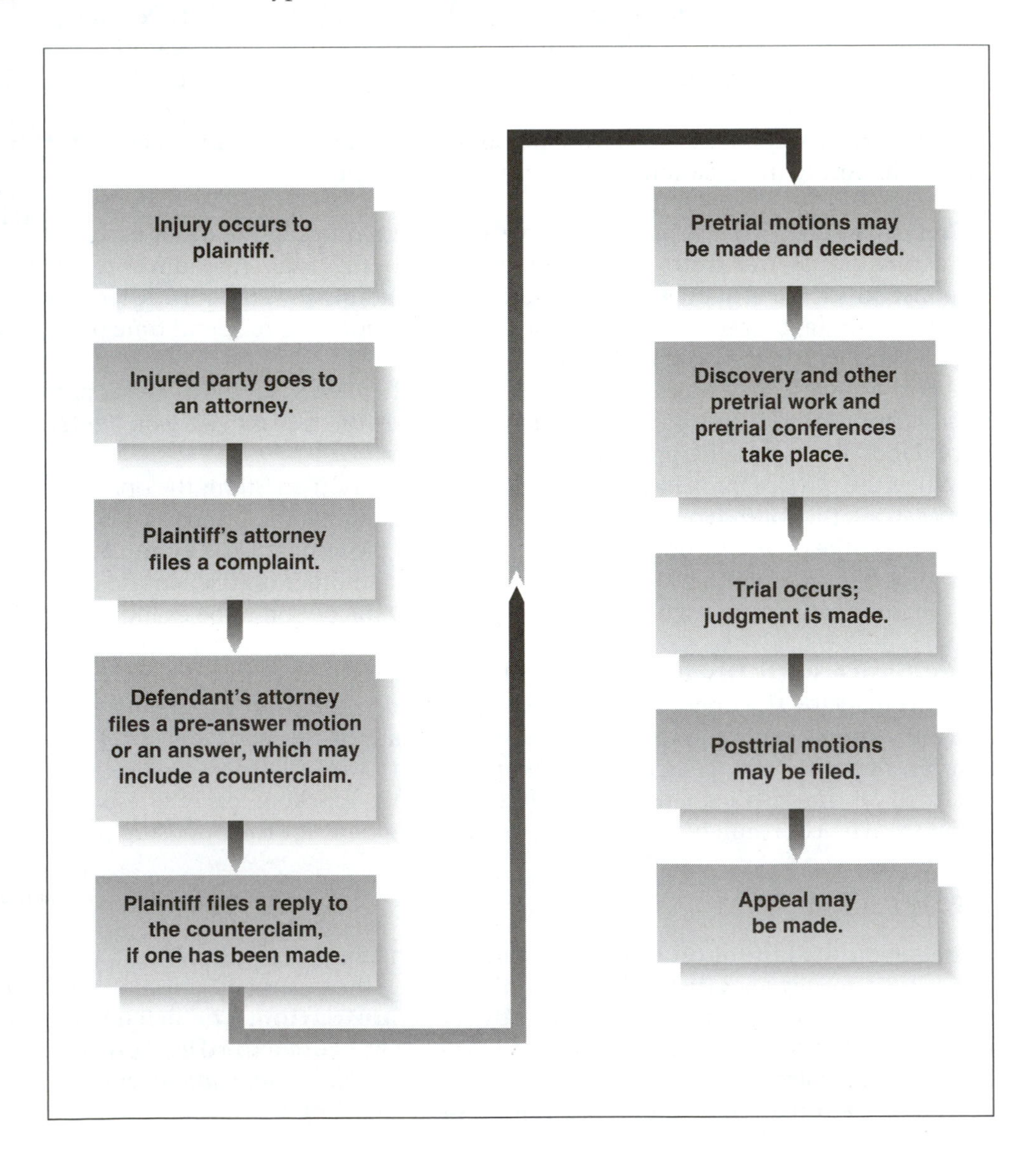

THE APPEAL

A party who appeals is known as the **appellant,** or petitioner. His or her attorney files in the reviewing court the record on appeal, which includes trial testimony and the evidence. The party in opposition to the appellant is the **appellee,** or the respondent. Attorneys for both sides file **briefs** with the reviewing court. A brief contains, among other things, arguments on a party's behalf that cite applicable statutes and relevant cases to support affirming or reversing the judgment of the lower court. The attorneys may also present oral arguments.

A court of appeals does not hear any evidence. Its decision in a case is based on the record and the briefs. In general, appellate courts review the record for errors of law. If the reviewing court believes that an error was committed, the judgment will be *reversed.* Sometimes the case will be *remanded* (sent back to the court that originally heard the case) for a new trial. In most cases, the judgment of the lower court is *affirmed,* resulting in the enforcement of the court's judgment.

If the reviewing court is an intermediate appellate court, the losing party normally may appeal to the state supreme court. If this court agrees to hear the case, new briefs must be filed and there may again be oral arguments. The supreme court may reverse or affirm the appellate court's decision, or remand the case. At this point, unless a federal question is at issue, the case has reached its end.

APPELLANT
The party who takes an appeal from one court to another; sometimes referred to as the petitioner.

APPELLEE
The party against whom an appeal is taken—that is, the party who opposes setting aside or reversing the judgment; sometimes referred to as the respondent.

BRIEF
A written summary or statement prepared by one side in a lawsuit to explain its case to the judge; a typical brief has a facts summary, a law summary, and an argument about how the law applies to the facts.

TERMS AND CONCEPTS FOR REVIEW

CHAPTER SUMMARY • THE ROLE OF COURTS IN OUR LEGAL SYSTEM

Jurisdiction	**1.** Territorial boundaries within which a court has the power to decide cases concerning a defendant or a defendant's property. **2.** A court's authority over the subject matter of a case.
Types of Courts	**1.** *Trial courts*—Where an action is initiated. All states have trial courts. In the federal system, the district courts are trial courts. **2.** *Intermediate appellate courts*—Courts of appeal and review. Many states have an intermediate appellate court; in the federal system, the circuit courts of appeals are the intermediate appellate courts. **3.** *Highest appellate courts*—Each state has a high court from which appeal to the United States Supreme Court is possible only if a federal question is involved. The United States Supreme Court is the highest court in the federal system and the final arbiter of the Constitution and federal law.

CHAPTER SUMMARY • *Continued*

Procedure	Civil court procedure in a state court involves the following steps: **1.** *The pleadings:* **a.** Complaint—A statement of the facts, the issues, and the parties involved, filed with the court by the plaintiff. A summons and a copy of the complaint are delivered to the defendant. **b.** Pre-answer motion—Such as a motion to dismiss, which may be made by the defendant; granted if the plaintiff failed to state a claim for which the law can grant relief. **c.** Answer—Can admit or deny the allegations in the complaint and may include a counterclaim. **2.** *Dismissal or judgment before trial:* **a.** Motion for judgment on the pleadings—May be made by either party; granted if no facts are disputed. In considering the motion, the court looks only at the pleadings. **b.** Motion for summary judgment—May be made by either party; granted if no facts are disputed. In considering the motion, the court can look at evidence outside the pleadings. **3.** *Discovery*—The process of gathering evidence concerning the case; involves depositions (sworn testimony by a party to the lawsuit or any witness) and *interrogatories* (written answers to questions made by parties to the action with the aid of their attorneys). **4.** *Trial*—Involves opening statements from both parties' attorneys, each party's presentation of its side of the case (with the introduction and examination of witnesses and evidence), the plaintiff's rebuttal, the defendant's rejoinder, closing arguments from both sides, various motions (such as a motion for a directed verdict) from both parties, and the court's verdict. **5.** *Posttrial and prejudgment options:* **a.** Motion for a new trial—Will be granted if the judge is convinced that the jury was in error. **b.** Appeal—Either party can appeal the trial court's judgment to an appropriate court of appeals. Briefs are filed, a hearing is held, and the court renders an opinion.

HYPOTHETICAL QUESTIONS

3–1. Jurisdiction. Marya Callais, a citizen of Florida, was walking near a busy street in Tallahassee one day when a large crate flew off a passing truck and hit her, resulting in numerous injuries to Callais. She incurred a great deal of pain and suffering plus numerous medical expenses, and she could not work for six months. She wishes to sue the trucking firm for $300,000 in damages. The firm's headquarters are in Georgia, although the company does business in Florida. In what court may Marya bring suit—a Florida state court, a Georgia state court, or a federal court? What factors might influence her decision?

3–2. Jurisdiction. Shem and Nadine Maslov, who live in Massachusetts, saw an advertisement in the *Boston Globe* for vacationers that was sponsored by a national hotel chain: "Stay in Maximum Inns' beachfront hotel in Puerto Rico for one week for only $400; continental breakfast included." The Maslovs decided to accept the offer and spent a week at the hotel. On the last day, Nadine fell on a wet floor in the hotel lobby and sustained multiple fractures to her left ankle and hip. Because of her injuries, which were subsequently complicated by infections, she was unable to work at her job as an airline flight attendant for ten months. The hotel chain does not do business in Massachusetts. If Nadine sues Maximum Inns in a Massachusetts state court, can the court exercise jurisdiction over Maximum Inns? What factors should the court consider in deciding this jurisdictional issue?

REAL WORLD CASE PROBLEM

3–3. Motion for a New Trial. Washoe Medical Center, Inc., admitted Shirley Swisher for the treatment of a fractured pelvis. During her stay, Swisher suffered a fatal fall from her hospital bed. Gerald Parodi, the administrator of her estate, and others, filed an action against Washoe in which they sought damages for the alleged lack of care in treating Swisher. During the questioning of prospective jurors, when the plaintiffs' attorney returned a few minutes late from a break, the trial judge led the prospective jurors in a standing ovation. The judge joked with one of the prospective jurors, whom he had known in college, about the judge's fitness to serve as a judge and personally endorsed another prospective juror's business. After the trial, the jury returned the verdict in favor of Washoe. The plaintiffs filed a motion for a new trial, but the judge denied the motion. The plaintiffs then appealed, arguing that the tone set by the judge prejudiced their right to a fair trial. Should the appellate court agree? Why or why not? [*Parodi v. Washoe Medical Center, Inc.,* 111 Nev. 365, 892 P2d 588(1995)]

For updated links to resources available on the Web, as well as a variety of other materials, visit this text's Web site at **http://blte.westbuslaw.com**.

The decisions of the United States Supreme Court and of all of the U.S. courts of appeals are now published online shortly after the decisions are rendered (often within hours). You can find these decisions and obtain information about the federal court system by accessing the Federal Court Locator at

http://vls.law.vill.edu/Locator/fedcourt.html

For information on the justices of the United States Supreme Court, links to opinions they have authored, and other information about the Supreme Court, go to

http://oyez.nwu.edu

The Web site for the federal courts offers information on the federal court system and links to all federal courts at

http://www.uscourts.gov

The National Center for State Courts (NCSC) offers links to the Web pages of all state courts. Go to

http://www.ncsc.dni.us/court/sites/courts.htm

ONLINE LEGAL RESEARCH

Go to **http://blte.westbuslaw.com,** the Web site that accompanies this text. Select "Internet Applications," and then click on "Chapter 3." There you will find the following Internet exercises that you can perform to learn more about the court procedures involved in civil lawsuits and in small claims courts:

Activity 3–1: Civil Procedure

Activity 3–2: Small Claims Courts

Chapter 3 ■ WORK SET

TRUE-FALSE QUESTIONS

_____ **1.** Generally, a court can exercise jurisdiction over the residents of the state in which the court is located.

_____ **2.** All state trial courts have general jurisdiction.

_____ **3.** The decisions of a state's highest court on all questions of state law are final.

_____ **4.** Federal district courts have original jurisdiction in federal matters.

_____ **5.** Federal courts may refuse to enforce a state or federal statute that violates the U.S. Constitution.

_____ **6.** The United States Supreme Court can hear appeals on federal questions from state and federal courts.

_____ **7.** Pleadings consist of a complaint, an answer, and a motion to dismiss.

_____ **8.** If a party does not deny the truth of a complaint, he or she is in default.

_____ **9.** Business conduct that was considered acceptable in the past is entirely acceptable today.

MULTIPLE-CHOICE QUESTIONS

_____ **1.** National Computers, Inc., was incorporated in Nebraska, has its main office in Kansas, and does business in Missouri. National is subject to the jurisdiction of

a. Nebraska, Kansas, or Missouri.
b. Nebraska or Kansas, but not Missouri.
c. Nebraska or Missouri, but not Kansas.
d. Kansas or Missouri, but not Nebraska.

_____ **2.** Alpha, Inc., sues Beta, Inc., in state court. Alpha loses and files an appeal with the state appeals court. The appeals court will

a. not retry the case, because the appropriate place for the retrial of a state case is a federal court.
b. not retry the case, because an appeals court examines the record of a case, looking at questions of law and procedure for errors by the trial court.
c. retry the case, because after a case is tried a party has a right to an appeal.
d. retry the case, because Alpha and Beta do not agree on the result of the trial.

_____ **3.** A suit can be brought in a federal court if it involves

a. a question under the Constitution, a treaty, or a federal law.
b. citizens of different states, a foreign country and a U.S. citizen, or a foreign citizen and an American citizen, and the amount in controversy is more than $75,000.
c. either a or b.
d. none of the above.

_____ **4.** Concurrent jurisdiction exists when

a. only state courts have the power to hear a case.
b. only federal courts have the power to hear a case.
c. both state and federal courts have the power to hear a case.
d. neither state nor federal courts have the power to hear a case.

_____ **5.** Ann sues Carla in a state trial court. Ann loses the suit. If Ann wants to appeal, the most appropriate court in which to file the appeal is

a. the state appellate court.
b. the nearest federal district court.
c. the nearest federal court of appeals.
d. the United States Supreme Court.

_____ **6.** The first step in a lawsuit is the filing of pleadings, and the first pleading filed is the complaint. The complaint contains

a. a statement alleging jurisdictional facts.
b. a statement of facts entitling the complainant to relief.
c. a statement asking for a specific remedy.
d. all of the above.

_____ **7.** The purposes of discovery include

a. saving time.
b. narrowing the issues.
c. preventing surprises at trial.
d. all of the above.

_____ **8.** Jim and Bill are involved in an automobile accident. Sue is a passenger in Bill's car. Jim's attorney wants to ask Sue, as a witness, some questions concerning the accident. Sue's answers to the questions are given in

a. a deposition.
b. a response to interrogatories.
c. a rebuttal.
d. none of the above.

_____ **9.** After the entry of a judgment, who can appeal?

a. Only the winning party.
b. Only the losing party.
c. Either the winning party or the losing party.
d. None of the above.

ISSUE SPOTTERS

1. Ron wants to sue Art's Supply Company for Art's failure to deliver supplies that Ron needed to prepare his work for an appearance at a local Artists Fair. What must Ron establish before a court will hear the suit?

2. Carlos, a citizen of California, is injured in an automobile accident in Arizona. Alex, the driver of the other car, is a citizen of New Mexico. Carlos wants Alex to pay Carlos's $125,000 in medical expenses and car repairs. Can Carlos sue in federal court?

Torts

4

LEARNING OBJECTIVES

When you finish this chapter, you should be able to:

1. State the purpose of tort law.
2. Explain how torts and crimes differ.
3. Identify intentional torts against persons.
4. Name the four elements of negligence.
5. Define strict liability, and list circumstances in which it will be applied.

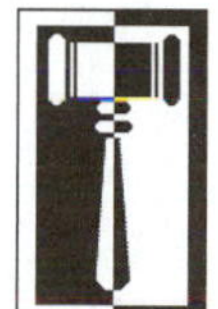

FACING A LEGAL PROBLEM

Joe is walking down the street, minding his own business, when suddenly Albert attacks him. In the ensuing struggle, Albert stabs Joe several times, seriously injuring Joe. A police officer restrains and arrests Albert. Albert is subject to criminal prosecution by the state. *May Albert also be subject to a lawsuit by Joe?*

A **tort** is wrongful conduct—a civil, as opposed to a criminal, wrong not arising from a breach of contract. Through tort law, society compensates those who have suffered injuries as a result of the wrongful conduct of others.

TORT
A civil wrong not arising from a breach of contract. A breach of a legal duty that proximately causes harm or injury to another.

Tort law covers a wide variety of injuries. Tort law provides remedies for acts that cause physical injury or that interfere with physical security and freedom of movement. Tort law provides remedies for acts that cause destruction or damage to property. Society also recognizes an interest in protecting personal privacy, family relations, reputation, and dignity, and tort law provides remedies for invasion of these protected interests.

LEARNING OBJECTIVE NO. 1
Stating the Purpose of Tort Law

Certain torts normally occur only in the business context. The important area of business torts will be treated in Chapter 5. In this chapter, we discuss torts that can occur in any context, including the business environment.

The Basis of Tort Law

LEARNING OBJECTIVE NO. 2
Explaining How Torts and Crimes Differ

Tort law recognizes that some acts are wrong because they cause injuries to others. A tort is not the only type of wrong that exists in the law; crimes also involve wrongs. A crime is an act so reprehensible that it is considered a wrong against society as a whole, as well as against the individual victim. Therefore, the *state* prosecutes and punishes (through fines, imprisonment, and possibly death) persons who commit criminal acts. A tort action, in contrast, is a civil action in which one person brings a personal suit against another to obtain compensation (money **damages**) or other relief for the harm suffered.

DAMAGES
Money sought as a remedy for a breach of contract or for a tortious act.

In the legal problem set out at the beginning of this chapter, Albert attacks and stabs Joe. A police officer arrests Albert, who is subject to criminal prosecution by the state. *May Albert also be subject to a lawsuit by Joe?* Yes. Here, Albert has committed the torts of assault and battery (to be discussed shortly). Some torts, such as assault and battery, provide a basis for a criminal prosecution as well as a tort action.

Exhibit 4–1 illustrates how the same wrongful act can result in both civil (tort) and criminal actions against the wrongdoer.

Intentional Torts against Persons

LEARNING OBJECTIVE NO. 3
Identifying Intentional Torts against Persons

An **intentional tort** requires intent. The **tortfeasor** (the one committing the tort) must intend to commit an act, the consequences of which interfere with the interests of another in a way not permitted by law. An evil or harmful motive is not required—intent only means that the actor intended the consequences of his or her act or knew with substantial certainty that certain consequences would result from the act. It is assumed that individuals intend the *normal* consequences of their actions. Thus, forcefully pushing another is an intentional tort (if injury results), because the object of a strong push can ordinarily be expected to go flying.

INTENTIONAL TORT
A wrongful act knowingly committed.

TORTFEASOR
One who commits a tort.

This section discusses intentional torts against persons, which include assault and battery, false imprisonment, defamation, invasion of the right to privacy, and misrepresentation.

EXHIBIT 4–1
Tort Lawsuit and Criminal Prosecution for the Same Act

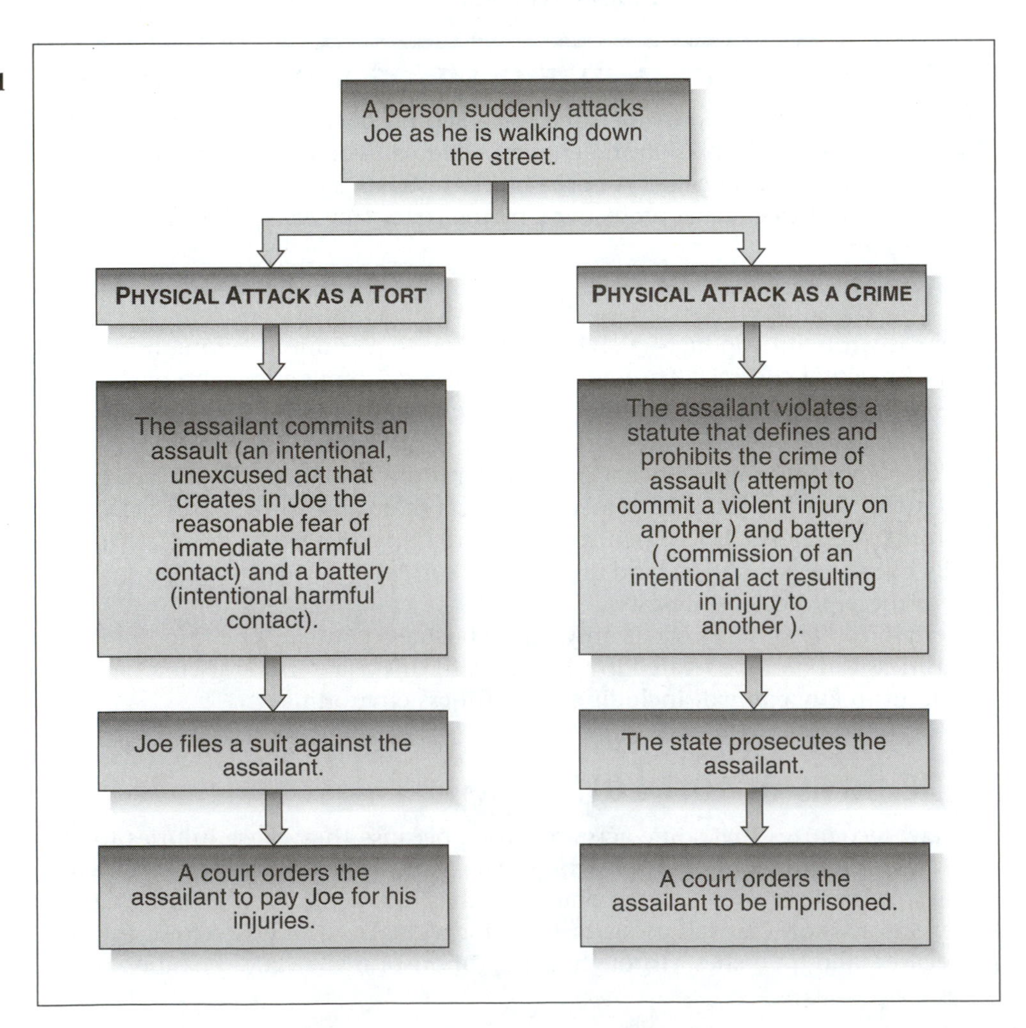

ASSAULT AND BATTERY

An intentional, unexcused act that creates in another person a reasonable apprehension or fear of immediate harmful or offensive contact is an **assault.** Apprehension is not the same as fear. If a contact is such that a reasonable person would want to avoid it, and there is a reasonable basis for believing that the contact will occur, the plaintiff suffers apprehension whether or not he or she is afraid.

ASSAULT
Any word or action intended to make another person fearful of immediate physical harm; a reasonably believable threat.

The *completion* of the act that caused the apprehension, if it results in harm to the plaintiff, is a **battery**—an unexcused and harmful or offensive physical contact *intentionally* performed. The contact can be harmful, or it can be merely offensive (such as an unwelcome kiss). The contact can involve any part of the body or anything attached to it—for example, an item of clothing or a car in which one is sitting. Whether the contact is offensive or not is determined by the *reasonable person* standard (which is discussed in more detail later in this chapter). The contact can be made by the defendant or by some force the defendant sets in motion—for example, a rock thrown.

BATTERY
The unprivileged, intentional touching of another.

IN THE COURTROOM

Ivan threatens Jean with a gun, then shoots her. *Which of these acts is an assault? Which is a battery?* The pointing of the gun at Jean is an assault; the firing of the gun (if the bullet hits Jean) is a battery. The law concerning assault protects us from having to expect harmful or offensive contact. Apprehension of such contact is enough to justify compensation. The law concerning battery protects us from being subject to harmful or offensive contact. The contact can be made by another person or by some force the other person sets in motion—for example, a bullet fired from a gun.

Defenses to Assault and Battery. A number of **defenses** (reasons why plaintiffs should not obtain what they are seeking) can be raised by a defendant who is sued for assault or battery, or both:

DEFENSE
That which a defendant offers and alleges in an action or suit as a reason why the plaintiff should not recover or establish what he or she seeks.

1. *Consent.* When a person consents to the act that damages him or her, there is generally no liability (legal responsibility) for the damage.
2. *Self-defense.* An individual who is defending his or her life or physical well-being can claim self-defense. In situations of both *real* and *apparent* danger, a person may use whatever force is reasonably necessary to prevent harmful contact.
3. *Defense of others.* An individual can act in a reasonable manner to protect others who are in real or apparent danger.
4. *Defense of property.* Reasonable force may be used to remove intruders from one's home, although force that is likely to cause death or great bodily injury can never be used just to protect property.

FALSE IMPRISONMENT

False imprisonment is the intentional confinement or restraint of another person without justification. The confinement can be accomplished through the use of physical barriers, physical restraint, or threats of physical force. Moral pressure or threats of future harm do not constitute false imprisonment.

Businesspersons are often confronted with suits for false imprisonment after they have attempted to confine a suspected shoplifter for questioning. In some states, a merchant can use the defense of *probable cause* to justify delaying a suspected shoplifter. Probable cause exists when the evidence to support the belief that a person is guilty outweighs the evidence against that belief. The detention, however, must be conducted in a reasonable manner and for only a *reasonable* length of time.

Employees who handle shoplifters should be appropriately trained in the proper procedure for apprehending and detaining someone suspected of shoplifting. Print out a short list of rules and have it checked by a local attorney familiar with recent court decisions in your area.

DEFAMATION

DEFAMATION
Anything published or publicly spoken that causes injury to another's good name, reputation, or character.

SLANDER
Defamation in oral form.

LIBEL
Defamation in written form.

Defamation of character involves wrongfully hurting a person's good reputation. Doing so orally involves the tort of **slander;** doing it in writing involves the tort of **libel.** Defamation also occurs when a false statement is made about a person's product, business, or title to property. We deal with these torts in the following chapter.

There are four types of false utterances that are considered torts *per se* (meaning no proof of injury or harm is required for these false utterances to be actionable):

1. A statement that another has a loathsome communicable disease.
2. A statement that another has committed improprieties while engaging in a profession or trade.
3. A statement that another has committed or has been imprisoned for a serious crime.
4. A statement that an unmarried woman is unchaste.

The Publication Requirement. The basis of the tort of defamation is the *publication* of a statement that holds an individual up to contempt, ridicule, or hatred. Publication means that a statement is communicated to a person other than the defamed party. If Peters calls Gordon incompetent when no one else is around, the statement is not slander because it was not communicated to a third party.

Dictating a letter to a secretary constitutes publication. If a third party overhears a statement by chance, this is also publication. Defamatory statements made via the Internet are also actionable (capable of providing the basis for a lawsuit). An individual who republishes or repeats defamatory statements is liable even if that person reveals the source of the statements.

IN THE COURTROOM

Jack and Donna are exchanging thoughts online via the Internet. Donna accuses her boss of sexual misconduct. *Does this statement constitute defamation?* Yes. This is because what may seem like a private online "conversation" between just two persons is, in fact, a very public exchange, potentially accessible to millions of people. The fact that Jack and Donna are unseen at the time a defamatory statement is made makes no difference. The person defamed (the boss, in this example) could suffer serious harm from the statement—loss of reputation and perhaps even the loss of a job. Donna could be sued in tort for damages.

PRIVILEGE
In tort law, privilege may be raised as a defense to defamation.

ACTUAL MALICE
In a defamation suit, a statement made about a public figure normally must be made with actual malice (with either knowledge of its falsity or a reckless disregard of the truth) for liability.

Defenses against Defamation. Truth is normally an absolute defense against a defamation charge. Furthermore, there may be a **privilege** involved in certain communications. For example, statements made by attorneys and judges during a trial are privileged and cannot be the basis for a defamation charge. Members of Congress making statements on the floor of Congress have an absolute privilege.

In general, defamatory statements that are made in the press about *public figures* (those who exercise substantial governmental power and any persons in the public limelight) are privileged if they are made without **actual malice.** To be made with actual malice, a statement must be made *with either knowledge of falsity or a reckless disregard for the truth.* Public figures must prove actual malice because statements made about them are usually related to matters of public interest. Also, public figures generally have access to a public medium, such as television or radio, for answering falsehoods; private individuals do not.

INVASION OF THE RIGHT TO PRIVACY

Four acts qualify as an invasion of privacy:

1. The use of a person's name, picture, or other likeness for commercial purposes without permission. This tort—the tort of *appropriation*—will be examined in the next chapter.
2. Intrusion in an individual's affairs or seclusion in an area in which the person has a reasonable expectation of privacy.
3. Publication of information that places a person in a false light. This could be a story that a person did something that he or she did not actually do. (Publishing such a story could also constitute defamation.)
4. Public disclosure of private facts about an individual that an ordinary person would find objectionable.

MISREPRESENTATION—FRAUD (DECEIT)

Misrepresentation leads another to believe in a condition that is different from a condition that actually exists. The tort of **fraudulent misrepresentation,** or fraud, involves intentional deceit for personal gain. The tort includes several elements:

FRAUDULENT MISREPRESENTATION
Any misrepresentation, either by misstatement or omission of a material fact, knowingly made with the intention of deceiving another and on which a reasonable person would and does rely to his or her detriment.

1. Misrepresentation of facts or conditions with knowledge that they are false or with reckless disregard for the truth.
2. Intent to induce another to rely on the misrepresentation.
3. Justifiable reliance by the deceived party.
4. Damages suffered as a result of reliance.
5. Causal connection between the misrepresentation and the injury.

For fraud to occur, more than mere **puffery,** or *seller's talk,* must be involved. Fraud exists only when a person represents as a fact something he or she knows is untrue. For example, it is fraud to claim that a building does not leak when one knows it does. Facts are objectively ascertainable, whereas seller's talk is not. "I am the best accountant in town" is seller's talk. The speaker is not trying to represent something as fact, because the term *best* is a subjective, not an objective, term. We examine fraudulent misrepresentation in further detail in Chapter 12, in the context of contract law.

PUFFERY
A salesperson's often exaggerated claims concerning the quality of property offered for sale. Such claims involve opinions rather than facts and are not considered to be legally binding promises or warranties.

Intentional Torts against Property

Intentional torts against property include trespass to land, trespass to personal property, and conversion. Land is *real property,* which also includes things "permanently" attached to the land (see Chapter 36). *Personal property* consists of all other items, which are basically movable (see Chapter 35). Thus, a house and lot are real property, whereas the furniture inside a house is personal property.

TRESPASS TO LAND

A **trespass to land** occurs when a person, without permission, enters onto, above, or below the surface of land that is owned by another; causes anything to enter onto the land; remains on the land; or permits anything to remain on it. Actual harm to the land is not required. Common types of trespass to land include walking or driving on the land, shooting a gun over the land, throwing rocks at a building that belongs to someone else, building a dam across a river and thus causing water to back up on someone else's land, and placing part of one's building on an adjoining landowner's property.

TRESPASS TO LAND
The entry onto, above, or below the surface of land owned by another without the owner's permission or legal authorization.

In some jurisdictions, a trespasser is liable for damage caused to the property and generally cannot hold the owner liable for injuries sustained on the premises.

Other jurisdictions apply a "reasonable duty" rule; for example, a landowner may have a duty to post a notice that property is patrolled by guard dogs. Trespassers normally can be removed from the premises through the use of reasonable force without the owner's being liable for assault and battery.

There is a defense to charges of trespass if the trespass is warranted, as when a trespasser enters to assist someone in danger. Another defense is to show that the purported owner did not actually have the right to possess the land in question.

TRESPASS TO PERSONAL PROPERTY

TRESPASS TO PERSONAL PROPERTY
The unlawful taking or harming of another's personal property; interference with another's right to the exclusive possession of his or her personal property.

When an individual unlawfully harms the personal property of another or otherwise interferes with the owner's right to exclusive possession and enjoyment of that property, **trespass to personal property** occurs. If one student takes another's business law book and hides it so that the owner cannot find it for several days prior to a final examination, the student has committed trespass to personal property.

If it can be shown that trespass to personal property was warranted, then a complete defense exists. Most states, for example, allow automobile repair shops to hold a customer's car (under what is called an *artisan's lien,* discussed in Chapter 32) if the customer refuses to pay for repairs already completed.

CONVERSION

CONVERSION
The wrongful taking, using, or retaining possession of personal property that belongs to another.

When personal property is wrongfully taken from its rightful owner or possessor and placed in the service of another, the act of **conversion** occurs. Conversion is any act depriving an owner of personal property without that owner's permission and without just cause. When conversion occurs, trespass to personal property usually occurs as well. If the initial taking of the property is unlawful, there is trespass; keeping the property is conversion. (If the initial taking of the property is not a trespass, failing to return it may still be conversion.) Conversion is the civil side of crimes related to theft. A store clerk who steals merchandise from the store commits a crime and engages in the tort of conversion at the same time.

A successful defense against the charge of conversion is that the purported owner does not in fact own the property or does not have a right to possess it that is superior to the right of the holder. Necessity is another possible defense against conversion. If Abrams takes Mendoza's cat, Abrams is guilty of conversion. If Mendoza sues Abrams, Abrams must return the cat or pay damages. If, however, the cat has rabies and Abrams took the cat to protect the public, Abrams has a valid defense—necessity (and perhaps even self-defense, if he can prove that he was in danger because of the cat).

Unintentional Torts (Negligence)

NEGLIGENCE
The failure to exercise the standard of care that a reasonable person would exercise in similar circumstances.

The tort of **negligence** occurs when someone suffers injury because of another's failure to live up to a required *duty of care.* It is not required that the tortfeasor wish to bring about the consequences of the act or believe that they will occur. It is required only that the actor's conduct create a *risk* of such consequences. If no risk is created, there is no negligence.

Many of the actions discussed in the section on intentional torts would constitute negligence if the element of intent were missing. For example, if Juarez intentionally shoves Natsuyo, who falls and breaks an arm as a result, Juarez will have committed an intentional tort. If Juarez carelessly bumps into Natsuyo, however, and she falls and breaks an arm as a result, Juarez's action will constitute negligence. In either situation, Juarez has committed a tort.

In examining a question of negligence, one should ask four questions:

1. Did the defendant owe a duty of care to the plaintiff?
2. Did the defendant breach that duty?
3. Did the plaintiff suffer a legally recognizable injury as a result of the defendant's breach of the duty of care?
4. Did the defendant's breach cause the plaintiff's injury?

Each of these elements of neligence is discussed below.

LEARNING OBJECTIVE NO. 4
Naming the Four Elements of Negligence

The Duty of Care and Its Breach

The basic principle underlying the **duty of care** is that people are free to act as they please so long as their actions do not infringe on the interests of others. When someone fails to comply with the duty of exercising reasonable care, a potentially tortious act may have been committed. Failure to live up to a standard of care may be an act (setting fire to a building) or an omission (neglecting to put out a campfire). It may be an intentional act, a careless act, or a carefully performed but nevertheless dangerous act that results in injury.

Duty of Care
The duty of all persons, as established by tort law, to exercise a reasonable amount of care in their dealings with others.

The Reasonable Person Standard. In determining whether a duty of care has been breached, the courts ask how a reasonable person would have acted in the same circumstances. It is not necessarily how a particular person would act. It is society's judgment on how people *should* act. If the so-called reasonable person existed, he or she would be careful, conscientious, even tempered, and honest. What constitutes reasonable care varies with the circumstances.

Duty of Landowners. Landowners are expected to exercise reasonable care to protect from harm persons coming onto their property. As mentioned earlier, in some jurisdictions, landowners are held to owe a duty to protect even trespassers against certain risks. Landowners who rent or lease premises to tenants are expected to exercise reasonable care to ensure that the tenants and their guests are not harmed in common areas, such as stairways (see Chapter 37).

Retailers and other firms that explicitly or implicitly invite persons to come onto their premises are usually charged with a duty to exercise reasonable care to protect those **business invitees.**

Business Invitees
Those people, such as customers or clients, who are invited onto business premises by the owner of those premises for business purposes.

IN THE COURTROOM

Don enters Select Foods, a supermarket. There is no sign warning that the floor is wet where one of the employees has finished cleaning. Don slips on the wet floor and sustains injuries as a result. *Is Select Foods liable for damages?* Yes. A court would hold that Select Foods was negligent because the employee failed to exercise reasonable care in protecting the store's customers against foreseeable risks that the employee knew or *should have known* about. That a patron might slip on a wet floor and be injured as a result was a foreseeable risk, and the employee should have taken care to avoid this risk or to warn the customer of it. The store also has a duty to discover and remove any hidden dangers that might injure a customer or other invitee.

Some risks are so obvious that no warning is necessary. For example, a business owner does not need to warn customers to open a door before attempting to walk through it. Other risks, however, may not be so obvious in the eyes of some persons, such as children. For example, a store owner may not think it is necessary to warn customers that a ladder leaning against the back wall of the store could fall down and harm them. It is possible, though, that a child would not see the danger.

A businessperson should assume that the worst can happen and post warnings near all potential hazards no matter how obvious they seem.

You can locate the professional standards for various professional organizations at

http://www.lib.uwaterloo.ca/society/standards.html

Duty of Professionals. If an individual has knowledge, skill, or intelligence superior to that of an ordinary person, the individual's conduct must be consistent with that status. Professionals—including doctors, architects, accountants, and others—must have a standard minimum level of special knowledge and ability. In determining what constitutes reasonable care in the case of professionals, their training and expertise is taken into account. In other words, an accountant cannot defend against a lawsuit for negligence by stating, "I was not familiar with that principle of accounting."

THE INJURY REQUIREMENT

For a tort to have been committed, the plaintiff must have suffered a *legally recognizable* injury. To recover damages (receive compensation), the plaintiff must have suffered some loss, harm, wrong, or invasion of a protected interest. If no harm or injury results from an action, there is nothing to compensate—and no tort exists. For example, if you carelessly bump into a passerby, who stumbles and falls as a result, you may be liable in tort if the passerby is injured in the fall. If the person is unharmed, however, there normally could be no suit for damages, because no injury was suffered.

CAUSATION

Another element necessary to a tort is *causation*. If a person fails in a duty of care and someone suffers injury, the wrongful activity must have caused the harm for a tort to have been committed.

Causation in Fact and Proximate Cause. In deciding whether there is causation, the court must address two questions:

1. *Is there causation in fact?* Did the injury occur because of the defendant's act? If an injury would not have occurred without the defendant's act, then there is causation in fact. **Causation in fact** can usually be determined by the use of the *but for* test: "but for" the wrongful act, the injury would not have occurred.
2. *Was the act the proximate cause of the injury?* As a practical matter, the law establishes limits through the concept of proximate cause. **Proximate cause** exists when the connection between an act and an injury is strong enough to justify imposing liability. Consider an example. Ackerman carelessly leaves a campfire burning. The fire not only burns down the forest but also sets off an explosion in a nearby chemical plant that spills chemicals into a river, killing all the fish for a hundred miles downstream and ruining the economy of a tourist resort. Should Ackerman be liable to the resort owners? To the tourists whose vacations were ruined? These are questions of proximate cause that a court must decide.

CAUSATION IN FACT
An act or omission without which an event would not have occurred.

PROXIMATE CAUSE
Legal cause; exists when the connection between an act and an injury is strong enough to justify imposing liability.

Foreseeability. *Foreseeability* is the test for proximate cause. If the victim of the harm or the consequences of the harm are unforeseeable, there is no proximate cause. How far a court stretches foreseeability is determined in part by the extent to which the court is willing to stretch the defendant's duty of care.

IN THE COURTROOM

Jim checks into Travelers Inn. During the night, a fire is started by an arsonist. The inn has a smoke detector, sprinkler, and alarm system, which alert the guests, but there are no emergency lights or clear exits. Attempting to escape, Jim finds the first-floor doors and windows locked. He forces open a second-floor window and jumps out. To recover for his injuries, he files a suit against Travelers Inn, on the ground of negligence. Travelers Inn responds that harm caused by arson is not a reasonably foreseeable risk. *Is the harm caused by a fire set by an arsonist a reasonably foreseeable risk?* Yes. In this case, the possibility of fire was foreseen and guarded against with smoke detectors and sprinkler and alarm systems. The duty to protect others against unreasonable risks of harm extends to risks arising from acts of third persons, even criminals. Travelers' failure to provide adequate lighting and exits created a foreseeable risk that a fire, however it started, would harm its guests.

Defenses to Negligence

The basic defenses in negligence cases are assumption of risk and comparative negligence.

Assumption of Risk. A plaintiff who voluntarily enters into a risky situation, knowing the risk involved, will not be allowed to recover. This is the defense of **assumption of risk.** The requirements of this defense are (1) knowledge of the risk and (2) voluntary assumption of the risk. For example, a driver entering a race knows there is a risk of being injured in a crash. The driver assumes this risk.

Assumption of Risk
A defense against negligence that can be used when the plaintiff is aware of a danger and voluntarily assumes the risk of injury from that danger.

Of course, a person does not assume a risk different from or greater than a risk normally carried by an activity. In our example, the driver assumes the risk of being injured in the race but not the risk that the banking in the curves of the racetrack will give way during the race because of a construction defect.

Comparative Negligence. Most states allow recovery based on the doctrine of **comparative negligence.** Under this doctrine, both the plaintiff's and the defendant's negligence is computed and the liability distributed accordingly. Some jurisdictions have a "pure" form of comparative negligence that allows a plaintiff to recover even if the extent of his or her fault is greater than that of the defendant. For example, if a plaintiff is 80 percent at fault and a defendant 20 percent at fault, the plaintiff may recover 20 percent of his or her damages. Many states, however, have a "50 percent" rule by which the plaintiff recovers nothing if he or she was more than 50 percent at fault.

Comparative Negligence
A doctrine in tort law under which the liability for injuries resulting from negligent acts is shared by all parties who were negligent (including the injured party), on the basis of each person's proportionate negligence.

IN THE COURTROOM

Brian is an experienced all-terrain-vehicle (ATV) rider. Without putting on a helmet, Brian takes his ATV for a drive. It flips, and Brian strikes his head, causing injuries. He files a suit against the ATV's manufacturer, American ATV Company. During the trial, it is proved that Brian's failure to wear a helmet was responsible for essentially all his injuries. Brian's state has a "50 percent" rule. *Under these circumstances, is the manufacturer liable for any of the damage sustained?* No. In a "50 percent" rule state, if a plaintiff is found to be at least equally responsible for whatever damage is sustained, he or she can recover nothing. The evidence that Brian's failure to wear a helmet is responsible for essentially all the damage is fatal to his case.

Strict Liability
Liability regardless of fault.

Strict Liability

LEARNING OBJECTIVE NO. 5
Defining Strict Liability, and Listing Circumstances in Which It Will Be Applied

Another category of torts is **strict liability,** or *liability without fault.* Strict liability for damages proximately caused by an abnormally dangerous activity is one application of this doctrine. Strict liability applies in such a case because of the extreme risk of the activity. For example, even if blasting with dynamite is performed with all reasonable care, there is still a risk of injury. Balancing that risk against the potential for harm, it is fair to ask the person engaged in the activity to pay for any injury caused by it. A significant application of strict liability is in the area of *product liability*—liability of manufacturers and sellers for harmful or defective products. We will discuss product liability in greater detail in Chapter 19.

IN THE COURTROOM

All-Pests Fumigation, Inc., fumigates an apartment building. The residents are evacuated for the procedure, but the occupants of a neighboring building are not. After the fumigation, residents of the neighboring building become ill and are treated for pesticide poisoning. It is discovered that the fire wall between the two buildings is defective and contains an open space through which the pesticide had passed. The occupants of the neighboring building sue All-Pests, alleging that it is strictly liable for their injuries. *Can All-Pests be liable for damages when the negligence of others (including building contractors) made the injuries possible?* Yes. Fumigation is an ultrahazardous activity because it involves a risk of serious harm that cannot be eliminated by the exercise of utmost care. All-Pests is thus liable regardless of how careful it was in the fumigating. That a third party was also negligent does not relieve All-Pests from liability for a hazard it created.

TERMS AND CONCEPTS FOR REVIEW

CHAPTER SUMMARY • TORTS

Intentional Torts against Persons	1. *Assault and battery*—An assault is an unexcused and intentional act that causes another person to be apprehensive of immediate harm. A battery is an assault that results in physical contact. 2. *False imprisonment*—The intentional confinement or restraint of another person's movement without justification. 3. *Defamation (libel or slander)*—A false statement of fact, not made under privilege, that is communicated to a third person and that causes damage to a person's reputation. For public figures, the plaintiff must also prove actual malice. 4. *Invasion of the right to privacy*—The use of a person's name or likeness for commercial purposes without permission, wrongful intrusion into a person's private activities, publication of information that places a person in a false light, or disclosure of private facts that an ordinary person would find objectionable. 5. *Misrepresentation—fraud (deceit)*—A false representation made by one party, through misstatement of facts or through conduct, with the intention of deceiving another and on which the other reasonably relies to his or her detriment.

CHAPTER SUMMARY • *Continued*

Intentional Torts against Property	**1.** *Trespass to land*—The invasion of another's real property without consent or privilege. Specific rights and duties apply once a person is expressly or impliedly established as a trespasser. **2.** *Trespass to personal property*—Unlawfully damaging or interfering with the owner's right to use, possess, or enjoy his or her personal property. **3.** *Conversion*—A wrongful act in which personal property is taken from its rightful owner or possessor and placed in the service of another.
Unintentional Torts—Negligence	**1.** *Negligence*—The careless performance of a legally required duty or the failure to perform a legally required act. Elements include that a legal duty of care exists, that the defendant breached that duty, and that the breach caused damage or injury to another. **2.** *Defenses to negligence*—The basic defenses in negligence cases are assumption of risk and comparative negligence.
Strict Liability	Under the doctrine of strict liability, a person may be held liable, regardless of the degree of care exercised, for damages or injuries caused by his or her product or activity. Strict liability includes liability for harms caused by abnormally dangerous activities and by defective products.

HYPOTHETICAL QUESTIONS

4–1. Defenses to Negligence. Corinna was riding her bike on a city street. While she was riding, she frequently looked behind her to verify that the books that she had fastened to the rear part of her bike were still attached. On one occasion while she was looking behind her, she failed to notice a car that was entering an intersection just as she was crossing it. The car hit her, causing her to sustain numerous injuries. Three eye witnesses stated that the driver of the car had failed to stop at the stop sign before entering the intersection. Corinna sued the driver of the car for negligence. What defenses might the defendant driver raise in this lawsuit? Discuss fully.

4–2. Liability to Business Invitees. Kim went to Ling's Market to pick up a few items for dinner. It was a rainy, windy day, and the wind had blown water through the door of Ling's Market each time the door opened. As Kim entered through the door, she slipped and fell in the approximately one-half inch of rainwater that had accumulated on the floor. The manager knew of the weather conditions but had not posted any sign to warn customers of the water hazard. Kim injured her back as a result of the fall and sued Ling's for damages. Can Ling's be held liable for negligence in this situation? Discuss.

REAL WORLD CASE PROBLEM

4–3. Duty to Business Invitees. George Ward entered a K-Mart department store in Champaign, Illinois, through a service entrance near the home improvements department. After purchasing a large mirror, Ward left the store through the same door. On his way out the door, carrying the large mirror in front and somewhat to the side of him, he collided with a concrete pole located just outside the door about a foot and a half from the outside wall. The mirror broke, and the broken glass cut Ward's right cheek and eye, resulting in reduced vision in that eye. He later stated that he had not seen the pole, had not realized what was happening, and only knew that he felt "a bad pain, and then saw stars." Ward sued K-Mart Corp. for damages, alleging that the store was negligent. What was the nature of K-Mart's duty of care to Ward? Did it breach that duty by placing the concrete pole just outside the door? What factors should the court consider when deciding whether K-Mart should be held liable for Ward's injuries? Discuss fully. [*Ward v. K-Mart Corp.*, 136 Ill.2d 132, 554 N.E.2d 223, 143 Ill.Dec. 288 (1990)]

For updated links to resources available on the Web, as well as a variety of other materials, visit this text's Web site at **http://blte.westbuslaw.com**.

You can find cases and articles on torts, including business torts, in the tort law library at the Internet Law Library's Web site. Go to

http://www.lawguru.com/ilawlib

ONLINE LEGAL RESEARCH

Go to **http://blte.westbuslaw.com**, the Web site that accompanies this text. Select "Internet Applications," and then click on "Chapter 4." There you will find the following Internet research exercises that you can perform to learn more about privacy rights in an online world and the elements of negligence:

Activity 4–1: Privacy Rights in Cyberspace

Activity 4–2: Negligence and the *Titanic*

Chapter 4 ■ WORK SET

TRUE-FALSE QUESTIONS

____ **1.** One function of tort law is to provide an injured person with a remedy.

____ **2.** To be guilty of an intentional tort, a person must intend the consequences of his or her act or know with substantial certainty that certain consequences will result.

____ **3.** Immediate harmful or offensive contact is an element of assault.

____ **4.** Immediate harmful or offensive contact is an element of battery.

____ **5.** The tort of defamation does not occur unless a defamatory statement is made in writing.

____ **6.** Ed tells customers that he is "the best plumber in town." This is fraudulent misrepresentation, unless Ed actually believes that he is the best.

____ **7.** A person who borrows a friend's car and fails to return it at the friend's request is guilty of conversion.

____ **8.** To avoid liability for negligence, the same duty of care must be exercised by all individuals, regardless of their knowledge, skill, or intelligence.

____ **9.** Under the doctrine of strict liability, liability is imposed for reasons other than fault.

MULTIPLE-CHOICE QUESTIONS

____ **1.** Tom owns Tom's Computer Store. Tom sees Nan, a customer, pick up software from a shelf and put it in her bag. As Nan is about to leave, Tom tells her that she can't leave until he checks her bag. If Nan sues Tom for false imprisonment, Nan will

a. win, because a merchant cannot delay a customer on a mere suspicion.
b. win, because Nan did not first commit a tort.
c. lose, because a merchant may delay a suspected shoplifter for a reasonable time based on probable cause.
d. lose, because Tom did not intend to commit the tort of false imprisonment.

____ **2.** Walking in Don's air-conditioned market on a hot day with her sisters, four-year-old Silvia drops her ice cream on the floor near the dairy case. Two hours later, Jan stops to buy milk, slips on the ice cream puddle, and breaks her arm. Don is

a. liable, because a merchant is always liable for customers' actions.
b. liable, if Don failed to take all reasonable precautions against Jan's injury.
c. not liable, because Jan's injury was her own fault.
d. not liable, because Jan's injury was the fault of Silvia's sisters.

_____ **3.** Joe, a 99-pound weakling, clenches his fist, stands as if ready to throw a punch, and orally threatens to hit a 360-pound lineman for the Chicago Bears. Joe is

a. not guilty of assault, because words alone are not enough.
b. not guilty of assault, because it is unlikely that the lineman is afraid of Joe.
c. guilty of assault, because the words are accompanied by a threatening act.
d. guilty of assault, because a professional football player is a public figure.

_____ **4.** Gus sends a letter to Jose in which he accuses Jose of embezzling. Jose's secretary, Tina, reads the letter. If Jose sues Gus for defamation, Jose will

a. win, because Tina's reading of the letter satisfies the publication element.
b. win, because Gus's writing of the letter satisfies the publication element.
c. lose, because the letter is not proof that Jose is an embezzler.
d. lose, because the publication element is not satisfied.

_____ **5.** During a trial, a judge calls an attorney unethical. If the attorney sues the judge for defamation, the attorney will

a. win, because the attorney is a public figure.
b. win, if the attorney can prove the statement was made with actual malice.
c. lose, because the judge's statement was privileged.
d. lose, because the judge is a public figure.

_____ **6.** Al, a landlord, installs two-way mirrors in his tenants' rooms through which he watches them without their knowledge. Al is guilty of

a. using another's likeness for commercial purposes without permission.
b. public disclosure of private facts about another.
c. publication of information that places another in false lights.
d. intrusion into another's affairs or seclusion.

_____ **7.** Fred returns home from work to find Barney camped in Fred's backyard. Fred says, "Get off my property." Barney says, "I'm not leaving." Fred forcibly drags Barney off the property. If Barney sues Fred, Barney will

a. win, because Fred used too much force.
b. win, because Barney told Fred that he was not leaving.
c. lose, because Fred used only reasonable force.
d. lose, because Barney is a trespasser.

_____ **8.** Driving his car negligently, Paul crashes into a light pole. The pole falls, smashing through the roof of a house onto Karl, who is killed. But for Paul's negligence, Karl would not have died. Regarding Karl's death, Paul's crash is the

a. cause in fact.
b. proximate cause.
c. intervening cause.
d. superseding cause.

ISSUE SPOTTERS

1. Adam kisses the sleeve of Eve's blouse, to which she did not consent. Is Adam guilty of a tort?

2. If a student takes another student's business law textbook as a practical joke and hides it for several days before the final examination, has a tort been committed?

Business Torts, Intellectual Property, and Cyberlaw

5

LEARNING OBJECTIVES

When you finish this chapter, you should be able to:

1. Identify two kinds of business torts involving wrongful interference.
2. Discuss the law's protection for trademarks.
3. Describe the protection that the law provides for patents.
4. State the law's protection for copyrights.
5. Define the law's protection for trademarks on the Internet.
6. Discuss how the law can protect patents on the Internet.

FACING A LEGAL PROBLEM

In the 1850s in England, an opera singer, Joanna Wagner, was under contract to sing for a man named Lumley in Lumley's London theater for a specified period of years. A man named Gye, who knew of this contract, nonetheless "enticed" Wagner to refuse to carry out the agreement. Wagner began to sing in Gye's theater instead. *Did Gye's action constitute a ground for a lawsuit?*

Businesses may, generally speaking, engage in whatever is *reasonably* necessary to obtain a fair share of a market or to recapture a share that has been lost. They are not allowed, however, to use the motive of complete elimination of competition to justify certain business activities.

As explained in Chapter 4, a *tort* is a civil (as opposed to criminal) wrong not arising from a breach of contract. **Business torts** are defined as wrongful interference with another's business rights. Those who enter into business should be acquainted with the point at which zealous competition might be construed by a court of law to cross over into tortious interference with the business rights of others.

BUSINESS TORT
A tort occurring within the business context.

After an examination of business torts, we turn to the subject of intellectual property. *Trademarks, patents,* and *copyrights* are all forms of intellectual property. The study of intellectual property law is important because intellectual property has taken on an increasing importance not only within the United States but globally as well.

Wrongful Interference

Business torts involving wrongful interference are generally divided into two categories: wrongful interference with a contractual relationship and wrongful interference with a business relationship.

WRONGFUL INTERFERENCE WITH A CONTRACTUAL RELATIONSHIP

LEARNING OBJECTIVE NO. 1

Identifying Two Kinds of Business Torts Involving Wrongful Interference

Three elements are necessary for wrongful interference with a contractual relationship to occur:

1. A valid, enforceable *contract* (a promise constituting an agreement) must exist between two parties.
2. A third party must *know* that this contract exists.
3. The third party must *intentionally* cause either of the two parties to break the contract.

The contract may be between a firm and its employees or a firm and its customers. Sometimes a competitor of a firm may draw away one of the firm's key employees. If the original employer can show that the competitor induced the former employee to break the contract, damages can be recovered from the competitor.

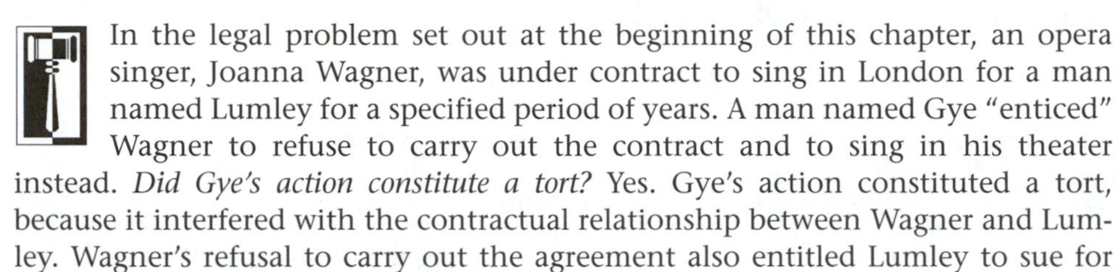

In the legal problem set out at the beginning of this chapter, an opera singer, Joanna Wagner, was under contract to sing in London for a man named Lumley for a specified period of years. A man named Gye "enticed" Wagner to refuse to carry out the contract and to sing in his theater instead. *Did Gye's action constitute a tort?* Yes. Gye's action constituted a tort, because it interfered with the contractual relationship between Wagner and Lumley. Wagner's refusal to carry out the agreement also entitled Lumley to sue for breach of contract.

WRONGFUL INTERFERENCE WITH A BUSINESS RELATIONSHIP

Businesspersons devise countless schemes to attract customers. They are forbidden by the courts, however, to interfere unreasonably in another's business in their attempts to gain a share of the market. There is a difference between *competition* (which is legal) and *predatory behavior* (which is illegal). The distinction usually depends on whether a business is attempting to attract customers in general or to solicit only those customers who have shown an interest in a similar product or service of a specific competitor. If a shopping center contains two shoe stores, for example, an employee of Store A cannot be positioned at the entrance of Store B for the purpose of diverting customers to Store A. This activity constitutes the tort of wrongful interference with a business relationship, which is commonly considered to be an unfair trade practice.

DEFENSES TO WRONGFUL INTERFERENCE

Justification is the defense used most often against the accusation of the tort of wrongful interference with a contractual or business relationship. For example, legitimate competitive behavior is permissible even if it results in the breaking of a contract. If Antonio's Meats advertises so effectively that it induces Alex's Restaurant to break its contract with Alvarez Meat Company, Alvarez Meat Company will be unable to recover from Antonio's Meats on a wrongful interference theory, because advertising is legitimate competitive behavior.

Disparagement of Property

DISPARAGEMENT OF PROPERTY
Economically injurious falsehoods made about another's product or property. A general term for torts that are more specifically referred to as slander of quality or slander of title.

Disparagement of property occurs when economically injurious falsehoods (lies) are made about another's *product* or *property.* Disparagement of property is a general term for torts that can be more specifically referred to as *slander of quality* or *slander of title.*

SLANDER OF QUALITY

Publication of false information about another's product, alleging that it is not what its seller claims, constitutes the tort of **slander of quality.** This tort has also been given the name *trade libel.* The plaintiff must prove that actual damages resulted from the slander of quality. That is, it must be shown not only that a third person refrained from dealing with the plaintiff because of the improper publication but also that there were associated damages.

SLANDER OF QUALITY
Publication of false information about another's product, alleging it is not what its seller claims; also referred to as trade libel.

SLANDER OF TITLE

When a publication denies or casts doubt on another's legal ownership of any property, and when this results in financial loss to that property's owner, the tort of **slander of title** may exist. Usually, this is an intentional tort in which someone knowingly publishes an untrue statement about property with the intent of discouraging a third person from dealing with the person slandered. For example, it would be difficult for a car dealer to attract customers after competitors published a notice that the dealer's lot consisted of only stolen autos.

SLANDER OF TITLE
The publication of a statement that denies or casts doubt upon another's legal ownership of any property, causing financial loss to that property's owner.

Trademark, Patent, and Copyright Infringement

Laws protecting patents, trademarks, and copyrights are explicitly designed to protect and reward inventive and artistic creativity. For example, trademark law provides incentives to companies to invest in the development of goodwill (the good reputation that a business has in the eyes of the public) by ensuring that others will not steal and profit from their trade symbols.

TRADEMARKS AND RELATED PROPERTY

LEARNING OBJECTIVE NO. 2
Discussing the Law's Protection for Trademarks

A **trademark** is a distinctive mark, motto, device, or implement that a manufacturer stamps, prints, or otherwise affixes to the goods it produces so that they may be identified on the market and their origin vouched for. Clearly, if one uses the trademark of another, it leads consumers to believe that one's goods were made by the other. For instance, if an independent jeans maker uses the trademark red tag used by the makers of Levi's, it leads consumers to believe that its products are Levi's brand jeans, even when they are not. The law seeks to avoid this kind of confusion. The tort of trademark infringement occurs when one who does not own a trademark copies it to a substantial degree or uses it in its entirety.

TRADEMARK
A word or symbol that has become sufficiently associated with a good (at common law) or has been registered with a government agency. Once a trademark is established, the owner has exclusive use of it and has the right to bring a legal action against those who infringe upon the protection given the trademark.

Trademark Protection. Generally, the more distinctive a trademark is, the less likely it is that it will be confused with other trademarks. Therefore, the extent to which the law protects a trademark is normally determined by how distinctive the trademark is. Fanciful, arbitrary, or suggestive trademarks are inherently distinctive (that is, they need no proof of their distinctiveness) and are protected by law. Fanciful trademarks include invented words, such as Xerox for one manufacturer's copiers and Kodak for another company's photographic products. Arbitrary trademarks include actual words used with products that have no literal connection to the words, such as English Leather used as a name for an aftershave lotion (and not for leather processed in England). Suggestive trademarks are those that suggest something about a product without describing the product directly. For example, Dairy Queen suggests an association between its products and milk, but it does not describe ice cream directly.

When choosing a trademark, be sure that it is not confusingly similar to an existing trademark.

Descriptive terms, geographical terms, and personal names are not inherently distinctive and do not receive protection under the law until they acquire a secondary meaning. A secondary meaning may arise when customers begin to associate a specific trademark with the source of the trademarked product. For example, the name Calvin Klein is a strong trademark because consumers associate that name with goods marketed by Calvin Klein or licensed distributors of Calvin Klein products. Whether a secondary meaning becomes attached to a term or name usually depends on how extensively the product is advertised, the market for the product, the number of sales, and other factors. Once a secondary meaning is attached to a term or name, a trademark is considered distinctive and is protected. Of course, geographical terms and personal names used in fanciful or arbitrary ways are inherently distinctive. Generic terms, such as *bicycle* or *computer,* receive no protection, even if they acquire a secondary meaning.

There are two ways to own a trademark—being the first to use it or being the first to register it with the U.S. Patent and Trademark Office.

Trademark Registration. The state and federal governments provide for the registration of trademarks. Once a trademark has been registered, a firm is entitled to its exclusive use for marketing purposes. The owner of the trademark need not register it to obtain protection from the tort of trademark infringement, but registration does furnish proof of the date of inception of its use. Registration is renewable between the fifth and sixth years after the initial registration and every twenty years thereafter (ten years for marks registered after 1989), as long as the mark remains distinctive and is used.

SERVICE MARK
A mark used in the sale or the advertising of services, such as to distinguish the services of one person from the services of others.

Protection for Service, Certification, and Collective Marks. A **service mark** is similar to a trademark, but is used to distinguish the services of one person from those of another. For example, each airline has a particular mark or symbol associated with its name. Titles or character names used in radio and television are frequently registered as service marks.

Other marks protected by law include certification marks and collective marks. A *certification mark* is used by one or more persons other than the owner to certify the region, materials, mode of manufacture, quality, or accuracy of the owner's goods or services. When used by members of a cooperative, association, or other organization, it is referred to as a *collective mark*. Examples of certification marks are the "Good Housekeeping Seal of Approval" and "UL Tested." Collective marks appear at the ends of the credits of movies to indicate the various associations and organizations that participated in the making of the films. The union marks found on the tags of certain products are also collective marks.

TRADE NAME
A name used in commercial activity to designate a particular business, a place at which a business is located, or a class of goods.

Protection for Trade Names. Trademarks are not the same as trade names. The term **trade name** is used to indicate part or all of a business's name, whether the business is a sole proprietorship, a partnership, or a corporation. Generally, a trade name is directly related to a business and its goodwill. As with trademarks, words must be unusual or fancifully used if they are to be protected as trade names. The word *Safeway* was held by the courts to be sufficiently fanciful to obtain protection as a trade name for a grocery store chain.

PATENTS

PATENT
A government grant that gives an inventor the exclusive right or privilege to make, use, or sell his or her invention for a limited time period.

LEARNING OBJECTIVE NO. 3
Describing the Protection that the Law Provides for Patents

A **patent** is a grant from the government that conveys to, and secures for, an inventor the exclusive right to make, use, and sell an invention for a period of twenty years. Patents for fourteen years are given for designs, as opposed to inventions. For either a regular patent or a design patent, the applicant must demonstrate to the satisfaction of the patent office that the invention, discovery, or design is genuine, novel, useful, and not obvious in light of current technology. A patent holder gives notice to all that an article or design is patented by placing on it the word "Patent" or "Pat." plus the patent number.

If a firm makes, uses, or sells another's patented design, product, or process without the patent owner's permission, the tort of patent infringement exists. Patent infringement may exist even though not all features or parts of an invention are copied. (With respect to a patented process, however, all steps or their equivalent must be copied for infringement to exist.) Often, litigation for patent infringement is so costly that the patent holder will instead offer to sell to the infringer a license to use the patented design, product, or process. Indeed, in many cases the costs of detection, prosecution, and monitoring are so high that patents are valueless to their owners, because the owners cannot afford to protect them.

COPYRIGHTS

A **copyright** is an intangible right granted by statute to the author or originator of certain literary or artistic productions. These works are protected by the federal government's Copyright Act. Works created after January 1, 1978, are automatically given copyright protection for the life of the author plus 70 years. For copyrights owned by publishing houses, the copyright expires 95 years from the date of publication or 120 years from the date of creation, whichever is first. For works by one or more authors, the copyright expires 70 years after the death of the last surviving author. A copyright owner no longer needs to place a © or R on the work to have the work protected against infringement. Chances are that if somebody created it, somebody owns it.

COPYRIGHT
The exclusive right of "authors" to publish, print, or sell an intellectual production for a statutory period of time. A copyright applies to works of art, literature, and other works of authorship (including computer programs).

What Is Protected Expression? Works that are copyrightable include books, records, films, artworks, architectural plans, menus, music videos, and product packaging. To obtain protection under the Copyright Act, a work must be original and fall into one of the following categories: (1) literary works; (2) musical works; (3) dramatic works; (4) pantomimes and choreographic works; (5) pictorial, graphic, and sculptural works; (6) films and other audiovisual works; (7) sound recordings; and (8) computer software. To be protected, a work must be "fixed in a durable medium" from which it can be perceived, reproduced, or communicated. Protection is automatic. Registration is not required.

The U.S. Patent and Trademark Office provides online access to a broad range of U.S. and international trademark resources at

http://www.uspto.gov/

The Copyright Act excludes copyright protection for any "idea, procedure, process, system, method of operation, concept, principle or discovery, regardless of the form in which it is described, explained, illustrated, or embodied." Note that it is not possible to copyright an *idea*. The underlying ideas embodied in a work may be freely used by others. What is copyrightable is the particular way in which an idea is *expressed*. Whenever an idea and an expression are inseparable, the expression cannot be copyrighted (a standard calendar, for instance, cannot be copyrighted).

IN THE COURTROOM

Alpha Company, a video game manufacturer, develops a gladiators video game with distinctive graphics. When the new game proves to be popular in the marketplace, Beta, Inc., one of Alpha's competitors, comes out with its own video game based on gladiators. GammaCo, another competitor, copies the graphics of Alpha's game to market a third new game. *Does Alpha have any recourse against Beta for producing another game that is based on gladiators?* No. Under the copyright law, a developer cannot prevent a competitor from producing another game that is based on gladiators. An idea (a game based on gladiators) is not copyrightable. *Can Alpha prevent GammaCo from copying the graphics?* Yes. An idea is not copyrightable, but the way in which the idea is expressed (the graphics of the game) is.

LEARNING OBJECTIVE NO. 4
Stating the Law's Protection for Copyrights

Copyright Infringement. Whenever the form or expression of an idea is copied, an infringement of copyright occurs. The production does not have to be exactly the same as the original, nor does it have to reproduce the original in its entirety. Penalties or remedies can be imposed on those who infringe copyrights. These include requiring the payment of damages and subjecting an infringer to criminal proceedings for willful violations (which may result in fines, imprisonment, or both).

An exception to liability for copyright infringement is made under the "fair use" doctrine. A person or organization can reproduce copyrighted material without paying royalties for purposes such as criticism, comment, news reporting, teaching (including multiple copies for classroom use), scholarship, or research. In determining whether the use made of a work in a particular case is a fair use, a court considers (1) the purpose of the use, (2) the nature of the copyrighted work, (3) how much of the original is copied, and (4) the effect of the use on the market for the copyrighted work.

Trade Secrets

TRADE SECRETS
Information or processes that give a business an advantage over competitors who do not know the information or processes.

Some business processes and information that are not, or cannot be, patented, copyrighted, or trademarked are nevertheless protected against appropriation by competitors as trade secrets. **Trade secrets** consist of customer lists, plans, research and development, pricing information, marketing techniques, production techniques, and generally anything that makes an individual company unique and that would have value to a competitor.

Thus, if a salesperson tries to solicit the company's customers for noncompany business, or if an employee copies the employer's unique method of manufacture, he or she has appropriated a trade secret. Theft of confidential business data by industrial espionage, as when a business taps into a competitor's computer, is a theft of trade secrets.

The Economic Espionage Act of 1996 made the theft of trade secrets a federal crime. An individual who violates the act can be imprisoned for up to ten years and fined up to $500,000. If a corporation or other organization violates the act, it can be fined up to $5 million. Any property acquired as a result of the violation and any property used in the commission of the violation is subject to forfeiture—meaning that the government can take the property. A theft of trade secrets conducted via the Internet, for example, could result in the forfeiture of every computer, printer, or other device used to commit or facilitate the violation.

Cyberlaw: Protecting Intellectual Property in Cyberspace

VIRTUAL PROPERTY
Intellectual property that exists on the Internet.

The legal issues relating to **virtual property**—property in cyberspace—are essentially legal questions involving intellectual property. In the context of cyberspace, a fundamental issue has to do with the degree of legal protection that should be given to virtual property. If the protection is inadequate, the incentive to make new works available online will be reduced. If the protection is too strict, the free flow and fair use of data will be impaired.

CYBER MARKS

CYBER MARK
A trademark in cyberspace.

DOMAIN NAME
The series of letter and symbols used to identify site operators on the Internet; Internet "addresses."

In cyberspace, trademarks are sometimes referred to as **cyber marks.** Many issues relating to cyber marks concern the right of a mark's owner to use it as part of a **domain name.** A domain name is an Internet address such as "westlaw.com." The top-level domain (the part of the name to the right of the period) indicates the type of entity that is using the name ("com" is an abbreviation for "commercial"). The second-level domain often consists of the name of the entity that owns the site.

LEARNING OBJECTIVE NO. 5

Defining the Law's Protection for Trademarks on the Internet

Trademark Infringement. In the real world, one business can often use the same name as another without causing any conflict, particularly if the businesses are small, their goods or services are different, and the areas within which they do business are separate. In cyberspace, however, no two businesses can use the same domain name. In other words, although two or more businesses can own the trademark Acme, only one business can operate on the Internet with the domain name "acme.com." Because of this restrictive feature of domain names, the courts have held that the unauthorized use of another's mark in a domain name constitutes trademark infringement if the use would likely cause customer confusion.

Cybersquatting. Cybersquatting occurs when a person registers a domain name that is the same as, or confusingly similar to, the trademark of another and then offers to sell the domain name back to the mark's owner. (Registration of domain names is discussed in the next section.)

Under the Anticybersquatting Consumer Reform Act (ACRA) of 1999, a federal law, it is illegal for a person to "register, traffic in, or use" a domain name if the name is identical or confusingly similar to another's mark and if the one registering, trafficking in, or using the name has a "bad faith intent" to profit from that mark. In deciding whether bad faith exists, courts consider the other person's rights, the intent to divert consumers in a way that could harm the goodwill represented by the mark, whether there is an offer to transfer or sell the domain name to the mark's owner, and whether there is an intent to use the domain name to offer goods and services.

A mark's owner may file a suit under the ACRA against an alleged cybersquatter. A successful plaintiff may obtain, in addition to a transfer or cancellation of the domain name, actual damages and profits, or statutory damages of from $1,000 to $100,000.

Resolving Domain Name Disputes. The Internet Corporation for Assigned Names and Numbers (ICANN) is a nonprofit corporation that the federal government set up to oversee the distribution of domain names. ICANN has authorized other organizations to register the names. As part of the registration application, a party must state that his or her use of the name will not infringe on another's rights. If it does, the name may be transferred or canceled.

ICANN operates an online arbitration system to resolve domain name disputes. When trademark infringement involves a domain name, instead of, or in addition to, filing a suit, a party may submit a complaint to an ICANN-approved dispute resolution provider. These disputes are resolved according to ICANN's Uniform Domain Name Dispute Resolution Policy (UDRP) and a set of accompanying rules.

ICANN's UDRP lists three elements that must be proved to have a domain name transferred or canceled. First, the challenged domain name must be identical or confusingly similar to a mark in which the complainant has rights. Second, the party against whom the complaint is made must have no rights or legitimate interests in the domain name. Third, the challenged domain name must be registered and be used in bad faith.

A party who participates in an ICANN-approved proceeding but who is not satisfied with the result may appeal to a court.

IN THE COURTROOM

Alpha, Inc., makes computer-related products under the brand name "Beta," which Alpha registers as a trademark. Gamma Corporation registers "beta.com" as a domain name and uses it briefly. Alpha offers Gamma $5,000 for the name, but Gamma refuses and offers the name to other companies for a higher price. *Is Gamma in violation of ICANN's Uniform Dispute Resolution Policy?* Yes. Alpha has rights in the Beta mark, and Beta is not a name by which Gamma is commonly known. Gamma's use of the Beta name to attract Internet users to its Web site creates a likelihood of confusion with Alpha's mark and is evidence of bad faith. Also, Gamma's offer to sell the name indicates bad faith.

PATENTS FOR CYBERPRODUCTS

Cyberproducts to meet the needs of Internet users and online service providers are being developed and patented at an unprecedented rate. Cyberproducts include data-compression software, encryption programs, software facilitating information linking and retrieval systems, and other forms of network software.

The problem faced by the developers of cyberproducts, who normally invest a lot of time and money resources in the research and development of those products, is how to protect their exclusive rights to the use of the products. Patent law provides the greatest protection for these products.

A patent owner whose product is featured on the Internet may find it particularly difficult to prevent the unauthorized use of the patented property. For example, a video game maker might agree to provide part of a game on the Internet, through a third party's Web site, to give potential purchasers a sample of the product. How can the game maker prevent the third party from using, or letting others use, the product for other purposes (such as making and selling illegal copies of the game)?

LEARNING OBJECTIVE NO. 6
Discussing How the Law Can Protect Patents on the Internet

Licensing the use of a product is one of the best ways to protect intellectual property on the Internet. In the context of a patent, a *license* is permission granted by the patent owner to another (the *licensee*) to make, sell, or use the patented item. Any license that a patent holder grants can be restricted to certain specified purposes and can be limited to the licensee only. Because the Internet does not have any geographical boundaries, a licensing agreement should be made in consideration of all U.S., foreign, and international laws. These same principles apply to the owners and licensees of other intellectual property, including copyrights and trademarks. (See Chapter 21 for more on the law concerning the licensing of computer information such as software.)

COPYRIGHTS IN DIGITAL INFORMATION

Copyright law is probably the most important form of intellectual property protection on the Internet. This is because much of the material on the Internet consists of works of authorship (including multimedia presentations, software, and database information). These works are the traditional focus of copyright law. Copyright law is also important because the nature of the Internet requires that data be "copied" before being transferred online. Copies are a significant part of the traditional controversies arising in this area of the law.

Copyright Infringement. Selling a copy of a work without the permission of the copyright holder constitutes copyright infringement.

Because of the nature of cyberspace, one controversy has been determining at what point an electronic "copy" of a work is made. The courts have held that loading a file or program into a computer's random access memory, or RAM, constitutes the making of a "copy" for purposes of copyright law. RAM is a portion of a computer's memory into which a file, for example, is loaded so that it can be accessed (read or written over). Thus, a copyright is infringed when, for example, a party downloads software into RAM if that party does not own the software or otherwise have a right to download it.

Another controversy has been an issue relating to sales of "collective works," such as magazines. Magazines and newspapers buy and publish articles written by freelance writers. Besides circulating hard copies of their periodicals, these publishers sell the contents to e-publishers for inclusion in online databases and other electronic sources. Most recently, a court has held that publishers must have the writers' permission to make these sales.

IN THE COURTROOM

Global News Corporation, the publisher of *PC Monthly* magazine and other periodicals, buys an article from Terry, a freelance writer. Without Terry's permission, Global News includes the article on a CD-ROM that contains all of the editions of *PC Monthly* and other Global News periodicals, and offers the CD-ROM for sale. *Has Global News committed copyright infringement?* Yes. To put the contents of their periodicals into e-databases and onto CD-ROMs, publishers such as Global News need the permission of the writers whose contributions are included in the periodicals.

Software Circumvention. The Digital Millennium Copyright Act of 1998 provides civil and criminal penalties for anyone who circumvents encryption software or other technological anti-piracy protection. Also prohibited are the manufacture, import, sale, or distribution of devices or services for circumvention.

There are exceptions to fit the needs of libraries, scientists, universities, and others. In general, the "fair use" of circumvention for educational and other noncommercial purposes is permitted. For example, circumvention is allowed if the purpose is to test computer security, to conduct encryption research, to protect personal privacy, or to allow parents to monitor their children's journeys over the Internet.

Service Providers' Liability. Under the Digital Millennium Copyright Act mentioned in the previous section, an Internet service provider (ISP) is not liable for any copyright infringement by its customer if the ISP is unaware of the subscriber's violation. An ISP may be held liable only after learning of the violation and failing to take action to shut the subscriber down. A copyright holder has to act promptly, however, by pursuing a claim in court, or the subscriber has the right to be restored to online access.

The Cyberspace Law Institute (CLI) offers articles and information on topics such as copyright infringement, trademarks, and domain names at

http://www.cli.org

Global Copyright Protection. Technology, especially the Internet, offers new outlets for creative products. It also makes them easier to steal. Copyrighted works can be pirated and distributed around the world quickly and efficiently. To curb this crime, in 1996 the World Intellectual Property Organization (WIPO) enacted the WIPO Copyright Treaty. The purpose was to upgrade global standards of copyright protection, particularly for the Internet.

Special provisions of the treaty relate to rights in digital data. The treaty strengthens some rights for copyright owners, in terms of their application in cyberspace, but leaves other questions unresolved. For example, the treaty does not make clear what, for purposes of international law, constitutes the making of a "copy" in electronic form. The United States signed the WIPO treaty in 1996 and implemented its terms in the Digital Millennium Copyright Act.

TERMS AND CONCEPTS FOR REVIEW

business tort 55
copyright 59
cyber mark 60
disparagement of property 56
domain name 60
patent 58
service mark 58
slander of quality 57
slander of title 57
trade name 58
trade secret 60
trademark 57
virtual property 60

CHAPTER SUMMARY • Business Torts, Intellectual Property, and Cyberlaw

Wrongful Interference	1. *Wrongful interference with a contractual relationship*—Intentional interference with a valid, enforceable contract by a third party. 2. *Wrongful interference with a business relationship*—Unreasonable interference by one party in another's business relationship.
Disparagement of Property	Slanderous or libelous statements made about another's product or property; more specifically referred to as slander of quality and slander of title.
Trademark, Patent, and Copyright Infringement	1. *Infringement of trademarks and related property*—When one uses, without permission, the protected trademark, service mark, or trade name of another when marketing goods or services. 2. *Patent infringement*—When one uses or sells another's patented design, product, or process without the patent owner's permission. 3. *Copyright infringement*—Whenever the form or expression of an idea is copied without the permission of the copyright holder.
Protecting Intellectual Property in Cyberspace	1. *Trademark protection*—Trademark law applies to the use of domain names on the Internet. The unauthorized use of another's trademark in a domain name constitutes trademark infringement. 2. *Patent protection*—Licensing the use of a product is one of the best ways to protect it on the Internet. The license can be restricted to certain purposes and can be limited to the licensee only. 3. *Copyright protection*—Online providers may be liable for the unauthorized copying, distribution, and performance or display of copyrighted work. Intentionally taking and distributing pirated, copyrighted works to others over the Internet is illegal.

HYPOTHETICAL QUESTIONS

5–1. Copyright Infringement. In which of the following situations would a court likely hold Maruta liable for copyright infringement?

(a) At the library, Maruta photocopies ten pages from a scholarly journal relating to a topic on which she is writing a term paper.

(b) Maruta makes leather handbags and sells them in her small leather shop. She advertises her handbags as "Vutton handbags," hoping customers might mistakenly assume that they were made by Vuitton, the well-known maker of high-quality luggage and handbags.

(c) Maruta owns a video store. She purchase the latest videos from various video manufacturers, but buys only one copy of each video. Then, using blank videotapes, she makes copies to rent or sell to her customers.

(d) Maruta teaches Latin American history at a small university. She has a videocassette recorder (VCR) and frequently tapes television programs relating to Latin America. She then takes the videos to her classroom so that her students can watch them.

5–2. Wrongful Interference. Jennings owns a bakery shop. He has been trying to obtain a long-term contract with the owner of Julie's Tea Salon for some time. Jennings starts a local advertising campaign on radio and television and in the newspaper. The campaign is so persuasive that Julie decides to break the contract she has had for some time with Orley's Bakery so that she can patronize Jenning's bakery. Is Jennings liable to Orley's Bakery for the tort of wrongful interference with a contractual relationship? Is Julie liable for this tort? For anything?

REAL WORLD CASE PROBLEM

5–3. Trademark Infringement. CBS, Inc., owns and operates Television City, a television production facility in Los Angeles. Home to many television series, the name "Television City" is broadcast each week in connection with each show. CBS sells T-shirts, pins, watches, and so on emblazoned with "CBS Television City." CBS registered "Television City" with the U.S. Patent and Trademark Office as a service mark "for television production services." David and William Liederman wished to open a restaurant in New York City using the name "Television City." Besides food, the restaurant would sell television memorabilia such as T-shirts, sweatshirts, and posters. When CBS learned of the Liederman's plans, it asked a federal district court to order them not to use "Television City" in connection with their restaurant. Does CBS's registration of "Television City" ensure its exclusive use in all markets and all products? If not, what factors might the court consider to determine whether the Liedermans can use "Television City" in connection with their restaurant? [*CBS, Inc. v. Liederman,* 866 F.Supp. 763 (S.D.N.Y. 1994)]

For updated links to resources available on the Web, as well as a variety of other materials, visit this text's Web site at **http://blte.westbuslaw.com**.

Information on intellectual property law is available at the following site:

http://wbl.legal.net/intellct.htm

You can find answers to frequently asked questions (FAQs) about trademark and patent law—and links to registration forms, statutes, international patent and trademark offices, and numerous other related materials—at the Web site of the U.S. Patent and Trademark Office. Go to

http://www.uspto.gov

To access the federal database of registered trademarks directly, go to

www.uspto.gov/tmdb/index.html

To perform patent searches and to access information on the patenting process, go to

http://www.bustpatents.com

You can also access information on patent law at the following Internet site:

http://www.patents.com

For information on copyrights, go to the U.S. Copyright Office at

lcweb.loc.gov/copyright

You can find extensive information on copyright law—including United States Supreme Court decisions in this area and the texts of the Berne Convention and other international treaties on copyright issues—at the Web site of the Legal Information Institute at Cornell University's School of Law. Go to

http://www.law.cornell.edu/topics/copyright.html

An online magazine that deals, in part, with intellectual property issues is Law Technology Product News. The URL for this publication is

http://www.ljextra.com/ltpn

The Cyberspace Law Institute (CLI) offers articles and information on such topics as copyright infringement, privacy, trade secrets, and trademarks. To access the CLI's Web site, go to

http://www.cli.org

ONLINE LEGAL RESEARCH

Go to **http://blte.westbuslaw.com**, the Web site that accompanies this text. Select "Internet Applications," and then click on "Chapter 5." There you will find the following Internet research exercises that you can perform to learn more about intellectual property rights:

Activity 5–1: The Price of Free Speech

Activity 5–2: Gray-Market Goods

Chapter 5 ■ WORK SET

TRUE-FALSE QUESTIONS

_____ **1.** The tort of intentional interference with a contractual relationship requires a valid, enforceable contract between two parties.

_____ **2.** Bona fide competitive behavior does not constitute wrongful interference with a contractual relationship.

_____ **3.** Even if a person's interference with another's contractual relationship is justified, it constitutes wrongful interference.

_____ **4.** Slander of title requires publication of false information that denies or casts doubt on another's legal ownership of any property.

_____ **5.** To obtain a patent, a person must prove to the patent office that his or her invention is genuine, novel, useful, and not obvious in light of contemporary technology.

_____ **6.** To obtain a copyright, an author must prove to the copyright office that a work is genuine, novel, useful, and not a copy of another copyrighted work.

_____ **7.** A personal name can be trademarked if it has acquired a secondary meaning.

_____ **8.** Service, certification, and collective marks are covered by the same policies and restrictions that apply to copyrights.

_____ **9.** Principles of trademark law do not apply on the Internet.

_____ **10.** A copyright is infringed only if a work is copied in its entirety.

MULTIPLE-CHOICE QUESTIONS

_____ **1.** For years, Mark Corporation has used a monkey symbol in marketing its jeans but has not registered the symbol with a government office. Quick, Inc., recently decided to import jeans made abroad and sell them with the monkey symbol, which it also has not registered. Mark sues Quick. Quick is

a. liable, because it had no right to trade on Mark's goodwill.
b. not liable, because Mark did not register the symbol with the government.
c. not liable, because it did not manufacture the jeans; it only imported them.
d. not liable, because a monkey symbol cannot be a trademark.

_____ **2.** A salesperson for Woodco tells the owner of Pat's Lumber that Timber, Inc., does not sell mahogany. The salesperson knows the statement is false. Pat had intended to buy mahogany from Timber, but instead buys it from Woodco. If Timber sues Woodco for slander of quality, Woodco will be held

a. liable, if Timber proves that it suffered damages from Pat's decision.
b. liable, if Timber proves that Pat did not see Timber's salesperson.
c. not liable, if Woodco proves that its prices are competitive.
d. not liable, if Woodco proves that it made no profit on the deal.

_____ **3.** Bio Box Company advertises so effectively that Product Packaging, Inc., stops doing business with Styro Cartons, Inc. Bio is

a. liable to Styro for wrongful interference with a contractual relationship.
b. liable to Styro for wrongful interference with a business relationship.
c. liable to Styro for disparagement of property.
d. not liable.

_____ **4.** Ken invents a light bulb that lasts longer than ordinary bulbs. To prevent others from making, using, or selling the bulb or its design, he should obtain

a. a trademark.
b. a copyright.
c. a patent.
d. none of the above.

_____ **5.** Standard Products, Inc., obtains a patent on a laser printer. This patent is violated if the printer is copied

a. in its entirety only.
b. in part.
c. not at all.
d. none of the above.

_____ **6.** Bob works for Eagle Manufacturing Company, under a contract in which he agrees not to disclose any process he uses while in Eagle's employ. When Bob goes into business for himself, he copies some of Eagle's unique production techniques. Bob has committed

a. trademark infringement.
b. patent infringement.
c. copyright infringement.
d. theft of a trade secret.

_____ **7.** To identify its goods, Nationwide Products use a red, white, and blue symbol that combines the letter N and a map of the United States. This symbol is protected by

a. trademark law.
b. copyright law.
c. patent law.
d. all of the above.

_____ **8.** Clothes made by members of the Union of Clothing Workers are sold with tags that identify this fact. This tag is a

a. service mark.
b. certification mark.
c. collective mark.
d. trade name.

ISSUE SPOTTERS

1. A video game manufacturer develops a gladiators video game with distinctive graphics. Can the developer prevent a competitor from producing another game based on gladiators? Can the developer prevent competitors from copying the graphics?

2. Global Products develops new software for engineers and architects that it would like to publicize through an online service on the Internet. How can Global give potential customers a look at its product and protect against patent infringement?

Criminal Law

LEARNING OBJECTIVES

When you finish this chapter, you should be able to:

1. Explain the difference between crimes and other types of wrongful conduct.
2. Indicate the essential elements of criminal liability.
3. Describe the constitutional safeguards that protect the rights of persons accused of crimes.
4. Define the crimes that affect business.
5. Summarize the defenses to criminal liability.

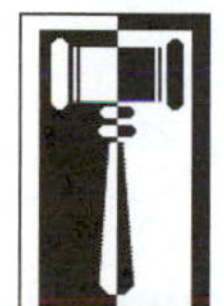

FACING A LEGAL PROBLEM

Ray steals a purse from an unattended car at a gas station. Because the purse contains money and a handgun, Ray is convicted of grand theft of property (cash), and grand theft of a firearm. On appeal, Ray claims that he is not guilty of grand theft of a firearm because he did not know that the purse contained a gun. *Can Ray be convicted of the crime of grand theft of a firearm even though he did not know that a gun was in the purse?*

Sanctions are used to bring about a society in which individuals engaged in business can compete and prosper. These sanctions include damages for torts (as discussed in Chapters 4 and 5) and breaches of contract (to be discussed in Chapter 15). Other sanctions are imposed under criminal law.

In this chapter, following a brief summary of the major differences between criminal and civil law, we look at how crimes are classified and what elements must be present for criminal liability to exist. We then examine criminal procedural law. Finally, we focus on crimes affecting business and the defenses that can be raised to avoid liability for criminal actions.

Civil Law and Criminal Law

Civil law spells out the duties that exist between persons or between citizens and their governments, excluding the duty not to commit crimes. Contract law, for example, is part of civil law. The whole body of tort law, which deals with the infringement by one person on the legally recognized rights of another, is also an area of civil law.

Criminal law, in contrast, has to do with crime. A **crime** is a wrong against society proclaimed in a statute and, if committed, punishable by society through

CRIME
A wrong against society proclaimed in a statute and, if committed, punishable by society through fines and/or imprisonment—and, in some cases, death.

LEARNING OBJECTIVE NO. 1
Explaining the Difference between Crimes and Other Types of Wrongful Conduct

FELONY
A crime that carries the most severe sanctions, usually ranging from one year in a state or federal prison to the forfeiture of one's life.

MISDEMEANOR
A lesser crime than a felony, punishable by a fine or imprisonment for up to one year in other than a state or federal penitentiary.

fines, imprisonment, and, in some cases, death. Because crimes are *offenses against society as a whole,* they are prosecuted by a public official, not by victims. Exhibit 6–1 presents additional ways in which criminal and civil law differ.

Classification of Crimes

Crimes are classified as felonies or misdemeanors. **Felonies** are serious crimes punishable by death or by imprisonment in a federal or state penitentiary for more than a year.

Under federal law and in most states, any crime that is not a felony is a **misdemeanor.** Misdemeanors are crimes punishable by a fine or by confinement for up to a year. If incarcerated (imprisoned), the guilty party goes to a local jail instead of a penitentiary. Disorderly conduct and trespass are common misdemeanors.

What Constitutes Criminal Liability?

Two elements must exist for a person to be convicted of a crime: (1) the performance of a prohibited act and (2) a specified state of mind or intent on the part of the actor.

THE CRIMINAL ACT

LEARNING OBJECTIVE NO. 2
Indicating the Essential Elements of Criminal Liability

Every criminal statute prohibits certain behavior. Most crimes require an act of *commission;* that is, a person must do something to be accused of a crime. In some cases, an act of *omission* can be a crime, but only when a person has a legal duty to perform the omitted act. Failure to file a tax return is an example of an omission that is a crime.

INTENT TO COMMIT A CRIME

A wrongful mental state is as necessary as a wrongful act in establishing criminal liability. What constitutes such a mental state varies according to the wrongful action. For murder, the act is the taking of a life, and the mental state is the intent to take life. For theft, the guilty act is the taking of another person's property, and the mental state involves both the knowledge that the property belongs to another and the intent to deprive the owner of it.

EXHIBIT 6–1
Civil and Criminal Law Compared

ISSUE	CIVIL LAW	CRIMINAL LAW
Area of concern	Rights and duties between individuals	Offenses against society as a whole
Wrongful act	Harm to a person	Violation of a statute that prohibits some type of activity
Party who brings suit	Person who suffered harm	The state
Standard of proof	Preponderance of the evidence	Beyond a reasonable doubt
Remedy	Damages to compensate for the harm	Punishment (fine or imprisonment)

In the legal problem set out at the beginning of this chapter, Ray steals a purse that contains money and a handgun. He is convicted of grand theft of property (cash) and grand theft of a firearm. He appeals, arguing that he is not guilty of grand theft of a firearm because he did not know that a gun was in the purse. *Can Ray be convicted of grand theft of a firearm even though he did not know that a gun was in the purse?* No. A separate crime occurs only when there are separate distinct acts of seizing the property of another. Ray committed the crime of grand theft because of the value of property in the purse, including the value of the gun. Only one crime of theft occurred, however. Ray saw the purse and took it without knowing what it contained: there was one intent and one act.

Constitutional Safeguards

LEARNING OBJECTIVE NO. 3
Describing the Constitutional Safeguards That Protect the Rights of Persons Accused of Crimes

Criminal law brings the force of the state, with all its resources, to bear against the individual. The U.S. Constitution provides safeguards to protect the rights of individuals and to prevent the arbitrary use of power on the part of the government. The United States Supreme Court has ruled that most of these safeguards apply not only in federal but also in state courts. They include the following:

1. The Fourth Amendment protection from unreasonable searches and seizures.
2. The Fourth Amendment requirement that no warrants for a search or an arrest can be issued without probable cause.
3. The Fifth Amendment requirement that no one can be deprived of "life, liberty, or property without due process of law."
4. The Fifth Amendment prohibition against **double jeopardy** (trying someone twice for the same criminal offense).
5. The Fifth Amendment requirement that no person can be required to be a witness against (incriminate) himself or herself.
6. The Sixth Amendment guarantees of a speedy trial, trial by jury, a public trial, the right to confront witnesses, and the right to a lawyer at various stages in some proceedings.
7. The Eighth Amendment prohibitions against excessive bail and fines and cruel and unusual punishment.

DOUBLE JEOPARDY
A situation occurring when a person is tried twice for the same criminal offense; prohibited by the Fifth Amendment to the Constitution.

THE EXCLUSIONARY RULE

Under the **exclusionary rule,** all evidence obtained in violation of the constitutional rights spelled out in the Fourth, Fifth, and Sixth Amendments normally must be excluded, as well as all evidence derived from the illegally obtained evidence. Evidence derived from illegally obtained evidence is known as "fruit of the poisonous tree." For example, if a confession is obtained after an illegal arrest, the arrest would be "the poisonous tree," and the confession, if "tainted" by the arrest, would be the "fruit." The purpose of the exclusionary rule is to deter police from misconduct.

EXCLUSIONARY RULE
A rule under which any evidence that is obtained in violation of the accused's constitutional rights guaranteed by the Fourth, Fifth, and Sixth Amendments, as well as any evidence derived from illegally obtained evidence, will not be admissible in court.

IN THE COURTROOM

During a routine traffic stop, a police officer arrests Evan on the ground that there is an outstanding warrant for his arrest. In fact, there is no warrant and the officer knows it. The police search Evan's car and discover marijuana. Evan is charged with possession of marijuana. He moves to suppress the evidence (marijuana), on the ground that the arrest was unlawful. *Is evidence admissible in a criminal trial if it is obtained during an arrest made on the basis of a warrant that does not exist?* No. The exclusionary rule was designed as a means of deterring police misconduct. Application of the exclusionary rule in this case could deter police officers' misconduct by indicating that they must act reasonably in such situations.

For information on the criminal justice system, go to the U.S. Department of Justice's home page at

http://usdoj.gov

INFORMING SUSPECTS OF THEIR RIGHTS

Individuals who are arrested must be informed of certain constitutional rights, including their right to remain silent and their right to counsel. If the arresting officer fails to inform a criminal suspect of these rights, any statement the suspect makes will not be admissible in court.

There are some exceptions. In federal cases, for example, a voluntary confession can be used in evidence even if the accused was not informed of his or her rights. In some cases, juries may accept confessions without being convinced of their voluntariness.

IN THE COURTROOM

Jean is arrested by state police officers for the theft of corporate funds. The officers obtain her written confession without informing her of her rights. When the prosecution tries to admit the confession into evidence at the trial, Jean objects. She claims that she would not have confessed if she had been advised of her right to remain silent and to have an attorney. *Were Jean's constitutional rights violated?* Yes. When individuals are taken into custody, they must be warned before questioning that they have the right to remain silent, that anything they say can be used against them in a court of law, that they have the right to the presence of an attorney, and that if they cannot afford an attorney one will be appointed for them prior to questioning. *Is Jean's confession admissible at her trial?* No. An accused can waive his or her rights, but the government must show that the waiver was made knowingly and intelligently. Jean was not informed of her rights, so she could not have waived them.

Crimes Affecting Business

LEARNING OBJECTIVE NO. 4

Defining the Crimes That Affect Business

Numerous forms of crime occur in a business context. Many of these are referred to as **white-collar crimes.** The term is used to mean an illegal act or series of acts committed by an individual or business using some nonviolent means to obtain a personal or business advantage. In this section, we focus on white-collar property crimes, computer crimes, and violations of the Racketeer Influenced and Corrupt Organizations Act (RICO) that affect business.

WHITE-COLLAR CRIME
Nonviolent crime committed by individuals or corporations to obtain a personal or business advantage.

FORGERY

The fraudulent making or altering of any writing in a way that changes the legal rights and liabilities of another is **forgery.** If, without authorization, Severson signs Bennett's name to the back of a check made out to Bennett, Severson is committing forgery. Forgery also includes changing trademarks, falsifying public records, counterfeiting, and altering a legal document.

FORGERY
The fraudulent making or altering of any writing in a way that changes the legal rights and liabilities of another.

ROBBERY

Robbery is forcefully and unlawfully taking personal property of any value from another. The use of force or intimidation is usually necessary for an act of theft to be considered a robbery. Thus, picking pockets is not robbery, because the action is unknown to the victim.

ROBBERY
The act of forcefully and unlawfully taking personal property of any value from another; force or intimidation is usually necessary for an act of theft to be considered a robbery.

LARCENY

Any person who wrongfully or fraudulently takes and carries away another person's personal property is guilty of **larceny.** Larceny includes the fraudulent

LARCENY
The wrongful taking and carrying away of another person's personal property with the intent to permanently deprive the owner of the property.

intent to deprive an owner permanently of property. Many business-related larcenies entail fraudulent conduct. Whereas robbery involves force or fear, larceny does not. Therefore, picking pockets is larceny, not robbery.

Stealing computer programs may constitute larceny even though the "property" consists of magnetic impulses. Stealing computer time can also constitute larceny. Intercepting cellular phone calls to obtain another's phone card number—and then using that number to place long-distance calls, often overseas—is a form of property theft.

Embezzlement

When a person entrusted with another person's property or money fraudulently appropriates it, **embezzlement** occurs. Typically, this involves an employee who steals money. Banks face this problem, and so do businesses in which company officers or accountants "doctor" the books to cover up the fraudulent conversion of money for their own benefit. Embezzlement is not larceny, because the wrongdoer does not physically take the property from the possession of another, and it is not robbery, because force or fear is not used.

Embezzlement
The fraudulent appropriation of money or other property by a person to whom the money or property has been entrusted.

In the Courtroom

While hauling a load of refrigerators from San Diego to New York in a truck owned by National Appliance Company, Fred departs from his route and stops in Las Vegas, where he tries to sell some of the refrigerators. No one buys them and they never leave the truck, but to display them Fred breaks the truck's seals, enters the cargo compartment, and opens two refrigerator cartons. Fred is arrested and charged with embezzlement. Fred claims that there are no grounds for the charge, because he never took anything off the truck. *Does the charge of embezzlement apply when property is not physically removed from the owner's possession?* Yes. If a person has control over the property of another and has the intent of converting the goods to his or her own use, then embezzlement occurs. By leaving his route to sell the refrigerators and keep the proceeds, Fred exercised control over the property, with the intent to convert it to his own use.

Mail and Wire Fraud

One of the most potent weapons against white-collar criminals is the Mail Fraud Act of 1990. Under this act, it is a federal crime to use the mails to defraud the public. Illegal use of the mails must involve (1) mailing or causing someone else to mail a writing—something written, printed, or photocopied—for the purpose of executing a scheme to defraud and (2) a contemplated or an organized scheme to defraud by false pretenses. If, for example, Johnson advertises by mail the sale of a cure for cancer that he knows to be fraudulent because it has no medical validity, he can be prosecuted for fraudulent use of the mails.

Federal law also makes it a crime to use wire, radio, or television transmissions to defraud. Violators may be fined up to $1,000, imprisoned for up to five years, or both. If the violation affects a financial institution, the violator may be fined up to $1 million, imprisoned up to thirty years, or both.

Computer Crime

The American Bar Association defines **computer crime** as any act that is directed against computers and computer parts, that uses computers as instruments of

Computer Crime
Any act that is directed against computers and computer parts, that uses computers as instruments of crime, or that involves computers and constitutes abuse.

crime, or that involves computers and constitutes abuse. In this section, we look at some of the ways in which computers are used in criminal activity.

Financial Crimes. A large number of computer crimes fall into the broad category of financial crimes. In addition to using computers for information storage and retrieval, businesses use computers to conduct financial transactions. These circumstances provide opportunities for employees and others to commit crimes that can involve serious economic losses. For example, some employees can transfer monies among accounts with little effort and without the risk involved in transactions evidenced by paperwork.

Software Piracy. Considerable sums often are invested in research and development to create new, innovative software programs. Once marketed, new software requires that user support be provided during its life on the market. Given these expenses, many individuals and businesses have been tempted to steal software by decoding and making unauthorized copies of it. This is known as *software piracy.* Under most state laws, this is a crime. At the federal level, laws protecting intellectual property (such as patent and copyright laws) cover computer programs.

Property Theft. The theft of computer equipment (hardware) has become easier as computer components have become smaller in size and more readily transportable. Another kind of computer-related property theft may involve goods that are controlled and accounted for by means of a computer applications program. For example, an employee in a company's accounting department could manipulate inventory records to funnel orders for goods through a phony account and ship the merchandise elsewhere. The theft of computer equipment and the theft of goods with the aid of computers are subject to the same criminal and tort laws as thefts of other property.

Vandalism and Destructive Programming. On occasion, political activists, terrorists, and disgruntled employees have physically damaged hardware or ruined software. These acts have included such conduct as smashing computer equipment with a crowbar. Other destructive acts have required greater technical awareness and facility, and a knowledgeable individual can do a considerable amount of damage. For example, a computer program (referred to popularly as a *virus*) can be designed to rearrange, replace, or even destroy data.

Theft of Data or Services. Most people would agree that when an individual uses another's computer or computer information system without authorization, the individual is stealing. For example, an employee who uses a computer system or data stored in a computer system for private gain and without the employer's authorization would likely be considered a thief. Under a number of revised criminal codes or broad judicial interpretations of existing statutes, the unauthorized use of computer data or services is considered larceny.

IN THE COURTROOM

Peter works for the U.S. Defense Intelligence Agency (DIA) with access to the DIA's computers. Peter is also involved in amateur ballroom dancing. Over a five-year period, Peter uses the DIA's computers to create hundreds of documents, including newsletters and mailing lists, relating to his ballroom dance activities. Peter is arrested and charged with converting to his own use government computer time and storage under a statute that makes it illegal for any person to "knowingly convert to his or her use any thing of value of the United States." Peter argues that the statute does not cover intangible property (property that, such as computer data and services, does not have a physical existence). *Does the statute cover the theft of such intangible property as computer time and storage?* Yes. The statute covers "any thing of value." This prohibits the misappropriation of anything belonging to the federal government, including intangible property.

Detecting and Prosecuting Computer Crime. One of the challenges presented by computer crime is its relative invisibility. Such crime is often difficult to detect and may go undetected for some time. Even when it is apparent that a crime has occurred, tracing it to the individual who committed it can be difficult. The individual's identity is "hidden" by the anonymous nature of the computer system. Even when crimes are detected and reported, the complexities of the computer systems involved have often frustrated the attempts of attorneys, police officers, jurors, and others to comprehend the offenses and prosecute the offenders successfully.

To protect against computer crimes, limit employees' access to computer data with a system of security clearances, change passwords frequently, encrypt the data, and store a copy in outside facilities.

To control computer crime, government at both the federal and state levels has undertaken protective measures. At the federal level, the Counterfeit Access Device and Computer Fraud and Abuse Act of 1984 prohibits unauthorized access to certain types of information, such as restricted government information, information in a financial institution's financial records, and information in a credit reporting agency's files on consumers. Penalties for violations include up to five years' imprisonment and a fine of up to $250,000 or twice the amount that was gained or lost as a result of the crime.

BRIBERY

Basically, three types of bribery are considered crimes: bribery of public officials, commercial bribery, and bribery of foreign officials.

Bribery of Public Officials. The attempt to influence a public official to act in a way that serves a private interest is a crime. The bribe can be anything the recipient considers to be valuable. The commission of the crime occurs when the bribe is offered. The recipient does not have to agree to perform whatever action is desired by the person offering the bribe, nor does the recipient have to accept the bribe.

Commercial Bribery. Typically, people make commercial bribes to obtain proprietary information, cover up an inferior product, or secure new business. Industrial espionage sometimes involves commercial bribes. For example, a person in one firm may offer an employee in a competing firm some type of payoff in exchange for trade secrets and pricing schedules. So-called kickbacks or payoffs for special favors or services are a form of commercial bribery in some situations.

Bribery of Foreign Officials. Bribing foreign officials to obtain favorable business contracts is a crime. The Foreign Corrupt Practices Act of 1977 was passed to curb the practice of bribery by American businesspersons in securing foreign contracts.

RICO

The Racketeer Influenced and Corrupt Organizations Act (RICO) was passed by Congress in 1970. The purpose of RICO was to curb the apparently increasing entry of organized crime into the legitimate business world. Under RICO, it is a federal crime (1) to use income obtained from racketeering activity to purchase any interest in an enterprise, (2) to acquire or maintain an interest in an enterprise through racketeering activity, (3) to conduct or participate in the affairs of an enterprise through racketeering activity, or (4) to conspire to do any of the preceding acts.

The Federal Bureau of Investigation offers abundant information and statistics on crime at

http://www.fbi.gov

Racketeering activity is not a new type of crime created by RICO. Rather, RICO incorporates twenty-six separate types of federal crimes and nine types of state felonies and indicates that if a person commits two or more of these offenses, he or she is guilty of "racketeering activity." Most of the criminal RICO offenses have little, if anything, to do with normal business activities, for they involve gambling, arson, and extortion. Securities fraud (involving the sale of stocks and bonds) and mail fraud, however, are also criminal RICO violations, and RICO has become an effective tool in attacking these white-collar crimes. Under criminal provisions of RICO, any individual found guilty of a violation is subject to a fine of up to $25,000 per violation, imprisonment for up to twenty years, or both.

RICO also permits the government to require a defendant found guilty of a violation to sell his or her interest in a business or to close down the business. In some cases, private individuals are allowed to recover three times their actual loss (treble damages), plus attorneys' fees, for business injuries caused by a violation of the statute. Plaintiffs have used RICO in numerous commercial fraud cases. Frequent targets of civil RICO lawsuits are insurance companies, employment agencies, banks, and stock brokerage firms.

IN THE COURTROOM

Rollo commits federal crimes that injure others' businesses and qualify as racketeering activity, subject to prosecution under the Racketeer Influenced Corrupt Organizations Act (RICO). Rollo invests the profits in a video rental business. Rollo is later charged, arrested, tried, and convicted for the RICO violations. The businesses that Rollo injured then sue him for damages. *How much can they recover?* Under RICO, persons may recover three times their actual loss, plus attorneys' fees. The government can also impose other penalties on RICO criminals such as Rollo.

Defenses to Criminal Liability

LEARNING OBJECTIVE NO. 5

Summarizing the Defenses to Criminal Liability

Even if both elements of criminal liability are present, there are defenses that the law deems sufficient to excuse a defendant's criminal behavior. Among the most important defenses to criminal liability are infancy, insanity, entrapment, and immunity. Also, in some cases, defendants are given *immunity* and thus relieved, at least in part, of criminal liability for crimes they committed. We look at each of these defenses here.

Infancy

The term *infant,* as used in the law, refers to any person who has not reached the age of majority (see Chapter 10). In all states, special courts handle cases involving children who are alleged to have violated the law. In some states, a child is treated as an adult and tried in a regular court if he or she is above a certain age (usually fourteen) and is guilty of a felony, such as murder.

Insanity

Someone suffering from a mental illness is sometimes judged incapable of the state of mind required to commit a crime. Different courts use different tests for legal insanity. Almost all federal courts and some state courts do not hold a person responsible for criminal conduct if, as a result of mental disease or defect, the person lacked the capacity to appreciate the wrongfulness of the conduct or to obey the law.

Some states use a test under which a criminal defendant is not responsible if, at the time of the offense, he or she did not know the nature and quality of the act or did not know that the act was wrong. Other states use the irresistible-impulse test. A person operating under an irresistible impulse may know an act is wrong but cannot refrain from doing it.

ENTRAPMENT

Entrapment is a defense designed to prevent police officers or other government agents from encouraging crimes in order to apprehend persons wanted for criminal acts. In the typical entrapment case, an undercover agent *suggests* that a crime be committed and somehow pressures or induces an individual to commit it. The agent then arrests the individual for the crime. The crucial issue is whether a person who committed a crime was predisposed to commit the crime or did so because the agent induced it.

ENTRAPMENT
In criminal law, a defense in which the defendant claims that he or she was induced by a public official—usually an undercover agent or police officer—to commit a crime that he or she would otherwise not have committed.

IMMUNITY

Accused persons cannot be forced to give information if it will be used to prosecute them. This privilege is granted by the Fifth Amendment to the Constitution. To obtain information from a person accused of a crime, the state can grant immunity from prosecution or agree to prosecute for a less serious offense in exchange for the information. Once immunity is given, the person can no longer refuse to testify.

TERMS AND CONCEPTS FOR REVIEW

computer crime 73
crime 69
double jeopardy 71
embezzlement 73
entrapment 77
exclusionary rule 71
felony 70
forgery 72
larceny 72
misdemeanor 70
robbery 72
white-collar crime 72

CHAPTER SUMMARY • CRIMINAL LAW

Civil Law and Criminal Law	**1.** *Civil law*—Spells out the duties that exist between persons or between citizens and their governments, excluding the duty not to commit crimes. **2.** *Criminal law*—Has to do with crimes, which are defined as wrongs against society proclaimed in statutes and, if committed, punishable by society through fines, imprisonment, and, in some cases, death. Because crimes are *offenses against society as a whole,* they are prosecuted by a public official, not by victims. (See Exhibit 6–1 on page 70 for a summary of how criminal and civil laws differ.)
Classification of Crimes	**1.** *Felonies*—Serious crimes punishable by death or by imprisonment in a penitentiary for more than a year. **2.** *Misdemeanors*—Under federal law and in most states, any crime that is not a felony.
Elements of Criminal Liability	**1.** *Guilty act*—In general, some form of harmful act must be committed for a crime to exist. **2.** *Intent*—An intent to commit a crime, or a wrongful mental state, is required for a crime to exist.

CHAPTER SUMMARY • *Continued*

Constitutional Safeguards	The rights of accused persons are protected under the Constitution, particularly by the Fourth, Fifth, Sixth, and Eighth Amendments. Under the exclusionary rule, evidence obtained in violation of the constitutional rights of the accused will not be admissible in court. Individuals must be informed of their constitutional rights (such as their rights to counsel and to remain silent) on being taken into custody.
Crimes Affecting Business	**1.** *Forgery*—The fraudulent making or altering of any writing in a way that changes the legal rights and liabilities of another. **2.** *Robbery*—The forceful and unlawful taking of personal property of any value from another. **3.** *Larceny*—The wrongful or fraudulent taking and carrying away of another's personal property with the intent to deprive the owner permanently of the property. **4.** *Embezzlement*—The fraudulent appropriation of another person's property or money by a person to whom it was entrusted. **5.** *Mail and wire fraud*—Using the mails, wires, radio, or television to defraud the public. **6.** *Computer crime*—Any act that is directed against computers and computer parts, that uses computers as instruments of crime, or that involves computers and constitutes abuse. **7.** *Bribery*—The crime of bribery is committed when the bribe is tendered. **8.** *RICO*—The Racketeer Influenced and Corrupt Organizations Act (RICO) of 1970 makes it a federal crime (1) to use income obtained from racketeering activity to purchase any interest in an enterprise, (2) to acquire or maintain an interest in an enterprise through racketeering activity, (3) to conduct or participate in the affairs of an enterprise through racketeering activity, or (4) to conspire to do any of the preceding acts.
Defenses to Criminal Liability	**1.** *Infancy.* **2.** *Insanity.* **3.** *Entrapment.* **4.** *Immunity.*

HYPOTHETICAL QUESTIONS

6–1. Types of Crimes. Determine from the facts below what type of crime has been committed in each situation.

(a) Carlos is walking through an amusement park when his wallet, with $2,000 in it, is "picked" from his pocket.

(b) Carlos walks into a camera shop. Without force and without the owner's noticing, Carlos walks out with a camera.

6–2. Theft. The head of CompTac Corporation's accounting department, Roy Olson, has to pay his daughter's college tuition within a week, or his daughter will not be able to continue taking classes. The payment due is over $20,000. Roy would be able to make the payment in two months, but cannot do so until then. The college refuses to wait that long. In desperation, Roy—through a fictitious bank account and some clever accounting—"borrows" funds from CompTac. Before Roy can pay back the borrowed funds, an auditor discovers what Roy did. CompTac's president alleges that Roy has "stolen" company funds and informs the police of the theft. Has Roy committed a crime? If so, what crime did he commit? Explain.

REAL WORLD CASE PROBLEM

6–3. Criminal Liability. In January 1988, David Ludvigson was hired as chief executive officer of Leopard Enterprises, a group of companies that owned funeral homes and cemeteries in Iowa and sold "preneed" funeral contracts. Under Iowa law, 80 percent of monies obtained under such a contract must be set aside in trust until the death of the person for whose benefit the funds were paid. Shortly after Ludvigson was hired, the firm began having financial difficulties. Ludvigson used money from these contracts to pay operating expenses until the company went bankrupt and was placed in receivership. Ludvigson was charged and found guilty on five counts of second degree theft stemming from the misappropriation of these funds. He appealed, alleging, among other things, that because none of the victims whose trust funds were used to cover operating expenses was denied services, no injury was done and thus no crime was committed. Will the court agree with Ludvigson? Explain. [*State v. Ludvigson*, 482 N.W.2d 419 (Iowa 1992)]

For updated links to resources available on the Web, as well as a variety of other materials, visit this text's Web site at **http://blte.westbuslaw.com**.

The Bureau of Justice Statistics in the U.S. Department of Justice offers an impressive collection of statistics on crime at the following Web site:

http://www.ojp.usdoj.gov/bjs

For summaries of famous criminal cases and documents relating to these trials, go to Court TV's Web site at

http://www.courttv.com/index.html

If you would like to learn more about criminal procedures, the following site offers an "Anatomy of a Murder: A Trip through Our Nation's Legal Justice System":

http://tqd.advanced.org/2760/home.htm

At the above site, you can also find a glossary of terms used in criminal law, view actual forms that are filled out during the course of an arrest, and learn about some controversial issues in criminal law.

Many state criminal codes are now online. To find your state's code, go to

http://www.findlaw.com

and select "State" under the link to "Laws: Cases and Codes."

You can learn about some of the constitutional questions raised by various criminal laws and procedures by going to the Web site of the American Civil Liberties Union at

http://www.aclu.org

The text of the U.S. Sentencing Guidelines Manual is online at

http://www.ussc.gov

ONLINE LEGAL RESEARCH

Go to **http://blte.westbuslaw.com**, the Web site that accompanies this text. Select "Internet Applications," and then click on "Chapter 6." There you will find the following Internet research exercise that you can perform to learn more about criminal procedures:

Activity 6–1: Revisiting *Miranda*

Chapter 6 ■ WORK SET

TRUE-FALSE QUESTIONS

_____ **1.** A crime is a wrong against society proclaimed in a statute.

_____ **2.** A person can be convicted simply for intending to commit a crime.

_____ **3.** If a crime is punishable by death, it must be a felony.

_____ **4.** Children over age fourteen are presumed competent to stand trial.

_____ **5.** A person who has been granted immunity from prosecution cannot be compelled to answer any questions.

_____ **6.** Robbery is the taking of another's personal property, from his or her person or immediate presence.

_____ **7.** Stealing a computer program is not a crime.

_____ **8.** Fraudulently altering a public document can be forgery.

_____ **9.** Racketeering activity is a new type of crime created by RICO.

_____ **10.** Persons suffering from mental illness are sometimes judged incapable of the state of mind required to commit a crime.

MULTIPLE-CHOICE QUESTIONS

_____ **1.** Which of the following statements is true?

a. Criminal defendants are prosecuted by the state.
b. Criminal defendants must prove their innocence.
c. Criminal law actions are intended to give the victims financial compensation.
d. A crime is never a violation of a statute.

_____ **2.** Crime requires

a. the performance of a prohibited act.
b. the intent to commit a crime.
c. both a and b.
d. none of the above.

_____ **3.** Helen, an undercover police officer, pressures Pete to buy stolen goods. When he does so, he is arrested and charged with dealing in stolen goods. Pete will likely be

a. acquitted, because he was entrapped.
b. acquitted, because Helen was entrapped.
c. acquitted, because both parties were entrapped.
d. convicted.

_____ **4.** Police officer Berry arrests John on suspicion of burglary. Berry advises John of his rights. These rights include that

a. John has the rights to remain silent and to consult with an attorney.
b. anything said can and will be used against John in court.
c. both a and b.
d. none of the above.

_____ **5.** In a jewelry store, April takes a diamond ring from the counter and puts it in her pocket. She walks three steps toward the door before the manager stops her. April is arrested and charged with larceny. She will likely be

a. acquitted, because she was entrapped.
b. acquitted, because she only took three steps.
c. acquitted, because she did not leave the store.
d. convicted.

_____ **6.** Kevin takes home the company-owned laptop computer that he uses in his office. He has no intention of returning it. Kevin has committed

a. larceny.
b. embezzlement.
c. robbery.
d. none of the above.

_____ **7.** Police detective Howard suspects Carol of a crime. Howard may be issued a warrant to search Carol's premises if he can show

a. probable cause.
b. proximate cause.
c. causation in fact.
d. intent to search the premises.

_____ **8.** Double jeopardy (trying someone twice for the same crime) is

a. permitted only if the verdict in the first trial is not guilty.
b. permitted only if the verdict in the first trial is guilty.
c. permitted regardless of the verdict in the first trial.
d. prohibited.

_____ **9.** Police officer Katy obtains a confession from criminal suspect Bart after an illegal arrest. At Bart's trial, the confession would likely be

a. admitted as proof of Bart's guilt.
b. admitted as evidence of Bart's crime.
c. admitted as support for Katy's suspicions.
d. excluded.

ISSUE SPOTTERS

1. With Jim's permission, Lee signs Jim's name to several traveler's checks that were issued to Jim and cashes them. Jim reports that the checks were stolen and receives replacements. Has Lee committed forgery?

2. Carl appears on television talk shows touting a cure for AIDS that he knows is fraudulent, because it has no medical validity. He frequently mentions that he needs funds to make the cure widely available, and donations pour into local television stations to be forwarded to Carl. Has Carl committed a crime? If so, what?

UNIT TWO
CONTRACTS

UNIT OUTLINE

7 Introduction to Contracts

LEARNING OBJECTIVES

When you finish this chapter, you should be able to:

1. Define the objective theory of contracts.
2. List the basic requirements of a contract.
3. Contrast express and implied contracts.
4. Summarize the difference between executed and executory contracts.
5. State the differences among valid, void, voidable, and unenforceable contracts.

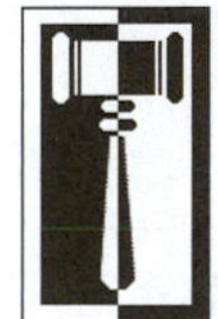

FACING A LEGAL PROBLEM

Jack offers to pay Simone $10 if she walks across the entire span of the Golden Gate Bridge. *If Simone says nothing but simply walks across the bridge, do she and Jack have a contract? If Simone says no and turns and walks away, are there any legal consequences? If, without saying a word, Barry rather than Simone starts to walk across, do Jack and Barry have a contract?*

PROMISE
A declaration that binds the person who makes it (promisor) to do or not to do a certain act. The person to whom the promise is made (promisee) has a right to expect or demand the performance of some particular thing.

PROMISOR
A person who makes a promise.

PROMISEE
A person to whom a promise is made.

CONTRACT
A set of promises constituting an agreement between parties, giving each a legal duty to the other and also the right to seek a remedy for the breach of the promises/duties.

Contract law assures the parties to private agreements that the **promises** they make will be enforceable. A *promise* is a declaration that something either will or will not happen in the future. Sometimes the promises exchanged create *moral* rather than *legal* obligations. Failure to perform a moral obligation, such as an agreement to take a friend to lunch, does not usually create a legal liability. Some promises may create both a moral and a legal obligation, such as a father's promise to pay for his daughter's college education.

Clearly, many promises are kept because of a sense of duty, or because keeping them is in the mutual self-interest of the parties involved, not because the **promisor** (the person making the promise) or the **promisee** (the person to whom the promise is made) is conscious of the rules of contract law. Nevertheless, the rules of contract law are often followed in business agreements to avoid potential problems.

Definition of a Contract

A **contract** is an agreement that can be enforced in a court. It is formed by two or more parties who agree to perform or refrain from performing some act now or in the future. Generally, contract disputes arise when there is a promise of future performance. If the contractual promise is not fulfilled, the party who made it is subject to the sanctions of a court (see Chapter 15). That party may be required to pay money damages for failing to perform. In limited instances, the party may be required to perform the promised act.

In determining whether a contract has been formed, the element of intent is of prime importance. In contract law, intent is determined by what is called the **objective theory of contracts,** not by the personal or subjective intent, or belief, of a party. The theory is that a party's intention to enter into a contract is judged by outward, objective facts as interpreted by a *reasonable* person, rather than by the party's own secret, subjective intentions. Objective facts include (1) what the party said when entering into the contract, (2) how the party acted or appeared, and (3) the circumstances surrounding the transaction. As will be discussed later in this chapter, in the section on express versus implied contracts, intent to form a contract may be manifested not only in words (oral or written) but also by conduct.

LEARNING OBJECTIVE NO. 1
Defining the Objective Theory of Contracts

OBJECTIVE THEORY OF CONTRACTS
The view that contracting parties shall only be bound by terms that can objectively be inferred from promises made.

The Basic Requirements of a Contract

The following list describes the requirements of a contract. Each will be explained more fully in the chapters indicated.

LEARNING OBJECTIVE NO. 2
Listing the Requirements of a Contract

1. *Agreement.* An agreement includes an *offer* and an *acceptance.* One party must offer to enter into a legal agreement, and another party must accept the terms of the offer (Chapter 8).
2. *Consideration.* Any promises made by parties must be supported by legally sufficient and bargained-for *consideration* (something of value received or promised, to convince a person to make a deal) (Chapter 9).
3. *Contractual capacity.* Both parties entering into the contract must have the contractual *capacity* to do so. The law must recognize them as possessing characteristics that qualify them as competent parties (Chapter 10).
4. *Legality.* The contract's purpose must be to accomplish some goal that is *legal* and not against public policy (Chapter 11).
5. *Genuineness of assent.* The apparent consent of both parties must be *genuine* (Chapter 12).
6. *Form.* The contract must be in whatever *form* the law requires. For example, some contracts must be in writing to be enforceable (Chapter 13).

The first four items in this list are formally known as the *elements of a contract.* The last two are possible *defenses to the formation or the enforcement of a contract.*

Types of Contracts

There are numerous types of contracts, and each has a legal significance as to formation, enforceability, or performance. The best method of explaining each is to compare one type of contract with another.

BILATERAL VERSUS UNILATERAL CONTRACTS

Every contract involves at least two parties. The **offeror** is the party making the offer. The **offeree** is the party to whom the offer is made. The offeror always promises to do or not to do something and thus is also a promisor. Whether the contract is classified as *unilateral* or *bilateral* depends on what the offeree must do to accept the offer and to bind the offeror to a contract.

OFFEROR
A person who makes an offer.

OFFEREE
A person to whom an offer is made.

If to accept the offer, the offeree must only *promise* to perform, the contract is a **bilateral contract.** Hence, a bilateral contract is a "promise for a promise." No performance, such as the payment of money or delivery of goods,

BILATERAL CONTRACT
A contract that includes the exchange of a promise for a promise.

need take place for a bilateral contract to be formed. The contract comes into existence at the moment the promises are exchanged. If the offer is phrased so that the offeree can accept only by completing the contract performance, the contract is a **unilateral contract.** Hence, a unilateral contract is a "promise for an act."

UNILATERAL CONTRACT
A contract that includes the exchange of a promise for an act.

In the legal problem set out at the beginning of this chapter, Jack offers to pay Simone $10 if she walks across the Golden Gate Bridge. *If, without saying a word, Simone walks across the bridge, do she and Jack have a contract?* Yes. They have a unilateral contract, which can be accepted only by performance. *If Simone tells Jack no and turns and walks away, are there any legal consequences?* No. A unilateral contract is a "promise for an act." Without the act, there is no contract and thus no consequences for not acting. *If no one says anything more, but Barry rather than Simone starts to walk across, do Jack and Barry have a contract?* No. Only if the person to whom the offer is made walks completely across the bridge is the offer accepted.

Contests, lotteries, and other prize-winning competitions are examples of offers for unilateral contracts. If a person complies with the rules of the contest—such as submitting the right lottery number at the right place and time—a unilateral contract is formed, binding the organization offering the prize to a contract to perform as promised in the offer.

The 'Lectric Law Library provides information on contract law, including a definition of a contract, the elements required for a contract, and so on. Go to

http://www.lectlaw.com

Then go to Laypeople's Law Lounge, and scroll down to Contracts.

A problem arises in unilateral contracts when the promisor attempts to *revoke* (cancel) the offer after the promisee has begun performance but before the act has been completed. The promisee can accept the offer only upon full performance, and offers are normally *revocable* (capable of being taken back, or canceled) until accepted. The modern-day view, however, is that the offer becomes irrevocable once performance has begun. Thus, even though the offer has not yet been accepted, the offeror is prohibited from revoking it for a reasonable time.

IN THE COURTROOM

Mai offers to buy Harry's sailboat, moored in San Francisco, upon delivery of the boat to Mai's dock in Newport Beach, 300 miles south of San Francisco. Harry rigs the boat and sets sail. Shortly before his arrival at Newport Beach, Harry receives a radio message from Mai withdrawing her offer. *Does Mai's message terminate the offer, or because Harry has begun performing, is the offer irrevocable?* Mai's offer is part of a unilateral contract, and only Harry's delivery of the sailboat at her dock is an acceptance. Ordinarily, her revocation would terminate the offer, but because performance—sailing almost 300 miles—had been substantially completed by Harry, her offer is irrevocable. Harry can deliver the boat and bind Mai to the contract.

The problem of performance of unilateral contracts often arises in sales of real estate. A broker, for example, may invest substantial effort in finding a buyer for someone who has listed his or her property for sale and then learn that the seller is canceling the brokerage agreement.

LEARNING OBJECTIVE NO. 3
Contrasting Express and Implied Contracts

EXPRESS VERSUS IMPLIED CONTRACTS

An **express contract** is one in which the terms of the agreement are fully and explicitly stated in words, oral or written. A signed lease for an apartment or a house is an express written contract. If a classmate calls you on the phone and agrees to buy your textbooks from last semester for $50, an express oral contract has been made.

EXPRESS CONTRACT
A contract that is oral and/or written (as opposed to an implied contract).

A contract that is implied from the conduct of the parties is called an **implied-in-fact contract,** or an implied contract. This contract differs from an express contract in that the *conduct* of the parties, rather than their words, creates and defines the terms of the contract.

IMPLIED-IN-FACT CONTRACT
A contract formed in whole or in part from the conduct of the parties (as opposed to an express contract).

IN THE COURTROOM

Suppose you need a tax consultant or an accountant to fill out your tax return this year. You look through the Yellow Pages and find both an accountant and a tax consultant at an office in your neighborhood, so you drop by to see them. You go into the office and explain your problem, and they tell you what their fees are. The next day you return, giving the secretary all the necessary information and documents, such as canceled checks, W-2 forms, and so on. You say nothing expressly to the secretary. Rather, you walk out the door. *Have you entered into an implied-in-fact contract to pay the tax consultant and accountant the usual and reasonable fees for their services?* Yes. The contract is implied by your conduct and by their conduct. They expect to be paid for completing your tax return. By bringing in the records they will need to do the work, you have implied an intent to pay them.

The following three steps establish an implied-in-fact contract:

1. The party furnished some goods or services.
2. The party furnishing the goods or services expected to be paid, and the party to whom the goods or services were provided knew or should have known that payment was expected (by using the objective-theory-of-contracts test, discussed previously).
3. The party to whom the goods or services were provided had a chance to reject them and did not.

Promises made in an employment manual may create an implied-in-fact employment contract.

QUASI CONTRACTS—CONTRACTS IMPLIED IN LAW

Quasi contracts, or contracts *implied in law,* are wholly different from actual contracts. Express contracts and implied-in-fact contracts are actual, or true, contracts. Quasi contracts, as their name suggests, are not true contracts. They do not arise from any agreement, express or implied, between the parties themselves. Rather, quasi contracts are fictional contracts implied by courts and imposed on parties in the interests of fairness and justice. Usually, quasi contracts are imposed to avoid the *unjust enrichment* of one party at the expense of another.

QUASI CONTRACT
An obligation or contract imposed by law, in the absence of agreement, to prevent unjust enrichment. Sometimes referred to as an implied-in-law contract (a legal fiction) to distinguish it from an implied-in-fact contract.

IN THE COURTROOM

Larrissa enters into a contract with Pavel, agreeing to work for Pavel for one year. At the end of the year, Larrissa is to be paid $18,000. Larrissa works for ten months and then leaves voluntarily, without cause. Pavel refuses to pay her for the ten months she worked, so Larrissa sues in quasi contract for the value of services rendered. *Will the court allow Larrissa to recover her salary for the ten months worked?* Very likely, yes—minus any damages caused to Pavel by her early departure.

There are situations in which the party obtaining the unjust enrichment is not liable. Basically, the quasi-contractual principle cannot be invoked by a party who has conferred a benefit on someone else unnecessarily or as a result of misconduct or negligence.

IN THE COURTROOM

You take your car to the local car wash and ask to have it run through the washer and to have the gas tank filled. While it is being washed, you go to a nearby shopping center for two hours. In the meantime, one of the workers at the car wash mistakenly believes that your car is the one that he is supposed to hand wax. When you come back, you are presented with a bill for a full tank of gas, a wash job, and a hand wax. *Do you have to pay for the hand wax?* Clearly, a benefit has been conferred on you. This benefit, however, has been conferred because of a mistake by the car-wash employee. You have not been *unjustly* enriched. People cannot normally be forced to pay for benefits "thrust" on them.

The doctrine of quasi contract generally cannot be used when there is an actual contract that covers the area in controversy. For example, Martinez contracts with Stevenson to deliver a furnace to a building project owned by Richards. Martinez delivers the furnace, but Stevenson never pays Martinez. Stevenson has been unjustly enriched in this situation, to be sure. Martinez cannot collect from Richards in quasi contract, however, because Martinez had an existing contract with Stevenson. Martinez already has a remedy—he can sue for breach of contract to recover the price of the furnace from Stevenson. No quasi contract need be implied by the court in this instance to achieve justice.

FORMAL VERSUS INFORMAL CONTRACTS

FORMAL CONTRACT
An agreement or contract that by law requires for its validity a specific form, such as executed under seal.

Formal contracts require a special form or method of creation (formation) to be enforceable. They include (1) contracts under seal, (2) recognizances, (3) negotiable instruments, and (4) letters of credit. *Contracts under seal* are documents with a special seal attached. The significance of the seal has lessened, although about ten states require no consideration when a contract is under seal. A *recognizance* is an acknowledgment in court by a person that he or she will pay a certain sum if a certain event occurs or that he or she will perform some specified obligation. One form of recognizance is the personal recognizance bond used as bail in a criminal matter. Negotiable instruments and letters of credit are special methods of payment designed for use in many commercial settings (they are discussed at length in subsequent chapters). *Negotiable instruments* include checks, notes, drafts, and certificates of deposit. *Letters of credit* are agreements to pay contingent on the purchaser's receipt of invoices and bills of lading (documents evidencing receipt of, and title to, goods shipped).

INFORMAL CONTRACT
A contract that does not require a specified form or formality for its validity.

EXECUTED CONTRACT
A contract that has been completely performed by both parties.

EXECUTORY CONTRACT
A contract that has not as yet been fully performed.

Informal contracts (also called *simple contracts*) include all contracts other than formal contracts. No special form is required (except for certain types of contracts that must be in writing), because the contracts are usually based on their substance rather than on their form.

EXECUTED VERSUS EXECUTORY CONTRACTS

LEARNING OBJECTIVE NO. 4
Summarizing the Difference between Executed and Executory Contracts

Contracts are also classified according to their state of performance. A contract that has been fully performed on both sides is called an **executed contract.** A contract that has not been fully performed on either side is called an **executory contract.** If one party has fully performed but the other has not, the contract is said to be executed on the one side and executory on the other, but the contract is still classified as executory.

IN THE COURTROOM

Assume you agree to buy ten tons of coal from the Western Coal Company. Western delivers the coal to your steel mill, where it is now being burned. You have not yet paid for the coal. *Is the contract executed, executory, or both?* At this point, the contract is executed on the part of Western and executory on your part. After you pay, the contract will be executed on both sides.

VALID, VOID, VOIDABLE, AND UNENFORCEABLE CONTRACTS

LEARNING OBJECTIVE NO. 5
Stating the Differences among Valid, Void, Voidable, and Unenforceable Contracts

A **valid contract** has the necessary elements to entitle at least one of the parties to enforce it in court. Those elements consist of an offer and an acceptance that are supported by legally sufficient consideration, for a legal purpose, and made by parties who have the legal capacity to enter into the contract. Each element is discussed in detail in the following chapters.

VALID CONTRACT
A properly constituted contract having legal strength or force.

A **void contract** is no contract at all. The terms *void* and *contract* are contradictory. A void contract produces no legal obligations by any of the parties. For example, a contract can be void because one of the parties was adjudged by a court to be legally insane or because the purpose of the contract was illegal.

VOID CONTRACT
A contract having no legal force or binding effect.

A **voidable contract** is a *valid* contract in which one (or both) of the parties has (have) the option of avoiding the legal obligations arising under the contract. The party having the option can elect to avoid any duty to perform or can elect to *ratify* (make valid) the contract. If the contract is avoided, both parties are released from it. If it is ratified, both parties must fully perform their respective legal obligations.

VOIDABLE CONTRACT
A contract that may be legally annulled at the option of one of the parties.

As a general rule, but subject to exceptions, contracts made by minors are voidable at the option of the minor (see Chapter 10). Contracts entered into under fraudulent conditions are voidable at the option of the innocent party. In addition, contracts entered into because of mistakes and those entered into under legally defined duress or undue influence are voidable (see Chapter 12).

An **unenforceable contract** is one that cannot be enforced because of certain legal defenses against it. It is not unenforceable because a party failed to satisfy a legal requirement of the contract; rather, it is a valid contract rendered unenforceable by law. For example, certain contracts must be in writing (see Chapter 13). If they are not, they will not be enforceable except under certain exceptional circumstances.

UNENFORCEABLE CONTRACT
A valid contract having no legal effect or force in a court action.

TERMS AND CONCEPTS FOR REVIEW

bilateral contract 85
contract 84
executed contract 88
executory contract 88
express contract 86
formal contract 88
implied-in-fact contract 87
informal contract 88
objective theory of contracts 85
offeree 85
offeror 85
promise 84
promisee 84
promisor 84
quasi contract 87
unenforceable contract 89
unilateral contract 86
valid contract 89
void contract 89
voidable contract 89

CHAPTER SUMMARY • INTRODUCTION TO CONTRACTS

Requirements of a Contract	1. *Agreement.* 2. *Consideration.* 3. *Contractual capacity.* 4. *Legality.*
Possible Defenses to the Enforcement of a Contract	1. *Genuineness of assent.* 2. *Form.*
Types of Contracts	1. *Bilateral*—A promise for a promise. 2. *Unilateral*—A promise for an act (acceptance is the completed performance of the act). 3. *Express*—Formed by words (oral, written, or a combination). 4. *Implied in fact*—Formed by the conduct of the parties. 5. *Quasi contract* (implied in law)—Imposed by law to prevent unjust enrichment. 6. *Formal*—Requires a special form for creation. 7. *Informal*—Requires no special form for creation (unless required to be in writing). 8. *Executed*—A fully performed contract. 9. *Executory*—A contract not fully performed. 10. *Valid*—A contract with the necessary contractual elements of offer and acceptance, consideration, parties with legal capacity, and made for a legal purpose. 11. *Void*—No contract exists or there is a contract without legal obligations. 12. *Voidable*—One party has the option of avoiding or enforcing the contractual obligation. 13. *Unenforceable*—A contract exists, but it cannot be enforced because of a legal defense.

HYPOTHETICAL QUESTIONS

7–1. Express versus Implied Contracts. Suppose that McDougal, a local businessperson, is a good friend of Krunch, the owner of a local candy store. Every day at his lunch hour McDougal goes into Krunch's candy store and spends about five minutes looking at the candy. After examining Krunch's candy and talking with Krunch, McDougal usually buys one or two candy bars. One afternoon, McDougal goes into Krunch's candy shop, looks at the candy, and picks up a $1 candy bar. Seeing that Krunch is very busy, he waves the candy bar at Krunch without saying a word and walks out. Is there a contract? If so, classify it within the categories presented in this chapter.

7–2. Contract Classification. High-Flying Advertising, Inc., contracted with Big Burger Restaurants to fly an advertisement above the Connecticut beaches. The advertisement offered $5,000 to any person who could swim from the Connecticut beaches to Long Island across the Long Island Sound in less than a day. McElfresh saw the streamer and accepted the challenge. He started his marathon swim that same day at 10 A.M. After he had been swimming for four hours and was about halfway across the sound, McElfresh saw another plane pulling a streamer that read, "Big Burger revokes." Is there a contract between McElfresh and Big Burger? If there is a contract, what type(s) of contract is (are) formed?

REAL WORLD CASE PROBLEM

7–3. Recovery for Services Rendered. After Walter Washut had suffered a heart attack and could no longer take care of himself, he asked Eleanor Adkins, a friend who had previously refused Washut's proposal to marry him, to move to his ranch. For the next twelve years, Adkins lived with Washut, although she retained ownership of her own house and continued to work full-time at her job. Adkins took care of Washut's personal needs, cooked his meals, cleaned and maintained his house, cared for the livestock, and handled other matters for Washut. According to Adkins, Washut told her on numerous occasions that "everything would be taken care of" and that she would never have to leave the ranch. After Washut's death, Adkins sought to recover in quasi contract for the value of the services she had rendered to Washut. Adkins stated in her deposition that she performed the services because she loved Washut, not because she expected to be paid for them. What will the court decide and why? [*Adkins v. Lawson*, 892 P.2d 128 (Wyo. 1995)]

For updated links to resources available on the Web, as well as a variety of other materials, visit this text's Web site at **http://blte.westbuslaw.com**.

The 'Lectric Law Library provides information on contract law, including a definition of a contract, the elements required for a contract, and so on. Go to

http://www.lectlaw.com

Then go to the Laypeople's Law Lounge, and scroll down to Contracts.

You can keep abreast of recent and planned revisions of the *Restatements of the Law,* including the *Restatement (Second) of Contracts,* by accessing the American Law Institute's Web site at

http://www.ali.org

ONLINE LEGAL RESEARCH

Go to **http://blte.westbuslaw.com**, the Web site that accompanies this text. Select "Internet Applications," and then click on "Chapter 7." There you will find the following Internet research exercises that you can perform to learn more about contracts and contract provisions:

Activity 7–1: Contracts and Contract Provisions

Activity 7–2: Contracts in Ancient Mesopotamia

Chapter 7 ■ WORK SET

TRUE-FALSE QUESTIONS

_____ **1.** All contracts involve promises, and every promise is a legal contract.

_____ **2.** An agreement includes an offer and an acceptance.

_____ **3.** Consideration, in contract terms, refers to the competency of a party to enter into a contract.

_____ **4.** A unilateral contract involves performance instead of promises.

_____ **5.** Formal contracts are contracts between parties who are in formal relationships—employer-employee relationships, for example.

_____ **6.** An unenforceable contract is a contract in which one or both of the parties has the option of avoiding his or her legal obligations.

_____ **7.** A quasi contract is imposed by a court to avoid the unjust enrichment of one party at the expense of another.

_____ **8.** An express contract is one in which the terms are fully stated in words.

MULTIPLE-CHOICE QUESTIONS

_____ **1.** Don contracts with Jan to paint Jan's townhouse while she's on vacation. By mistake, Don paints Mick's townhouse. Mick sees Don painting but says nothing. From whom can Don recover?

a. Jan, because she was the party with whom Don contracted.
b. Jan, under the theory of quasi contract.
c. Mick, because his house was painted.
d. Mick, under the theory of quasi contract.

_____ **2.** Brian offers to sell Ashley his CD-ROM collection, forgetting that he does not want to sell some of the disks. Unaware of Brian's forgetfulness, Ashley accepts. Is there a contract including all of Brian's disks?

a. Yes, according to the objective theory of contracts.
b. Yes, according to the subjective theory of contracts.
c. No, because Brian did not intend to sell his favorite disks.
d. No, because Ashley had no reason to know of Brian's forgetfulness.

_____ **3.** Greg promises to imprint four thousand t-shirts with Rona's logo. Rona pays in advance. Before Greg delivers the shirts, the contract is classified as

a. executory, because it is executory on Greg's part.
b. executory, because it is executory on Rona's part.
c. executed, because it is executed on Greg's part.
d. none of the above.

_____ **4.** Without agreeing as to payment, Mary accepts the services of Lee, an accountant, and is pleased with the work. Is there a contract between them?

a. Yes, there is an express contract.
b. Yes, there is an implied-in-fact contract.
c. No, because they made no agreement concerning payment.
d. Yes, there is an implied-in-law contract.

_____ **5.** The requirements of a contract include

a. agreement.
b. consideration.
c. agreement and consideration.
d. none of the above.

_____ **6.** Sam contracts with Hugo's Sports Equipment to buy a jet ski and to pay for it in installments. Sam is a minor, and so he can choose to avoid his contractual obligations. The contract between Sam and Hugo is

a. valid.
b. void.
c. voidable.
d. both a and c.

_____ **7.** A contract consists of promises between two or more parties to

a. refrain from performing some act.
b. perform some act in the future.
c. perform some act now.
d. any of the above.

_____ **8.** Dick tells Ben that he will pay Ben $1,500 to set fire to Dick's store, so that Dick can collect money under his fire insurance policy. Ben sets fire to the store, but Dick refuses to pay. Their deal is

a. an enforceable contract.
b. a voidable contract.
c. a void contract.
d. a valid contract.

_____ **9.** Rita calls Rick on the phone and agrees to buy his laptop computer for $200. This is

a. an express contract.
b. an implied-in-fact contract.
c. an implied-in-law contract.
d. no contract.

ISSUE SPOTTERS

1. Jay signs and returns a letter from Bill referring to a certain saddle and its price. When Bill delivers the saddle, Jay sends it back, claiming that they have no contract. Bill claims that they do have a contract. Do they?

2. Alison receives from the local tax collector a notice of property taxes due. The notice is for tax on Jerry's property, but Alison believes that the tax is hers and pays it. Can Alison recover from Jerry the amount that she paid?

Offer and Acceptance

LEARNING OBJECTIVES

When you finish this chapter, you should be able to:

1. Identify the requirements of an offer.
2. Recognize a counteroffer.
3. Identify the requirements of a valid acceptance.
4. Describe how an offer can be accepted.

FACING A LEGAL PROBLEM

You and three co-workers ride to work each day in Julio's automobile, which has a market value of $8,000. One cold morning the four of you get into the car, but Julio cannot get it started. He yells in anger, "I'll sell this car to anyone for $500!" You drop $500 in his lap. *Is the car yours?*

Essential to any contract is that the parties agree on the terms of the contract. **Agreement** exists when an offer made by one party is accepted or assented to by the other. Ordinarily, agreement is evidenced by an *offer* and an *acceptance.* One party offers a certain bargain to another party, who then accepts that bargain. Because words often fail to convey the precise meaning intended, the law of contracts generally adheres to the *objective theory of contracts,* as discussed in Chapter 7. Under this theory, a party's words and conduct are held to mean whatever a reasonable person in the offeree's position would think they mean.

AGREEMENT
A meeting of two or more minds. Often used as a synonym for contract.

Requirements of the Offer

An **offer** is a promise or commitment to perform or refrain from performing some specified act in the future. As discussed in Chapter 7, the party making an offer is called the *offeror,* and the party to whom the offer is made is called the *offeree.*

OFFER
An offeror's proposal to do something, which creates in the offeree accepting the offer a legal power to bind the offeror to the terms of the proposal by accepting the offer.

Three elements are necessary for an offer to be effective:

1. There must be a *serious, objective* (readily recognizable and accepted by others) *intention* by the offeror.
2. The terms of the offer must be reasonably *certain* or *definite* so that the parties and the court can ascertain the terms of the contract.
3. The offer must be communicated to the offeree.

LEARNING OBJECTIVE NO. 1
Identifying the Requirements of an Offer

INTENTION

The first requirement for an effective offer to exist is a serious, objective intention on the part of the offeror. Intent is not determined by the *subjective* (personal, unspoken) intentions, beliefs, or assumptions of the offeror. It is determined by what a reasonable person in the offeree's position would conclude the offeror's words and actions meant. Offers made in obvious anger, jest, or undue excitement do not meet the serious-and-objective-intent test. Because these offers are not effective, an offeree's acceptance does not create an agreement.

In the legal problem set out at the beginning of this chapter, Julio angrily yelled that he would sell his $8,000 car to anyone for $500. *Would a reasonable person conclude that this was a serious offer?* No. A reasonable person, taking into consideration Julio's frustration and the obvious difference in value between the car's market price and the purchase price, would conclude that his offer was not made with serious and objective intent. Thus, even if you dropped $500 in Julio's lap at the moment of his angry "offer," you would not have an agreement.

Expressions of Opinion. An expression of opinion is not an offer. It does not evidence an intention to enter into a binding agreement.

IN THE COURTROOM

Hawkins took his son to McGee, a doctor, and asked McGee to operate on the son's hand, which had been scarred in an accident. McGee said the boy would be in the hospital three or four days and that the hand would *probably* heal within a few days. The hand became infected, and the son was hospitalized for three months. *Did the father win a suit for breach of contract?* No. The court held that McGee did not make an offer to heal the son's hand in three or four days. He merely expressed an opinion as to when the hand would heal.

Preliminary Negotiations. A request or invitation to negotiate is not an offer. It is only an expression of a willingness to discuss the possibility of entering into a contract. Examples are statements such as "Will you sell your three-bedroom house?" or "I wouldn't sell my car for less than $1,000." A reasonable person in the offeree's position would not conclude that these statements evidence an intention to enter into a binding obligation. Likewise, when the government and private firms need to have construction work done, contractors are invited to submit bids. The *invitation* to submit bids is not an offer, and a contractor does not bind the government or private firm by submitting a bid. (The bids that the contractors submit are *offers,* however, and the government or private firm can bind the contractor by accepting the bid.)

Advertisements, Catalogues, and Circulars. In general, mail-order catalogues and circular letters (meant for the general public) are not considered evidence of an intention to enter into a contract but are considered invitations to negotiate.

IN THE COURTROOM

Tartop & Company advertises a used paving machine. The ad is mailed to hundreds of firms and reads, "Used Case Construction Co. paving machine. Builds curbs and finishes cement work all in one process. Price $11,250." *If General Paving, Inc., calls Tartop and says, "We accept your offer," is an enforceable contract formed?* No. A reasonable person would conclude that Tartop was not promising to sell the paving machine, but rather was inviting buyers to offer to buy at that price. A seller never has an unlimited supply of goods. If advertisements were offers, then everyone who "accepted" after the retailer's supply was exhausted could sue for breach of contract.

Price lists are another form of invitation to negotiate or trade. A seller's price list is not an offer to sell at that price. It merely invites the buyer to offer to buy at that price. In fact, a seller usually puts "prices subject to change" on a price list. Only in rare circumstances will a price quotation be construed as an offer.

Auctions. In an auction, a seller "offers" goods for sale through an auctioneer. This is not, however, an offer for purposes of contract. The seller is really only expressing a willingness to sell. Unless the terms of the auction are explicitly stated to be *without reserve,* the seller (through the auctioneer) may withdraw the goods at any time before the auctioneer closes the sale by announcement or by fall of the hammer. The seller's right to withdraw goods characterizes an auction *with reserve.* All auctions are assumed to be of this type unless a clear statement to the contrary is made. In auctions with reserve, the bidder is actually the offeror. Before the auctioneer strikes the hammer, which constitutes acceptance of a bid, a bidder may revoke his or her bid, or the auctioneer may reject that bid or all bids. At auctions without reserve, the goods cannot be withdrawn and must be sold to the highest bidder.

Definiteness

The second requirement for an effective offer is the definiteness of its terms. An offer must have reasonably definite (determined or fixed) terms so that a court can determine if a breach has occurred and give an appropriate remedy. An offer may invite an acceptance to be worded in such specific terms that the contract is made definite. Thus, if someone offers to sell you "from one to ten quarts of oil for your car" and asks you to state the desired number in your acceptance, your agreement to buy two quarts is an enforceable contract—the quantity is specified and the terms are definite.

A term in an offer such as "Price to be determined later" may allow the offeree, after acceptance, to claim that a contract was never formed, because the price term was too indefinite.

Communication

A third requirement for an effective offer is communication, resulting in the offeree's knowledge of the offer. For example, if a reward is offered for the return of a lost cat, a person who does not know about the reward cannot claim it, even if he or she finds the cat and returns it.

Termination of the Offer

The communication of an effective offer to an offeree gives the offeree the power to transform the offer into a binding, legal obligation (a contract). This power of acceptance, however, does not continue forever. It can be terminated by *action of the parties or by operation of the law.*

Termination by Action of the Parties

An offer can be terminated by the action of the parties in any of the three ways discussed below.

Revocation of the Offer. The offeror's act of withdrawing an offer is called **revocation.** Unless an offer is irrevocable, the offeror usually can revoke the offer (even if he or she promises to keep the offer open), as long as the revocation

Revocation
In contract law, the withdrawal of an offer by an offeror; unless the offer is irrevocable, it can be revoked at any time prior to acceptance without liability.

is communicated to the offeree before the offeree accepts. Revocation may be accomplished by expressly repudiating the offer (a statement such as "I withdraw my previous offer of October 17" would be an express repudiation) or by performing acts inconsistent with the existence of the offer, which are made known to the offeree.

IN THE COURTROOM

Geraldine offers to sell some land to Manuel. Before Manuel accepts the offer, however, he learns from his friend Konstantine that Geraldine has in the meantime sold the property to Fenwick. *Could Manuel still "accept" the offer and then sue Geraldine for breach of contract?* No. Manuel's knowledge of Geraldine's sale of the land to Fenwick, even though Manuel learned of it through a third party, effectively revokes Geraldine's offer to sell the land to Manuel. Geraldine's sale of the land to Fenwick is inconsistent with the offer to Manuel, and thus the offer to Manuel is revoked.

The general rule followed by most states is that a revocation becomes effective when the offeree or offeree's agent actually receives it. Therefore, a letter of revocation mailed on April 1 and delivered at the offeree's residence or place of business on April 3 becomes effective on April 3.

An offer made to the public can be revoked in the same manner the offer was originally communicated. For example, a store offers a reward for information leading to the arrest and conviction of persons who burglarized it. The store publicizes the offer by advertising it in three local papers for four days. To revoke the offer, the store must normally publish the revocation in the same papers for the same number of days.

Although most offers are revocable, some can be made irrevocable. Increasingly, courts refuse to allow an offeror to revoke an offer when the offeree had changed position because of justifiable reliance on the offer (see the discussion of promissory estoppel in Chapter 9). In some circumstances, offers made by merchants may also be considered irrevocable offers, or "firm offers" (see Chapter 16).

OPTION CONTRACT
A contract under which the offeror cannot revoke his or her offer for a stipulated time period, and the offeree can accept or reject the offer during this period without fear of the offer's being made to another person. The offeree must give consideration for the option (the irrevocable offer) to be enforceable.

Another form of irrevocable offer is an **option contract.** An option contract is created when an offeror promises to hold an offer open for a specified period of time in return for a payment (consideration) given by the offeree. An option contract takes away the offeror's power to revoke the offer for the period of time specified in the option. If no time is specified, then a reasonable period of time is implied.

IN THE COURTROOM

Assume that you are in the business of writing movie scripts. Your agent contacts the head of development at New Line Cinema and offers to sell New Line your new movie script. New Line likes your script and agrees to pay you $5,000 for an option to buy the script within the next six months. According to the terms, for the next six months you cannot sell the script to anyone without offering it to New Line first. In this situation, you (through your agent) are the offeror, and New Line is the offeree. *Can you revoke your offer to sell New Line your script within the next six months?* No. The offer to sell the script has become a contract—an option contract. If after six months no contract to buy the script is formed, however, New Line loses the $5,000, and you are free to sell the script to another firm.

Rejection of the Offer by the Offeree. The offer may be rejected by the offeree, in which case the offer is terminated. A rejection is ordinarily accomplished by words or by conduct evidencing an intent not to accept the offer. As with revocation, rejection of an offer is effective only when it is actually received by the offeror or the offeror's agent.

IN THE COURTROOM

Growgood Farms mailed a letter to Bell's Soup Company offering to sell carrots at ten cents a pound. *What are Bell's Soup Company's options at that point?* Bell's could reject the offer by writing or telephoning Growgood Farms and expressly rejecting the offer, or by mailing the offer back to Growgood, evidencing an intent to reject it. Or Bell's could offer to buy the carrots at eight cents per pound (a counteroffer), necessarily rejecting the original offer.

Merely inquiring about an offer does not constitute rejection. When the offeree merely inquires as to the firmness of the offer, there is no reason to presume that he or she intends to reject it. Thus, if your friend offers to buy your computer's hard drive for $200 and you respond, "Is that your best offer?" or "Will you pay $250?" a reasonable person would conclude that you did not reject the offer but merely made an inquiry. You could still accept and bind your friend to the $200 price.

Counteroffer by the Offeree. A **counteroffer** is usually a rejection of the original offer and the simultaneous making of a new offer, giving the original offeror (now the offeree) the power of acceptance. For example, if a homeowner offers to sell her home to a certain prospective buyer for $115,000, and the prospective buyer says, "The price is too high. I'll pay $110,000," the response is a counteroffer—it terminates the original offer and creates a new offer by the prospective buyer.

At common law, the **mirror image rule** requires that the offeree's acceptance match the offeror's offer exactly. In other words, the terms of acceptance must "mirror" those of the offer. If the acceptance materially changes or adds to the terms of the original offer, it will not be considered an acceptance but rather a counteroffer.

LEARNING OBJECTIVE NO. 2
Recognizing a Counteroffer

COUNTEROFFER
An offeree's response to an offer in which the offeree rejects the original offer and at the same time makes a new offer.

MIRROR IMAGE RULE
A common law rule that requires, for a valid contractual agreement, that the terms of the offeree's acceptance adhere exactly to the terms of the offeror's offer.

TERMINATION BY OPERATION OF THE LAW

The offeree's power to transform an offer into a binding obligation can be terminated by the operation of the law in the following circumstances.

Lapse of Time. An offer terminates automatically by law when the period of time specified in the offer has passed. The time period normally begins to run when the offer is actually received by the offeree, not when it is sent or drawn up. When the offer is delayed, the period begins to run from the date the offeree would have received the offer, but only if the offeree knows or should know that the offer is delayed. Thus, an offer specified to be held open for twenty days will lapse at the end of twenty days. If the offeror mails the offer to the wrong address, and the offeree knows it, the offer will lapse twenty days after the day the offeree would have received the offer if the offeror had mailed it correctly.

If no time for acceptance is specified in the offer, the offer terminates at the end of a *reasonable* period of time. A reasonable period of time is determined by the subject matter of the contract, business and market conditions, and other relevant circumstances. An offer to sell farm produce, for example, will terminate sooner than an offer to sell farm equipment, because farm produce is perishable and subject to greater fluctuations in market value.

Death or Incompetence of the Offeror or Offeree. An offeree's power of acceptance is terminated when the offeror or offeree dies or is deprived of legal capacity (characteristics, such as sanity, that a party must possess to be considered competent) to enter into the proposed contract. For example, an offeror who has been adjudged mentally incompetent and had a guardian appointed for him or her by a court would not be considered competent to enter into contracts. An offer normally cannot pass to an offeror's or offeree's heirs, guardian, or estate. This is true even if the other party did not know of the death or incompetence.

Supervening Illegality of the Proposed Contract. A statute or court decision that makes an offer illegal will automatically terminate the offer. For example, an offer to lend money at an interest rate of 15 percent will automatically terminate if, before the offer is accepted, a statute is enacted prohibiting loans at interest rates greater than 14 percent.

Acceptance

LEARNING OBJECTIVE NO. 3

Identifying the Requirements of an Acceptance

Acceptance is a voluntary act (which may consist of words or conduct) by the offeree that shows assent (agreement) to the offer. The acceptance must be unequivocal and must be communicated to the offeror. Thus, an acceptance has three requirements:

1. An offer must be accepted by the offeree, not by a third person.
2. The acceptance must be uneqivocal.
3. In most cases, the acceptance must be communicated to the offeror.

Who Can Accept?

Generally, a third person cannot be a substitute for the offeree and effectively accept the offer. After all, the identity of the offeree is as much a condition of a bargaining offer as any other term. Thus, except in special circumstances, only the person to whom the offer is made (or that person's agent) can accept the offer and create a binding contract. For example, Lotte makes an offer to Paul. Paul is not interested, but Paul's friend José says, "I accept the offer." No contract is formed.

Unequivocal Acceptance

To exercise the power of acceptance effectively, the offeree must accept without adding or changing any terms. This is the *mirror image rule* previously discussed. If the acceptance is subject to new conditions, or if the terms of the acceptance materially change the original offer, the acceptance may be deemed a counteroffer that implicitly rejects the original offer.

Silence as Acceptance

Ordinarily, silence cannot be acceptance, even if the offeror states, "By your silence and inaction, you will be deemed to have accepted this offer." This general rule applies because an offeree should not be put under a burden of liability to act affirmatively in order to reject an offer.

Communication of Acceptance

Whether the offeror must be notified of the acceptance depends on the nature of the contract. In a bilateral contract, communication of acceptance is necessary, because acceptance is in the form of a promise (not performance). The bilateral contract is formed when the promise is made (rather than when the act is performed). In a unilateral contract, in contrast, the full performance of some act is called for. Acceptance is usually evident, and notification is therefore unnecessary (unless the law requires it or the offeror asks for it).

Mode and Timeliness of Acceptance

In a bilateral contract, the general rule is that acceptance is timely if it is effective within the duration of the offer. Problems arise, however, when the parties involved are not dealing face to face. In such cases, the offeree may use an authorized mode of communication. Acceptance takes effect, thus completing formation of the contract, at the time the communication is sent via the mode expressly or impliedly authorized by the offeror. This is the so-called **mailbox rule,** also called the "deposited acceptance rule," which the majority of courts uphold. Under this rule, if the authorized mode of communication is via the mail, then an acceptance becomes valid when it is dispatched—not when it is received by the offeror. (This is an exception to the rule that acceptance requires a completed communication in bilateral contracts.)

Mailbox Rule
A rule providing that an acceptance of an offer becomes effective upon dispatch (upon being placed in a mailbox), if mail is, expressly or impliedly, an authorized means of communication of acceptance to the offeror.

Most offerors do not specify *expressly* the means by which the offeree is to accept. Thus, the common law recognizes the following *impliedly* authorized means of acceptance:

1. The means chosen by the offeror in making the offer implies that the offeree is authorized to use the *same* or *faster* means for acceptance.
2. When two parties are at a distance, *mailing* is impliedly authorized.

LEARNING OBJECTIVE NO. 4
Describing How an Offer Can Be Accepted

Several factors determine whether a means of acceptance is reasonable. These factors include the nature of the circumstances at the time the offer was made, the means used by the offeror to transmit the offer to the offeree, and the reliability of the offer's delivery. If, for instance, an offer was sent by Federal Express overnight delivery because an acceptance was required urgently, then the offeree's attempt to accept via fax would be deemed reasonable.

There are three basic exceptions to the rule that a contract is formed when acceptance is sent by authorized means:

1. If the acceptance is not properly dispatched (if a letter is incorrectly addressed, for example, or is without the proper postage), in most states it will not be effective until it is received by the offeror.
2. If the offeror specifically conditions his or her offer upon the receipt of an acceptance by a certain time, it must be received before that time.
3. Sometimes an offeree sends a rejection first, then later changes his or her mind and sends an acceptance. Obviously, this chain of events could cause confusion and even detriment to the offeror, depending on whether the rejection or the acceptance arrived first. In such cases, the law cancels the rule of acceptance upon dispatch, and the first communication received by the offeror determines whether a contract is formed. If the rejection comes first, there is no contract.

Findlaw's directory of law-related Web sites offers numerous links to aspects of contract law. Findlaw's URL is

http://www.findlaw.com/

Look in the index of legal subjects for Contracts, and you will find information ranging from a "Layman's Guide to Drafting and Signing Contracts" to contract law in cyberspace to sample contract forms.

TERMS AND CONCEPTS FOR REVIEW

CHAPTER SUMMARY • OFFER AND ACCEPTANCE

Offer—Requirements	**1.** *Intent*—There must be a serious, objective intention by the offeror to become bound by the offer. Nonoffer situations include (a) expressions of opinion; (b) preliminary negotiations; and (c) advertisements, catalogues, and circulars. **2.** *Definiteness*—The terms of the offer must be sufficiently definite to be ascertainable by the parties or by a court. **3.** *Communication*—The offer must be communicated to the offeree.
Offer—Termination	**1.** *By action of the parties*— **a.** *Revocation*—Unless the offer is irrevocable, it can be revoked at any time before acceptance without liability. Revocation is not effective until received by the offeree or the offeree's agent. Some offers, such as the merchant's firm offer and option contracts, are irrevocable. **b.** *Rejection*—Accomplished by words or actions that demonstrate a clear intent not to accept or consider the offer further; not effective until received by the offeror or offeror's agent. **c.** *Counteroffer*—A rejection of the original offer and the making of a new offer. **2.** *By operation of law*— **a.** *Lapse of time*—The offer terminates (1) at the end of the time period specified in the offer, or (2) if no time period is stated in the offer, at the end of a reasonable time period. **b.** *Death or incompetence*—Terminates the offer unless the offer is irrevocable. **c.** *Illegality*—Supervening illegality terminates the offer.
Acceptance	**1.** Can be made only by the offeree or the offeree's agent. **2.** Must be unequivocal. If new terms or conditions are added to the acceptance, it will be considered a counteroffer (mirror image rule). **3.** Acceptance of a unilateral offer is effective upon full performance of the requested act. Generally, no communication is necessary. **4.** Acceptance of a bilateral offer can be communicated by the offeree by any authorized mode of communication and is effective upon dispatch. Unless the mode of communication is expressly specified by the offeror, the following methods are impliedly authorized: **a.** The same mode used by the offeror, or a faster mode. **b.** Mailing, when the two parties are at a distance.

HYPOTHETICAL QUESTIONS

8–1. Offer. Chernek, operating a sole proprietorship, has a large piece of used farm equipment for sale. He offers to sell the equipment to Bollow for $10,000. Discuss the legal effects of the following events on the offer.

(a) Chernek dies prior to Bollow's acceptance, and at the time she accepts, Bollow is unaware of Chernek's death.

(b) Bollow pays $100 for a thirty-day option to purchase the equipment. During this period Chernek dies, and later Bollow accepts the offer, knowing of Chernek's death.

(c) Bollow pays $100 for a thirty-day option to purchase the equipment. During this period Bollow dies, and Bollow's estate accepts Chernek's offer within the stipulated time period.

8–2. Offer and Acceptance. Carrie offered to sell a set of legal encyclopedias to Antonio for $300. Antonio said that he would think about her offer and let her know his decision the next day. Norvel, who had overheard the conversation between Carrie and Antonio, said to Carrie, "I accept your offer" and gave her $300. Carrie gave Norvel the books. The next day, Antonio, who had no idea that Carrie had already sold the books to Norvel, told Carrie that he accepted her offer. Has Carrie breached a valid contract with Antonio? Explain.

REAL WORLD CASE PROBLEM

8–3. Offer and Acceptance. Cora Payne was involved in an automobile accident with Don Chappell, an employee of E & B Carpet Cleaning, Inc. E & B's insurance company offered Payne $18,500 to settle her claim against E & B. Payne did not accept the offer at that time, but instead filed suit against E & B and its insurance company (the defendants). Later Payne offered to settle the case for $50,000, but the defendants refused her offer. Ultimately, Payne told the defendants that she would accept the insurance company's original settlement of $18,500, but the insurance company stated that the offer was no longer open for acceptance. When Payne sought to compel the defendants to perform the original settlement offer, the defendants contended that Payne's filing of her lawsuit terminated the insurance company's earlier settlement offer. Will the court agree with the defendants? Discuss. [*Payne v. E & B Carpet Cleaning, Inc.*, 896 S.W.2d 650 (Mo.App.1995)]

For updated links to resources available on the Web, as well as a variety of other materials, visit this text's Web site at **http://blte.westbuslaw.com**.

You can find articles and information on various areas of law—including contracts—at the Law Office's Web site. Go to

http://lawoffice.com

Select the topic of Business and Commercial Law from the Law Knowledgebase list on the right-hand side of the home page.

To view the terms of a sample contract, go to the "forms" pages of the 'Lectric Law Library at

http://www.lectlaw.com/form.htm

ONLINE LEGAL RESEARCH

Go to **http://blte.westbuslaw.com**, the Web site that accompanies this text. Select "Internet Applications," and then click on "Chapter 8." There you will find the following Internet research exercise that you can perform to learn more about contract terms:

Activity 8–1: Contract Terms

Chapter 8 ■ WORK SET

TRUE-FALSE QUESTIONS

_____ **1.** The seriousness of an offeror's intent is determined by what a reasonable offeree would conclude the offeror's words and actions meant.

_____ **2.** A contract providing that Joe is to pay Bill "a fair share of the profits" will be enforced.

_____ **3.** A simple rejection of an offer will terminate it.

_____ **4.** Offers that must be kept open for a period of time include advertisements.

_____ **5.** The mirror image rule is an old rule that no longer applies.

_____ **6.** If an offeree is silent, he or she can never be considered to have accepted an offer.

_____ **7.** An offer terminates when the time specified in the offer has passed and the offeror has given one last chance to the offeree to accept.

_____ **8.** Anyone who is aware of an offer can accept it and create a binding contract.

_____ **9.** Acceptance is timely if it is made before an offer terminates.

MULTIPLE-CHOICE QUESTIONS

_____ **1.** Julio offers to sell Christine a used computer for $400. Which of the following replies would constitute an acceptance?

a. "I accept. Please send a written contract."
b. "I accept, if you send a written contract."
c. "I accept, if I can pay in monthly installments."
d. None of the above.

_____ **2.** In a letter, Vern offers to sell his car to Lee, stating that the offer will stay open for thirty days. Vern

a. cannot revoke the offer for thirty days.
b. can revoke the offer only in another letter.
c. can revoke the offer any time before Lee accepts.
d. can revoke the offer any time within thirty days, even after Lee accepts.

_____ **3.** Digit Computers places an ad announcing a sale of its inventory at public auction. At the auction, Digit's auctioneer holds up a high-speed modem and asks, "What am I bid for this item?" Which of the following is TRUE?

a. The first bid is an acceptance subject to no other bid being received.
b. Each bid is an acceptance subject to no higher bid being received.
c. Each bid is an offer that may be accepted or rejected.
d. Each bid is an offer that must be accepted if no higher bid is received.

____ **4.** Ed sends to Sax, Inc., a written order for software to be specially designed, offering a certain amount of money. If Sax does not respond, it can be considered to have accepted the offer

a. after a reasonable time has passed.
b. if Ed knows that Sax accepts all offers unless it sends notice to the contrary.
c. only when Sax begins the work.
d. none of the above.

____ **5.** Paul makes an offer to Lynn in a letter, saying nothing about how her acceptance should be sent. Lynn indicates her acceptance in a return letter. Lynn 's acceptance is effective when

a. Lynn decides to accept.
b. Lynn sends the letter.
c. Paul receives the letter.
d. none of the above.

____ **6.** Cindy makes an offer to Neal in a fax. Neal indicates his acceptance in a return fax. Neal's acceptance is effective when

a. Neal decides to accept.
b. Neal sends the fax.
c. Cindy receives the fax.
d. none of the above.

____ **7.** Kelly mails to Pat an offer to sell her computer, stating that Pat has thirty days to accept. Pat immediately mails a letter of rejection. After reconsidering, Pat mails a letter of acceptance within the time permitted by the offer. Which of the following is TRUE?

a. The rejection is effective because Pat mailed it first.
b. The acceptance is effective if Kelly receives it first.
c. The acceptance has no effect, because a rejection when mailed voids a deal.
d. None of the above.

____ **8.** Icon Properties, Inc., makes an offer in a letter to Bob to sell a certain lot for $30,000, with the offer to stay open for thirty days. Bob would prefer to pay $25,000, if Icon would sell at that price. What should Bob reply to Icon to leave room for negotiation without rejecting the offer?

a. "I will not pay $30,000."
b. "Will you take $25,000?"
c. "I will pay $25,000."
d. "I will pay $27,500."

ISSUE SPOTTERS

1. One morning, when Jane's new car—with an $18,000 market value—doesn't start, she yells in anger, "I'd sell this car to anyone for $500." If you drop $500 in her lap, is the car yours?

2. Fidelity Corporation offers to hire Ron to replace Monica, who has given Fidelity a month's notice of intent to quit. Fidelity gives Ron a week to decide whether to accept. Two days later, Monica signs an employment contract with Fidelity for another year. The next day, Monica tells Ron of the new contract. Ron immediately sends a formal letter of acceptance to Fidelity. Do Fidelity and Ron have a contract?

Consideration

9

LEARNING OBJECTIVES

When you finish this chapter, you should be able to:

1 List the elements of consideration.

2 State the preexisting duty rule.

3 Identify the exceptions to the preexisting duty rule.

4 Understand the concept of promissory estoppel.

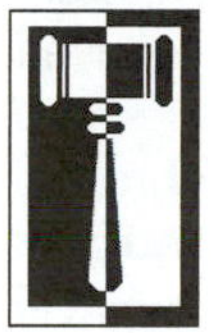

FACING A LEGAL PROBLEM

Antonio says to his son, "When you finish painting the garage, I will pay you $100." Antonio's son paints the garage. The act of painting the garage is the consideration that creates the contractual obligation of Antonio to pay his son $100. *If, instead, Antonio had said to his son, "In consideration of the fact that you are not as wealthy as your brothers, I will pay you $500," would this promise have been enforceable?*

CONSIDERATION
That which motivates the exchange of promises or performance in a contractual agreement. The consideration, which must be present to make the contract legally binding, must result in a detriment to the promisee (something of legal value, legally sufficient, and bargained for) or a benefit to the promisor.

LEARNING OBJECTIVE NO. 1
Listing the Elements of Consideration

In every legal system, there are promises that will be enforced and promises that will not be enforced. Just because a party has made a promise does not mean it is enforceable. Under the common law, a primary basis for the enforcement of promises is **consideration.** Consideration distinguishes contracts from gifts.

Consideration is usually defined as the value (such as money) given in return for a promise (such as the promise to sell you a computer upon receipt of your payment). Often consideration is broken down into two parts: (1) something of *legal value* must be given in exchange for the promise, and (2) there must be a *bargained-for* exchange. The "something of legal value" may consist of a return promise that is bargained for. If the "something of legal value" consists of performance, that performance may be (1) an act (other than a promise); (2) a forbearance (a refraining from action); or (3) the creation, modification, or destruction of a legal relationship.

In the legal problem set out at the beginning of this chapter, Antonio said to his son, "When you finish painting the garage, I will pay you $100." Antonio's son painted the garage. This act is the consideration that creates the obligation of Antonio to pay the $100. *If Antonio had instead said to his son, "In consideration of the fact that you are not as wealthy as your brothers, I will pay you $500," would this promise have been enforceable?* No. Antonio's son would not have given any consideration for it. Antonio would have simply stated his motive for giving his son $500. Using the word consideration does not, alone, make it consideration.

To learn more about the requirements of a valid contract, including consideration, you can access the Law Office's site at

http://www.lawoffice.com

Legal Sufficiency of Consideration

For a binding contract to be created, consideration not only must exist but also must be legally sufficient. To be *legally sufficient,* consideration for a promise must be legally *beneficial to the promisor* or *detrimental to the promisee.* In this connection, *detriment* means that in return for the promise, the promisee has (1) done, or promised to do, something that he or she had no prior legal duty to do or (2) refrained from, or promised to refrain from, doing something that he or she had no prior legal duty to refrain from doing (forbearance).

IN THE COURTROOM

In the 1850s, when the age of majority was considerably younger than twenty-one, William Story, Sr., promised his fifteen-year-old nephew, William Story II, that if the nephew refrained from alcohol, tobacco, and gambling until the age of twenty-one, he would pay him $5,000. The nephew agreed. Following his twenty-first birthday, the nephew wrote to his uncle that he had performed his part of the bargain and was thus entitled to the $5,000. They agreed that the uncle would invest the money for the nephew. Four years later, when the uncle died, the executor of the uncle's estate refused to pay the nephew, contending that the contract was invalid. The executor argued that there was no consideration, and therefore no contract, because the uncle had received nothing, and the nephew had actually benefited by fulfilling the uncle's wishes. *Did the uncle and nephew have an enforceable contract?* Yes. The money belonged to the nephew. Before the uncle's intervention, the nephew had used tobacco and had occasionally drunk liquor. On the strength of the uncle's promise, the nephew dropped his bad habits. This was the consideration that made the contract—on the faith of the agreement, the nephew refrained from doing something that he was otherwise entitled to do.

The law can be flexible, but this flexibility can lead to uncertainty in predicting the results in particular cases.

Adequacy of Consideration

Legal sufficiency of consideration means that consideration must be something of value in the eyes of the law. Adequacy of consideration refers to "how much" consideration is given. Essentially, adequacy of consideration concerns the fairness of the bargain. On the surface, fairness would appear to be an issue when the values of items exchanged are unequal. In general, however, courts do not question the adequacy of consideration if the consideration is legally sufficient.

Under the doctrine of freedom of contract, parties are usually free to bargain as they wish. If people could sue merely because they entered into an unwise contract, the courts would be overloaded with frivolous suits. In extreme cases, a court of law may look to the amount or value (the adequacy) of the consideration, because apparently inadequate consideration can indicate fraud, duress (unlawful threats or coercion causing someone to do something he or she would not otherwise have done), or undue influence (unlawful persuasion causing someone to do something he or she would not otherwise have done). In cases in which the consideration is grossly inadequate, the courts may declare the contract unenforceable on the ground that it is *unconscionable*—that is, generally speaking, it is so one sided under the circumstances as to be unfair. (Unconscionability is discussed further in Chapter 11.)

Preexisting Duty

LEARNING OBJECTIVE NO. 2
Stating the Preexisting Duty Rule

Under most circumstances, a later promise to do what one already has a legal duty to do is not legally sufficient consideration because no legal detriment or benefit has been incurred. This is the *preexisting duty rule.* The preexisting legal duty may be imposed by law or may arise out of a previous contract. A sheriff, for example, cannot collect a reward for information leading to the capture of a criminal if the sheriff already has a legal duty to capture the criminal. Likewise, if a party is already bound by contract to perform a certain duty, that duty cannot serve as consideration for a second contract.

IN THE COURTROOM

Bauman-Bache, Inc., begins construction on a seven-story office building and after three months demands an extra $75,000 on its contract. If the extra $75,000 is not paid, it will stop working. The owner of the land, having no one else to complete construction, agrees to pay the extra $75,000. *If the owner later refuses to pay the extra money, could Bauman-Bache successfully sue to enforce the agreement?* No. The agreement is not enforceable because it is not supported by legally sufficient consideration; Bauman-Bache was under a preexisting contract to complete the building.

Unforeseen Difficulties

LEARNING OBJECTIVE NO. 3
Identifying the Exceptions to the Preexisting Duty Rule

In the interests of fairness and equity, the courts sometimes allow exceptions to the preexisting duty rule. A court may decide not to apply the preexisting duty rule when a party to a contract confronts extraordinary difficulties that were totally unforeseen at the time the contract was formed. For example, an honest contractor who has contracted with a landowner to build a house runs into extraordinary difficulties, and the landowner agrees to pay extra compensation to overcome them. A court may then enforce the agreement to pay more. If the difficulties are the types of risks ordinarily assumed in business, however, the court will likely assert the preexisting duty rule (and not enforce the agreement to pay more).

Rescission and New Contract

The law recognizes that two parties can mutually agree to rescind their contract, at least to the extent that it is executory (still to be carried out). **Rescission** is defined as the unmaking of a contract so as to return the parties to the positions they occupied before the contract was made. When rescission and the making of a new contract take place at the same time, the courts frequently are given a choice of applying the preexisting duty rule (as in the earlier Bauman-Bache example) or allowing rescission and the new contract to stand.

Rescission
A remedy whereby a contract is terminated and the parties are returned to the positions they occupied before the contract was made; may be effected through the mutual consent of the parties, by their conduct, or by the decree of a court of equity.

Past Consideration

Promises made in return for actions or events that have already taken place are unenforceable. These promises lack consideration in that the element of bargained-for exchange is missing. In short, you can bargain for something to take place now or in the future, but not for something that has already taken place. Therefore, **past consideration** is no consideration. For example, if a real estate agent sells her friend's house without charging a commission and the friend later

Past Consideration
An act done before the contract is made, which ordinarily, by itself, cannot be consideration for a later promise to pay for the act.

promises to pay the agent $3,000 "for your generous act," the promise is not enforceable, because the "act" has already taken place. (In effect, the friend is expressing her intention to give the agent a gift.)

IN THE COURTROOM

Ellen, a nurse, spent many years living with, and looking after, her parents. Shortly after her parents died, her brother told her, in the presence of several other people, that he was so grateful to her for the care she gave their parents that he would take care of her for the rest of her life. When her brother fails to keep his promise, Ellen brings an action to have the promise enforced. *Will the court hold that a contract exists?* No, because Ellen had already provided the services to her parents before her brother made his promise. Therefore, Ellen's consideration for her brother's promise was not a promise to do something in the future but something she had done in the past. Past consideration is no consideration. Ellen could not enforce the contract, therefore, because no contract existed.

The 'Lectric Law Library provides information on contract law, including consideration, at

http://www.lectlaw.com/bul02.htm

Problems Concerning Consideration

Problems concerning consideration usually fall into one of the following categories:

1. Promises exchanged when total performance by the parties is uncertain.
2. Settlement of claims.
3. Certain promises enforceable without consideration (under the doctrine of promissory estoppel).

The courts' solutions to these types of problems can give you insight into how the law views the complex concept of consideration.

Uncertain Performance

If the terms of the contract express such uncertainty of performance that the promisor has not definitely promised to do anything, the promise is said to be *illusory*—it is without consideration and unenforceable. For example, a promise by the president of a company to pay all employees a 10 percent bonus at the end of the year "if management thinks it is warranted" is illusory because performance depends solely on the discretion of management. There is no bargained-for consideration. The statement declares merely that management may or may not do something in the future. The president is not obligated (incurs no detriment) now or in the future.

Option-to-cancel clauses in contracts sometimes present problems in regard to consideration. An employment "contract" in which the employer reserves the right to cancel before performance begins is an illusory contract—there is no consideration in the form of any detriment to the employer. If the right to cancel requires thirty days' notice, however, the employer relinquishes the right to hire someone else for thirty days. If the employer cancels the contract, the employee has an enforceable claim for thirty days' salary.

Settlement of Claims

There are several ways in which businesspersons or others can settle legal claims, and it is important to understand the nature of consideration given in these kinds of settlement agreements, or contracts. A common means of settling a claim is through an *accord and satisfaction,* in which one who owes a debt offers to pay a lesser amount than the amount that is owed. We will discuss the concept of accord and satisfaction in Chapter 15 in the context of discharging contractual obligations. Here we look at two other methods that are commonly used to settle claims, a release and a covenant not to sue.

Release. A **release** bars any further recovery beyond the terms stated in the release. Releases will generally be binding if they are (1) given in good faith, (2) stated in a signed writing (required by many states), and (3) accompanied by consideration. Clearly, you are better off if you know the extent of your injuries or damages before signing a release.

RELEASE
The relinquishment, concession, or giving up of a right, claim, or privilege, by the person in whom it exists or to whom it accrues, to the person against whom it might have been enforced or demanded.

IN THE COURTROOM

Suppose that you are involved in an automobile accident caused by Raoul's negligence. Raoul offers to give you $1,000 if you will release him from further liability resulting from the accident. You believe that this amount will cover your damages, so you agree to the release. Later you discover that it will cost $1,200 to repair your car. *Can you collect the balance from Raoul?* The answer is normally no; you are limited to the $1,000 in the release. *Why?* Because a valid contract existed. You and Raoul both assented to the bargain (hence, agreement existed), and sufficient consideration was present. The consideration was the legal detriment you suffered (by releasing Raoul from liability, you forfeited your right to sue to recover damages, should they be more than $1,000).

Covenant Not to Sue. A **covenant not to sue,** in contrast to a release, does not always bar further recovery. The parties simply substitute a contractual obligation for some other type of action. Thus, in the previous situation, if you agreed with Raoul not to sue for damages in a tort action if he would pay for the damage to your car and Raoul fails to pay, you can bring an action for breach of contract.

COVENANT NOT TO SUE
An agreement to substitute a contractual obligation for some other type of action.

PROMISSORY ESTOPPEL

Sometimes individuals rely on promises, and such reliance may form a basis for contract rights and duties. Under the doctrine of **promissory estoppel** (also called *detrimental reliance*), a person who has reasonably relied on the promise of another can often hope to obtain some measure of recovery. For the doctrine of promissory estoppel to be applied, a number of elements are required:

1. There must be a promise.
2. The promisee must justifiably rely on the promise.
3. The reliance normally must be of a substantial and definite character.
4. Justice will be better served by the enforcement of the promise.

PROMISSORY ESTOPPEL
When a promisor reasonably expects a promise to induce definite and substantial action or forbearance by the promisee, and it does induce such action or forbearance in reliance thereon, the promise is binding if injustice can be avoided only by enforcing it.

LEARNING OBJECTIVE NO. 4
Understanding the Concept of Promissory Estoppel

IN THE COURTROOM

Your uncle tells you, "I'll pay you $150 a week so you won't have to work anymore." You quit your job, but your uncle refuses to pay you. *Would a court enforce your uncle's promise?* Possibly yes, under the doctrine of promissory estoppel. There was a promise, in reliance on which you quit your job (quitting a job is of a substantial and definite character), and justice might be best served by enforcing the promise. Later, your uncle makes a promise to give you $10,000 with which to buy a car. *If you buy the car and he does not pay you, would a court enforce the promise?* You may once again be able to enforce the promise under the doctrine of promissory estoppel. Your uncle, the promisor (the offeror), may be **estopped** (barred, or impeded) from revoking the promise.

ESTOP
To bar, impede, or preclude.

TERMS AND CONCEPTS FOR REVIEW

CHAPTER SUMMARY • CONSIDERATION

Legal Sufficiency of Consideration	To be legally sufficient, consideration must involve a legal detriment to the promisee—doing (or refraining from doing) something that one had no prior legal duty to do (or refrain from doing)—or a legal benefit to the promisor, or both. Consideration is not legally sufficient if one is either by law or by contract under a *preexisting duty* to perform the action being offered as consideration for a new contract.
Adequacy of Consideration	Adequacy of consideration relates to "how much" consideration is given and whether a fair bargain was reached. Courts will inquire into the adequacy of consideration (if the consideration is legally sufficient) only when fraud, undue influence, duress, or unconscionability may be involved.
Problems Concerning Consideration	**1.** *Uncertain performance*—When the nature or extent of performance is uncertain, too much uncertainty renders the promise illusory (without consideration and unenforceable). **2.** *Settlement of claims*— **a.** Release—An agreement in which, for consideration, a party is barred from further recovery beyond the terms specified in the release. **b.** Covenant not to sue—An agreement not to sue on a present, valid claim. **3.** *Promissory estoppel*—A doctrine that applies when (a) there is a promise, (b) the promisee justifiably relies on the promise, (c) the reliance is of a substantial and definite character, and (d) justice is better served by enforcing the promise.

HYPOTHETICAL QUESTIONS

9–1. Contract Modification. Tabor is the buyer of widgets manufactured by Martin. Martin's contract with Tabor calls for delivery of 10,000 widgets at $1 per widget in ten equal installments. After delivery of two installments, Martin informs Tabor that because of inflation, Martin is losing money and will promise to deliver the remaining 8,000 widgets only if Tabor will pay $1.20 per widget. Tabor agrees in writing. Discuss whether Martin can legally collect the additional $200 on delivery to Tabor of the next installment of 1,000 widgets.

9–2. Contract Modification. Bernstein owns a lot and wants to build a house according to a particular set of plans and specifications. She solicits bids from building contractors and receives three bids: one from Carlton for $60,000, one from Friend for $58,000, and one from Shade for $53,000. She accepts Shade's bid. One month after construction of the house has begun, Shade contacts Bernstein and informs her that because of inflation and a recent price hike in materials, he will not finish the house unless Bernstein agrees to pay an extra $3,000. Bernstein reluctantly agrees to pay the additional sum. After the house is finished, however, Bernstein refuses to pay the additional $3,000. Discuss whether Bernstein is legally required to pay this additional amount.

REAL WORLD CASE PROBLEM

9–3. Past Consideration. Rivendell Forest Products, Ltd., had a computer program—the *Quote Screen* system—that allowed it to quote prices to its customers many times faster than its competitors. To keep the *Quote Screen* system a secret, Rivendell insisted that all of its employees, including Timothy Cornwell, sign a confidentiality agreement in 1988. Cornwell was employed by Rivendell from 1987 to 1990, when he left Rivendell to work as a marketing manager for the Georgia-Pacific Corp., a competitor. Cornwell introduced Georgia-Pacific to Rivendell's *Quote Screen* system. Rivendell sued Cornwell for, among other things, breach of the confidentiality agreement. The trial court held that the confidentiality agreement was not a valid contract because Rivendell had failed to provide consideration, such as salary increase or promotion, in exchange for Cornwell's promise to keep the *Quote Screen* system a secret. If Cornwell had signed the confidentiality agreement when he was first hired, would the result have been the same? Explain. [*Rivendell Forest Products, Ltd. v. Georgia-Pacific Corp.*, 824 F.Supp. 961 (D.Colo. 1993)]

For updated links to resources available on the Web, as well as a variety of other materials, visit this text's Web site at **http://blte.westbuslaw.com**.

A good way to learn more about how the courts decide such issues as whether consideration was lacking for a particular contract is to look at relevant case law. To find recent cases on contract law decided by the United States Supreme Court and the federal appellate courts, access Cornell University's School of Law site at

http://www.law.cornell.edu/topics/contracts.html

The New Hampshire Consumer's Sourcebook provides information on contract law, including consideration, from a consumer's perspective. You can access this site at

http://www.state.nh.us/nhdoj/Consumer/cpb.html

ONLINE LEGAL RESEARCH

Go to **http://blte.westbuslaw.com**, the Web site that accompanies this text. Select "Internet Applications," and then click on "Chapter 9." There you will find the following Internet research exercise that you can perform to learn more about contracts that are enforceable without consideration:

Activity 9–1: Promissory Estoppel

Chapter 9 ■ WORK SET

TRUE-FALSE QUESTIONS

_____ **1.** Ordinarily, courts evaluate the adequacy or fairness of consideration even if the consideration is legally sufficient.

_____ **2.** A promise to do what one already has a legal duty to do is not legally sufficient consideration under most circumstances.

_____ **3.** Promises made with consideration based on events that have already taken place are fully enforceable.

_____ **4.** Rescission is the unmaking of a contract so as to return the parties to the positions they occupied before the contract was made.

_____ **5.** A promise has no legal value as consideration.

_____ **6.** A covenant not to sue is an agreement to substitute a contractual obligation for some other type of action.

_____ **7.** Consideration is the value given in return for a promise.

_____ **8.** Promissory estoppel may prevent a party from using lack of consideration as a defense.

MULTIPLE-CHOICE QUESTIONS

_____ **1.** Dwight offers to buy a book owned by Lee for $40. Lee accepts and hands the book to Dwight. The transfer and delivery of the book constitute performance. Is this performance consideration for Dwight's promise?

a. Yes, because performance always constitutes consideration.
b. Yes, because Dwight sought it in exchange for his promise, and Lee gave it in exchange for that promise.
c. No, because performance never constitutes consideration.
d. No, because Lee already had a duty to hand the book to Dwight.

_____ **2.** Max agrees to supervise a construction project for Al for a certain fee. In mid-project, without an excuse, Max removes the plans from the site and refuses to continue. Al promises to increase Max's fee. Max returns to work. Is going back to work consideration for the promise to increase the fee?

a. Yes, because performance always constitutes consideration.
b. Yes, because Al sought it in exchange for his promise.
c. No, because performance never constitutes consideration.
d. No, because Max already had a duty to supervise the project.

_____ **3.** Shannon contracts with Dan to build two houses on two lots. After building the first house, they decide that they would prefer to build a garage instead of a house on the second lot. Under these circumstances

a. they must build the second house—a contract must be fully executed.
b. they can rescind their contract and make a new contract to build a garage.
c. the contract to build two houses is illusory.
d. none of the above.

_____ **4.** Ed has a cause to sue Mary in a tort action, but agrees not to sue her if she will pay for the damage. If she fails to pay, Ed can bring an action against her for breach of contract. This is an example of

a. promissory estoppel.
b. a release.
c. a covenant not to sue.
d. an unenforceable contract.

_____ **5.** John's car is hit by Ben's truck. A doctor tells John that he will be disabled only temporarily. Ben's insurance company offers John $5,000 to settle his claim. John accepts and signs a release. Later, John learns that he is permanently disabled. John sues Ben and the insurance company. John will

a. win, because John did not know when he signed the release that the disability was permanent.
b. win, because Ben caused the accident.
c. lose, because John signed a written release—no fraud was involved, and consideration was given.
d. none of the above.

_____ **6.** Mike promises that next year he will sell Kim a certain house, allowing her to live in it until then. Kim completely renovates the house, repairs the heating system, and entirely landscapes the property. The next year, Mike tells Kim he's decided to keep the house. Who is entitled to the house?

a. Kim, under the doctrine of promissory estoppel.
b. Kim, because Mike's decision to keep the house is an unforeseen difficulty.
c. Mike, because his promise to sell Kim the house was illusory.
d. Mike, because he initially stated only his intention to sell.

_____ **7.** Deb has a cause to sue Jim in a tort action. Jim offers Deb $5,000 not to sue, and she agrees. This an example of

a. promissory estoppel.
b. a release.
c. a covenant not to sue.
d. an unenforceable contract.

ISSUE SPOTTERS

1. In September, Sharon agrees to work for Cole Productions, Inc., at $500 a week for a year beginning January 1. In October, Sharon is offered the same work at $600 a week by Quintero Shows, Ltd. When Sharon tells Cole about the other offer, they tear up their contract and agree that Sharon will be paid $575. Is the new contract binding?

2. Before Maria starts her first year of college, Fred promises to give her $5,000 when she graduates. She goes to college, borrowing and spending far more than $5,000. At the beginning of the spring semester of her senior year, she reminds Fred of the promise. Fred sends her a note that says, "I revoke the promise." Is Fred's promise binding?

Capacity

LEARNING OBJECTIVES

When you finish this chapter, you should be able to:

1. Understand the right of minors to disaffirm their contracts.
2. Identify obligations that minors cannot avoid.
3. Recognize when a minor has ratified a voidable contract.
4. Explain how intoxication affects the liability on a contract.
5. Discuss the effects of mental incompetency on contractual liability.

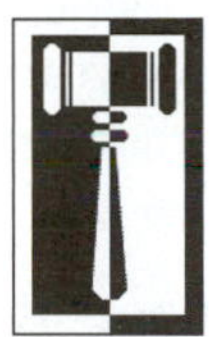

FACING A LEGAL PROBLEM

Jaime Perez, who is seventeen years old, purchases a computer from Radio Shack. While transporting the computer to his home, Perez negligently drops it, breaking the plastic casing. The next day he returns the computer to Radio Shack and disaffirms the contract. *Does Perez have to pay for the damaged casing?*

Although the parties to a contract must assume certain risks, the law indicates that neither party should be allowed to benefit from the other party's lack of **contractual capacity**—the legal ability to enter into a contractual relationship. For this reason, contracts entered into by persons lacking the *contractual capacity* to do so may not be enforced.

CONTRACTUAL CAPACITY The capacity required by the law for a party who enters into a contract to be bound by that contract.

Courts generally presume the existence of contractual capacity. There are some situations, however, in which capacity is lacking or may be questionable. A person *adjudged by a court* to be mentally incompetent, for example, cannot form a legally binding contract with another party. In other situations, a party may have the capacity to enter into a valid contract but also have the right to avoid liability under it. For example, minors usually are not legally bound by contracts.

In this chapter, we look at the effect of youth, mental incompetence, and intoxication on contractual capacity. Other factors also may affect the capacity to form an enforceable contract, but the question of legal capacity most often involves minors, intoxicated persons, or mentally incompetent persons.

Minors

Under the common law, a minor was defined as a male who had not attained the age of twenty-one or a female who was not yet eighteen. Today, in most states the *age of majority* (when a person is no longer a minor) for contractual purposes is eighteen years for both sexes. In addition, some states provide for the termination of minority upon marriage.

Subject to certain exceptions, the contracts entered into by a minor are voidable at the option of that minor. The minor has the choice of *ratifying* (accepting and validating) the contract, thus making it enforceable, or *disaffirming* (renouncing) the contract and setting aside the contract and all legal obligations arising from it. An adult who enters into a contract with a minor, however, cannot avoid his or her contractual duties on the ground that the minor can do so. Unless the minor exercises the option to disaffirm the contract (to be discussed shortly), the adult party is bound by it.

DISAFFIRMANCE

The general rule is that a minor can enter into any contract an adult can, provided that the contract is not one prohibited by law for minors (for example, the sale of alcoholic beverages). Although minors have the right to disaffirm their contracts, there are exceptions (to be discussed later).

LEARNING OBJECTIVE NO. 1

Understanding the Right of Minors to Disaffirm Their Contracts

DISAFFIRMANCE
The repudiation of an obligation.

Disaffirmance in General. For a minor to exercise the option to avoid a contract, he or she need only manifest an intention not to be bound by it. The minor "avoids" the contract by "disaffirming" it. The technical definition of **disaffirmance** is the legal avoidance, or setting aside, of a contractual obligation. Words or conduct may serve to express this intent. The contract can ordinarily be disaffirmed at any time during minority or for a reasonable time after the minor comes of age. In some states, however, when there is a contract for the sale of land by a minor, the minor cannot disaffirm the contract until he or she reaches the age of majority.

It is important that disaffirmance be timely. If, for example, an individual wishes to disaffirm a contract made as a minor but fails to do so until two years after he or she has reached the age of majority, a court will likely hold that the contract has been ratified (see the discussion of ratification below).

Duty of Restitution. When a contract has been executed, minors cannot disaffirm it without returning whatever goods they may have received or paying for their reasonable use. The majority of courts hold that the minor need only return the goods (or other consideration), provided such goods are in the minor's possession or control.

In the legal problem set out at the beginning of this chapter, Jaime Perez, a minor, buys a computer from Radio Shack. Taking the computer home, Perez drops it, breaking the plastic casing. The next day he takes the computer back to Radio Shack and disaffirms the contract. *Is there anything else that he must do, considering that he damaged the computer?* In most states, the answer is no. In those states, returning the computer fulfilled Perez's duty, even though the computer was damaged.

RESTITUTION
A remedy under which a person is restored to his or her original position prior to a contract.

A few states, however, either by statute or by court decision, place an additional duty on the minor—the duty of **restitution.** This rule recognizes the legitimate interests of those who deal with minors. The theory is that the adult should be returned to the position he or she held before the contract was made.

IN THE COURTROOM

Jaime Perez, a minor, bought a computer from Radio Shack, dropped it and broke it on the way home, and returned it the next day, disaffirming the contract to buy it. *If Perez lived in a state that recognized the duty of restitution, is there anything else that he would need to do in light of the fact that he damaged the computer?* Yes. He would be required not only to return the computer but also to pay Radio Shack for the damage to it.

If a minor disaffirms a contract, he or she must disaffirm the *entire* contract. The minor cannot decide to keep part of the goods contracted for and return the remainder. When a minor disaffirms, all property that he or she has transferred to the adult as consideration (or its equivalent in money) can be recovered.

Misrepresentation of Age. Suppose that a minor tells a seller she is twenty-one years old when she is really seventeen. Ordinarily, the minor can disaffirm the contract even though she has misrepresented her age. Moreover, the minor is not liable in certain jurisdictions for the tort of deceit for such misrepresentation, the rationale being that such a tort judgment might indirectly force the minor to perform the contract.

Many jurisdictions, however, do find circumstances under which a minor can be bound by a contract when his or her age has been misrepresented. First, several states have enacted statutes for precisely this purpose. In these states, misrepresentation of age is enough to prohibit disaffirmance.

Second, some courts refuse to allow minors to disaffirm executed (fully performed) contracts unless they can return the consideration received. The combination of the minors' misrepresentation and their unjust enrichment has persuaded several courts to *estop* (prevent) minors from asserting contractual incapacity.

Third, some courts allow a misrepresenting minor to disaffirm the contract, but they hold the minor liable for damages. Here, the defrauded party may sue the minor for misrepresentation or fraud. A split in authority exists on this point, because some courts, as previously noted, have recognized that allowing a suit in tort is equivalent to the indirect enforcement of the minor's contract.

Basically, a minor's ability to avoid a contractual obligation is allowed by the law as a shield for the minor's defense, not as a sword for his or her unjust enrichment.

Access to the Internet

To find recent cases on contract law decided by the United States Supreme Court and the federal appellate courts, access Cornell University's School of Law site at

http://www.law.cornell.edu/topics/contracts.html

IN THE COURTROOM

Jennifer Lee was twenty years old when she contracted to purchase an automobile from Haydocy Pontiac, Inc., but she told the salesperson that she was twenty-one. Lee financed most of the purchase price. Immediately following delivery of the automobile, she turned the car over to a third person and never thereafter had possession. She made no further payments on the contract and attempted to rescind (cancel) it. She made no offer to return the car. Haydocy sued Lee for the balance owed. *Could Haydocy recover the balance, given the fact that Lee was a minor who had misrepresented her age?* The court allowed Haydocy to recover the fair market value of the automobile from Lee, although the fair market value could not exceed the original purchase price of the automobile. Lee was estopped (precluded) from rescinding the contract on the ground that she was a minor, because she induced the sale by misrepresenting her age.

LEARNING OBJECTIVE NO. 2

Identifying Obligations That Minors Cannot Avoid

Liability for Necessaries, Insurance, and Loans. A minor who enters into a contract for **necessaries** (such items as food, clothing, and shelter) may disaffirm the contract but remains liable for the reasonable value of the goods. The legal duty to pay a reasonable value does not arise from the contract itself but is imposed by law under a theory of quasi contract. One theory is that the minor should not be unjustly enriched and should therefore be liable for purchases that fulfill basic needs. Another theory is that the minor's right to disaffirm a contract has economic ramifications in that a seller is likely to refuse to deal with minors because of this right. If minors can at least be held liable for the reasonable value of the goods, a seller's reluctance to enter into contracts with minors may be offset. This theory explains why the courts narrow the subject matter to necessaries—without such a rule, minors might be denied the opportunity to purchase necessary goods.

NECESSARIES
Necessities required for life, such as food, shelter, clothing, and medical attention; normally, necessaries are also considered to include items or services appropriate to an individual's circumstances and condition in life.

When in doubt about the age of a customer to whom you are about to sell major consumer durable goods or anything other than necessaries, require legal proof of age.

Traditionally, insurance has not been viewed as a necessary, so minors can ordinarily disaffirm their contracts and recover all premiums paid. Some jurisdictions, however, prohibit the right to disaffirm such contracts—for example, when minors contract for life insurance on their own lives.

Financial loans are seldom considered to be necessaries, even if the minor spends the money borrowed on necessaries. If, however, a lender makes a loan to a minor for the express purpose of enabling the minor to purchase necessaries, and the lender personally makes sure the money is so spent, the minor normally is obligated to repay the loan.

RATIFICATION

RATIFICATION
The approval or validation of a previous action. In contract law, the confirmation of a voidable act (that is, an act that without ratification would not be an enforceable contractual obligation).

In contract law, **ratification** is the act of accepting and giving legal force to an obligation that previously was not enforceable. A minor who has reached the age of majority can ratify a contract in three ways—by express ratification, by conduct, or by a failure to disaffirm the contract within a reasonable period of time after reaching the age of majority.

Express ratification takes place when the minor, upon reaching the age of majority, states orally or in writing that he or she intends to be bound by the contract. If a minor, on reaching the age of majority, manifests an intent to ratify the contract by conduct (by enjoying the benefits of the contract, for example), this may also constitute ratification, particularly if the adult party to the contract has performed his or her part of the bargain.

LEARNING OBJECTIVE NO. 3
Recognizing When a Minor Has Ratified a Voidable Contract

A minor's failure to disaffirm a contract within a reasonable time after reaching the age of majority may also be deemed by the courts to constitute ratification when the contract is executed (performed by both parties). If the contract is still executory (not yet performed or only partially performed), however, failure to disaffirm the contract will not necessarily imply ratification. Generally, the courts base their determination on whether the minor, after reaching the age of majority, has had ample opportunity to consider the nature of the contractual obligations he or she entered into as a minor and the extent to which the adult party to the contract has performed.

PARENTS' LIABILITY

As a general rule, parents are not liable for the contracts made by their minor children acting on their own. This is why businesses ordinarily require parents to sign any contract made with a minor. The parents then become personally obligated under the contract to perform the conditions of the contract, even if their child avoids liability.

Generally, a minor is held personally liable for the torts he or she commits. Therefore, minors cannot disaffirm their liability for their tortious conduct. The parents of the minor can *also* be held liable under certain circumstances. For example, if the minor commits the tort under the direction of a parent or while performing an act requested by a parent, the injured party can hold the parent liable. In addition, parents are liable in many states up to a statutory amount for malicious acts committed by a minor living in the home of the parents.

EMANCIPATION

EMANCIPATION
In regard to minors, the act of being freed from parental control. The parents renounce parental duties and surrender the right to the custody and earnings of the minor.

The release of a minor by his or her parents is known as **emancipation.** Emancipation involves completely relinquishing the right to the minor's control, care, custody, and earnings. It is a repudiation of parental obligations. Emancipation may be express or implied, absolute or conditional, total or partial. Several jurisdictions permit minors to petition for emancipation themselves. In those states, a grant of emancipation may also remove a minor's lack of capacity to contract. Generally, however, emancipation does not affect a minor's contractual capacity.

Intoxicated Persons

LEARNING OBJECTIVE NO. 4
Explaining How Intoxication Affects Liability on a Contract

A contract entered into by an intoxicated person can be either voidable or valid. If the person was sufficiently intoxicated to lack mental capacity, the transaction is voidable at the option of the intoxicated person, even if the intoxication was purely voluntary. For the contract to be voidable, it must be proved that the intoxicated person's reason and judgment were impaired to the extent that he or she did not comprehend the legal consequences of entering into the contract. If the person was intoxicated but understood these legal consequences, the contract is enforceable. Simply because the terms of the contract are foolish or are obviously favorable to the other party does not mean the contract is voidable. Under any circumstances, an intoxicated person is liable for the reasonable value of any necessaries he or she receives.

Problems often arise in determining whether a party was sufficiently intoxicated to avoid legal duties. Many courts prefer looking at factors other than the intoxicated party's mental state (for example, whether the other party fraudulently induced the person to become intoxicated).

Mentally Incompetent Persons

LEARNING OBJECTIVE NO. 5
Discussing How Mental Incompetency Affects Contractual Liability

Contracts made by mentally incompetent persons can be either void, voidable, or valid. If a person has been adjudged mentally incompetent by a court of law and a guardian has been appointed, any contract made by the mentally incompetent person is *void*—no contract exists. Only the guardian can enter into a binding legal duty on behalf of the person.

Mentally incompetent persons not previously so adjudged by a court may enter into *voidable* contracts if they do not know they are entering into the contract, or if they lack the mental capacity to comprehend its subject matter, nature, and consequences. In such situations, the contracts are voidable at the option of the mentally incompetent person but not the other party. Whenever there is no prior adjudication of mental incompetence, most courts examine whether the party was able to understand the nature, purpose, and consequences of his or her act at the time of the transaction. The contract may be disaffirmed or ratified. Ratification must occur after the person is mentally competent or after a guardian is appointed and ratifies the contract. Like minors and intoxicated persons, mentally incompetent persons are liable for the reasonable value of any necessaries they receive.

A contract entered into by a mentally incompetent person may also be *valid*. A person can understand the nature and effect of entering into a certain contract yet simultaneously lack capacity to engage in other activities. In such situations, the contract is valid, because the person is not legally mentally incompetent for contractual purposes.

TERMS AND CONCEPTS FOR REVIEW

contractual capacity 117
disaffirmance 118
emancipation 120
necessaries 119
ratification 120
restitution 118

CHAPTER SUMMARY • CAPACITY

Minors	A minor is a person who has not yet reached the age of majority. In most states, the age of majority is eighteen for contract purposes. Contracts with minors are voidable at the option of the minor. On reaching the age of majority, a minor may *disaffirm* or *ratify* contracts made when he or she was a minor. **1.** *Disaffirmance*— **a.** Can take place (in most states) at any time during minority and within a reasonable time after the minor has reached the age of majority. **b.** When disaffirming executed contracts, the minor has a duty of restitution to return received goods if they are still in the minor's control and (in some states) to pay for any damage to the goods. **c.** If a minor disaffirms a contract, the entire contract must be disaffirmed. **d.** A minor who has committed an act of fraud (such as misrepresentation of age) will be denied the right to disaffirm by some courts. **e.** A minor may disaffirm a contract for necessaries but remains liable for the reasonable value of the goods. **2.** *Ratification*—May be express or implied. **a.** *Express*—Exists when the minor, through a written or an oral agreement, explicitly assumes the obligations imposed by the contract. **b.** *Implied*—Exists when the conduct of the minor is inconsistent with disaffirmance. **3.** *Parents' liability*—Generally, parents are not liable for the contracts made by their minor children acting on their own, nor are parents liable for minors' torts except in certain circumstances. **4.** *Emancipation*—Occurs when parents completely relinquish the right to the minor's control, care, custody, and earnings. Emancipation may be express or implied, absolute or conditional, total or partial. In some jurisdictions, minors are permitted to petition for emancipation themselves. Generally, emancipation does not affect a minor's contractual capacity.
Intoxicated Persons	**1.** A contract entered into by an intoxicated person is *voidable* at the option of the intoxicated person if the person was sufficiently intoxicated to lack mental capacity, even if the intoxication was voluntary. **2.** A contract with an intoxicated person is *enforceable* if, despite being intoxicated, the person understood the legal consequences of entering into the contract.
Mentally Incompetent Persons	**1.** A contract made by a person adjudged by a court to be mentally incompetent is *void*. **2.** A contract made by a mentally incompetent person not adjudged by a court to be mentally incompetent is *voidable* at the option of the mentally incompetent person.

HYPOTHETICAL QUESTIONS

10–1. Intoxication. After Kira had had several drinks one night, she sold Charlotte a diamond necklace worth thousands of dollars for one hundred dollars. The next day, Kira offered the one hundred dollars to Charlotte and requested the return of her necklace. Charlotte refused to accept the one hundred dollars or return the necklace, claiming that they had a valid contract of sale. Kira explained that she had been intoxicated at the time the bargain was made and thus the contract was voidable at her option. Was Kira correct? Explain.

10–2. Mental Incompetence. Two physicians, Devito and Burke, leased an office suite for five years and agreed to share the rent payments equally—even if one of them moved out or was unable to occupy his part of the premises as a result of disability or for any other reason. Two weeks later, Devito consulted a neurologist about his increasing absent-mindedness and forgetfulness and discussed the possibility of giving up his practice. A few months later, Devito was diagnosed as suffering from presenile dementia (premature deterioration of the brain). The condition had been developing slowly for a matter of years, resulting in the progressive loss of memory and other mental abilities. The following year, Devito was so impaired mentally that he had to close his practice and retire. Burke later sued Devito for his share of the remaining rent under the lease. Devito claimed that he had been mentally incompetent at the time he signed the agreement to share the rent and hence the agreement was voidable at his option. Will Devito prevail in court? Discuss.

REAL WORLD CASE PROBLEM

10–3. Contracts by Minors. When he was seventeen years old, Sean Power bought an automobile insurance policy from Allstate Insurance Co. At the time, he rejected Allstate's offer of underinsured motorist coverage. Three months later, Power was injured in an automobile accident. The other driver's insurance was not enough to pay for Power's injuries. Power filed a suit in a South Carolina state court against Allstate, claiming that he could disaffirm the part of his insurance contract in which he had rejected the underinsured motorist coverage. Will the court allow Power to disaffirm his contract only in part? Why or why not? [*Power v. Allstate Insurance Co.,* 312 S.C. 381, 440 S.E.2d 406 (1994)]

For updated links to resources available on the Web, as well as a variety of other materials, visit this text's Web site at **http://blte.westbuslaw.com**.

For access to state statutory provisions governing the emancipation of minors, go to

http://www.law.cornell.edu/topics/Table_Emancipation.htm

ONLINE LEGAL RESEARCH

Go to **http://blte.westbuslaw.com**, the Web site that accompanies this text. Select "Internet Applications," and then click on "Chapter 10." There you will find the following Internet research exercise that you can perform to learn more about the law governing minors:

Activity 10–1: Minors and the Law

Chapter 10 ■ WORKSET

TRUE-FALSE QUESTIONS

_____ **1.** An adult who enters into a contract with a minor cannot generally avoid the contract.

_____ **2.** When a minor disaffirms a contract, whatever the minor transferred as consideration (or its value) normally must be returned.

_____ **3.** A person who is so intoxicated as to lack mental capacity when he or she enters into a contract must perform the contract even if the other party has reason to know of the intoxication.

_____ **4.** Emancipation has no effect on a minor's contractual capacity.

_____ **5.** If an individual who has not been judged mentally incompetent understands the nature and effect of entering into a certain contract, the contract is normally valid.

_____ **6.** The age of majority for contractual purposes is twenty-one for males and eighteen for females.

_____ **7.** Some states' statutes restrict minors from avoiding certain contracts, including certain insurance contracts and loans for education or medical care.

_____ **8.** Generally, parents are liable for contracts made by their minor children.

_____ **9.** In most cases, a person, to disaffirm a contract entered into when he or she was intoxicated, must return any consideration received.

MULTIPLE-CHOICE QUESTIONS

_____ **1.** Troy, a minor, sells to Vern his collection of sports memorabilia for $250. On his eighteenth birthday, Troy learns that the collection may have been worth at least $2,500. Troy can

a. disaffirm, because the contract has not been fully performed.
b. disaffirm, if Troy does so within a reasonable time of attaining majority.
c. not disaffirm, because Troy has already attained majority.
d. not disaffirm, because the contract has been fully performed.

_____ **2.** Doug has been drinking heavily. Joe offers to buy Doug's farm for a fair price. Believing the deal is a joke, Doug writes and signs an agreement to sell and gives it to Joe. Joe believes the deal is serious. The contract is

a. enforceable, if the circumstances indicate Doug understands what he did.
b. enforceable, because Joe believes that the transaction is serious.
c. unenforceable, because the intoxication permits Doug to avoid the contract.
d. unenforceable, because Doug thinks it is a joke.

_____ **3.** Ed is adjudged mentally incompetent. Irwin is appointed to act as Ed's guardian. Irwin signs a contract to sell some of Ed's property to pay for Ed's care. On regaining competency, Ed can

a. disaffirm, because he was mentally incompetent.
b. disaffirm, because he is no longer mentally incompetent.
c. not disaffirm, because Irwin could enter into contracts on his behalf.
d. not disaffirm, because he may become mentally incompetent again.

_____ **4.** Adam, a sixteen-year-old minor, enters into a contract for necessaries, which his parents could provide but do not. Adam disaffirms the contract. Adam's parents

a. must pay the reasonable value of the goods.
b. must pay more than the reasonable value of the goods.
c. can pay less than the reasonable value of the goods.
d. do not have to pay anything for the goods.

_____ **5.** First Bank loans money to Patty, a sixteen-year-old minor. Patty must repay the loan if

a. the loan is for the express purpose of buying necessaries.
b. First Bank makes sure the money is spent on necessaries.
c. both a and b.
d. none of the above.

_____ **6.** Eve, a fifteen-year-old minor, buys a computer from SP Computers. The contract is fully executed. Eve now wants to disaffirm it. To do so, she

a. must return the computer to SP.
b. must return only the computer components that she does not want.
c. need not return anything to SP.
d. none of the above.

_____ **7.** Neal is adjudged mentally incompetent and a guardian is appointed. Neal later signs an investment contract with Mary. This contract is

a. valid.
b. voidable.
c. void.
d. none of the above.

_____ **8.** Jeff, a fifteen-year-old minor, contracts with Online, Inc., for Internet access services. Considering that Jeff is a minor, which of the following is TRUE?

a. Online can disaffirm the contract.
b. Jeff can disaffirm the contract.
c. Both a and b.
d. None of the above.

ISSUE SPOTTERS

1. Joan, who is sixteen years old, moves out of her parents' home and signs a one-year lease for an apartment at Kenwood Apartments. Joan's parents tell her that she can return to live with them at any time. Unable to pay the rent, Joan moves to her parents' home two months later. Can Kenwood enforce the lease against Joan?

2. Nina, a minor, buys a motorcycle from Buto Motorcycles. She pays $500 as a down payment and agrees to pay the balance in monthly $100 installments. She uses the motorcycle for a month then takes it back to Buto and demands the return of the $500. Can she get the money back without accounting for wear and tear on the motorcycle?

The Legality of Agreements

LEARNING OBJECTIVES

When you finish this chapter, you should be able to:

1. Identify contracts that are contrary to federal or state statutes.
2. Identify contracts that are contrary to public policy.
3. State circumstances in which covenants not to compete are enforceable.
4. Understand the consequences of entering into an illegal agreement.

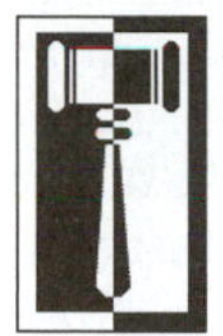

FACING A LEGAL PROBLEM

Isaacson tries to take out a life insurance policy on Donohue, as well as insurance policies on Donohue's auto and home, naming himself as beneficiary under each policy. An examination shows that Isaacson has no insurable interest in Donohue's life but is simply gambling on how long Donohue will live. The only interest that Isaacson has in any of Donohue's property is a mortgage on the house. *Will any of Isaacson's requests for insurance be accepted?*

To this point, we have discussed three of the requirements for a valid contract to exist—agreement (offer and acceptance), consideration, and contractual capacity. Now we examine a fourth: legality. For a contract to be valid and enforceable, it must be formed for a legal purpose. A contract to do something that is prohibited by federal or state statutory law is illegal. As such, it is void from the outset and thus unenforceable. Also, a contract that is tortious (pronounced *tor*-shus) or calls for an action contrary to public policy is illegal and unenforceable. Note that a contract, or a clause in a contract, may be illegal even in the absence of a specific statute prohibiting the action promised by the contract.

Contracts Contrary to Statute

Statutes often prescribe the terms of contracts. In some instances, the laws are specific, even providing for the inclusion of certain clauses and their wording (such as in insurance policies). Other statutes prohibit certain contracts on the basis of their subject matter, the time at which they are entered into, or the status of the contracting parties. In this section, we examine several ways in which contracts may be contrary to statute and thus illegal.

LEARNING OBJECTIVE NO. 1
Identifying Contracts that Are Contrary to Federal or State Statutes

USURY

USURY
Charging an illegal rate of interest.

Virtually every state has a statute that sets the maximum rate of interest that can be charged for different types of transactions, including ordinary loans. A lender who makes a loan at an interest rate above the lawful maximum commits **usury.** The maximum rate of interest varies from state to state.

GAMBLING

In general, wagers and games of chance are illegal. All states have statutes that regulate gambling—defined as any scheme that involves distribution of property by chance among persons who have paid valuable consideration for the opportunity to receive the property. Gambling is the creation of risk for the purpose of assuming it. A few states do permit gambling, and a number of states have recognized the substantial revenues that can be obtained from legal, state-operated lotteries.

Sometimes it is difficult to distinguish a gambling contract from the risk sharing inherent in almost all contracts. Thus, for example, insurance contracts can be entered into only by someone with an *insurable interest.* An insurable interest (discussed in Chapters 17 and 34) is a property or ownership right wherein the insured derives a financial benefit or advantage from the preservation of that right or suffers a financial loss or damage from its destruction.

In the legal problem set out at the beginning of this chapter, Isaacson tried to take out insurance policies on Donohue's life, auto, and home, naming himself as beneficiary. Isaacson had no insurable interest in Donohue's life, and the only interest he has in any of Donohue's property is a mortgage on Donohue's house. *Will any of Isaacson's requests for insurance be accepted?* Yes. Because Isaacson has a mortgage on Donohue's house, he can take out an insurance policy based on this property interest. Isaacson's request for insurance on Donohue's life will be denied, however. Similarly, Isaacson cannot take out an insurance policy on Donohue's auto, because Isaacson does not have an insurable interest in it.

Futures contracts, or contracts for the future purchase or sale of commodities (such as corn and wheat), are not illegal gambling contracts—although it might appear that a person selling or buying a futures contract is essentially gambling on the future price of the commodity. Because the seller of the futures contract either already has a property interest in the commodity or can purchase the commodity elsewhere and deliver the commodity as required in the futures contract, courts have upheld the legality of such contracts.

SABBATH (SUNDAY) LAWS

Statutes called Sabbath (Sunday) laws prohibit the formation or performance of certain contracts on a Sunday. Under the common law, such contracts are legal in the absence of this statutory prohibition. Under some state statutes, all contracts entered into on a Sunday are illegal. Statutes in other states prohibit only the sale of merchandise, particularly alcoholic beverages, on a Sunday.

BLUE LAWS
State or local laws that make the performance of commercial activities on Sunday illegal.

These statutes, which date back to colonial times, are often called **blue laws.** Blue laws get their name from the blue paper on which New Haven, Connecticut, printed its Sabbath ordinance in 1781. The ordinance prohibited all work on Sunday and required all shops to close on the "Lord's Day." A number of states enacted laws forbidding the carrying on of "all secular labor and business on the Lord's Day."

Exceptions to Sunday laws permit contracts for necessities (such as food) and works of charity. A fully executed (performed) contract entered into on a Sunday cannot be rescinded (canceled). Many states do not enforce Sunday laws, and some of these laws have been held to be unconstitutional on the ground that they are contrary to the freedom of religion.

LICENSING STATUTES

All states require that members of certain professions or callings obtain licenses allowing them to practice. Doctors, lawyers, real estate brokers, architects, electricians, and stockbrokers are but a few of the people who must be licensed. Some licenses are obtained only after extensive schooling and examinations, which indicate to the public that a special skill has been acquired. Others require only that the particular person be of good moral character.

Generally, business licenses provide a means of regulating and taxing certain businesses and protecting the public against actions that could threaten the general welfare. For example, in nearly all states, a stockbroker must be licensed and must file a bond (a promise obtained from a professional bonding company to pay a certain amount of money if the stockbroker commits theft). The bond is filed with the state to protect the public from fraudulent transactions in stock. Similarly, a plumber must be licensed and bonded to protect the public against incompetent plumbers and to protect the public health. Only persons or businesses possessing the qualifications and complying with the conditions required by statute are entitled to licenses. Typically, for example, an owner of a saloon or tavern is required to sell food as a condition for obtaining a license to sell liquor for consumption on the premises.

When a person enters into a contract with an unlicensed individual, the contract may still be enforceable depending on the nature of the licensing statute. Some states expressly provide that the lack of a license in certain occupations bars the enforcement of work-related contracts. If the statute does not expressly state this, one must look to the underlying purpose of the licensing requirements for a particular occupation. If the purpose is to protect the public from unauthorized practitioners, a contract involving an unlicensed individual is illegal and unenforceable. If, however, the underlying purpose of the statute is to raise government revenues, a contract entered into with an unlicensed practitioner is enforceable—although the unlicensed person is usually fined.

Contracts Contrary to Public Policy

Although contracts involve private parties, some are not enforceable because of the negative impact they would have on society. These contracts are said to be *contrary to public policy.* Examples include a contract to commit an immoral act and a contract that prohibits marriage.

LEARNING OBJECTIVE NO. 2
Identifying Contracts that Are Contrary to Public Policy

IN THE COURTROOM

Everett offers Dennis $500 if Dennis refrains from marrying Everett's daughter Pearl. Dennis accepts the $500, but marries Pearl anyway. *Can Everett succeed in a lawsuit against Dennis for breach of contract?* No. The contract to refrain from marrying Pearl is void (no contract ever existed), as are all contracts that prohibit marriage. Everett cannot sue Dennis for breach of contract.

CONTRACTS IN RESTRAINT OF TRADE

LEARNING OBJECTIVE NO. 3
Stating Circumstances in Which Covenants Not to Compete Are Enforceable

Contracts in restraint of trade usually adversely affect the public (which favors competition in the economy) and typically violate one or more federal or state statutes. An exception is recognized when the restraint is reasonable and an

If you buy a business, negotiate for a covenant not to compete.

integral part of a contract. Many such exceptions involve a type of restraint called a *covenant not to compete.*

Covenants not to compete are often contained in contracts concerning the sale of an ongoing business. A covenant not to compete is created when a seller agrees not to open a new store in a certain geographical area surrounding the old store. Such agreements enable the seller to sell, and the purchaser to buy, the "goodwill" and "reputation" of an ongoing business. If, for example, a well-known merchant sells his or her store and opens a competing business a block away, many of the merchant's customers will likely do business at the new store. This, in turn, renders valueless the good name and reputation sold to the new merchant for a price.

Agreements not to compete can also be contained in employment contracts. It is common for many people in middle-level and upper-level management positions to agree not to work for competitors or not to start a competing business for a specified period of time after terminating employment. Such agreements are legal so long as the specified period of time is not excessive in duration and the geographical restriction is reasonable. Basically, the restriction on competition must be reasonable—that is, no greater than necessary to protect a legitimate business interest.

Unconscionable Contracts or Clauses

Ordinarily, a court does not look at the fairness or equity of a contract; in other words, it does not inquire into the adequacy of consideration. Persons are assumed to be reasonably intelligent, and the court does not come to their aid just because they have made an unwise or foolish bargain. In certain circumstances, however, bargains are so oppressive that the courts relieve innocent parties of part or all of their duties. Such a bargain is an **unconscionable contract or clause.** (*Unconscionable* means unethical or unfair.) Both the Uniform Commercial Code and the Uniform Consumer Credit Code embody the unconscionability concept—the former with regard to the sale of goods and the latter with regard to consumer loans.

Unconscionable Contract or Clause
A contract or clause that is void on the basis of public policy because one party, as a result of his or her disproportionate bargaining power, is forced to accept terms that are unfairly burdensome and that unfairly benefit the dominating party.

Recent court decisions have distinguished between procedural and substantive unconscionability. Procedural unconscionability has to do with how a term becomes part of a contract. It relates to factors bearing on a party's lack of knowledge or understanding of the contract terms because of inconspicuous print, unintelligible language ("legalese"), lack of opportunity to read the contract, lack of opportunity to ask questions about the contract's meaning, and other factors.

Substantive unconscionability describes those contracts, or portions thereof, that are oppressive or overly harsh. Courts generally focus on provisions that deprive one party of the benefits of the agreement or leave that party without remedy for nonperformance by the other.

Contracts entered into because of one party's vastly superior bargaining power may be deemed unconscionable. These situations usually involve an **adhesion contract,** which is a contract drafted by one party (such as a dishonest retail dealer) and then presented to another (such as an uneducated consumer) on a "take it or leave it" basis. Another example of an unconscionable contract is one in which the terms of the agreement "shock the conscience" of the court.

Adhesion Contract
A "standard form" contract, such as that between a large retailer and a consumer, in which the stronger party dictates the terms.

IN THE COURTROOM

Smith, a welfare recipient with a fourth-grade education, agrees to purchase a refrigerator from A-Plus Appliances for $2,000, signing a two-year installment contract. The same type of refrigerator usually sells for $400 on the market. After paying $900, Smith refuses to pay more, and A-Plus sues to collect the balance. *Is the court likely to require Smith to pay the remaining*

$1,100? Some courts have held this type of contract to be unconscionable. These courts look at such factors as the buyer's lack of education, the disparity of bargaining power between the parties, and the price of the goods (despite the general rule that courts will not inquire into the adequacy of consideration).

EXCULPATORY CLAUSES

Often closely related to the concept of unconscionability are **exculpatory clauses.** These are clauses that release a party from liability in the event of monetary or physical injury, *no matter who is at fault.* (*Exculpatory* means attempting to clear of blame.) Indeed, some courts refer to such clauses in terms of unconscionability. In any event, exculpatory clauses that relieve a party from liability for harm caused by simple negligence normally are unenforceable when they are asserted by an employer against an employee.

EXCULPATORY CLAUSE
A clause that releases a party (to a contract) from liability for his or her wrongful acts.

IN THE COURTROOM

Madison Manufacturing Company asked Juan, a new employee, to sign a contract that included a clause exculpating Madison from liability for harm caused "by accidents or injuries in the factory, or which may result from defective machinery or carelessness or misconduct of himself or any other employee in service of the employer." *If Juan is injured in a factory accident, can Madison use the clause to avoid responsibility?* Probably not. The provision attempts to remove Madison's potential liability for injuries occurring to employees, and it would ordinarily be held contrary to public policy.

Also, exculpatory clauses asserted by a public utility, such as a railroad or an electric company, regarding harm caused during the public utility's operations are usually unenforceable. A railroad, for example, cannot use an exculpatory clause to avoid liability for the negligent maintenance of its trains.

In general, the courts have shown a mixed response to exculpatory clauses used by landlords (regarding a landlord's liability for defective premises), by amusement parks, and by horse-rental and golf-cart concessions.

The Effect of Illegality

LEARNING OBJECTIVE NO. 4
Understanding the Consequences of Entering into an Illegal Agreement

In general, an illegal contract is void: the contract is deemed never to have existed, and the courts will not aid either party. In most illegal contracts, both parties are considered to be equally at fault—*in pari delicto.* If a contract is executory (not yet fulfilled), neither party can enforce it. If it is executed, there can be neither contractual nor quasi-contractual recovery.

That one wrongdoer in an illegal contract is unjustly enriched at the expense of the other is of no concern to the law—except under certain circumstances (to be discussed shortly). The major justification for this hands-off attitude is that it is improper to place the machinery of justice at the disposal of a plaintiff who has broken the law by entering into an illegal bargain. Another justification is the hoped-for deterrent effect of this general rule. A plaintiff who suffers a loss because of an illegal bargain should presumably be deterred from entering into similar illegal bargains in the future.

Some persons are excepted from the general rule that neither party to an illegal bargain can sue for breach and neither can recover for performance rendered.

Justifiable Ignorance of the Facts

When one of the parties is relatively innocent, that party can often obtain restitution (recovery of benefits conferred) in a partially executed contract. The courts do not enforce the contract but do allow the parties to return to their original positions. It is also possible for an innocent party who has fully performed under the contract to enforce the contract against the guilty party.

IN THE COURTROOM

Debbie contracts with Tucker to purchase ten crates of goods that legally cannot be sold or shipped. Tucker hires a trucking firm to deliver the shipment to Debbie and agrees to pay the firm the normal fee of $500. *If the trucking firm delivers the goods as agreed, but Tucker fails to pay, can the trucking firm recover the $500 from Tucker?* Yes. Although the law specifies that the shipment and sale of the goods were illegal, the carrier, being an innocent party, can legally collect the $500 from Tucker.

Members of Protected Classes

When a statute protects a certain class of people, a member of that class can enforce an illegal contract even though the other party cannot. For example, there are statutes that prohibit certain employees (such as flight attendants) from working more than a specified number of hours per month. An employee who works more than the maximum can recover for those extra hours of service.

Blue Sky Law
State law that regulates the offer and sale of securities.

Another example of statutes designed to protect a particular class of people are **blue sky laws,** which are state laws that regulate and supervise investment companies for the protection of the public. Such laws are intended to stop the sale of stock in fly-by-night concerns, such as visionary oil wells and distant gold mines. Investors are protected as a class and can sue to recover the purchase price of stock issued in violation of such laws.

Most states also have statutes regulating the sale of insurance. If an insurance company violates a statute when selling insurance, the purchaser can nevertheless enforce the policy and recover from the insurer.

Withdrawal from an Illegal Agreement

If the illegal part of a bargain has not yet been performed, the party tendering performance can withdraw from the bargain and recover the performance or its value.

IN THE COURTROOM

Martha and Francisco decide to wager (illegally) on the outcome of a boxing match. They each deposit money with a stakeholder, who agrees to pay the winner of the bet. Before the boxing match is held, Francisco changes his mind about the bet. *Can he get his money back?* Yes. At this point, each party has performed part of the agreement, but the illegal part of the agreement will not occur until the money is paid to the winner. Before such payment occurs, either party is entitled to withdraw from the agreement by giving notice of repudiation to the stakeholder.

ILLEGAL CONTRACT THROUGH FRAUD, DURESS, OR UNDUE INFLUENCE

Whenever a plaintiff has been induced to enter into an illegal bargain as a result of fraud, duress, or undue influence, he or she can either enforce the contract or recover for its value.

REFORMATION OF AN ILLEGAL COVENANT NOT TO COMPETE

On occasion, when a covenant not to compete is unreasonable in its essential terms, the court may *reform* the covenant not to compete, converting its terms into reasonable ones. Instead of declaring the covenant not to compete illegal and unenforceable, the court reasons that the parties intended their contract to contain reasonable terms and changes the contract so that this basic intent can be enforced. This presents a problem, however, in that, by rewriting the contract, the judge becomes a party to it. Consequently, contract **reformation** is usually carried out by a court only when it is necessary to prevent undue burdens or hardships.

REFORMATION
A court-ordered correction of a written contract so that it reflects the true intentions of the parties.

TERMS AND CONCEPTS FOR REVIEW

adhesion contract 130
blue law 128
blue sky law 132
exculpatory clause 131
reformation 133
unconscionable contract or clause 130
usury 128

CHAPTER SUMMARY • THE LEGALITY OF AGREEMENTS

Contracts Contrary to Statute	**1.** *Usury*—It is illegal to make a loan at an interest rate that exceeds the maximum rate established by state law. **2.** *Gambling*—Gambling contracts that contravene (go against) state statutes are deemed illegal and thus void. **3.** *Sabbath (Sunday) laws*—Laws prohibiting the formation or the performance of certain contracts on Sunday vary widely from state to state. **4.** *Licensing statutes*—Contracts entered into by persons who do not have a license, when one is required by statute, will not be enforceable unless the underlying purpose of the statute is to raise government revenues (and not to protect the public from unauthorized practitioners).
Contracts Contrary to Public Policy	**1** *Contracts in restraint of trade*—Contracts to reduce or restrain free competition are illegal unless the restraint is reasonable. Most of these contracts are now prohibited by statutes. An exception is a *covenant not to compete.* It is usually enforced by the courts if the terms are reasonable as to time and area of restraint, especially when the covenant is part of a contract for the sale of a business and the goodwill and reputation of the firm are essential to the contract. **2.** *Unconscionable contracts and exculpatory clauses*—When a contract or contract clause is so unfair that it is oppressive to one party, it can be deemed unconscionable by a court; as such, it is illegal and cannot be enforced.
Effect of Illegality	**1.** In general, an illegal contract is void, and the courts will aid neither party when both parties are considered to be equally at fault *(in pari delicto)*. If the contract is executory, neither party can enforce it. If the contract is executed, there can be neither contractual nor quasi-contractual recovery. **2.** Exceptions (that is, situations in which recovery is allowed): **a.** When one party to the contract is relatively innocent. **b.** When one party to the contract is a member of a group of persons protected by statute. **c.** When one party was induced to enter into an illegal bargain through fraud, duress, or undue influence.

HYPOTHETICAL QUESTIONS

11–1. Covenants Not to Compete. Joseph, who owns the only pizza parlor in Middletown, learns that Giovanni is about to open a competing pizza parlor in the same small town, just a few blocks from Joseph's restaurant. Joseph offers Giovanni $10,000 in return for Giovanni's promise not to open a pizza parlor in the Middletown area. Giovanni accepts the $10,000 but goes ahead with his plans, in spite of the agreement. When Giovanni opens his restaurant for business, Joseph sues to enjoin (prevent) Giovanni's continued operation of his restaurant or to recover the $10,000. The court denies recovery. On what basis?

11–2. Licensing Statutes. State X requires that persons who prepare and serve liquor in the form of drinks at commercial establishments be licensed by the state to do so. The only requirement for obtaining a yearly license is that the person be at least twenty-one years old. Mickey, aged thirty-five, is hired as a bartender for the Southtown Restaurant. Gerald, a staunch alumnus of a nearby university, brings twenty of his friends to the restaurant to celebrate a football victory one afternoon. Gerald orders four rounds of drinks, and the bill is nearly $200. Gerald learns that Mickey has failed to renew his bartender's license, and Gerald refuses to pay, claiming that the contract is unenforceable. Discuss whether Gerald is correct.

REAL WORLD CASE PROBLEM

11–3. Gambling Contracts. No law prohibits citizens in a state that does not sponsor a state-operated lottery from purchasing lottery tickets in a state that does have such a lottery. Because Georgia did not have a state-operated lottery, Talley and several other Georgia residents allegedly agreed to purchase a ticket in a lottery sponsored by Kentucky and to share the proceeds if they won. They did win, but apparently Talley had difficulty collecting his share of the proceeds. In Talley's suit to obtain his share of the funds, a Georgia trial court held that the "gambling contract" was unenforceable because it was contrary to Georgia's public policy. On appeal, how should the court rule on this issue? Discuss. [*Talley v. Mathis,* 265 Ga. 179, 453 S.E.2d 704 (1995)]

For updated links to resources available on the Web, as well as a variety of other materials, visit this text's Web site at **http://blte.westbuslaw.com**.

If you are interested in learning about some "Sunday laws" in colonial America, go to

http://www.natreformassn.org/statesman/99/charactr.html

Chapter 11 ■ WORK SET

TRUE-FALSE QUESTIONS

_____ **1.** An exculpatory clause may not be enforced.

_____ **2.** An adhesion contract will never be deemed unconscionable.

_____ **3.** An illegal contract is valid unless it is executory.

_____ **4.** If the purpose of a licensing statute is to protect the public from unlicensed practitioners, a contract entered into with an unlicensed practitioner is unenforceable.

_____ **5.** Covenants not to compete are never enforceable.

_____ **6.** Usury is charging an illegal rate of interest.

_____ **7.** There is no difference between gambling and the risk that underlies most contracts.

_____ **8.** All states have statutes that regulate gambling.

MULTIPLE-CHOICE QUESTIONS

_____ **1.** At the start of the football season, Bob bets Murray about the results of the next SuperBowl. Adam holds their money. By the time of the divisional play-offs, Bob changes his mind and asks for his money back. Gambling on sports events is illegal in their state. Can Bob be held to the bet?

a. Yes. It would be unconscionable to let Bob back out so late in the season.
b. Yes. No party to the contract is innocent, and thus, no party can withdraw.
c. No. If an illegal agreement is still executory, either party can withdraw.
d. No. The only party who can be held to the bet is Murray.

_____ **2.** Al sells his business to Dan and, as part of the agreement, promises not to engage in a business of the same kind within thirty miles for three years. Competition within thirty miles would hurt Dan's business. Al's promise

a. violates public policy, because it is part of the sale of a business.
b. violates public policy, because it unreasonably restrains Al from competing.
c. does not violate public policy, because it is no broader than necessary.
d. none of the above.

_____ **3.** Luke practices law without an attorney's license. The state requires a license to protect the public from unauthorized practitioners. Clark hires Luke to handle a legal matter. Luke cannot enforce their contract because

a. it is illegal.
b. Luke has no contractual capacity.
c. Luke did not give consideration.
d. none of the above.

_____ **4.** Amy contracts to buy Kim's business. Kim agrees not to compete with Amy for one year in the same county. Six months later, Kim opens a competing business six blocks away. Amy

a. cannot enforce the contract because it is unconscionable.
b. cannot enforce the contract because it is a restraint of trade.
c. can enforce the contract because all covenants not to compete are valid.
d. can enforce the contract because it is reasonable in scope and duration.

_____ **5.** Sam signs an employment contract that contains a clause absolving the employer of any liability if Sam is injured on the job. If Sam is injured on the job due to the employer's negligence, the clause will

a. protect the employer from liability.
b. likely not protect the employer from liability.
c. likely be held unconscionable.
d. both b and c.

_____ **6.** A fully executed contract that was entered into on a Sunday

a. must be rescinded.
b. may be rescinded.
c. is unconstitutional.
d. none of the above.

_____ **7.** Ann contracts with Bob, a financial planner who is required by the state to have a license. Bob does not have a license. Their contract is enforceable if

a. the purpose of the statute is to protect the public from unlicensed practitioners.
b. the purpose of the statute is to raise government revenue.
c. Bob does not know that he is required to have a license.
d. Ann does not know that Bob is required to have a license.

_____ **8.** A contract that is full of inconspicuous print and unintelligible language and that is presented without an opportunity to read it is

a. always unenforceable.
b. always enforceable.
c. unenforceable under some circumstances.
d. void.

_____ **9.** An illegal contract may serve as a basis for recovery for a plaintiff who

a. suffers a loss.
b. is induced to enter into the contract as a result of fraud.
c. unjustly enriches the other party to the contract.
d. all of the above.

ISSUE SPOTTERS

1. Diane bets Tex $1,000 that the Dallas Cowboys will win the SuperBowl. A state law prohibits gambling. Do Diane and Tex have an enforceable contract?

2. Potomac Airlines prints on the backs of its tickets that it is not liable for any injury to a passenger caused by Potomac's negligence. Ron buys a ticket and boards the plane. On takeoff, the plane crashes, and Ron is injured. If the cause of the accident is found to be Potomac's negligence, can Potomac use the clause as defense to liability?

Mistakes and Other Contract Defects

12

LEARNING OBJECTIVES

When you finish this chapter, you should be able to:

1. State the difference between mistakes as to facts and mistakes as to judgment of market conditions.
2. List the elements of fraudulent misrepresentation.
3. Contrast misrepresentation of fact and misrepresentation of law.
4. Recognize the difference between undue influence and duress.

FACING A LEGAL PROBLEM

Jud Wheeler signs a contract to purchase ten acres of land in Idaho. If Jud believes that the land is owned by the Mittens, when it actually belongs to the Krauses, a court may allow the contract to be avoided because Jud made a mistake of fact. *If, however, Jud is aware that the land belongs to the Krauses but wants to buy it because he believes that he can resell the land at a profit to Bart, can Jud escape his contractual obligations if it later turns out that Bart does not want to buy it?*

A contract has been entered into between two parties, each with full legal capacity and for a legal purpose. The contract is supported by consideration. Nonetheless, the contract may be unenforceable if the parties have not truly agreed to the terms. This lack of genuine agreement, or genuine assent, can occur if one or more of the parties is mistaken about an important fact concerning the subject matter of the contract. Parties are also considered to lack genuine assent if a contract has been entered into as a result of fraudulent misrepresentation, undue influence, or duress. Lack of genuine assent is a defense to the enforcement of a contract.

Mistakes

We all make mistakes, and it is not surprising that mistakes are made when contracts are created. In certain circumstances, contract law allows a contract to be avoided on the basis of mistake. Realize, though, that the concept of mistake in contract law has to do with mistaken assumptions relating to contract formation. The concept does not have to do with various mistakes we make that may relate to a contract. For example, if you sent an installment payment due under a loan

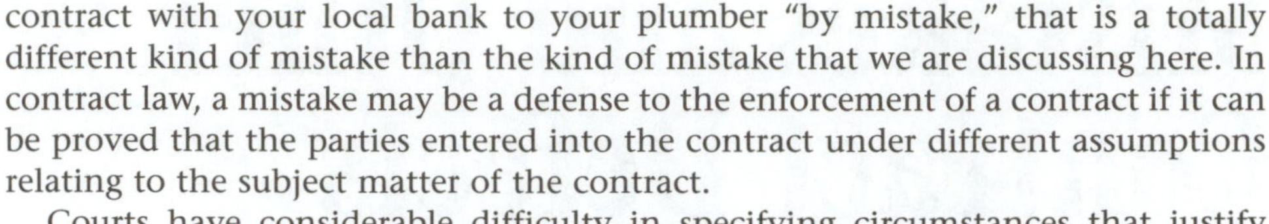

contract with your local bank to your plumber "by mistake," that is a totally different kind of mistake than the kind of mistake that we are discussing here. In contract law, a mistake may be a defense to the enforcement of a contract if it can be proved that the parties entered into the contract under different assumptions relating to the subject matter of the contract.

LEARNING OBJECTIVE NO. 1

Stating the Difference between Mistakes as to Facts and Mistakes as to Judgment of Market Conditions

Courts have considerable difficulty in specifying circumstances that justify allowing a mistake to invalidate a contract. Thus, the results in cases with similar facts can be different, and finding clearly defined rules governing the effects of mistakes can be difficult. Generally, though, courts distinguish between *mistakes as to judgment of market conditions* and *mistakes as to fact*. *Market conditions* are such factors as the possible future worth of the subject matter of a contract, such as a plot of land, and the identity of parties who might someday be interested in buying it. These are *ordinary business risks*. The location of the land and the identity of the parties who own it now are *facts*. Only *mistakes as to facts* have legal significance.

Law Guru, which allows you to access more than 160 legal search engines and indexes from a single location, can lead you to other sources on contract law. Go to

http://lawguru.com/lawlinks.html

In the legal problem set out at the beginning of this chapter, Jud Wheeler signed a contract to buy ten acres of land in Idaho. *If Jud wanted to buy the land because he believed that he could resell it at a profit to Bart, could Jud avoid the contract if it later turned out that he was mistaken?* Not likely. Jud's overestimation of the value of the land or of Bart's interest in it is an ordinary risk of business, for which a court will not normally provide relief.

In contract formation, mistakes can occur in two forms—*unilateral* and *bilateral (mutual)*. A unilateral mistake is made by only one of the contracting parties. A mutual mistake is made by both.

Unilateral Mistakes

A unilateral mistake involves some *material fact*—a fact that is important and central to the subject matter of the contract. In general, a unilateral mistake does not afford the mistaken party any right to relief from the contract. In other words, the contract normally is enforceable. Thus, in a letter to your friend offering to sell your car, if you mistakenly include a slightly lower price than you intended and your friend accepts the terms in the letter, you will be bound to the price.

Read a contract before signing it. In most states, the courts hold that a peson who signs a contract is bound to it, even if the person did not read it before signing it.

There are at least two exceptions. The contract may not be enforceable (1) if the *other* party to the contract knows or should have known that a mistake was made or (2) if the error was due to a mathematical mistake in addition, subtraction, division, or multiplication and was done inadvertently and without gross negligence (intentional failure to perform a duty in reckless disregard of the consequences). Of course, the mistake must still involve some *material* fact.

IN THE COURTROOM

Odell Construction Company made a bid to install the plumbing in an apartment building. When Herbert Odell, the president, added up his costs, his secretary forgot to give him the figures for the pipe fittings. Because of the omission, Odell's bid was $6,500 below that of the other bidders. The prime contractor, Sunspan, Inc., accepted and relied on Odell's bid. *Is the bid enforceable?* If Sunspan was not aware of Odell's mistake and could not reasonably have been aware of it, the bid will be enforceable, and Odell will be required to install the plumbing at the bid price. If, however, it can be shown that Odell's secretary mentioned her error to Sunspan, or if Odell's bid was so far below the others that, as a contractor, Sunspan should reasonably have known the bid was a mistake, the bid can be rescinded. Sunspan would not be allowed to accept the offer knowing it was made by mistake. The law of contracts protects only *reasonable* expectations.

MUTUAL MISTAKES

When both parties are mistaken about the same material fact, the contract can be rescinded by either party. As stated earlier, the mistake must be about a *material fact* (one that is important and central to the contract). If, instead, a mutual mistake concerns the later market *value* or *quality* of the object of the contract, the contract normally can be enforced by either party. This rule is based on the theory that both parties assume certain risks when they enter into a contract. Without this rule, almost any party who did not receive what he or she considered was a fair bargain could argue bilateral mistake. In essence, this would make *adequacy* of consideration a factor in determining whether a contract existed, and, as discussed previously, the courts normally do not inquire into the adequacy of consideration. Thus, the sale of an item cannot be rescinded simply because, at the time, neither party knew that it was worth much more than the sale price.

A word or term in a contract may be subject to more than one reasonable interpretation. In that situation, if the parties to the contract attach materially different meanings to the term, their mutual misunderstanding may allow the contract to be rescinded.

Fraudulent Misrepresentation

Although fraud is a tort, the presence of fraud also affects the genuineness of the innocent party's consent to the contract. Thus, the transaction is not voluntary in the sense required by "mutual assent." When an innocent party consents to a contract with fraudulent terms, the contract usually can be voided because the innocent party has not *voluntarily* consented. Normally, the innocent party can either rescind (cancel) the contract and be restored to the original position or enforce the contract and seek damages for injuries resulting from the fraud.

Typically, there are three elements of **fraud:**

1. A misrepresentation of a material fact must occur.
2. There must be an intent to deceive.
3. The innocent party must justifiably rely on the misrepresentation.

To recover damages, the innocent party must also suffer an injury.

FRAUD
Any misrepresentation, either by misstatement or omission of a material fact, knowingly made with the intention of deceiving another and on which a reasonable person would and does rely to his or her detriment.

LEARNING OBJECTIVE NO. 2
Listing the Elements of Fraudulent Misrepresentation

MISREPRESENTATION MUST OCCUR

The first element of proving fraud is to show that misrepresentation of a *material fact* has occurred. This misrepresentation can be in words or actions. An art gallery owner's statement "This painting is a Picasso" is an express misrepresentation if the painting was done by another artist.

A statement of *opinion* is generally not subject to a claim of fraud. Claims such as "This computer will never break down" or "This car will last for years and years" are statements of opinion, not fact. Contracting parties should recognize them as such and not rely on them. A fact is objective and verifiable; an opinion is usually subject to debate. Therefore, a seller is allowed to "huff and puff his or her wares" without being liable for fraud.

In certain cases, however—particularly when a naïve purchaser relies on a so-called expert's opinion—the innocent party may be entitled to rescission or reformation. Reformation is an equitable remedy granted by a court in which the terms of a contract are altered to reflect the true intentions of the parties. (Reformation of an illegal covenant not to compete is discussed in Chapter 11.)

Misrepresentation by Conduct. Misrepresentation need not be expressly made through the words or writings of another; it can also occur by conduct. For example, if a seller, by his or her actions, prevents a buyer from learning of some fact that is material to the contract, such an action constitutes misrepresentation by conduct. Thus, concealing a horse's blind eye, in a sale of the horse, would constitute fraud.

Another example of misrepresentation by conduct is the false denial of knowledge or information concerning facts that are material to the contract when such knowledge or information is requested.

Misrepresentation of Law. Misrepresentation of law does not ordinarily entitle the party to be relieved of a contract. People are assumed to know the law.

IN THE COURTROOM

Mercedes has a parcel of property that she is trying to sell to Carlos. Mercedes knows that a local ordinance prohibits building anything higher than three stories on the property. Nonetheless, she tells Carlos, "You can build a condominium fifty stories high if you want to." Carlos buys the land and later discovers that Mercedes's statement is false. *Can Carlos avoid the contract?* Normally, Carlos cannot avoid the contract, because under the common law, people are assumed to know easily researched state and local laws.

LEARNING OBJECTIVE NO. 3
Contrasting Misrepresentation of Fact and Misrepresentation of Law

Also, a person should not rely on a nonlawyer's statement about a point of law. Exceptions to this rule occur, however, when the misrepresenting party is in a profession known to require greater knowledge of the law than the average citizen possesses.

Misrepresentation by Silence. Ordinarily, neither party to a contract has a duty to come forward and disclose facts, and a contract normally will not be set aside because certain pertinent information is not volunteered. Thus, you do not have to tell potential buyers that a car you are selling has been in an accident (unless they ask).

Generally, if a *serious* defect or a *serious* potential problem is known to the seller but cannot reasonably be suspected by the buyer, the seller may have a duty to speak. For example, if a city fails to disclose to bidders subsoil conditions that will cause great expense in constructing a sewer, the city is guilty of fraud. Also, when the parties are in a fiduciary relationship (one of trust, such as partners, doctor and patient, or attorney and client), there is a duty to disclose material facts. Failure to do so may constitute fraud.

INTENT TO DECEIVE

SCIENTER
Knowledge by the misrepresenting party that material facts have been falsely represented or omitted with an intent to deceive.

The second element of fraud is knowledge on the part of the misrepresenting party that facts have been falsely represented. This element, normally called ***scienter*** (pronounced sy-*en*-ter), or "guilty knowledge," usually signifies that there was an *intent to deceive. Scienter* clearly exists if a party knows that a fact is not as stated. *Scienter* also exists if a party makes a statement that he or she believes not to be true or makes a statement recklessly, without regard to whether it is true or false. Finally, this element is met if a party says or implies that a statement is made on some basis, such as personal knowledge or personal investigation, when it is not.

IN THE COURTROOM

Rolando, when selling a house to Cariton, tells Cariton that the plumbing includes pipe of a certain high quality. Rolando knows nothing about the quality of the pipe but does not really believe it to be as she is representing it to be (and in fact it is not as she says it is). Rolando's statement induces Cariton to buy the house. *Can Cariton avoid the contract?* Normally, yes. Cariton can probably avoid the contract on the basis of Rolando's statement. Rolando's statement is a misrepresentation because Rolando does not believe the truth of what she said and because she knows that she does not have any basis for making the statement.

Reliance on the Misrepresentation

The third element of fraud is reasonably *justifiable reliance* on the misrepresentation of fact. The deceived party must have a justifiable reason for relying on the misrepresentation, and the misrepresentation must be an important factor (but not necessarily the sole factor) in inducing the party to enter into the contract. Reliance is not justified if the innocent party knows the true facts or relies on obviously extravagant statements. Thus, if the defects in a piece of property are obvious, the buyer cannot justifiably rely on the seller's representations. If the defects are hidden or latent (that is, not apparent on examination), the buyer is justified in relying on the seller's statements.

IN THE COURTROOM

Merkel, a bank director, induces O'Connell, a co-director, into signing a statement that the bank's assets will satisfy its liabilities by stating, "We have plenty of assets to satisfy our creditors." *If O'Connell knows that the true facts are otherwise, is he justified in relying on Merkel's statement?* No. If O'Connell does not know the true facts, however, *and has no way of finding them out,* he may be justified in relying on the statement.

Injury to the Innocent Party

For a person to *recover damages* caused by fraud, proof of an injury is required. The measure of damages is ordinarily equal to the property's value had it been delivered as represented, less the actual price paid for the property. In actions based on fraud, courts often award *punitive,* or *exemplary, damages*—which are granted to a plaintiff over and above the proved, actual compensation for the loss. Punitive damages are based on the public-policy consideration of *punishing* the defendant or setting an example for similar wrongdoers.

Most courts do not require a showing of injury when the action is to *rescind* or *cancel* the contract. Because rescission returns the parties to the position they were in prior to the contract, a showing of injury to the innocent party is unnecessary.

Undue Influence

Undue influence arises from relationships in which one party can greatly influence another party, thus overcoming that party's free will. Minors and elderly people are often under the influence of guardians. If a guardian induces a young or elderly *ward* (a person placed by a court under the care of a guardian) to enter into a contract that benefits the guardian, undue influence may have been exerted. Undue influence can arise from a number of confidential relationships or relationships founded on trust, including attorney-client, doctor-patient, guardian-ward, parent-child, husband-wife, and trustee-beneficiary relationships. The essential feature of undue influence is that the party being taken advantage of does not, in reality, exercise free will in entering into a contract. A contract entered into under excessive or undue influence lacks genuine assent and is therefore voidable.

UNDUE INFLUENCE
Persuasion that is less than actual force but more than advice and that induces a person to act according to the will or purposes of the dominating party.

LEARNING OBJECTIVE NO. 4

Recognizing the Difference between Undue Influence and Duress

Duress

Assent to the terms of a contract is not genuine if one of the parties is *forced* into the agreement. Recognizing this, the courts allow that party to rescind the contract. Forcing a party to enter into a contract under the fear of threats is legally defined as **duress.** Duress is both a defense to the enforcement of a contract and a ground for rescission (cancellation) of a contract. Therefore, the party upon whom the duress is exerted can choose to carry out the contract or to avoid the entire transaction. (The wronged party usually has this choice when assent is not real or genuine.)

DURESS
Unlawful pressure brought to bear on a person, overcoming that person's free will and causing him or her to do (or refrain from doing) what he or she otherwise would not (or would) have done.

Economic need is generally not sufficient to constitute duress, even when one party exacts a very high price for an item the other party needs. If the party exacting the price also creates the need, however, economic duress may be found.

IN THE COURTROOM

The Internal Revenue Service (IRS) assesses a large tax and penalty against Weller. Weller retains Eyman, an attorney, to resist the assessment. Two days before the deadline for filing a reply with the IRS, Eyman declines to represent Weller unless Weller signs a contract to pay a very high fee for Eyman's services. *If Weller signs the contract but later refuses to pay Eyman the higher fee, can Eyman enforce the agreement?* No. The agreement is unenforceable. Although Eyman threatened only to withdraw his services, something that he was legally entitled to do, he alone was responsible for delaying his withdrawal until the last days. Because it would have been impossible at that late date to obtain adequate representation elsewhere, Weller was forced into either signing the contract or losing his right to challenge the IRS assessment.

TERMS AND CONCEPTS FOR REVIEW

duress 142
fraud 139
scienter 140
undue influence 141

CHAPTER SUMMARY • MISTAKES AND OTHER CONTRACT DEFECTS

Mistakes	**1.** *Unilateral*—Generally, the mistaken party is bound by the contract *unless* (a) the other party knows or should have known of the mistake, or (b) the mistake is an inadvertent mathematical error—such as an error in addition, subtraction, etc.—committed without gross negligence. **2.** *Mutual*—When both parties' mistake concerns a material fact, either party can avoid the contract. If the mistake concerns value or quality, either party can enforce the contract.
Misrepresentation	**1.** *Fraud*—When fraud occurs, usually the innocent party can enforce or avoid the contract. The elements necessary to establish fraud follow: **a.** A misrepresentation of a material fact must occur. **b.** There must be an intent to deceive. **c.** The innocent party must justifiably rely on the misrepresentation. **2.** *Damages*—For damages, the innocent party must suffer an injury. **3.** *Other*—Usually, the innocent party can rescind the contract but cannot seek damages unless he or she has suffered an injury due to the misrepresentation. A misrepresentation of law generally does not permit a person to avoid the contract.

CHAPTER SUMMARY • *Continued*

Undue Influence	Undue influence arises from special relationships, such as fiduciary or confidential relationships, in which one party's free will has been overcome by the undue influence exerted by the other party. Usually, the contract is voidable.
Duress	Duress is forcing a party to enter into a contract under the fear of a threat—for example, the threat of violence or serious economic loss. The party forced to enter the contract can rescind the contract.

HYPOTHETICAL QUESTIONS

12–1. Genuineness of Assent. Jerome is an elderly man who lives with his nephew, Philip. Jerome is totally dependent on Philip's support. Philip tells Jerome that unless Jerome transfers a tract of land he owns to Philip for a price 15 percent below market value, Philip will no longer support and take care of him. Jerome enters into the contract. Discuss fully whether Jerome can set aside this contract.

12–2. Fraudulent Misrepresentation. Larry offered to sell Stanley his car and told Stanley that the car had been driven only 25,000 miles and had never been in an accident. Stanley hired Cohen, a mechanic, to appraise the condition of the car, and Cohen said that the car probably had at least 50,000 miles on it and probably had been in an accident. In spite of this information, Stanley still thought the car would be a good buy for the price, so he purchased it. Later, when the car developed numerous mechanical problems, Stanley sought to rescind the contract on the basis of Larry's fraudulent misrepresentation of the auto's condition. Will Stanley be able to rescind his contract? Discuss.

REAL WORLD CASE PROBLEM

12–3. Genuineness of Assent. Linda Lorenzo purchased Lurlene Noel's home in 1988 without having it inspected. The basement started leaking in 1989. In 1991, Lorenzo had the paneling removed from the basement walls and discovered that the walls were bowed inward and cracked. Lorenzo then had a civil engineer inspect the basement walls, and he found that the cracks had been caulked and painted over before the paneling was installed. He concluded that the "wall failure" had existed for "at least thirty years" and that the basement walls were "structurally sound." Does Lorenzo have a cause of action against Noel? If so, on what ground? Discuss. [*Lorenzo v. Noel,* 206 Mich.App. 682, 522 N.W.2d 724 (1994)]

For updated links to resources available on the Web, as well as a variety of other materials, visit this text's Web site at **http://blte.westbuslaw.com**.

For an illustration of how fraudulent misrepresentation can occur in the sale of real estate, go to

http://www.legaljournal.com/html/default_misrepresentation.htm

ONLINE LEGAL RESEARCH

Go to **http://blte.westbuslaw.com**, the Web site that accompanies this text. Select "Internet Applications," and then click on "Chapter 12." There you will find the following Internet research exercise that you can perform to learn more about fraud and unconscionability:

Activity 12–1: Fraudulent Misrepresentation

Chapter 12 ■ WORK SET

TRUE-FALSE QUESTIONS

_____ **1.** Under a mistake of fact, a contract can sometimes be avoided.

_____ **2.** When parties to both sides of a contract are mistaken as to the same fact, the contract cannot be rescinded by either party.

_____ **3.** To commit fraudulent misrepresentation, one party must intend to mislead another.

_____ **4.** In an action to rescind a contract for fraudulent misrepresentation, proof of injury is required to collect damages.

_____ **5.** The essential feature of undue influence is that the party taken advantage of does not exercise free will.

_____ **6.** If a person believes a statement to be true, he or she cannot be held liable for misrepresentation.

_____ **7.** A seller has no duty to disclose to a buyer a defect that is known to the seller but could not reasonably be suspected by a buyer.

_____ **8.** When both parties make a mistake as to the future market value of the object of their contract, the contract can be rescinded by either party.

MULTIPLE-CHOICE QUESTIONS

_____ **1.** Metro Transport asks for bids on a construction project. Metro estimates that the cost will be $200,000. Most bids are about $200,000, but EZ Construction bids $150,000. In adding a column of figures, EZ mistakenly omitted a $50,000 item. Because Metro had reason to know of the mistake

a. Metro can enforce the contract.
b. EZ can increase the price and enforce the contract at the higher price.
c. EZ can avoid the contract.
d. none of the above.

_____ **2.** To induce Sam to buy a lot in Mel's development, Mel tells Sam that he intends to add a golf course. The terrain is suitable, and there is enough land, but Mel has no intention of adding a golf course. Sam is induced by the statement to buy a lot. Sam's reliance on Mel's statement is justified because

a. Mel is the owner of the development.
b. Sam does not know the truth and has no way of finding it out.
c. Sam did not buy the golf course.
d. the golf course had obviously not been built yet.

_____ **3.** Bob agrees to sell to Pam ten shares of Eagle Corporation stock. Neither party knows whether the stock will increase or decrease in value. Pam believes that it will increase in value. If she is mistaken, her mistake will

a. justify voiding the contract.
b. not justify voiding the contract.
c. warrant a refund to her from Bob of the difference.
d. warrant a payment from her to Bob of the difference.

_____ **4.** In a letter offering to sell amplifiers to Gina for her theater, Dick describes the 120-watt amplifiers as "210 watts per channel." This is fraudulent misrepresentation if

a. the number of watts is a material fact.
b. Dick intended to deceive Gina.
c. Gina relies on the description.
d. all of the above.

_____ **5.** Ken, who is not a real estate broker, sells Global Associates some land. Which of the following statements by Ken, with the accompanying circumstance, would be a fraudulent misrepresentation in that sale?

a. "This acreage offers the most spectacular view of the valley." From higher up the mountain, more of the valley is visible.
b. "You can build an office building here." The county requires the property to be exclusively residential, but neither Ken nor Global know that.
c. "This property includes ninety acres." Ken knows it is only eighty acres.
d. "The value of this property will triple in five years." Ken does not know whether the value of the property will triple in five years.

_____ **6.** Ron enters into a contract with American Suppliers, Inc., under what Ron later learns to have been misrepresented facts. Ron has not yet suffered an injury. He can

a. obtain damages from American Suppliers.
b. rescind the contract.
c. both a and b.
d. none of the above.

_____ **7.** To sell a warehouse to A&B Enterprises, Ray does not disclose that the foundation was built on unstable pilings. A&B may later avoid the contract on the ground of

a. misrepresentation.
b. undue influence.
c. duress.
d. none of the above.

ISSUE SPOTTERS

1. Brad, an accountant, files Dina's tax returns. When the Internal Revenue Service assesses a large tax against Dina, she retains Brad to resist the assessment. The day before the deadline for replying to the IRS, Brad tells Dina that unless she pays a higher fee, he will withdraw. If Dina agrees to pay, is the contract enforceable?

2. In selling a house, Matt tells Ann that the wiring, fixtures, and appliances are of a certain quality. Matt knows nothing about the quality, but it is not as specified. Ann buys the house. On learning the true quality, Ann confronts Matt, who says he wasn't trying to fool her, he was only trying to make a sale. Can she rescind the deal?

Written Contracts

13

LEARNING OBJECTIVES

When you finish this chapter, you should be able to:

1. Identify contracts that must be in writing under the Statute of Frauds.
2. Describe what satisfies the writing requirement under the Statute of Frauds.
3. State the parol evidence rule.
4. List circumstances in which parol evidence is admissible.

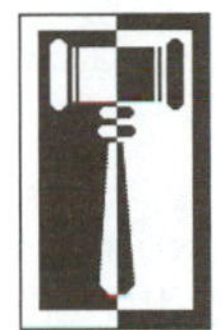

FACING A LEGAL PROBLEM

Suppose that you graduate from college on June 1. The same day, an employer calls you on the telephone and orally contracts to hire you immediately (June 1) for one year at $2,000 per month. You go to work, but after three months the employer tells you that she is letting you go. You remind her of your contract. She says, "If you've got nothing in writing, there is no enforceable contract. Clean out your desk." Is she right? *Does this contract have to be in writing to be enforceable?*

A contract that is otherwise valid may be unenforceable if it is not in the proper **form** (that is, in writing). Certain types of contracts are required by law to be in writing. If there is no written evidence of the contract, it may not be enforceable. In this chapter, we examine the kinds of contracts that require a writing under what is called the *Statute of Frauds.* The chapter concludes with a discussion of the *parol evidence rule,* under which courts determine the admissibility at trial of evidence extraneous (external) to written contracts.

FORM
The manner observed in creating a legal agreement, as opposed to the substance of the agreement.

The Statute of Frauds—Requirement of a Writing

On April 12, 1677, the English Parliament passed a law known as the **Statute of Frauds.** The intention of the law was to prevent harm to innocent parties by requiring written evidence of agreements concerning important transactions. In the United States, nearly every state has a statute of frauds modeled after the British act.

STATUTE OF FRAUDS
A state statute under which certain types of contracts must be in writing to be enforceable.

Essentially, the Statute of Frauds requires certain contracts to be in writing. If a contract is oral when it is required to be in writing, it will not, as a rule, be enforced by the courts. Although the statutes vary slightly from state to state, all require the following types of contracts to be in writing or evidenced by a written memorandum:

LEARNING OBJECTIVE NO. 1
Identifying Contracts That Must Be in Writing under the Statute of Frauds

1. Contracts involving interests in land.
2. Contracts that cannot *by their terms* be performed within one year from the date of formation.
3. Collateral contracts, such as promises to answer for the debt or duty of another.
4. Promises made in consideration of marriage.
5. Contracts for the sale of goods priced at $500 or more.

Certain exceptions are made to the applicability of the Statute of Frauds in some circumstances. These exceptions are discussed later in this section.

Contracts Involving Interests in Land

Under the Statute of Frauds, a contract involving an interest in land must be in writing. Land is real property and includes all physical objects that are permanently attached to the land, such as buildings, plants, and trees. A contract calling for the sale of land is not enforceable unless it is in writing or evidenced by a written memorandum. Thus, a party to an oral contract involving an interest in land cannot force the other party to buy or sell the property that is the subject of the contract. The Statute of Frauds is a *defense* to the enforcement of this type of oral contract.

A contract for the sale of land ordinarily involves the entire interest in the real property, including buildings, growing crops, vegetation, minerals, timber, and anything else affixed to the land. Therefore, a **fixture** (personal property so affixed or so used as to become a part of the real property) is treated as real property. Anything else, however, such as a couch, is treated as personal property.

Fixture
A thing that was once personal property but that has become attached to real property in such a way that it takes on the characteristics of real property and becomes part of that real property.

The Statute of Frauds requires written contracts not just for the sale of land but also for the transfer of other interests in land, such as mortgages and leases. These other interests are described in Chapter 36.

The One-Year Rule

A contract that cannot, *by its own terms,* be performed within one year from the date the contract is formed must be in writing to be enforceable. Because disputes over such contracts are unlikely to occur until some time after the contracts are made, resolution of these disputes is difficult unless the contract terms have been put in writing. The idea behind this rule is that a witness's memory is not to be trusted for longer than a year.

For a particular contract to fall into this category, contract performance must be, by its terms, *objectively impossible* to perform within a year from the date of contract formation. A contract to provide five crops of tomatoes to be grown on a specific farm in Illinois, for instance, would be impossible to perform within a year, because it is impossible to grow five crops of tomatoes in a single year in Illinois.

If the contract, by its terms, makes performance within the year *possible* (even if not probable), the contract is not within the Statute of Frauds and need not be in writing. A contract to provide security services for a warehouse for as long as the warehouse needs it could be fully performed within a year, because the warehouse could go out of business within twelve months.

The one-year period begins to run *the day after the contract is made.* Exhibit 13–1 illustrates the one-year rule.

In the legal problem set out at the beginning of this chapter, an employer orally contracted to hire you—beginning immediately—for one year at $2,000 per month. *Does such a contract have to be in writing to be enforceable?* No. Under the Statute of Frauds, this contract need not be in writing to be enforceable, because the one-year period to measure performance begins on June 2. Because your performance of one year can begin immediately, it would take you exactly one year from the date of entering the contract to complete the performance.

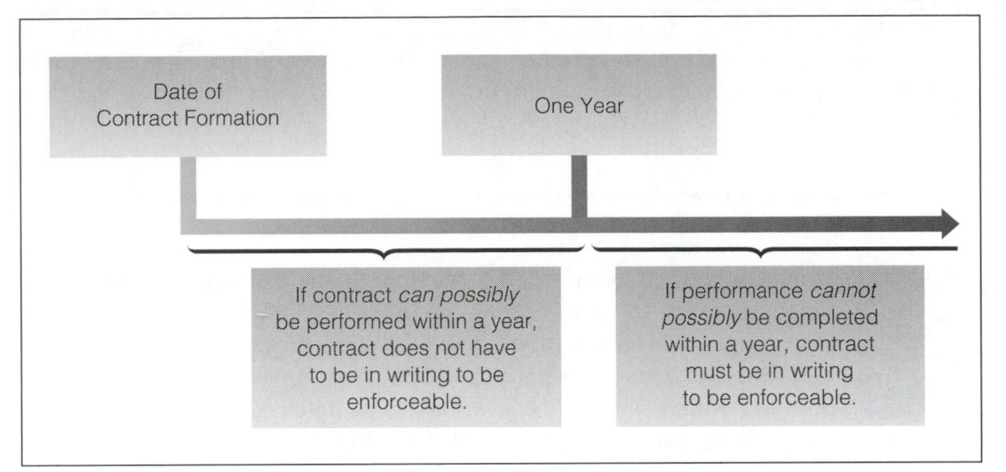

EXHIBIT 13–1
The One-Year Rule

COLLATERAL PROMISES

A **collateral promise,** or secondary promise, is one that is ancillary to a principal transaction or primary contractual relationship. In other words, a collateral promise is one made by a third party to assume the debts or obligations of a primary party to a contract if the primary party does *not* perform. Any collateral promise of this nature falls under the Statute of Frauds and therefore must be in writing to be enforceable.

COLLATERAL PROMISE
A secondary promise that is ancillary to a principal transaction or primary contractual relationship, such as a promise made by one person to pay the debts or discharge the duties of another if the latter fails to perform. A collateral promise normally must be in writing to be enforceable.

Primary versus Secondary Obligations. To understand this concept, it is important to distinguish between primary and secondary promises and obligations. You commit yourself to a primary obligation when you agree to pay for something. You commit yourself to a secondary obligation when you agree to pay for something *on the condition that* a certain other party does not make the payment.

IN THE COURTROOM

Pablo contracts with Joanne's Floral Boutique to send his mother a dozen roses for Mother's Day. Pablo promises to pay for the roses when he receives the bill. On the same day, Pablo's mother borrows $1,000 from the Medford Bank. Pablo promises the bank that he will pay the $1,000 if his mother does not repay the loan on time. *Which of these promises must be in writing to be enforceable under the Statute of Frauds?* Pablo's promise to repay his mother's debt is a secondary obligation and must be in writing if the bank wants to enforce it. Pablo, in this situation, becomes a *guarantor* of the loan. That is, he guarantees that he will pay back the loan if his mother fails to do so. In contracting for the roses, Pablo incurred a *primary* obligation. This contract does not fall under the Statute of Frauds and does not have to be in writing to be enforceable. If Pablo fails to pay the florist and the florist sues him for payment, Pablo cannot raise the Statute of Frauds as a defense. He cannot claim that the contract is unenforceable because it was not in writing.

We will return to the concept of guaranty and the distinction between primary and secondary obligations in Chapter 32, in the context of creditors' rights.

An Exception—The "Main Purpose" Rule. An oral promise to answer for the debt of another is covered by the Statute of Frauds *unless* the guarantor's main purpose in accepting secondary liability is to secure a personal benefit. This type of contract need not be in writing. The assumption is that a court can infer from the circumstances of a case whether the main, or "leading," objective of the promisor was to secure a personal benefit and thus, in effect, to answer for his or her own debt.

IN THE COURTROOM

Frances contracts with Machio Manufacturing Company to have some machines made to specifications for her factory. She promises Allrite Supply Company, Machio's supplier, that if Allrite continues to deliver materials to Machio, Frances will guarantee payment. *Under the Statute of Frauds, does this promise need to be in writing to be enforceable?* No. This promise need not be in writing, even though the effect may be to pay the debt of another, because Frances's main purpose is to secure a benefit for herself.

Another typical application of the so-called main purpose doctrine is when one creditor guarantees the debtor's debt to another creditor to forestall litigation. This allows the debtor to remain in business long enough to generate profits sufficient to pay *both* creditors.

PROMISES MADE IN CONSIDERATION OF MARRIAGE

PRENUPTIAL AGREEMENT An agreement entered into in contemplation of marriage, specifying the rights and ownership of the parties' property.

A unilateral promise to pay a sum of money or to give property in consideration of a promise to marry must be in writing. If a father promises to pay a young man $10,000 if the young man agrees to marry the father's daughter, the promise must be in writing. The same rule applies to **prenuptial agreements.** These agreements, which are also sometimes called *antenuptial agreements,* are agreements made before marriage that define each partner's ownership rights in the other partner's property. For example, a prospective wife may wish to limit the amount her prospective husband could obtain if the marriage ended in divorce. Prenuptial arrangements made in consideration of marriage must be in writing to be enforceable.

Generally, courts tend to give more credence to prenuptial agreements that are accompanied by consideration. Thus, if prospective spouses sign a prenuptial agreement setting out limits for alimony should they divorce, a court is likely to uphold the agreement if it is accompanied by a significant payment (the consideration) when it is signed.

To add certainty to the enforceability of prenuptial agreements, the National Conference of Commissioners on Uniform State Laws issued the Uniform Prenuptial Agreements Act (UPAA) in 1983. The UPAA provides that prenuptial agreements must be in writing to be enforceable and that the agreements become effective when the parties marry.

CONTRACTS FOR THE SALE OF GOODS

The Uniform Commercial Code (UCC) requires a writing or memorandum for a sale of goods priced at $500 or more. (See UCC 2–201—Section 2–201 of the UCC—which is included in Appendix B.) A writing that will satisfy the UCC requirement need only state the quantity term. Other terms agreed on need not be stated "accurately" in the writing, as long as they adequately reflect both parties' intentions. The contract will not be enforceable, however, for any quantity greater than that set forth in the writing. In addition, the writing must be signed by the person to be charged—that is, by the person who refuses to perform or the one being sued. Beyond these two requirements, the writing need not designate the buyer or the seller, the terms of payment, or the price.

EXCEPTIONS TO THE STATUTE OF FRAUDS

Exceptions to the applicability of the Statute of Frauds are made in the situations described below.

Partial Performance. In cases involving contracts relating to the transfer of interests in land, if the purchaser has paid part of the price, taken possession, and made permanent improvements to the property (such as having built a house on the land), and the parties cannot be returned to the positions they held before their contract, a court may grant *specific performance* (performance of the contract according to its precise terms).

Whether the courts will enforce an oral contract for an interest in land when partial performance has taken place is usually determined by the degree of injury that would be suffered if the court chose not to enforce the oral contract. In some states, mere reliance on an oral contract is enough to remove it from the Statute of Frauds.

Under the UCC, an oral contract is enforceable to the extent that a seller accepts payment or a buyer accepts delivery of the goods. Thus, if a buyer orders by telephone twenty items from a seller and repudiates the contract after ten have been delivered and accepted, the seller could enforce the contract to the extent of the ten items already accepted by the buyer.

Admissions. In some states, if a party against whom enforcement of an oral contract is sought "admits" in pleadings, testimony, or otherwise in court that a contract for sale was made, the contract will be enforceable. A contract subject to the UCC will be enforceable, but only to the extent of the quantity admitted. Thus, if a buyer admits under oath that an oral agreement was made with a seller for twenty items, the agreement will be enforceable to that extent.

Promissory Estoppel. In some states, an oral contract that would otherwise be unenforceable under the Statute of Frauds may be enforced under the doctrine of promissory estoppel, or detrimental reliance. Recall from Chapter 9 that if a promisor makes a promise on which the promisee justifiably relies to his or her detriment, a court may *estop* (prevent) the promisor from denying that a contract exists. In these circumstances, an oral promise can be enforceable if two requirements are met. First, the person making the promise must foresee that the promisee will rely on it. Second, there must be no way to avoid injustice except to enforce the promise. For example, if you orally promise to give the manager of your farm a certain plot of land in return for her attaining a specific level of success with your farm, once she has performed, you can be held to the promise.

Special Exceptions under the UCC. Special exceptions to the applicability of the Statute of Frauds apply to sales contracts. Oral contracts for customized goods may be enforced in certain circumstances. Another exception has to do with oral contracts *between merchants* that have been confirmed in writing. These exceptions will be examined in detail in the discussion of the UCC provisions regarding the Statute of Frauds in Chapter 16. (See also UCC 2–201 in Appendix B.)

The Statute of Frauds—Sufficiency of the Writing

To be safe, all contracts should be fully set forth in a writing signed by all the parties. This ensures that if any problems arise concerning performance of the contract, a written agreement fully specifying the performance promised by each party can be introduced into court. The Statute of Frauds requires either a written contract or a *written memorandum* signed by the party against whom enforcement is sought.

If you enter into an oral contract over the telephone, fax or e-mail a written confirmation outlining your understanding of the oral contract.

LEARNING OBJECTIVE NO. 2
Describing What Satisfies the Writing Requirement under the Statute of Frauds

A written memorandum can consist of any confirmation, invoice, sales slip, check, or fax. Any one or combination of these items may constitute a writing that satisfies the Statute of Frauds. The entire writing does not have to consist of a single document to constitute an enforceable contract. One document may incorporate another document by expressly referring to it. Several documents may form a single contract if they are physically attached, by staple, paper clip, or glue. Several documents may form a single contract even if they are only placed in the same envelope. The signature need not be placed at the end of the document but can be anywhere in the writing; it can even be initials rather than the full name.

IN THE COURTROOM

Sam orally agrees to sell to Lee some land next to a shopping mall. Sam gives to Lee an unsigned memo that contains a legal description of the property, and Lee gives to Sam an unsigned first draft of their contract. Sam writes a signed letter to Lee that refers to the memo and to the first and final drafts of the contract. Lee sends to Sam an unsigned copy of the final draft of the contract with a signed check stapled to it. *Do Sam and Lee have a writing sufficient to satisfy the Statute of Frauds?* Yes. Together, the documents constitute a writing sufficient to satisfy the Statute of Frauds and bind both parties to the terms of the contract.

Access to the Internet

You can find a report on electronic contracts at

http://www.uchastings.edu/plri/fall94/whipple.html

The report discusses satisfying the writing requirements of the Statute of Frauds.

A memorandum evidencing the oral contract need only contain the essential terms of the contract. Under the UCC, for the sale of goods the writing need only name the quantity term and be signed by the party being charged. Under most provisions of the Statute of Frauds, the writing must name the parties, subject matter, consideration, and quantity. Contracts for the sale of land, in some states, require that the memorandum also state the *essential* terms of the contract (such as location and price) with sufficient clarity to allow the terms to be determined from the memo, without reference to any outside sources.

Only the party to be held liable on the contract need sign the writing. Therefore, a contract may be enforceable by one of its parties but not by the other. Thus, a party who signs a letter setting out the essential terms of an oral contract can be held to those terms. The other party, who signed nothing, can plead the Statute of Frauds as a defense, and the contract cannot be enforced against him or her.

PAROL EVIDENCE RULE
A rule of contracts under which a court will not receive into evidence prior statements or contemporaneous oral statements that contradict a written agreement when the court finds that the written agreement was intended by the parties to be a final, complete, and unambiguous expression of their agreement.

The Parol Evidence Rule

LEARNING OBJECTIVE NO. 3
Stating the Parol Evidence Rule

The **parol evidence rule** prohibits the introduction at trial of evidence of the parties' prior negotiations or agreements or contemporaneous (occurring during the same period of time) oral agreements if that evidence contradicts or varies the terms of written contracts. The written contract is ordinarily assumed to be the complete embodiment of the parties' agreement. Because of the rigidity of the parol evidence rule, however, courts make several exceptions.

LEARNING OBJECTIVE NO. 4
Listing Circumstances in Which Parol Evidence Is Admissible

1. Evidence of a *subsequent modification* of a written contract can be introduced into court. Keep in mind that the oral modifications may not be enforceable if they come under the Statute of Frauds—for example, if they increase the price of the goods for sale to $500 or more or increase the term for performance to more than one year. Also, oral modifications will not be enforceable if the original contract provides that any modification must be in writing.
2. Oral evidence can be introduced in all cases to show that the contract was voidable or void (for example, induced by mistake, fraud, or misrepresentation). In this case, if deception led one of the parties to agree to the terms of a written

contract, oral evidence attesting to fraud should not be excluded. Courts frown upon bad faith and are quick to allow such evidence when it establishes fraud.

3. When the terms of a written contract are ambiguous, evidence is admissible to show the meaning of the terms.
4. Evidence is admissible when the written contract is incomplete in that it lacks one or more of the essential terms. The courts allow evidence to "fill in the gaps."
5. Under the UCC, evidence can be introduced to explain or supplement a written contract by showing a prior dealing, course of performance, or usage of trade. These terms will be discussed in further detail in Chapter 16, in the context of sales contracts. Here, it is sufficient to say that when buyers and sellers deal with each other over extended periods of time, certain customary practices develop. These practices are often overlooked when writing the contract, so courts allow the introduction of evidence to show how the parties have acted in the past.
6. The parol evidence rule does not apply if the existence of the entire written contract is subject to an orally agreed-on condition. Proof of the condition does not *alter* or *modify* the written terms but involves the *enforceability* of the written contract.

IN THE COURTROOM

Suppose you agree with your friend Amy to buy her car for $4,000, but only if your brother, Frank, inspects it and approves of your purchase. Amy agrees to this condition. Because she is leaving town for the weekend and you want to use the car (if you buy it) before she returns, however, you write up a contract of sale, and both of you sign it. Frank does not approve of the purchase. When you do not buy the car, Amy sues you, alleging that you breached the contract. *Can you introduce proof of the oral condition regarding Frank's inspection and approval of the car?* Yes. In this case, your oral agreement does not alter or modify the terms of your written agreement. Instead, it concerns whether or not the contract exists at all.

7. When an *obvious* or *gross* clerical (or typographic) error exists that clearly would not represent the agreement of the parties, parol evidence is admissible to correct the error. Thus, if a written lease provides for monthly rent of $30 rather than the $300 orally agreed to by the parties, parol evidence would be admissible to correct the obvious mistake.

The key in determining whether evidence will be allowed basically is whether the written contract is intended to be a complete and final embodiment of the terms of the agreement. If it is so intended, it is referred to as an **integrated contract,** and extraneous (outside) evidence is excluded. If it is only partially integrated, evidence of consistent additional terms is admissible to supplement the written agreement.

Integrated Contract
A written contract that constitutes the final expression of the parties' agreement. If a contract is integrated, evidence extraneous to the contract that contradicts or alters the meaning of the contract in any way is inadmissible.

TERMS AND CONCEPTS FOR REVIEW

collateral promise 149
fixture 148
form 147
integrated contract 153
parol evidence rule 152
prenuptial agreement 150
Statute of Frauds 147

CHAPTER SUMMARY • WRITTEN CONTRACTS

Contracts Subject to the Statute of Frauds	**1.** *Applicability*—The following types of contracts fall under the Statute of Frauds and must be in writing to be enforceable: **a.** *Contracts involving interests in land*—Statute applies to any contract for an interest in realty, such as a sale, a lease, or a mortgage. **b.** *Contracts whose terms cannot be performed within one year*—Statute applies only to contracts objectively impossible to perform fully within one year from the day after the contract's formation. **c.** *Collateral promises*—Statute applies only to express contracts made between the guarantor and the creditor, whose terms make the guarantor secondarily liable. Exception: main purpose rule. **d.** *Promises made in consideration of marriage*—Statute applies to promises to pay money or give property in consideration of a promise to marry and to prenuptial agreements made in consideration of marriage. **e.** *Contracts for the sale of goods priced at $500 or more*—Under the UCC. **2.** *Exceptions*—Partial performance; admissions; promissory estoppel; other exceptions under the UCC.
Sufficiency of the Writing	To constitute an enforceable contract under the Statute of Frauds, a writing must be signed by the party against whom enforcement is sought, name the parties, identify the subject matter, and state with reasonable certainty the essential terms. In a sale of land, the price and a description of the property may need to be stated with sufficient clarity to be determined without reference to outside sources. Under the UCC, a contract for a sale of goods is not enforceable beyond the quantity of goods shown.
Parol Evidence Rule	Prohibits the introduction at trial of evidence of the parties' prior negotiations or agreements or contemporaneous oral agreements if that evidence contradicts or varies the terms of written contracts. The written contract is assumed to be the complete embodiment of the parties' agreement. Exceptions are made in the following circumstances: **1.** To show that the contract was subsequently modified. **2.** To show that the contract was voidable or void. **3.** To clarify the meaning of ambiguous terms. **4.** To clarify the terms of the contract when the written contract lacks one or more of its essential terms. **5.** Under the UCC, to explain the meaning of contract terms in light of a prior dealing, course of performance, or usage of trade. **6.** To show that the entire contract is subject to an orally agreed-on condition. **7.** When an obvious clerical or typographic error was made.

HYPOTHETICAL QUESTIONS

13–1. Collateral Promises. Gemma promises a local hardware store that she will pay for a lawn mower that her brother is purchasing on credit if the brother fails to pay the debt. Must this promise be in writing to be enforceable? Why or why not?

13–2. Statute of Frauds. William Rowe, suffering from the effects of a severe gastric hemorrhage, was admitted to General Hospital. On the day Rowe was admitted, Rowe's son told the doctor, "We want you to do everything you can to save his life, and we don't want you to spare any expense. Whatever he needs, Doctor, you go ahead and get it, and I will pay you." After Rowe was discharged from the hospital, his son refused to pay his medical bills. Can the hospital enforce the son's oral promise? Discuss fully.

REAL WORLD CASE PROBLEM

13–3. One-Year Rule. Adam Curry worked as a videodisc jockey for MTV Networks (MTVN). In discussions during 1993, Curry and MTVN executives agreed that Curry could develop, at his own expense, an Internet site address ("mtv.com") and that MTVN would not interfere with Curry's development of the site. By early 1994, Curry's mtv.com address had been accessed by millions of Internet users, in part because of a computer bulletin board (developed by Curry) that facilitated communication between performers and other music professionals. In the meantime, MTVN decided to offer online services through America Online, Inc. These services were to include a bulletin board similar to that developed by Curry. In mid-January 1994, MTVN requested that Curry cease using the mtv.com address. A dispute ensued, and eventually MTVN sued Curry on several grounds. Curry counterclaimed that MTVN had breached its oral contract with him. MTVN argued that because the contract could not be performed within one year, the Statute of Frauds barred its enforcement. How should the court decide this issue? Explain. [*MTV Networks, A Division of Viacom International, Inc. v. Curry*, 867 F.Supp. 202 (S.D.N.Y. 1994)]

For updated links to resources available on the Web, as well as a variety of other materials, visit this text's Web site at **http://blte.westbuslaw.com.**

The online version of UCC Section 2–201 on the Statute of Frauds includes links to definitions of certain terms used in the section. To access this site, go to

http://www.law.cornell.edu/ucc/2/2-201.html

Professor Eric Talley of the University of Southern California provides an interesting discussion of the history and current applicability of the Statute of Frauds, both internationally and in the United States, at the following Web site:

http://www-bcf.usc.edu/~etalley/frauds.html

ONLINE LEGAL RESEARCH

Go to **http://blte.westbuslaw.com**, the Web site that accompanies this text. Select "Internet Applications," and then click on "Chapter 13." There you will find the following Internet research exercise that you can perform to learn more about the Statute of Frauds:

Activity 13–1: The Statute of Frauds

Chapter 13 ■ WORK SET

TRUE-FALSE QUESTIONS

_____ **1.** Contracts for transfers, other than sales, of interests in land need not be in writing to be enforceable under the Statute of Frauds.

_____ **2.** A contract for a sale of goods of over $300 must be in writing to be enforceable under the Statute of Frauds.

_____ **3.** An oral contract that should be in writing to be enforceable under the Statute of Frauds may be enforceable if it has been partially performed.

_____ **4.** The only writing sufficient to satisfy the Statute of Frauds is a typewritten form, signed at the bottom by all parties, with the heading "Contract" at the top.

_____ **5.** Under the parol evidence rule, virtually any evidence is admissible to prove or disprove the terms of a contract.

_____ **6.** A promise to answer for the debt of another must be in writing to be enforceable, unless the guarantor's main purpose is to obtain a personal benefit.

_____ **7.** A contract that makes performance within one year possible need not be in writing to be enforceable.

_____ **8.** A promise to pay a sum of money in consideration of a promise to marry must be in writing.

MULTIPLE-CHOICE QUESTIONS

_____ **1.** Walt sells his pick-up truck to Bob. When Walt starts to remove the camper, Bob says, "Wait. We agreed the camper was included." Walt points to their written contract and says, "No, we didn't." The contract says nothing about the camper. The camper is

a. part of the deal under the parol evidence rule.
b. not part of the deal under the parol evidence rule.
c. part of the deal because Bob thought it was.
d. not part of the deal because Walt thought it was not.

_____ **2.** On March 1, the chief engineer for the software design division of Uni Products orally contracts to hire Lee for one year, beginning March 4. Lee works for Uni for five months. When sales decline, Lee is discharged. Lee sues Uni for reinstatement or seven months' salary. Lee will

a. win, because the contract can be performed within one year.
b. win, because employment contracts need not be in writing to be enforceable.
c. lose, because the contract cannot be performed within one year.
d. lose, because employment contracts must be in writing to be enforceable.

_____ **3.** National Properties, Inc., orally contracts for a sale of its lot and warehouse to U.S. Merchants, Inc., then later decides not to go through with the sale. The contract is most likely enforceable against

a. both National and U.S. Merchants.
b. National only.
c. U.S. Merchants only.
d. neither National nor U.S. Merchants.

_____ **4.** Hans owes Bell Credit Company $10,000. Chris orally promises Bell that he will pay Hans's debt if Hans does not. This promise is

a. not enforceable because it is not in writing.
b. enforceable under the "main purpose rule" exception.
c. not enforceable because the debt is Hans's.
d. enforceable under the part performance exception.

_____ **5.** Which of the following constitutes a writing that satisfies the Statute of Frauds?

a. A signed sales slip.
b. A blank invoice.
c. An empty envelope.
d. All of the above.

_____ **6.** Terry signs a letter setting out the essential terms of an oral contract with Adrian. Those terms are most likely enforceable against

a. both Terry and Adrian.
b. Terry only.
c. Adrian only.
d. neither Terry nor Adrian.

_____ **7.** Jim orally promises to work for Pat, and Pat orally promises to employ Jim at a rate of $500 a week. This contract must be in writing to be enforceable if Jim promises to work for

a. his entire life.
b. at least five years.
c. five years, but either party may terminate the contract on thirty-days' notice.
d. both a and c.

_____ **8.** Tom orally agrees to be liable for Meg's debt to Ace Loan Company. If Tom's purpose for this guaranty is to obtain a personal benefit, the guaranty is

a. enforceable whether or not it is in writing.
b. enforceable only if it is in writing.
c. unenforceable if it is in writing.
d. unenforceable unless it is in writing.

ISSUE SPOTTERS

1. GamesCo orders $800 worth of game pieces from Midstate Plastic, Inc. Midstate delivers, and GamesCo pays for, $450 worth. GamesCo then says it wants no more pieces from Midstate. GamesCo and Midstate have never dealt with each other before and have nothing in writing. Can Midstate enforce a deal for $350 more?

2. Paula orally agrees with Next Corporation to work in New York City for Next for two years. Paula moves her family to New York and begins work. Three months later, Paula is fired for no stated cause. She sues for reinstatement or pay. Next argues that there is no written contract between them. What will the court say?

Third Party Rights

14

LEARNING OBJECTIVES

When you finish this chapter, you should be able to:

1 State what a contract assignment is.

2 Define a contract delegation.

3 Identify noncontracting parties who have rights in a contract.

4 Explain when a third party beneficiary's rights in a contract vest.

FACING A LEGAL PROBLEM

Wayne attends Metro Community College in Riverside. To pay tuition, buy books, and meet other expenses, Wayne obtains a loan from the First National Bank of Riverside. Six months later, Wayne receives a letter from the bank, which states that it has transferred its rights to receive Wayne's payments on the loan to the Educational Loan Collection Agency (ELCA). The letter tells Wayne that when he begins making payments, he should make them directly to the ELCA. *Should Wayne pay the bank or the ELCA?*

Because a contract is a private agreement between the parties who have entered into it, it is fitting that these parties alone should have rights and liabilities under the contract. This is referred to as **privity of contract.** *Privity* refers to the parties' relationship, which is considered sufficiently direct to uphold a legal claim between them. Privity of contract establishes the basic concept that third parties have no rights in a contract to which they are not a party. Thus, if I offer to sell you my watch and you accept, but I later refuse to deliver it and you decide to overlook the breach, your friend who is outraged by my behavior cannot successfully sue me—she was not a party to the contract.

PRIVITY OF CONTRACT
The relationship that exists between the promisor and the promisee of a contract.

There are two exceptions to the rule of privity of contract. One exception allows a party to a contract to transfer the rights arising from the contract to another and/or to free himself or herself from the duties of a contract by having another person perform them. Legally, such an action is referred to as an *assignment of rights* and/or a *delegation of duties.* A second exception to the rule of privity of contract involves a *third party beneficiary* contract. Here, the rights of a third party against the promisor (the party making a promise) arise from the contract because the parties normally make the contract with the intent to benefit the third party. The law relating to assignments, delegations, and third party beneficiary contracts is discussed in this chapter.

Within the legal interest group on the commercial service America Online, there is a subcategory on torts and contracts. If you subscribe to America Online the key word is:
legal

Assignments and Delegations

When third parties acquire rights or assume duties arising from a contract to which they were not parties, the rights are transferred to them by *assignment,* and the duties are transferred by *delegation.* Assignment and delegation occur *after* the original contract is made, when one of the parties transfers to another party a right or duty under the contract.

LEARNING OBJECTIVE NO. 1
Stating What a Contract Assignment Is

ASSIGNMENTS

ASSIGNMENT
The act of transferring to another all or part of one's rights arising under a contract.

In a bilateral contract, the two parties have corresponding rights and duties. One party (the obligee) has a *right* to require the other to perform some task, and the other party (the obligor) has a *duty* to perform it. The transfer of *rights* to a third person is known as an **assignment.** When rights under a contract are assigned unconditionally, the rights of the *assignor* (the party making the assignment) are extinguished. The third party (the *assignee,* or party receiving the assignment) has a right to demand performance from the other original party to the contract (the *obligor*).

These relationships are illustrated in Exhibit 14–1. As shown in the exhibit, once Alessio has assigned to Cabrera her rights under the original contract with Bren, Cabrera can enforce the contract against Bren if Bren fails to perform. The assignee takes only those rights that the assignor originally had. If Bren owes Alessio $50, and Alessio assigns to Cabrera the right to receive the $50, a valid assignment of a debt exists. Cabrera is entitled to enforce payment in a court if Bren does not pay her the $50.

Furthermore, the assignee's rights are subject to the defenses that the obligor has against the assignor. If Alessio leases an apartment from Bren for one year but fails to pay the seventh month's rent, and the next day Alessio assigns the lease to Cabrera, Bren can evict Alessio and Cabrera, even though Cabrera is innocent of the failure to pay the rent.

Retailers usually sell their rights to receive payment at a discount because of the risk of noncollection from some debtors.

Assignments are important because they are involved in much business financing. Probably the most common contractual right that is assigned is the right to the payment of money. For instance, to obtain funds to buy additional inventory, a retailer may assign the rights to receive payments from his or her credit customers to a financing agency, which would then give the retailer cash. Depending on the terms of the assignment, the agency could insist that the customers pay it directly, or it may have nothing to do with such payments unless the retailer fails to repay the agency. Millions of dollars change hands daily in the business world in the form of assignments of rights in contracts. If it were not possible to transfer (assign) contractual rights, many businesses could not continue to operate.

EXHIBIT 14–1
Assignment Relationships

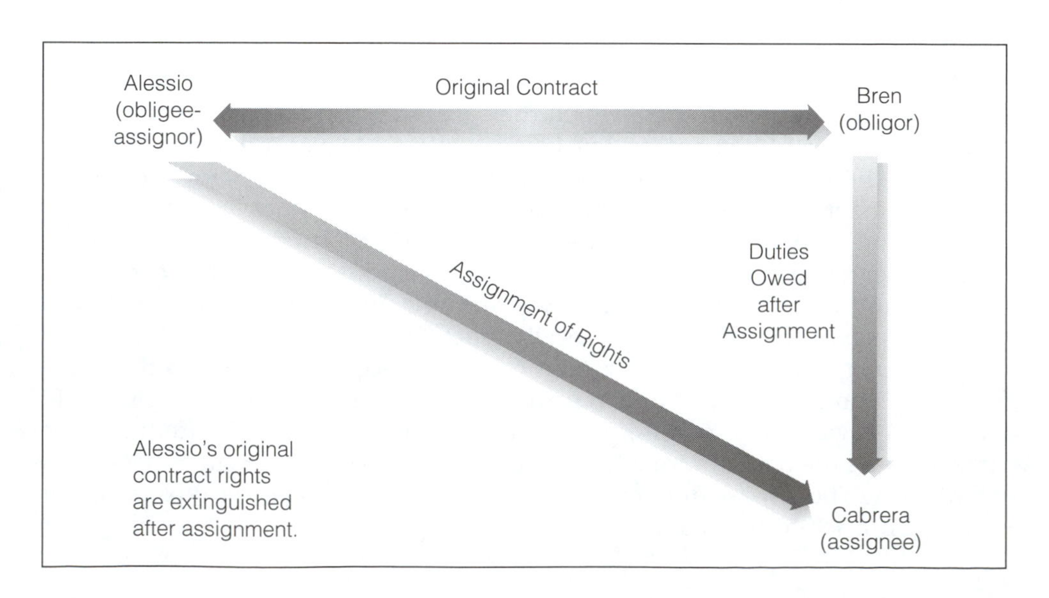

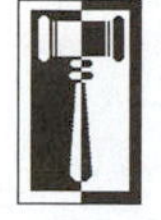

In the legal problem set out at the beginning of this chapter, Wayne obtains a student loan from a bank and is later notified that the bank has transferred its right to receive Wayne's payments to a business agency. *What is this transfer? Should Wayne pay the bank or the agency?* The transfer is an assignment. The agency may have purchased the right to receive Wayne's payments. The agency can insist that Wayne make his payments directly to the agency.

Rights That Cannot Be Assigned. As a general rule, all rights can be assigned, except in the special circumstances listed below.

1. If a statute expressly prohibits assignment, the particular right in question cannot be assigned. For instance, if the assignment of future workers' compensation benefits is prohibited by state statute, a worker cannot assign all benefits due her should she be injured on the job.
2. When a contract is *personal* in nature, the rights under the contract cannot be assigned unless all that remains is a money payment. For instance, if you hire someone to tutor you, you cannot assign the tutor's services to someone else. It would change the nature of the tutor's obligation.
3. A right cannot be assigned if assignment will materially increase or alter the risk or duties of the obligor. For this reason, an insurance policy cannot be assigned. Insurance companies evaluate the particular risk of a certain party and tailor their policies to fit that risk. If the policy is assigned to a third party, the insurance risk may be materially altered.
4. If a contract stipulates that the rights cannot be assigned, then *ordinarily* they cannot be assigned. Thus, if a contract provides that "any assignment renders this contract void, and all rights hereunder will thereupon terminate," the rights cannot effectively be assigned.

There are several exceptions to the fourth rule stated above (that an assignment can be prohibited by contract). First, a contract cannot prevent an assignment of the right to receive money. This exception exists to encourage the free flow of money and credit in modern business settings. Second, the assignment of rights in real estate often cannot be prohibited, because such a prohibition is contrary to public policy. These prohibitions are called restraints against **alienation** (transfer of land ownership). Third, the assignment of *negotiable instruments* (see Chapter 22) cannot be prohibited. Fourth, in a contract for the sale of goods, the right to receive damages for breach of contract or for payment of an account owed may be assigned even though the sales contract prohibits such assignment.

ALIENATION
The process of transferring land.

Notice of Assignment. Once a valid assignment of rights has been made to a third party, the third party should notify the obligor—the original party to the contract—of the assignment (see Bren in Exhibit 14–1). This is not legally necessary to establish the validity of the assignment, because an assignment is effective immediately, whether or not notice is given. Two major problems arise, however, when notice of the assignment is not given to the obligor:

1. If the assignor assigns the same right to two different persons, the question arises as to which one has priority (right) to the performance by the obligor. Although the rule most often observed in the United States is that the first assignment in time is the first in right, some states follow the English rule, which basically gives priority to the first assignee who gives notice. Thus, if Bren owes Alessio $1,000 and Alessio assigns the claim first to Cabrera, without notice to Bren, and then to Dorman, who notifies Bren, in most states Cabrera would have priority to payment. In some states Dorman would have priority, because Dorman gave first notice.
2. Until the obligor has notice of assignment, the obligor can discharge his or her obligation by performance to the assignor, and performance by the obligor to the assignor constitutes a discharge to the assignee. Once the obligor receives proper notice, only performance to the assignee can discharge the obligor's obligations.

IN THE COURTROOM

Pryor owes Tomás $1,000 on a contractual obligation. Tomás assigns this monetary claim to Maria. No notice of assignment is given to Pryor. Pryor pays Tomás the $1,000. *Was the assignment valid? Did Pryor's payment discharge the debt, or does Pryor also have to pay Maria?* Although the assignment was valid, Pryor's payment to Tomás discharged the debt, and Maria's failure to give notice to Pryor of the assignment caused Maria to lose the right to collect the money from Pryor. If Maria had given Pryor notice, Pryor's payment to Tomás would not have discharged the debt, and Maria would have had a legal right to require payment from Pryor.

DELEGATIONS

LEARNING OBJECTIVE NO. 2
Defining a Contract Delegation

DELEGATION
The transfer of a contractual duty to a third party. The party delegating the duty (the delegator) to the third party (the delegatee) is still obliged to perform on the contract if the delegatee fails to perform.

Just as a party can transfer rights through an assignment, a party can also transfer duties. A transfer of duties is called a **delegation.** (Delegation relationships are graphically illustrated in Exhibit 14–2.) Normally, a delegation of duties does not relieve the party making the delegation (the *delegator*) of the obligation to perform in the event that the party to whom the duty has been delegated (the *delegatee*) fails to perform. No special form is required to create a valid delegation of duties. As long as the delegator expresses an intention to make the delegation, it is effective; the delegator need not even use the word *delegate.*

Duties That Cannot Be Delegated. As a general rule, any duty can be delegated. There are, however, some exceptions to this rule. Delegation is prohibited in the following circumstances:

1. When performance depends on the *personal* skill or talents of the obligor. Thus, a specific tutor who is known for her expertise in finance and who is hired to teach the various aspects of financial underwriting and investment banking could not delegate this duty.
2. When special trust has been placed in the obligor.
3. When performance by a third party will vary materially from that expected by the obligee (the one to whom performance is owed) under the contract.
4. When the contract expressly prohibits delegation.

EXHIBIT 14–2
Delegation Relationships

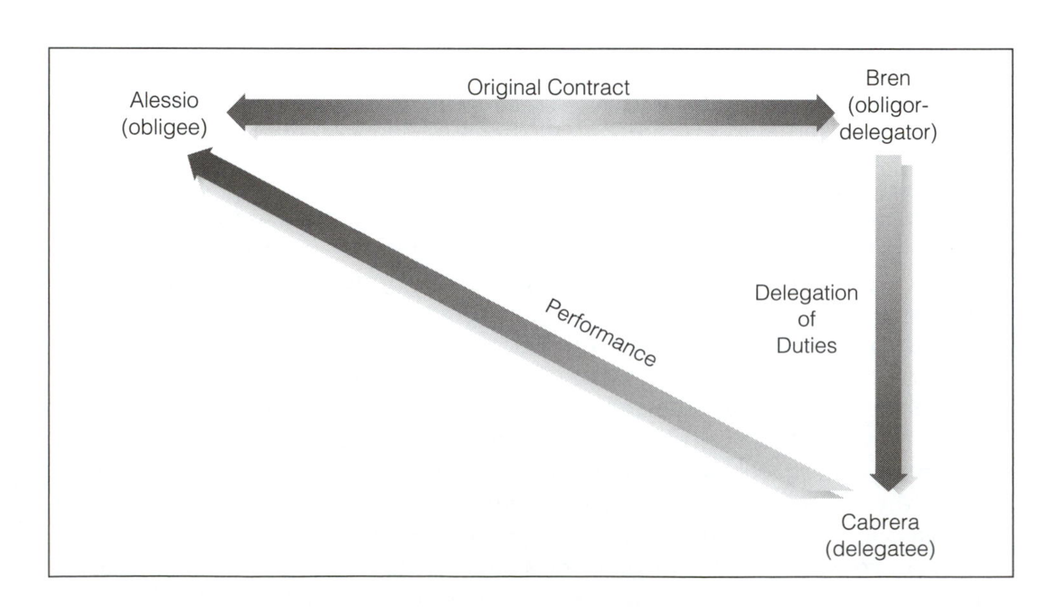

IN THE COURTROOM

Sue contracts with Karl to pick up and deliver some heavy construction machinery. Sue delegates this duty to Frank, who is in the business of delivering heavy machinery. *Is the delegation effective?* Yes. The performance required is of a routine and nonpersonal nature and does not change Karl's expectancy under the contract.

Effect of a Delegation. If a delegation of duties is enforceable, the *obligee* (the one to whom performance is owed) must accept performance from the delegatee. The obligee can legally refuse performance from the delegatee only if the duty is one that cannot be delegated. A valid delegation of duties does not relieve the delegator of obligations under the contract. If the delegatee fails to perform, the delegator is still liable to the obligee.

Liability of the Delegatee. Can the obligee hold the delegatee liable if the delegatee fails to perform? If the delegatee has made a promise of performance that will directly benefit the obligee, there is an "assumption of duty." Breach of this duty makes the delegatee liable to the obligee.

IN THE COURTROOM

Leo contracts to build Donna a house according to Donna's blueprint. Leo becomes seriously ill and contracts to have Hal build the house for Donna (the obligee). Hal fails to build the house. *Can Donna sue Leo? Can Donna sue Hal?* Because the delegatee, Hal, contracted with Leo (the obligor) to build the house for the benefit of Donna (the obligee), Donna can sue Leo, Hal, or both. Although there are many exceptions, the general rule is that the obligee can sue both the delegatee and the obligor.

Assignment of "All Rights"

When a contract provides for an "assignment of all rights," this wording may also be treated as providing for an "assumption of duties" on the part of the assignee. Therefore, when general words are used (for example, "I assign the contract" or "I assign all my rights under the contract"), the contract is construed as implying both an assignment of rights and a delegation of duties.

Third Party Beneficiaries

To have contractual rights, a party normally must be a party to the contract. As mentioned earlier in this chapter, an exception exists when the original parties to the contract intend at the time of contracting that the contract performance directly benefit a third person. In this situation, the third person becomes a *beneficiary* of the contract and has legal rights.

The law distinguishes between two types of **third party beneficiaries:** *intended* beneficiaries and *incidental* beneficiaries. Only intended beneficiaries acquire legal rights in a contract.

LEARNING OBJECTIVE NO. 3
Identifying Noncontracting Parties Who Have Rights in a Contract

THIRD PARTY BENEFICIARY
One who is not a party to a contract but for whose benefit a promise is made in the contract.

Intended Beneficiaries

An **intended beneficiary** is one who can sue the promisor directly for breach of a contract made for the beneficiary's benefit. Who, however, is the promisor?

INTENDED BENEFICIARY
A third party for whose benefit a contract is formed; intended beneficiaries can sue the promisor if such a contract is breached.

In bilateral contracts, both parties to the contract are promisors, because they both make promises that can be enforced. In third party beneficiary contracts, courts will determine the identity of the promisor by asking which party made the promise that benefits the third party—that person is the "promisor." Allowing a third party to sue the promisor directly in effect circumvents the "middle person" (the promisee) and thus reduces the burden on the courts. Otherwise, a third party would sue the promisee, who would then sue the promisor.

The most common intended beneficiary contract is a life insurance contract. In a typical contract, the promisee pays premiums to a life insurance company, and the insurance company (the promisor) promises to pay a certain amount of money on the promisee's death to anyone the promisee designates as a beneficiary. The designated beneficiary is a third party beneficiary under the policy and can enforce the promise made by the company to pay on the promisee's death.

An intended third party beneficiary cannot enforce a contract against the original parties until the rights of the third party have *vested,* which means the rights have taken effect and cannot be taken away. Until these rights have vested, the original parties to the contract—the promisor and the promisee—can modify or rescind the contract without the consent of the third party. When do the rights of third parties vest? Generally, the rights of an intended beneficiary vest when either of the following occurs:

1. When the third party demonstrates *manifest assent* to the contract, such as by sending a letter or note consenting to a contract formed for his or her benefit.
2. When the third party materially alters his or her position in *detrimental reliance* on the contract.

LEARNING OBJECTIVE NO. 4
Explaining When the Rights of a Third Party Beneficiary Vest

If the contract expressly reserves the right to cancel, rescind, or modify the contract, the rights of the third party beneficiary are subject to any changes that result. In such a case, the vesting of the third party's rights does not terminate the power of the original contracting parties to alter their legal relationships. This is particularly true in most life insurance contracts, in which the right to change the beneficiary is reserved to the policyowner.

Incidental Beneficiaries

Incidental Beneficiary
A third party who incidentally benefits from a contract but whose benefit was not the reason the contract was formed; an incidental beneficiary has no rights in a contract and cannot sue the promisor if the contract is breached.

The benefit that an **incidental beneficiary** receives from a contract between two parties is unintentional. Therefore, an incidental beneficiary cannot enforce a contract to which he or she is not a party. In determining whether a third party beneficiary is an intended or an incidental beneficiary, the courts generally use the *reasonable person* test. That is, a beneficiary will be considered an intended beneficiary if a reasonable person in the position of the third party beneficiary would believe that the promisee *intended* to confer upon the beneficiary the right to bring suit to enforce the contract.

Several other factors must also be examined to determine whether a party is an intended or an incidental beneficiary. The presence of one or more of the factors listed here strongly indicates an *intended* (rather than an incidental) benefit to a third party:

1. Performance rendered directly to the third party.
2. The right of the third party to control the details of performance.
3. Express designation in the contract.

IN THE COURTROOM

Jules contracts with Vivian to build a cottage on Vivian's land. Jules's plans specify that Super Insulation Company's insulation materials must be used when constructing the house. *Can Super Insulation enforce the contract against Jules by requiring that Jules buy its insulation materials?* No. Super Insulation Company is an incidental beneficiary. An incidental beneficiary has no rights in the contract and cannot enforce it against the promisor.

TERMS AND CONCEPTS FOR REVIEW

CHAPTER SUMMARY • THIRD PARTY RIGHTS

Assignment	**1.** An assignment is the transfer of rights under a contract to a third party. The *rights* of the assignor (the person making the assignment) may be extinguished. The assignee (the person to whom the rights are assigned) has a right to performance from the obligor (the other original party to the contract). **2.** Generally, all rights can be assigned, except in the following circumstances: **a.** When assignment is expressly prohibited by statute (for example, workers' compensation benefits). **b.** When a contract calls for the performance of personal services. **c.** When the assignment will materially increase or alter the duties of the obligor. **d.** When the contract itself stipulates that the rights cannot be assigned (except a money claim). **3.** Notice of the assignment should be given by the assignee to the obligor. **a.** If the assignor assigns the same right to two different persons, generally the first assignment in time is the first in right, although in some states the first assignee to give notice takes priority. **b.** Until the obligor is notified of the assignment, an obligor can tender performance to the assignor, and if performance is accepted by the assignor, the obligor's duties under the contract are discharged without benefit to the assignee.
Delegation	**1.** A delegation is the transfer of duties under a contract to a third party whereby the delegatee (the third party) assumes the obligation of performing the contractual duties previously held by the delegator (the one making the delegation). **2.** As a general rule, any duty can be delegated, except in the following circumstances: **a.** When performance depends on the personal skill or talents of the obligor. **b.** When special trust has been placed in the obligor. **c.** When performance by a third party will vary materially from that expected by the obligee (the one to whom the duty is owed) under the contract. **d.** When the contract expressly prohibits delegation. **3.** A valid delegation of duties does not relieve the delegator of obligations under the contract. If the delegatee fails to perform, the delegator is still liable to the obligee. **4.** An "assignment of all rights" is often construed to mean that both the rights and duties of a contract are transferred to a third party.
Third Party Beneficiary Contract	A third party beneficiary contract is one made for the purpose of benefiting a third party. **1.** *Intended beneficiary*—One for whose benefit a contract is created. When the promisor (the one making the contractual promise that benefits a third party) fails to perform as promised, the third party can sue the promisor directly. **2.** *Incidental beneficiary*—A third party who indirectly (incidentally) benefits from a contract but for whose benefit the contract was not specifically intended. Incidental beneficiaries have no rights to the benefits received and cannot sue the promisor to have them enforced.

HYPOTHETICAL QUESTIONS

14–1. Third Party Beneficiaries. Wilken owes Rivera $2,000. Howie promises Wilken to pay Rivera the $2,000 in return for Wilken's promise to give Howie's children guitar lessons. Is Rivera an intended beneficiary of the Howie-Wilken contract? Explain.

14–2. Delegation. Inez has a specific set of plans to build a sailboat. The plans are detailed in nature, and any boatbuilder can build the boat. Inez secures bids, and the low bid is made by the Whale of a Boat Corp. Inez contracts with Whale to build the boat for $4,000. Whale then receives unexpected business from elsewhere. To meet the delivery date in the contract with Inez, Whale delegates its obligation to build the boat, without Inez's consent, to Quick Brothers, a reputable boatbuilder. When the boat is ready for delivery, Inez learns of the delegation and refuses to accept delivery, even though the boat is built to specifications. Discuss fully whether Inez is obligated to accept and pay for the boat. Would your answer be any different if Inez had not had a specific set of plans but had instead contracted with Whale to design and build a sailboat for $4,000? Explain.

REAL WORLD CASE PROBLEM

14–3. Assignment. Joseph LeMieux, of Maine, won #373,000 in a lottery operated by the Tri-State Lotto Commission. The lottery is sponsored by the three northern New England states and is administered in Vermont. In accordance with its usual payment plan, Tri-State was to pay the $373,000 to LeMieux in annual installments over a twenty-year period. LeMieux assigned his rights to the lottery installment payments for the years 1996 through 2006 to Singer Freidlander Corp., for the sum of $80,000. LeMieux and Singer Freidlander (the plaintiffs) sought a court judgment authorizing the assignment agreement between them despite Tri-State's regulation barring the assignment of lottery proceeds. The trial court granted Tri-State's motion for summary judgment. On appeal, the plaintiffs argued that Tri-State's regulation was invalid. Is it? Discuss fully. [*LeMieux v. Tri-State Lotto Commission,* 666 A.2d 1170 (Vt. 1995)]

For updated links to resources available on the Web, as well as a variety of other materials, visit this text's Web site at **http://blte.westbuslaw.com.**

You can find a summary of the law governing assignments, as well as "SmartAgreement" forms that you can use for various types of contracts, at

http://www.smartagreements.com/gen1/lp75.htm

A *New York Law Journal* article discussing *Lawrence v. Fox* and other leading decisions from the New York Court of Appeals is online at

http://www.nylj.com/links/150sterk.html

ONLINE LEGAL RESEARCH

Go to **http://blte.westbuslaw.com,** the Web site that accompanies this text. Select "Internet Applications," and then click on "Chapter 14." There you will find the following Internet research exercise that you can perform to learn more about third party rights in contracts:

Activity 14–1: Third Party Beneficiaries

Chapter 14 ■ WORK SET

TRUE-FALSE QUESTIONS

_____ **1.** Intended beneficiaries have no legal rights under a contract.

_____ **2.** The party who makes an assignment is the assignee.

_____ **3.** All rights can be assigned.

_____ **4.** If a contract contains a clause that prohibits assignment of the contract, then ordinarily the contract cannot be assigned.

_____ **5.** A right to the payment of money may be assigned.

_____ **6.** An assignment is not effective without notice.

_____ **7.** No special form is required to create a valid delegation of duties.

_____ **8.** Only intended beneficiaries acquire legal rights in a contract.

_____ **9.** A contract cannot prevent an assignment of a right to receive money.

MULTIPLE-CHOICE QUESTIONS

_____ **1.** Gary contracts with Dan to buy Dan a new car manufactured by General Motors Corporation (GMC). GMC is

a. an intended beneficiary.
b. an incidental beneficiary.
c. not a third party beneficiary.
d. both a and b.

_____ **2.** Bernie has a right to $100 against Holly. Bernie assigns the right to Tom. Tom's rights against Holly

a. include the right to demand performance from Holly.
b. are subject to any defenses Holly has against Bernie.
c. do not vest until Holly assents to the assignment.
d. both a and b.

_____ **3.** Frank owes Jim $100. Frank contracts with Ron to pay the $100 and notifies Jim of the contract by fax. Jim replies by fax that he agrees. After Frank receives Jim's reply, Ron and Frank send Jim a fax stating that they decided to rescind their contract. Jim's rights under the contract

a. vested when Jim learned of the contract and manifested assent to it.
b. vested when Frank and Ron formed their contract.
c. will not vest because Ron and Frank rescinded their contract.
d. could never vest because Jim is an incidental beneficiary.

_____ **4.** Jenny sells her Value Auto Parts store to Burt and makes a valid contract not to compete. Burt wants to sell the store to Discount Auto Centers and assign to Discount the right to have Jenny not compete. Burt can

a. sell the business and assign the right.
b. sell the business but not assign the right.
c. assign the right but not sell the business.
d. neither assign the right nor sell the business.

_____ **5.** Dick contracts with Jane to cut the grass on Jane's lawn. Dick delegates performance of the duty to Sally with Jane's assent. Who owes Jane a duty to cut her grass?

a. Dick, but not Sally.
b. Sally, but not Dick.
c. Both Dick and Sally.
d. Neither Dick nor Sally.

_____ **6.** Nick contracts with Kathy to paint Nick's portrait. Kathy's right to receive payment for the work

a. cannot be assigned.
b. can be assigned if the duty to paint the portrait is delegated.
c. can be assigned if Nick agrees.
d. can be assigned under any circumstances.

_____ **7.** A contract for a sale of goods between John and Mary provides that the right to receive damages for its breach cannot be assigned. This clause

a. is not effective.
b. is effective only before the contract is executed.
c. is effective only after the contract is executed.
d. is effective under all circumstances.

_____ **8.** Fred unconditionally assigns to Ellen his rights under a contract with Paul. Fred's rights under the contract

a. continue until the contract is fully executed.
b. continue until Paul performs his obligations under the contract.
c. continue until Ellen receives Paul's performance.
d. are extinguished.

_____ **9.** Ann has a right to receive payment under a contract with Bill. Without notice, Ann assigns the right first to Carl and then to Diane. In most states, the party with priority to the right would be

a. Ann.
b. Bill.
c. Carl.
d. Diane.

ISSUE SPOTTERS

1. Brian owes Jeff $100. Ed tells Brian to give him the money and he'll pay Jeff. Brian gives Ed the money. Ed never pays Jeff. Can Jeff successfully sue Ed for the money?

2. A&B Construction Company contracts to build a house for Mike. The contract states that "any assignment of this contract renders the contract void." After A&B builds the house, but before Mike pays, A&B assigns its right to payment to Ace Credit Company. Can Ace enforce the contract against Mike?

Contract Discharge and Remedies

LEARNING OBJECTIVES

When you finish this chapter, you should be able to:

1. Explain the difference between complete and substantial contractual performance.
2. Describe how parties can discharge their contract by agreement.
3. Identify different types of damages.
4. Define the remedy of rescission and restitution.
5. Explain the remedy of specific performance.

FACING A LEGAL PROBLEM

The DeLeons contract with a construction company to build a house. The contract specifies Brand X plasterboard. The builder cannot obtain Brand X, and the DeLeons are on holiday hiking in the mountains in France and are unreachable. The builder decides to install Brand Y instead, which she knows is identical in quality and durability to Brand X. All other aspects of construction conform to the contract. *Does this deviation constitute a breach of contract? Can the DeLeons avoid their obligation to pay the builder because Brand Y plasterboard was used instead of Brand X?*

Parties to a contract need to know when their contract is terminated. In other words, the parties need to know when their contractual duties are at an end. This chapter deals first with the *discharge* of a contract, which is normally accomplished when both parties have performed the acts promised in the contract. We look at the degree of *performance* required and at some other ways in which discharge can occur.

When it is no longer advantageous for a party to fulfill his or her contractual obligations, breach of contract may result. A **breach of contract** occurs when a party fails to perform part or all of the required duties under a contract. Once this occurs, the other party—the nonbreaching party—can choose one or more of several remedies. These remedies are discussed in the last part of this chapter.

Breach of Contract
Failure, without legal excuse, of a promisor to perform the obligations of a contract.

Discharge
The termination of one's obligation. In contract law, discharge occurs when the parties have fully performed their contractual obligations or when events, conduct of the parties, or operation of the law releases the parties from further performance.

Performance
In contract law, the fulfillment of one's duties arising under a contract with another; the normal way of discharging one's contractual obligations.

Contract Discharge

The most common way to **discharge** (terminate) one's contractual duties is by **performance** (fulfillment) of those duties. In addition to performance, there are numerous other ways in which a contract can be discharged, including discharge by agreement of the parties and discharge based on impossibility of performance.

DISCHARGE BY PERFORMANCE

TENDER
A timely offer or expression of willingness to pay a debt or perform an obligation.

The contract comes to an end when both parties fulfill their respective duties by performance of the acts they have promised. Performance can also be accomplished by tender. **Tender** is an unconditional offer to perform by a person who is ready, willing, and able to do so. Therefore, a seller who places goods at the disposal of a buyer has tendered delivery and can demand payment according to the terms of the agreement. A buyer who offers to pay for goods has tendered payment and can demand delivery of the goods. Once performance has been tendered, the party making the tender has done everything possible to carry out the terms of the contract. If the other party refuses to perform, the party making the tender can consider the duty discharged and sue for breach of contract.

LEARNING OBJECTIVE NO. 1
Explaining the Difference between Complete and Substantial Contractual Performance

Complete versus Substantial Performance. It is important to distinguish between *complete performance* and *substantial performance.* Normally, conditions expressly stated in the contract must fully occur in all aspects for complete (or strict) performance to take place. Any deviation breaches the contract and discharges the other party's obligation to perform. Although in most contracts the parties fully discharge their obligations by complete performance, sometimes a party fails to fulfill all of the duties or completes the duties in a manner contrary to the terms of the contract. The issue then arises as to whether the performance was sufficiently substantial to discharge the contractual obligations.

To qualify as substantial, the performance must not vary greatly from the performance promised in the contract. It must result in substantially the same benefits as those promised in the contract. If performance is substantial, the other party's duty to perform remains absolute (less damages, if any, for the minor deviations). If performance is not substantial, there is a *material breach*—the nonbreaching party is excused from performance and can sue for damages caused by the breach.

In the legal problem set out at the beginning of this chapter, a contract specified Brand X plasterboard, but the builder substituted Brand Y, which is identical in quality and durability. *Does this deviation from the contract constitute a breach? Can the buyers (the DeLeons) avoid the contract on this basis?* Very likely, a court would hold that the builder had substantially performed her end of the bargain, and the buyers are therefore obligated to pay. *What if the plasterboard substituted for Brand X had been inferior in quality, reducing the value of the house by $3,000?* A court would likely hold that the contract had been substantially performed and the contract price should be paid, less the $3,000.

Performance to the Satisfaction of Another. Contracts often state that completed work must personally satisfy one of the parties or a third person.

When the subject matter of the contract is personal, performance must actually satisfy the party whose satisfaction is required. For example, contracts for portraits, works of art, medical or dental work, and tailoring are personal. Only the personal satisfaction of the party is sufficient to fulfill the contract—unless the party expresses dissatisfaction only to avoid payment or otherwise is not acting in good faith.

If you cannot perform a contract, consider making a cash offer to "buy" a release. If anything other than an insignificant amount of money is involved, however, work with an attorney in making the offer.

Contracts that involve mechanical fitness, utility, or marketability (such as "the pump must be mounted on a platform") need only be performed to the satisfaction of a reasonable person unless they *expressly state otherwise.* When contracts require performance to the satisfaction of a third party (such as "the road must be graded to the satisfaction of the supervising engineer"), the courts are divided. A majority of courts require the work to be satisfactory to a reasonable person, but some courts hold that the personal satisfaction of the third party must be met.

Discharge by Agreement

Any contract can be discharged by the agreement of the parties. This agreement can be in the original contract, or the parties can form a new contract for the express purpose of discharging the original contract.

LEARNING OBJECTIVE NO. 2
Describing Methods by Which Parties Can Discharge Their Contract by Agreement

Discharge by Rescission. *Rescission* is the process in which the parties cancel the contract and are returned to the positions they occupied prior to the contract's formation. For *mutual rescission* to take place, the parties must make another agreement that also satisfies the legal requirements for a contract—there must be an *offer,* an *acceptance,* and *consideration.* Ordinarily, if the parties agree to rescind the original contract, their promises *not* to perform those acts promised in the original contract will be legal consideration for the second contract. This occurs when the contract is executory on *both* sides (that is, neither party has completed performance). Contracts that are *executed* on *one* side (one party has performed) can be rescinded only if the party who has performed receives consideration for the promise to call off the deal.

Discharge by Novation. The process of **novation** substitutes a third party for one of the original parties. Essentially, the parties to the original contract and one or more new parties all get together and agree to the substitution. The requirements of a novation are as follows:

NOVATION
The substitution, by agreement, of a new contract for an old one, with the rights under the old one being terminated. Typically, there is a substitution of a new person who is responsible for the contract and the removal of the original party's rights and duties under the contract.

1. The existence of a previous, valid obligation.
2. Agreement by all the parties to a new contract.
3. The extinguishing of the old obligation (discharge of the prior party).
4. A new, valid contract.

IN THE COURTROOM

You contract with A. Logan Enterprises to sell it your office-equipment business under an installment sales contract requiring twelve monthly payments. Logan later decides not to buy the business but knows of another party, MBI Corporation, interested in doing so. All three of you get together and agree to a new contract under which MBI agrees to purchase your business. *Is the original contract discharged and replaced with the new contract?* As long as the new contract is supported by consideration, the novation discharges the original contract between you and Logan and replaces it with the new contract between you and MBI. Logan prefers the novation over an assignment, because it discharges all the liabilities stemming from its contract with you. If Logan had merely assigned the contract to MBI, Logan would have remained liable to you for the payments if MBI defaulted.

Discharge by Substituted Agreement. A *substituted agreement* is a new contract between the same parties that expressly or impliedly revokes and discharges a prior contract. The parties involved may simply want a new agreement with somewhat different terms, so they expressly state in a new contract that the old contract is now discharged. They can also make the new contract without expressly stating that the old contract is discharged. If the parties do not expressly discharge the old contract, it will be *impliedly* discharged by the different terms of the new contract.

ACCORD AND SATISFACTION
An agreement and payment (or other performance) between two parties, one of whom has a right of action against the other. After the agreement has been made and payment or other performance has been tendered, the "accord and satisfaction" is complete.

Discharge by Accord and Satisfaction. In an **accord and satisfaction,** the parties agree to accept performance different from the performance originally promised. An *accord* is defined as an executory contract (one that has not yet been performed) to perform some act in order to satisfy an existing contractual duty. The duty is not yet discharged. A *satisfaction* is the performance of the accord. An *accord* and its *satisfaction* (performance) discharge the original contractual obligation.

Once the accord has been made, the original obligation is merely suspended unless the accord agreement is breached. Thus, the obligor can discharge the obligation by performing the obligation agreed to in the accord. Likewise, if the obligor refuses to perform the accord, the obligee can bring an action on the original obligation.

IN THE COURTROOM

Shea obtains a judgment against Marla for $4,000 in cash. Later both parties agree that the judgment can be satisfied by Marla's transfer of her automobile to Shea. This agreement to accept the auto in lieu of $4,000 in cash is the accord. *If Marla transfers her automobile to Shea, this performance is the satisfaction. If Marla refuses to transfer her car, is the accord breached? Would Shea have any recourse against Marla?* Yes, to both questions. Marla's refusal to transfer the car would be a breach of the accord. Because the original obligation is merely suspended, Shea can bring an action to enforce the judgment for $4,000 in cash.

When Performance Is Impossible or Impracticable

Impossibility of Performance
A doctrine under which a party to a contract is relieved of his or her duty to perform when performance becomes impossible or totally impracticable (through no fault of either party).

After a contract has been made, performance may become impossible in an objective sense. This is known as **impossibility of performance** and may discharge a contract. This *objective impossibility* ("It can't be done") must be distinguished from *subjective impossibility* ("I simply can't do it"). Examples of *subjective* impossibility include contracts in which goods cannot be delivered on time because of freight car shortages and contracts in which money cannot be paid on time because the bank is closed. In effect, the party in these cases is saying, "It is impossible for *me* to perform," not "It is impossible for *anyone* to perform." Accordingly, such excuses do not discharge a contract, and the nonperforming party is normally held in breach of contract.

Impossibility of Performance. Certain situations generally qualify under the objective-impossibility rules to discharge contractual obligations:

1. When one of the parties to a personal contract *dies or becomes incapacitated prior to performance.* For example, Fred, a famous dancer, contracts with Ethereal Dancing Guild to play a leading role in its new ballet. Before the ballet can be performed, Fred becomes ill and dies. His personal performance was essential to the completion of the contract. Thus, his death discharges the contract.
2. When the *specific* subject matter of the contract is destroyed. For example, A-1 Farm Equipment agrees to sell Gudgel a specific tractor on its lot and promises to have it ready for Gudgel to pick up on Saturday. On Friday night, a bus veers off the nearby highway and smashes into the tractor, destroying it beyond repair. The accident renders A-1's performance impossible.
3. When a change in the *law* renders performance illegal. An example is a contract to loan money at 20 percent, when the legal interest rate is changed to make loans in excess of 12 percent illegal. Another example is a contract to build an apartment building, when the zoning laws are changed to prohibit the construction of residential rental property. Both changes render the contracts impossible to perform.

Commercial Impracticability. Performance becomes *commercially impracticable* when it turns out to be more difficult or expensive than anticipated. This is known as the doctrine of **commercial impracticability.** For example, in one case, a court held that a contract was discharged because a party would have to pay ten times more than the original estimate to excavate (remove from the ground) a certain amount of gravel.

Caution should be used in invoking the doctrine of commercial impracticability. The added burden of performing must be *extreme* and must *not* be foreseeable by the parties at the time the contract is made.

COMMERCIAL IMPRACTICABILITY
A doctrine under which a party may be excused from performing a contract when (1) a contingency occurs, (2) the contingency's occurrence makes performance impracticable, and (3) the nonoccurrence of the contingency was a basic assumption on which the contract was made.

Temporary Impossibility. An occurrence or event (such as war) that makes it temporarily impossible to perform the act for which a party has contracted operates to *suspend* performance until the impossibility ceases. Then, ordinarily, the parties must perform the contract as originally agreed. If, however, the lapse of time and the change in circumstances make it substantially more burdensome for the parties to perform the promised acts, the contract is discharged.

Contract Remedies

A **remedy** is the relief provided for an innocent party when the other party has breached the contract. It is the means employed to enforce a right or to redress an injury. The most common remedies are *damages, rescission and restitution,* and *specific performance.*

REMEDY
The relief given to innocent parties, by law or by contract, to enforce a right or to prevent or compensate for the violation of a right.

DAMAGES

A breach of contract entitles the nonbreaching party to sue for damages (money). **Damages** are designed to compensate the nonbreaching party for the loss of the bargain. Generally, innocent parties are to be placed in the position they would have occupied had the contract been performed. Different types of damages are discussed in the sections that follow.

LEARNING OBJECTIVE NO. 3
Identifying Different Types of Damages

DAMAGES
Money sought as a remedy for a breach of contract or for a tortious act.

Compensatory Damages. Damages compensating the nonbreaching party for the loss of the bargain are known as **compensatory damages.** These damages compensate the injured party only for injuries actually sustained and proved to have arisen directly from the loss of the bargain due to the breach of contract. Compensatory damages simply replace the loss caused by the wrong or injury.

COMPENSATORY DAMAGES
A money award equivalent to the actual value of injuries or damages sustained by the aggrieved party.

The amount of compensatory damages is the difference between the value of the breaching party's promised performance and the value of his or her actual performance. This amount is reduced by any loss that the injured party has avoided, however. Expenses or costs that are caused directly by a breach of contract—such as those incurred to obtain performance from another source—are *incidental damages.* For example, if you are hired to perform certain services during August for $3,000, but the employer breaches the contract and you find another job that pays only $500, you can recover $2,500 as compensatory damages, plus the expenses to find the other job as incidental damages.

The measurement of compensatory damages varies by type of contract. In a contract for a sale of goods, the usual measure of compensatory damages is an amount equal to the difference between the contract price and the market price (at the time and place of delivery).

For a discussion of how "smart contracts" in the future might make breach of contract expensive to the breaching party, go to

http://www.best.com/~szabo/smart.contracts.2.html

IN THE COURTROOM

MediQuick Laboratories contracts with Cal Computer Industries to purchase ten Model X-15 computer workstations for $8,000 each. *If Cal Computer fails to deliver the ten workstations, and the current market price of the workstations is $8,150 each, what would be MediQuick's measure of damages?* MediQuick's measure of damages is $1,500 (10 x $150), plus incidental damages. In cases in which the breach is by the buyer, and the seller has not as yet produced the goods, compensatory damages normally equal the lost profits on the sale, not the difference between the contract price and the market price.

CONSEQUENTIAL DAMAGES
Special damages that compensate for a loss that is not direct or immediate (for example, lost profits). The special damages must have been reasonably foreseeable at the time the breach or injury occurred.

Consequential Damages. **Consequential damages,** which are also referred to as *special damages,* are foreseeable damages that result from a party's breach of contract. They differ from compensatory damages in that they are caused by special circumstances beyond the contract itself. When a seller does not deliver goods, knowing that a buyer is planning to resell those goods immediately, consequential damages are awarded for the loss of profits from the planned resale. For a nonbreaching party to recover consequential damages, the breaching party must know (or have reason to know) that special circumstances will cause the nonbreaching party to suffer an additional loss.

IN THE COURTROOM

Gilmore contracts to have a specific item shipped to her—one that she desperately needs to repair her printing press. Gilmore tells the shipper that she must receive the item by Monday or she will not be able to print her paper and will lose $750. *If the shipper is late, what can Gilmore recover?* Gilmore can recover the consequential damages caused by the delay (the $750 in losses).

MITIGATION OF DAMAGES
A rule requiring a plaintiff to have done whatever was reasonable to minimize the damages caused by the defendant.

Mitigation of Damages. In most situations, when a breach of contract occurs, the injured party has a duty to mitigate, or reduce, the damages that he or she suffers. Under this doctrine of **mitigation of damages,** the required action depends on the nature of the situation. For example, in the majority of states, a wrongfully terminated employee has a duty to mitigate damages suffered by the employers' breach. The damages they will be awarded are their salaries less the incomes they would have received in similar jobs obtained by reasonable means.

PUNITIVE DAMAGES
Compensation in excess of actual or consequential damages. They are awarded in order to punish the wrongdoer and usually will be awarded only in cases involving willful or malicious misconduct.

Punitive Damages. **Punitive damages,** which are also known as *exemplary damages,* are generally not recoverable in an action for breach of contract. Punitive damages are designed to punish and make an example of a wrongdoer for the purpose of deterring similar conduct in the future. Such damages have no legitimate place in contract law because they are, in essence, penalties, and a breach of contract is not unlawful in a criminal sense. A contract is a civil relationship between the parties. The law may compensate one party for the loss of bargain—no more and no less.

In a few situations, a person's actions can cause both a breach of contract and a tort. For example, the parties can establish by contract a certain reasonable standard or duty of care. Failure to live up to that standard is a breach of contract, and the act itself may constitute negligence. An intentional tort (such as fraud) may also be tied to a breach of contract. In such a case, it is possible for the nonbreaching party to recover punitive damages for the tort in addition to compensatory and consequential damages for the breach of contract.

LIQUIDATED DAMAGES
An amount, stipulated in the contract, that the parties to a contract believe to be a reasonable estimation of the damages that will occur in the event of a breach.

PENALTY
A sum inserted into a contract, not as a measure of compensation for its breach but rather as punishment for a default. The agreement as to the amount will not be enforced, and recovery will be limited to actual damages.

Liquidated Damages. A **liquidated damages** provision in a contract specifies a certain amount of money to be paid in the event of a future default or breach of contract. (*Liquidated* means determined, settled, or fixed.) Liquidated damages differ from penalties. A **penalty** specifies a certain amount to be paid in the event of a default or breach of contract and is *designed to penalize* the breaching party. Liquidated damage provisions normally are enforceable; penalty provisions are not.

To determine whether a particular provision is for liquidated damages or for a penalty, answer two questions: First, were the potential damages that would be incurred if the contract were not performed on time difficult to estimate when the contract was formed? Second, was the amount set as damages a reasonable estimate of those potential damages? If both answers are yes, the provision is for liquidated damages and will be enforced. If either answer is no, the provision is for a penalty and normally will not be enforced.

RESCISSION AND RESTITUTION

LEARNING OBJECTIVE NO. 4
Defining the Remedy of Rescission and Restitution

Rescission is essentially an action to undo, or cancel, a contract—to return nonbreaching parties to the positions that they occupied prior to the transaction. When fraud, mistake, duress, or failure of consideration is present, rescission is available. The failure of one party to perform entitles the other party to rescind the contract. The rescinding party must give prompt notice to the breaching party. To rescind a contract, both parties must make **restitution** to each other by returning goods, property, or money previously conveyed.

RESTITUTION
A remedy under which a person is restored to his or her original position prior to a contract.

If the goods or property can be returned, they must be. If the goods or property have been consumed, restitution must be an equivalent amount of money. Essentially, restitution refers to the recapture of a benefit conferred on the defendant through which the defendant has been unjustly enriched.

IN THE COURTROOM

Alima pays $10,000 to Milos in return for Milos's promise to design a house for her. The next day Milos calls Alima and tells her that he has taken a position with a large architectural firm in another state and cannot design the house. Alima decides to hire another architect that afternoon. *If Alima sues Milos for restitution, what can Alima recover?* Alima can get restitution of $10,000, because an unjust benefit of $10,000 was conferred on Milos.

SPECIFIC PERFORMANCE

LEARNING OBJECTIVE NO. 5
Explaining the Remedy of Specific Performance

The equitable remedy of **specific performance** calls for the performance of the act promised in the contract. This remedy is quite attractive to the nonbreaching party, because it provides the exact bargain promised in the contract. It also avoids some of the problems inherent in a suit for money damages. First, the nonbreaching party need not worry about collecting the judgment. Second, the nonbreaching party need not look around for another contract. Third, the actual performance may be more valuable than the money damages. Although the equitable remedy of specific performance is often preferable to other remedies, it is not granted unless the party's legal remedy (money damages) is inadequate.

SPECIFIC PERFORMANCE
An equitable remedy requiring exactly the performance that was specified in a contract. Usually granted only when money damages would be an inadequate remedy and the subject matter of the contract is unique (for example, real property).

For example, contracts for the sale of goods, such as wheat or corn, that are readily available on the market rarely qualify for specific performance. Damages ordinarily are adequate in such situations because substantially identical goods can be bought or sold in the market. If the goods are unique, however, a court of equity will decree specific performance. For example, paintings, sculptures, or rare books or coins are so unique that damages will not enable a buyer to obtain substantially identical goods in the market. The same principle applies to contracts relating to sales of land or interests in land—each parcel of land is unique.

The following site offers information on contract law, including breach of contract and remedies: **http://www.nolo.com/Chunkcm/CM9.html**

Courts of equity normally refuse to grant specific performance of personal-service contracts. Public policy strongly discourages involuntary servitude. Moreover, the courts do not want to monitor a personal-service contract. For example, if you contract with a brain surgeon to perform brain surgery on you, and the surgeon refuses to perform, the court would not compel (and you certainly would not want) the surgeon to perform under these circumstances. There is no way the court can ensure meaningful performance in such a situation.

TERMS AND CONCEPTS FOR REVIEW

accord and satisfaction 171
breach of contract 169
commercial impracticability 173
compensatory damages 173
consequential damages 174
damages 173
discharge 169
impossibility of performance 172
liquidated damages 174
mitigation of damages 174
novation 171
penalty 174
performance 169
punitive damages 174
remedy 173
restitution 175
specific performance 175
tender 170

CHAPTER SUMMARY • CONTRACT DISCHARGE AND REMEDIES

Discharge	**1.** *Discharge by performance*—A contract may be discharged by complete (strict) or substantial performance. Totally inadequate performance constitutes a material breach of contract. In some cases, performance must be to the satisfaction of another. **2.** *Discharge by agreement of the parties*—Parties may agree to discharge their contractual obligations in several ways: (a) by mutually agreeing to rescind (cancel) the contract; (b) by novation, in which a new party is substituted for one of the primary parties to a contract; (c) by substituted agreement, in which the parties make a new contract that revokes the prior contract; and (d) by accord and satisfaction, in which the parties agree to render performance different from that originally agreed upon. **3.** *Discharge by objective impossibility of performance owing to one of the following:* **a.** The death or incapacity of a person whose performance is essential to the completion of the contract. **b.** The destruction of the specific subject matter of the contract. **c.** A change in the law that renders illegal the performance called for by the contract. **4.** *Discharge by commercial impracticability of performance.*
Damages	A legal remedy designed, on the breach of a contract, to compensate the nonbreaching party for the loss of the bargain by placing the parties in the positions that they would have occupied had the contract been fully performed. **1.** *Compensatory damages*—Damages that compensate a nonbreaching party for the loss of the bargain. In contracts for sales of goods, the usual measure of such damages is the difference between the contract price and the market price. **2.** *Consequential damages*—Damages resulting from special circumstances beyond the contract. The breaching party must have known at the time the contract was formed that special circumstances existed and that the nonbreaching party would incur additional loss on breach of the contract. **3.** *Punitive damages*—Damages awarded to punish the breaching party. Usually not awarded unless a tort is involved. **4.** *Liquidated damages*—Damages that may be specified in a contract as the amount to be paid to the nonbreaching party if the contract is breached. Such clauses are enforced if the damages were difficult to estimate at the time the contract was formed and if the amount stipulated is reasonable. If construed to be a penalty, the clause cannot be enforced.
Rescission and Restitution	**1.** *Rescission*—An action by prompt notice to cancel the contract and return the parties to the positions that they occupied prior to the transaction. Available when fraud, mistake, duress, or failure of consideration is present.

CHAPTER SUMMARY • *Continued*

Rescission and Restitution—continued	**2.** *Restitution*—When a contract is rescinded, both parties must make restitution to each other by returning the goods, property, or money previously conveyed.
Specific Performance	An equitable remedy calling for the performance of the act promised in the contract. Only available in special situations—such as those involving contracts for the sale of unique goods or land—and when damages would be an inadequate remedy.

HYPOTHETICAL QUESTIONS

15–1. Novation versus Accord and Satisfaction. Doug owes creditor Cartwright $1,000, which is due and payable on June 1. Doug has a car accident, misses several months of work, and consequently does not have the money to pay Cartwright on June 1. Doug's father, Bert, offers to pay Cartwright $1,100 in four equal installments if Cartwright will discharge Doug from any further liability on the debt. Cartwright accepts. In view of these events, answer the following questions:

(a) Is the transaction a novation, or is it an accord and satisfaction? Explain.

(b) Does the contract between Bert and Cartwright have to be in writing to be enforceable? (Review the Statute of Frauds.) Explain.

15–2. Impossibility of Performance. Millie contracted to sell Frank 1,000 bushels of corn to be grown on Millie's farm. Owing to drought conditions during the growing season, Millie's yield was much less than anticipated, and she could deliver only 250 bushels to Frank. Frank accepted the lesser amount but sued Millie for breach of contract. Can Millie defend successfully on the basis of objective impossibility of performance? Explain.

REAL WORLD CASE PROBLEM

15–3. Mitigation of Damages. Charles Kloss had worked for Honeywell, Inc. for over fifteen years when Honeywell decided to transfer the employees at its Ballard facility to its Harbour Pointe facility. Honeywell planned to hire a medical person at the Harbour Pointe facility and promised Kloss that if he completed a nursing program and became a registered nurse (RN), the company would hire him for the medical position. When Kloss graduated from his RN program, however, Honeywell did not assign him to a nursing or medical position. Instead, the company game Kloss a job in its maintenance department. Shortly thereafter, Kloss left the company and eventually sued Honeywell for damages (lost wages) resulting from Honeywell's breach of the employment contract. One of the issues facing the court was whether Kloss, by voluntarily leaving the maintenance job at Honeywell, had failed to mitigate his damages. How should the court rule on this issue? Discuss. [*Kloss v. Honeywell, Inc.*, 77 Wash.App. 294, 890 P.2d 480 (1995)]

For updated links to resources available on the Web, as well as a variety of other materials, visit this text's Web site at **http://blte.westbuslaw.com**.

The following site offers information on contract law, including breach of contract and remedies:

http://www.law.cornell.edu/topics/contracts.html

ONLINE LEGAL RESEARCH

Go to **http://blte.westbuslaw.com**, the Web site that accompanies this text. Select "Internet Applications," and then click on "Chapter 15." There you will find the following Internet research exercise that you can perform to learn more about breach of contract and damages:

Activity 15–1: Contract Damages and Contract Theory

Chapter 15 ■ WORK SET

TRUE-FALSE QUESTIONS

_____ **1.** Complete performance occurs when a contract's conditions are fully satisfied.

_____ **2.** A material breach of contract does not discharge the other party's duty to perform.

_____ **3.** An executory contract cannot be rescinded.

_____ **4.** Normal damages compensate a nonbreaching party for the loss of the contract or give a nonbreaching party the benefit of the contract.

_____ **5.** Punitive damages are usually not awarded for a breach of contract.

_____ **6.** Liquidated damages are uncertain in amount.

_____ **7.** Consequential damages are awarded for foreseeable losses caused by special circumstances beyond the contract.

_____ **8.** Specific performance is available only when damages are also an adequate remedy.

MULTIPLE-CHOICE QUESTIONS

_____ **1.** Sam owes Lyle $10,000. Sam promises, in writing, to give Lyle a video-game machine in lieu of payment of the debt. Lyle agrees and Sam delivers the machine. Substituting and performing one duty for another is

a. a rescission.
b. an accord and satisfaction.
c. a novation.
d. none of the above.

_____ **2.** C&D Services contracts with Ace Concessions, Inc., to service Ace's vending machines. Later, C&D wants Dean Vending Services to assume the duties under a new contract. Ace consents. This is

a. a rescission.
b. an accord and satisfaction.
c. an alteration of contract.
d. a novation.

_____ **3.** Kate contracts with Bob to transport Bob's goods to his stores. If this contract is discharged like most contracts, it will be discharged by

a. performance.
b. agreement.
c. operation of law.
d. none of the above.

_____ **4.** Alan contracts with Pam to build a shopping mall on Pam's land. Before construction begins, the city enacts a law that makes it illegal to build a mall in Pam's area. Performance of this contract is

a. not affected.
b. temporarily suspended.
c. discharged.
d. discharged on Pam's obligations only.

_____ **5.** Mix Corporation contracts to sell to Frosty Malts, Inc., eight steel mixers. When Mix refuses to deliver, Frosty buys mixers from MaxCo, for 25 percent more than the contract price. Frosty is entitled to damages equal to

a. what Mix's profits would have been.
b. the price Frosty would have had to pay Mix.
c. the difference between what Frosty would have had to pay Mix and what Frosty did pay MaxCo.
d. what Frosty paid MaxCo.

_____ **6.** Dave contracts with Paul to buy six computers. Dave tells Paul that if the goods are not delivered on Monday, he will lose $12,000 in business. Paul does not deliver the goods on Monday. Dave is forced to rent computers on Tuesday. Paul delivers four computers on Friday. Dave is entitled to

a. compensatory damages.
b. incidental damages.
c. consequential damages.
d. all of the above.

_____ **7.** Jay agrees in writing to sell a warehouse and the land on which it is located to Nora. When Jay refuses to go through with the deal, Nora sues. Jay must transfer the land and warehouse to Nora if she is awarded

a. rescission and restitution.
b. specific performance.
c. reformation.
d. none of the above.

_____ **8.** Jake agrees to hire Teresa. Their contract provides that if Jake fires Teresa, she is to be paid whatever amount would have been payable if she had worked for the full term. This clause is

a. a liquidated damages clause.
b. a penalty clause.
c. both a and b.
d. none of the above.

ISSUE SPOTTERS

1. George contracts to build a storage shed for Ron. Ron pays George in full, but George completes only half the work. Ron pays Paula $500 to finish the shed. If Ron sues George, what would be the measure of recovery?

2. Amy contracts to sell her ranch to Mark, who is to take possession on June 1. Amy delays the transfer until August 1. Mark incurs expenses in providing for cattle that he bought to stock the ranch. When they made the contract, Amy had no reason to know of the cattle. Is Amy liable for Mark's expenses in providing for the cattle?

UNIT THREE
SALES, LEASES, AND E-COMMERCE

UNIT OUTLINE

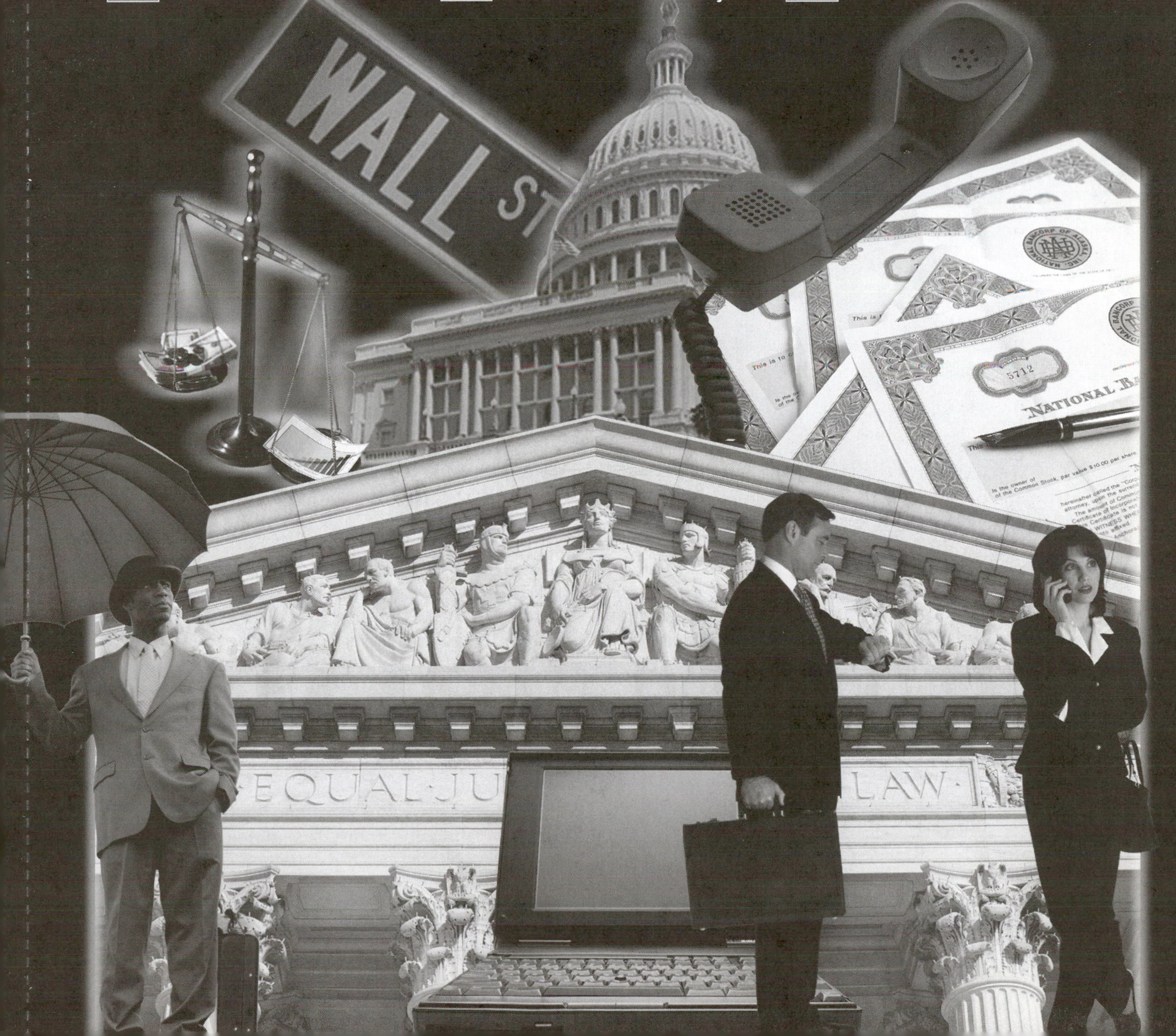

Introduction to Sales and Lease Contracts

LEARNING OBJECTIVES

When you finish this chapter, you should be able to:

1. State the scope of Article 2 of the UCC.
2. Identify how the UCC deals with open contract terms.
3. Explain whether a contract under the UCC contains any additional terms included in the offeree's acceptance.
4. Discuss UCC exceptions to the Statute of Frauds.
5. Describe what a court can do when confronted with an unconscionable contract or clause.

FACING A LEGAL PROBLEM

Advent Systems, Ltd., developed a computerized document management system that Unisys Corporation agreed to sell in the marketplace. When Unisys canceled the arrangement, Advent sued for breach of contract. One of the issues was whether the contract involved primarily a sale of goods. Advent argued that software is not a "good" and that therefore the contract was primarily for services (and thus not subject to the Uniform Commercial Code, which covers only contracts for sales of goods). *How should the court rule?*

When we focus on sales and lease contracts, we move away from common law principles and into the area of statutory law. The state statutory law governing such transactions is based on the Uniform Commercial Code (UCC). The UCC facilitates commercial transactions by making the laws governing sales and lease contracts clearer, simpler, and more readily applicable to the numerous difficulties that can arise during such transactions. Excerpts from the most recent version of the Uniform Commercial Code are included as Appendix B in this text.

SALES CONTRACT
A contract to sell goods.

LEARNING OBJECTIVE NO. 1
Stating the Scope of Article 2 of the UCC

Sales of Goods

A contract for a sale of goods, or **sales contract,** is governed by the common law principles applicable to all contracts, and you should reexamine these principles when studying sales. The law of sales is based both on Article 2 of the UCC and the relevant common law that has not been modified by the UCC. The relationship between general contract law and the law governing contracts for the sales of goods is illustrated in Exhibit 16–1.

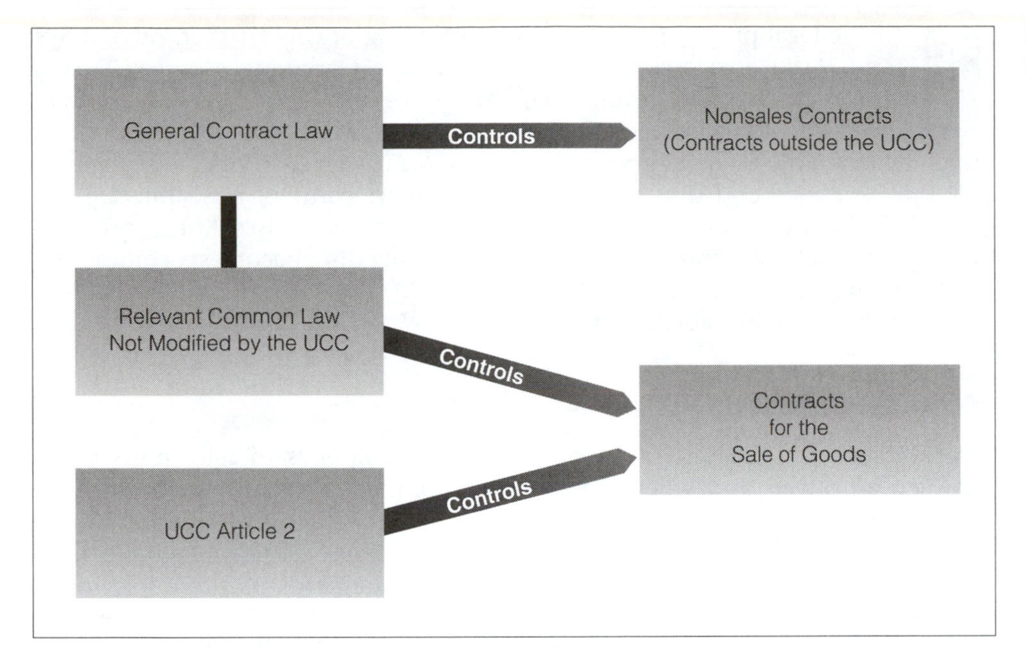

EXHIBIT 16–1
Law Governing Contracts

WHAT IS A SALE?

The UCC states that Article 2 "applies to transactions in goods." This implies a broad scope—covering leases, gifts, bailments (temporary deliveries of personal property), and purchases of goods. In this chapter, however, we treat Article 2 as being applicable only to an actual sale (as would most authorities and courts). A **sale** is officially defined as "the passing of title from the seller to the buyer for a price," where title refers to the formal right of ownership of property. The price may be payable in money or in other goods, services, or realty (real estate).

SALE
The passing of title to property from the seller to the buyer for a price.

WHAT ARE GOODS?

To be characterized as a *good,* an item of property must be *tangible,* and it must be *movable.* **Tangible property** has physical existence—it can be touched or seen. Intangible property—such as corporate stocks and bonds, patents and copyrights, and ordinary contract rights—has only conceptual existence and thus does not come under Article 2. A *movable* item can be carried from place to place.

TANGIBLE PROPERTY
Property that has physical existence (such as a car).

"Things Attached to the Land." Real estate is excluded from Article 2. Real estate includes land, interests in land, and things permanently attached to the land. A contract for the sale of minerals or the like (including oil and gas) or a structure (such as a building) is a contract for a sale of goods *if they are to be severed from the land by the seller.* A sale of growing crops or timber to be cut is a contract for a sale of goods *regardless of who severs them.* Other "things attached" to realty but capable of severance without material harm to the land (such as counters in a restaurant) are considered goods *regardless of who severs them.*

Goods and Services. The majority of courts treat services as being excluded by the UCC. In cases in which goods and services are combined, courts disagree. For example, is the blood furnished to a patient during an operation a "sale of goods" or the "performance of a medical service"? Some courts say it is a good; others say it is a service. Because the UCC does not provide the answer, the courts try to determine which factor is predominant—the good or the service. The UCC does stipulate, however, that serving food or drink to be consumed either on or off restaurant premises is a "sale of goods," at least for the purpose of an implied warranty of merchantability (see Chapter 19).

In the legal problem set out at the beginning of this chapter, Advent Systems, Ltd., developed software that Unisys Corporation agreed to sell. Unisys canceled the arrangement, and Advent sued for breach of contract. One issue was whether software is a good and thus whether the contract involved primarily a sale of goods. *How should the court rule?* The court ruled that software is a good and thus that the Advent-Unisys contract was subject to the UCC. The court compared computer programs to compact discs. Music in itself is not a good but, when transferred to a laser-readable disc, becomes a commodity. A computer program, transferred to a diskette, CD-ROM, or DVD-ROM is tangible, movable, and available for sale.

WHO IS A MERCHANT?

MERCHANT
Under the UCC, a person who deals in goods of the kind involved (see UCC 2–104).

Article 2 governs the sale of goods in general. It applies to sales transactions between all buyers and sellers. In a limited number of instances, however, the UCC presumes that in certain phases of sales transactions involving **merchants,** special business standards ought to be imposed because of the merchants' relatively high degree of commercial expertise. Such standards do not apply to the casual or inexperienced ("consumer") seller or buyer. Under the UCC, a merchant is a person who deals in goods of the kind involved in the sales contract or who, by occupation, holds himself or herself out as having knowledge and skill unique to the practices or goods involved in the transaction.

Leases of Goods

Consumers and business firms lease automobiles, industrial equipment, items for use in the home (such as floor sanders), and many other types of goods. Article 2A of the UCC covers any transaction that creates a lease of goods. Article 2A is essentially a repetition of Article 2, except that it applies to leases of goods, rather than sales of goods, and thus varies to reflect differences between sale and lease transactions.

LEASE AGREEMENT
In regard to the lease of goods, an agreement in which one person (the lessor) agrees to transfer the right to the possession and use of the property to another person (the lessee) in exchange for rental payments.

LESSOR
A person who sells the right to the possession and use of goods to another in exchange for rental payments.

LESSEE
A person who acquires the right to the possession and use of another's goods in exchange for rental payments.

Article 2A defines a **lease agreement** as the lessor and lessee's bargain, as found in their language and as implied by other circumstances, including course of dealing and usage of trade or course of performance. A **lessor** is one who sells the right to the possession and use of goods under a lease. A **lessee** is one who acquires the right to the possession and use of goods under a lease.

Sales and Lease Contracts

The following sections summarize the ways that UCC provisions *change* the effect of the general law of contracts. It is important to remember that parties to sales and lease contracts are free to establish whatever terms they wish. The UCC comes into play when the parties have left a term out of their contract and that omission later gives rise to a dispute.

THE OFFER

In general contract law, the moment a definite offer is met by an unqualified acceptance, a binding contract is formed. In commercial sales transactions, the verbal exchanges, the correspondence, and the actions of the parties may not reveal exactly when a binding contract arises. The UCC states that an agreement sufficient to constitute a contract can exist even if the moment of its making is undetermined.

Open Terms. According to contract law, an offer must be definite enough for the parties (and the courts) to ascertain its essential terms when it is accepted. The

UCC states that a sales or lease contract will not fail for indefiniteness even if one or more terms are left open as long as (1) the parties intended to make a contract and (2) there is a reasonably certain basis for the court to grant an appropriate remedy.

Although the UCC has radically lessened the requirements for definiteness of terms, it has not removed the common law requirement that the contract be at least definite enough for the court to identify the agreement, so as to enforce the contract or award appropriate damages in the event of breach.

The UCC provides numerous *open-term* provisions that can be used to fill the gaps in a contract. Thus, in the case of a dispute, all that is necessary to prove the existence of a contract is an indication (such as a purchase order) that there is a contract. Missing terms can be proved by evidence, or it will be presumed that what the parties intended was whatever is reasonable. The *quantity* of goods involved must be expressly stated, however. If the quantity term is left open, the courts will have no basis for determining a remedy.

For information on the Uniform Commercial Code, go to

http://www.law.cornell.edu/ucc/ucc.table.html

LEARNING OBJECTIVE NO. 2

Identifying How the UCC Deals with Open Contract Terms

Merchant's Firm Offer. Under regular contract principles, an offer can be revoked at any time before acceptance. The UCC has an exception that applies only to **firm offers** for the sale or lease of goods made by a *merchant* (regardless of whether or not the offeree is a merchant). A firm offer exists if a merchant gives *assurances* in a *signed writing* that his or her offer will remain open. A firm offer is irrevocable without the necessity of consideration for the stated period or, if no definite period is stated, for a reasonable period (neither to exceed three months).

FIRM OFFER
An offer (by a merchant) that is irrevocable without consideration for a period of time (not longer than three months). A firm offer by a merchant must be in writing and must be signed by the offeror.

ACCEPTANCE

The following sections examine the UCC provisions covering acceptance. As you will see, acceptance of an offer to buy, sell, or lease goods generally may be made in any reasonable manner and by any reasonable means.

Methods of Acceptance. The common law rule is that an offeror can specify a particular means of acceptance, making that means the only one effective for contract formation. Unauthorized means are effective as long as the acceptance is received by the specified deadline.

When the offeror does not specify a means of acceptance, the UCC provides that acceptance can be made by any means of communication reasonable under the circumstances.

The UCC permits acceptance of an offer to buy goods for current or prompt shipment by either a *promise* to ship or *prompt shipment* of the goods to the buyer. If the seller does not promise to ship the goods that the buyer ordered but instead ships goods that differ from the buyer's order in some way (a different color or size, for example), this shipment constitutes both an *acceptance* (a contract) and a *breach*. This rule does not apply if the seller seasonably (within a reasonable amount of time) notifies the buyer that the nonconforming shipment is offered only as an accommodation or as a favor. The notice of accommodation must clearly indicate to the buyer that the shipment does not constitute an acceptance and that, therefore, no contract has been formed.

IN THE COURTROOM

McIntosh orders five thousand *blue* widgets from Halderson. Halderson ships five thousand *black* widgets to McIntosh, notifying McIntosh that, as Halderson only has black widgets in stock, these are sent as an accommodation. *Is the shipment of black widgets an acceptance or an offer?* The shipment is an offer. A contract will be formed only if McIntosh accepts the black widgets. If Halderson ships black widgets *without* notifying McIntosh that the goods are being sent *as an accommodation,* Halderson's shipment is both an acceptance of McIntosh's offer and a breach of the resulting contract. McIntosh may sue Halderson for any appropriate damages.

Notice of Acceptance. Under the common law, because a unilateral offer invites acceptance by performance, the offeree need not notify the offeror of the performance unless the offeror would not otherwise know about it (see Chapter 8). Under the UCC, however, if a sales contract is unilateral, the offeror must be notified of the offeree's performance (acceptance) within a reasonable time, or the offeror can treat the offer as having lapsed.

Additional Terms. Under the common law, variations in terms between the offer and the offeree's acceptance violate the mirror image rule, which requires that the terms of an acceptance exactly mirror the offer (see Chapter 8). This rule causes considerable problems in commercial transactions, particularly when different standardized purchase order forms are used. Exhibit 16–2 indicates the kinds of terms and conditions that may be included in a standard purchase order form.

LEARNING OBJECTIVE NO. 3

Explaining Whether a Contract under the UCC Contains Any Additional Terms Included in the Offeree's Acceptance

To avoid these problems, the UCC dispenses with the mirror image rule. Under the UCC, a contract is formed if the offeree makes a definite expression of acceptance (such as signing the form in the appropriate location), even though the terms of the acceptance modify or add to the terms of the original offer.

What happens to these new terms? The answer depends on whether the parties are nonmerchants or merchants.

When One or Both Parties Are Nonmerchants. If one (or both) of the parties is a *nonmerchant,* the contract is formed according to the terms of the original offer submitted by the original offeror and not according to the additional terms of the acceptance.

IN THE COURTROOM

Tolsen offers in writing to sell his personal computer to Valdez for $600. Valdez faxes a reply to Tolsen in which Valdez states, "I accept your offer to purchase your computer for $600. I would like a box of computer paper and ten diskettes to be included in the purchase price." *Has Valdez given Tolsen a definite expression of acceptance (creating a contract)?* Yes, he has, even though Valdez's acceptance also suggests an added term for the offer. Because Tolsen is not a merchant, the additional term is merely a proposal (suggestion). Tolsen is not legally obligated to comply with it.

A seller and buyer who frequently do business with each other can agree ahead of time on the general terms and conditions that will apply to all transactions.

When Both Parties Are Merchants. When both parties to the contract are merchants, the additional terms automatically become part of the contract unless (1) the original offer expressly required acceptance of its terms, (2) the new or changed terms materially alter the contract, or (3) the offeror rejects the new or changed terms within a reasonable time.

Modifications Subject to the Offeror's Consent. Regardless of merchant status, the offeree's expression cannot be construed as an acceptance if the modifications are subject to the offeror's assent. For instance, when an offeree says, "I accept your offer if you agree to include ten more units," this is not an acceptance because it includes modifications ("ten more units") subject to the offeror's assent.

EXHIBIT 16–2
An Example of a Purchase Order (Front)

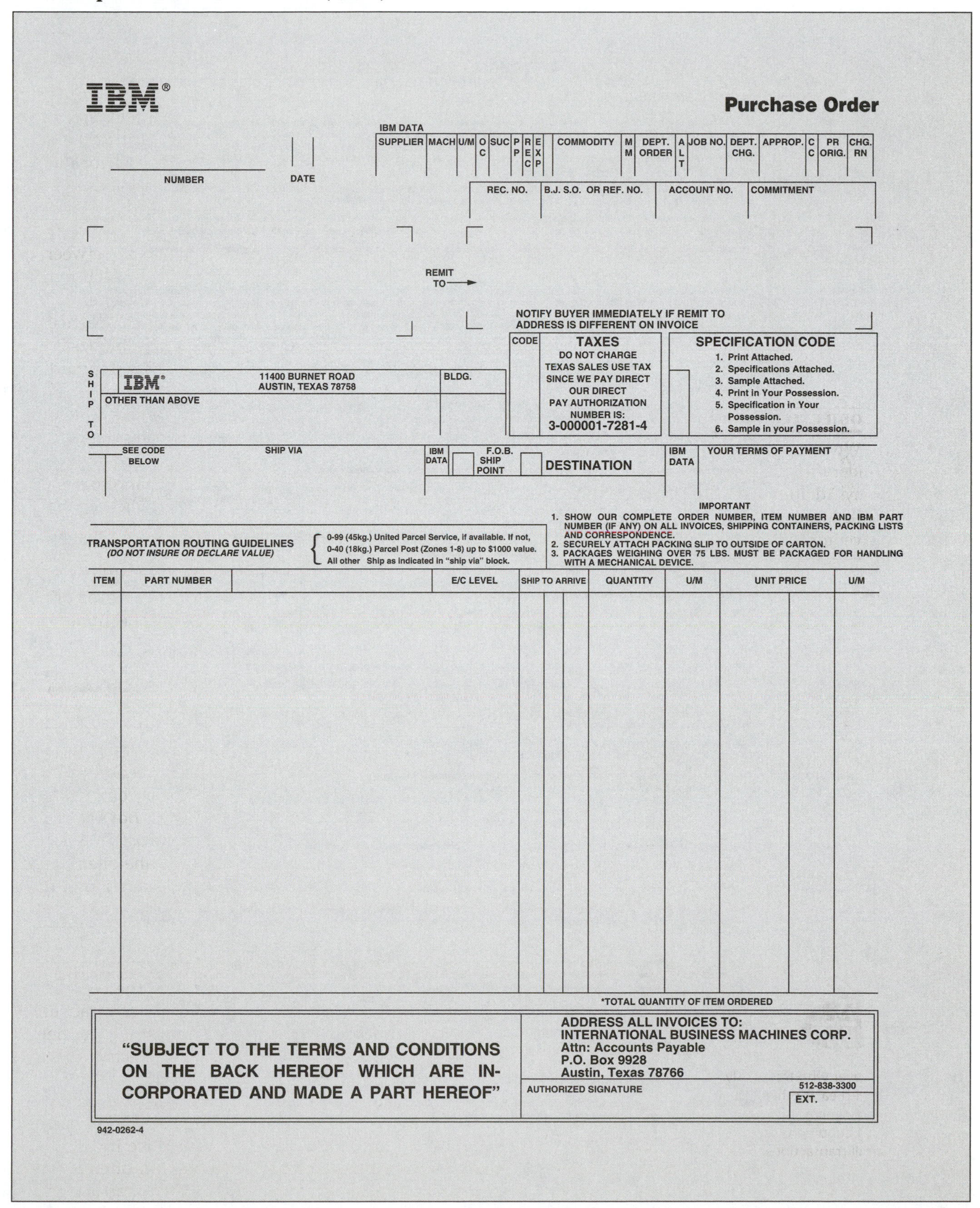

IBM®

Purchase Order

NUMBER   DATE

IBM DATA

SUPPLIER	MACH	U/M	OC	SUC	PPC	REC	EXP	COMMODITY	MM	DEPT. ORDER	ALT	JOB NO.	DEPT. CHG.	APPROP.	CC	PR ORIG.	CHG. RN

REC. NO.	B.J. S.O. OR REF. NO.	ACCOUNT NO.	COMMITMENT

REMIT TO →

NOTIFY BUYER IMMEDIATELY IF REMIT TO ADDRESS IS DIFFERENT ON INVOICE

SHIP TO: IBM® 11400 BURNET ROAD AUSTIN, TEXAS 78758 BLDG.
OTHER THAN ABOVE

CODE
TAXES
DO NOT CHARGE TEXAS SALES USE TAX SINCE WE PAY DIRECT OUR DIRECT PAY AUTHORIZATION NUMBER IS:
3-000001-7281-4

SPECIFICATION CODE
1. Print Attached.
2. Specifications Attached.
3. Sample Attached.
4. Print in Your Possession.
5. Specification in Your Possession.
6. Sample in your Possession.

SEE CODE BELOW | SHIP VIA | IBM DATA | F.O.B. SHIP POINT | DESTINATION | IBM DATA | YOUR TERMS OF PAYMENT

IMPORTANT
1. SHOW OUR COMPLETE ORDER NUMBER, ITEM NUMBER AND IBM PART NUMBER (IF ANY) ON ALL INVOICES, SHIPPING CONTAINERS, PACKING LISTS AND CORRESPONDENCE.
2. SECURELY ATTACH PACKING SLIP TO OUTSIDE OF CARTON.
3. PACKAGES WEIGHING OVER 75 LBS. MUST BE PACKAGED FOR HANDLING WITH A MECHANICAL DEVICE.

TRANSPORTATION ROUTING GUIDELINES
(DO NOT INSURE OR DECLARE VALUE)
0-99 (45kg.) United Parcel Service, if available. If not,
0-40 (18kg.) Parcel Post (Zones 1-8) up to $1000 value.
All other Ship as indicated in "ship via" block.

ITEM	PART NUMBER	E/C LEVEL	SHIP TO ARRIVE	QUANTITY	U/M	UNIT PRICE	U/M

*TOTAL QUANTITY OF ITEM ORDERED

"SUBJECT TO THE TERMS AND CONDITIONS ON THE BACK HEREOF WHICH ARE INCORPORATED AND MADE A PART HEREOF"

ADDRESS ALL INVOICES TO:
INTERNATIONAL BUSINESS MACHINES CORP.
Attn: Accounts Payable
P.O. Box 9928
Austin, Texas 78766

AUTHORIZED SIGNATURE   512-838-3300   EXT.

942-0262-4

Source: Reprinted with the permission of the IBM Corp. © 1985. Copyright: IBM.

EXHIBIT 16–2—Continued
An Example of a Purchase Order (Back)

STANDARD TERMS AND CONDITIONS

IBM EXPRESSLY LIMITS ACCEPTANCE TO THE TERMS SET FORTH ON THE FACE AND REVERSE SIDE OF THIS PURCHASE ORDER AND ANY ATTACHMENTS HERETO:

PURCHASE ORDER CONSTITUTES COMPLETE AGREEMENT	This Purchase order, including the terms and conditions on the face and reverse side hereof and any attachments hereto, contains the complete and final agreement between International Business Machines Corporation (IBM) and Seller. Reference to Seller's bids or proposals, if noted on this order, shall not affect terms and conditions hereof, unless specifically provided to the contrary herein, and no other agreement or quotation in any way modifying any of said terms and conditions will be binding upon IBM unless made in writing and signed by IBM's authorized representative.
ADVERTISING	Seller shall not, without first obtaining the written consent of IBM, in any manner advertise, publish or otherwise disclose the fact that Seller has furnished, or contracted to furnish to IBM, the material and/or services ordered hereunder.
APPLICABLE LAW	The agreement arising pursuant to this order shall be governed by the laws of the State of New York. No rights, remedies and warranties available to IBM under this contract or by operation of law are waived or modified unless expressly waived or modified by IBM in writing.
CASH DISCOUNT OR NET PAYMENT PERIOD	Calculations will be from the date an acceptable invoice is received by IBM. Any other arrangements agreed upon must appear on this order and on the invoice.
CONFIDENTIAL INFORMATION	Seller shall not disclose to any person outside of its employ, or use for any purpose other than to fulfill its obligations under this order, any information received from IBM pursuant to this order, which has been disclosed to Seller by IBM in confidence, except such information which is otherwise publicly available or is publicly disclosed by IBM subsequent to Seller's receipt of such information or is rightfully received by Seller from a third party. Upon termination of this order, Seller shall return to IBM upon request all drawings, blueprints, descriptions or other material received from IBM and all materials containing said confidential information. Also, Seller shall not disclose to IBM any information which Seller deems to be confidential, and it is understood that any information received by IBM, including all manuals, drawings and documents will not be of a confidential nature or restrict, in any manner, the use of such information by IBM. Seller agrees that any legend or other notice on any information supplied by Seller, which is inconsistent with the provisions of this article, does not create any obligation on the part of IBM.
GIFTS	Seller shall not make or offer gifts or gratuities of any type to IBM employees or members of their families. Such gifts or offerings may be construed as Seller's attempt to improperly influence our relationship.
IBM PARTS	All parts and components billed by IBM to Seller for incorporation in work being performed for IBM shall be used solely for such purposes.
OFF-SPECIFICATION	Seller shall obtain from IBM written approval of all off-specification work.
PACKAGES	Packages must bear IBM's order number and show gross, tare and net weights and/or quantity.
PATENTS	Seller will settle or defend, at Seller's expense (and pay any damages, costs or fines resulting from), all proceedings or claims against IBM, its subsidiaries and affiliates and their respective customers, for infringement, or alleged infringement, by the goods furnished under this order, or any part or use thereof of patents (including utility models and registered designs) now or hereafter granted in the United States or in any country where Seller, its subsidiaries or affiliates, heretofore has furnished similar goods. Seller will, at IBM's request, identify the countries in which Seller, its subsidiaries or affiliates, heretofore has furnished similar goods.
PRICE	If price is not stated on this order, Seller shall invoice at lowest prevailing market price.
QUALITY	Material is subject to IBM's inspection and approval within a reasonable time after delivery. If specifications are not met, material may be returned at Seller's expense and risk for all damages incidental to the rejection. Payment shall not constitute an acceptance of the material nor impair IBM's right to inspect or any of its remedies.
SHIPMENT	Shipment must be made within the time stated on this order, failing which IBM reserves the right to purchase elsewhere and charges Seller with any loss incurred, unless delay in making shipment is due to unforeseeable causes beyond the control and without the fault or negligence of Seller.
SUBCONTRACTS	Seller shall not subcontract or delegate its obligations under this order without the written consent of IBM. Purchase of parts and materials normally purchased by Seller or required by this order shall be construed as subcontracts or delegations.
(NON-U.S. LOCATIONS ONLY)	Seller further agrees that during the process of bidding or production of goods and services hereunder, it will not re-export or divert to others any IBM specifications, drawing or other data, or any product of such data.
TAXES	Unless otherwise directed, Seller shall pay all sales and use taxes imposed by law upon or on account of this order. Where appropriate, IBM will reimburse Seller for this expense.
TOOLS	IBM owned tools held by Seller are to be used only for making parts for IBM. Tools of any kind held by Seller for making IBM's parts must be repaired and renewed by Seller at Seller's expense.
TRANSPORTATION	<u>Routing</u>—As indicated in transportation routing guidelines on face of this order. <u>F.O.B.</u>—Unless otherwise specified, ship collect, F.O.B. origin. <u>Prepaid Transportation (when specified)</u>—Charges must be supported by a paid freight bill or equivalent. <u>Cartage</u>) No charge allowed <u>Premium Transportation</u>) unless authorized <u>Insurance</u>) by IBM <u>Consolidation</u>—Unless otherwise instructed, consolidate all daily shipments to one destination on one bill of lading.
COMPLIANCE WITH LAWS AND REGULATIONS	Seller shall at all times comply with all applicable Federal, State and local laws, rules and regulations.
EQUAL EMPLOYMENT OPPORTUNITY	There are incorporated in this order the provisions of Executive Order 11246 (as amended) of the President of the United States on Equal Employment Opportunity and the rules and regulations issued pursuant thereto with which the Seller represents that he will comply, unless exempt.
EMPLOYMENT AND PROCUREMENT PROGRAMS	There are incorporated in this order the following provisions as they apply to performing work under Government procurement contracts: Utilization of Small Business Concerns (if in excess of $10,000) (Federal Procurement Regulation (FPR) 1-1.710-3(a)); Small Business Subcontracting Program (if in excess of $500,000) (FPR 1-1.710-3 (b)); Utilization of Labor Surplus Area Concerns (if in excess of $10,000) (FPR 1-1.805-3(a)); Labor Surplus Area Subcontracting Program (if in excess of $500,000) (FPR 1-1.805-3 (b)); Utilization of Minority Enterprises (if in excess of $10,000) (FPR 1-1.1310-2 (a)); Minority Business Enterprises Subcontracting Program (if in excess of $50,000) (FPR 1-1.1310-2(b)); Affirmative Action for Handicapped Workers (if $2,500 or more) (41 CFR 60-741.4); Affirmative Action for Disabled Veterans and Veterans of the Vietnam Era (if $10,000 or more) (41 CFR 60-250.4); Utilization of Small Business Concerns and Small Business Concerns Owned and Controlled by Socially and Economically Disadvantaged Individuals (if in excess of $10,000) (44 Fed. Reg. 23610 (April 20, 1979)); Small Business and Small Disadvantaged Business Subcontracting Plan (if in excess of $500,000) (44 Fed. Reg. 23610 (April 20, 1979)).
WAGES AND HOURS	Seller warrants that in the performance of this order Seller has complied with all of the provisions of the Fair Labor Standards Act of 1938 of the United States as amended.
WORKERS' COMPENSATION, EMPLOYERS' LIABILITY INSURANCE	If Seller does not have Workers' Compensation or Employer's Liability Insurance, Seller shall indemnify IBM against all damages sustained by IBM resulting from Seller's failure to have such insurance.

CONSIDERATION

The UCC radically changes the common law rule that contract modification must be supported by new consideration. Under the UCC, an agreement modifying a contract needs no consideration to be binding.

Modifications Must Be Made in Good Faith. Of course, contract modification must be sought in good faith. Good faith in the case of a merchant means honesty in fact and the observance of reasonable commercial standards of fair dealing in the trade. Modifications *extorted* from the other party are in bad faith and unenforceable.

IN THE COURTROOM

Jim agrees to manufacture and sell certain goods to Louise for a stated price. Subsequently, a sudden shift in the market makes it difficult for Jim to sell the items to Louise at the agreed price without suffering a loss. Jim tells Louise of the situation, and Louise agrees to pay an additional sum for the goods. *Can Louise later refuse to pay more than the original price?* No. A shift in the market is a good faith reason for contract modification. Under the UCC, Louise's promise to modify the contract needs no consideration to be binding. Thus, Louise is bound to the modified contract.

When Modification without Consideration Requires a Writing. In some situations, modification without consideration must be written to be enforceable. The contract may prohibit any changes unless they are in a signed writing. Also, any modification that brings a sales contract under the Statute of Frauds (which requires that a contract for a sale of goods priced at $500 or more must be in writing to be enforceable) will usually require that the modification be written. Thus, if an oral contract for a sale of goods priced at $400 is modified so that the goods are priced at $600, the modification must be in writing to be enforceable. Unlike Article 2, Article 2A does not say whether a lease as modified needs to satisfy the Statute of Frauds.

STATUTE OF FRAUDS

The UCC contains a Statute of Frauds provision that applies to contracts for the sale or lease of goods. As stated above, this requires that if the price is $500 or more, there must be a writing for the contract to be enforceable. The parties can have an initial oral agreement, however, and satisfy the Statute of Frauds by having a subsequent written memorandum of their oral agreement. In each case, the writing must be signed by the party against whom enforcement is sought.

Sufficiency of the Writing. A writing or a memorandum will be sufficient as long as it indicates that the parties intended to form a contract and as long as it is signed by the party against whom enforcement is sought. The contract will not be enforceable beyond the quantity of goods shown in the writing, but all other terms can be proved in court by oral testimony. For leases, the writing must reasonably identify and describe the goods leased and the lease term.

LEARNING OBJECTIVE NO. 4
Discussing UCC Exceptions to the Statute of Frauds

Written Confirmation between Merchants. Merchants can satisfy the requirements of a writing for the Statute of Frauds if, after the parties have agreed orally, one of the merchants sends a signed written confirmation to the other merchant. Unless the merchant who receives the confirmation gives written notice of objection to its contents within ten days after receipt, the writing is sufficient against the receiving merchant, even though he or she has not signed anything.

IN THE COURTROOM

Alfonso is a merchant buyer in Cleveland. He contracts over the telephone to purchase $4,000 worth of goods from Goldstein, a New York City merchant seller. Two days later Goldstein sends written confirmation detailing the terms of the oral contract, and Alfonso subsequently receives it. *Is Alfonso bound to the contract?* If Alfonso does not give Goldstein written notice of objection to the contents of the written confirmation within ten days of receipt, Alfonso cannot raise the Statute of Frauds as a defense against the enforcement of the contract.

Exceptions. There are three other UCC exceptions to the UCC Statute of Frauds requirement. An oral contract for a sale of goods priced at $500 or more or a lease of goods involving total payments of $1,000 or more will be enforceable despite the absence of a writing in the following circumstances.

Specially Manufactured Goods. An oral contract is enforceable if it is for (1) goods that are specially manufactured for a particular buyer or specially manufactured or obtained for a particular lessee, (2) these goods are not suitable for resale or lease to others in the ordinary course of the seller's or lessor's business, and (3) the seller or lessor has substantially started to manufacture the goods or has made commitments for the manufacture or procurement of the goods. In this situation, once the seller or lessor has taken action, the buyer or lessee cannot repudiate the agreement claiming the Statute of Frauds as a defense.

Admissions. An oral contract is enforceable if the party against whom enforcement of a contract is sought admits in pleadings (written answers), testimony, or other court proceedings that a contract was made. In this case, the contract will be enforceable even though it was oral, but enforceability is limited to the quantity of goods admitted.

Partial Performance. An oral contract is enforceable if payment has been made and accepted or goods have been received and accepted. This is the "partial performance" exception. The oral contract will be enforced at least to the extent that performance *actually* took place.

PAROL EVIDENCE

If the parties to a contract set forth its terms in a confirmatory memorandum (a writing expressing offer and acceptance of the deal) or in a writing intended as their final expression, the terms of the contract cannot be contradicted by evidence of any prior agreements or contemporaneous oral agreements. The terms of the contract may, however, be explained or supplemented by *consistent additional terms* or by *course of dealing, usage of trade, or course of performance.*

Consistent Additional Terms. If the court finds an ambiguity in a writing that is supposed to be a complete and exclusive statement of the agreement between the parties, it may accept evidence of consistent additional terms to clarify or remove the ambiguity. The court will not, however, accept evidence of contradictory terms. This is the rule under both the UCC and the common law of contracts.

Course of Dealing and Usage of Trade. The UCC has determined that the meaning of any agreement, evidenced by the language of the parties and by their actions, must be interpreted in light of commercial practices and other surrounding circumstances. In interpreting a commercial agreement, the court will assume that the *course of dealing* between the parties and the *usage of trade* were taken into account when the agreement was phrased.

A **course of dealing** is a sequence of previous actions and communications between the parties to a particular transaction that establishes a common basis for their understanding. A course of dealing is restricted, literally, to the sequence of actions and communications between the parties that occurred prior to the agreement in question.

COURSE OF DEALING
A sequence of previous conduct between the parties to a particular transaction that establishes a common basis for their understanding.

Usage of trade is any practice or method of dealing having such regularity of observance in a place, vocation, or trade as to justify an expectation that it will be observed with respect to the transaction in question. Further, the express terms of an agreement and an applicable course of dealing or usage of trade will be interpreted to be consistent with each other whenever reasonable. When such interpretation is *unreasonable,* however, the express terms in the agreement will prevail.

USAGE OF TRADE
Any practice or method of dealing having such regularity of observance in a place, vocation, or trade as to justify an expectation that it will be observed with respect to the transaction in question.

Course of Performance. A **course of performance** is the conduct that occurs under the terms of a particular agreement. The parties know best what they meant by their words, and the course of performance actually undertaken is the best indication of what they meant.

COURSE OF PERFORMANCE
The conduct that occurs under the terms of a particular agreement; such conduct indicates what the parties to an agreement intended it to mean.

IN THE COURTROOM

In separate contracts over a period of time, Janson's Lumber Company agrees to sell Barrymore specified numbers of "two-by-fours." The lumber in fact does not measure 2 inches by 4 inches but rather 1⅞ inches by 3¾ inches. *If Barrymore objects to the lumber delivered in the final delivery under the last contract, can Janson's enforce the deal?* Yes. Janson's can prove that two-by-fours are never exactly 2 inches by 4 inches by applying usage of trade, course of dealing, or both. Janson's can show that in previous transactions, Barrymore took lumber measuring 1⅞ inches by 3¾ inches without objection. In addition, Janson's can show that in the trade, two-by-fours are commonly 1⅞ inches by 3¾ inches. Also, Barrymore's acceptance, without objection, of other contract deliveries (course of performance) is relevant.

UNCONSCIONABILITY

As discussed in Chapter 11, an unconscionable contract is one that is so unfair and one-sided that it would be unreasonable to enforce it. The UCC allows a court to evaluate a contract or any clause in a contract, and if the court deems it to be unconscionable *at the time it was made,* the court can (1) refuse to enforce the contract, (2) enforce the contract without the unconscionable clause, or (3) limit the application of any unconscionable clauses to avoid an unconscionable result.

LEARNING OBJECTIVE NO. 5
Describing What a Court Can Do When Confronted with an Unconscionable Contract or Clause

TERMS AND CONCEPTS FOR REVIEW

CHAPTER SUMMARY • INTRODUCTION TO SALES AND LEASE CONTRACTS

Offer and Acceptance	**1.** The acceptance of unilateral offers can be made by a promise to ship or by shipment itself. **2.** Not all terms have to be included for a contract to result. **3.** Particulars of performance can be left open. **4.** Firm written offers by a *merchant* for three months or less cannot be revoked. **5.** Acceptance by performance requires notice within a reasonable time; otherwise, the offer can be treated as lapsed. **6.** Acceptance may be made by any reasonable means of communication; it is effective when dispatched.
Consideration	A modification of a contract for the sale of goods does not require consideration.
Requirements under the Statute of Frauds	**1.** All contracts for the sale of goods priced at $500 or more must be in writing. A writing is sufficient as long as it indicates a contract between the parties and is signed by the party against whom enforcement is sought. A contract is not enforceable beyond the quantity shown in the writing. **2.** Exceptions to the requirement of a writing exist in the following situations: **a.** When written confirmation of an oral contract *between merchants* is not objected to in writing by the receiver within ten days. **b.** When the oral contract is for specially manufactured goods not suitable for resale to others, and the seller has substantially started to manufacture the goods. **c.** When the defendant admits in pleadings, testimony, or other court proceedings that an oral contract for the sale of goods was made. In this case, the contract will be enforceable to the extent of the quantity of goods admitted. **d.** When payment has been made and accepted under the terms of an oral contract. The oral agreement will be enforceable to the extent that such payment has been received and accepted or to the extent that goods have been received and accepted.
Parol Evidence Rule	**1.** The terms of a clearly and completely worded written contract cannot be contradicted by evidence of prior agreements or contemporaneous oral agreements. **2.** Evidence is admissible to clarify the terms of a writing in the following situations: **a.** If the contract terms are ambiguous. **b.** If evidence of course of dealing, usage of trade, or course of performance is necessary to learn or to clarify the intentions of the parties to the contract.
Unconscionability	An unconscionable contract is one that is so unfair and one sided that it would be unreasonable to enforce it. If the court deems a contract to be unconscionable at the time it was made, the court can (1) refuse to enforce the contract, (2) refuse to enforce the unconscionable clause of the contract, or (3) limit the application of any unconscionable clauses to avoid an unconscionable result.

HYPOTHETICAL QUESTIONS

16–1. Statute of Frauds. Fresher Foods, Inc., orally agreed to purchase from Dale Vernon, a farmer, one thousand bushels of corn for $1.25 per bushel. Fresher Foods paid $125 down and agreed to pay the remainder of the purchase price upon delivery, which was scheduled for one week later. When Fresher Foods tendered the balance of $1,125 on the scheduled day of delivery and requested the corn, Vernon refused to deliver it. Fresher Foods sued Vernon for damages, claiming that Vernon had breached their oral contract. Can Fresher Foods recover? If so, to what extent?

16–2. Merchant's Firm Offer. On September 1, Jennings, a used-car dealer, wrote a letter to Wheeler in which he stated, "I have a 1955 Thunderbird convertible in mint condition that I will sell you for $13,500 at any time before October 9. [signed] Peter Jennings." By September 15, having heard nothing from Wheeler, Jennings sold the Thunderbird to another party. On September 29, Wheeler accepted Jennings's offer and tendered $13,500. When Jennings told Wheeler he had sold the car to another party, Wheeler claimed Jennings had breached their contract. Is Jennings in breach? Explain.

REAL WORLD CASE PROBLEM

16–3. Goods and Services Combined. Jane Pittsley contracted with Donald Houser, who was doing business as the Hilton Contract Carpet Co., for the installation of carpet in her home. Following installation, Pittsley complained to Hilton that some seams were visible, gaps appeared, the carpet did not lie flat in all areas, and the carpet failed to reach the wall in certain locations. Although Hilton made various attempts to fix the installation by attempting to stretch the carpet and other methods, Pittsley was not satisfied with the work and eventually sued Hilton to recover the $3,500 she had paid toward the $4,319.50 contract price for the carpet and its installation. Hilton paid the installers $700 for the work done in laying Pittsley's carpet. One of the issues before the court was whether the contract was a contract for the sale of goods or a contract for the sale of services. How should the court decide this issue? Discuss fully. [*Pittsley v. Houser,* 125 Idaho 820, 875 P.2d 232 (1994)]

For updated links to resources available on the Web, as well as a variety of other materials, visit this text's Web site at **http://blte.westbuslaw.com**.

For information about the National Conference of Commissioners (NCC) on Uniform State Laws and links to online uniform acts, go to

http://www.nccusl.org

The NCC, in association with the University of Pennsylvania Law School, now offers an official site for in-process and final drafts of uniform and model acts. For an index of in-process drafts, go to

http://www.law.upenn.edu/bll/ulc/ulc.htm

For an index of final drafts, go to

http://www.law.upenn.edu/bll/ulc/ulc_final.htm

Cornell University's Legal Information Institute offers online access to the UCC, as well as to UCC articles as enacted by particular states and proposed revisions to articles, at

http://www.law.cornell.edu/ucc/ucc.table.html

The Pace University School of Law's Institute of International Commercial Law maintains a Web site that contains the full text of the CISG, as well as relevant cases and discussions of the law. Go to

http://cisgw3.law.pace.edu

ONLINE LEGAL RESEARCH

Go to **http://blte.westbuslaw.com**, the Web site that accompanies this text. Select "Internet Applications," and then click on "Chapter 16." There you will find the following Internet research exercise that you can perform to learn more about sales contracts:

Activity 16–1: Is It a Contract?

Chapter 16 ■ WORK SET

TRUE-FALSE QUESTIONS

_____ **1.** If the subject of a sale is goods, Article 2 of the UCC applies.

_____ **2.** A contract for a sale of goods is subject to the same traditional principles that apply to all contracts.

_____ **3.** If the subject of a transaction is a service, Article 2 of the UCC applies.

_____ **4.** The UCC requires that an agreement modifying a contract must be supported by new consideration to be binding.

_____ **5.** Under the UCC's Statute of Frauds, a writing must include all material terms except quantity.

_____ **6.** An unconscionable contract is a contract so one-sided and unfair, at the time it is made, that enforcing it would be unreasonable.

_____ **7.** A lease agreement is a bargain between a lessor and a lessee, as shown by their words and conduct.

_____ **8.** Under the UCC, acceptance can be made by any means of communication reasonable under the circumstances.

MULTIPLE-CHOICE QUESTIONS

_____ **1.** Under UCC Article 2, the price of a sale may be payable in

a. money only.
b. goods only.
c. money or goods only.
d. money, goods, services, or real estate.

_____ **2.** Morro Beverage Company has a surplus of carbon dioxide (which is what puts the bubbles in Morro beverages). Morro agrees to sell the surplus to the Rock Ale Company. Morro is a merchant with respect to

a. carbon dioxide but not Morro beverages.
b. Morro beverages but not carbon dioxide.
c. both Morro beverages and carbon dioxide.
d. neither Morro beverages nor carbon dioxide.

_____ **3.** Marina Shipyard agrees to build a barge for MaxCo Shipping. The contract includes an option for up to five more barges, but states that the prices of the other barges could be higher. Marina and MaxCo have

a. a binding contract for at least one barge and up to six barges.
b. a binding contract for one barge only.
c. no contract, because the terms of the option are too indefinite.
d. no contract, because both parties are merchants with respect to barges.

_____ **4.** Mike and Rita orally agree to a sale of 100 pair of hiking boots at $50 each. Rita gives Mike a check for $500 as a down payment. Mike takes the check. At this point, the contract is enforceable

a. to the full extent because it is for specially made goods.
b. to the full extent because it is oral.
c. to the extent of $500.
d. none of the above.

_____ **5.** Med Labs sends Kraft Instruments a purchase order for scalpels. The order states that Med will not be bound by any additional terms. Kraft ships the scalpels with an acknowledgment that includes an additional, materially different term. Med is

a. not bound by the term, because the offer expressly states that no other terms will be accepted.
b. not bound by the term, because the additional term constitutes a material alteration.
c. both a and b.
d. bound by the term.

_____ **6.** Under the parol evidence rule, evidence of contradictory prior agreements or contemporaneous oral agreements is inadmissible EXCEPT

a. that consistent terms can clarify or remove an ambiguity in the writing.
b. that commercial practices can be used to interpret the contract.
c. both a and b.
d. none of the above.

_____ **7.** Lena, a car dealer, writes to Sam that "I have a 1992 Honda Civic that I will sell to you for $4,000. This offer will be kept open for one week." Six days later, Todd tells Sam that Lena sold the car that morning for $5,000. Who violated the terms of the offer?

a. Lena
b. Sam
c. Todd
d. No one

_____ **8.** Stron Computers agrees to buy an unspecified quantity of microchips from SmartCorp. The quantity that a court would order Stron to buy under this contract is

a. the amount that Stron would buy during a normal year.
b. the amount that SmartCorp would make in a normal year.
c. the amount that SmartCorp actually makes this year.
d. none of the above.

ISSUE SPOTTERS

1. Brad orders 150 computer desks. Fred ships 150 printer stands. Is this an acceptance of Brad's offer or a counteroffer? If it is an acceptance, is it a breach of the contract? What if Fred told Brad, "I'm sending printer stands as an accommodation"?

2. Smith & Sons, Inc., sells truck supplies to J&B, which services trucks. Over the phone, J&B and Smith negotiate for the sale of eighty-four sets of tires. Smith sends a letter to J&B detailing the terms. Smith ships the tires two weeks later. J&B refuses to pay. Is there an enforceable contract between them?

Title and Risk of Loss

17

LEARNING OBJECTIVES

When you finish this chapter, you should be able to:

1. Explain the concept of identifying goods to a contract.
2. Identify when title passes under a contract for a sale of goods.
3. State what happens when persons who acquire goods without title attempt to resell the goods.
4. Discuss who bears the loss if goods are damaged, destroyed, or lost, or if the contract is breached.
5. Pinpoint who has an insurable interest in goods.

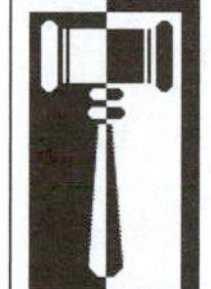

FACING A LEGAL PROBLEM

Anselm, Brad, and Cord are farmers. They deposit, respectively, 5,000 bushels, 3,000 bushels, and 2,000 bushels of the same grade and quality of grain in a bin. The three become owners in common, with Anselm owning 50 percent of the 10,000 bushels, Brad 30 percent, and Cord 20 percent. *If Anselm contracts to sell 5,000 bushels of grain to Tarey, do those bushels have to be removed from the bin?*

Anything can happen between the time a contract is signed and the time the goods are transferred to the buyer's or lessee's possession. For example, in a sale of oranges to be delivered after the harvest, fire, flood, or frost may destroy the orange groves, or the oranges may be damaged or lost in transit. Because of these possibilities, it is important to know the rights and liabilities of the parties. The rules of the Uniform Commercial Code (UCC) about these rights and liabilities are discussed in the sections that follow. (Excerpts from the UCC are included in Appendix B.) In most situations, rights and liabilities are determined not by who has title (the formal right of ownership of property) but by three other concepts: identification, risk of loss, and insurable interest.

Identification

Before any interest in goods can pass from the seller or lessor to the buyer or lessee, two conditions must prevail: (1) the goods must be in existence, and (2) they must be identified as the specific goods designated in the contract. If either condition is lacking, only a contract to *sell* (not a sale) exists. Goods that are *not* both existing and identified to the contract are called "future goods." For

IDENTIFICATION
In the sale or lease of goods, the express designation of the goods provided for in the contract.

LEARNING OBJECTIVE NO. 1
Explaining the Concept of Identifying Goods to a Contract

example, a contract to purchase next year's crop of hay would be a contract for future goods—a crop yet to be grown. For passage of title, the goods must be identified in a way that will distinguish them from all similar goods.

Identification is a designation of goods as the subject matter of the sales or lease contract. In many cases, identification is simply a matter of specific designation. For example, you contract to purchase a fleet of five cars by the serial numbers listed for the cars, or you agree to purchase all the wheat in a specific bin at a stated price per bushel. Identification is significant because it gives the buyer or lessee the right to obtain insurance on the goods and the right to recover from third parties who damage the goods.

PURCHASING GOODS FROM A LARGER MASS

Goods that are part of a larger mass are identified when the goods are marked, shipped, or somehow designated by the seller or lessor as the particular goods to pass under the contract. Suppose that a buyer orders 1,000 cases of beans from a 10,000-case lot. Until the seller separates the 1,000 cases of beans from the 10,000-case lot, title and risk of loss remain with the seller (if anything happens to the beans, the seller will have to pay for them).

FUNGIBLE GOODS
Goods that are alike by physical nature, by agreement, or by trade usage. Examples of fungible goods are wheat, oil, and wine that are identical in type and quality.

The most common exception deals with fungible goods. **Fungible goods** are goods that are alike naturally or by agreement or trade usage. Examples are wheat, oil, and wine, when all such goods are of like grade and quality. If these goods are held or intended to be held by owners in common (owners with an undivided share of the whole), a seller-owner can pass title and risk of loss to the buyer without a separation. The buyer replaces the seller as an owner in common.

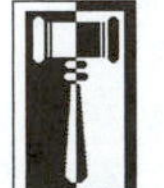

In the legal problem set out at the beginning of this chapter, farmers Anselm, Brad, and Cord deposit, respectively, 5,000 bushels, 3,000 bushels, and 2,000 bushels of the same grade and quality of grain in a bin. As owners in common, Anselm owns 50 percent of the 10,000 bushels, Brad 30 percent, and Cord 20 percent. *If Anselm contracts to sell his bushels of grain to Tarey, do those 5,000 bushels need to be removed?* No. Because the goods are fungible, title and risk of loss can pass to Tarey without physically separating the bushels. Tarey becomes an owner in common with Brad and Cord.

WHEN IDENTIFICATION OCCURS

In their contract, parties can agree on when identification will take place. But if they do not so specify, the following additional rules apply:

1. Identification takes place at the time the contract is made *if the contract calls for the sale or lease of specific goods already existing.*
2. If the sale involves unborn animals that will be born within twelve months from the time of the contract, or if it involves crops to be harvested within twelve months (or the next harvest season occurring after contracting, whichever is longer), identification will take place, in the first case, when the unborn animals are conceived and, in the second case, when the crops are planted or begin to grow. If a lease involves any unborn animals, identification occurs when the animals are conceived.
3. In other cases, identification takes place when the goods are marked, shipped, or somehow designated by the seller or lessor as the particular goods to pass under the contract.

LEARNING OBJECTIVE NO. 2
Identifying When Title Passes under a Contract for a Sale of Goods

Passage of Title

Once goods exist and are identified, title can be determined. Under the UCC, any explicit understanding between the buyer and the seller determines when title passes. If there is no such agreement, title passes to the buyer at the time and the place the seller *physically* delivers the goods. The delivery arrangements determine when this occurs.

In lease contracts, of course, title to the goods is retained by the lessor-owner of the goods. Hence, the UCC's provisions relating to passage of title do not apply to leased goods.

Shipment and Destination Contracts

In a **shipment contract,** the seller is required or authorized to ship goods by carrier, such as a trucking company or an air freight company. Under a shipment contract, the seller is required only to deliver the goods into the hands of a carrier. Title passes to the buyer at the time and place of shipment.

Shipment Contract
A contract for the sale of goods in which the buyer assumes liability for any losses or damage to the goods on the seller's delivery of the goods to a carrier.

In a **destination contract,** the seller is required to deliver the goods to a particular destination, usually directly to the buyer. Title passes to the buyer when the goods are *tendered* at that destination. A tender of delivery is the seller's placing or holding of the goods at the buyer's disposition (with any necessary notice) so that the buyer can take delivery. For example, a seller in New York agrees to deliver goods to a buyer's warehouse in Los Angeles by truck. When the truck arrives in Los Angeles, the seller calls the buyer to tell her that the goods are in the city and to ask her to open the warehouse, so that she can take delivery.

Destination Contract
A contract for the sale of goods in which the seller assumes liability for any losses or damage to the goods until they are tendered at the destination specified in the contract.

Generally, *all contracts are assumed to be shipment contracts if nothing to the contrary is stated in the contract.*

Delivery without Movement of the Goods

Some contracts of sale do not call for the seller's shipment or delivery (the buyer is to pick up the goods). The passage of title in this situation depends on whether the seller must deliver a **document of title,** such as a bill of lading or a warehouse receipt, to the buyer. A *bill of lading* is a receipt for goods that is signed by a carrier and that serves as a contract for the transportation of the goods. A *warehouse receipt* is a receipt issued by a warehouser for goods stored in a warehouse. (See Exhibits 17–1 and 17–2 on pages 200 and 201.) When a document of title is required, title passes to the buyer *when and where the document is delivered.* Thus, if the goods are stored in a warehouse, title passes to the buyer when the appropriate documents are delivered to the buyer. The goods never move.

Document of Title
Paper exchanged in the regular course of business that evidences the right to possession of goods (for example, a bill of lading or warehouse receipt).

When no documents of title are required and delivery is made without moving the goods, title passes at the time and place the sales contract was made, if the goods have already been identified. If the goods have not been identified, title does not pass until identification occurs.

To review bills of lading, access the following Web site:

http://www.showtrans.com/bl.htm

IN THE COURTROOM

Rogers sells lumber to Boudakian. It is agreed that Boudakian will pick up the lumber at the yard. *When does title to the lumber pass to Boudakian?* If the lumber has been identified (segregated, marked, or in any other way distinguished from all other lumber), title will pass to Boudakian when the contract is signed. If the lumber is still in storage bins at the mill, title will not pass until the particular lumber to be sold under this contract is identified.

LEARNING OBJECTIVE NO. 3
Stating What Happens When Persons Who Acquire Goods without Title Attempt to Resell the Goods

Sales or Leases by Nonowners

Problems relating to passage of title occur when persons who acquire goods with imperfect titles attempt to sell or lease the goods. What are the rights of two

EXHIBIT 17–1
A Sample Bill of Lading

UNIFORM MOTOR CARRIER ORDER BILL OF LADING

1st Sheet

Original—Domestic

Shipper's No. ______

Agent's No. ______

CENTRAL FREIGHT LINES INC.

RECEIVED, subject to the classifications and tariffs in effect on the date of the issue of this Bill of Lading,

From ______ Date ______ 19

At ______ Street ______ City ______ County ______ State

the property described below, in apparent good order, except as noted (contents and condition of contents of packages unknown) marked, consigned and destined as shown below, which said company (the word company being understood throughout this contract as meaning any person or corporation in possession of the property under the contract) agrees to carry to its usual place of delivery at said destination, if within the scope of its lawful operations, otherwise to deliver to another carrier on the route to said destination. It is mutually agreed, as to each carrier of all or any of said property over all or any portion of said route to destination, and as to each party at any time interested in all or any of said property, that every service to be performed hereunder shall be subject to all the conditions not prohibited by law, whether printed or written, herein contained, including the conditions on back hereof, which are hereby agreed to by the shipper and accepted for himself and his assigns.

The surrender of this Original ORDER Bill of Lading properly indorsed shall be required before the delivery of the property. Inspection of property covered by this bill of lading will not be permitted unless provided by law or unless permission is indorsed on this original Bill of lading or given in writing by the shipper.

Consigned to Order of ______

Destination ______ Street, ______ City, ______ County, ______ State

Notify ______

At ______ Street, ______ City, ______ County, ______ State

I.C.C. No. ______ Vehicle No. ______

Routing ______

No. Packages	Description of Articles, Special Marks, and Exceptions	*Weight (Subject to Correction)	Class or Rate	Check Column
	SAMPLE			

Subject to Section 7 of Conditions, if this shipment is to be delivered to the consignee without recourse on the consignor, the consignor shall sign the following statement:

The carrier shall not make delivery of this shipment without payment of freight and all other lawful charges.

______
(signature of consignor.)

If charges are to be prepaid write or stamp here, "To be Prepaid."

Received $ ______ to apply in prepayment of the charges of the property described hereon.

______
Agent or Cashier.

Per ______
(the signature here acknowledges only the amount prepaid.)

Charges advanced:

$ ______

*If the shipment moves between two ports by a carrier by water, the law requires that the bill of lading shall state whether it is "carrier's or shipper's weight."

Note--Where the rate is dependent on value, shippers are required to state specifically in writing the agreed or declared value of the property.

The agreed or declared value of the property is hereby specifically stated by the shipper to be not exceeding

______ per ______

Shipper ______ Agent.

Per ______ Per ______

Permanent address of Shipper ______ Street ______ City, ______ State

MOORE BUSINESS FORMS, INC. WACO, TEX. M

Source: Reprinted with permission of Central Freight Lines, Inc. © 1985 Central Freight Lines, Inc. Note: This form is printed in yellow to warn holders that it is a bill of lading. The back of the form permits negotiation by indorsement.

EXHIBIT 17–2
A Sample Warehouse Receipt

HART

Warehouse Receipt – Not Negotiable

Agreement No. ________ Vault No. ______________________________

Service Order ________ ______________________________

Receipt and
Lot Number ________ Date of Issue ______________ 19____

Received for the account of and deliverable to • ______________________________

whose latest known address is ______________________________

SAMPLE

______________________ the goods enumerated on the inside or attached schedule to be

stored in Company warehouse, located at ______________________________
which goods are accepted only upon the following conditions set forth below:

READ CAREFULLY That the value of all goods stored, including the contents of any container, and all goods hereafter stored for Depositor's account to be not over $ per pound† per article unless a higher value is noted in the schedule, for which an additional monthly storage charge of ________¢ on each $________ valuation in excess of $ per pound † per article or fraction thereof will be made.

If there are any items enumerated in this receipt valued in excess of the above limitations per pound per article and not so noted in the schedule, return this receipt within 10 days with proper values so indicated in writing in order that the receipt may be re-issued and proper higher storage rates assessed.

OWNERSHIP. The Customer, Shipper, Depositor, or Agent represents and warrants that he is lawfully possessed of goods to be stored and/or has the authority to store or ship said goods. (If the goods are mortgaged, notify the Company the name and address of the mortgagee.)

PAYMENT OF CHARGES. Storage bills are payable monthly in advance for each month's storage or fraction thereof. Labor charges, cartage and other services rendered are payable upon completion of work. All charges shall be paid at the warehouse location shown hereon, and if delinquent, shall incur interest monthly at the rate of per cent ( ) per year.

The Depositor will pay reasonable attorney's fee incurred by The Company in collecting delinquent accounts.

LIABILITY OF COMPANY. The company shall be liable for any loss or injury to the goods caused by its failure to exercise such care as a reasonably careful man would exercise under like circumstances. The company will not be liable for loss or damage to fragile articles not packed, or articles packed or unpacked by other than employees of this company. Depositor specifically agrees that the warehouse will not be liable for contamination of or for insect damage to articles placed in drawer of furniture by the depositor. Periodic spraying of the warehouse premises shall constitute ordinary and proper care, unless the depositor requests in writing and pays for anti-infestation treatment of articles in drawers and compartments of stored furniture.

CHANGE OF ADDRESS. Notice of change of address must be given the Company in writing, and acknowledged in writing by the Company.

TRANSFER OR WITHDRAWAL OF GOODS. The warehouse receipt is not negotiable and shall be produced and all charges must be paid before delivery to the Depositor, or transfer of goods to another person; however, a written direction to the Company to transfer the goods to another person or deliver the goods may be accepted by the Company at its option without requiring tender of the warehouse receipt

ACCESS TO STORAGE PARTIAL WITHDRAWAL. A signed order from the person in whose name the receipt is issued is required to enable others to remove or have access to goods. A charge is made for stacking and unstacking, and for access to stored goods.

BUILDING-FIRE-WATCHMAN. The Company does not represent or warrant that its building cannot be destroyed by fire or that the contents of said buildings including the said property cannot be destroyed by fire. The Company shall not be required to maintain a watchman or sprinkler system and its failure to do so shall not constitute negligence.

CLAIMS OR ERRORS. All claims for non-delivery of any article or articles and for damage, breakage, etc., must be made in writing within ninety (90) days from delivery of goods stored or they are waived. Failure to return the warehouse receipt for correction within ( ) days after receipt thereof by the depositor will be conclusive that it is correct and delivery will be made only in accordance therewith.

FUTURE SERVICE. This Contract shall extend and apply to future services rendered to the Depositor by the Company and to any additional goods deposited with the Company by the Depositor.

WAREHOUSEMAN'S LIEN. The Company reserves the right to sell the goods stored, in accordance with the provisions of the Uniform Commercial Code (Business and Commerce Code if stored in Texas), for all lawful charges in arrears.

TERMINATION OF STORAGE. The Company reserves the right to terminate the storage of the goods at any time by giving to the Depositor thirty (30) days' written notice of its intention so to do, and, unless the Depositor removes such goods within that period, the Company is hereby empowered to have the same removed at the cost and expense of the Depositor, or the Company may sell them at auction in accordance with state law.

DEPOSITOR WILL PAY REASONABLE LEGAL FEES INCURRED BY WAREHOUSE IN COLLECTING DELINQUENT CHARGES.

THIS DOCUMENT CONTAINS THE WHOLE CONTRACT BETWEEN THE PARTIES AND THERE ARE NO OTHER TERMS, WARRANTIES, REPRESENTATIONS, OR AGREEMENTS OF EITHER DEPOSITOR OR COMPANY NOT HEREIN CONTAINED.

Storage per month or fraction thereof. . . .	$________
Warehouse labor	$________
Cartage.	$________
Packing at residence . . .	$________
Wrapping and preparing for storage.	$________
Charges advanced	$________
________________	$________
________________	$________

By ______________________________

• Insert "Mr. and/or Mrs." or, if military personnel, appropriate rank or grade.
†Delete the words "per pound" if the declared value is per article.
For goods stored for military personnel under PL 245, the contractor's liability for care of goods is as provided in Basic Agreement with U.S. Goverment

THIS PROPERTY HAS NOT BEEN INSURED BY THIS COMPANY FOR FIRE OR ANY OTHER CASUALTY
SCHEDULE OF GOODS ON FOLLOWING PAGE OR ATTACHED

HART HART

W-1 (9-81) Approved by SW WT4© Re-order from Hart Graphics, Austin, Texas parties who lay claim to the same goods when those goods are sold or leased with imperfect titles?

Void Title. A buyer acquires at least whatever title the seller has to the goods sold. A buyer may unknowingly purchase goods from a seller who is not the owner of the goods. If the seller is a thief, the seller's title is *void*—legally, no title exists. Thus, the buyer acquires no title, and the real owner can reclaim the goods from the buyer. (Of course, the buyer can then try to recover from the thief!)

The same result would occur if the goods were leased. Generally, a lessee acquires only whatever right to possess and use the goods that the lessor has or has the power to transfer, subject to the lease contract. If the lessor has no rights to transfer, the lessee acquires no rights.

IN THE COURTROOM

Jim steals goods owned by Margaret. He sells the goods to Sandra, who acts in good faith and honestly was not aware that the goods were stolen. *Can Margaret reclaim the goods from Sandra?* Yes. Jim had *void title* to those goods. Margaret can reclaim them from Sandra even though Sandra acted in good faith and honestly was not aware that the goods were stolen.

INSOLVENT
When a person's liabilities exceed the value of his or her assets, or when a person either has stopped paying his or her debts in the ordinary course of business or cannot pay the debts as they come due.

GOOD FAITH PURCHASER
A purchaser who buys without notice of any circumstance that would put a person of ordinary prudence on inquiry as to whether the seller has valid title to the goods being sold.

Voidable Title. A seller has *voidable title* if the goods that he or she is selling were obtained by fraud; paid for with a check that is later dishonored; purchased from a minor; or purchased on credit, when the seller was **insolvent.** Under the UCC, a person is insolvent when that person ceases to pay his or her debts, cannot pay the debts as they become due, or is insolvent within the meaning of federal bankruptcy law (see Chapter 33). Purchasers of such goods acquire all title that their transferors either had or had the power to transfer, but no more.

In contrast to a seller with void title, a seller with *voidable title* has the power to transfer a good title to a **good faith purchaser.** A good faith purchaser is a buyer who is unaware of circumstances that would make a person of ordinary prudence inquire about the validity of the seller's title to the goods. The real owner cannot recover goods from a good faith purchaser. If the buyer of the goods is not a good faith purchaser, then the actual owner of the goods can reclaim them from the buyer (or from the seller, if the goods are still in the seller's possession). Exhibit 17–3 illustrates these concepts.

The same rules apply in circumstances involving leases. A lessor with voidable title has the power to transfer a valid leasehold interest to a good faith lessee for value. The real owner cannot recover the goods, except as permitted by the terms of the lease. The real owner can, however, receive all proceeds arising from the lease, as well as a transfer of all rights, title, and interest as lessor under the lease, including the lessor's interest in the return of the goods when the lease expires.

The Entrustment Rule. Entrusting goods to a merchant *who deals in goods of that kind* gives the merchant the power to transfer all rights to a *buyer in the ordinary course of business*. Entrusting includes both delivering the goods to the merchant and leaving the purchased goods with the merchant for later delivery or pickup. A buyer in the ordinary course of business is a person who, in good faith and without knowledge that the sale violates the ownership rights of a third party, buys in the normal course of business from a person (other than a pawnbroker) in the business of selling goods of that kind. The good faith buyer, however, obtains only those rights held by the person entrusting the goods.

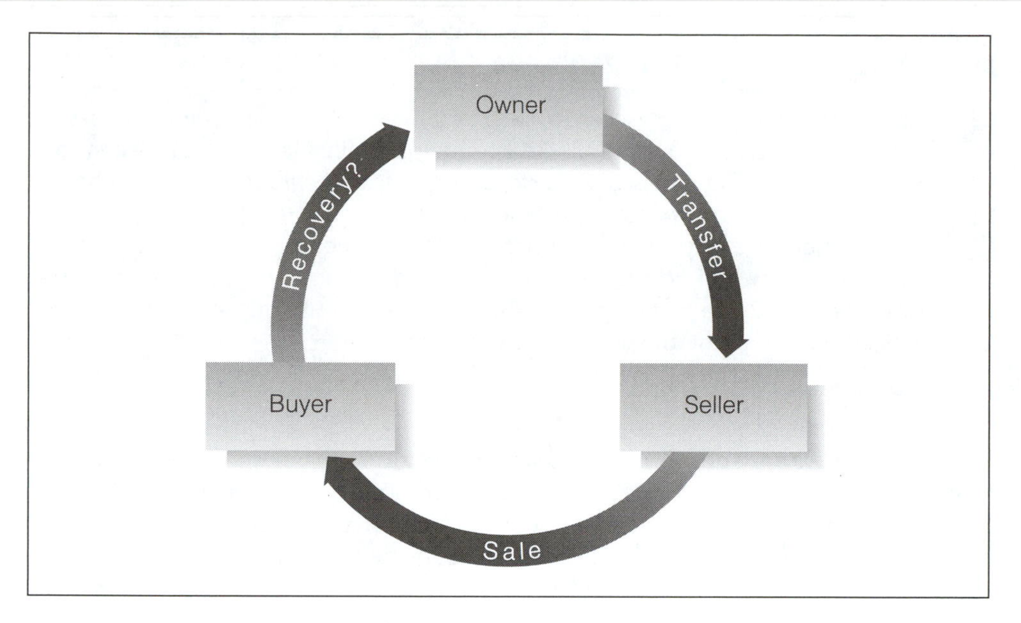

EXHIBIT 17–3
Void and Voidable Title
If goods are transferred from their owner to another by theft, the thief acquires no ownership rights. Because the thief's title is *void,* a later buyer can acquire no title, and the owner can recover the goods. If the transfer occurs by fraud, the transferee acquires a *voidable* title. A later good faith purchaser for value can acquire good title, and the original owner cannot recover the goods.

Article 2A provides a similar rule for leased goods. If a lessor entrusts goods to a lessee-merchant who deals in goods of that kind, the lessee-merchant has the power to transfer all of the rights the lessor had in the goods to a buyer or sublessee in the ordinary course of business.

IN THE COURTROOM

Jan's watch is stolen by Selena. Selena leaves the watch with a jeweler for repairs. The jeweler sells the watch to Ben, who does not know that the jeweler has no right to sell it. *Against whom does Ben get good title?* Ben gets good title against Selena, who entrusted the watch to the jeweler, but not against Jan, who neither entrusted the watch to Selena nor authorized Selena to entrust it. Therefore, Ben is a buyer in the ordinary course of business as to Selena but not as to Jan, who can recover the watch from Ben.

Risk of Loss

LEARNING OBJECTIVE NO. 4
Discussing Who Bears the Loss If Goods Are Damaged, Destroyed, or Lost, or If the Contract is Breached

Under the UCC, the question of who suffers a financial loss if goods are damaged, destroyed, or lost is not necessarily determined by title. Who bears the risk of loss can be determined through an agreement by the parties. Who suffers the loss may also depend on whether the sales or lease contract has been breached at the time of loss.

Delivery with Movement of the Goods—Carrier Cases

When there is no other specification in the agreement, the following rules apply to cases involving movement of the goods (carrier cases).

Shipment Contracts. In a shipment contract, if the seller or lessor is required or authorized to ship goods by carrier (but not required to deliver them to a particular destination), risk of loss passes to the buyer or lessee when the goods are delivered to the carrier. (Buyers and lessees have recourse against carriers, and they also usually buy insurance to cover the goods.)

IN THE COURTROOM

Russell Orchards, a seller in Houston, Texas, sells five hundred cases of grapefruit to Grocers Fruit Brokers, a buyer in New York. The contract states that the sale is "F.O.B. Houston" (*free on board* in Houston—that is, the *buyer* pays the transportation charges from Houston). The contract authorizes a shipment by carrier. It does not require that the seller tender the grapefruit in New York. *If the goods are damaged in transit, who suffers the loss—the seller or the buyer?* The loss is the buyer's. Risk passes to the buyer when conforming goods are placed in the possession of the carrier.

A contract clause could provide that risk will not pass until the goods are "delivered, installed, inspected, and tested (or in running order for a period of time)."

Destination Contracts. In a destination contract, the risk of loss passes to the buyer or lessee when the goods are *tendered* to the buyer or lessee at that destination. In the preceding example, if the contract had been F.O.B. New York, risk of loss during transit to New York would have been the seller's.

DELIVERY WITHOUT MOVEMENT OF THE GOODS

BAILEE
One to whom goods are entrusted by a bailor.

The UCC also addresses situations in which the seller or lessor is required neither to ship nor to deliver the goods. Frequently, the buyer or lessee is to pick up the goods from the seller or lessor, or the goods are held by a **bailee.** Under the UCC, a bailee is a party who, by a bill of lading, warehouse receipt, or other document of title, acknowledges possession of goods and contracts to deliver them. A warehousing company, for example, or a trucking company that normally issues documents of title for goods it receives is a bailee. (Bailments are discussed in more detail in Chapter 35.)

Goods Held by the Seller or Lessor. If the goods are held by the seller or lessor, a document of title is usually not used. If the seller or lessor is a merchant, risk of loss to goods held by the seller or lessor passes to the buyer or lessee when he or she *takes physical possession of the goods.* If the seller or lessor is not a merchant, the risk of loss passes to the buyer or lessee upon *tender of delivery.*

Goods Held by a Bailee. When a bailee is holding goods for a person who has contracted to sell them and the goods are to be delivered without being moved, the goods are usually represented by a negotiable or nonnegotiable document of title (a bill of lading or a warehouse receipt—see Exhibits 17–1 and 17–2).

Negotiable and *nonnegotiable* refer to the capability of a document of title to transfer the rights to goods that the document covers. With a negotiable document of title, a party can transfer the rights by signing and delivering, or in some situations simply delivering, the document. For example, when a seller signs a negotiable document of title that covers certain goods and delivers it to a buyer, the buyer may acquire *all* rights to the goods (and, by signing and delivering the document, transfer those rights to someone else).

When goods are held by a bailee, risk of loss passes to the buyer when (1) the buyer receives a negotiable document of title for the goods, (2) the bailee acknowledges the buyer's right to possess the goods, or (3) the buyer receives a nonnegotiable document of title *and* has had a *reasonable time* to present the document to the bailee and demand the goods. If the bailee refuses to honor the document, the risk of loss remains with the seller.

In respect to leases, if goods held by a bailee are to be delivered without being moved, the risk of loss passes to the lessee on acknowledgment by the bailee of the lessee's right to possession of the goods.

Conditional Sales

Buyers and sellers sometimes form sales contracts that are conditioned either on the buyer's approval of the goods or on the buyer's resale of the purchased goods. The UCC states that (unless otherwise agreed) if the goods are for the buyer to use, the transaction is a *sale on approval*. If the goods are for the buyer to resell, the transaction is a *sale or return*.

Sale on Approval. When a seller offers to sell goods to a buyer and permits the buyer to take the goods on a trial basis, a **sale on approval** is made. Title and risk of loss (from causes beyond the buyer's control) remain with the seller until the buyer accepts (approves) the offer. Acceptance can be made expressly, by any act inconsistent with the *trial* purpose or seller's ownership (such as reselling the goods), or by the buyer's election not to return the goods within the trial period. If the buyer does not wish to accept, the buyer may notify the seller. The return is then at the seller's expense and risk. Goods held on approval are not subject to the claims of the buyer's creditors until acceptance.

Sale on Approval
A type of conditional sale that becomes absolute only when the buyer approves, or is satisfied with, the good(s) sold. Besides express approval of goods, approval may be inferred if the buyer keeps the goods beyond a reasonable time or uses the goods in any way that is inconsistent with the seller's ownership.

Sale or Return. In a **sale or return,** a seller delivers a quantity of goods to a buyer on the understanding that if the buyer wishes to retain any portion of those goods, the buyer will consider the portion retained as having been sold to him or her and will pay accordingly. The balance will be returned to the seller or will be held by the buyer as a bailee subject to the seller's order. For instance, if a diamond wholesaler delivers gems to a retailer on the understanding that the retailer can return any unsold gems at the end of six months, the transaction is a sale or return.

Sale or Return
A type of conditional sale wherein title and possession pass from the seller to the buyer; however, the buyer retains the option to rescind or return the goods during a specified period even though the goods conform to the contract.

When the buyer receives possession at the time of sale, the title and risk of loss pass to the buyer. Both remain with the buyer until the buyer returns the goods to the seller within the specified time. If the buyer fails to return the goods within this time, the sale is finalized. The return of the goods is at the buyer's risk and expense. Goods held under a sale-or-return contract are subject to the claims of the buyer's creditors while they are in the buyer's possession.

The UCC treats a **consignment** as a sale or return. Under a consignment, the owner of goods (the *consignor*) delivers them to another (the *consignee*) for the consignee to sell. If the consignee sells the goods, he or she must pay the consignor for them. If the goods are not sold, they may simply be returned to the consignor. While the goods are in the possession of the consignee, the consignee holds title, and creditors of the consignee will prevail in any action to repossess the goods. For instance, if a jewelry maker delivers some earrings to a retail arts and crafts store on consignment, the earrings (like all of the retailer's inventory) are subject to the claims of the retailer's creditors.

Consignment
A transaction in which an owner of goods (the consignor) delivers the goods to another (the consignee) for the consignee to sell. The consignee pays the consignor for the goods when the consignee sells the goods.

Risk of Loss When a Sales or Lease Contract Is Breached

There are many ways to breach a sales or lease contract. The transfer of risk operates differently depending on which party breaches. Generally, the party in breach bears the risk of loss.

When the Seller or Lessor Breaches. If the goods are so nonconforming that the buyer has the right to reject them, the risk of loss does not pass to the buyer until the defects are **cured** (repaired, replaced, or discounted in price by the seller) or until the buyer accepts the goods in spite of their defects (thus waiving the right to reject). For example, a buyer orders blue widgets, but the seller ships red ones. The risk of loss remains with the seller, unless the buyer accepts the widgets in spite of their color.

Cure
The right of a party who tenders nonconforming performance to correct his or her performance within the contract period.

If a buyer accepts a shipment of goods and later discovers a defect, acceptance can be revoked. Revocation allows the buyer to pass the risk of loss back to the seller, at least to the extent that the buyer's insurance does not cover the loss.

There is a similar rule for leases. If the lessor or supplier tenders goods that are so nonconforming that the lessee has the right to reject them, the risk of loss remains with the lessor or the supplier until cure or acceptance. If the lessee, after acceptance, revokes his or her acceptance of nonconforming goods, the revocation passes the risk of loss back to the seller or supplier, to the extent that the lessee's insurance does not cover the loss.

When the Buyer or Lessee Breaches. When a buyer or lessee breaches a contract, the general rule is that the risk of loss *immediately* shifts to the buyer or lessee. There are three important limitations to this rule:

1. The seller or lessor must have already identified the goods under the contract.
2. The buyer or lessee bears the risk for only a *commercially reasonable time* after the seller or lessor learns of the breach. What is a commercially reasonable time depends on the circumstances.
3. The buyer or lessee is liable only to the extent of any *deficiency* in the seller's insurance coverage.

Insurable Interest

LEARNING OBJECTIVE NO. 5
Pinpointing Who Has an Insurable Interest in Goods

Parties to sales or lease contracts often obtain insurance coverage to protect against damage, loss, or destruction of goods. Any party purchasing insurance, however, must have a "sufficient interest" in the insured item to obtain a valid policy. Insurance laws—not the UCC—determine "sufficiency." The UCC is helpful, however, because it contains certain rules regarding the buyer's and seller's insurable interest in goods.

Insurable Interest of the Buyer or Lessee

Insurable Interest
An interest either in a person's life or well-being or in property that is sufficiently substantial that insuring against injury to the person or damage to the property does not amount to a mere wagering (betting) contract.

Buyers and lessees have an **insurable interest** in *identified goods*. The moment goods are identified to the contract by the seller or lessor, the buyer or lessee has an interest that allows him or her to obtain necessary insurance coverage for those goods even before the risk of loss passes.

IN THE COURTROOM

In March, a farmer sells a cotton crop that he hopes to harvest in October. After the crop is planted, the buyer insures it against hail damage. In September, a hailstorm ruins the crop. The buyer files a claim under her insurance policy. The insurer refuses to pay, asserting that the buyer has no insurable interest in the crop. *Is the insurer correct?* No. The buyer acquired an insurable interest when the crop was planted, because she had a contract to buy it.

Insurable Interest of the Seller or Lessor

A seller has an insurable interest in goods as long as he or she retains title to the goods. Even after title passes to a buyer, a seller who has a "security interest" in the goods (a right to secure payment) still has an insurable interest and can insure the goods. Hence, a buyer and a seller can have an insurable interest in identical goods at the same time. In all cases, one must sustain a loss to recover from an insurance company. A lessor retains an insurable interest in leased goods until an option to buy has been exercised by the lessee and the risk of loss has passed to the lessee.

TERMS AND CONCEPTS FOR REVIEW

CHAPTER SUMMARY • TITLE AND RISK OF LOSS

Shipment Contracts	In the absence of an agreement, title and risk pass on the seller's or lessor's delivery of conforming goods to the carrier.
Destination Contracts	In the absence of an agreement, title and risk pass on the seller's or lessor's *tender* of delivery of conforming goods to the buyer or lessee at the point of destination.
Delivery without Physical Movement of the Goods	**1.** In the absence of an agreement, if the goods are not represented by a document of title— **a.** Title passes on the formation of the contract. **b.** Risk passes to the buyer or lessee, if the seller or lessor is a merchant, on the buyer's or lessee's receipt of the goods. If the seller or lessor is a nonmerchant, risk passes on the seller's or lessor's *tender* of delivery of the goods. **2.** In the absence of an agreement, if the goods are represented by a document of title— **a.** If negotiable, and goods are held by a bailee, title and risk pass on the buyer's receipt of the document. **b.** If nonnegotiable, and goods are held by a bailee, title passes on the buyer's receipt of the document. Risk does not pass, however, until the buyer has had a reasonable time to present the document to demand the goods. **3.** In the absence of an agreement, if the goods are held by a bailee and no document of title is transferred, risk passes to the buyer when the bailee acknowledges the buyer's right to possession. **4.** In respect to leases, if goods held by a bailee are to be delivered without being moved, the risk of loss passes to the lessee upon acknowledgement by the bailee of the lessee's right to possession of the goods.
Sales by Nonowners	Between the owner and a good faith purchaser or sublessee— **1.** Void title—Owner prevails. **2.** Voidable title—Buyer prevails. **3.** Entrusting to a merchant—Buyer or sublessee prevails.
Sale-on-Approval Contracts	Title and risk of loss (from causes beyond the buyer's control) remain with the seller until the buyer approves (accepts) the offer.
Sale-or-Return Contracts	When the buyer receives possession of the goods, title and risk of loss pass to the buyer, and the buyer has the option to return to the seller the goods, title, and risk.
Passage of Risk of Loss in a Breached Sales or Lease Contract	**1.** If the seller or lessor breaches by tendering nonconforming goods that are rejected by the buyer or lessee, the risk of loss does not pass to the buyer or lessee until the defects are cured (unless the buyer or lessee accepts the goods in spite of their defects, thus waiving the right to reject).

CHAPTER SUMMARY • *Continued*

Passage of Risk of Loss in a Breached Sales or Lease Contract—continued	**2.** If the buyer or lessee breaches the contract, the risk of loss to identified goods immediately shifts to the buyer or lessee. Limitations are— **a.** The buyer or lessee bears the risk for only a commercially reasonable time after the seller or lessor learns of the breach. **b.** The buyer or lessee is liable only to the extent of any deficiency in the seller's or lessor's insurance coverage.
Buyer's or Lessee's Insurable Interest	Buyers and lessees have an insurable interest in goods the moment the goods are identified to the contract by the seller or lessor.
Seller's or Lessor's Insurable Interest	Sellers and lessors have an insurable interest in goods as long as they have (1) title to the goods or (2) a security interest in the goods.

HYPOTHETICAL QUESTIONS

17–1. Sales by Nonowners. In the following situations, two parties lay claim to the same goods sold. Discuss which of the parties would prevail in each situation.

(a) Terry steals Dom's television set and sells the set to Blake, an innocent purchaser, for value. Dom learns that Blake has the set and demands its return.

(b) Karlin takes her television set for repair to Orken, a merchant who sells new and used television sets. By accident, one of Orken's employees sells the set to Grady, an innocent purchaser-customer, who takes possession. Karlin wants her set back from Grady.

17–2. Risk of Loss. When will risk of loss pass from the seller to the buyer under each of the following contracts, assuming the parties have not expressly agreed on when risk of loss would pass?

(a) A New York seller contracts with a San Francisco buyer to ship goods to the buyer F.O.B. San Francisco.

(b) A New York seller contracts with a San Francisco buyer to ship goods to the buyer in San Francisco. There is no indication as to whether the shipment will be F.O.B. New York or F.O.B. San Francisco.

(c) A seller contracts with a buyer to sell goods located on the seller's premises. The buyer pays for the goods and makes arrangements to pick them up the next week at the seller's place of business.

(d) A seller contracts with a buyer to sell goods located in a warehouse.

REAL WORLD CASE PROBLEM

17–3. Entrustment Rule. Ron Rasmus was a farmer in the business of buying, selling, and raising exotic animals, including ostriches. When Gene Baker began buying flightless birds for investment purposes, he entered into an agreement with Rasmus to board the animals at Rasmus's farm. Mike Pickard bought two pairs of adult breeding ostriches from Rasmus, unaware that they were Baker's. Pickard sold one of the pairs to Gary Prenger. Both Pickard and Prenger arranged to board the ostriches with Rasmus. When Baker removed the birds from Rasmus's farm, Pickard and Prenger filed a suit in an Iowa state court against him, seeking in part to recover the birds. To whom do the birds belong? Discuss fully. [*Prenger v. Baker,* 542 N.W.2d 805 (Iowa 1995)]

Expanded Access to the Internet

For updated links to resources available on the Web, as well as a variety of other materials, visit this text's Web site at **http://blte.westbuslaw.com.**

To find information on the UCC, including the UCC provisions discussed in this chapter, refer to the Web sites listed in the *Expanded Access to the Internet* in Chapter 16.

Information on current commercial law topics, including some of the topics discussed in this chapter, is available at the Web site of the law firm of Hale and Dorr. Go to

http://www.haledorr.com

ONLINE LEGAL RESEARCH

Go to **http://blte.westbuslaw.com,** the Web site that accompanies this text. Select "Internet Applications," and then click on "Chapter 17." There you will find the following Internet research exercise that you can perform to learn more about passage of title:

Activity 17–1: Passage of Title

Chapter 17 ■ WORK SET

TRUE-FALSE QUESTIONS

_____ **1.** Identification occurs when goods are shipped by the seller.

_____ **2.** Unless the parties agree otherwise, title passes at the time and place that the buyer accepts the goods.

_____ **3.** Unless a contract provides otherwise, it is normally assumed to be a shipment contract.

_____ **4.** A buyer and a seller cannot both have an insurable interest in the same goods at the same time.

_____ **5.** In a sale on approval, the risk of loss passes to the buyer as soon as the buyer takes possession.

_____ **6.** A buyer can acquire valid title to stolen goods if he or she does not know that the goods are stolen.

_____ **7.** Under a destination contract, title passes at time and place of shipment.

_____ **8.** If a seller is a merchant, the risk of loss passes when a buyer takes possession of the goods.

MULTIPLE-CHOICE QUESTIONS

_____ **1.** Bob contracts to sell to the Marcos University Bookstore 10,000 black felt-tipped pens. Bob identifies the pens by boxing the order, attaching labels with Marcos's address to the cartons, and leaving the boxes on the loading dock for shipping. Between Bob and Marcos,

a. the risk of loss has passed with respect to all of the pens.
b. the risk of loss has passed with respect to half of the pens.
c. the risk of loss has passed with respect to the pens with labels on the boxes.
d. none of the above.

_____ **2.** Popco in Akron agrees to ship one hundred popcorn poppers to Fine Stores in Dayton under a shipment contract. On Monday, Popco delivers the poppers to Capitol Transport to take to Dayton, where they arrive on Tuesday. On Wednesday, Capitol tells Fine that it can pick the goods up at Capitol's warehouse. On Thursday, the warehouse burns to the ground. On Friday, Fine learns about the fire. The risk of loss passed to Fine on

a. Monday.
b. Tuesday.
c. Friday.
d. none of the above.

_____ **3.** On Monday, Stan buys a mountain bike from Tom, his neighbor, who says, "Take the bike." Stan says, "I'll leave it in your garage until Friday." On Tuesday, Rosie steals the bike from Tom's garage. Who bore the risk?

a. Stan.
b. Tom.
c. Both a and b.
d. None of the above.

_____ **4.** On Monday, Craft Computers in Seattle delivers five hundred keyboards to Pac Transport to take to Portland under a destination contract with Comp Stores. The keyboards arrive in Portland on Tuesday, and Pac tells Comp they are at Pac's warehouse. On Thursday, the warehouse burns down. On Friday, Comp learns of the fire. The risk of loss passed to Comp on

a. Monday.
b. Tuesday.
c. Friday.
d. none of the above.

_____ **5.** Alpha Comm agrees to sell one hundred cellular phones to Beta Electronics. Alpha identifies the goods by marking the crates with red stripes. Title has not yet passed to Beta. Who has an insurable interest in the goods?

a. Only Alpha.
b. Only Beta.
c. Both Alpha and Beta.
d. None of the above.

_____ **6.** Under a contract with QT Corp., Gold Media ships sixty hard drives. When QT opens the crates, it discovers that the drives are the wrong model, but agrees to accept them anyway. The risk of loss passed to QT when

a. Gold shipped the drives.
b. QT opened the crates.
c. QT discovered that the goods were the wrong model.
d. QT accepted the drives.

_____ **7.** Apple Bike Makers agrees to sell forty mountain bikes to Orange Mountain Recreation, under a shipment contract. Apple delivers the goods to Sugar Trucking to take to Orange Mountain. Sugar delivers the goods. Title to the goods passed when

a. Apple agreed to sell the goods.
b. Apple delivered the goods to Sugar.
c. Sugar delivered the goods to Orange Mountain.
d. none of the above.

ISSUE SPOTTERS

1. Adams Textiles in Kansas City sells certain fabrics to Silk n' Satin Stores in Oklahoma City. Adams packs the fabric and ships it by rail to Silk. In transit across Kansas, a tornado derails the train and scatters and shreds the fabric across miles of cornfields. What are the consequences if Silk bore the risk? If Adams bore the risk?

2. Paula boards her horse Blaze at Gold Spur Stables. She sells the horse to George and calls Gold Spur to say, "I sold Blaze to George." Gold Spur says, "Ok." That night, Blaze is kicked in the head by another horse and dies. Who pays for the loss?

Performance and Breach

18

LEARNING OBJECTIVES

When you finish this chapter, you should be able to:

1. Explain the seller's and lessor's major obligation under a contract.
2. Identify the buyer's or lessee's major duties under a contract.
3. List the remedies available to a seller or lessor when the buyer or lessee is in breach.
4. State the remedies available to a buyer or lessee when the seller or lessor is in breach.

FACING A LEGAL PROBLEM

In San Francisco, Rogers contracts to sell Aguirre five used trucks, which both parties know are located in a warehouse in Chicago. The parties expect that Aguirre will pick up the trucks, but nothing about a place of delivery is specified in the contract. *What is the place for delivery of the trucks? Can Rogers "deliver" the trucks without moving them? If so, how?*

To understand the *performance* that is required of the parties under a sales or lease contract, it is necessary to know the duties and obligations each party has assumed under the terms of the contract. In this chapter, after first looking at the general requirement of good faith, we examine the basic performance obligations of the parties under a sales or lease contract.

Sometimes circumstances make it difficult for a person to carry out the promised performance. In this situation, the contract may be breached. When breach occurs, the aggrieved party looks for remedies—which are dealt with in the second half of this chapter.

Good Faith and Commercial Reasonableness

The obligations of good faith and commercial reasonableness underlie every contract within the UCC. These standards are read into every contract. They also provide a framework in which the parties can specify particulars of performance. For instance, a contract may specify the city in which goods are to be delivered but leave open the particular address. The buyer is obliged to specify the address before the delivery date. If he or she fails to do so, the seller is excused from any resulting delay.

Obligations of the Seller or Lessor

LEARNING OBJECTIVE NO. 1

Explaining the Seller's and Lessor's Major Obligation under a Contract

The seller's or lessor's major obligation under a sales contract is to *tender* conforming goods to the buyer or lessee.

Tender of Delivery

Tender of delivery requires that the seller or lessor hold *conforming* goods at the buyer's or lessee's disposal and give the buyer or lessee whatever notification is reasonably necessary to enable the buyer or lessee to take delivery.

Tender must occur at a *reasonable hour* and in a *reasonable manner.* In other words, a seller cannot call the buyer at 2:00 A.M. and say, "The goods are ready. I'll give you twenty minutes to get them." Unless the parties have agreed otherwise, the goods must be tendered for delivery at a reasonable time and kept available for a reasonable period of time to enable the buyer to take possession of them.

All goods called for by a contract must be tendered in a single delivery unless the parties agree otherwise or the circumstances are such that either party can rightfully request delivery in lots. Hence, an order for 1,000 shirts cannot be delivered two at a time. If the seller and the buyer understand that the shirts are to be delivered as they are produced in four lots of 250 each, however, and the price can be apportioned accordingly, it may be commercially reasonable to deliver in lots.

Place of Delivery

The UCC provides for the place of delivery under a contract if the contract does not state or otherwise indicate a place.

Noncarrier Cases. If the contract does not designate the place of delivery for the goods, and the buyer is expected to pick them up, the place of delivery is the *seller's place of business* or, if the seller has none, the *seller's residence.* If the contract involves the sale of *identified goods,* and the parties know when they enter into the contract that these goods are located somewhere other than at the seller's place of business (such as at a warehouse), then the *location of the goods* is the place for delivery.

In the legal problem set out at the beginning of this chapter, in San Francisco, Rogers contracts to sell Aguirre trucks located in a warehouse in Chicago. Nothing is said about delivery, although the parties expect Aguirre to pick up the trucks. *What is the place for delivery?* Chicago. *How can Rogers "deliver" the trucks without moving them?* Aguirre will need some type of document to show the bailee (the warehouser to whom the goods are entrusted) that Aguirre is entitled to the trucks. Rogers can tender delivery without moving the trucks by either giving Aguirre a *negotiable document of title* or obtaining the *bailee's (warehouser's) acknowledgment* that Aguirre is entitled to possession.

Carrier Cases. In many instances, attendant circumstances or delivery terms in the contract make it apparent that the parties intend that a carrier, such as a trucking company, be used to move the goods. There are two ways a seller can complete performance of the obligation to deliver the goods in carrier cases: through a shipment contract or through a destination contract.

Shipment Contracts. Recall from Chapter 17 that a *shipment contract* requires or authorizes the seller to ship goods by a carrier. The contract does not require that the seller deliver the goods at a particular destination. Unless otherwise agreed, the seller must do the following:

1. Put the goods into the hands of the carrier.
2. Make a contract for their transportation that is reasonable according to the nature of the goods and their value. (For example, certain types of goods, such as frozen beef, need refrigeration in transit.)
3. Obtain and promptly deliver or tender to the buyer any documents necessary to enable the buyer to obtain the goods from the carrier.
4. Promptly notify the buyer that shipment has been made.

If the seller fails to notify the buyer that shipment has been made or fails to make a proper contract for transportation, and a *material loss* of the goods or a *delay* results, the buyer can reject the shipment.

Destination Contracts. Under a *destination contract,* the seller agrees to see that conforming goods will be duly tendered to the buyer at a particular destination. The goods must be tendered at a reasonable hour and held at the buyer's disposal for a reasonable length of time. The seller must also give the buyer appropriate notice. In addition, the seller must provide the buyer with any documents of title necessary to enable the buyer to obtain delivery from the carrier.

The Perfect Tender Rule

If the goods or the tender of delivery fail in any respect to conform to the contract, the buyer or lessee has the right to accept the goods, reject the entire shipment, or accept part and reject part.

To obtain information on performance requirements in relation to contracts for the international sale of goods, you can access the Institute of International Commercial Law at Pace University at:

http://cisgw3.law.pace.edu

Exceptions to the Perfect Tender Rule

Because of the rigidity of the perfect tender rule, several exceptions to the rule have been created, some of which are discussed here.

Agreement of the Parties. If the parties have agreed that, for example, defective goods or parts will not be rejected if the seller or lessor is able to repair or replace them within a reasonable period of time, the perfect tender rule does not apply.

Cure. The term *cure* refers to the seller's or lessor's right to repair, adjust, or replace defective or nonconforming goods. When any tender or delivery is rejected because of *nonconforming goods* and the time for performance has *not yet expired,* the seller or lessor can notify the buyer or lessee promptly of the intention to cure and can then do so *within the contract time for performance.* Once the time for performance under the contract has expired, the seller or lessor can still exercise the right to cure if he or she had *reasonable grounds to believe that the nonconforming tender would be acceptable to the buyer or lessee.*

IN THE COURTROOM

In the past, Reddy Electronics frequently allowed the Topps Company to substitute certain electronic supplies when the goods Reddy ordered were not available. Under a new contract for the same type of goods, Reddy rejects the substitute supplies on the last day Topps can perform the contract. *Does Topps have the right to cure?* Yes. Topps had reasonable grounds to believe Reddy would accept a substitute. Therefore, Topps can cure within a reasonable time, even though conforming delivery will occur after the actual time limit for performance allowed under the contract.

The right to cure substantially restricts the right of the buyer or lessee to reject. For example, if the buyer refuses a tender of goods as nonconforming but does not disclose the nature of the defect to the seller, the buyer cannot later assert the defect as a defense if the defect is one that the seller could have cured. Generally, buyers and lessees must act in good faith and state specific reasons for refusing to accept the goods.

Substitution of Carriers. An agreed-on manner of delivery (such as which carrier will be used to transport the goods) may become impracticable or unavailable through no fault of either party. If a commercially reasonable substitute is available, this substitute performance is sufficient.

INSTALLMENT CONTRACT
A contract in which payments due are made periodically. Also may allow for delivery of goods in separate lots with payment made for each.

Installment Contracts. An **installment contract** is a single contract that requires or authorizes delivery in two or more separate lots to be accepted and paid for separately. In an installment contract, a buyer or lessee can reject an installment *only if the nonconformity substantially impairs the value* of the installment and cannot be cured. For instance, if a seller is to deliver fifteen freezers in lots of five each, and in the first lot, four of the freezers have defective cooling units that cannot be repaired, the buyer can reject the entire lot. An entire installment contract is breached only when one or more nonconforming installments *substantially* impair the value of the *whole contract.*

Commercial Impracticability. Whenever occurrences unforeseen by either party when the contract was made render performance commercially impracticable, the rule of perfect tender no longer holds. The unforeseen contingency must be one that would have been impossible to imagine in a given business situation.

IN THE COURTROOM

A major oil company that receives its supplies from the Middle East has a contract to supply a buyer with 100,000 gallons of oil. After the contract is entered into, an oil embargo by the Organization of Petroleum Exporting Countries (OPEC) prevents the seller from securing oil supplies to meet the terms of the contract. Because of the same embargo, the seller cannot secure oil from any other source. *Does this situation come under the commercial-impracticability exception to the perfect tender doctrine?* Yes. Of course, the embargo must have been unforeseen by either party when the contract was made.

Destruction of Identified Goods. When a casualty (such as a fire) totally destroys *identified goods* under a contract through no fault of either party and *before risk passes to the buyer or lessee,* the parties are excused from performance. If the goods are only partially destroyed, the buyer or lessee can inspect them and either treat the contract as void or accept the damaged goods with a reduction of the contract price.

LEARNING OBJECTIVE NO. 2
Identifying the Buyer's or Lessee's Major Duties under a Contract

Obligations of the Buyer or Lessee

Once the seller or lessor has tendered delivery, the buyer or lessee is obligated to accept the goods and pay for them according to the terms of the contract. In the absence of any specific agreements, the buyer or lessee must do the following:

1. Furnish facilities reasonably suited for receipt of the goods.
2. Make payment at the time and place the buyer *receives* the goods.

Payment

Payment can be made by any means agreed on between the parties—cash or any other method of payment generally acceptable in the commercial world. If the seller demands cash, the seller must permit the buyer reasonable time to obtain it. When a sale is made on credit, the buyer is obliged to pay according to the specified terms (for example, ninety days). The credit period usually begins on the *date of shipment.*

Right of Inspection

Unless otherwise agreed, or for C.O.D. (collect on delivery) goods, the buyer or lessee has the right to verify, before making payment, that the goods tendered or delivered conform to the contract. If the goods are not what the buyer or lessee ordered, he or she has no duty to pay. Unless otherwise agreed, inspection can take place at any reasonable place and time and in any reasonable manner. Generally, what is reasonable is determined by custom of the trade, past practices of the parties, and the like.

Revocation of Acceptance

After a buyer or lessee accepts a lot or a commercial unit, any return of the goods must be by *revocation of acceptance.* (*Revocation* means "withdrawal.") Acceptance can be revoked if a nonconformity *substantially* impairs the value of the unit or lot and if one of the following factors is present:

1. If acceptance was predicated on the reasonable assumption that the nonconformity would be cured, and it has not been cured within a reasonable period of time.
2. If the buyer or lessee does not discover the nonconformity until after acceptance, either because it was difficult to discover before acceptance or because the seller's or lessor's assurance that the goods were conforming kept the buyer or lessee from inspecting the goods.

Anticipatory Repudiation

What if, before the time for performance, one party clearly communicates to the other the intention not to perform? Such an action is a breach of the contract by *anticipatory repudiation* (refusal to acknowledge the party's obligations under the contract). When anticipatory repudiation occurs, the aggrieved party can do the following:

1. Await performance by the repudiating party, hoping that he or she will decide to honor the contract.
2. Resort to any remedy for breach.
3. In either case, *suspend performance* or proceed with the seller's right to resell the goods or to salvage unfinished goods (see below).

Remedies of the Seller or Lessor

LEARNING OBJECTIVE NO. 3
Listing the Remedies Available to a Seller or Lessor When the Buyer or Lessee Is in Breach

Numerous remedies are available to a seller or lessor when the buyer or lessee is in breach under the UCC. Many of these remedies—including the rights to withhold delivery, to reclaim the goods, to resell the goods, to recover the purchase price, and to recover damages—are discussed here.

The Right to Withhold Delivery

In general, sellers and lessors can withhold or stop performance of their obligations under a contract when buyers or lessees are in breach. If a buyer or lessee has wrongfully rejected or revoked acceptance, failed to make proper and timely payment, or repudiated a part of the contract, the seller or lessor can withhold delivery of the goods. If a breach results from the buyer's or lessee's *insolvency* (see Chapter 17), the seller or lessor can refuse to deliver the goods unless the buyer or lessee pays in cash.

The Right to Reclaim the Goods

Under a sales contract, if a seller discovers that the buyer has *received* goods on credit and is insolvent, the seller can demand return of the goods, if the demand is made within ten days of the buyer's receipt of the goods. The seller can demand and reclaim the goods at any time if the buyer misrepresented his or her solvency in writing within three months prior to the delivery.

In regard to lease contracts, if the lessee is in default (fails to make payments that are due, for example), the lessor may reclaim the leased goods that are in the possession of the lessee.

The Right to Resell the Goods

Sometimes a buyer or lessee breaches or repudiates a contract when the seller or lessor is still in possession of the goods (or when the goods have been delivered to a carrier or bailee, but the buyer or lessee has not yet received them). In this event, the seller or lessor can resell or dispose of the goods. When the goods contracted for are unfinished at the time of breach, the seller or lessor can do one of two things: (1) cease manufacturing the goods and resell them for scrap or salvage value, or (2) complete the manufacture of the goods and resell or dispose of them. In any case, the seller or lessor can recover any deficiency between the resale price and the contract price, along with **incidental damages** (those costs to the seller or lessor resulting from the breach).

Incidental Damages
Damages resulting from a breach of contract, including all reasonable expenses incurred because of the breach.

The Right to Recover the Price

An unpaid seller or lessor can bring an action to recover the purchase price or payments due under the lease contract, and incidental damages, but only under one of the following circumstances:

1. When the buyer or lessee has accepted the goods and has not revoked acceptance.
2. When conforming goods have been lost or damaged after the risk of loss has passed to the buyer or lessee.
3. When the buyer or lessee has breached the contract after the contract goods have been identified and the seller or lessor is unable to resell the goods.

If a seller or lessor sues for the contract price of goods that he or she has been unable to resell or dispose of, the goods must be held for the buyer or lessee. The seller or lessor can resell at any time prior to collection (of the judgment) from the buyer or lessee, but the net proceeds from the sale must be credited to the buyer or lessee.

IN THE COURTROOM

Southern Realty contracts with Gem Point, Inc., to purchase one thousand pens with Southern Realty's name inscribed on them. Gem Point delivers the pens, but Southern Realty refuses to accept. *Does Gem Point have, as a proper remedy, an action for the purchase price?* Yes. Gem Point could not sell to anyone else the pens inscribed with Southern Realty's business name.

THE RIGHT TO RECOVER DAMAGES

If a buyer or lessee repudiates a contract or wrongfully refuses to accept the goods, a seller or lessor can bring an action to recover the damages that were sustained. Ordinarily, the amount of damages equals the difference between the contract price lease payments and the market price (at the time and place of tender of the goods) plus incidental damages.

Before filing a lawsuit, assess how successful you might be and determine whether a negotiated settlement is preferable.

If the difference between the contract price or lease payments and the market price is too small to place the seller or lessor in the position that he or she would have been in if the buyer or lessee had fully performed, the proper measure of damages is the seller's or lessor's lost profits, including a reasonable allowance for overhead and other incidental expenses. For instance, if a car dealer contracts to sell a car for $5,000 to a buyer who repudiates, and the seller later sells the car to another buyer for $5,000, the seller can recover the profit that he or she would have made on the second sale (if the first buyer had not breached, the seller would have sold two cars instead of one).

Remedies of the Buyer or Lessee

LEARNING OBJECTIVE NO. 4

Stating the Remedies Available to a Buyer or Lessee When the Seller or Lessor Is in Breach

Under the UCC, there are numerous remedies available to the buyer or lessee. Here we treat some of them—including the rights to reject the goods, to obtain specific performance, to obtain cover, and to recover damages.

THE RIGHT OF REJECTION

If either the goods or the tender of the goods by the seller or lessor fails to conform to the contract *in any respect,* the buyer or lessee normally can reject the goods. If some of the goods conform to the contract, the buyer or lessee can keep the conforming goods and reject the rest.

Timeliness and Reason for Rejection Required. Goods must be rejected within a reasonable amount of time, and the seller or lessor must be **seasonably** (in a timely fashion; at the proper time) notified. Failure to do so precludes the buyer or lessee from using those defects to justify rejection or to establish breach when the seller or lessor could have cured the defects if they had been stated seasonably.

SEASONABLY
Within a specified time period, or if no time is specified, within a reasonable time.

Duties of Merchant Buyers and Lessees When Goods Are Rejected. If a *merchant buyer or lessee* rightfully rejects goods, he or she is required to follow any reasonable instructions received from the seller or lessor with respect to the goods controlled by the buyer or lessee. For instance, the seller or lessor might ask the buyer or lessee to store the goods in the buyer's or lessee's warehouse until the next day when the seller or lessor can retrieve them. If there are no instructions, the buyer or lessee may store the goods or reship them to the seller or lessor. In any of these situations, the buyer or lessee is entitled to reimbursement for the costs involved.

THE RIGHT TO OBTAIN SPECIFIC PERFORMANCE

A buyer or lessee can obtain specific performance—that is, exactly what was contracted for—when the goods are unique or when the buyer's or lessee's remedy at law (money damages) is inadequate. When the contract is for the purchase of a particular work of art, a copyright, or a similarly unique item, money damages may not be sufficient.

IN THE COURTROOM

Sutherlin contracts to sell his antique car to Fenwick for $30,000, with delivery and payment due on June 14. Fenwick tenders payment on June 14, but Sutherlin refuses to deliver. *If Fenwick sues Sutherlin, can Fenwick obtain the car?* Because the antique car is unique, Fenwick can probably obtain specific performance of the contract from Sutherlin.

The Right of Cover

Cover
Under the UCC, a remedy that allows the buyer or lessee, on the seller's or lessor's breach, to purchase or lease the goods from another seller or lessor and substitute them for the goods due under the contract. If the cost of cover exceeds the cost under the contract, the breaching party will be liable to the buyer or lessee for the difference.

In certain situations, buyers and lessees can protect themselves by obtaining **cover**—that is, by substituting goods for those that were due under the contract. This option is available to a buyer or lessee who has rightfully rejected goods or revoked acceptance. The option is also available when the seller or lessor repudiates the contract or fails to deliver the goods. After purchasing substitute goods, the buyer or lessee can recover from the seller or lessor the difference between the cost of cover and the contract price, plus incidental and consequential damages less the expenses (such as delivery costs) that were saved as a result of the breach. Consequential damages include any loss suffered by the buyer or lessee that the seller or lessor could have foreseen (had reason to know about) at the time of the contract. For instance, if a contractor tells a heavy equipment manufacturer that the contractor needs a certain piece of equipment by July 1 to close a $10,000 deal, the manufacturer can foresee that if the equipment is not delivered by that date, the contractor will suffer consequential damages.

The Right to Recover Damages

If a seller or lessor repudiates the contract or fails to deliver the goods, the buyer or lessee can sue for damages. The measure of recovery is the difference between the contract price and the market price of the goods (at the place the seller or lessor was supposed to deliver) at the time the buyer or lessee *learned* of the breach. The buyer or lessee can also recover incidental and consequential damages less expenses that were saved as a result of the seller's or lessor's breach.

IN THE COURTROOM

Schilling orders 10,000 bushels of wheat from Valdone for $5 a bushel, with delivery due on June 14 and payment due on June 20. Valdone does not deliver on June 14. On June 14 the market price of wheat is $5.50 per bushel. Schilling chooses to do without the wheat. He sues Valdone for damages for nondelivery. *How much can Schilling recover?* Schilling can recover $0.50 × 10,000, or $5,000, plus any expenses the breach may have caused him to incur. (Any expenses saved by the breach would be deducted.)

When the seller or lessor breaches a warranty, the measure of damages equals the difference between the value of the goods as accepted and their value if they had been delivered as warranted. For this and other types of breaches in which the buyer or lessee has accepted the goods, the buyer or lessee is entitled to recover for any loss resulting in the ordinary course of events.

Statute of Limitations

An action brought by a party for breach of contract must be commenced under the UCC *within four years after the cause of action arises.* By agreement in the contract, the parties can reduce this period to not less than one year but cannot extend it beyond four years. A cause of action arises for breach of warranty when the seller makes *tender* of delivery. This is the rule even if the aggrieved party is unaware of the breach.

TERMS AND CONCEPTS FOR REVIEW

cover 220
incidental damages 218
installment contract 216
seasonably 219

CHAPTER SUMMARY • PERFORMANCE AND BREACH

Seller's or Lessor's Performance	**1.** The seller or lessor must ship or tender *conforming* goods to the buyer. Tender must take place at a *reasonable hour* and in a *reasonable manner.* Under the perfect tender doctrine, the seller or lessor must tender goods that exactly conform to the terms of the contract. **2.** If the seller or lessor tenders nonconforming goods and the buyer or lessee rejects them, the seller or lessor may *cure* (repair or replace the goods) within the contract time for performance (or for a reasonable time beyond the contract time, if the seller or lessor had reasonable grounds to believe that the buyer or lessee would accept the nonconforming goods). **3.** If the agreed-on means of delivery becomes impracticable or unavailable, the seller or lessor must substitute an alternative means (such as a different carrier) if one is available. **4.** If a seller or lessor tenders nonconforming goods in any one installment under an installment contract, the buyer or lessee may reject the installment only if its value is substantially impaired and cannot be cured. The entire contract is breached when one or more installments *substantially* impair the value of the *whole* contract. **5.** When performance becomes commercially impracticable owing to circumstances unforeseen when the contract was formed, the perfect tender rule no longer holds.
Buyer's or Lessee's Performance	**1.** Upon tender of delivery by the seller or lessor, the buyer or lessee must furnish facilities reasonably suited for receipt of the goods. **2.** The buyer or lessee must pay for the goods at the time and place the buyer or lessee *receives* them, even if the place of shipment is the place of delivery, unless the sale is made on credit. Payment may be by any method generally acceptable in the commercial world. **3.** Unless otherwise agreed, the buyer or lessee has an absolute right to inspect the goods before acceptance. **4.** The buyer or lessee may revoke acceptance only if a nonconformity *substantially* impairs the value of the unit or lot and if one of the following is present: **a.** Acceptance was predicated on the reasonable assumption that the nonconformity would be cured, and it was not cured within a reasonable time. **b.** The buyer or lessee did not discover the nonconformity before acceptance, either because it was difficult to discover before acceptance or because the seller's or lessor's assurance that the goods were conforming kept the buyer or lessee from inspecting the goods.
Anticipatory Repudiation	If, before the time for performance, either party clearly indicates to the other an intention not to perform, the aggrieved party may (a) await performance by the repudiating party or (b) resort to any remedy for breach. In either situation, the aggrieved party may *suspend performance* or proceed with the seller's or lessor's right to resell or to dispose of the goods, or to salvage unfinished goods.

CHAPTER SUMMARY • *Continued*

Seller's or Lessor's Remedies for Breach	**1.** If the goods are in the seller's or lessor's possession, the seller or lessor may withhold delivery, resell the goods, or sue for damages. **2.** If the goods are in the buyer's or lessee's possession, the seller or lessor may (a) reclaim goods from an insolvent buyer or lessee if the demand is made within ten days of receipt or (b) sue for the price under the contract.
Buyer's or Lessee's Remedies for Breach	**1.** If the seller or lessor refuses to deliver or the seller or lessor tenders nonconforming goods and the buyer or lessee rejects them, the buyer or lessee may cover or sue for damages. **2.** If the seller or lessor tenders nonconforming goods and the buyer or lessee accepts them, the buyer or lessee, with notice, may sue for damages. **3.** If the seller or lessor refuses delivery and the buyer or lessee wants the goods, the buyer or lessee may sue for specific performance.
Statute of Limitations	There is a four-year statute of limitations for actions for breach of contract. By agreement, the parties can reduce this period to not less than one year, but they cannot extend it beyond four years.

HYPOTHETICAL QUESTIONS

18–1. Remedies. Genix, Inc., has contracted to sell Larson five hundred washing machines of a certain model at list price. Genix is to ship the goods on or before December 1. Genix produces one thousand washing machines of this model but has not yet prepared Larson's shipment. On November 1, Larson repudiates the contract. Discuss the remedies available to Genix in this situation.

18–2. Anticipatory Repudiation. Moore contracted in writing to sell her 1994 Ford Taurus to Hammer for $8,500. Moore agreed to deliver the car on Wednesday, and Hammer promised to pay the $8,500 on the following Friday. On Tuesday, Hammer informed Moore that he would not be buying the car after all. By Friday, Hammer had changed his mind again and tendered $8,500 to Moore. Moore, although she had not sold the car to another party, refused the tender and refused to deliver. Hammer claimed that Moore had breached their contract. Moore contended that Hammer's repudiation released her from her duty to perform under the contract. Who is correct and why?

REAL WORLD CASE PROBLEM

18–3. Remedies of the Buyer or Lessee. Marine Indemnity Insurance Co. of America purchased a "toploader" (a piece of ship-loading equipment) from Hapag-Lloyd, A.G. (A.G. is an abbreviation of the German *Aktiengesellschaft*—the German equivalent of the English term *company*.) Marine Indemnity was aware of the fact that the wiring in the toploader's engine was defective but nevertheless used the equipment in its defective state without notifying the seller. After Marine Indemnity had used the toploader for about four weeks, the wiring caused an explosion in the engine, which severely damaged the equipment. Marine Indemnity then sued Hapag-Lloyd for breach of express warranty. The trial court held for Marine Indemnity. Hapag-Lloyd appealed, contending that Marine Indemnity's failure to give timely notice of the breach barred it from pursuing any remedy. Will the appellate court agree with Hapag-Lloyd? Discuss fully. [*Hapag-Lloyd, A.G. v. Marine Indemnity Insurance Co. of America,* 576 So.2d 1330 (Fla.App.3d 1991)]

Expanded Access to the Internet

For updated links to resources available on the Web, as well as a variety of other materials, visit this text's Web site at **http://blte.westbuslaw.com**.

To find information on the UCC, including the UCC provisions discussed in this chapter, refer to the Web sites listed in the *Expanded Access to the Internet* in Chapter 16.

The Boeing Company has posted online a summary of the contract rights and duties of parties forming sales contracts with that company. To view the summary, go to

http://www.boeing.com/companyoffices/doingbiz/tcmdhs/sect7_97.htm#c

Online Legal Research

Go to **http://blte.westbuslaw.com**, the Web site that accompanies this text. Select "Internet Applications," and then click on "Chapter 18." There you will find the following Internet research exercise that you can perform to learn more about performance requirements in the international context:

Activity 18–1: International Performance Requirements

Chapter 18 ■ WORK SET

TRUE-FALSE QUESTIONS

_____ **1.** Performance of a sales contract is controlled by the agreement between the seller and the buyer.

_____ **2.** If identified goods are destroyed through no fault of either party, and risk has not passed to the buyer, the parties are excused from performance.

_____ **3.** Payment is always due at the time of delivery.

_____ **4.** A buyer or lessee can always reject delivered goods on discovery of a defect, regardless of previous opportunities to inspect.

_____ **5.** If a buyer or lessee is in breach, the seller or lessor can cancel the contract and sue for damages.

_____ **6.** If a seller or lessor cancels a contract without justification, he or she is in breach, and the buyer or lessee can sue for damages.

_____ **7.** A buyer's principal obligation is to tender delivery.

_____ **8.** In an installment contract, a buyer can reject any installment for any reason.

MULTIPLE-CHOICE QUESTIONS

_____ **1.** Standard Office Products orders one hundred computers from National Suppliers. National promises to deliver on Tuesday. The delivery must be

a. at a reasonable hour, but it can be in any manner.
b. in a reasonable manner, but it can be at any time.
c. at a reasonable hour and in a reasonable manner.
d. none of the above.

_____ **2.** Bill delivers six satellite dishes to Tom, according to their contract. The contract says nothing about payment. Tom must pay for the goods

a. within thirty days of the seller's request for payment.
b. within ten days.
c. within ten business days.
d. on delivery.

_____ **3.** Neal contracts to sell five laser printers to Laura. Under either a shipment or a destination contract, Neal must give Laura

a. the documents necessary to obtain the goods.
b. appropriate notice regarding delivery.
c. both a and b.
d. none of the above.

_____ **4.** World Globe Company agrees to sell to Tom's Map Shop fifty globes. World tenders delivery, but Tom refuses to accept or to pay for the globes. If World sues Tom for damages, World could recover the difference between the contract price and the market price at the time and place of

a. contracting.
b. tender.
c. rejection.
d. none of the above.

_____ **5.** Alto Corporation agrees to buy one hundred hard drives from Gopher Equipment. When Gopher fails to deliver, Alto is forced to cover. Alto sues Gopher. Alto can recover from Gopher

a. the cover price, less the contract price.
b. incidental and consequential damages.
c. both a and b.
d. none of the above.

_____ **6.** Pep Paints agrees to sell to Monar Painters Grade A-1 latex outdoor paint to be delivered September 8. On September 7, Pep tenders Grade B-2 paint. Monar rejects the Grade B-2 paint. If, two days later, Pep tenders Grade C-3 paint with an offer of a price allowance, Pep will have

a. one day to cure.
b. a reasonable time to cure.
c. additional, unlimited time to cure.
d. none of the above.

_____ **7.** Roy's Game Town orders virtual reality helmets from VR, Inc. VR delivers, but Roy rejects the shipment without telling VR the reason. If VR had known the reason, it could have corrected the problem within hours. Roy sues VR for damages. Roy will

a. win, because VR's tender did not conform to the contract.
b. win, because VR made no attempt to cure.
c. lose, because Roy's rejection was unjustified—VR could have cured.
d. lose, because a buyer cannot reject goods and sue for damages.

_____ **8.** AdamCo agrees to sell the latest version of the Go! CD-ROMs to Cutter Computers. AdamCo delivers an outdated version of Go! (nonconforming goods). Cutter's possible remedies may include

a. recovering damages.
b. revoking acceptance.
c. rejecting part or all of the goods.
d. all of the above.

ISSUE SPOTTERS

1. Mike agrees to sell 1,000 espresso makers to Jenny to be delivered on May 1. Due to a strike in the last week of April, there is a temporary shortage of delivery vehicles. Mike can deliver the espresso makers 200 at a time over a period of ten days, with the first delivery on May 1. Does Mike have the right to deliver the goods in five lots?

2. Pic Post-Stars agrees to sell Ace Novelty 5,000 posters of celebrities, to be delivered on April 1. On March 1, Pic tells Ace, "The deal's off." Ace says, "I expect you to deliver. I'll be waiting." Can Ace sue Pic without waiting until April 1?

Warranties and Product Liability

19

LEARNING OBJECTIVES

When you finish this chapter, you should be able to:

1 State when express warranties arise in a sales or lease contract.

2 Identify the implied warranties that arise in a sales or lease contract.

3 Discuss negligence as the basis of product liability.

4 List the requirements of strict product liability.

FACING A LEGAL PROBLEM

Shari steals merchandise from the inventory room in Miguel's Electronics Store and sells a CD-ROM drive and a computer monitor to Cory, who does not know that they are stolen. If Miguel discovers that Cory has the goods, Miguel has the right to reclaim them from her. *If that happens, does Cory have any recourse against Shari?*

In sales and lease law, a warranty is an assurance by one party of the existence of a fact upon which the other party can rely. The Uniform Commercial Code (UCC) has numerous rules governing the concept of product warranty as it occurs in a sales or lease contract. That will be the subject matter of the first part of this chapter. A natural addition to the discussion is *product liability:* Who is liable to consumers, users, and bystanders for physical harm and property damage caused by a particular good or the use of that good? That is the subject of the second part of this chapter.

Warranties

The UCC designates several warranties that can arise in a sales or lease contract, including warranties of title, express warranties, and implied warranties.

WARRANTIES OF TITLE

Title warranty arises automatically in most sales contracts. There are three types of warranties of title.

Good Title. In most cases, sellers warrant that they have valid title to the goods sold and that transfer of the title is rightful.

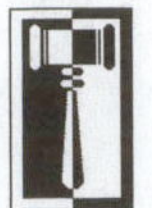

In the legal problem set out at the beginning of this chapter, Shari steals goods from Miguel and sells them to Cory, who does not know about the theft. If Miguel discovers that Cory has the goods, Miguel can reclaim them. *Does Cory have any recourse against Shari?* Yes. Under the UCC, Cory can sue Shari for breach of warranty, because a thief has no title to stolen goods and thus cannot give good title. When Shari sold Cory the goods, Shari *automatically* warranted to her that the title conveyed was valid and that its transfer was rightful. Because this was not in fact the case, Shari breached the warranty of title. Shari is therefore liable to Cory for the appropriate damages.

No Liens. A second warranty of title provided by the UCC protects buyers who are *unaware* of any encumbrances (claims, charges, or liabilities—usually called **liens**) against goods at the time the contract was made. This protects buyers who, for example, unknowingly buy goods that are subject to a creditor's security interest (see Chapter 31). If a creditor repossesses the goods from a buyer who *had no knowledge of the security interest,* the buyer can recover from the seller for breach of warranty.

LIEN
An encumbrance upon a property to satisfy or protect a claim for payment of a debt.

The buyer who has *actual knowledge* of a security interest has no recourse against a seller. If the seller is a merchant and the buyer is a "buyer in the ordinary course of business," however, the buyer is free of the security interest even if he or she knows of it. An exception is if the buyer knows the sale is in violation of the security interest; then he or she is subject to it. This protection for buyers is discussed in Chapter 31.

No Infringements. A third type of title warranty is a warranty against infringement of any patent, trademark, or copyright. In other words, a merchant is deemed to warrant that the goods delivered are free from any patent, trademark, or copyright claims of a third person. If this warranty is breached and the buyer is sued by the claim holder, the buyer *must notify the seller* of the lawsuit within a reasonable time to enable the seller to decide whether to participate in the defense against it.

Disclaimer of Title Warranty. In an ordinary sales transaction, the title warranty can be disclaimed or modified only by *specific language* in a contract. For example, sellers can assert that they are transferring only the rights, title, and interest that they actually have in the goods.

In certain cases, the circumstances of the sale are sufficient to indicate clearly to a buyer that no assurances as to title are being made. The classic example is a sheriff's sale. At a sheriff's sale, buyers know that the goods have been seized to satisfy debts. It is apparent that the goods are not the property of the person conducting the sale.

EXPRESS WARRANTIES

EXPRESS WARRANTY
A promise, ancillary to an underlying sales or lease agreement, that is included in the written or oral terms of the agreement under which the promisor assures the quality, description, or performance of the goods.

LEARNING OBJECTIVE NO. 1
Stating When Express Warranties Arise in a Sales or Lease Contract

A seller or lessor can create an **express warranty** by making representations about the quality, condition, or performance potential of the goods. Express warranties arise when a seller or lessor indicates any of the following:

1. That the goods conform to any *affirmation or promise* of fact that the seller or lessor makes to the buyer or lessee about the goods. Statements such as "These drill bits will *easily* penetrate stainless steel" are express warranties.
2. That the goods conform to any *description.* For example, a label that reads "crate contains one diesel engine" creates an express warranty.
3. That the goods conform to any *sample or model.* For example, if a sports equipment salesperson shows you sample baseballs and you order a hundred, the balls that are delivered must conform to the samples.

Basis of the Bargain. To create an express warranty, the seller or lessor does not need to use formal words such as *warrant* or *guarantee* or to state that he or she has a specific intention to make a warranty. The UCC requires only that the affirmation, promise, description, or sample must become part of the "basis of the bargain." Just what constitutes the basis of the bargain is hard to say. The UCC does not define the concept. It is a question of fact in each case whether a representation was made at such a time and in such a way that it induced the buyer or lessee to enter the contract.

If you do not intend to make an express warranty, do not make a promise or an affirmation of fact concerning the performance or quality of a product you are selling.

Statements of Opinion. If the seller or lessor makes a statement that relates to the value or worth of the goods, or makes a statement of opinion or recommendation about the goods, the seller or lessor is not creating an express warranty. For instance, a seller might say that the quality of her products is "excellent and unsurpassed." This is known as "puffing" and creates no warranty.

If the seller or lessor is an expert and gives an opinion as an expert, however, then a warranty can be created. For example, if an art dealer and expert in seventeenth-century paintings says to a purchaser that a particular painting is a Rembrandt, and the purchaser buys the painting, the dealer has warranted the accuracy of the opinion.

The reasonableness of the buyer's or lessee's reliance is the controlling criterion in many cases. For example, a salesperson's statements that a ladder "will never break" and will "last a lifetime" are so clearly improbable that no reasonable buyer should rely on them.

IN THE COURTROOM

A salesperson for a car dealer claims about one of the cars, "This is the best used car to come along in years; it has four new tires and a 350-horsepower engine just rebuilt this year. It's worth a fortune—anywhere else you'd pay $10,000 for it." *Which of these statements are express warranties, and which are only opinions?* The salesperson's *affirmations of fact* create a warranty: the automobile has an engine; it has 350 horsepower; it was rebuilt this year; there are four tires on the car; and the tires are new. The salesperson's opinion that the vehicle is "the best used car to come along in years," however, creates no warranty. Similarly, the statements relating to the possible value of the goods ("It's worth a fortune—anywhere else you'd pay $10,000 for it") do not create a warranty.

LEARNING OBJECTIVE NO. 2

Identifying the Implied Warranties That Arise in a Sales or Lease Contract

IMPLIED WARRANTIES

An **implied warranty** is one that *the law derives* by implication from the nature of the transaction or the situation or circumstances of the parties.

IMPLIED WARRANTY
A warranty that the law implies through either the situation of the parties or the nature of the transaction.

Implied Warranty of Merchantability. An **implied warranty of merchantability** automatically arises in every sale or lease of goods made *by a merchant* who deals in goods of the kind sold. Thus, a retailer of ski equipment makes an implied warranty of merchantability every time the retailer sells a pair of skis, but a neighbor selling his or her skis at a garage sale does not.

IMPLIED WARRANTY OF MERCHANTABILITY
A presumed promise by a merchant seller or lessor of goods that the goods are reasonably fit for the general purpose for which they are sold or leased, are properly packaged and labeled, and are of proper quality.

This warranty imposes on a merchant liability for the safe performance of a product. It makes no difference whether the merchant knew of or could have discovered a defect that makes the product unsafe.

Goods that are *merchantable* are "reasonably fit for the ordinary purposes for which such goods are used." They must be of at least average, fair, or medium-grade quality. The quality must be comparable to quality that will pass without objection in the trade or market for goods of the same description. The goods must be adequately packaged and labeled. They also must conform to the promises or affirmations of fact made on the container or label, if any.

Some examples of nonmerchantable goods are light bulbs that explode when switched on, pajamas that burst into flames upon slight contact with a stove burner, high heels that break off shoes under normal use, and shotgun shells that explode prematurely.

IN THE COURTROOM

Joplin buys an ax at Gershwin's Hardware Store. No express warranties are made. The first time she chops wood with it, the ax handle breaks, and Joplin is injured. She immediately notifies Gershwin. Examination shows that the wood in the handle was rotten but that the rottenness could not have been noticed by either Gershwin or Joplin. Nonetheless, Joplin notifies Gershwin that she will hold him responsible for the medical bills. *Can Gershwin be held liable?* Yes. Gershwin is responsible because a merchant seller of goods warrants that the goods he or she sells are fit for normal use. This ax was obviously not fit for normal use.

Implied Warranty of Fitness for a Particular Purpose. The implied warranty of fitness for a particular purpose arises when *any seller or lessor* (merchant or nonmerchant) knows the particular purpose for which a buyer or lessee will use the goods *and* knows that the buyer or lessee is relying on the seller's skill and judgment to select suitable goods.

A "particular purpose of the buyer or lessee" differs from the "ordinary purpose for which goods are used" (merchantability). Goods can be merchantable but unfit for a buyer's or lessee's particular purpose. Say, for example, that you need a gallon of paint to match the color of your office walls—a light shade somewhere between coral and peach. You take a sample to your local hardware store and request a gallon of paint of that color. Instead, you are given a gallon of bright blue paint. Here, the salesperson has not breached any warranty of implied merchantability—the bright blue paint is of high quality and suitable for interior walls—but he or she has breached an implied warranty of fitness for a particular purpose.

A seller or lessor does not need to have actual knowledge of the buyer's or lessee's particular purpose. It is sufficient if a seller or lessor "has reason to know" the purpose. The buyer or lessee, however, must have *relied* on the seller's or lessor's skill or judgment in selecting or furnishing suitable goods.

IN THE COURTROOM

Bloom buys a short-wave radio from Radio Shop, telling the salesperson that she wants a set strong enough to pick up Radio Luxembourg, which is eight thousand miles away. Radio Shop sells Bloom a Model X set. The set works, but it does not pick up Radio Luxembourg. *Can Bloom recover her money?* Yes. The salesperson knew specifically that Bloom wanted a set that would pick up Radio Luxembourg. Bloom relied on the salesperson to furnish a radio that would fulfill this purpose. Because Radio Shop did not do so, it breached the implied warranty of fitness for a particular purpose.

Other Implied Warranties. The UCC recognizes that implied warranties can arise (or be excluded or modified) from course of dealing, course of performance, or usage of trade. *Course of dealing* is a sequence of conduct between the parties to a transaction that establishes a common basis for their understanding. *Course of performance* is the conduct that occurs under an agreement, indicating what the parties to the agreement intended for it to mean.

Usage of trade is a practice or method of dealing so regularly observed as to justify an expectation that it will be observed in a particular transaction. Thus, in the absence of evidence to the contrary, when both parties to a contract have knowledge of a well-recognized trade custom, the courts will infer that they both intended for that custom to apply to their contract. For example, if an industry-wide custom is to lubricate a new car before it is delivered, and a dealer fails to do so, the dealer can be liable to a buyer for breach of implied warranty.

Third Party Beneficiaries of Warranties

One of the general principles of contract law is that unless you are one of the parties to a contract, you have no rights under the contract. The relationship between the parties to a contract is referred to as *privity*. Generally, privity must exist between a plaintiff and a defendant to bring an action based on a contract.

With warranties, however, there is sharp disagreement over how far liability should extend. To satisfy opposing views, the drafters of the UCC proposed three alternatives, eliminating the requirement of privity in various circumstances. All three alternatives are intended to eliminate the privity requirement with respect to certain enumerated types of injuries (personal versus property) for certain beneficiaries (for example, household members or bystanders). The law in each state depends on which alternative that state adopted.

Warranty Disclaimers

Because each warranty is created in a special way, the manner in which each one can be disclaimed or qualified by the seller varies.

Express Warranties. Express warranties can be excluded or limited by specific and unambiguous language, provided that this is done in a manner that protects the buyer or lessee from surprise. Therefore, a written disclaimer in language that is clear and conspicuous, and called to a buyer's or lessee's attention *at the time the sales contract is formed,* could negate all oral express warranties not included in the written sales contract.

Implied Warranties. Generally speaking, unless circumstances indicate otherwise, implied warranties (merchantability and fitness) are disclaimed by the expressions "as is," "with all faults," or other similar expressions that in common understanding for *both* parties call the buyer's attention to the fact that there are no implied warranties.

The UCC also permits a seller or lessor to disclaim specifically the implied warranty either of fitness or of merchantability. To disclaim the implied warranty of fitness, the disclaimer *must* be in writing and be conspicuous. The word *fitness* does not have to be mentioned. It is sufficient if, for example, the disclaimer states, "There are no warranties that extend beyond the description on the face hereof." A *merchantability disclaimer* must be more specific; it must mention *merchantability*. It need not be written. If it is, however, the writing must be conspicuous.

As a seller, you might wish to have the buyer sign a statement certifying that he or she has read all of your warranty disclaimer provisions.

Buyer's or Lessee's Refusal to Inspect. If a buyer or lessee actually examines the goods (or a sample or model) as fully as desired before entering into a contract, or if the buyer or lessee refuses to examine the goods, *there is no implied warranty with respect to defects that a reasonable examination would reveal. Failing* to examine the goods is not a *refusal* to examine them. A refusal occurs only when the seller *demands* that the buyer or lessee examine the goods.

The seller or lessor remains liable for any latent (hidden) defects that ordinary inspection would not reveal. What the examination ought to reveal depends on a buyer's or lessee's skill and method of examination. For example, an auto mechanic purchasing a car should be responsible for discovering defects that a nonexpert would not be expected to find. The circumstances determine what defects an inspection should reveal.

MAGNUSON-MOSS WARRANTY ACT

If you wish to limit warranties, do so by means of a carefully worded and prominently placed written or printed provision that a reasonable person would understand and accept.

The Magnuson-Moss Warranty Act of 1975 was designed to prevent deception in warranties by making them easier to understand. Under the act, no seller or lessor is *required* to give an express written warranty for consumer goods. If a seller or lessor chooses to do so, however, and the cost of the consumer goods is more than $10, the warranty must be labeled as "full" or "limited." In addition, if the cost of the goods is more than $15, the warrantor must make certain disclosures fully and conspicuously in a single document in "readily understood language." These disclosures include the names and addresses of the warrantor(s), what specifically is warranted, procedures for enforcement of the warranty, any limitations on relief, and the fact that the buyer has legal rights.

A full warranty requires free repair or replacement of any defective part. If the product cannot be repaired within a reasonable time, the consumer has the choice of either a refund or a replacement without charge. The full warranty frequently does not have a time limit on it. Any limitation on consequential damages (damages that compensate for a loss that is not direct, such as lost profits) must be *conspicuously* stated. A *limited warranty* arises when the written warranty fails to meet one of the requirements of a full warranty.

Product Liability

PRODUCT LIABILITY
The legal liability of manufacturers and sellers to buyers, users, and sometimes bystanders for injuries or damages suffered because of defects in goods purchased.

Manufacturers and sellers of goods can be held liable to consumers, users, and bystanders for physical harm or property damage that is caused by the goods. This is called **product liability.** Product liability may be based on the warranty theories just discussed, as well as on the theories of *negligence, misrepresentation,* and *strict liability.*

NEGLIGENCE

NEGLIGENCE
The failure to exercise the standard of care that a reasonable person would exercise in similar circumstances.

LEARNING OBJECTIVE NO. 3
Discussing Negligence as the Basis of Product Liability

Negligence is the failure to use the degree of care that a reasonable, prudent person would have used under the circumstances. If a seller fails to exercise such reasonable care and an injury results, he or she may be sued for negligence.

Because a failure to exercise reasonable care is negligence, a manufacturer must exercise "due care" to make a product safe. Due care must be exercised in designing the product, in selecting the materials, in using the appropriate production process, in assembling and testing the product, and in placing adequate warnings on the label informing the user of dangers of which an ordinary person might not be aware. The duty of care also extends to the inspection and testing of any components that are bought from other manufacturers and used in the final product.

An action based on negligence does not require privity of contract between the plaintiff and the defendant. A manufacturer is liable for its failure to exercise due care to any person who sustains an injury caused by a negligently made (defective) product.

MISREPRESENTATION

When a fraudulent misrepresentation has been made to a user or consumer and that misrepresentation ultimately results in an injury, the basis of liability may be the tort of fraud. Examples are the intentional mislabeling of packaged cosmetics or the intentional concealment of a product's defects. A more interesting basis of liability is nonfraudulent misrepresentation, which occurs when a merchant *innocently* misrepresents the character or quality of goods.

IN THE COURTROOM

A manufacturer, Winthrop Laboratories, a division of Sterling Drug, Inc., innocently indicated to the medical profession that a prescription medication called Talwin was not physically addictive. Using this information, a physician prescribed the drug for his patient, who developed an addiction that turned out to be fatal. *Could the manufacturer be held liable?* Yes. Although the misrepresentation was innocent and the addiction was a highly unusual reaction resulting from the victim's unusual susceptibility to this product, the drug company was still held liable.

STRICT LIABILITY

Under the doctrine of strict liability, people are liable for the results of their acts regardless of their intentions or their exercise of reasonable care. For example, a company that uses dynamite to blast for a road is strictly liable for any damages that it causes, even if the company takes reasonable and prudent precautions to prevent the damages.

In the area of product liability, the doctrine applies to the sellers of goods (including manufacturers, processors, assemblers, packagers, bottlers, wholesalers, distributors, and retailers). Liability does not depend on privity of contract—the injured party does not have to be the buyer or a third party beneficiary.

Requirements of Strict Product Liability. Just because a person is injured by a product does not mean he or she will have a cause of action against the manufacturer. The following requirements must be met:

LEARNING OBJECTIVE NO. 4
Listing the Requirements of Strict Product Liability

1. The product must be in a defective condition when the defendant sells it.
2. The defendant must normally be engaged in the business of selling that product.
3. The product must be unreasonably dangerous to the user or consumer because of its defective condition (in most states).
4. The plaintiff must incur physical harm to self or property by use or consumption of the product.
5. The defective condition must be the proximate cause of the harm.
6. The goods must not have been substantially changed from the time the product was sold to the time the injury was sustained.

A product may be so defective as to be **unreasonably dangerous** if either (1) the product was dangerous beyond the expectation of the ordinary consumer or (2) a less dangerous alternative was economically feasible for the manufacturer, but the manufacturer failed to produce it.

UNREASONABLY DANGEROUS
In product liability, defective to the point of threatening a consumer's health or safety, dangerous beyond the expectation of the ordinary consumer, or when a less dangerous alternative is economically feasible for a manufacturer but the manufacturer fails to use it.

Less Dangerous Alternatives. When determining whether a less dangerous alternative was economically feasible for the manufacturer, courts will consider a number of factors, including the following:

1. A product's utility and desirability.
2. The availability of other, safer products.
3. The dangers that have been identified prior to an injured user's suit.
4. The obviousness of the dangers.
5. The normal expectation of danger, particularly for established products.

6. The probability of injury and its likely seriousness.
7. The avoidability of injury by care in the product's use, including the contribution of instructions and warnings.
8. The viability of eliminating the danger without appreciably impairing the product's function or making the product "too" expensive.

Thus, a court may consider a snowblower without a safety guard over the opening through which the snow is blown to be in a condition that is unreasonably dangerous, even if it carries warnings to stay clear of the opening. The danger may be within the users' expectations. The court, however, will also consider the likelihood of injury and its probable seriousness, as well as the cost of putting a guard over the opening and the guard's effect on the blower's operation.

Suppliers of Component Parts. Under the rule of strict liability in tort, the basis of liability includes suppliers of component parts. For example, General Motors buys brake pads from a subcontractor and puts them in Chevrolets without changing their composition. If those pads are defective, both the supplier of the brake pads and General Motors will be held strictly liable for the damages caused by the defects.

Defenses to Product Liability

Frequently, negligent misconduct or misuse of a product by the harmed person or a third party, coupled with the product's defect, causes damage or injury. A plaintiff's misconduct or misuse of the product may be a defense to reduce the claimant's recovery or to bar it altogether.

Assumption of Risk. Assumption of risk can sometimes be used as a defense in an action based on strict liability in tort. For such a defense to be established, the defendant must show that

1. The plaintiff voluntarily engaged in the risk while realizing the potential danger.
2. The plaintiff knew and appreciated the risk created by the defect in the product.
3. The plaintiff's decision to undertake the known risk was unreasonable.

Product Misuse. Similar to the defense of assumption of risk is that of product misuse. Here the injured party does not know that the product is dangerous for a particular use, but that use is not the one for which the product was designed. The defense of product misuse has been severely limited by the courts. Suppliers are generally required to expect reasonably foreseeable misuses and to design products that are either safe when misused or marketed with some protective device, such as a childproof cap.

Comparative Negligence A theory under which the liability for injuries resulting from negligent acts is shared by all persons who were guilty of negligence (including the injured party), on the basis of each person's proportionate carelessness.

Comparative Negligence. Most states consider the negligent or intentional actions of the plaintiff in the apportionment of liability and damages. This is the doctrine of **comparative negligence.** Under this doctrine, the amount of the defendant's liability is reduced in proportion to the amount by which the plaintiff's injury or damage was caused by the plaintiff's own negligence.

TERMS AND CONCEPTS FOR REVIEW

CHAPTER SUMMARY • WARRANTIES AND PRODUCT LIABILITY

Warranty of Title	**1.** Upon transfer of title, the seller warrants— **a.** The right to pass good and rightful title. **b.** That the goods are free from unstated liens or encumbrances. **c.** If a merchant, that the goods do not infringe on another's patent, copyright, or trademark. **2.** *Defenses*—Exclusion or modification only by specific language or circumstances.
Express Warranty	**1.** As part of the basis of a sale or lease, arises when the seller or lessor— **a.** Makes an affirmation or promise of fact. **b.** Provides a description of the goods. **c.** Shows a sample or model. **2.** Under the Magnuson-Moss Warranty Act, an express written warranty for goods priced at more than $10 must be— **a.** Full—Free repair or replacement of defective parts; refund or replacement of goods that cannot be repaired. **b.** Limited—When less than a full warranty is offered. **3.** *Defenses*— **a.** Opinion (puffing). **b.** Exclusion or limitation.
Implied Warranty of Merchantability	**1.** When the seller or lessor is a merchant who deals in goods of the kind sold, the seller or lessor warrants that the goods sold are properly packaged and labeled, are of proper quality, and are reasonably fit for the ordinary purposes for which such goods are used. **2.** *Defenses*— **a.** A specific disclaimer that mentions merchantability and, if in writing, is conspicuous. **b.** Goods stated to be "as is" or "with all faults." **c.** If the buyer or lessee examines, the buyer or lessee is bound by all defects that are found or that should have been found. If the buyer or lessee refuses to examine, he or she is bound by obvious defects.
Implied Warranty of Fitness for a Particular Purpose	**1.** Arises when the buyer's or lessee's purpose or use is known by the seller or lessor, and the buyer or lessee purchases in reliance on the seller's or lessor's selection. **2.** *Defenses*— **a.** A specific disclaimer must be in writing and be conspicuous. **b.** Same as for implied warranty of merchantability (above, 2b and 2c).
Implied Warranty from Course of Dealing or Trade Usage	**1.** Arises through prior dealings or usage of trade. **2.** *Defense*—Exclusion by specific language.
Product Liability Based on Negligence or Misrepresentation	**1.** Due care must be used by the manufacturer in designing the product, selecting materials, using the appropriate production process, assembling and testing the product, and placing adequate warnings on the label or product. **2.** Privity of contract is not required. A manufacturer is liable for failure to exercise due care to any person who sustains an injury proximately caused by a negligently made (defective) product. **3.** Misrepresentation of a product may result in liability.
Requirements of Strict Product Liability	**1.** The defendant must sell the product in a defective condition. **2.** The defendant must normally be engaged in the business of selling that product. **3.** The product must be unreasonably dangerous to the user or consumer because of its defective condition (in most states). **4.** The plaintiff must incur physical harm to self or property by use or consumption of the product. **5.** The defect must be the proximate cause of the harm. **6.** The goods must not have been substantially changed from the time the product was sold to the time the injury was sustained.

CHAPTER SUMMARY • *Continued*

Possible Defenses to Product Liability	**1.** Assumption of risk on the part of the user or consumer. **2.** Misuse of the product by the user or consumer in a way unforeseeable by the manufacturer. **3.** Liability may be allocated between plaintiff and defendant (comparative negligence).

HYPOTHETICAL QUESTIONS

19–1. Warranty Disclaimers. Tandy purchased a washing machine from Marshall Appliances. The sale contract included a provision explicitly disclaiming all express or implied warranties, including the implied warranty of merchantability. The disclaimer was printed in the same size and color as the rest of the contract. The machine turned out to be a "lemon" and never functioned properly. Tandy sought a refund of the purchase price, claiming that Marshall had breached the implied warranty of merchantability. Can Tandy recover her money, notwithstanding the warranty disclaimer in the contract? Explain.

19–2. Implied Warranties. Sam, a farmer, needs to place a two-thousand-pound piece of equipment in his barn. The equipment must be lifted thirty feet into a hayloft. Sam goes to Durham Hardware and tells Durham that he needs some heavy-duty rope to be used on his farm. Durham recommends a one-inch-thick nylon rope, and Sam purchases two hundred feet of it. Sam ties the rope around the piece of equipment, puts it through a pulley, and with the aid of a tractor lifts the equipment off the ground. Suddenly, the rope breaks. In the crash to the ground, the equipment is extensively damaged. Sam files suit against Durham for breach of the implied warranty of fitness for a particular purpose. Discuss how successful Sam will be with his suit.

REAL WORLD CASE PROBLEM

19–3. Product Liability. John Whitted bought a Chevrolet Nova from General Motors Corp. (GMC). Six years later, Whitted crashed the Nova into two trees. During the impact, the seat belt broke, and Whitted was thrust against the steering wheel, which broke, and the windshield, which shattered. He suffered fractures in his left arm and cuts to his forehead. Whitted sued GMC, asserting, among other things, that because the seat belt broke, the defendants were strictly liable for his injuries. What does Whitted have to show in order to prove his case? [*Whitted v. General Motors Corp.,* 58 F.3d 1200 (7th Cir. 1995)]

For updated links to resources available on the Web, as well as a variety of other materials, visit this text's Web site at **http://blte.westbuslaw.com**.

To find information on the UCC, including the UCC provisions discussed in this chapter, refer to the Web sites listed in the *Expanded Access to the Internet* in Chapter 16.

For an example of an "as is" clause, see the warranty disclaimer provided by the University of Minnesota for one of its research software products at

http://www.cmrr.drad.umn.edu/stimulate/stimUsersGuide/node7.html

For information on the *Restatements of the Law,* including the *Restatement (Second) of Torts* and the *Restatement (Third) of Torts: Products Liability,* go to the Web site of the American Law Institute at

http://www.ali.org

For information on product-liability suits against tobacco companies and recent settlements, go to

http://www.usatoday.com/news/smoke/smoke00.htm

A discussion of the "demise of privity" with respect to product liability in leading cases decided by the New York Court of Appeals can be found at the following Web page within the site offered by the *New York Law Journal:*

http://www.nylj.com/links/150sterk.html

Law Journal EXTRA! has articles on current cases and issues in the area of product liability, as well as proposed legislation, at

http://www.ljx.com/practice/productliability/index.html

Online Legal Research

Go to **http://blte.westbuslaw.com**, the Web site that accompanies this text. Select "Internet Applications," and then click on "Chapter 19." There you will find the following Internet research exercises that you can perform to learn more about warranty and product liability law:

Activity 19–1: Warranties

Activity 19–2: Product-Liability Litigation

Chapter 19 ■ WORK SET

TRUE-FALSE QUESTIONS

____ **1.** A contract cannot involve both an implied warranty of merchantability and an implied warranty of fitness for a particular purpose.

____ **2.** A seller's best protection from being held accountable for express statements is not to make them in the first place.

____ **3.** A clear, conspicuous, written statement brought to a buyer's attention when a contract is formed can disclaim all warranties not in a written contract.

____ **4.** To disclaim the implied warranty of merchantability, a merchant must mention "merchantability."

____ **5.** Whether or not a buyer examines goods before entering into a contract, there is an implied warranty with respect to defects that an examination would reveal.

____ **6.** Privity of contract is required to hold a manufacturer liable in a product liability action based on negligence.

____ **7.** In a defense of comparative negligence, an injured party's failure to take care against a known defect will be considered in apportioning liability.

____ **8.** Under the doctrine of strict liability, a defendant is liable for the results of his or her acts only if he or she intended those results.

MULTIPLE-CHOICE QUESTIONS

____ **1.** Noel's Ski Shop sells a pair of skis to Fred. When he first uses the skis, they snap in two. The cause is something that Noel did not know about and could not have discovered. If Fred sues Noel, he will likely

a. win, because Noel breached the merchant's implied duty of inspection.
b. win, because Noel breached the implied warranty of merchantability.
c. lose, because Noel knew nothing about the defect that made the skis unsafe.
d. lose, because consumers should reasonably expect to find on occasion that a product will not work as warranted.

____ **2.** Tyler Desk Corporation writes in its contracts, in large red letters, "There are no warranties that extend beyond the description on the face hereof." The disclaimer negates the implied warranty of

a. merchantability.
b. fitness for a particular purpose.
c. title.
d. all of the above.

_____ **3.** Eagle Equipment sells motor vehicle parts to dealers. In response to a dealer's order, Eagle ships a crate with a label that reads, "Crate contains one 150-horsepower diesel engine." This statement is

a. an express warranty.
b. an implied warranty of merchantability.
c. an implied warranty of fitness for a particular purpose.
d. none of the above.

_____ **4.** B&B Autos sells cars, trucks, and other motor vehicles. A B&B salesperson claims, "This is the finest car ever made." This statement is

a. an express warranty.
b. an implied warranty of merchantability.
c. an implied warranty of fitness for a particular purpose.
d. none of the above.

_____ **5.** Sam is injured in an accident involving a defective tractor. Sam sues the maker of the tractor. To successfully claim assumption of risk as a defense, the defendant must show

a. Sam voluntarily engaged in the risk while realizing the potential danger.
b. Sam knew and appreciated the risk created by the defect.
c. Sam's decision to undertake the known risk was unreasonable.
d. all of the above.

_____ **6.** T&T, Inc., designs a product that is safe when used properly. Bob uses the product for an unforeseeable, improper use. If Bob sues T&T, the manufacturer will likely be held

a. liable for negligence or misrepresentation.
b. strictly liable.
c. either a or b.
d. none of the above.

_____ **7.** Jane buys a defective product from Valu-Mart and is injured as a result of using the product. If Jane sues Valu-Mart based on strict liability, to recover damages she must prove that Valu-Mart

a. was in privity of contract with Jane.
b. was engaged in the business of selling the product.
c. failed to exercise due care.
d. defectively designed the product.

ISSUE SPOTTERS

1. General Construction Company (GCC) tells Industrial Supplies, Inc., that it needs an adhesive to do a particular job. Industrial provides a five-gallon bucket of a certain brand. When it does not perform to GCC's specifications, GCC sues Industrial, which claims, "We didn't expressly promise anything." What should GCC argue?

2. Anchor, Inc., makes prewrapped mattress springs. Through an employee's carelessness, an improperly wrapped spring is sold to Bloom Company, which uses it in the manufacture of a mattress. Bloom sells the mattress to Beds Unlimited, which sells it to Kay. While sleeping on the mattress, Kay is stabbed in the back by the spring. The wound becomes infected, and Kay becomes seriously ill. Can Anchor be held liable?

Consumer Protection

LEARNING OBJECTIVES

When you finish this chapter, you should be able to:

1. Define what is and what is not deceptive advertising.
2. Recognize what information must be included on labels.
3. Discuss the regulation of credit in consumer transactions.
4. Describe federal health and safety protection.

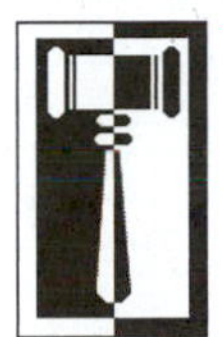

FACING A LEGAL PROBLEM

The makers of Campbell's soups advertised that "most" Campbell's soups were low in fat and cholesterol and thus were helpful in fighting heart disease. What the ad did not say was that Campbell's soups are high in sodium, and high-sodium diets may increase the risk of heart disease. *Does this omission make the advertising deceptive?*

State and federal legislation regulates the manner in which businesses may advertise, engage in mail-order transactions, package and label their products, and so on. In addition, numerous local, state, and federal agencies exist to aid the consumer in settling his or her grievances with sellers and producers. In this chapter, we will examine some of the sources of consumer protection and some of the major issues.

Deceptive Advertising

Numerous government agencies, both federal and state, are empowered to protect consumers from **deceptive advertising.** The most important federal agency regulating advertising is the Federal Trade Commission (FTC). The Federal Trade Commission Act empowers the FTC to determine what constitutes a deceptive practice under that act.

DECEPTIVE ADVERTISING Advertising that misleads consumers.

DEFINING DECEPTIVE ADVERTISING

LEARNING OBJECTIVE NO. 1
Defining What Is and What Is Not Deceptive Advertising

As defined by the FTC, deceptive advertising generally means that the advertisement may be interpreted in more than one way and that one of those interpretations is false or misleading. False or deceptive advertising comes in many forms. Deception may arise from a false statement or claim about a company's own products or competitors' products. The deception may concern a product's quality, effects, price, origin, or availability. It also may arise from an omission of important information about the product. Some advertisements contain "half-truths," meaning that the presented information is true, but incomplete, leading consumers to a false conclusion.

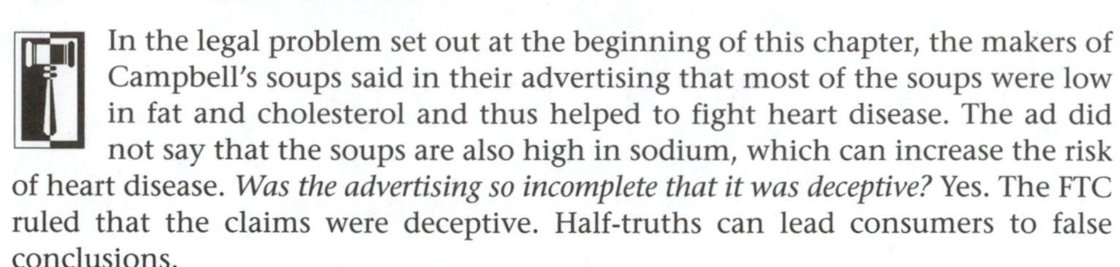

In the legal problem set out at the beginning of this chapter, the makers of Campbell's soups said in their advertising that most of the soups were low in fat and cholesterol and thus helped to fight heart disease. The ad did not say that the soups are also high in sodium, which can increase the risk of heart disease. *Was the advertising so incomplete that it was deceptive?* Yes. The FTC ruled that the claims were deceptive. Half-truths can lead consumers to false conclusions.

Other ads contain statements not supported by adequate scientific evidence. These may or may not be considered deceptive. When the claim is incapable of measurement—as in "When you're out of Schlitz, you're out of beer"—no problem of deception is perceived by the FTC. In addition, an ad may be deceptive even though it is literally true.

BUSINESS TiP

Remember that a seller's puffery—his or her opinion about the goods—is not a legally binding warranty or promise.

IN THE COURTROOM

An ad for "Teak Tables" may be for tables manufactured by a firm named "Teak," and thus the advertiser could claim the ad was truthful. *Could the ad nonetheless be considered deceptive?* Yes, because most consumers would be led to assume that the ad referred to teak wood. As a general rule, the test for whether an ad is deceptive is *if a reasonable consumer would be deceived.*

Access to the Internet

To view the FTC's Web site, go to:

http://www.ftc.gov

Bait-and-Switch Advertising

One of the FTC's important rules is contained in its "Guides against Bait Advertising." The rule is designed to prohibit advertisements that specify a very low price for a particular item that will likely be unavailable to the consumer, who will then be encouraged to purchase a more expensive item. The low price is the "bait" to lure the consumer into the store. The salesperson is instructed to "switch" the consumer to a different item. According to the FTC guidelines, **bait-and-switch advertising** occurs if the seller refuses to show the advertised item, fails to have reasonably adequate quantities of it available, fails to promise to deliver the advertised item within a reasonable time, or discourages employees from selling the item.

Bait-and-Switch Advertising
Advertising a product at a very attractive price (the "bait") and then informing the consumer, once he or she is in the store, that the advertised product is either not available or is of poor quality; the customer is then urged to purchase ("switched" to) a more expensive item.

FTC Actions against Deceptive Advertising

The FTC receives complaints from many sources, including competitors of alleged violators, consumers, consumer organizations, trade associations, Better Business Bureaus, government organizations, and state and local officials. If complaints are widespread, the FTC will investigate and perhaps take action. If, after its investigations, the FTC believes that a given advertisement is unfair or deceptive, it drafts a formal complaint, which is sent to the alleged offender.

If the company does not agree to settle a complaint, the FTC can conduct a hearing before an administrative law judge (see the discussion of administrative law in Chapter 39). If the FTC succeeds in proving that an advertisement is unfair or deceptive, it usually issues a **cease-and-desist order** requiring that the challenged advertising be stopped. It might also require a sanction known as **counteradvertising** by requiring the company to advertise anew—in print, on radio, and on television—to inform the public about the earlier misinformation.

Cease-and-Desist Order
An administrative or judicial order prohibiting a person or business firm from conducting activities that an agency or court has deemed illegal.

Counteradvertising
New advertising that is undertaken pursuant to a Federal Trade Commission order for the purpose of correcting earlier false claims that were made about a product.

Labeling and Packaging Laws

A number of federal and state labeling and packaging laws have been passed to provide the consumer with accurate information or warnings about products or their possible misuse. The Fur Products Labeling Act of 1951, the Wool Products Labeling Act of 1939, the Flammable Fabrics Act of 1953, the Federal Food, Drug and Cosmetic Act of 1938, the Fair Packaging and Labeling Act of 1966, and the Smokeless Tobacco Health Education Act of 1986 are a few of the acts that have been enacted to reduce the amount of incorrect labeling and packaging.

LEARNING OBJECTIVE NO. 2
Recognizing What Information Must Be Included on Labels

In general, labels must be accurate, which means that they must use words as they are ordinarily understood by consumers. For example, a regular-size box of cereal cannot be labeled "giant" if that word would exaggerate the amount of cereal in the box. Labels often must specify the raw materials used in a product, such as the percentage of cotton, nylon, or other fibers used in a shirt. Consumer goods must have labels that identify the product, the manufacturer, the packer or distributor and its place of business, the net quantity of the contents, and the quantity of each serving if the number of servings is stated.

There are also rules that govern package descriptions and savings claims, information disclosure for ingredients in nonfood products, and standards for the partial filling of packages. The provisions are enforced by the Federal Trade Commission and the Department of Health and Human Services.

Consumer Sales and Credit

A number of statutes that protect the consumer in sales transactions concern the disclosure of certain terms in sales. Others provide rules governing door-to-door sales, mail-order transactions, and unsolicited merchandise. The Federal Reserve Board of Governors, for example, has issued **Regulation Z,** which governs credit provisions associated with sales contracts. Numerous states have passed laws governing the remedies available to consumers in home sales. Furthermore, states have adopted a number of consumer protection provisions by incorporating the Uniform Commercial Code and the Uniform Consumer Credit Code (discussed later in this chapter) into their statutory codes.

REGULATION Z
A set of rules promulgated by the Federal Reserve System's board of governors to implement the provisions of the Truth-in-Lending Act.

In 1968, Congress passed the first of a series of statutes regarding the content of credit information contained in written and oral messages. If, for instance, certain credit terms are used in an advertisement, other credit information is also required. Thus, if a car dealer states in a newspaper advertisement that individuals have thirty-six months to pay, the ad must also include the cash price of the automobiles, the down payment required, the finance charge, the amount of each periodic payment, and the annual percentage rate of interest.

To protect consumers who purchase goods and services on credit, federal legislation imposes numerous procedural requirements on creditors that must be met when credit is being extended to a consumer. These requirements are discussed below.

Door-to-Door Sales

Door-to-door sales are singled out for special treatment in the laws of most states. A number of states have passed what are known as **"cooling off" laws,** which permit the buyers of goods sold door-to-door to cancel their contracts within a specified period of time, usually two to three days after the sale. A Federal Trade Commission regulation also requires sellers to give consumers three days to cancel any sale (and to tell them that they have three days to cancel). Because this rule applies in addition to the relevant state statutes, consumers are given the most favorable benefits of the FTC rule and their own state statute. Also, the FTC

"COOLING OFF" LAW
A law that allows a buyer a period of time (typically three days) in which to cancel a door-to-door sales contract.

rule requires that a consumer be informed in Spanish of the three-day rule if the sale is conducted in Spanish.

MAIL-ORDER SALES

Heading the list of consumer complaints received by the nation's Better Business Bureaus are problems stemming from product sales by telephone or mail. Many mail-order houses are outside the buyer's state, and it is more costly to seek **redress** (relief) for grievances in such situations.

REDRESS
Satisfaction for damage caused by the wrongdoing of another.

A federal statute prevents the use of mails to defraud individuals. In addition, several states have passed statutes governing practices by sellers, including insurance companies, that solicit through the mails. The state statutes parallel the federal statutes governing mail fraud.

The Postal Reorganization Act of 1970 provides that unsolicited merchandise sent by U.S. mail may be retained, used, discarded, or disposed of in any manner deemed appropriate, without the individual's incurring any obligation to the sender. In addition, the mailing of unordered merchandise (except for free samples) constitutes an unfair trade practice and is not permitted. (Exceptions are mailings by charitable agencies and those made by mistake.)

FTC REGULATION OF SPECIFIC INDUSTRIES

The FTC targets certain sales practices on an industry-wide basis. In 1984, for example, the FTC enacted a rule that requires used-car dealers to affix a "Buyer's Guide" label to all cars sold on their lots. The label must disclose the following information: (1) the car's warranty or a statement that the car is being sold "as is," (2) information regarding any service contract or promises being made by the dealer, and (3) a suggestion that the purchaser obtain both an inspection of the car and a written statement of any promises made by the dealer.

In 1984, the FTC also enacted rules requiring that funeral homes provide customers with itemized prices of all charges incurred for a funeral. In addition, the regulations prohibit funeral homes from requiring specific embalming procedures or specific types of caskets for bodies that are to be cremated.

TRUTH-IN-LENDING ACT

LEARNING OBJECTIVE NO. 3
Discussing the Regulation of Credit in Consumer Transactions

One of the most significant statutes regulating the credit and credit-card industry is the Truth-in-Lending Act (TILA), the name commonly given to Title 1 of the Consumer Credit Protection Act (CCPA), which was passed by Congress in 1974. The TILA is basically a *disclosure law.* The TILA is administered by the Federal Reserve Board and requires sellers and lenders to disclose credit terms or loan terms so that individuals can shop around for the best financing arrangements. TILA requirements apply only to persons who, in the ordinary course of their business, lend money, sell on credit, or arrange for the extension of credit. Thus, sales or loans made between two consumers do not come under the protection of the act. Also, only debtors who are *natural* persons (as opposed to the artificial "person" of a corporation) are protected by this law.

The disclosure requirements are found in Regulation Z, which, as mentioned previously, was promulgated by the Federal Reserve Board. If the contracting parties are subject to the TILA, the requirements of Regulation Z apply to any transaction involving an installment sales contract in which payment is to be made in more than four installments. These transactions typically include installment loans, retail and installment sales, car loans, home improvement loans, and certain real estate loans if the amount of financing is less than $25,000.

Amendments to the TILA apply to those who lease or arrange to lease consumer goods in the ordinary course of their business, if the goods are priced at

$25,000 or less and if the lease term exceeds four months. For consumers who lease automobiles and other goods, lessors are required to disclose in writing all of the material terms of the lease.

Under the provisions of the TILA, all of the terms of a credit instrument must be fully disclosed. The TILA also provides for contract rescission if a creditor fails to follow *exactly* the procedures required.

EQUAL CREDIT OPPORTUNITY ACT

In 1974, Congress enacted the Equal Credit Opportunity Act (ECOA) as an amendment to the Consumer Credit Protection Act. The ECOA prohibits the denial of credit solely on the basis of race, religion, national origin, color, sex, marital status, or age. The act also prohibits credit discrimination on the basis of whether an individual receives certain forms of income, such as public assistance benefits. Creditors are prohibited from requesting any information from a credit applicant that could be used for the type of discrimination covered in the act and its amendments. Under the ECOA, a creditor may not require the signature of an applicant's spouse, other than a joint applicant, on a credit instrument if the applicant qualifies under the creditor's standards of creditworthiness for the amount and terms of the credit requested.

CREDIT-CARD RULES

Under the TILA, the liability of a credit cardholder is limited to $50 per card for unauthorized charges made prior to the time the the creditor is notified. A credit-card company cannot bill a consumer for unauthorized charges if the credit card was improperly issued by the credit-card company or bank.

IN THE COURTROOM

Joann, a consumer, receives an unsolicited credit card in the mail. The card is later stolen by Fred, who uses the card to make purchases. *Will Joann be liable for the unauthorized charges?* No. The card was not issued at Joann's request and was thus improperly issued. The TILA prohibits a credit-card company from billing a consumer for any unauthorized charges if the credit card is improperly issued.

If a debtor thinks that an error has occurred in billing, or wishes to withhold payment for a faulty product purchased by credit card, the TILA outlines specific procedures for settling the dispute.

FAIR CREDIT REPORTING ACT

To ensure that consumers can determine and alter any inaccurate information about their credit records, Congress passed the Fair Credit Reporting Act (FCRA) in 1970. The FCRA covers all credit bureaus, investigative reporting companies, detective and collection agencies, and computerized information-reporting companies. The consumer has the right to be notified of reporting activities; to have access to information contained in consumer reports; and to have corrected any erroneous information upon which a denial of credit, employment, or insurance might have been based. Upon request and proper identification, any consumer is entitled to know the nature and substance of information about him or her that is contained in the agency's file, as well as the sources of the information and the identity of those who have received a consumer credit report, such as businesses that may wish to extend credit to the consumer. An investigative report cannot be prepared on an individual consumer unless that person is notified and given the right to request information on the nature and scope of the investigation.

FAIR DEBT COLLECTION PRACTICES ACT

In 1977, Congress passed the Fair Debt Collection Practices Act (FDCPA) in an attempt to curb what were perceived to be abuses by collection agencies. The act applies only to specialized debt-collection agencies that, usually for a percentage of the amount owed, regularly attempt to collect debts on behalf of someone else. Creditors who attempt to collect debts are not covered unless, by misrepresenting themselves to the debtor, they cause the debtor to believe that they are a collection agency.

The act prohibits the following debt-collection practices:

1. Contacting the consumer at his or her place of employment if the employer objects, contacting the consumer at inconvenient or unusual times, or contacting the consumer if he or she has an attorney.
2. Contacting third parties other than parents, spouses, or financial advisers about the payment of a debt unless authorized by a court.
3. Using harassment and intimidation (such as using abusive language), or using false or misleading information (such as posing as a police officer).
4. Communicating with the consumer after receipt of a notice that the consumer is refusing to pay the debt, except to advise the consumer of further action to be taken by the collection agency.

The FDCPA also requires collection agencies to include a "validation notice" whenever they initially contact a debtor for payment of a debt or within five days of that initial contact. The notice must state that the debtor has thirty days within which to dispute the debt and to request a written verification of the debt from the collection agency. The debtor's request for debt validation must be in writing.

The enforcement of the FDCPA is primarily the responsibility of the Federal Trade Commission. The act allows debtors to recover civil damages, as well as attorneys' fees, in an action against a collection agency that violates provisions of the act.

Health Protection

LEARNING OBJECTIVE NO. 4

Describing Federal Health and Safety Protection

For information on the Food and Drug Administration, access

http://www.fda.gov/

In 1906, Congress passed the Pure Food and Drug Act, which was the first step toward protecting consumers against adulterated and misbranded food and drug products. In 1938, the Federal Food, Drug, and Cosmetic Act was passed to strengthen the protective features of the 1906 legislation. These acts and subsequent amendments established standards for foods, specified safe levels of potentially dangerous food additives, and created classifications of foods and food advertising. Drugs must be proved to be effective as well as safe before they can be marketed. Food additives that can be shown to be carcinogenic (cancer causing) to humans or animals are forbidden. In general, food and drug laws make manufacturers responsible for ensuring that the food they offer for sale contains no substances that could cause injury to health. Most of the statutes involving food and drugs are monitored and enforced by the Food and Drug Administration.

Also in 1906, Congress passed the Meat Inspection Act, the beginning of legislation establishing inspection requirements for all meat and poultry sold for human consumption. The Food Safety and Quality Service of the Department of Agriculture enforces statutes relating to meat and poultry inspection.

Congress has enacted a number of statutes in an attempt to protect individuals from harmful products as well. In response to public concern over the dangers of cigarette smoking, Congress has required warnings to be placed on cigarette and little-cigar packages, as well as on containers of smokeless tobacco. Major-brand cigarette producers are required to rotate four warning labels on a quarterly basis. Smaller companies may use any of the four warnings interchangeably on a random basis. Each warning begins, "Surgeon General's Warning" and then states one of the following:

1. Smoking Causes Lung Cancer, Heart Disease, Emphysema, and May Complicate Pregnancy.
2. Quitting Smoking Now Greatly Reduces Serious Risks to Your Health.
3. Smoking by Pregnant Women May Result in Fetal Injury, Premature Birth, and Low Birth Weight.
4. Cigarette Smoke Contains Carbon Monoxide.

The Smokeless Tobacco Health Education Act of 1986 requires producers, packagers, and importers of smokeless tobacco to label their products conspicuously with one of three warnings:

1. WARNING: This product may cause mouth cancer.
2. WARNING: This product may cause gum disease and tooth loss.
3. WARNING: This product is not a safe alternative to cigarettes.

All advertising, except outdoor billboards, must include these warnings.

Consumer Product Safety

The trend toward increased government regulation in the area of public health has been mirrored in the area of consumer product safety. Legislation in this area began in 1953 with the enactment of the Flammable Fabrics Act, which prohibits the sale of highly flammable clothing or materials. Between 1953 and 1972, Congress enacted legislation regulating specific classes of products, product design, or product composition rather than regulating the overall safety of consumer products. Finally, as a result of 1970 recommendations of the National Commission on Product Safety, the Consumer Product Safety Act was passed in 1972 in an attempt to protect consumers from unreasonable risk of injury from hazardous products. The act created the Consumer Product Safety Commission (CPSC).

Generally, the CPSC was authorized to set standards for consumer products and to ban the manufacture and sale of any product deemed potentially hazardous to consumers. The commission has the authority to remove products from the market if they are deemed imminently hazardous and to require manufacturers to report information about any products already sold or intended for sale that have proved to be hazardous. The CPSC was also given the authority to administer other acts relating to product safety, such as the Child Protection and Toy Safety Act of 1969, the Hazardous Substances Labeling Act of 1960, and the Flammable Fabrics Act of 1953.

The Consumer Product Safety Commission (CPSC) provides online versions of CPSC publications, such as its *Consumer Product Safety Review,* on its Website at

http://www.cpsc.gov

State Consumer Protection Laws

Consumers are afforded the protections offered by sections in the Uniform Commercial Code (UCC) on express and implied warranties. The UCC also restricts the ability of sellers to limit their liability for personal injuries caused by defective products. Perhaps the most significant consumer protection provision of the UCC, however, is the provision that recognizes the principle of unconscionability. This provision prohibits the enforcement of any contracts that are so one sided and unfair that they "shock the conscience" of the court.

In 1968, the National Conference of Commissioners on Uniform State Laws issued the Uniform Consumer Credit Code (UCCC). The UCCC has been adopted by only a few states, although bits and pieces of it have been included in numerous state statutes. The UCCC is an attempt to establish a comprehensive body of rules governing the most important aspects of consumer credit. The UCCC focuses on truth-in-lending disclosures, maximum credit ceilings, door-to-door sales, and referral sales. The UCCC is also concerned with fine-print clauses and provisions for creditor remedies. In those states that have adopted the UCCC, it replaces previous state consumer credit laws, as well as acts dealing with installment loans, interest rates, and retail installment sales.

Despite the variation among state consumer protection laws, a common thread runs through most of them. Typically, state consumer protection laws are directed at deceptive trade practices, such as a seller's providing false or misleading information to the consumer. Some of the legislation is quite broad. A prime example is the Texas Deceptive Trade Practices Act of 1973, which forbids a seller from selling to a buyer anything that the buyer does not need or cannot afford.

TERMS AND CONCEPTS FOR REVIEW

bait-and-switch advertising 242
cease-and-desist order 242
"cooling off" law 243
counteradvertising 242
deceptive advertising 241
redress 244
Regulation Z 243

CHAPTER SUMMARY • CONSUMER PROTECTION

Advertising	**1.** *Deceptive advertising*—Advertising that is false or may be misleading to consumers is prohibited. **2.** *Bait-and-switch advertising*—Advertising a lower-priced product when the intention is not to sell the advertised product but to lure consumers into the store and convince them to buy a higher-priced product is prohibited. **3.** *Federal Trade Commission actions against deceptive ads*— **a.** Cease-and-desist order—Requires the advertiser to stop the challenged advertising. **b.** Counteradvertising—Requires the advertiser to advertise to correct the earlier misinformation.
Labeling and Packaging	Manufacturers must comply with labeling or packaging requirements for their specific products. In general, all labels must be accurate and not misleading.
Sales and Credit	**1.** *Credit terms*—If certain credit terms pertaining to the purchase of a product are advertised, other relevant credit and sale terms (such as cash price, down payment, payments, other charges, and annual percentage rate of interest) must be included. **2.** *Door-to-door sales*—Consumers have three days to cancel. **3.** *Mail-order sales*—Federal and state statutes prohibit the use of the mails to defraud individuals. **4.** *Unsolicited merchandise sent by mail*—May be retained, used, discarded, or disposed of in any manner by the recipient. The recipient incurs no contractual obligation. **5.** *Truth-in-Lending Act (Title I of the Consumer Credit Protection Act)*—Requires sellers and lenders to disclose credit terms and loan terms. Also provides for the following: **a.** Equal credit opportunity (prohibits creditors from discriminating on the basis of race, gender, and so on). **b.** Credit-card protection (limits liability of cardholders prior to notice to $50 for unauthorized charges and protects consumers from liability for unauthorized charges made on unsolicited credit cards). **c.** Credit-card rules (allow credit-card users to withhold payment for a faulty product or for an error in billing).

CHAPTER SUMMARY • *Continued*

Sales and Credit—Continued	**6.** *Fair Credit Reporting Act*—Entitles consumers to be informed of a credit investigation, to request verification of the accuracy of the report, and to have corrected erroneous information in their files. **7.** *Fair Debt Collection Practices Act*—Prohibits debt collectors from using unfair debt-collection practices (such as contacting the debtor at his or her place of employment if the employer objects, contacting third parties about the debt, harassment, intimidation, and so on). **8.** *Uniform Consumer Credit Code*—A comprehensive body of rules governing the most important aspects of consumer credit; adopted by only a minority of states.
Health Protection	Laws govern the processing and distribution of food and drugs. Explicit warnings about hazards are required for some products (such as tobacco).
Product Safety	The Consumer Product Safety Act of 1972 seeks to protect consumers from risk of injury from hazardous products. The Consumer Product Safety Commission has the power to remove products that are deemed imminently hazardous from the market and to ban the manufacture and sale of hazardous products.

HYPOTHETICAL QUESTIONS

20–1. Sales. On June 28, a sales representative for Renowned Books called on the Guevaras at their home. After listening to a very persuasive sales pitch, the Guevaras agreed in writing to purchase a twenty-volume set of historical encyclopedias from Renowned Books for a total of $299. An initial down payment of $35 was required, with the remainder of the price to be paid in monthly payments over a one-year period. Two days later, the Guevaras, having second thoughts about the purchase, contacted the book company and stated that they had decided to rescind the contract. Renowned Books said this would be impossible. Has Renowned Books violated any consumer law by not allowing the Guevaras to rescind their contract? Explain.

20–2. Credit Protection. Maria Ochoa receives two new credit cards on May 1. She had solicited one of them from Midtown Department Store, and the other had arrived unsolicited from High-Flying Airlines. During the month of May, Ochoa made numerous credit-card purchases from Midtown Store, but she does not use the High-Flying Airlines card. On May 31, a burglar breaks into Ochoa's home and steals both credit cards, along with other items. Ochoa notifies the Midtown Department Store of the theft on June 2, but she fails to notify High-Flying Airlines. Using the Midtown credit card, the burglar makes a $500 purchase on June 1 and a $200 purchase on June 3. The burglar then charges a vacation flight on the High-Flying Airlines card for $1,000 on June 5. Ochoa receives the bills for these charges and refuses to pay them. Discuss Ochoa's liability in these situations.

REAL WORLD CASE PROBLEM

20–3. Debt Collection. Equifax A.R.S., a debt-collection agency, sent Donna Russell a notice about one of her debts. The front of the notice stated that "[i]f you do not dispute this claim (see reverse side) and wish to pay it within the next 10 days we will not post this collection to your file." The reverse side set out Russell's rights under the Fair Debt Collection Practices Act (FDCPA), including that she had thirty days to decide whether to contest the claim. Russell filed a suit in a federal district court against Equifax. The court ruled against Russell, who appealed. On what basis might Russell argue that Equifax violated the FDCPA? [*Russell v. Equifax A.R.S.*, 74 F.3d 30 (2d Cir. 1996)]

For updated links to resources available on the Web, as well as a variety of other materials, visit this text's Web site at **http://blte.westbuslaw.com**.

For current articles concerning consumer issues, go to the Alexander Law Firm's "Consumer Law Page," which is online at

http://consumerlawpage.com/intro.html

The law firm of Arent Fox offers extensive information relating to advertising law at

http://www.advertisinglaw.com

The Virtual Law Library of the Indiana University School of Law provides numerous links to online environmental law sources. Go to

http://www.law.indiana.edu

ONLINE LEGAL RESEARCH

Go to **http://blte.westbuslaw.com**, the Web site that accompanies this text. Select "Internet Applications," and then click on "Chapter 20." There you will find the following Internet research exercise that you can perform to learn more about consumer law:

Activity 20–1: Consumer Law

Chapter 20 ■ WORK SET

TRUE-FALSE QUESTIONS

_____ **1.** Advertising will be deemed deceptive if a consumer would be misled by the advertising claim.

_____ **2.** In general, labels must be accurate—they must use words as those words are understood by the ordinary consumer.

_____ **3.** Under no circumstances can a consumer rescind a contract freely entered into.

_____ **4.** The TILA applies to creditors who, in the ordinary course of business, lend money or sell goods on credit to consumers.

_____ **5.** Consumers may have more protection under state laws than federal laws.

_____ **6.** The Fair Debt Collection Practices Act applies to anyone who attempts to collect a debt.

_____ **7.** There are no federal agencies that regulate sales.

_____ **8.** One who leases consumer goods in the ordinary course of their business does not, under any circumstances, have to disclose all material terms in writing.

MULTIPLE-CHOICE QUESTIONS

_____ **1.** General Tobacco Corporation (GTC) sells tobacco products. On the packages of its smokeless tobacco products, GTC must include

a. warnings about health hazards associated with cigarettes.
b. warnings about health hazards associated with smokeless products.
c. warnings about health hazards associated with tobacco generally.
d. none of the above.

_____ **2.** The ordinary business of Ace Credit Company is to lend money to consumers. Ace must disclose all credit terms clearly and conspicuously in

a. no credit transaction.
b. any credit transaction in which payments are to be made in more than four installments.
c. any credit transaction in which payments are to be made in more than one installment.
d. all credit transactions.

_____ **3.** ABC Corporation sells a variety of consumer products. Generally, the labels on its products must

a. only be accurate.
b. only use words as they are ordinarily understood by consumers.
c. be accurate and use words as they are ordinarily understood by consumers.
d. none of the above.

_____ **4.** Rich Foods Company advertises that its cereal, "Fiber Rich," reduces cholesterol. After an investigation and a hearing, the FTC finds no evidence to support the claim. To correct the public's impression of Fiber Rich, which of the following would be most appropriate?

a. Counteradvertising.
b. Cease-and-desist order.
c. Civil fine.
d. Criminal fine.

_____ **5.** Maria does not speak English. Burt comes to her home and, after a long presentation in Spanish, sells her a vacuum cleaner. He hands her a paper that contains only in English a notice of the right to cancel a sale within three days. This transaction was

a. proper, because the salesperson gave the buyer notice of her rights.
b. not proper, because the deal was in Spanish but the notice was in English.
c. proper, because ignorance of your rights is no defense.
d. not proper, because ignorance of your rights is a defense.

_____ **6.** Bob takes out a student loan from the First National Bank. After graduation, Bob goes to work, but he does not make payments on the loan. The bank agrees with Ace Collection Agency that if Ace collects the debt, it can keep a percentage of the amount. To collect the debt, Ace can contact

a. Bob at his place of employment, even if his employer objects.
b. Bob at unusual or inconvenient times or any time if he retains an attorney.
c. third parties, including Bob's parents, unless ordered otherwise by a court.
d. Bob only to advise him of further action that Ace will take.

_____ **7.** National Foods, Inc., sells many kinds of breakfast cereals. Under the Fair Packaging and Labeling Act, National must include on the packages

a. the identity of the product only.
b. the net quantity of the contents and number of servings only.
c. the identity of the product, the net quantity of the contents, and number of servings.
d. none of the above.

_____ **8.** American Doll Company begins marketing a new doll with clothes and hair that is highly flammable, and accessories small enough to choke a little child. The Consumer Product Safety Commission may

a. order that the doll be removed from store shelves.
b. warn consumers but cannot order that the doll be removed from stores.
c. ban the doll's manufacture but cannot order it removed from stores.
d. do nothing.

ISSUE SPOTTERS

1. Top Electronics, Inc., advertises GEM computers at a low price. Top keeps only a few in stock and tells its sales staff to switch consumers attracted by the price to more expensive brands. Top tells its staff that if all else fails, refuse to show the GEMs, and if a consumer insists on buying one, do not promise delivery. Has Top violated a law?

2. Sweet Candy Company wants to sell its candy in a normal-sized package labeled "Gigantic Size." Fine Fabrics, Inc., wants to advertise its sweaters as having "That Wool Feel," but does not want to specify on labels that the sweaters are 100 percent polyester. What stops these firms from marketing their products as they would like?

E-Commerce

21

LEARNING OBJECTIVES

When you finish this chapter, you should be able to:

1. Discuss whether shrink-wrap agreements are enforceable.
2. Define the legal validity of an electronic signature.
3. Describe the potential legal effects of using electronic agents.
4. Summarize the coverage of the Uniform Computer Information Transactions Act (UCITA).
5. Identify the similarities of the Uniform Computer Information Transactions Act (UCITA) and the Uniform Electronic Transactions Act (UETA).

FACING A LEGAL PROBLEM

Delta Company buys accounting software from Omega Corporation. On the outside of the software box, on the inside cover of the instruction manual, and on the first screen that appears each time the program is used is a license that claims to cover the use of the product. The license also includes a limitation on Omega's liability arising from the use of the software. One year later, Delta discovers that the software has a bug that has cost Delta a financial loss. Delta files a suit against Omega. *Is the limitation-on-liability clause on the software box enforceable?*

E-commerce (doing business over the Internet) may involve businesses selling goods and services to consumers in business-to-consumer, or B2C, transactions. An increasing percentage of the deals transacted in cyberspace, however, involve business-to-business (B2B) transactions. Does engaging in e-commerce create any special contract problems or call for any other changes in the law as it has traditionally applied to contracts?

E-Commerce
Business transacted in cyberspace.

Many observers argue that the development of cyberspace is revolutionary and that new legal theories, and new law, are needed to govern **e-contracts,** or contracts entered into in e-commerce. To date, most courts have applied traditional common law principles to cases arising in the e-environment. New laws have been drafted, however, to apply in situations in which old laws have sometimes been thought inadequate. This chapter considers some of the circumstances that exist in the computer industry and in e-commerce and some of the new laws that apply in those circumstances.

E-Contract
A contract entered into in e-commerce.

Shrink-Wrap Agreements

In the real world, the terms of a contract are frequently negotiated at the beginning of a business deal, before either party has started to perform. Sometimes, however, the parties start to perform before they have agreed on the contract's terms.

SHRINK-WRAP AGREEMENT An agreement whose terms are expressed inside a box in which goods are packaged. Sometimes called a *shrink-wrap license.*

In the computer industry, this occurs in the form of a **shrink-wrap agreement** (or *shrink-wrap license,* as it is sometimes called)—an agreement whose terms are expressed inside a box in which the goods are packaged. (The term *shrink-wrap* refers to the plastic that covers the box.) Usually, the party who opens the box is informed that he or she agrees to the terms by keeping whatever is in the box.

In most cases, this agreement is not between a seller and a buyer, but between the manufacturer of the hardware or software and its user. The terms of the agreement generally concern warranties, remedies, and other issues associated with the use of the product.

ENFORCEABLE CONTRACT TERMS

LEARNING OBJECTIVE NO. 1
Discussing Whether Shrink-wrap Agreements are Enforceable

In many cases, the courts have enforced the terms of shrink-wrap agreements the same as the terms of other contracts. Sometimes, the courts have reasoned that by including the terms with the product, the seller proposed a contract that the buyer could accept by using the product after having had an opportunity to read the terms (whether or not the buyer actually read them).

Also, it seems practical from a business's point of view to enclose a full statement of the legal terms of a sale with the product rather than to read the statement over the phone, for example, when a buyer calls in an order for the product.

In the legal problem set out at the beginning of this chapter, Delta Company buys from Omega Corporation software that includes a limitation-on-liability clause on the box. *Is the clause enforceable?* Yes. The shrink-wrap license is enforceable, and its limitation on Omega's liability caused by use of the software is valid. The parties are both businesses, and the terms of the license are set forth in several locations. Those terms are enforceable unless they are objectionable on grounds that apply to contracts in general.

PROPOSALS FOR ADDITIONAL TERMS

Not all of the terms presented in shrink-wrap agreements have been enforced. One important consideration is whether the parties form their contract before or after the seller communicates the terms of the shrink-wrap agreement to the buyer. If a court finds that the buyer learned of the shrink-wrap terms *after* the parties entered into a contract, the court might conclude that those terms were proposals for additional terms, which were not part of the contract unless the buyer expressly agreed to them.

IN THE COURTROOM

Whenever it sells a computer, Digital Products, Inc., includes a copy of its "Standard Terms and Conditions Agreement" in the box. At the top of the first page is the following: "NOTE TO THE CUSTOMER: By keeping your computer system beyond five (5) days after the date of delivery, you accept these Terms and Conditions." Beth buys a Digital computer and keeps it for more than five days. *Are the "Standard Terms" enforceable?* Yes, if they are considered to be part of the contract for the sale of the computer. If Digital tells each customer that Digital's acceptance of a sale is conditioned on the customer's agreeing to the terms, for example, the terms are enforceable.

Click-On Agreements

A **click-on agreement** (or *click-on license* or *click-wrap agreement,* as it is sometimes called) occurs when a buyer, completing a transaction on a computer, is required to indicate his or her assent to be bound by the terms of an offer by clicking on a button that says, for example, "I agree." The terms may be contained on a Web site through which the buyer is obtaining goods or services, or they may appear on a computer screen when software is loaded.

CLICK-ON AGREEMENT
This occurs when a buyer, completing a transaction on a computer, is required to indicate his or her assent to be bound by the terms of an offer by clicking on a button that says, for example, "I agree." Sometimes referred to as a *click-on license* or a *click-wrap agreement.*

Exhibit 21–1 contains the language of a click-on disclaimer that accompanies a package of software made and marketed by Adobe Systems, Inc.

Under the Uniform Commercial Code (UCC), businesses or consumers can make a contract for a sale of goods "in any manner sufficient to show agreement, including conduct by both parties which recognizes the existence of a contract." The *Restatement (Second) of Contracts* states that parties may agree to a contract "by written or spoken words or by other action or by failure to act." With these provisions in mind, it seems that a binding contract can be created over the Internet by clicking on an "I agree" button.

IN THE COURTROOM

Mail Online Corporation provides free e-mail service to those subscribers who click on an "I accept" button to agree to Mail Online's "Terms of Services." The terms prohibit a subscriber from using the service to send spam (unsolicited commercial bulk e-mail). EZ Investment Company, a subscriber, uses the service to send to other subscribers spam peddling "get rich quick" schemes. *Has EZ Investment breached a contract with Mail Online?* Yes. An online service agreement, with a click-on acceptance button, is an enforceable contract.

E-Signatures

As discussed in Chapter 13, in many cases a contract, to be enforced, requires the signature of the party against whom enforcement is sought. Before the days when most people could write, they signed documents with an "X." Then came the handwritten signature, followed by typed signatures, printed signatures, and, most recently, electronic signatures, or **e-signatures.**

E-SIGNATURE
An electronic sound, symbol, or process attached to or logically associated with a record and executed or adopted by a person with the intent to sign the record, according to the Uniform Electronic Transactions Act.

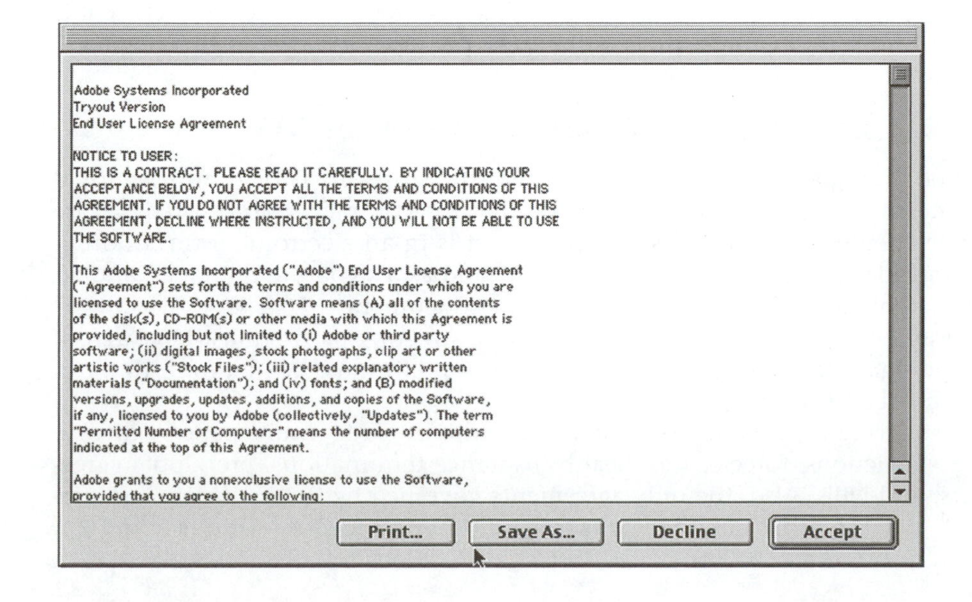

EXHIBIT 21–1
A Click-On Disclaimer

Throughout the evolution of signature technology, debates over what constitutes a valid signature have occurred, and with good reason: without some agreement on what constitutes a valid signature, little business or legal work could be accomplished. A significant issue in the context of e-commerce is the legal effect of e-signatures.

E-Signature Technologies

Today, there are numerous technologies that allow electronic documents to be signed. These include digital signatures and alternative technologies.

The most common e-signature technology is the *asymmetric cryptosystem,* which creates an e-signature using two different (asymmetric) "keys." A person attaches an e-signature to a document using a private key, or code. The key has a public counterpart. Anyone with the appropriate software can use the public key to verify that an e-signature was made using the private key. A **cybernotary,** or legally recognized certification authority, issues the keys, identifies the owner, and certifies the validity of the public key.

Cybernotary
A legally recognized certification authority that issues the keys for digital signatures, identifies their owners, certifies their validity, and serves as a repository for public keys.

Other forms of e-signatures have been—or are now being—developed as well. For example, some e-signatures use "smart cards." A smart card is a credit-card size device that is embedded with code and other data. As with credit and debit cards, this smart card can be inserted into computers to transfer information. Unlike those other cards, however, a smart card could be used to establish a person's identity as validly as a signature on a piece of paper.

State Laws Governing E-Signatures

Most states have laws governing e-signatures. The problem is that the state e-signature laws are not uniform.

In an attempt to create more uniformity among the states, the National Conference of Commissioners on Uniform State Laws promulgated the Uniform Electronic Transactions Act (UETA) in 1999. The UETA defines an *e-signature* as "an electronic sound, symbol, or process attached to or logically associated with a record and executed or adopted by a person with the intent to sign the record." A **record** is "information that is inscribed on a tangible medium or that is stored in an electronic or other medium and is retrievable in perceivable form."

Record
Information that is inscribed in either a tangible medium or stored in an electronic or other medium and that is retrievable, according to the Uniform Electronic Transactions Act. The Uniform Computer Information Transaction Act uses *record* instead of *writing.*

This definition of *e-signature* includes encrypted digital signatures, names (intended as signatures) at the ends of e-mail, and a click on a Web page if the click includes the identification of the person. The UETA also states, among other things, that a signature may not be denied legal effect or enforceability solely because it is in electronic form. (Other aspects of the UETA are discussed later in this chapter.)

Federal Law on E-Signatures and E-Documents

LEARNING OBJECTIVE NO. 2
Defining the Legal Validity of an Electronic Signature

In 2000, Congress enacted the Electronic Signatures in Global and National Commerce Act (E-SIGN Act) to provide that no contract, record, or signature may be "denied legal effect" solely because it is in an electronic form. In other words, under this law, an e-signature is as valid as a signature on paper, and an e-document can be as enforceable as a paper document.

For an e-signature to be enforceable, the contracting parties must have agreed to use e-signatures. For an e-document to be valid, it must be in a form that can be retained and accurately reproduced.

Contracts and documents that are exempt include court papers, divorce decrees, evictions, foreclosures, health insurance terminations, prenuptial agreements, and wills. Also, the only agreements governed by the Uniform Commercial Code (UCC) that fall under this law are those covered by Articles 2 and 2A, and UCC 1–107 and 1–206.

Despite the limitations, the E-SIGN Act expands enormously the possibilities for contracting online. From a remote location, a businessperson might open an account with a financial institution, obtain a mortgage or other loan, buy insurance, and purchase real estate over the Internet. Payments and transfers of funds could be done entirely online. This can avoid the time and costs associated with producing, delivering, signing, and returning paper documents.

E-Agents

As you will learn in Chapter 25, an *agency* relationship is one in which one party (called the *agent*) agrees to represent or act for the other (called the *principal*). An electronic agent, or **e-agent,** is not a person but a semiautonomous computer program that is capable of executing specific tasks. Examples of e-agents in e-commerce include software that can search through many databases and retrieve only relevant information for the user.

E-AGENT
A computer program, or electronic or other automated means used to independently initiate an action or to respond to electronic messages or performances without review by an individual.

Some e-agents are used to make purchases on the Internet. An Internet user might use one of the following e-agents to search the Web for a particular book: PriceScan, MX Bookfinder, and Bestbookbuys. Any one of these e-agents will scour the Web for the lowest price for that particular book title. Once found, the e-agent usually offers links to the appropriate Web sites. Other shopping e-agents locate other specific products in online catalogues and actually negotiate product acquisition, as well as delivery.

HOW MUCH AUTHORITY?

An important aspect of agency law is the scope of an agent's authority to act on behalf of his or her principal. Under traditional agency law, contracts formed by an agent normally are legally binding on the principal *if* the principal authorized the agent, either expressly or impliedly, to form the contracts. One of the controversies involving e-agents concerns the extent of an e-agent's authority to act on behalf of its principal.

POSSIBLE SOLUTIONS

To avoid problems created by the use of e-agents, some online stores have blocked e-agents from accessing pricing information. Other online stores are developing click-on agreements that can be understood by a computer and that are therefore more conspicuous for e-agents.

LEARNING OBJECTIVE NO. 3
Describing the Potential Legal Effects of Using Electronic Agents

The Uniform Computer Information Transactions Act (UCITA), a proposed law issued in 1999, and discussed in detail in the next section, specifically addresses the issue of e-agents. The UCITA provides that any individual or company that uses an e-agent "is bound by the operations of the electronic agent, even if no individual was aware of or reviewed the agent's operations or the results of the operations." The liability of individuals and companies for the acts of e-agents, however, is qualified. Under the UCITA, "a court may grant appropriate relief if the operations resulted from fraud, electronic mistake, or the like."

For information on the National Conference of Commissioners of Uniform State Laws (NCCUSL), see the NCCUSL Web site at

http://www.nccusl.org

The Uniform Computer Information Transactions Act

Among the proposed new laws that go beyond the existing law is the Uniform Computer Information Transactions Act (UCITA). The UCITA is a draft of legislation suggested to the states by the National Conference of Commissioners of Uniform State Laws (NCCUSL) and the American Law Institute (ALI). These organizations have initiated many of the most significant laws that apply to traditional commerce, including the Uniform Commercial Code (UCC).

Coverage and Content

LEARNING OBJECTIVE NO. 4
Summarizing the Coverage of the Uniform Computer Information Transactions Act (UCITA)

The UCITA establishes a comprehensive set of rules covering contracts involving computer information. **Computer information** is "information in electronic form obtained from or through use of a computer, or that is in digital or equivalent form capable of being processed by a computer."

Computer Information
Information in electronic form obtained from or through use of a computer, or that is in digital or an equivalent form capable of being processed by a computer.

Under this definition, the act covers contracts to license or purchase software, contracts to create a computer program, contracts for computer games, contracts for online access to databases, contracts to distribute information on the Internet, "diskettes" that contain computer programs, online books, and other similar contracts.

The UCITA May Apply to Only Part of a Transaction. The UCITA does not apply generally to the sale of goods even if software is embedded in or used in the production of the goods (except a computer). This includes television sets, stereos, books, and automobiles as examples. It also does not apply to traditional movies, records, or cable. These industries are specifically excluded for the most part.

When a transaction includes computer information as defined in the act and subject matter other than computer information, the UCITA generally provides that if the primary subject matter deals with computer and information rights, the act applies to the entire transaction. If this is not the primary subject matter, then the act applies only to the part "of the transaction involving computer information, informational rights in it and creation or modification of it."

Parties Can "Opt Out." As with most other uniform acts that apply to business, the UCITA allows the parties to waive or vary the provisions of the act by a contract. The parties may even agree to "opt-out" of the act and, for contracts not covered by the act, to "opt-in." In other words, the UCITA expressly recognizes the freedom to contract and supports the idea that this is a basic principle of contract law.

The UCITA stresses the parties' agreement (similar to the emphasis in UCC Article 2), and the act's provisions apply in the absence of an agreement. These provisions are called **default rules.** As with other uniform statutes, rules relating to good faith, diligence, public policy, unconscionability, and related principles cannot be varied or deleted by agreement.

Default Rules
Under the Uniform Computer Information Transaction Act, rules that apply only in the absence of an agreement between contracting parties to the contrary.

Rights and Restrictions. The licensing of information is the primary method used for transferring computer information in business today. A license contract involves a transfer of computer information, such as software, from a seller (the licensor) to a buyer (the licensee). The licensee is given certain rights to use and control the computer information during the license period. Title does not pass, and quite often the license places restrictions on the licensee's use of, and rights to copy and control, the computer information. Many of the sections of the UCITA deal with the rights and restrictions that can be imposed on the parties in the license.

From Contract Formation to Contract Remedies. The UCITA, which consists of nine "parts," covers everything from the formation of a contract to remedies for breach of contract. To give you an idea of the extent of the act's coverage, we list the titles of the parts and subparts of the act in Exhibit 21–2.

Highlights

The UCITA resembles UCC Article 2. Both acts have similar general provisions, including definitions (approximately sixty-six) and formal requirements (such as

EXHIBIT 21–2
The UCITA—Titles of Parts and Subparts

UNIFORM COMPUTER INFORMATION TRANSACTIONS ACT	
PART I GENERAL PROVISIONS [SUBPART A. SHORT TITLE AND DEFINITIONS] [SUBPART B. GENERAL SCOPE AND TERMS] PART 2 FORMATION AND TERMS [SUBPART A. FORMATION OF CONTRACT] [SUBPART B. TERMS OF RECORDS] [SUBPART C. ELECTRONIC CONTRACTS: GENERALLY] PART 3 CONSTRUCTION [SUBPART A. GENERAL] [SUBPART B. INTERPRETATION] PART 4 WARRANTIES PART 5 TRANSFER OF INTERESTS AND RIGHTS [SUBPART A. OWNERSHIP AND TRANSFERS] [SUBPART B. FINANCING ARRANGEMENTS]	PART 6 PERFORMANCE [SUBPART A. GENERAL] [SUBPART B. PERFORMANCE IN DELIVERY OF COPIES] [SUBPART C. SPECIAL TYPES OF CONTRACTS] [SUBPART D. LOSS AND IMPOSSIBILITY] [SUBPART E. TERMINATION] PART 7 BREACH OF CONTRACT [SUBPART A. GENERAL] [SUBPART B. DEFECTIVE COPIES] [SUBPART C. REPUDIATION AND ASSURANCES] PART 8 REMEDIES [SUBPART A. GENERAL] [SUBPART B. DAMAGES] [SUBPART C. REMEDIES RELATED TO PERFORMANCE] PART 9 MISCELLANEOUS PROVISIONS

a Statute of Frauds, which, in the case of the UCITA, requires a written memorandum when a contract requires a payment of $5,000 or more). Other comparable provisions include rules for offer and acceptance, unconscionable contracts or terms, parol evidence, and other principles.

The UCITA goes further, however, with provisions covering the contracting parties' choice of law and choice of forum, the UCITA's relationship to federal law and other state laws, and many others. These provisions make the UCITA more comprehensive in scope than UCC Article 2.

Described in the next sections are some of the UCITA's highlights. As you will note, most of them address situations that arise due to the unique nature of licensing computer information.

Mass-Market Licenses. Basically, a *mass-market* transaction is either (1) a consumer contract or (2) a transaction in which the computer information is directed to the general public and the end-user licensee acquires the information in a retail transaction.

A **mass-market license** is an electronic form contract that is usually presented with a package of computer information purchased. We commonly get these licenses by having the license contract shrink-wrapped or, in the case of an online transaction, click-wrapped with the computer information (when a certain link is clicked on).

These licenses are different from negotiated licenses in that mass-market licenses are automatically enforceable, as long as the terms are readily available and the licensee has had an opportunity to review the license terms.

If the licensee does not want the computer information for any reason, the UCITA allows the licensee to return the computer information for a refund and recover any reasonable expenses incurred in making the removal and return of the

It is especially important, when forming an e-contract, to include a forum-selection clause. This helps to make the outcome of any dispute more predictable when the parties to the contract are in distant locations subject to different laws.

MASS-MARKET LICENSE
An e-contract that is presented with a package of computer information in the form of a *click-on license* or a *shrink-wrap license*.

computer information. The UCITA provides that these rights of return and entitlement to reasonable expenses cannot be waived or disclaimed by the licensor.

Warranties. The UCITA provides for basically the same warranties as provided for in UCC Article 2. Thus, the licensor's affirmations of fact or promises concerning the computer information (as a basis for the bargain) constitute express warranties. Implied warranties are also provided for by the act (and can be disclaimed, as under UCC Article 2). The UCITA's implied warranties of merchantability and fitness are closely tailored to the information content and the "compatibility of the computer systems."

Authentication and Attribution. Before the emergence of electronic contracting, parties generally knew each other, and many contracts contained the signatures of the parties. Today, we deal with electronic signatures, or e-signatures. We want to be sure that the "person" sending the electronic message is in fact the person whose electronic message is being transmitted. For this reason, like the revisions of other statutes, the UCITA's rules were revised to provide for the authentication of e-signatures.

AUTHENTICATE
To sign a record, or with the intent to sign a record, to execute, or to adopt an electronic sound, symbol, or the like to link with the record. See *record.*

To **authenticate** means to sign a record, or with the intent to sign a record, to execute, or to adopt an electronic sound, symbol, or the like to link with the record. As noted earlier in this chapter, a record is information that is inscribed in either a tangible medium or stored in an electronic or other medium and that is retrievable. The UCITA uses the word *record* instead of *writing.*

To ensure that the person sending the electronic computer information is the same person whose e-signature accompanies the information, the UCITA has a procedure, referred to as the *attribution procedure,* that sets forth steps for identifying a person that sends the electronic communication. These steps, which can be specified by the contracting parties, can be simple or complex as long as they are commercially reasonable.

Attribution procedures can also have an effect on liability for errors in the message content. If the attribution procedure is in place to detect errors, the party who conforms to the procedure is not bound by the error. Consumers who make unintended errors are not bound as long as the consumer notifies the other party promptly, returns the computer information received, and has not benefited from its use.

Under the UCITA, as under previous law, there is no requirement that all of the parties read all of the terms in a contract for those terms to be effective.

IN THE COURTROOM

Tech News, Inc., is an online computer news service. To become a Tech News subscriber, a prospective customer views a computer screen that includes a "Subscription Agreement" in a scrollable window. Next to the window are boxes providing the choices "I Agree" and "I Don't Agree." Prospective customers have the option to click either of the boxes at any time. Without reading the agreement or even scrolling through the window, Carl clicks "I Agree." *Is Carl bound to the terms of the "Subscription Agreement"?* Yes. The agreement is valid and enforceable because Carl had a sufficient opportunity to view it.

ACCESS CONTRACT
A contract to obtain by electronic means access to, or information from, another person's information processing system, or the equivalent of such access, according to the Uniform Computer Information Transactions Act.

Access Contracts. The UCITA defines an **access contract** as "a contract to obtain by electronic means access to, or information from an information processing system of another person, or the equivalent of such access." This is important for most of us, if for no other reason than our ability to use the

Internet. The UCITA, however, has special rules governing available times and manner of access.

Support and Service Contracts to Correct Performance Problems. The UCITA covers licensor support and service contracts, but no licensor is required to provide such support and service. Computer software support contracts are common, and once made, the licensor is obligated to comply with the express terms of the support contract or, if the contract is silent on an issue, to do what is reasonable in light of ordinary business standards.

Electronic Self-Help. The UCITA allows the licensor to cancel, repossess, prevent continued use, and take similar actions on a licensee's breach of a license. The act permits the licensor to undertake "electronic self-help" to enforce the licensor's rights through electronic means.

Outside the UCITA, "self-help" refers to the right of a lessor, for example, under Article 2A of the UCC, which deals with the lease of goods, to repossess a leased computer if the lessee fails to make payments according to the terms of the lease. A lender may have this same right under Article 9, which covers secured transactions (transactions in which collateral is given as security for a loan) if a borrower fails to make payments on a loan secured by a computer.

In a transaction governed by the UCITA, electronic self-help includes the right of a software licensor to install a "turn-off" function in the software so that if the licensee violates the terms of the license, the software can be disabled from a distance. This right is most important to a small firm that licenses its software to a much larger company. Electronic self-help may be the licensor's only practical remedy if the license is breached.

There are some limitations on this right. For example, the amendments to the UCITA passed in August 2000 prohibit electronic self-help in mass-market transactions. In addition, the remedy is not available unless the parties agree to permit electronic self-help. The licensor must give notice of the intent to use the self-help remedy at least fifteen days before doing so, along with full disclosure of the nature of the breach and information to enable the licensee to cure the breach or to communicate with the licensor concerning the situation.

A licensor is entitled on a licensee's breach to incidental and consequential damages. Of course, a licensor must attempt to mitigate those damages, but electronic self-help cannot be used if the licensor "has reason to know that its use will result in substantial injury or harm to the public health or safety or grave harm to the public interest affecting third persons involved in the dispute."

These limitations on the use of electronic self-help cannot be waived or varied by contract.

The Uniform Electronic Transactions Act

As mentioned earlier in this chapter, another uniform law proposed by the National Conference of Commissioners on Uniform State Laws (NCCUSL) concerning e-commerce is the Uniform Electronic Transactions Act (UETA). The goal of the UETA is not to create rules for electronic transactions—for example, the act does not require digital signatures—but to support the enforcement of e-contracts.

The Validity of E-Contracts

Under the UETA, contracts entered into online, as well as other electronic documents, are presumed valid. In other words, a contract is not unenforceable simply because it is in an electronic form. The UETA does not apply to transactions governed by the UCC or the UCITA, or to wills or testamentary trusts.

THE UETA AND THE UCITA COMPARED

The UETA and the UCITA have many similarities. The drafters of the laws attempted to make them consistent. Both proposals provide for such items as the following:

- The equivalency of records and writings.
- The validity of e-signatures.
- The formation of contracts by e-agents.
- The formation of contracts between an e-agent and a natural person.
- The attribution of an electronic act to a person if it can be proved that the act was done by the person or his or her agent.
- A provision that parties do not need to participate in e-commerce to make binding contracts.

LEARNING OBJECTIVE NO. 5

Identifying the Similarities of the UCITA and the Uniform Electronic Transactions Act (UETA)

These two uniform laws also have differences. Those differences include the following.

- The UETA supports all electronic transactions, but it does not create rules for them. The UCITA concerns only contracts that involve computer information, but for those contracts, the UCITA imposes rules.
- The UETA does not apply unless contracting parties agree to use e-commerce in their transactions. The UCITA applies to any agreement that falls within its scope.

To read one of the drafts of the UCITA or the UETA, go to a Web site that the NCCUSL maintains with the University of Pennsylvania Law School at

http://www.law.upenn.edu/bll/ulc/ucita/citam99.htm

In sum, the chief difference between the UETA and the UCITA is that the UCITA addresses e-commerce issues that the UETA does not. Those issues, and how the UCITA deals with them, were discussed in the previous sections.

TERMS AND CONCEPTS FOR REVIEW

CHAPTER SUMMARY • E-CONTRACTS

Shrink-Wrap Agreements	1. *Definition*—An agreement whose terms are expressed inside a box in which the goods are packaged. 2. *Enforceability*—The courts have often enforced shrink-wrap agreements, even if the purchaser-user of the goods did not read the terms of the agreement. A court may deem a shrink-wrap agreement unenforceable, however, if the buyer learns of the shrink-wrap terms after the parties entered into the agreement.
Click-on Agreements	1. *Definition*—An agreement created when a buyer, completing a transaction on a computer, is required to indicate his or her assent to be bound by the terms of an offer by clicking on a button that says, for example, "I agree." 2. *Enforceability*—The courts have enforced click-on agreements, holding that by clicking "I agree," the offeree has indicated acceptance by conduct.

CHAPTER SUMMARY • *Continued*

E-Signatures	**1.** *Definition*—An electronic sound, symbol, or process attached to or logically associated with a record and executed or adopted by a person with the intent to sign the record. **2.** *State laws governing e-signatures*—Most states have laws governing e-signatures, and although these laws are not uniform, they generally provide for the validity of e-signatures. **3.** *Federal Law on e-signatures and e-documents*—The Electronic Signatures in Global and National Commerce Act (E-SIGN Act) of 2000 gives validity to e-signatures.
E-Agents	**1.** *Definition*—A semiautonomous computer program capable of executing specific tasks, such as software that can search through databases and retrieve relevant information for the agent's principal. **2.** *Scope of authority*—Under agency law, a principal normally is not bound by a contract formed by an agent who lacks the authority to form that contract. One of the problems posed by e-agents is the extent to which the e-agent is authorized to form e-contracts through, for example, click-on agreements. The Uniform Computer Information Transactions Act (UCITA) addresses this problem by including specific provisions relating to e-agents.
The Uniform Computer Information Transactions Act (UCITA)	**1.** *Purpose*—To govern transactions involving the licensing of intangible property, such as computer information, which are not covered by Article 2 of the Uniform Commercial Code (UCC). **2.** *Coverage and content*—The UCITA applies to contracts involving computer information, such as contracts to license or purchase software. Computer information is defined as "information in electronic form obtained from or through use of a computer, or that is in digital or equivalent form capable of being processed by a computer." As with most other uniform acts that apply to business, the UCITA allows the parties to waive or vary its provisions by contract or even agree to "opt-out" or "opt-in" to UCITA provisions. The UCITA covers all aspects of e-contracts involving computer information, from contract formation to contract remedies.
The Uniform Electronic Transactions Act (UETA)	**1.** *Purpose*—To create rules to support the enforcement of e-contracts. Under the UETA, contracts entered into online are presumed valid. The UETA does not apply to transactions governed by the UCC or the UCITA. **2.** *The UETA and the UCITA compared*—The chief difference between the UETA and the UCITA is that the latter addresses e-commerce issues that the UETA does not.

HYPOTHETICAL QUESTIONS

21–1. Click-On Agreements. Paul is a financial analyst for King Investments, Inc., a brokerage firm. Paul uses the Internet to investigate the background and activities of companies that might be good investments for King's customers. While visiting the Web site of Business Research, Inc., Paul sees on his screen a message that reads, "Welcome to business-research.com. By visiting our site, you have been entered as a subscriber to our e-publication, *Companies Unlimited.* This publication will be sent to you daily at a cost of $7.50 per week. An invoice will be included with *Companies Unlimited* every four weeks. You may cancel your subscription at any time." Has Paul entered into an enforceable contract to pay for *Companies Unlimited?* Why or why not? (To answer this question fully, you might want to review the elements of a contract discussed in Chapter 7.)

21–2. E-Agents. Alpha Business Products, Inc., sells software on its Web site through an online ordering system, an e-agent. Through this system, Beth, a purchasing agent for Medical Insurance Company, orders an upgrade for Medical's word-processing software. Before completing the order, Beth enters, in a "Comments" box, the following. "We will accept this upgrade if we are satisfied with the software after ten days' trial use." Do Alpha and Medical have a contract under the UCITA? Do they have a contract under the UETA? Discuss.

REAL WORLD CASE PROBLEM

21–3. License Agreement. Management Computer Controls, Inc. (known as "MC 2"), is a Tennessee corporation in the business of selling software. Charles Perry Construction, Inc., is a Florida corporation. Perry entered into two contracts with MC 2 to buy software designed to perform estimating and accounting functions for construction firms. Each contract was printed on a standard order form containing a paragraph that referred to a license agreement. The license agreement included a choice-of-forum and choice-of-law provision: "Agreement is to be interpreted and construed according to the laws of the State of Tennessee. Any action, either by you or MC 2, arising out of this Agreement shall be initiated and prosecuted in the Court of Shelby County, Tennessee, and nowhere else." Each of the software packages arrived with the license agreement affixed to the outside of the box. Additionally, the boxes were sealed with an orange sticker bearing the following warning: "By opening this packet, you indicate your acceptance of the MC 2 license agreement." Alleging that the software was not suitable for use with Windows NT (Microsoft's network operating system), Perry filed a suit against MC 2 in a Florida state court. MC 2 filed a motion to dismiss the complaint on the ground that the suit should be heard in Tennessee. How should the court rule? Why? [*Management Computer Controls, Inc. v. Charles Perry Construction, Inc.*, 743 So.2d 627 (Fla.App. 1 Dist. 1999)]

For updated links to resources available on the Web, as well as a variety of other materials, visit this text's Web site at **http://blte.westbuslaw.com**.

For information on PriceScan, go to

http://www.pricescan.com

SelectSurf includes links to shopping e-agents at

http://www.selectsurf.com/shopping/compare

For a comprehensive review of the UCITA, go to

http://www.ucitaonline.com

The UETA is online at

http://www.law.upenn.edu/bll/ulc/uecicta/uetast84.htm

ONLINE LEGAL RESEARCH

Go to **http://blte.westbuslaw.com**, the Web site that accompanies this text. Select "Internet Applications," and then click on "Chapter 21." There you will find the following Internet research exercise that you can perform to learn more about electronic contracts.

Activity 21–1: E-Contracts

Chapter 21 ■ WORK SET

TRUE-FALSE QUESTIONS

___ **1.** Courts never enforce shrink-wrap agreements.

___ **2.** Courts often enforce click-on agreements

___ **3.** Most states have laws governing e-signatures.

___ **4.** There is no federal law governing e-signatures.

___ **5.** The Uniform Computer Information Transactions Act (UCITA) is a federal law.

___ **6.** The UCITA covers contracts involving *computer information.*

___ **7.** If the primary subject matter of a deal is not computer and information rights, the UCITA does not apply.

___ **8.** Under the Uniform Electronic Transactions Act (UETA), contracts entered into online, and other e-documents, are presumed valid.

MULTIPLE-CHOICE QUESTIONS

___ **1.** Beta Products, Inc., attempts to enter into a shrink-wrap agreement with Carol. A court would likely consider it a part of their contract if Beta communicated the terms to Carol

a. after they formed their contract.
b. before they formed their contract.
c. at any time.
d. at no time.

___ **2.** Gamma Goods, Inc., attempts to include the terms of a click-on agreement in its contract with Dan. A court would likely consider it a part of their contract if Gamma communicated the terms to Dan

a. after they formed their contract.
b. before they formed their contract.
c. at any time.
d. at no time.

___ **3.** Sam signs a contract to access an online scientific research database. Tina signs a contract to license business applications software for her firm. The Uniform Computer Information Transactions Act (UCITA) covers contracts

a. to access online databases only.
b. to license or purchase software only.
c. to access online databases or to license or purchase software.
d. none of the above.

___ **4.** American Box Corporation uses software to produce its goods. Best Car Company embeds software in its products. The UCITA applies to sales of

a. American's goods only.
b. Best's products only.
c. American's goods and Best's products.
d. none of the above.

___ **5.** Delta Company and Epsilon Corporation agree to a contract that would otherwise fall under the UCITA, but their contract says nothing about it. Kappa, Inc., and Omega, Inc., agree to a contract that expressly brings itself under the UCITA, which it would not otherwise cover. The UCITA applies to the contract between

a. Delta and Epsilon only.
b. Kappa and Omega only.
c. both Delta and Epsilon, and Kappa and Omega.
d. none of the above.

___ **6.** Digital Software, Inc., uses an e-signature to formalize a deal with Eagle Engineering Corporation. To authenticate the e-signature, the UCITA provides for steps that the parties

a. cannot vary.
b. can specify but they must be commercially reasonable.
c. can specify but they must be complex.
d. can specify but they must be simple.

___ **7.** New Software Corporation licenses its software. When a licensee breaches the terms of the license, New Software can use electronic self-help only if

a. the license is a mass-market license.
b. the license cannot be enforced in another way.
c. the parties agreed in advance.
d. all of the above.

___ **8.** International Investments, Inc., and Global Sales Corporation use e-agents to form a contract. The use of e-agents to form a contract is supported by

a. the UETA only.
b. the UCITA only.
c. the UETA and the UCITA.
d. none of the above.

ISSUE SPOTTERS

1. Applied Software Products, Inc., licenses its software in mass-market transactions. What is a mass-market transaction, and what are the rights of the licensees?

2. Computer Applications Corporation and Digitized Data, Inc., agree to a contract in e-commerce. Assuming the deal falls under both the UETA and the UCITA, what are the differences between those uniform acts as they might apply in this situation?

UNIT FOUR
NEGOTIABLE INSTRUMENTS

UNIT OUTLINE

The Essentials of Negotiability

LEARNING OBJECTIVES

When you finish this chapter, you should be able to:

1. Identify the basic types of negotiable instruments.
2. List the requirements of a negotiable instrument.
3. State what may constitute a signature.
4. Decide whether a variable-interest-rate note is negotiable.
5. Describe the process of negotiation.

FACING A LEGAL PROBLEM

Midwestern Style Fabrics sells $50,000 worth of fabric to D&F Clothiers, Inc., each fall on terms requiring payment to be made in ninety days. One year, however, Midwestern wants cash, but D&F wants the usual term of payment in ninety days. *What can Midwestern and D&F do so that both of their wants are satisfied?*

NEGOTIABLE INSTRUMENT A written and signed unconditional promise or order to pay a specified sum of money on demand or at a definite time to order (to a specific person or entity) or to bearer.

The vast number of commercial transactions that take place daily in the modern business world would be inconceivable without negotiable instruments. A **negotiable instrument** is any written promise or order to pay a sum of money. Drafts, checks, and promissory notes are typical examples. Negotiable instruments are transferred more readily than ordinary contract rights. Also, persons who acquire negotiable instruments are normally subject to less risk than the ordinary assignee of a contract right.

Negotiable Instruments and the UCC

Both Article 3 and Article 4 of the Uniform Commercial Code (UCC) apply to transactions involving negotiable instruments. To understand the applicability of Article 3, it is necessary to distinguish between *negotiable* and *nonnegotiable* instruments. To qualify as a negotiable instrument, an instrument must meet special requirements relating to form and content. These requirements will be discussed later in this chapter.

When an instrument is negotiable, its transfer from one person to another is governed by Article 3 of the UCC. Indeed, the UCC defines *instrument* as a "negotiable instrument." For that reason, whenever the term *instrument* is used in this book, it refers to a negotiable instrument. Transfers of nonnegotiable instruments are governed by rules of assignment of contract rights (see Chapter 14). Article 4 of the UCC governs bank deposits and collections.

Types of Instruments

LEARNING OBJECTIVE NO. 1
Identifying the Basic Types of Negotiable Instruments

The UCC specifies four types of negotiable instruments: *drafts, checks, notes,* and *certificates of deposit (CDs).* These are frequently divided into the two classifications that we will discuss in the following sections: *orders to pay* (drafts and checks) and *promises to pay* (promissory notes and CDs).

Negotiable instruments may also be classified as *demand instruments* or *time instruments.* A demand instrument (an instrument that is payable when payment is requested) either states that it is payable on demand (or "at sight") or does not state any time of payment. Because a check specifies no time of payment, a check is payable on demand. Therefore, checking accounts are sometimes called **demand deposits.** A demand instrument is payable immediately after it is *issued.* **Issue** is the first delivery of an instrument by the party who creates it to any party, for the purpose of giving rights in the instrument to any person. Time instruments are payable at a future date.

DEMAND DEPOSIT
Funds (accepted by a bank) subject to immediate withdrawal, in contrast to a time deposit, which requires that a depositor wait a specific time before withdrawing or pay a penalty for early withdrawal.

ISSUE
The first transfer, or delivery, of an instrument to a holder.

DRAFTS AND CHECKS (ORDERS TO PAY)

A **draft** is an unconditional written order that involves *three parties.* The party creating it (the **drawer**) orders another party (the **drawee**) to pay money, usually to a third party (the **payee**). Exhibit 22–1 shows a typical draft. The drawee must be obligated to the drawer, either by an agreement or through a debtor-creditor relationship, for the drawee to be obligated to the drawer to *honor* (pay) the order.

A *time draft* is payable at a definite future time. A *sight* (or demand) draft is payable on sight—that is, when it is presented for payment. A sight draft may be payable on acceptance. Acceptance is the drawee's written promise to pay the draft when it comes due. The usual manner of accepting is by writing the word *accepted* across the face of the instrument, followed by the date of acceptance and the signature of the drawee. A draft can be both a time and a sight draft; such a draft is one payable at a stated time after sight.

DRAFT
Any instrument drawn on a drawee (such as a bank) that orders the drawee to pay a certain sum of money.

DRAWER
A person who initiates a draft (including a check), thereby ordering the drawee to pay.

DRAWEE
The person who is ordered to pay a draft or check. With a check, a financial institution is always the drawee.

PAYEE
A person to whom an instrument is made payable.

EXHIBIT 22–1
A Typical Time Draft

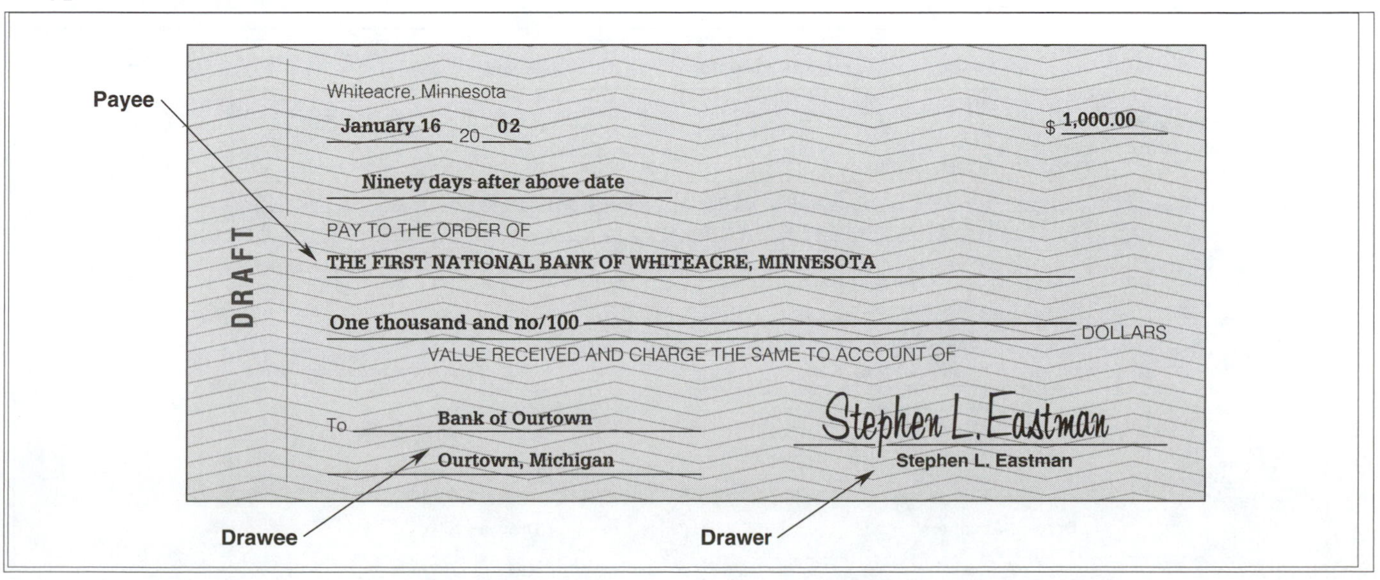

TRADE ACCEPTANCE
A draft drawn by the seller of goods on the purchaser and accepted by the purchaser's written promise to pay the draft. Once accepted, the purchaser becomes primarily liable to pay the draft.

A **trade acceptance** is a draft frequently used in the sale of goods. The seller is both the drawer and the payee on this draft. Essentially, the draft orders the buyer to pay a specified sum of money to the seller, usually at a stated time in the future. Trade acceptances are the standard credit instruments in sales transactions (see Exhibit 22–2).

In the legal problem set out at the beginning of this chapter, Midwestern Style Fabrics normally sells $50,000 worth of fabric to D&F Clothiers each fall on terms requiring payment in ninety days. One year Midwestern wants cash, but D&F wants the usual ninety-day term. *What can they do so that both of their wants are met?* Midwestern can draw a trade acceptance that orders D&F to pay $50,000 to the order of Midwestern Style Fabrics ninety days hence. D&F can accept by signing the face of the paper and returning it to Midwestern. The advantage to Midwestern of the trade acceptance is that D&F's acceptance creates an enforceable promise to pay the draft in ninety days. Midwestern can sell a trade acceptance to another party more easily than it can assign a debt to pay $50,000.

CHECK
A draft drawn by a drawer ordering the drawee bank or financial institution to pay a certain amount of money to the holder on demand.

The most commonly used type of draft is a **check.** The writer of the check is the drawer, the bank upon which the check is drawn is the drawee, and the person to whom the check is payable is the payee. With certain types of checks, such as *cashier's checks,* the bank is both the drawer and the drawee. The bank customer purchases a cashier's check from the bank—that is, pays the bank the amount of the check—and indicates to whom the check should be made payable. The bank, not the customer, is the drawer of the check (as well as the drawee). (Checks will be discussed more fully in Chapter 24.)

When *traveler's checks* are drawn on a bank, they are checks, but they require the purchaser's authorized signature before becoming payable. A negotiable instrument may be a check even though it states that it is something else—a *money order,* for example.

PROMISSORY NOTE
A written instrument signed by a maker unconditionally promising to pay a certain sum in money to a payee or a holder on demand or on a specified date.

MAKER
One who issues a promissory note or certificate of deposit (that is, one who promises to pay a certain sum to the holder of the note or CD).

BEARER
A person in the possession of an instrument payable to bearer or indorsed in blank.

PROMISSORY NOTES AND CDs (PROMISES TO PAY)

The **promissory note** is a written promise between *two parties.* One party is the **maker** of the promise to pay. The other is the payee, or the one to whom the promise is made. A promissory note, which is often referred to simply as a *note,* can be made payable at a definite time or on demand. It can name a specific payee or merely be payable to **bearer.** A bearer is a person in possession of an instru-

EXHIBIT 22–2
A Typical Trade Acceptance

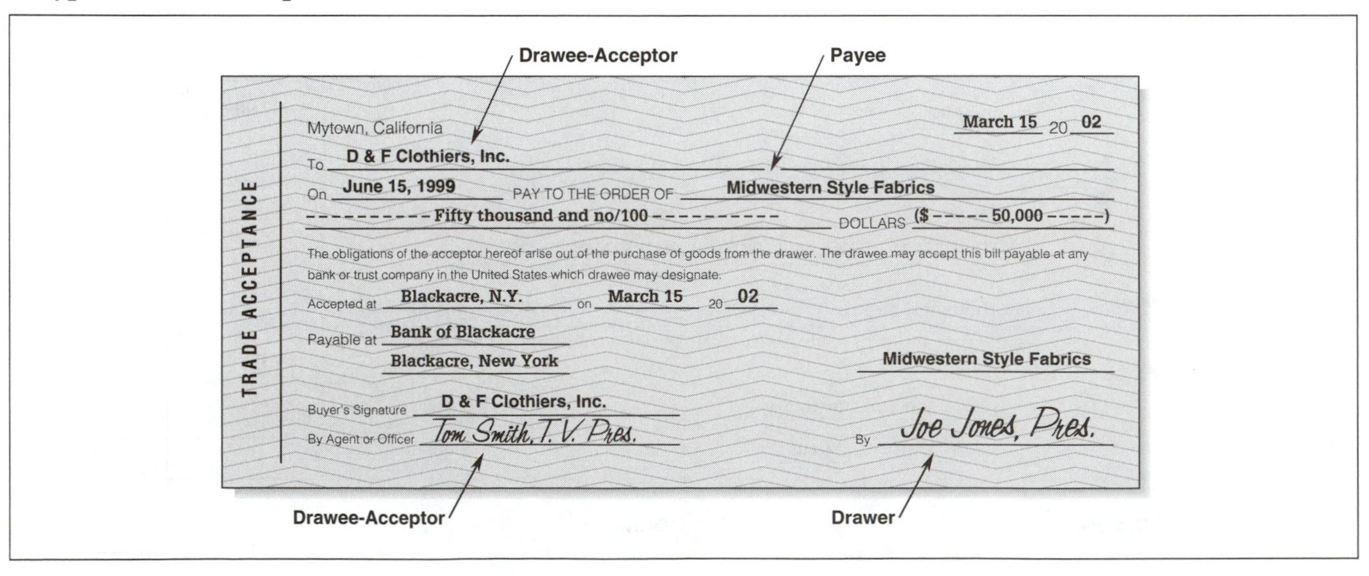

TRADE ACCEPTANCE
Mytown, California March 15 20 02
To D & F Clothiers, Inc.
On June 15, 1999 PAY TO THE ORDER OF Midwestern Style Fabrics
----------Fifty thousand and no/100---------- DOLLARS ($-----50,000-----)
The obligations of the acceptor hereof arise out of the purchase of goods from the drawer. The drawee may accept this bill payable at any bank or trust company in the United States which drawee may designate.
Accepted at Blackacre, N.Y. on March 15 20 02
Payable at Bank of Blackacre
Blackacre, New York
Midwestern Style Fabrics
Buyer's Signature D & F Clothiers, Inc.
By Agent or Officer Tom Smith, T.V. Pres.
By Joe Jones, Pres.

ment that is payable to bearer, is not payable to an identified person, does not state a payee, or is indorsed (signed) in blank—that is, signed without additional words. **Indorsements,** which are signatures with or without additional words or statements, are discussed later in this chapter. A typical promissory note is shown in Exhibit 22–3.

INDORSEMENT
A signature placed on an instrument for the purpose of transferring one's ownership rights in the instrument.

Notes are used in a variety of credit transactions and often carry the name of the transaction involved. For example, in real estate transactions, a promissory note for the unpaid balance on a house, secured by a mortgage on the property, is called a *mortgage note.* A note payable in installments, such as for payment for a television set over a twelve-month period, is called an *installment note.*

A note that is secured by personal property is called a *collateral note,* because the property pledged as security for the satisfaction of the debt is called *collateral.* To minimize the risk of loss when lending money, a creditor often requires the debtor to provide some collateral, or security, beyond a promise that the debt will be repaid. When this security takes the form of personal property (such as a motor vehicle), the creditor has an interest in the property known as a *security interest.* Security interests are discussed in more detail in Chapter 31.

A **certificate of deposit** (CD) is a bank's note. It is an acknowledgment by a bank that it has received a certain sum of money and that it promises to repay it. CDs in small denominations are often sold by savings and loan associations, savings banks, and commercial banks. They are called *small CDs* and are for amounts up to $100,000. Certificates of deposit for amounts over $100,000 are called *large* (or *jumbo*) *CDs.* Exhibit 22–4 on the next page shows a typical small CD.

CERTIFICATE OF DEPOSIT
An instrument evidencing a promissory acknowledgment by a bank of a receipt of money with an engagement to repay it.

What Is a Negotiable Instrument?

For an instrument to be negotiable, it must meet the following requirements:

LEARNING OBJECTIVE NO. 2
Listing the Requirements of a Negotiable Instrument

1. It must be in writing.
2. It must be signed by the maker or the drawer.
3. It must be an unconditional promise or order to pay.
4. It must state a fixed amount of money.
5. It must be payable on demand or at a definite time.
6. It must be payable to order or to bearer, unless it is a check.

EXHIBIT 22–3
A Typical Promissory Note

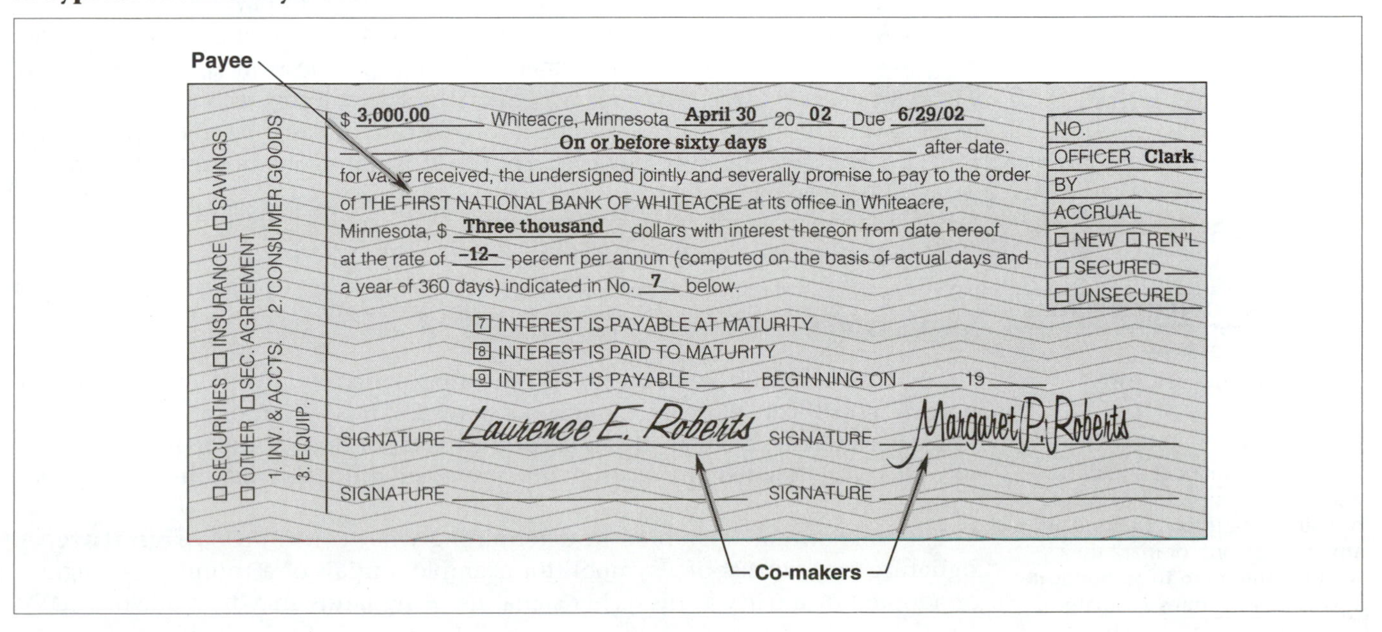

$ 3,000.00 Whiteacre, Minnesota April 30 20 02 Due 6/29/02
On or before sixty days after date.
for value received, the undersigned jointly and severally promise to pay to the order of THE FIRST NATIONAL BANK OF WHITEACRE at its office in Whiteacre, Minnesota, $ Three thousand dollars with interest thereon from date hereof at the rate of -12- percent per annum (computed on the basis of actual days and a year of 360 days) indicated in No. 7 below.

☑7 INTEREST IS PAYABLE AT MATURITY
☐8 INTEREST IS PAID TO MATURITY
☐9 INTEREST IS PAYABLE ____ BEGINNING ON ____ 19____

SIGNATURE Laurence E. Roberts SIGNATURE Margaret P. Roberts
SIGNATURE ____ SIGNATURE ____

NO.
OFFICER Clark
BY
ACCRUAL
☐ NEW ☐ REN'L
☐ SECURED
☐ UNSECURED

☐ SECURITIES ☐ INSURANCE ☐ SAVINGS
☐ OTHER ☐ SEC. AGREEMENT
1. INV. & ACCTS. 2. CONSUMER GOODS
3. EQUIP.

EXHIBIT 22–4
A Typical Small Certificate of Deposit

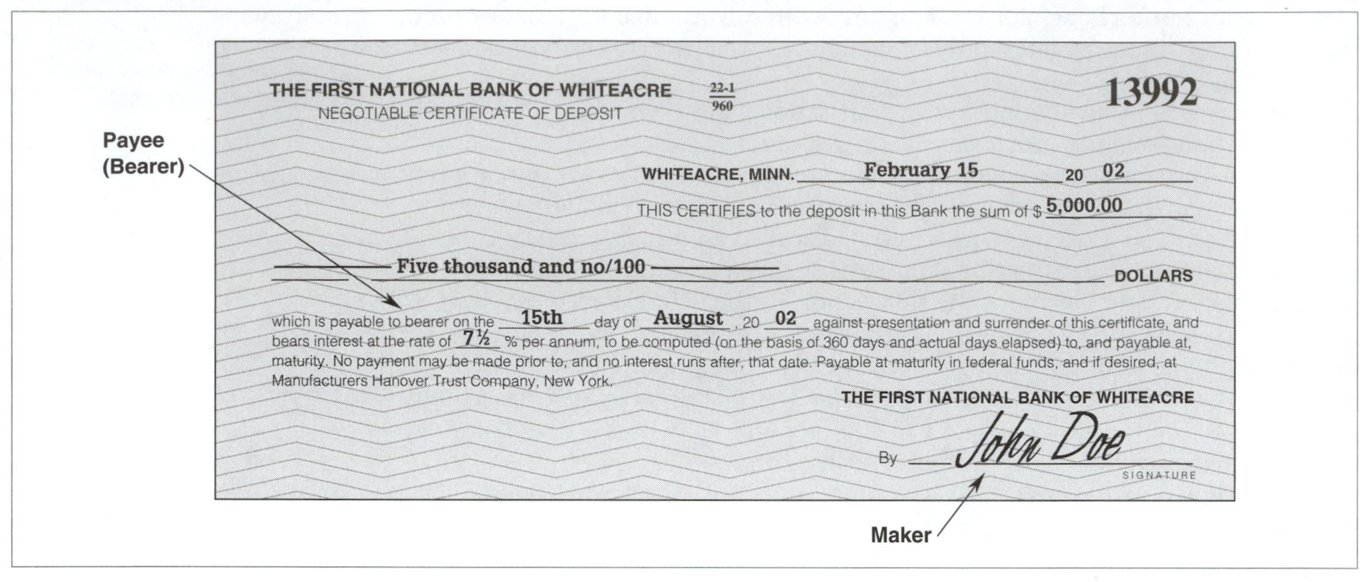
THE FIRST NATIONAL BANK OF WHITEACRE 22-1/960 13992
NEGOTIABLE CERTIFICATE OF DEPOSIT

WHITEACRE, MINN. February 15 20 02

THIS CERTIFIES to the deposit in this Bank the sum of $ 5,000.00

Five thousand and no/100 DOLLARS

which is payable to bearer on the 15th day of August, 20 02 against presentation and surrender of this certificate, and bears interest at the rate of 7½ % per annum, to be computed (on the basis of 360 days and actual days elapsed) to, and payable at, maturity. No payment may be made prior to, and no interest runs after, that date. Payable at maturity in federal funds, and if desired, at Manufacturers Hanover Trust Company, New York.

THE FIRST NATIONAL BANK OF WHITEACRE

By John Doe
SIGNATURE

Written Form

Negotiable instruments must be in written form. There are certain practical limitations concerning the writing and the substance on which the writing is placed:

1. The writing must be on material that lends itself to *permanence*. Instruments carved in blocks of ice or recorded on other impermanent surfaces would not qualify as negotiable instruments.
2. The writing must have *portability*. Although this is not a spelled-out legal requirement, if an instrument is not movable, it obviously cannot meet the requirement that it be freely transferable.

IN THE COURTROOM

Shanda writes in the sand, "I promise to pay $500 to the order of Jason." Cullen writes on the side of a cow, "I promise to pay Merrill $500." *Are either of these negotiable instruments?* Shanda's promise written in the sand is not a negotiable instrument. Although it is in writing, it lacks permanence. Cullen's promise written on the side of a cow technically meets the requirements of a negotiable instrument. A cow cannot easily be transferred in the ordinary course of business, however. Because it is not easily movable, the "instrument" is nonnegotiable.

LEARNING OBJECTIVE NO. 3
Stating What May Constitute a Signature

SIGNATURE
The name or mark of a person, written by that person or at his or her direction. In commercial law, any name, word, or mark used with the intention to authenticate a writing constitutes a signature.

Signatures

For an instrument to be negotiable, it must be signed by (1) the maker, if it is a note or a certificate of deposit, or (2) the drawer, if it is a draft or a check. If a person signs an instrument as the *agent* for the maker or drawer, the maker or drawer has effectively signed the instrument, provided the agent has the appropriate authority.

Extreme latitude is granted in determining what constitutes a **signature.** A signature may consist of a symbol (for example, initials or a thumbprint) signed or adopted by a party as his or her signature. A signature may be made manually or by means of a device (a rubber stamp) or a machine (such as those often used to write payroll checks).

The location of the signature on the document is unimportant. The usual place, however, is the lower right-hand corner. A *handwritten* statement in the body of the instrument, such as "I, Kammie Orlik, promise to pay Janel Tan," is sufficient to act as a signature.

UNCONDITIONAL PROMISE OR ORDER TO PAY

The terms of the promise or order must be included in writing in a negotiable instrument. These terms must not be conditioned on the occurrence or nonoccurrence of some other event or agreement.

Promise or Order. For an instrument to be negotiable, it must contain an express order or promise to pay. A mere acknowledgment of the debt, which might logically *imply* a promise, is not sufficient, because the promise must be an *affirmative,* written undertaking. For example, the traditional I.O.U. ("I.O.U. $10 [Signed] Bobby") might logically imply a promise. It is not a negotiable instrument, however, because it does not contain an express promise to repay the debt. If such words as "to be paid on demand" or "due on demand" are added, the need for an affirmative promise is satisfied. Similarly, if a buyer signs a promissory note that states, for example, "I promise to pay $500 to the order of the seller for the purchase of a Tectonics television set," then the requirement for a negotiable instrument is satisfied.

Unconditionality of a Promise or Order. Only unconditional promises or orders can be negotiable. A negotiable instrument's utility as a substitute for money or as a credit device would be dramatically reduced if it had conditional promises attached to it. It would be expensive and time consuming to investigate conditional promises. Therefore, the transferability of the negotiable instrument would be greatly restricted. Furthermore, the payee or any holder of the instrument would risk the possibility that the condition would not occur.

Cornell Law School's Legal Information Institute offers online access to the Uniform Commercial Code, including Articles 3 and 4, as enacted in several of the states, at

http://www.law.cornell.edu/uniform/ucc.html

Certain necessary conditions commonly used in business transactions do not make an otherwise negotiable instrument nonnegotiable, however. For example, many instruments state the terms of the underlying agreement or refer to the consideration paid for the investment as a matter of standard business practice. Such statements are not considered conditions and do not affect negotiability. Similarly, mere reference to another agreement does not affect negotiability. An instrument that is made subject to the other agreement, however, is nonnegotiable. Also, terms in an instrument that provide for payment only out of a particular fund or source do not render the instrument conditional—it remains negotiable. For instance, a note that restricts the source of payments to a certain account is negotiable.

A FIXED AMOUNT OF MONEY

Negotiable instruments must state with certainty a fixed amount of money to be paid at any time the instrument is payable. This requirement promises clarity and certainty in determining the value of the instrument. Also, to be negotiable, an instrument must be payable entirely in money. A promissory note that provides for payment in diamonds or forty hours of services is not payable in money and thus is nonnegotiable.

Fixed Amount. The term *fixed amount* means an amount that is ascertainable from the instrument. A demand note payable with 12 percent interest, for example, meets the requirement of fixed amount because its amount can be determined at the time it is payable.

The amount or rate of interest may be determined with reference to information that is not contained in the instrument but that is readily ascertainable by reference to a formula or a source described in the instrument. For example, when an instrument is payable at the *legal rate of interest* (a rate of interest fixed by statute), at a *judgment rate of interest* (a rate of interest fixed by statute that is applied to a monetary judgment awarded by a court until the judgment is paid or terminated), or as fixed by state law, the instrument is negotiable.

LEARNING OBJECTIVE NO. 4
Deciding Whether a Variable-Interest-Rate Note is Negotiable

Mortgage notes tied to a variable rate of interest (fluctuating as a result of market conditions) have become popular because these notes protect lenders when rates rise and benefit borrowers when rates decline. A variable-rate note can be negotiable. Only the principal is subject to the requirement that to be negotiable a writing must contain a promise or order to pay a fixed amount. The interest may be stated as a variable amount.

Payable in Money. Only instruments payable entirely in money are negotiable. The UCC defines money as "a medium of exchange authorized or adopted by a domestic or foreign government as a part of its currency." An instrument payable in government bonds or in shares of Microsoft stock is not negotiable, because neither is a medium of exchange recognized by the U.S. government.

PAYABLE ON DEMAND OR AT A DEFINITE TIME

A negotiable instrument must be payable on demand or at a definite time. Clearly, to ascertain the value of a negotiable instrument, it is necessary to know when the maker, drawee, or acceptor is required to pay. It is also necessary to know when the obligations of secondary parties will arise. Furthermore, it is necessary to know when an instrument is due in order to calculate when the statute of limitations may apply. Finally, with an interest-bearing instrument, it is necessary to know the exact interval during which the interest will accrue to determine the present value of the instrument.

Payable on Demand. Instruments that are payable on demand include those that contain the words "payable at sight" or "payable on demand" and those that say nothing about when payment is due. The nature of the instrument may indicate that it is payable on demand. For example, a check, by definition, is payable on demand. If no time for payment is specified, and if the person responsible for payment must pay when the instrument is presented, then the instrument is payable on demand.

Payable at a Definite Time. If an instrument is not payable on demand, to be negotiable it must be payable at a definite time specified on the face (front) of the instrument. The maker or drawee is under no obligation to pay until the specified time.

IN THE COURTROOM

An instrument dated February 1, 2002, states, "One year after the death of my grandfather, James Ezersky, I promise to pay to the order of Henry Ling $500. [Signed] Mary Ezersky." *Is this instrument negotiable?* No. Because the date of the grandfather's death is uncertain, the maturity date is uncertain, even though the event is bound to occur. Even if the grandfather has already died, the instrument is not negotiable because it does not specify the time for payment.

When an instrument is payable on or before a stated date ("payable on or before February 1, 2002"), it is clearly payable at a definite time, although the maker has the option of paying before the stated maturity date. This uncertainty does not violate the definite time requirement. In contrast, an instrument that is undated and made payable "one month after date" is clearly nonnegotiable. There is no way to determine the maturity date from the face of the instrument.

PAYABLE TO ORDER OR TO BEARER

To ensure a proper transfer, the instrument must be "payable to order or to bearer" at the time it is issued or first comes into the possession of the holder. Note, however, that a check that meets all other requirements for negotiability is a negotiable instrument even if the words "the order of" or "bearer" are missing.

A good rule of thumb is never to sign a blank check. Another good rule of thumb is never to write and sign a check payable to "cash" until you are actually at the bank.

Order Instruments. An instrument is an **order instrument** if it is payable to the order of an identified person ("Pay to the order of Buke") or to an identified person or order ("Pay to Itzhak or order"). This allows that person to transfer the instrument to whomever he or she wishes. Thus, the maker or drawer is agreeing to pay either the person specified or whomever that person might designate. In this way, the instrument retains its transferability.

To qualify as order paper, the person specified must be identified with certainty, because the transfer of an order instrument requires an indorsement. If an instrument states, "Pay to the order of my kissing cousin," the instrument is nonnegotiable, as a holder could not be sure which cousin was intended to indorse and properly transfer the instrument.

ORDER INSTRUMENT
A negotiable instrument that is payable "to the order of an identified person" or "to an identified person or order."

Bearer Instruments. A **bearer instrument** is an instrument that does not designate a specific payee. The maker or drawer of a bearer instrument agrees to pay anyone who presents the instrument for payment. An instrument containing any of the following terms is a bearer instrument:

- "Payable to the order of bearer."
- "Payable to James Jarrot or bearer."
- "Payable to bearer."
- "Payable to X."
- "Pay cash."
- "Pay to the order of cash."

BEARER INSTRUMENT
A negotiable instrument that is payable to the bearer, including instruments payable to "cash."

Transfer by Assignment or Negotiation

Once issued, a negotiable instrument can be transferred by *assignment* or by *negotiation.*

TRANSFER BY ASSIGNMENT

LEARNING OBJECTIVE NO. 5
Describing the Process of Negotiation

Recall from Chapter 14 that an assignment is a transfer of rights under a contract. Under general contract principles, a transfer by assignment to an assignee gives the assignee only those rights that the assignor had. As explained in Chapter 14, any defenses that can be raised against an assignor can normally be raised against the assignee. When a transfer fails to qualify as a negotiation, it becomes an assignment. The transferee is then an *assignee.*

TRANSFER BY NEGOTIATION

Negotiation is the transfer of an instrument in a form in which the transferee (the person to whom the instrument is transferred) becomes a **holder.** A holder is a person who possesses a negotiable instrument if the instrument is payable to bearer or, in the case of an instrument payable to an identified person, if the identified person is in possession.

NEGOTIATION
The transferring of a negotiable instrument to another in such form that the transferee becomes a holder.

HOLDER
The person who, by the terms of a negotiable instrument, is legally entitled to payment on it.

A holder, at the very least, receives the rights of the previous possessor. Unlike an assignment, a transfer by negotiation can make it possible for a holder to receive more rights in the instrument than the prior possessor had. (A holder who receives greater rights is known as a *holder in due course,* discussed in Chapter 23.) There are two methods of negotiating an instrument so that the receiver becomes a holder. The method used depends on whether the instrument is an order instrument or a bearer instrument.

Negotiating Order Instruments. If the instrument is an order instrument, it is negotiated by delivery with any necessary indorsements. An indorsement is a signature placed on an instrument for the purpose of transferring one's ownership in the instrument. An *indorsement in blank* specifies no particular indorsee and can consist of a mere signature. Types of indorsements and their consequences are listed in Exhibit 22–5.

IN THE COURTROOM

Carrington Corporation issues a payroll check "to the order of Elliot Goodseal." Goodseal takes the check to the supermarket, signs his name on the back (an indorsement), gives it to the cashier (a delivery), and receives cash. *Is the transfer of the check from Goodseal to the supermarket an assignment or a negotiation?* A negotiation. Goodseal "delivered" the check to the supermarket with the necessary indorsement (his signature).

Negotiating Bearer Instruments. If an instrument is payable to bearer, it is negotiated by delivery—that is, by transfer into another person's possession. Indorsement is not necessary. The use of bearer instruments involves more risk through loss or theft than the use of order instruments.

IN THE COURTROOM

Alan Tyson writes a check "Payable to cash" and hands it to Blaine Parrington (a delivery). Tyson has issued the check (a bearer instrument) to Parrington. Parrington places the check in his wallet, which is subsequently stolen. The thief has possession of the check. At this point, negotiation has not occurred, because delivery must be voluntary on the part of the transferor. *If the thief "delivers" the check to an innocent third person, however, will negotiation be complete?* Yes. Only delivery is necessary to negotiate a bearer instrument. If the thief delivers the check to an innocent third person, all rights to it pass to that third person. Parrington loses all rights to recover the proceeds of the check from that person. Of course, Parrington can recover his money from the thief if the thief can be found.

Converting an Order Instrument to a Bearer Instrument and Vice Versa. The method used for negotiation depends on the character of the instrument at the time the negotiation takes place. For example, a check originally payable to "cash" but subsequently indorsed with the words "Pay to Ernestine" must be negotiated as an order instrument (by indorsement and delivery), even though it was previously a bearer instrument. An instrument payable to the order of a named payee and indorsed in blank (by the holder's signature only, as will be discussed subsequently) becomes a bearer instrument.

EXHIBIT 22–5
Types of Indorsements and Their Consequences

WORDS CONSTITUTING THE INDORSEMENT	TYPE OF INDORSEMENT	INDORSER'S SIGNATURE LIABILITY[a]
"Rosemary White"	Blank	Unqualified signature liability on proper presentment and notice of dishonor.[b]
"Pay to Sam Wilson, Rosemary White"	Special	Unqualified signature liability on proper presentment and notice of dishonor.
"Without recourse, Rosemary White"	Qualified (blank for further negotiation)	No signature liability. Transfer warranty liability if breach occurs.[c]
"Pay to Sam Wilson, without recourse, Rosemary White"	Qualified (special for further negotiation)	No signature liability. Transfer warranty liability if breach occurs.
"Pay to Sam Wilson on condition he completes painting my house at 23 Elm Street by 9/1/99, Rosemary White"	Restrictive—conditional (special for further negotiation)	Signature liability only if condition is met. If condition is met, signature liability on proper presentment and notice of dishonor.
"Pay to Sam Wilson only, Rosemary White"	Restrictive—prohibitive (special for further negotiation)	Signature liability only on Sam Wilson receiving payment. If Wilson receives payment, signature liability on proper presentment and notice of dishonor.
"For deposit, Rosemary White"	Restrictive—for deposit (blank for further negotiation)	Signature liability only on White having amount deposited in her account. If deposit is made, signature liability on proper presentment and notice of dishonor.
"Pay to Ann South in trust for John North, Rosemary White"	Restrictive—trust (special for further negotiation)	Signature liability only on payment of Ann South for John North's benefit. If restriction is met, signature liability on proper presentment and notice of dishonor.

a. *Signature liability* refers to the liability of a party who signs an instrument. The basic questions include whether there is any liability and, if so, whether it is unqualified or restricted.
b. When an instrument is dishonored—that is, when, for example, a drawer's bank refuses to cash the drawer's check on proper presentment—an indorser of the check may be liable on it if he or she is given proper *notice of dishonor.*
c. The transferor of an instrument makes certain warranties to the transferee and subsequent holder, and thus, even if the transferor's signature does not render him or her liable on the instrument, he or she may be liable for breach of a transfer warranty. Transfer warranties are discussed in Chapter 23.

TERMS AND CONCEPTS FOR REVIEW

bearer 270
bearer instrument 275
certificate of deposit 271
check 270
demand deposit 269
draft 269
drawee 269
drawer 269
holder 275
indorsement 271
issue 269
maker 270
negotiable instrument 268
negotiation 275
order instrument 275
payee 269
promissory note 270
signature 272
trade acceptance 270

CHAPTER SUMMARY • THE ESSENTIALS OF NEGOTIABILITY

Types of Negotiable Instruments	Negotiable instruments may be classified by either of the following classification schemes: **1.** *Demand instruments versus time instruments*—A demand instrument is payable on demand (when the holder presents it to the maker or drawer). Time instruments are payable at a future date. **2.** *Orders to pay versus promises to pay*—Checks and drafts are *orders* to pay. Promissory notes and certificates of deposit (CDs) are *promises* to pay.
Requirements of Negotiability	To be negotiable, an instrument must meet the following requirements: **1.** *Must be in writing*—A writing can be on anything that is readily transferable and that has a degree of permanence. **2.** *Must be signed by the maker or drawer* **a.** It can be signed in a representative capacity. **b.** It can be in any form (such as a word, mark, or rubber stamp) that purports to be a signature and authenticates the writing. **c.** The signature can be anyplace on the instrument. **3.** *Must be a definite promise or order* **a.** A promise must be more than a mere acknowledgment of a debt. **b.** The words "I/we promise" or "pay" meet this criterion. **4.** *Must be unconditional* **a.** Payment cannot be expressly conditional on an event. **b.** Payment cannot be made subject to or governed by another agreement. **5.** *Must be an order or promise to pay a fixed amount*—An instrument may state a fixed sum even if payable with interest. **6.** *Must be payable in money* **a.** Any medium of exchange recognized as the currency of a government is money. **b.** The maker or drawer cannot retain the option to pay the instrument in money or in something else. **7.** *Must be payable on demand or at a definite time* **a.** Any instrument payable on sight, presentation, or issue or that does not state any time for payment is a demand instrument. **b.** An instrument is payable at a definite time, even if it is payable on or before a stated date or within a fixed period after sight, or if the drawer or maker has an option to extend it for a definite time. **8.** *Must be payable to order or bearer* **a.** An order instrument must identify the payee. **b.** An instrument with terms that intend payment to no particular person is payable to bearer. **c.** A check is negotiable even if the words "order" or "bearer" are omitted.
Types of Indorsements	**1.** Blank (for example, "Mark Deitsch"). **2.** Special (for example, "Pay to William Hsu, [signed] Jefferson Jones"). **3.** Qualified (for example, "Pay to Allison Jong, without recourse, [signed] Sarah Jacobs"). **4.** Restrictive (for example, "Pay to Stephanie Contento in trust for Ralph Zimmer, [signed] Ralph Zimmer").

HYPOTHETICAL QUESTIONS

22–1. Requirements by Negotiability. The following note is written by Muriel Evans on the back of an envelope: "I, Muriel Evans, promise to pay Karen Marvin or bearer $100 on demand." Is this a negotiable instrument? Discuss fully.

22–2. Indorsements. Bertram writes a check for $200, payable to "cash." He puts the check in his pocket and drives to the bank to cash the check. As he gets out of his car in the bank's parking lot, the check slips out of his pocket and falls to the pavement. Jerrod walks by moments later, picks up the check, and later that day delivers it to Amber, to whom he owes $200. Amber indorses the check "For deposit only. [Signed] Amber Dowel" and deposits it into her checking account. In light of these circumstances, answer the following questions:

(a) Is the check a bearer instrument or an order instrument?
(b) Did Jerrod's delivery of the check to Amber constitute a valid negotiation? Why or why not?
(c) What type of indorsement did Amber make?
(d) Does Bertram have a right to recover the $200 from Amber? Explain.

REAL WORLD CASE PROBLEM

22–3. Fixed Amount of Money. William Bailey and William Vaught, as officers for Bailey, Vaught, Robertson, and Co. (BVR), signed a promissory note to borrow $34,000 from the Forestwood National Bank. The interest rate was variable: "the lender's published prime rate" plus 1 percent. Forestwood went out of business, and ultimately, the note was acquired by Remington Investments, Inc. When BVR failed to make payments, Remington filed a suit in a Texas state court against BVR. BVR contended in part that the note was not negotiable because after Forestwood closed, there was no "published lender's prime rate" to use to calculate the interest. Did the note provide for payment of a "fixed amount of money"? [*Bailey, Vaught, Robertson, and Co. v. Remington Investments, Inc.*, 888 S.W.2d 860 (Tex.App.—Dallas, 1994)]

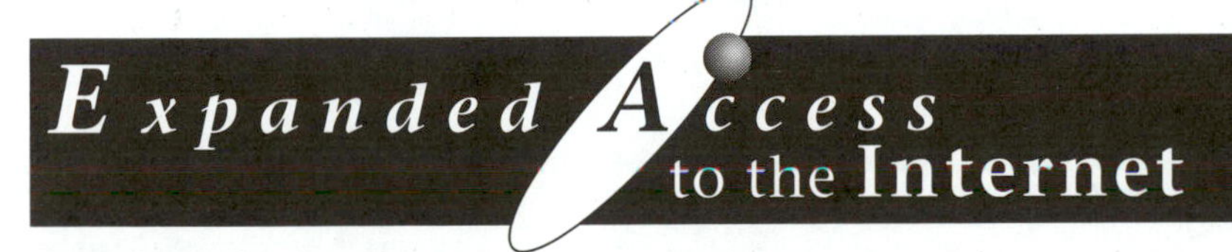

For updated links to resources available on the Web, as well as a variety of other materials, visit this text's Web site at **http://blte.westbuslaw.com**.

The National Conference of Commissioners on Uniform State Laws, in association with the University of Pennsylvania Law School, now offers an official site for in-process and final drafts of uniform and model acts. For an index of final acts, including UCC Articles 3 and 4, go to

http://www.law.upenn.edu/bll/ulc/ulc_final.htm

Cornell University's Legal Information Institute offers online access to the UCC, as well as to UCC articles as enacted by particular states and proposed revisions to articles, at

http://www.law.cornell.edu/ucc/ucc.table.html

British author Sir Alan Herbert has some fun with the "written form" requirement for a negotiable instrument in his entertaining (and fictitious) story entitled "The Negotiable Cow," which can be found online at

http://www.kmoser.com/herbert/herb04.htm

ONLINE LEGAL RESEARCH

Go to **http://blte.westbuslaw.com**, the Web site that accompanies this text. Select "Internet Applications," and then click on "Chapter 22." There you will find the following Internet research exercise that you can perform to learn more about negotiable instruments:

Activity 22–1: Overview of Negotiable Instruments

Chapter 22 ■ WORK SET

TRUE-FALSE QUESTIONS

_____ **1.** A negotiable instrument can be transferred only by negotiation.

_____ **2.** A bearer instrument is payable to whoever possesses it.

_____ **3.** To be negotiable, an instrument must be in writing.

_____ **4.** To be negotiable, an instrument must expressly state when payment is due.

_____ **5.** An instrument that does not designate a specific payee is an order instrument.

_____ **6.** Indorsements are required to negotiate order instruments.

_____ **7.** An order instrument is payable to whoever properly possesses it.

_____ **8.** Indorsements are required to negotiate bearer instruments.

MULTIPLE-CHOICE QUESTIONS

_____ **1.** Jasmine writes out a check payable to the order of Nancy. Nancy receives the check but wants to negotiate it further to her friend Max. Nancy can negotiate the check further by

a. indorsing it.
b. delivering it to the transferee.
c. both a and b.
d. none of the above.

_____ **2.** Kurt receives from Lee a check that is made out "Pay to the order of Kurt." Kurt turns it over and writes on the back, "Pay to Adam. [Signed] Kurt." Kurt's indorsement is a

a. blank indorsement.
b. special indorsement.
c. restrictive indorsement.
d. qualified indorsement.

_____ **3.** Ray is the owner of Espresso Express. Dan's Office Supplies sells Ray supplies for Espresso Express. To pay, Ray signs a check "Espresso Express" in the lower left-hand corner. The check is

a. not negotiable, because "Espresso Express" is a trade name.
b. not negotiable, because Ray signed the check in the wrong location.
c. negotiable, and Ray is bound.
d. negotiable, but Ray is not bound.

_____ **4.** Alex makes out a check "Pay to the order of Mel." Mel indorses the check on the back by signing his name. Before Mel signed his name, the check was

a. bearer paper.
b. order paper.
c. both a and b.
d. none of the above.

_____ **5.** Karen makes out a check "Pay to the order of Quinn." Quinn indorses the check on the back by signing his name. After Quinn signed his name, the check became

a. bearer paper.
b. order paper.
c. both a and b.
d. none of the above.

_____ **6.** Jules owes money to Vern. Vern owes money to Chris. Vern signs an instrument that orders Jules to pay to Chris the money that Jules owes to Vern. This instrument is a

a. note.
b. check.
c. certificate of deposit.
d. draft.

_____ **7.** Don's checks are printed "Pay to the order of" followed by a blank. On one of the checks, Don writes in the blank "Mac or bearer." The check is

a. a bearer instrument.
b. an order instrument.
c. both a and b.
d. none of the above.

_____ **8.** Lisa writes out a check payable to the order of Jeff. Negotiation occurs when Jeff receives the check. Jeff subsequently negotiates the check by

a. indorsing it only.
b. delivering it only.
c. indorsing and delivering it.
d. none of the above.

_____ **9.** Louis makes out a check "Pay to the order of Maria," and Maria indorses the check on the back by signing her name. With Maria's indorsement, the check is

a. a bearer instrument.
b. an order instrument.
c. both a and b.
d. none of the above.

ISSUE SPOTTERS

1. Jim owes Sherry $700. Sherry asks Jim to sign a negotiable instrument regarding the debt. Which of the following, if included on that instrument, would make it negotiable: "I.O.U. $700," "I promise to pay $700," or an instruction to Jim's bank stating, "I wish you would pay $700 to Sherry"?

2. Jack gets his paycheck from his employer, indorses the back ("Jack"), and goes to cash it at his credit union. On the way, he loses the check. Paige finds it. Has the check been negotiated to Paige? How might Jack have avoided any loss?

Transferability and Liability

23

LEARNING OBJECTIVES

When you finish this chapter, you should be able to:

1 State the difference between holders and holders in due course.

2 List the requirements for holder-in-due-course status.

3 Outline the liability of parties who sign negotiable instruments.

4 Identify transfer warranties, which extend to both signers and nonsigners of negotiable instruments.

5 List presentment warranties, which extend to both signers and nonsigners of negotiable instruments.

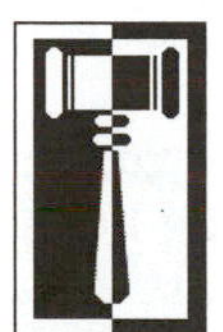

FACING A LEGAL PROBLEM

Marcia Morrison issues a $500 note payable to Reinhold Smith in payment for goods. Smith negotiates the note to Judy Larson, who promises to pay Smith for it in thirty days. During the next month, Larson learns that Smith has breached the contract by delivering defective goods and that Morrison will not honor the $500 note. Smith has left town. *Can Larson hold Morrison liable on the note?*

Problems arise when a holder seeking payment of a negotiable instrument learns that a defense to payment exists or that another party has a prior claim to the instrument. In such situations, for the person seeking payment, it becomes important to have the rights of a *holder in due course (HDC)*. An HDC takes a negotiable instrument free of all claims and most defenses of other parties.

We open this chapter by distinguishing between an ordinary holder and an HDC. We then examine the requirements for HDC status, the kinds of liability associated with negotiable instruments, and the defenses that parties may have to payment on an instrument. Our discussion concerns primarily negotiable instruments that already have been *negotiated*.

Holder versus Holder in Due Course

A *holder* is a person who possesses a negotiable instrument if the instrument is payable to bearer or, in the case of an instrument payable to an identified person, if the identified person is in possession. In other words, the holder is the person who, by the terms of the instrument, is legally entitled to payment. The

HOLDER IN DUE COURSE (HDC)
Any holder who acquires a negotiable instrument for value; in good faith; and without notice that the instrument is overdue, that it has been dishonored, or that any defense or claim to it exists on the part of any person.

LEARNING OBJECTIVE NO. 1
Stating the Difference between Holders and Holders in Due Course

LEARNING OBJECTIVE NO. 2
Listing the Requirements for Holder-in-Due-Course Status

holder of an instrument need not be its owner to enforce payment of it in his or her own name.

A transferee of a negotiable instrument who is characterized merely as a holder obtains only those rights that the predecessor-transferor had in the instrument. In the event that there is a conflicting, superior claim to or defense against the instrument, an ordinary holder will not be able to collect payment.

In contrast, a **holder in due course (HDC)** is a special-status transferee of a negotiable instrument who, by meeting certain acquisition requirements, takes the instrument *free* of most defenses and all claims to it. Stated another way, an HDC can normally acquire a higher level of immunity than can an ordinary holder in regard to defenses against payment on the instrument and claims of ownership to the instrument by other parties.

Requirements for HDC Status

An HDC must first be a holder of a negotiable instrument and must take the instrument (1) for value; (2) in good faith; and (3) without notice that it is overdue, that it has been dishonored, that any person has a defense against it or a claim to it, or that the instrument contains unauthorized signatures or alterations, or is so irregular or incomplete as to call into question its authenticity.

The underlying requirement of "due course" status is that a person must first be a holder on that instrument. Regardless of other circumstances surrounding acquisition, only a holder has a chance to become an HDC.

TAKING FOR VALUE

An HDC must have given *value* for the instrument. The concept of *value* in the law of negotiable instruments is not the same as the concept of *consideration* in the law of contracts (see Chapter 9). An *executory promise* (a promise to give value in the future) is valid consideration to support a contract. It does not, however, normally constitute value sufficient to make one an HDC.

Instead, a holder exchanging a promise for an instrument takes the instrument for value only to the extent that the promise has been performed. If the holder plans to pay for the instrument later or plans to perform the required services at some future date, the holder has not yet given value. In that case, the holder is not yet an HDC. To the extent that the holder has paid for the instrument or performed the promise, however, the holder is an HDC.

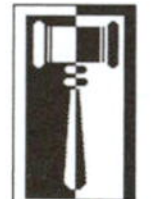

In the legal problem set out at the beginning of this chapter, Marcia Morrison gives a $500 note to Reinhold Smith to pay for goods. Smith delivers defective goods, and Morrison refuses to pay the note. In the meantime, Smith has negotiated the note to Judy Larson, who promised to pay Smith for it in thirty days. Larson learns of Smith's breach and Morrison's refusal to pay the $500 note. Smith has left town. *Can Larson hold Morrison liable on the note?* That will depend on whether Larson is an HDC. Because Larson had not yet given value at the time that she learned of Morrison's defense to payment of the note (breach of contract), Larson is a mere holder, not an HDC. Thus, Morrison's defense is valid against Larson. If Larson had paid Smith for the note at the time of transfer, she would be an HDC and could hold Morrison liable on the note.

A holder can take an instrument for value in one of five ways:

1. By performing the promise for which the instrument was issued or transferred.
2. By acquiring a security interest or other lien in the instrument (other than a lien obtained by a judicial proceeding). Security interests and other liens are discussed in Chapters 31 and 32.
3. By taking an instrument in payment of, or as security for, an antecedent (preexisting) debt.

4. By giving a negotiable instrument as payment.
5. By giving, as payment, a commitment that cannot be revoked (withdrawn or recalled).

A person who receives an instrument as a gift or who inherits it has not met the requirement of value. In these situations, the person becomes an ordinary holder and does not possess the rights of an HDC.

Taking in Good Faith

The second requirement for HDC status is that the holder take the instrument in *good faith*. This means that the purchaser-holder must have acted honestly in the process of acquiring the instrument. *Good faith* is honesty in fact and the observance of reasonable commercial standards of fair dealing. The good faith requirement *applies only to the holder.* It is immaterial whether the transferor acted in good faith. Thus, a person who in good faith takes a negotiable instrument from a thief may become an HDC.

Because of the good faith requirement, one must ask whether the purchaser, when acquiring the instrument, honestly believed that the instrument was not defective. One must also ask whether the purchaser, when taking the instrument, observed reasonable commercial standards (that is, conformed with what others might have done). If a person purchases a $10,000 note for $200 from a stranger on a street corner, the issue of good faith can be raised on the grounds of the suspicious circumstances as well as the grossly inadequate consideration.

Taking without Notice

The final requirement for HDC status involves a lack of notice that the instrument is defective. A person will not be afforded HDC protection if he or she acquires an instrument knowing, or having reason to know, that it is defective in any one of the following ways:

1. It is overdue.
2. It has been dishonored.
3. There is an uncured (uncorrected) default (failure to pay) with respect to another instrument issued as part of the same series.
4. The instrument contains an unauthorized signature or has been altered.
5. There is a defense against the instrument or a claim to the instrument.
6. The instrument is so irregular or incomplete as to call into question its authenticity.

Before buying a negotiable instrument, make sure that it has no defects—undertake a good faith attempt to determine whether the maker or drawer of the instrument might have a valid reason for refusing to pay.

What Constitutes Notice? Notice of a defective instrument is given whenever the holder has (1) actual knowledge of the defect; (2) receipt of a notice about a defect; or (3) reason to know that a defect exists, given all the facts and circumstances known at the time in question. The holder must also have received the notice at a time and in a manner that gives the holder a reasonable opportunity to act on it. Facts that a purchaser might know but that do not of themselves make an instrument defective, such as bankruptcy proceedings against the maker or drawer, do not constitute notice that the instrument is defective.

Overdue Instruments. Any negotiable instrument is either payable at a definite time *(time instrument)* or payable on demand *(demand instrument)*. What constitutes notice that an instrument is overdue will vary depending on whether it is a time or a demand instrument.

A holder of a time instrument who takes the paper the day after its expressed due date is *on notice* that it is overdue. Nonpayment by the due date should indicate to any purchaser who is obligated to pay that the primary party has a defense to payment. Thus, a promissory note due on May 15 must be acquired before midnight on May 15. If it is purchased on May 16, the purchaser will be an ordinary holder, not an HDC.

Sometimes instruments read, "Payable in thirty days." A note dated December 1 that is payable in thirty days is due by midnight on December 31. If the payment date falls on a Sunday or holiday, the instrument is payable on the next business day. If a debt is to be paid in installments or through a series of notes, the maker's default on any installment of principal (not interest) or on any one note of the series will constitute notice to the purchaser that the instrument is overdue.

A purchaser has notice that a demand instrument is overdue if he or she takes the instrument knowing that demand has been made the day before. A purchaser also has notice if he or she takes a demand instrument that has been outstanding for an unreasonable period of time after its date. A reasonable time for a check is ninety days or less. A reasonable time for other demand instruments depends on the circumstances.

Signature Liability

LEARNING OBJECTIVE NO. 3

Outlining the Liability of Parties Who Sign Negotiable Instruments

The key to liability on a negotiable instrument is a signature. A person is not liable on an instrument unless (1) the person signed the instrument, or (2) the person is represented by an agent or representative who signed the instrument and the signature is binding on the represented person. The following sections discuss the types of liability that exist in relation to negotiable instruments and the conditions that must be met before liability can arise.

Primary Liability

A person who is primarily liable on a negotiable instrument is absolutely required to pay the instrument, subject to certain defenses. Primary liability is unconditional. The primary party's liability is immediate when the instrument is signed or issued and effective when the instrument becomes due. No action by the holder of the instrument is required. Makers and acceptors are primarily liable.

The maker of a promissory note promises to pay the note. If the note is complete when the maker signs it, then the maker's obligation is to pay it according to its terms. If the note is incomplete when the maker signs it, then the maker's obligation is to pay it according to its terms when it is completed as authorized. If the completion is unauthorized but the note is negotiated to a holder in due course (HDC), then the maker must pay the HDC according to the unauthorized terms.

The drawee-acceptor of a draft or check is in virtually the same position as the maker of a promissory note. A drawee's acceptance of a draft, which it makes by signing the draft, guarantees that the drawee will pay the draft when it is presented later for payment. When a drawee accepts a draft, the drawee becomes an **acceptor** and is primarily liable to all subsequent holders. A drawee that refuses to accept a draft that requires the drawee's acceptance has dishonored the instrument.

Acceptor
The person (the drawee) who accepts a draft and who engages to be primarily responsible for its payment.

IN THE COURTROOM

Under a contract to buy five thousand pairs of imported jeans, Jones Outfitters, Inc., issues to Worldwide Importers a trade acceptance, payable ninety days after the jeans are shipped. When the jeans are shipped, Worldwide draws a draft on Jones in the amount of the price and forwards the draft to Jones. Jones signs it. *What does Jones guarantee by signing the draft?* When Jones signs it, Jones accepts it, guaranteeing that Jones will pay it when it is presented later for payment. The draft becomes a trade acceptance, which Worldwide can negotiate further. (Worldwide is the drawer of the draft, and Jones is the drawee.)

Secondary Liability

Drawers and indorsers have secondary liability. In the case of notes, an indorser's secondary liability does not arise until the maker, who is primarily liable, has defaulted on the instrument. With regard to drafts (and checks), a drawer's secondary liability does not arise until the drawee fails to pay or to accept the instrument, whichever is required. For example, Lo An writes a check on her account at Universal Bank payable to the order of Val Carerra. If Universal Bank does not pay the check when Carerra presents it for payment, then Lo An is liable to Carerra.

Parties who are secondarily liable on a negotiable instrument promise to pay on that instrument only if the following events occur:

1. The instrument is properly and timely presented.
2. The instrument is dishonored.
3. If the secondarily liable party is an *unqualified* indorser, timely notice of dishonor is given. For example, Oman writes a check on his account at State Bank payable to Bea. Bea indorses the check in blank and cashes it at Midwest Grocery, which transfers it to State Bank for payment. If State Bank refuses to pay it, Midwest must timely notify Bea to hold her liable.

Proper Presentment. Presentment by a holder must be made to the proper person, must be made in a proper manner, and must be timely.

The party to whom the instrument must be presented depends on what type of instrument is involved. A note or certificate of deposit must be presented to the maker for payment. A draft is presented by the holder to the drawee for acceptance, payment, or both, whichever is required. A check is presented to the drawee-bank for payment.

Presentment can be properly made in any of the following ways, depending on the type of instrument involved:

1. By any commercially reasonable means, including oral, written, or electronic communication (but presentment is not effective until the demand for payment or acceptance is received).
2. Through a clearinghouse procedure used by banks (see Chapter 24), such as for deposited checks.
3. At the place specified in the instrument for acceptance or payment.

One of the most crucial criteria for proper presentment is timeliness. Failure to present on time is the most common cause for the discharge of unqualified indorsers from secondary liability. See Exhibit 23–1.

Proper Notice. Once an instrument is dishonored, notice must be given to hold secondary parties liable. Notice may be given in any reasonable manner. This includes oral notice, written notice, or electronic notice (notice by fax, modem, e-mail, and the like) and notice written or stamped on the instrument itself. Any

EXHIBIT 23–1
Time for Proper Presentment

TYPE OF INSTRUMENT	TIME FOR ACCEPTANCE	TIME FOR PAYMENT
Time	On or before due date	On due date
Demand	Within a reasonable time (after date or issue or after secondary party becomes liable thereon)	
Check	Not applicable	Within thirty days of date to hold drawer secondarily liable Within thirty days of indorsement to hold indorser secondarily liable

necessary notice must be given by a bank before its midnight deadline (midnight of the next banking day after receipt). Notice by any party other than a bank must be given within thirty days following the day on which the person receives notice of dishonor.

UNAUTHORIZED SIGNATURES

People are not normally liable to pay on negotiable instruments unless their signatures appear on the instruments. The general rule is that an unauthorized signature is wholly inoperative and will not bind the person whose name is forged.

There are two exceptions to this rule:

1. Any unauthorized signature is wholly inoperative unless the person whose name is signed ratifies (affirms) it. For example, a signature made by an agent who exceeded the scope of his or her authority can be ratified by the principal, either expressly, by affirming the validity of the signature, or impliedly, by other conduct, such as keeping any benefits received in the transaction or failing to repudiate the signature.
2. A person may be precluded from denying the effectiveness of an unauthorized signature, however, if the person's negligence led to the unauthorized signature. For example, suppose that a person who writes and signs a check, leaves blank the amount and the name of the payee, and then leaves the check in a place available to the public. That person can be estopped (prevented), on the basis of negligence (that is, for failing to use reasonable care), from denying liability for its payment. Whatever loss occurs may be allocated, however, between certain parties on the basis of comparative negligence (that is, if two parties fail to use reasonable care, the amount of any loss can be apportioned between them according to the degree to which each was negligent).

An unauthorized signature operates as the signature of the unauthorized signer in favor of an HDC. For example, a person who forges a check can be held personally liable by an HDC.

SPECIAL RULES FOR UNAUTHORIZED INDORSEMENTS

Generally, when there is a forged or unauthorized indorsement, the burden of loss falls on the first party to take the instrument with such an indorsement. Two situations are possible, however, in which the loss falls on the maker or drawer. We look at those situations here.

IMPOSTER
One who, with the intent to deceive, pretends to be somebody else.

Imposters. An **imposter** is one who, by use of the mails, telephone, or personal appearance, induces a maker or drawer to issue an instrument in the name of an impersonated payee. If the maker or drawer believes the imposter to be the named payee at the time of issue, the indorsement by the imposter is not treated as unauthorized when the instrument is transferred to an innocent party. This is because the maker or drawer intended the imposter to receive the instrument.

In these situations, the unauthorized indorsement of a payee's name can be as effective as if the real payee had signed. The *imposter rule* provides that an imposter's indorsement will be effective—that is, not a forgery—insofar as the drawer goes.

IN THE COURTROOM

A man walks into Mark's sports equipment store and purports to be Jerry Lewis soliciting contributions in the fight against muscular dystrophy. Mark has heard of Lewis's charitable efforts but has never met or seen him. Wishing to support a worthy cause, Mark writes out a check for $250 payable to Jerry Lewis and hands it to the imposter. The imposter indorses the check in the name of Jerry Lewis and cashes it at a Stop and Shop convenience store.

Mark discovers the fraud and stops payment on the check, claiming that the payee's signature is forged. *Can Mark recover the amount of the check from Stop and Shop?* No. Mark cannot claim a forgery against the store but must seek redress from the imposter instead. If Mark had sent the check to the real Jerry Lewis, but the check had been stolen and negotiated to the store on a forged indorsement, the imposter rule would *not* apply. In that situation, Stop and Shop would have to seek redress against the forger.

The comparative-negligence standard mentioned in connection with the liability of banks paying over unauthorized signatures also applies in cases involving imposters. If, for example, a bank fails to exercise ordinary care in cashing a check made out to an imposter and this failure substantially contributes to the drawer's loss, the drawer may have a valid claim against the bank.

Fictitious Payees. The so-called **fictitious payee** rule deals with the intent of the maker or drawer to issue an instrument to a payee who has no interest in the instrument. This most often takes place when (1) a dishonest employee deceives the employer into signing an instrument payable to a party with no right to receive the instrument or (2) a dishonest employee or agent has the authority to issue an instrument on behalf of the employer. In these situations, the payee's indorsement is not treated as a forgery, and the employer can be held liable on the instrument by an innocent holder.

FICTITIOUS PAYEE
A payee on a negotiable instrument whom the maker or drawer does not intend to have an interest in the instrument. Indorsements by fictitious payees are not forgeries under negotiable instruments law.

IN THE COURTROOM

Dan Symes draws up the payroll list from which the salary checks for the Honsu Company's employees are written. He fraudulently adds the name Penny Trip (a friend not entitled to payment) to the payroll, thus causing checks to be issued to her. Trip cashes the checks at the Lone Star Grocery Store and shares the proceeds with Symes. *Can Lone Star hold Honsu liable on the checks?* Yes. Trip's indorsement is not treated as a forgery, and Honsu can be held liable on them by Lone Star.

Warranty Liability

In addition to the signature liability discussed in the preceding section, transferors make certain implied warranties regarding the instruments that they are negotiating. Liability under these warranties is not subject to the conditions of proper presentment, dishonor, and notice of dishonor. These warranties arise even when a transferor does not indorse the instrument (as in delivery of a bearer instrument). Warranties fall into two categories: those that arise from the transfer of a negotiable instrument and those that arise upon presentment.

TRANSFER WARRANTIES

LEARNING OBJECTIVE NO. 4
Identifying Transfer Warranties, Which Extend to Both Signers and Nonsigners of Negotiable Instruments

A person who transfers an instrument *for consideration* makes certain warranties to the transferee and, if the transfer is by *indorsement,* to all subsequent transferees and holders who take the instrument in good faith. There are five **transfer warranties.** They are as follows:

TRANSFER WARRANTIES
Guaranties made by any person who transfers a negotiable instrument for consideration to all subsequent transferees and holders who take the instrument in good faith.

1. The transferor is entitled to enforce the instrument.
2. All signatures are authentic and authorized.
3. The instrument has not been materially altered.
4. The instrument is not subject to a defense or claim of any party that can be asserted against the transferor.

5. The transferor has no knowledge of any insolvency proceedings against the maker, the acceptor, or the drawer of an unaccepted instrument.

Unless the person who transfers an instrument receives consideration, the manner of transfer and the negotiation that is used determine how far and to whom a transfer warranty will run. Transfer by indorsement and delivery of order paper extends warranty liability to any subsequent holder who takes the instrument in good faith. The warranties of a person who transfers without indorsement (by delivery of bearer paper) will extend only to the immediate transferee.

IN THE COURTROOM

Wylie forges Kim's name as a maker of a promissory note. The note is made payable to Wylie. Wylie indorses the note in blank, negotiates it to Bret, and then leaves the country. Bret, without indorsement, delivers the note to Fern. Fern, in turn without indorsement, delivers the note to Rick. On Rick's presentment of the note to Kim, the forgery is discovered. *Can Rick hold Fern (the immediate transferor) liable for breach of warranty that all signatures are genuine?* Yes. The note is bearer paper. Rick cannot hold Bret liable, however, because Bret is not Rick's immediate transferor but is a prior nonindorsing transferor.

PRESENTMENT WARRANTIES

LEARNING OBJECTIVE NO. 5
Listing Presentment Warranties, Which Extend to Both Signers and Nonsigners of Negotiable Instruments

Any person who obtains payment or acceptance of an instrument makes to any other person who in good faith pays or accepts the instrument the following warranties:

1. The person obtaining payment or acceptance is entitled to enforce the draft or is authorized to obtain payment or acceptance on behalf of a person who is entitled to enforce the draft. (This is, in effect, a warranty that there are no missing or unauthorized indorsements.)
2. The draft has not been altered.
3. The person obtaining payment or acceptance has no knowledge that the signature of the drawer of the draft is unauthorized.

PRESENTMENT WARRANTIES
Warranties made by any person who presents an instrument for payment or acceptance.

These warranties are often referred to as **presentment warranties,** because they protect the person to whom the instrument is presented. These warranties cannot be disclaimed with respect to checks. A claim for breach must be given to the warrantor within thirty days after the claimant knows, or has reason to know, of the breach and the identity of the warrantor.

The second and third presentment warranties do not apply in certain cases (to certain persons) in which the presenter is an HDC. It is assumed, for example, that a drawer or a maker will recognize his or her own signature and that a maker or an acceptor will recognize whether an instrument has been materially altered.

Defenses

Defenses can bar collection from persons who would otherwise be primarily or secondarily liable on an instrument. There are two general categories of defenses—universal defenses and personal defenses.

UNIVERSAL DEFENSES

UNIVERSAL DEFENSES
Defenses that can be used to avoid payment to all holders of a negotiable instrument, including a holder in due course (HDC). Also called real defenses.

Universal defenses (also called *real defenses*) are valid against all holders, including HDCs or holders who take through an HDC. Universal defenses include the following:

1. *Forgery of a signature on the instrument.*

2. *Fraud in the execution.* If a person is deceived into signing a negotiable instrument, believing that he or she is signing something other than a negotiable instrument (such as a receipt), fraud in the execution is committed against the signer.
3. *Material alteration.* An alteration is material if it changes the contract terms between any two parties in any way. Examples of material alterations include completing an instrument, adding words or numbers, or making any other change in an unauthorized manner that relates to the obligation of a party.
4. *Discharge in bankruptcy.* This is a defense on any instrument regardless of the status of the holder, because the purpose of bankruptcy is to settle finally all of the insolvent party's debts.
5. *Minority.* Minority is a universal defense only to the extent that state law recognizes it as a defense to a simple contract.
6. *Illegality, mental incapacity, or extreme duress.* When the law declares that an instrument is *void* because it was issued in connection with illegal conduct, by a person who was adjudged mentally incompetent by a court, or by a person under an immediate threat of force or violence (for example, at gunpoint), the defense is universal.

PERSONAL DEFENSES

Personal defenses are used to avoid payment to an ordinary holder. There are many personal defenses. They include the following:

PERSONAL DEFENSES
Defenses that can be used to avoid payment to an ordinary holder of a negotiable instrument. Personal defenses cannot be used to avoid payment to a holder in due course (HDC).

1. *Breach of contract or breach of warranty.* When there is a breach of warranty or a breach of the contract for which the instrument was issued, the maker of a note can refuse to pay it, or the drawer of a check can stop payment.
2. *Fraud in the inducement (ordinary fraud).* A person who issues a negotiable instrument based on false statements by the other party will be able to avoid payment, unless the holder is an HDC.
3. *Illegality, mental incapacity, or ordinary duress.* If the law declares that an instrument is *voidable* because it was issued in connection with illegal conduct, by a person who is mentally incompetent, or by a person under ordinary duress (an unlawful threat to induce the person to do something that he or she would not otherwise do), the defense is personal.
4. *Previous payment of the instrument.*

Discharge

Discharge from liability on an instrument can come from payment, cancellation, or as previously discussed, material alteration. The liability of all parties is discharged when the party primarily liable on an instrument pays to a holder the amount due in full. Payment by any other party discharges only the liability of that party and later parties.

The holder of a negotiable instrument can discharge any party to the instrument by cancellation. For example, writing the word "Paid" across the face of an instrument constitutes cancellation. Destruction or mutilation of a negotiable instrument is considered cancellation only if it is done with the intention of eliminating an obligation on the instrument. Thus, if destruction occurs by accident, the instrument is not discharged, and the original terms can be established.

TERMS AND CONCEPTS FOR REVIEW

acceptor 286
fictitious payee 289
holder in due course (HDC) 284
imposter 288
personal defense 291
presentment warranty 290
transfer warranty 289
universal defense 290

CHAPTER SUMMARY • TRANSFERABILITY AND LIABILITY

Requirements for Holder-in-Due-Course (HDC) Status—Must Be a Holder	A *holder* is a person who possesses a negotiable instrument if the instrument is payable to bearer or, in the case of an instrument payable to an identified person, if the identified person is in possession.
Requirements for HDC Status—Must Take for Value	A holder takes for *value:* **1.** By performing the promise for which the instrument was issued or transferred. **2.** By acquiring a security interest or other lien in the instrument (other than a lien obtained by a judicial proceeding). **3.** By taking an instrument in payment of, or as security for, an antecedent debt. **4.** By giving a negotiable instrument as payment. **5.** By giving an irrevocable commitment as payment.
Requirements for HDC Status—Must Take in Good Faith	*Good faith* is honesty in fact and the observance of reasonable commercial standards of fair dealing.
Requirements for HDC Status—Must Take without Notice	**1.** *That the instrument is overdue:* **a.** Time instruments are overdue if they are not paid by their due dates. **b.** Demand instruments are overdue if they are outstanding for an unreasonable period of time after their dates. **c.** Checks are overdue ninety days after their dates. **d.** A note is overdue if any part of the principal is not paid when due. **e.** If any acceleration of a time instrument has occurred, the instrument is overdue on the day after the accelerated due date. **2.** *That the instrument has been dishonored*—Actual knowledge or knowledge of facts that would lead a person to suspect that an instrument has been dishonored is notice of dishonor. **3.** *That a claim or defense exists*—Notice exists if (a) a person has actual knowledge of a claim to or defense against an instrument or (b) an instrument is so incomplete or is so irregular that a reasonable person would be put on notice from examination or from facts surrounding the transaction.
Signature Liability	**1.** *Primary liability*— **a.** The maker or acceptor is obligated to pay a negotiable instrument according to its terms. **b.** The drawee is primarily liable to the drawer to pay a negotiable instrument in accordance with the drawer's orders but owes no duty to the payee or any holder. **2.** *Secondary liability*—Drawers and unqualified indorsers promise to pay on an instrument only if: **a.** The instrument is properly and timely presented. **b.** The instrument is dishonored. **c.** Timely notice of dishonor is given to the secondarily liable party. **3.** *Unauthorized signatures*—An unauthorized signature will not bind the person whose name is forged. Exceptions: **a.** The person whose unauthorized signature was used will be bound by the signature if he or she ratifies the signature or is in some way precluded from denying it. **b.** An unauthorized signature will operate as the signature of the unauthorized signer in favor of a holder in due course. **4.** *Special rules for unauthorized indorsements*—The loss falls on the first party to take the instrument, *except* in the following situations, in which the loss falls on the drawer or maker: **a.** When an imposter induces the maker or drawer of an instrument to issue it to the imposter. **b.** When a person signs as or on behalf of a maker or drawer, intending the payee to have no interest in the instrument, or when an agent or employee of the maker or drawer supplies him or her with the name of the payee, also intending the payee to have no interest (fictitious payee rule).

CHAPTER SUMMARY • *Continued*

Warranty Liability	**1.** *Transfer warranties*—The following warranties extend to all subsequent holders (although they can be disclaimed in any instrument except a check): **a.** The transferor is entitled to enforce the instrument. **b.** All signatures are authentic and authorized. **c.** The instrument has not been materially altered. **d.** No defense of any party is good against the transferor. **e.** The transferor has no knowledge of insolvency proceedings against the maker, acceptor, or drawer of an unaccepted instrument. **2.** *Presentment warranties*—The following warranties are impliedly made by any person who seeks payment or acceptance of a negotiable instrument to any other person who in good faith pays or accepts the instrument (although these warranties can be disclaimed on any instrument except a check): **a.** The party is entitled to enforce the instrument. **b.** The instrument has not been altered. **c.** The party presenting has no knowledge that the signature of the drawer is unauthorized.
Defenses against Payment	**1.** *Universal (real) defenses*—Valid against all holders, including HDCs and holders with the rights of HDCs. **a.** Forgery. **b.** Fraud in the execution. **c.** Material alteration. **d.** Discharge in bankruptcy. **e.** Minority—depending on state law. **f.** Illegality, mental incapacity, or extreme duress—if the contract is void. **2.** *Personal defenses*—Valid against ordinary holders; not valid against HDCs or holders with rights of HDCs. **a.** Breach of contract or breach of warranty. **b.** Fraud in the inducement. **c.** Illegality, ordinary duress, and mental incapacity—if the contract is voidable. **d.** Previous payment of the instrument.
Discharge	All parties to a negotiable instrument will be discharged when the party primarily liable on it pays to a holder the amount due in full. Discharge can also occur if the instrument has been canceled or materially altered.

HYPOTHETICAL QUESTIONS

23–1. Defenses. Fox purchased a used car from Emerson for $1,000. Fox paid for the car with a check, written in pencil, payable to Emerson for $1,000. Emerson, through careful erasure and alterations, changed the amount on the check to read $10,000 and negotiated the check to Sanderson. Sanderson took the check for value, in good faith, and without notice of the alteration and thus met the UCC requirements for holder-in-due-course status. Can Fox successfully raise the universal defense of material alteration to avoid payment on the check? Explain.

23–2. Signature Liability. Marion makes a promissory note payable to the order of Perry. Perry indorses the note by writing "without recourse, Perry" (see Chapter 22) and transfers the note for value to Steven. Steven, in need of cash, negotiates the note to Harriet by indorsing it with the words "Pay to Harriet, Steven." On the due date, Harriet presents the note to Marion for payment, only to learn that Marion has filed for bankruptcy and will have all debts (including the note) discharged in bankruptcy. Discuss fully whether Harriet can hold Marion, Perry, or Steven liable on the note.

REAL WORLD CASE PROBLEM

23–3. Discharge. Richard and Coralea Triplett signed two promissory notes—one for $14,000 and one for $3,500—in favor of FirsTier Bank, N.A. The Tripletts sent the bank a check for $7,200 as payment on the notes. A clerk divided the $7,200 payment to pay the second note in full and to reduce the amount owed on the first note. The clerk then incorrectly stamped the first note "PAID," signed it, and mailed it to the Tripletts. Later, a different clerk stamped the second note "PAID," signed it, and returned it to the Tripletts. When FirsTier sued the Tripletts in a Nebraska state court for the rest of the money due on the first note, the Tripletts asserted that the bank had stamped "PAID" on the note and returned it. The bank contended that it had not intended to release both notes. In deciding whether the first note was discharged, what factors should the court take into consideration? [*FirsTier Bank, N.A. v. Triplett,* 242 Neb. 614, 497 N.W.2d 339 (1993)]

For updated links to resources available on the Web, as well as a variety of other materials, visit this text's Web site at **http://blte.westbuslaw.com**.

The National Conference of Commissioners on Uniform State Laws, in association with the University of Pennsylvania Law School, now offers an official site for in-process and final drafts of uniform and model acts. For an index of final acts, including UCC Articles 3 and 4, go to

http://www.law.upenn.edu/bll/ulc/ulc_final.htm

ONLINE LEGAL RESEARCH

Go to **http://blte.westbuslaw.com**, the Web site that accompanies this text. Select "Internet Applications," and then click on "Chapter 23." There you will find the following Internet research exercise that you can perform to learn more about fictitious payees:

Activity 23–1: Fictitious Payees

Chapter 23 ■ WORK SET

TRUE-FALSE QUESTIONS

_____ **1.** Every person who possesses an instrument is a holder.

_____ **2.** Anyone who takes an instrument for value, in good faith, and without notice is a holder in due course (HDC).

_____ **3.** Personal defenses can be raised to avoid payment to an HDC.

_____ **4.** For HDC status, good faith means an honest belief that an instrument is not defective.

_____ **5.** Knowing that an instrument has been dishonored puts a holder on notice, and he or she cannot become an HDC.

_____ **6.** Generally, no one is liable on an instrument unless his or her signature appears on it.

_____ **7.** Warranty liability is subject to the same conditions of proper presentment, dishonor, and notice of dishonor as signature liability.

_____ **8.** Drawers are secondarily liable.

_____ **9.** An unauthorized signature usually binds the person whose name is forged.

MULTIPLE-CHOICE QUESTIONS

_____ **1.** Don signs a note that states, "Payable in thirty days." The note is dated March 2, which means it is due April 1. Jo buys the note on April 12. She is

a. an HDC to the extent that she paid for the note.
b. an HDC to the extent that the note is not yet paid.
c. not an HDC.
d. none of the above.

_____ **2.** Jack's sister Paula steals one of Jack's checks, makes it payable to herself, signs Jack's name, and cashes it at First National Bank. Jack tells the bank that he will pay it. If Jack later changes his mind, he will

a. be liable on the check.
b. be liable only to the extent of the amount in his checking account.
c. not be liable on the check.
d. none of the above.

_____ **3.** Anna, who cannot read English, signs a promissory note after Ted, her attorney, tells her that it is a credit application. Anna has

a. a defense of fraud assertable against a holder or an HDC.
b. a defense of fraud assertable against a holder only.
c. a defense against payment on the note under FTC Rule 433.
d. no defense against payment on the note.

_____ **4.** Ben contracts with Amy to fix her roof, and Amy writes Ben a check, but Ben never makes the repairs. Carl knows Ben breached the contract, but cashes the check anyway. Carl cannot attain HDC status as regards

a. any defense Amy might have against payment.
b. only any personal defense Amy might have against payment.
c. only Ben's breach, which is Amy's personal defense against payment.
d. none of the above.

_____ **5.** Able Company issues a draft for $1,000 on July 1, payable to the order of the Baker Corporation. The draft is drawn on the First National Bank. Before the bank accepts the draft, who has primary liability for payment?

a. Able Company.
b. Baker Corporation.
c. First National Bank.
d. No one.

_____ **6.** Bill issues a check for $4,000, dated June 1, to Ed. The check is drawn on the First National Bank. Ed indorses the check and transfers it to Jane. Which of the following will trigger the liability of Bill and Ed on the check, based on their signatures?

a. Presentment only.
b. Dishonor only.
c. Both presentment and dishonor.
d. Neither presentment nor dishonor.

_____ **7.** Standard Company issues a draft for $500 on May 1, payable to the order of Ace Credit Corporation. The draft is drawn on the First State Bank. If the bank does not accept the draft, who is liable for payment?

a. Standard Company.
b. Ace Credit Corporation.
c. First State Bank.
d. No one.

_____ **8.** Tony signs a note payable to the order of Joan. Joan indorses the note and gives it to Sam as payment for a debt. Sam indorses the note and sells it to Donna. Donna presents it to Tony. Tony pays it. Tony's payment discharges

a. only himself.
b. only Donna.
c. none of the parties.
d. all of the parties.

ISSUE SPOTTERS

1. Adam issues a $500 note to Bill due six months from the date issued. One month later, Bill negotiates the note to Carol for $250 in cash and a check for $250. To what extent is Carol an HDC of the note?

2. Neal issues a check for $4,000, dated June 1, to Ed. The check is drawn on the First National Bank. Ed indorses the check and transfers it to Steven. What will trigger the liability of Neal and Ed on the check?

Checks and the Banking System

24

LEARNING OBJECTIVES

When you finish this chapter, you should be able to:

1 Determine the liability of parties regarding overdrafts.

2 Identify parties' responsibilities as to stop-payment orders.

3 State the rule regarding liability arising from forged drawers' signatures.

4 Outline the availability of funds deposited in a customer's account.

FACING A LEGAL PROBLEM

O'Banion was the owner and operator of Superior Construction. When Superior ran into financial problems, O'Banion arranged with Merchants Bank to honor overdrafts on the corporate account. O'Banion continued to write checks. When the account became overdrawn, however, the bank refused to pay the checks. O'Banion suffered from a bad credit reputation, and Superior eventually went out of business. *Can O'Banion hold the bank liable for failing to pay the checks?*

Checks are the most common kind of negotiable instruments regulated by the Uniform Commercial Code (UCC). It is estimated that sixty-five billion personal and commercial checks are written each year in the United States. Checks are more than a daily convenience—they are an integral part of the economic system.

This chapter identifies the legal characteristics of checks and the legal duties and liabilities that arise when a check is issued. Then it considers the check deposit-and-collection process—that is, the actual procedure by which checks move through banking channels, causing the underlying cash dollars to be shifted from one bank account to another.

Checks

The bank-customer relationship begins when the customer opens a checking account and deposits money that will be used to pay for checks written. The rights and duties of the bank and the customer are contractual and depend on the nature of the transaction.

A check does not operate as an immediate legal assignment of funds between the drawer and the payee. The money in the bank represented by that check does not immediately move from the drawer's account to the payee's account. Furthermore, no underlying debt is discharged until the drawee-bank honors the check and makes final payment. To transfer checkbook dollars among different banks, each bank acts as the agent of collection for its customer.

Whenever a bank-customer relationship is established, certain rights and duties arise. The respective rights and duties of banks and their customers are discussed in detail in the following sections.

Honoring Checks

When a bank provides checking services, it agrees to honor the checks written by its customers with the usual stipulation that there be sufficient funds available in the account to pay each check. When a drawee-bank *wrongfully* fails to honor a check, it is liable to its customer for damages resulting from its refusal to pay. When the bank properly dishonors a check for insufficient funds, it has no liability to the customer.

The customer's agreement with the bank includes a general obligation to keep sufficient money on deposit to cover all checks written. The customer is liable to the payee or to the holder of a check in a civil suit if a check is not honored. If intent to defraud can be proved, the customer can also be subject to criminal prosecution for writing a bad check.

Overdrafts

LEARNING OBJECTIVE NO. 1

Determining the Liability of Parties Regarding Overdrafts

Overdraft
A check written on a checking account in which there are insufficient funds to cover the check.

When the bank receives an item properly payable from its customer's checking account, but there are insufficient funds in the account to cover the amount of the check, the bank can do one of two things. It can dishonor the item, or it can pay the item and charge the customer's account, creating an **overdraft.** To hold the customer liable for the overdraft, the customer must have authorized the payment and the payment must not violate any bank-customer agreement. The bank can subtract the difference from the customer's next deposit. If there is a joint account, however, the bank cannot hold any joint-account customer liable for payment of an overdraft unless the customer has signed the item or has benefited from the proceeds of the item.

In the legal problem set out at the beginning of this chapter, when Superior Construction ran into financial problems, Merchants Bank agreed to honor Superior's overdrafts. O'Banion, Superior's owner and operator, continued to write checks. When the account became overdrawn, the bank refused to pay the checks. O'Banion suffered from a bad credit reputation, and Superior eventually went out of business. *Can O'Banion hold the bank liable for failing to pay the checks?* Yes. When a bank agrees with a customer to pay overdrafts, the bank's refusal to honor checks on an overdrawn account is a wrongful dishonor.

Stale Checks

Stale Check
A check, other than a certified check, that is presented for payment more than six months after its date.

The bank's responsibility to honor its customers' checks is not absolute. A bank is not obliged to pay an uncertified check presented for payment more than six months after its date. Commercial banking practice regards a check outstanding for longer than six months as a **stale check.** A bank has the option of paying or not paying on such a check without liability. The usual banking practice is to consult the customer, who can then ask the bank not to pay the check. If a bank pays in good faith without consulting the customer, it has the right to charge the customer's account for the amount.

Death or Incompetence of a Customer

Neither the death nor the mental incompetence of a customer revokes the bank's authority to pay an item until the bank knows of the situation and has had reasonable time to act on the notice. Even when a bank knows of the death of a customer, for ten days after the date of death, it can pay or certify checks drawn on or before the date of death—unless a person claiming an interest in that account, such as an heir or an executor of the estate, orders the bank to stop payment. Without this provision, banks would constantly be required to verify the continued life and competence of their drawers.

Stop-Payment Orders

Only a customer or any person authorized to draw on the account can order payment of a check (or any item payable by the bank) to be stopped—that is, ask for a **stop-payment order.** This right does not extend to holders—that is, payees or indorsees—because the drawee-bank's contract is not with them, but only with its drawers. Also, a stop-payment order must be received within a reasonable time and in a reasonable manner to permit the bank to act on it.

LEARNING OBJECTIVE NO. 2
Identifying the Parties' Responsibilities As to Stop-Payment Orders

Although a stop-payment order can be given orally, usually by phone, it is binding on the bank for only fourteen calendar days unless confirmed in writing. A written stop-payment order (see Exhibit 24–1) or an oral order confirmed in writing is effective for six months, at which time it must be renewed in writing. If the stop-payment order is not renewed, the check can be paid by the bank, as a stale check, without liability.

Stop-Payment Order
An order by the drawer of a draft or check directing the drawer's bank not to pay the check.

If the drawee-bank pays the check over the customer's properly instituted stop-payment order, the bank will be obligated to recredit the account of the drawer-customer for the actual loss suffered by the drawer because of the payment. This loss may include damages for the dishonor of subsequent items (that is, items that would have been paid if the stop-payment order had been honored).

Before asking for a stop-payment order, make sure that your stop-payment order will be honored by your bank prior to the time the payee cashes the check.

IN THE COURTROOM

Murano orders one hundred cellular telephones from Advanced Communications, Inc., at $50 each. Murano pays in advance for the phones with a check for $5,000. Later that day, Advanced Communications tells Murano that it will not deliver the phones as arranged. Murano immediately calls the bank and stops payment on the check, confirming by

EXHIBIT 24–1
A Stop-Payment Order

Bank of America

Checking Account
Stop-Payment Order

To: Bank of America NT&SA
I want to stop payment on the following check(s).

ACCOUNT NUMBER: [| | | | | – | | | | |]

SPECIFIC STOP

*ENTER DOLLAR AMOUNT: [ ] *CHECK NUMBER: [ ]

THE CHECK WAS SIGNED BY: ______

THE CHECK IS PAYABLE TO: ______

THE REASON FOR THIS STOP PAYMENT IS: ______

STOP RANGE (Use for lost or stolen check(s) only.)

DOLLAR AMOUNT: 000

*ENTER STARTING CHECK NUMBER: [ ] *END CHECK NUMBER: [ ]

THE REASON FOR THIS STOP PAYMENT IS: ______

BANK USE ONLY

TRANCODE:
☐ 21—ENTER STOP PAYMENT (SEE OTHER SIDE TO REMOVE)

NON READS: ______
UNPROC. STMT HIST: ______
PRIOR STMT CYCLE: ______
HOLDS ON COOLS: ______
REJECTED CHKS: ______
LARGE ITEMS: ______
FEE COLLECTED: ______
DATE ACCEPTED: ______
TIME ACCEPTED: ______

I agree that this order (1) is effective only if the above check(s) has (have) not yet been cashed or paid against my account, (2) will end six months from the date it is delivered to you unless I renew it in writing, and (3) is not valid if the check(s) was (were) accepted on the strength of my Bank of America courtesy-check guarantee card by a merchant participating in that program. I also agree (1) to notify you immediately to cancel this order if the reason for the stop payment no longer exists or (2) that closing the account on which the check(s) is (are) drawn automatically cancels this order.

IF ANOTHER BRANCH OF THIS BANK OR ANOTHER PERSON OR ENTITY BECOMES A "HOLDER IN DUE COURSE" OF THE ABOVE CHECK, I UNDERSTAND THAT PAYMENT MAY BE ENFORCED AGAINST THE CHECK'S MAKER (SIGNER).

*I CERTIFY THE AMOUNT AND CHECK NUMBER(S) ABOVE ARE CORRECT.

☐ I have written a replacement check (number and date of check).

______

(Optional—please circle one: Mr., Ms., Mrs., Miss) CUSTOMER'S SIGNATURE **X** ______ DATE ______ sending a fax. Two days later, in spite of this stop-payment order, the bank honors Murano's check to Advanced Communications. *Will the bank be liable to Murano for the full $5,000?* Yes. The bank paid the check over Murano's properly instituted stop-payment order.

Cashier's checks (see Chapter 22) are sometimes used in the business community as nearly the equivalent of cash. Except in very limited circumstances, payment will not be stopped on a cashier's check or a teller's check. Once such a check has been issued by a bank, the bank must honor it when it is presented for payment.

Payment on a Forged Signature of the Drawer

When a bank pays a check on which the drawer's signature is forged, generally the bank suffers the loss. A bank may be able to recover at least some of the amount of the loss, however, from a customer whose negligence contributed to the forgery, from the forger of the check, or from a holder who cashes the check.

LEARNING OBJECTIVE NO. 3
Stating the Rule Regarding Liability Arising from Forged Drawers' Signatures

The General Rule. A forged signature on a check has no legal effect as the signature of a drawer. For this reason, banks require signature cards from each customer who opens a checking account. The bank is responsible for determining whether the signature on a customer's check is genuine. The general rule is that the bank must recredit the customer's account when it pays on a forged signature.

Customer Negligence. When the customer's negligence substantially contributes to the forgery, the bank will not normally be obliged to recredit the customer's account for the amount of the check.

IN THE COURTROOM

Compu-Net, Inc., uses a check-writing machine to write its payroll and business checks. A Compu-Net employee—Mac Malto—uses the machine to write himself a check for $10,000. Compu-Net's bank subsequently honors it. *Under what circumstances can the bank refuse to recredit $10,000 to Compu-Net's account for incorrectly paying on a forged check?* If the bank can show that Compu-Net failed to take reasonable care in controlling access to the check-writing equipment, Compu-Net cannot require the bank to recredit its account for the amount of the forged check.

A customer's liability may be reduced, however, by the amount of a loss caused by negligence on the part of a bank. Thus, if a customer can show that the bank should have been alerted to possible fraud (for example, if the bank knew the customer's checks had been stolen), the loss may be allocated between the customer and the bank.

Timely Examination Required. A bank can either return canceled checks to the customer or provide the customer with information to allow him or her to reasonably identify the checks paid (number, amount, and date of payment). In the second situation, the bank must maintain the ability to furnish legible copies of the checks on the customer's request for a period of seven years.

A customer must examine monthly statements and canceled checks promptly and with reasonable care and report any forged signatures promptly. This includes forged signatures of indorsers. The failure to examine and report, or any carelessness by the customer that results in a loss to the bank, makes the customer liable for the loss. Even if the customer can prove that reasonable care was taken against forgeries, discovery of such forgeries and notice to the bank must take place within specific time frames for the customer to require the bank to recredit his or her account.

When a series of forgeries by the same wrongdoer takes place, the customer, to recover for all the forged items, must discover and report the first forged check to the bank within thirty calendar days of the receipt of the bank statement and canceled checks. Failure to notify the bank within this period of time discharges the bank's liability for all similar forged checks that it pays prior to notification.

When the Bank Is Also Negligent. If the customer can prove that the bank was also negligent, then the bank will also be liable. In this situation, an allocation of the loss between the bank and the customer will be made on the basis of comparative negligence. In other words, even though a customer may have been negligent, the bank may have to recredit the customer's account for a portion of the loss if the bank also failed to exercise ordinary care (*ordinary care* means the observance of reasonable commercial standards, with respect to the banking business in the area).

Regardless of the degree of care exercised by the customer or the bank, a customer who fails to report his or her forged signature within one year from the date that the statement and canceled checks were made available for inspection loses the right to have the bank recredit his or her account.

Other Parties from Whom the Bank May Recover. When a bank pays a check on which the drawer's signature is forged, the bank has a right to recover from the party who forged the signature.

The bank may also have a right to recover from the person (its customer or a collecting bank) who cashes a check bearing a forged drawer's signature. This right is limited, however. A drawee-bank cannot recover from a person who took the instrument in good faith and for value or who in good faith changed position in reliance on the payment or acceptance. This means that in most cases, a drawee-bank will not recover from the person paid, because usually there is a person who took the check in good faith and for value or who in good faith changed position in reliance on the payment or acceptance.

Accepting Deposits

A second fundamental service a bank provides for its checking-account customers is that of accepting deposits of cash and checks. This section focuses on the check after it has been deposited. Most deposited checks involve parties who do business at different banks, but sometimes checks are written between customers of the same bank. Either situation brings into play the bank collection process.

The Collection Process

The first bank to receive a check for payment is the **depositary bank.** For example, when a person deposits an Internal Revenue Service (IRS) tax-refund check into a personal checking account at the local bank, that bank is the depositary bank. The bank on which a check is drawn (the drawee-bank) is called the **payor bank.** Any bank (except the payor bank) that handles a check during some phase of the collection process is a **collecting bank.** Any bank (except the payor bank or the depositary bank) to which an item is transferred in the course of this collection process is called an **intermediary bank.**

During the collection process, any bank can take on one or more of the various roles of depositary, payor, collecting, and intermediary bank. To illustrate, a buyer in New York writes a check on her New York bank and sends it to a seller in San Francisco. The seller deposits the check in her San Francisco bank account.

Depositary Bank
The first bank to which an item is transferred for collection, even though it may also be the payor bank.

Payor Bank
A bank on which an item is payable as drawn (or is payable as accepted).

Collecting Bank
Any bank handling an item for collection, except the payor bank.

Intermediary Bank
Any bank to which an item is transferred in the course of collection, except the depositary or payor bank.

The seller's bank is both a *depositary bank* and a *collecting bank*. The buyer's bank in New York is the *payor bank*. As the check travels from San Francisco to New York, any collecting bank handling the item in the collection process (other than the ones already acting as depositary bank and payor bank) is also called an *intermediary bank*.

Check Collection between Customers of the Same Bank. An item that is payable by the depositary bank (also the payor bank) that receives it is called an "on-us item." If the bank does not dishonor the check by the opening of the second banking day following its receipt, the check is considered paid.

IN THE COURTROOM

Otterley and Merkowitz both have checking accounts at First State Bank. On Monday morning, Merkowitz deposits into his own checking account a $300 check from Otterley. That same day, the bank issues Merkowitz a provisional (temporary) credit for $300. *When is Otterley's check considered honored, and when is Merkowitz's provisional credit final?* When the bank opens on Wednesday, Otterley's check is considered honored, and Merkowitz's provisional credit becomes a final payment.

You can obtain a tremendous amount of information on banking regulation from the Federal Deposit Insurance Corporation (FDIC) at

http://www.fdic.gov

Check Collection between Customers of Different Banks. Once a depositary bank receives a check, it must arrange to present it, either directly or through intermediary banks, to the appropriate payor bank. Each bank in the collection chain must pass the check on before midnight of the next banking day following its receipt. Thus, for example, a collecting bank that receives a check on Monday must forward it to the next collection bank before midnight Tuesday.

Unless the payor bank dishonors the check or returns it by midnight on the next banking day following receipt, the payor bank is accountable for the face amount of the check. Deferred posting (entering on the bank's records) is permitted, however, so that checks received after a certain time (say, 2:00 P.M.) can be deferred until the next day. Thus, a check received by a payor bank at 3:00 P.M. on Monday would be deferred for posting until Tuesday. In this case, the payor bank's deadline would be midnight Wednesday.

FEDERAL RESERVE SYSTEM
A network of twelve central banks headed by a board of governors, with the advice of the Federal Advisory Council and the Federal Open Market Committee, to give the United States an elastic currency, supervise and regulate banking activities, and facilitate the flow and discounting of commercial paper. All national banks and state-chartered banks that voluntarily join the system are members.

How the Federal Reserve System Clears Checks. The **Federal Reserve System** is a network of twelve government banks in which private banks have accounts called *reserve accounts*. This system has greatly simplified the clearing of checks—that is, the method by which checks deposited in one bank are transferred to the banks on which they were written. Suppose that Pamela Moy of Philadelphia writes a check to Jeanne Sutton in San Francisco. When Jeanne receives the check in the mail, she deposits it in her bank. Her bank then deposits the check in the Federal Reserve Bank of San Francisco, which transfers it to the Federal Reserve Bank of Philadelphia. That Federal Reserve bank then sends the check to Moy's bank, which deducts the amount of the check from Moy's account. Exhibit 24–2 illustrates this process.

Encoding and Retention Warranties. As part of the collection process, checks may be encoded with information (such as the amount of the check) that is read and processed by other banks' computers. In some situations, a check may be retained at its place of deposit, and only its image or information describing it is presented for payment under a Federal Reserve agreement, clearinghouse rule, or truncation agreement (*truncation* is presentation of checks for payment by electronic means).

Any person who encodes information on a check, or with respect to a check, after the check has been issued warrants to any subsequent bank or payor that the encoded information is correct. This is also true for any person who retains a

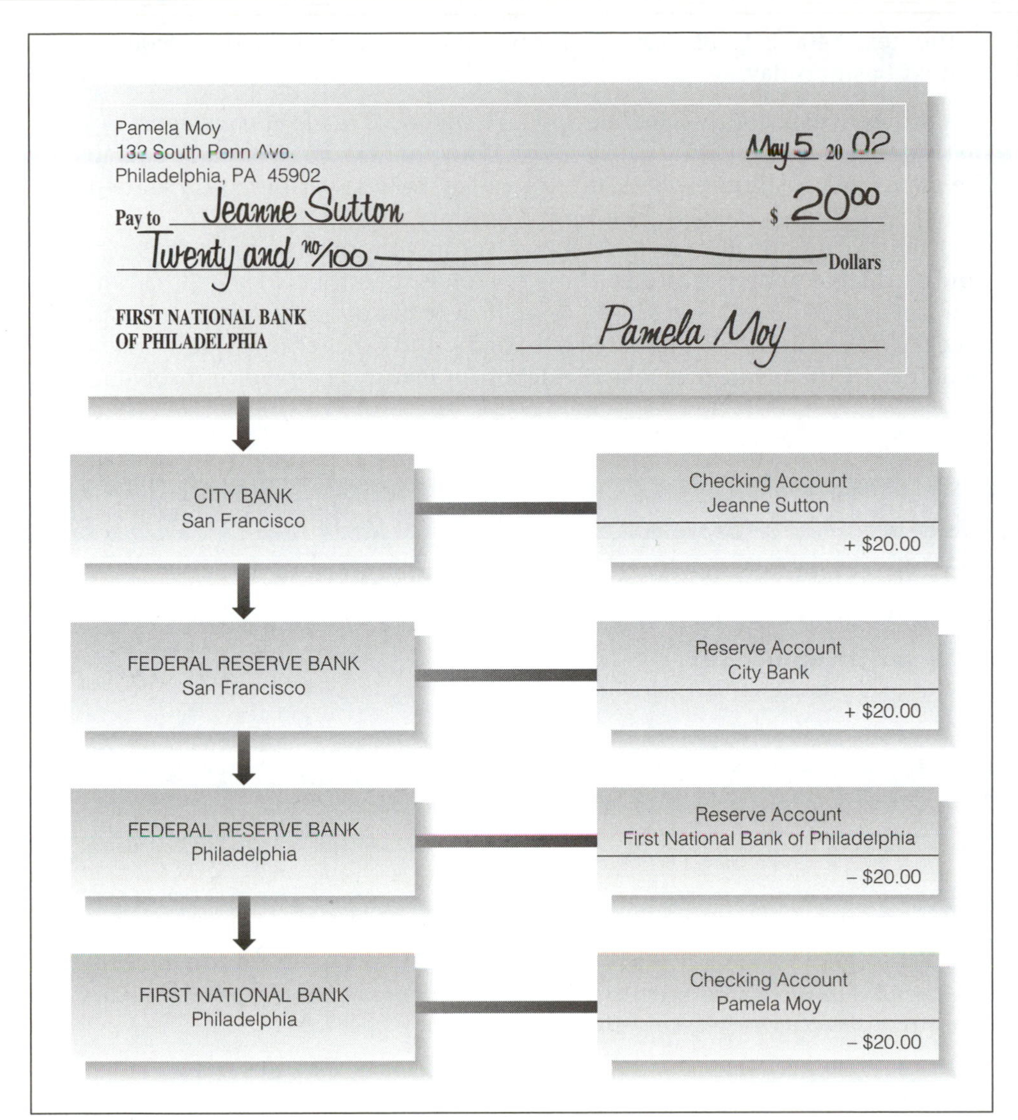

EXHIBIT 24–2
How a Check Is Cleared

check while transmitting its image or information describing it as presentation for payment. This person warrants that the retention and presentation of the item complies with the Federal Reserve or other agreement.

EXPEDITED FUNDS AVAILABILITY ACT

LEARNING OBJECTIVE NO. 4
Outlining the Availability of Funds Deposited in a Customer's Account

The Expedited Funds Availability Act of 1987 and Federal Reserve Regulation CC requires that any local check deposited must be available for withdrawal by check or as cash within one business day from the date of deposit. The Federal Reserve Board of Governors has designated check-processing regions. If the depositary and payor banks are located in the same region, the check is classified as a local check. For nonlocal checks, the funds must be available for withdrawal within not more than five business days.

In addition, the act requires the following:

1. The entire amount of certain deposits must be available (for withdrawal) on the *next business day*. These deposits include cash deposits, wire transfers, government checks, the first $100 of a day's check deposits, cashier's checks, certified checks, and checks for which the depositary and payor banks are branches of the same institution.
2. The first $100 of any other deposit must be available for cash withdrawal on the opening of the next business day after deposit. If a local check is deposited,

Additional information about banking can be obtained from the Federal Reserve System at **http://woodrow.mpls.frb.fed.us/info/policy**

the next $400 is to be available for withdrawal by no later than 5:00 P.M. the next business day.

A different availability schedule applies to deposits made at *nonproprietary* automated teller machines (ATMs). These are ATMs that are not owned or operated by the depositary institution. Basically, a five-day hold is permitted on all deposits, including cash deposits, made at nonproprietary ATMs.

Other exceptions also exist. A depositary institution has eight days to make funds available in new accounts (those open less than thirty days). It has an extra four days on deposits over $5,000 (except deposits of government and cashier's checks), on accounts with repeated overdrafts, and on checks of questionable collectibility (if the institution tells the depositor it suspects fraud or insolvency).

TERMS AND CONCEPTS FOR REVIEW

collecting bank 301
depositary bank 301
Federal Reserve System 302
intermediary bank 301
overdraft 298
payor bank 301
stale check 298
stop-payment order 299

CHAPTER SUMMARY • CHECKS AND THE BANKING SYSTEM

Honoring Checks	**1.** *Wrongful dishonor*—The bank is liable to its customer for actual damages proved to be due to wrongful dishonor. **2.** *Bank's charge against customer's account*—The bank has the right to charge a customer's account for any item properly payable, even if the charge results in an overdraft. **3.** *Stale checks*—The bank is not obligated to pay an uncertified check presented more than six months after its date, but the bank may do so in good faith without liability. **4.** *Death or incompetence of a customer*—So long as the bank does not know of the death or incompetence of a customer, the bank can pay an item without liability to the customer's estate. Even with knowledge of a customer's death, a bank can honor or certify checks (in the absence of a stop-payment order) for ten days after the date of the customer's death. **5.** *Stop-payment orders*—The customer must make a stop-payment order in time for the bank to have a reasonable opportunity to act. Oral orders are binding for only fourteen days unless they are confirmed in writing. Written orders are effective for only six months unless renewed in writing. The bank is liable for wrongful payment over a timely stop-payment order, but only to the extent of the loss suffered by the drawer-customer. **6.** *Unauthorized signature or alteration*—The customer has a duty to examine account statements with reasonable care on their receipt and to notify the bank promptly of any unauthorized signatures or alterations. On a series of unauthorized signatures or alterations by the same wrongdoer, examination and report must occur within thirty calendar days of receipt of the statement. Failure to comply releases the bank from any liability unless the bank failed to exercise reasonable care. Regardless of care or lack of care, the customer is estopped (barred) from holding the bank liable after one year for unauthorized customer signatures or alterations.
Accepting Deposits	**1.** *Check collection between customers of the same bank*—A check payable by the depositary bank that receives it is an "on-us item." If the bank does not dishonor the check by the opening of the second banking day following its receipt, the check is considered paid. **2.** *Check collection between customers of different banks*—Each bank in the collection process must pass the check on to the next appropriate bank before midnight of the next banking day following its receipt. **3.** *Role of the Federal Reserve System*—The Federal Reserve System facilitates the check-clearing process by serving as a clearinghouse for checks.

HYPOTHETICAL QUESTIONS

24–1. Forged Signatures. Gary goes grocery shopping and carelessly leaves his checkbook in his shopping cart. Dolores steals his checkbook, which has two blank checks remaining. On May 5, Dolores forges Gary's name on a check for $10 and cashes the check at Gary's bank, Citizens Bank of Middletown. Gary has not reported the theft of his blank checks to his bank. On June 1, Gary receives his monthly bank statement and canceled checks from Citizens Bank, including the forged check, but he does not examine the canceled checks. On June 20, Dolores forges Gary's last check. This check is for $1,000 and is cashed at Eastern City Bank, a bank with which Dolores has previously done business. Eastern City Bank puts the check through the collection process, and Citizens Bank honors it. On July 1, Gary receives his bank statement and canceled checks. On July 4, Gary discovers both forgeries and immediately notifies Citizens Bank. Dolores cannot be found. Gary claims that Citizens Bank must recredit his account for both checks, as his signature was forged. Discuss fully Gary's claim.

24–2. Death of Bank Customer/Stale Checks. Brian, on January 5, drafts a check for $3,000 drawn on the Southern Marine Bank and payable to his assistant, Shanta. Brian puts last year's date on the check by mistake. On January 7, before Shanta has had a chance to go to the bank, Brian is killed in an automobile accident. Southern Marine is aware of Brian's death. On January 10, Shanta presents the check to the bank, and the bank honors the check by payment to Shanta. Brian's widow, Joyce, claims that the bank wrongfully paid Shanta, because it knew of Brian's death and also paid a check that was by date over one year old. Joyce, as executor of Brian's estate and sole heir by his will, demands that Southern Marine recredit Brian's estate for the check paid to Shanta. Discuss fully Southern Marine's liability in light of Joyce's demand.

REAL WORLD CASE PROBLEM

24–3. Stale Checks. RPM Pizza, Inc., issued a $96,000 check to Systems Marketing but immediately placed a written stop-payment order on the check. Three weeks after the order expired, Systems cashed the check. Bank One Cambridge, RPM's bank, paid the check with funds from RPM's account. Because the check was more than six months old, it was stale and thus, according to standard bank procedures, as well as Bank One's own procedures, the signature on the check should have been specially verified. RPM filed a suit in a federal district court against Bank One to recover the amount of the check. What should the court consider in deciding whether the bank's payment of the check violated the UCC? [*RPM Pizza, Inc. v. Bank One Cambridge,* 69 F.Supp. 517 (E.D.Mich. 1994)]

For updated links to resources available on the Web, as well as a variety of other materials, visit this text's Web site at **http://blte.westbuslaw.com**.

You can obtain an extensive amount of information on banking regulation from the Federal Deposit Insurance Corporation (FDIC) at

http://www.fdic.gov

The American Bankers Association is the largest banking trade association in the United States. To learn more about the banking industry, go to

http://www.aba.com

ONLINE LEGAL RESEARCH

Go to **http://blte.westbuslaw.com**, the Web site that accompanies this text. Select "Internet Applications," and then click on "Chapter 24." There you will find the following Internet research exercises that you can perform to learn more about check fraud and smart cards:

Activity 24–1: Check Fraud

Activity 24–2: Smart Cards

Chapter 24 ■ WORK SET

TRUE-FALSE QUESTIONS

_____ **1.** If a bank pays a stale check in good faith without consulting the customer, the bank cannot charge the customer's account.

_____ **2.** If a bank receives an item payable from a customer's account in which there are insufficient funds, the bank cannot pay the item.

_____ **3.** A bank in the collection chain must normally pass a check on before midnight of the next banking day following receipt.

_____ **4.** The rights and duties of a bank and its customers are partially contractual.

_____ **5.** All funds deposited in all bank accounts must be available for withdrawal no later than the next business day.

_____ **6.** A forged drawer's signature on a check is effective as the signature of the person whose name is signed.

MULTIPLE-CHOICE QUESTIONS

_____ **1.** Jennifer receives a check from Mary for $300. The check is drawn on a local bank. If Jennifer deposits it in her bank, the $300 will be available to her

a. immediately.
b. the next business day.
c. within four days.
d. within eight days.

_____ **2.** Tom is paid with a check drawn on Pete's account at the First State Bank. The check has a forged drawer's signature. Tom indorses the check to Eve, who takes it in good faith and for value, and cashes it at the bank. When Pete discovers the forgery, he notifies the bank, which recredits his account. The bank can recover the amount of its loss from Eve

a. only if she has a bank account at any bank.
b. only if she has an account at the First State Bank.
c. under any circumstances.
d. under no circumstances.

_____ **3.** Ann buys three $300 television sets from Gail, paying with a check. That night, one of the sets explodes. Ann phones the City Bank, the drawee, and orders a stop payment. The next day, Gail presents the check to the bank for payment. If the bank honors the check, it must recredit Ann's account for

a. $300.
b. $900.
c. nothing, because the stop-payment order was oral.
d. nothing, because Gail did not present the check until the next day.

_____ **4.** Colin draws a check for $500 payable to the order of Mary. Mary indorses the check in blank and transfers it to Sam. Sam presents the check to the First National Bank, the drawee, for payment. If the bank does not pay the check, the bank is liable to

a. Sam.
b. Colin.
c. Mary.
d. none of the above.

_____ **5.** On July 1, Liz steals two blank checks from her employer, Dave's Market. On July 3, Liz forges Dave's signature and cashes the first check. The check is returned with Dave's monthly statement from the First National Bank on August 1. Dave does not examine the statement or the checks. On August 24, Liz forges Dave's signature and cashes the second check. This check is returned with Dave's monthly statement on September 1. Dave examines both statements, discovers the forgeries, and insists that the bank recredit the account for both checks. Assuming that the bank was not negligent in paying the checks, the bank must recredit Dave's account for

a. both checks.
b. the first check only.
c. the second check only.
d. neither of the checks.

_____ **6.** Delta Company uses its computer system to issue payroll checks. Ed, a Delta employee, uses the system without authorization to issue himself a check for $5,000. City Bank, Delta's bank, cashes the check. The bank need not recredit Delta's account for the entire $5,000 if

a. Delta owed Ed $5,000 in unpaid wages.
b. the bank did not take reasonable care to determine whether the check was good.
c. Delta did not take reasonable care to limit access to its payroll system.
d. none of the above.

_____ **7.** Jay arranges with the First National Bank to make automatic monthly payments on his student loan. More than three days before a scheduled payment, Jay can stop the automatic payments by notifying the bank

a. orally.
b. in writing.
c. in person.
d. any of the above.

ISSUE SPOTTERS

1. Lynn draws a check for $900 payable to the order of Jan. Jan indorses the check in blank and transfers it to Owen. Owen presents the check to the First National Bank, the drawee bank, for payment. If the bank does not honor the check, is Lynn liable to Owen? Could Lynn also be subject to criminal prosecution?

2. Herb steals a check from Kay's checkbook, forges Kay's signature, and transfers the check to Will for value. Unaware that the signature is not Kay's, Will presents the check to the First State Bank, the drawee. The bank cashes the check. Kay discovers the forgery and insists that the bank recredit her account. Can the bank refuse to recredit Kay's account? If not, can the bank recover the amount paid to Will?

UNIT FIVE
AGENCY AND EMPLOYMENT

UNIT OUTLINE

25 Agency

LEARNING OBJECTIVES

When you finish this chapter, you should be able to:

1. Explain the difference between employees and independent contractors.
2. Describe how an agency relationship is created.
3. Define the scope of an agent's authority.
4. Identify the parties' liability for contracts an agent makes with third parties.

FACING A LEGAL PROBLEM

Bruce is hired as a booking agent for a rock group, The Crash. As the group's agent, Bruce can negotiate and sign contracts for the rock group to appear at concerts. *Are the contracts binding and thus legally enforceable against the group?*

AGENCY
A relationship between two persons in which, by agreement or otherwise, one is bound by the words and acts of the other. The former is a principal; the latter is an agent.

AGENT
A person authorized by another to act for or in place of him or her.

PRINCIPAL
In agency law, a person who, by agreement or otherwise, authorizes an agent to act on his or her behalf in such a way that the acts of the agent become binding on the principal.

One of the most common, important, and pervasive legal relationships is that of **agency.** In an agency relationship between two parties, one of the parties, called the **agent,** agrees to represent or act for the other, called the **principal.** The principal has the right to control the agent's conduct in matters entrusted to the agent. By using agents, a principal can conduct multiple business operations simultaneously in various locations.

Agency Relationships

In a principal-agent relationship, the parties agree that the agent will act *on behalf and instead of* the principal in negotiating and transacting business with third persons. An agent is empowered to perform legal acts that are binding on the principal and can bind a principal in a contract with a third person.

In the legal problem set out at the beginning of this chapter, Bruce is hired as a booking agent for a rock group, The Crash. As the group's agent, Bruce negotiates and signs contracts for the rock group to appear at concerts. *Are these contracts legally enforceable against the group?* Yes. In their principal-agent relationship, the parties agreed that Bruce would act on behalf and instead of The Crash in negotiating and transacting business with third persons.

EMPLOYER-EMPLOYEE RELATIONSHIPS

An employee is one whose physical conduct is *controlled,* or subject to control, by the employer. Normally, all employees who deal with third parties are deemed to be agents.

All employment laws apply only to the employer-employee relationship. Statutes governing Social Security, withholding taxes, workers' compensation, unemployment compensation, workplace safety, and the like (see Chapter 26) are applicable only if there is an employer-employee status. *These laws do not apply to the independent contractor.*

EMPLOYER–INDEPENDENT CONTRACTOR RELATIONSHIPS

Independent contractors are not employees, because those who hire them have no control over the details of their physical performance. An **independent contractor** is a person who contracts with another (the principal) to do something but who is neither controlled by the other nor subject to the other's right to control with respect to the performance.

The relationship between a principal and an independent contractor may or may not involve an agency relationship. To illustrate: An owner of real estate who hires a real estate broker to negotiate a sale of his or her property has contracted with an independent contractor (the real estate broker) and has established an agency relationship for the specific purpose of assisting in the sale of the property. An owner of real estate who hires an appraiser to estimate the value of the property and who does not control the conduct of the work has contracted with an independent contractor (the appraiser) but has not established an agency relationship. The appraiser is not an agent, in part because he or she has no power to transact any business for the owner and is not subject to the owner's control over the conduct of the work.

In determining whether a person hired by another to do a job is an employee or an independent contractor, consider that generally, the greater the employer's control over the work, the more likely it is that the worker is an employee.

LEARNING OBJECTIVE NO. 1

Explaining the Difference between Employees and Independent Contractors

INDEPENDENT CONTRACTOR
One who works for, and receives payment from, an employer but whose working conditions and methods are not controlled by the employer. An independent contractor is not an employee but may be an agent.

Make sure that independent contractors do not represent themselves as your employees to the rest of the world.

Agency Formation

Generally, an agreement to enter into an agency relationship need not be in writing. There are two main exceptions: (1) whenever an agent is empowered to enter into a contract that the Statute of Frauds requires to be in writing (see Chapter 13), the agent's authority from the principal must be in writing (this is the *equal dignity rule,* discussed later in this chapter); and (2) a *power of attorney* (which is also discussed later in this chapter) must be in writing.

A principal must have legal capacity to enter into contracts. Any person can be an agent, however, regardless of whether he or she has the capacity to contract. An agency relationship can be created for any legal purpose. One created for an illegal purpose or contrary to public policy is unenforceable. For instance, it is illegal for medical doctors to employ unlicensed agents to perform professional actions.

The agency relationship can arise by acts of the parties in one of four ways: by agreement, by ratification, by estoppel, or by operation of law. These are discussed in the following sections.

LEARNING OBJECTIVE NO. 2

Describing How an Agency Relationship Is Created

AGENCY BY AGREEMENT

Because agency is a relationship to which both parties consent, it must be based on some *affirmative* indication that the agent agrees to act for the principal and the principal agrees to have the agent so act. An agency agreement can take the form of an express written contract or can be oral. An agency agreement can also be implied from conduct.

IN THE COURTROOM

A hotel expressly allows only Boris to park cars, but Boris has no employment contract there. The hotel's manager tells Boris when to work and where and how to park the cars. *What can be inferred from the hotel's conduct?* Such conduct amounts to a manifestation of the hotel's willingness to have Boris park its customers' cars. Boris can infer from the hotel's conduct that he has authority to act as a parking valet. It can be implied that he is an agent for the hotel, his purpose being to provide valet parking services for hotel guests.

AGENCY BY RATIFICATION

On occasion, a person who is in fact not an agent (or who is an agent acting outside the scope of his or her authority) may contract on behalf of another (a principal). If the principal approves or affirms that contract by word or by action, an agency relationship is created by **ratification.** Ratification is the affirmation of a previously unauthorized contract or act. The requirements for ratification are discussed later in this chapter.

RATIFICATION
In agency law, the confirmation by one person of an act or contract performed or entered into on his or her behalf by another, who assumed, without authority, to act as his or her agent.

AGENCY BY ESTOPPEL

A principal may cause a third person to believe reasonably that another person is his or her agent when the other person is in fact not an agent of the principal. In such a situation, the principal's actions create the *appearance* of an agency that does not in fact exist. If the third person deals with the supposed agent, the principal is estopped (barred) from denying the agency relationship in respect to that third person.

IN THE COURTROOM

Andrew accompanies Charles to call on a customer, Steve, the proprietor of the General Seed Store. Andrew is not employed by Charles at this time. Charles says to Steve that he wishes he had three more assistants "just like Andrew." This gives Steve reason to believe that Andrew is an agent for Charles. Steve then places seed orders with Andrew. *If Charles does not correct the impression that Andrew is an agent, will Charles be bound to fill the orders?* Yes. Charles's representation to Steve created the impression that Andrew was Charles's agent and had authority to solicit orders.

AGENCY BY OPERATION OF LAW

In some cases, the courts find an agency relationship in the absence of a formal agreement. This may occur in family relationships. For example, if one spouse purchases certain necessities and charges them to the other spouse's account, a court would find an agency relationship between the spouses. Sometimes, an agent has emergency powers to act under unusual circumstances (such as when the agent is unable to contact the principal) if failure to act would cause the principal substantial loss.

Rights and Duties in Agency Relationships

In this section, we examine the duties of agents and principals. In general, for every duty of the principal, the agent has a corresponding right, and vice versa.

Agent's Duties

The duties that an agent owes to a principal are set forth in the agency agreement or arise by operation of law. The duties are implied from the agency relationship *whether or not the identity of the principal is disclosed to a third party.* Generally, the agent owes the principal five duties.

Performance. An agent must use reasonable diligence and skill in performing the work. The degree of skill or care required of an agent is usually that expected of a reasonable person under similar circumstances. If an agent has represented himself or herself as possessing special skills (such as those that an accountant or attorney possesses), the agent is expected to use them.

Notification. An agent must notify the principal of all matters that come to his or her attention concerning the subject matter of the agency. What the agent actually tells the principal is not relevant. It is what the agent *should have told* the principal that is crucial. Under the law of agency, notice to the agent is notice to the principal. For example, the manager (the agent) of a grocery store is notified of a spilled gallon of milk in one of the aisles. If the manager fails to take steps to clean up the spill and a customer is injured, the store's owner (the principal) is liable for the injury.

The 'Lectric Law Library Lawcopedia contains a summary of agency laws at

http://www.lectlaw.com/d-a.htm

Scroll down through the A's and select the link to Agent for useful information on this area of the law.

Loyalty. The agent must act solely for the benefit of his or her principal and not in the interest of the agent or a third party.

Any information (such as a list of customers) acquired through the agency relationship is considered confidential. It would be a breach of loyalty to disclose such information during the agency relationship or after its termination.

Furthermore, an agent employed by a principal to buy cannot buy from himself or herself. For instance, if Verona asks Bob to buy an acre of land in a certain area of the city for her, Bob cannot take advantage of the relationship to sell his own acre in that area to her. Similarly, an agent employed to sell cannot become the purchaser without the principal's consent. Thus, if Gail asks Kurt to sell Gail's computer, Kurt cannot buy the computer without Gail's consent.

Obedience. When an agent is acting on behalf of the principal, the agent must follow all lawful and clearly stated instructions of the principal. During emergency situations, however, when the principal cannot be consulted, the agent may deviate from the instructions if the circumstances so warrant (such as when the principal would suffer a financial loss if the agent failed to act).

Accounting. The agent must keep for the principal an account of all property and money received and paid out on behalf of the principal. This includes gifts from third persons in connection with the agency. For example, a gift from a customer to a salesperson for prompt deliveries made by the salesperson's firm belongs to the firm. The agent must maintain separate accounts for the principal's funds and for the agent's personal funds. No intermingling is allowed.

Principal's Duties

The principal also has certain duties to the agent, either expressed or implied by law. Three such duties are discussed here.

Compensation. Whenever an amount of compensation is agreed on by the parties, the principal must pay it on completion of the agent's specified activities. If no amount is expressly agreed on, then the principal owes the agent the customary compensation for the agent's services.

Reimbursement and Indemnification. Whenever an agent disburses sums of money at the request of the principal, and whenever the agent disburses sums of money to pay for necessary expenses in the course of a reasonable performance of his or her agency duties, the principal must reimburse the agent. Agents cannot recover for expenses incurred by their own misconduct, however. For instance, an agent cannot recover for the expense of replacing stolen office supplies if it was the agent's responsibility to keep the supplies secure and he or she failed to do so.

A principal must also *indemnify* (compensate) an agent for liabilities incurred because of authorized acts and for losses suffered by the agent or others because of the principal's failure to perform any duties. For instance, if an agent orders supplies on the principal's behalf and the agent is held liable for the payment, the principal must indemnify the agent for the liability.

Cooperation. A principal must cooperate with and assist an agent in performing the agent's duties. The principal must do nothing to prevent such performance. For example, when a newspaper (the principal) grants its vendor (the agent) the right to sell its newspapers at a busy intersection to the exclusion of all of the newspaper's other vendors, the newspaper cannot grant another vendor the right to sell newspapers at that intersection.

Scope of Agent's Authority

LEARNING OBJECTIVE NO. 3
Defining the Scope of an Agent's Authority

An agent's authority to act can be either *actual* (express or implied) or *apparent*. If an agent contracts outside the scope of his or her authority, the principal may still become liable by ratifying the contract.

Express Authority

Equal Dignity Rule
In most states, a rule stating that express authority given to an agent must be in writing if the contract to be made on behalf of the principal is required to be in writing.

Express authority of an agent is embodied in that which the principal has engaged the agent to do. It can be given orally or in writing. The **equal dignity rule** in most states requires that if the contract being executed is or must be in writing, then the agent's authority must also be in writing.

IN THE COURTROOM

Zorba orally asks Parkinson to sell a ranch that Zorba owns. Parkinson finds a buyer and signs a sales contract (a contract for an interest in realty must be in writing) on behalf of Zorba to sell the ranch. *Can the buyer enforce the contract?* Not unless Zorba subsequently ratifies Parkinson's agency status *in writing.* Once the contract is ratified, either party can enforce rights under it.

Power of Attorney
A document or instrument authorizing another to act as one's agent or attorney.

Giving an agent a **power of attorney** confers express authority. A power of attorney normally is a written document. Like all agency relationships, a power of attorney can be special (permitting the agent to do specified acts only) or it can be general (permitting the agent to transact all business dealings for the principal). A sample power of attorney is shown in Exhibit 25–1.

EXHIBIT 25–1
Power of Attorney

POWER OF ATTORNEY

GENERAL

Know All Men by These Presents: That I, ____________________

____

the undersigned (jointly and severally, if more than one) hereby make, constitute and appoint ____________________

____

as a true and lawful Attorney for me and in my name, place and stead and for my use and benefit:

(a) To ask, demand, sue for, recover, collect and receive each and every sum of money, debt, account, legacy, bequest, interest, dividend, annuity and demand (which now is or hereafter shall become due, owing or payable) belonging to or claimed by me, and to use and take any lawful means for the recovery thereof by legal process or otherwise, and to execute and deliver a satisfaction or release therefore, together with the right and power to compromise or compound any claim or demand;

(b) To exercise any or all of the following powers as to real property, any interest therein and/or any building thereon: To contract for, purchase, receive and take possession thereof and or evidence of title thereto; to lease the same for any term or purpose, including leases for business, residence, and oil and/or mineral development; to sell, exchange, grant or convey the same with or without warranty; and to mortgage, transfer in trust, or otherwise encumber or hypothecate the same to secure payment of a negotiable or non-negotiable note or performance of any obligation or agreement;

(c) To exercise any or all of the following powers as to all kinds of personal property and goods, wares and merchandise, chooses in action and other property in possession or in action: To contract for, buy, sell, exchange, transfer and in any legal manner deal in and with the same; and to mortgage, transfer in trust, or otherwise encumber or hypothecate the same to secure payment of a negotiable or non-negotiable note or performance of any obligation or agreement;

(d) To borrow money and to execute and deliver negotiable or non-negotiable notes therefore with or without security; and to loan money and receive negotiable or non-negotiable notes therefore with such security as he shall deem proper;

(e) To create, amend, supplement and terminate any trust and to instruct and advise the trustee of any trust wherein I am or may be trustor or beneficiary; to represent and vote stock, exercise stock rights, accept and deal with any dividend, distribution or bonus, join in any corporate financing, reorganization, merger, liquidation, consolidation or other action and the extension, compromise, conversion, adjustment, enforcement or foreclosure, singly or in conjunction with others of any corporate stock, bond, note, debenture or other security; to compound, compromise, adjust, settle and satisfy any obligation, secured or unsecured, owing by or to me and to give or accept any property and/or money whether or not equal to or less in value than the amount owing in payment, settlement or satisfaction thereof;

(f) To transact business of any kind or class and as my act and deed to sign, execute, acknowledge and deliver any deed, lease, assignment of lease, covenant, indenture, indemnity, agreement, mortgage, deed of trust, assignment of mortgage or of the beneficial interest under deed of trust, extension or renewal of any obligation, subordination or waiver of priority, hypothecation, bottomry, charter-party, bill of lading, bill of sale, bill, bond, note, whether negotiable or non-negotiable, receipt, evidence of debt, full or partial release or satisfaction of mortgage, judgment and other debt, request for partial or full reconveyance of deed of trust and such other instruments in writing of any kind or class as may be necessary or proper in the premises.

Giving and Granting unto my said Attorney full power and authority to do so and perform all and every act and thing whatsoever requisite, necessary or appropriate to be done in and about the premises as fully to all intents and purposes as I might or could do if personally present, hereby ratifying all that my said Attorney shall lawfully do or cause to be done by virtue of these presents. The powers and authority hereby conferred upon my said Attorney shall be applicable to all real and personal property or interests therein now owned or hereafter acquired by me and wherever situate.

My said Attorney is empowered hereby to determine in his sole discretion the time when, purpose for and manner in which any power herein conferred upon him shall be exercised, and the conditions, provisions and covenants of any instrument or document which may be executed by him pursuant hereto; and in the acquisition or disposition of real or personal property, my said Attorney shall have exclusive power to fix the terms thereof for cash, credit and/or property, and if on credit with or without security.

The undersigned, if a married woman, hereby further authorizes and empowers my said Attorney, as my duly authorized agent, to join in my behalf, in the execution of any instrument by which any community real property or any interest therein, now owned or hereafter acquired by my spouse and myself, or either of us, is sold, leased, encumbered, or conveyed.

When the contest so requires, the masculine gender includes the feminine and/or neuter, and the singular number includes the plural.

WITNESS my hand this ________ day of ________________, 19___

____________________ ____________________

____________________ ____________________

State of California } SS.
County of ________________

On ____________________, before me, the undersigned, a Notary Public in and for said State, personally appeared ____________________

____

known to me by to be person ________ whose name ________________ subscribed to the within instrument and acknowledged that ________________ executed the same.

Witness my hand and official seal. (Seal) ____________________
Notary Public in and for said State.

Implied Authority

Implied authority of an agent can be (1) conferred by custom, (2) inferred from the position the agent occupies, or (3) inferred as being reasonably necessary to carry out express authority. Authority to manage a business, for example, implies authority to do what is reasonably required (as is customary, as can be inferred from a manager's position, or as is necessary to carry out the manager's express authority) to operate the business. Such actions include participating in contracts for employee help, for buying merchandise and equipment, and even for advertising the products sold in the store.

Apparent Authority and Estoppel

Actual authority of an agent arises from what the principal manifests *to the agent.* Apparent authority exists when the principal, by either word or action, causes a *third party* reasonably to believe that an agent has authority to act, even though the agent has no express or implied authority. If the third party changes his or her position in reliance on the principal's representations, the principal may be estopped (barred) from denying that the agent had authority.

IN THE COURTROOM

Emily Anderson, a salesperson for Gold Products, has no authority to collect payments for orders solicited from customers. A customer, Martin Huerta, pays Anderson for an order. Anderson takes the payment to Gold's accountant, who accepts the payment and sends Huerta a receipt. This procedure is followed for other orders by Huerta. One time, however, Anderson absconds with the money. *Can Huerta claim that the payment to Anderson was authorized and thus, in effect, a payment to Gold?* Yes. Gold's *repeated* acts of accepting Huerta's payment led him reasonably to expect that Anderson had authority to receive payments. Although Anderson did not have authority, Gold's conduct gave her *apparent* authority.

Ratification

As mentioned previously in this chapter, ratification is the affirmation of a previously unauthorized contract or act (involving the agent and a third party). Ratification can be express or implied. If the principal does not ratify, the principal is not bound. The requirements for ratification are as follows:

1. The one who acted as an agent must have acted on behalf of a principal who subsequently ratifies.
2. The principal must know of all material facts involved in the transaction.
3. The agent's act must be affirmed in its entirety by the principal.
4. The principal must have the legal capacity to authorize the transaction at the time the agent engages in the act and at the time the principal ratifies.
5. The principal's affirmance must occur prior to the withdrawal of the third party from the transaction or prior to the third party's change of position in reliance on the contract.
6. The principal must observe the same formalities when he or she approves the act purportedly done by the agent on his or her behalf as would have been required to authorize the act initially.

Liability in Agency Relationships

Frequently, the issue arises as to which party, the principal or the agent, should be held liable for the contracts formed by the agent or the torts committed by the agent. We look here at this aspect of agency law.

LIABILITY FOR AGENT'S CONTRACTS

An important consideration in determining liability for a contract formed by an agent is whether the identity of the principal was known to the third party at the time the contract was made. A **disclosed principal** is a principal whose identity is known by the third party at the time the contract is made by the agent. A **partially disclosed principal** is a principal whose identity is not known by the third party, but the third party knows that the agent is or may be acting for a principal at the time the contract is made. An **undisclosed principal** is a principal whose identity is totally unknown by the third party, and the third party has no knowledge that the agent is acting in an agency capacity at the time the contract is made.

If an agent, acting within the scope of his or her authority, contracts with a third party, a disclosed principal is liable to the third party (and ordinarily the agent is not liable). In the same circumstances, a partially disclosed principal would also be liable (and so would the agent). An undisclosed principal would be liable for the contract, unless (1) he or she was expressly excluded as a party in the contract; (2) the contract is a negotiable instrument, such as a check, signed by the agent with no indication of signing in a representative capacity; or (3) the performance of the agent is personal to the contract (for example, the contract requires the agent who is a famous musician to give a concert). In all cases, when the principal is undisclosed, the agent may be liable.

If the agent exceeds the scope of authority, and the principal fails to ratify the contract, the principal cannot be held liable to a contract by a third party. Hence, the agent is generally liable unless the third party knew of the agent's lack of authority.

LEARNING OBJECTIVE NO. 4
Identifying the Parties' Liability for Contracts an Agent Makes with Third Parties

DISCLOSED PRINCIPAL
A principal whose identity and existence as a principal is known by a third person at the time a transaction is conducted by an agent.

PARTIALLY DISCLOSED PRINCIPAL
A principal whose identity is unknown by a third person, but the third person knows that the agent is or may be acting for a principal at the time the contract is made.

UNDISCLOSED PRINCIPAL
A principal whose identity is unknown by a third person, and the third person has no knowledge that the agent is acting in an agency capacity at the time the contract is made.

LIABILITY FOR AGENT'S TORTS

A principal becomes liable for an agent's torts if the torts are committed within the scope of the agency or the scope of employment. The theory of liability used here involves the doctrine of ***respondeat superior*** (pronounced ree-*spahn*-dee-uht soo-*peer*-ee-your), a Latin term meaning "let the master respond." This doctrine is similar to the theory of strict liability discussed in Chapter 19. The doctrine imposes vicarious (indirect) liability on a principal without regard to the personal fault of the principal for torts committed by an agent in the scope of the agency. For instance, if a truck driver, the employee of a delivery firm, negligently runs a red light and injures a pedestrian, the owner of the truck is liable for the injury.

RESPONDEAT SUPERIOR
In Latin, "Let the master respond." A principle of law whereby a principal or an employer is held liable for the wrongful acts committed by agents or employees while acting within the scope of their agency or employment.

Termination of Agency

An agency can terminate by an act of the parties or by operation of law. Once the relationship between the principal and agent has ended, the agent no longer has the right to bind the principal.

TERMINATION BY ACT OF THE PARTIES

An agency may be terminated by act of the parties in several ways, as discussed below.

Lapse of Time. An agency agreement may specify the time period during which the agency relationship will exist. If so, the agency ends when that period expires. If no definite time is stated, then the agency continues for a reasonable time and can be terminated by either party.

Purpose Achieved. An agent can be employed to accomplish a particular objective, such as the purchase of stock for a cattle rancher. In that case, the agency automatically ends after the cattle have been purchased.

Occurrence of a Specific Event. An agency can be created to terminate upon the happening of a certain event. If a principal appoints an agent to handle the principal's business while the principal is away, for example, the agency automatically terminates when the principal returns.

Mutual Agreement. The parties can mutually agree to terminate their relationship. An agreement to terminate the agency effectively relieves the principal and the agent of the rights and duties in the relationship.

Termination by One Party. Either party can terminate an agency relationship. The agent's act of termination is a *renunciation* of authority (the agent abandons the right to act for the principal). The principal's act of termination is a *revocation* of authority (the principal takes back the right given to the agent to act on the principal's behalf).

Although both parties have the *power* to terminate, they may not each possess the *right.* Terminating an agency relationship may require breaking an agency contract, and no one has the right to break a contract. Such wrongful termination can subject the canceling party to a suit for damages.

Agency Coupled with an Interest. An agency *coupled with an interest* is a relationship created for the benefit of the agent. The agent actually acquires a beneficial interest in the subject matter of the agency. Under these circumstances, it is not equitable to permit a principal to terminate the relationship at will. Hence, this type of agency is *irrevocable.*

IN THE COURTROOM

Silvia Orta owns Green Hills. She needs some immediate cash, so she enters into an agreement with Jack Harrington. The agreement provides that Harrington will lend her $10,000, and she agrees to grant Harrington a one-half interest in Green Hills and "the exclusive right to sell" it with the loan to be repaid out of the sale's proceeds. Harrington is Orta's agent. *Is Harrington's agency coupled with an interest?* Yes. Harrington's power to sell Green Hills is coupled with a beneficial interest of one-half ownership in Green Hills created at the time of the loan for the purpose of supporting it and securing its repayment. The agency power is irrevocable.

Termination by Operation of Law

Termination of an agency by operation of law occurs in the following circumstances.

Death or Insanity. The death or mental incompetence of either the principal or the agent automatically and immediately terminates the ordinary agency relationship. Knowledge of the death is not required.

Impossibility. When the specific subject matter of an agency is destroyed or lost, the agency terminates. Thus, if an owner employs a broker to sell the owner's house but before the sale the premises are destroyed by fire, the agency terminates. When it is impossible for the agent to perform the agency lawfully, the agency terminates. For instance, if an agent is hired to buy oil for a U.S. firm from a foreign country on which Congress subsequently imposes an embargo, the agent cannot lawfully buy the oil and the agency terminates.

Changed Circumstances. When an event occurs that has such an unusual effect on the subject matter of the agency that the agent can reasonably infer that the principal will not want the agency to continue, the agency terminates. For instance, if an owner hires a realtor to sell a tract of land and the realtor learns that there is oil under the land, greatly increasing the value of the tract, the agency to sell the land is terminated.

Bankruptcy. Bankruptcy of the principal or the agent usually terminates the agency relationship. (Bankruptcy is discussed in Chapter 33.)

War. When the principal's country and the agent's country are at war with each other, the agency is terminated, or at least suspended.

NOTICE OF TERMINATION REQUIRED

When an agency terminates by operation of law because of the preceding reasons or some other unforeseen circumstance, there is no duty to notify third parties, unless the agent's authority is coupled with an interest. If the parties themselves have terminated the agency, however, it is the principal's duty to inform any third parties who know of the existence of the agency that it has been terminated. No particular form of notice of agency termination is required.

When termination of an agency requires notice to the agent, the principal can actually notify the agent, or the agent can learn of the termination through some other means (if the agent learns that the principal has gone out of business, for instance). If the agent's authority is written, however, it must be revoked in writing. The writing must be shown to all people who saw the original writing that established the agency relationship.

TERMS AND CONCEPTS FOR REVIEW

agency 310
agent 310
disclosed principal 317
equal dignity rule 314
independent contractor 311
partially disclosed principal 317
power of attorney 314
principal 310
ratification 312
***respondeat superior* 317**
undisclosed principal 317

CHAPTER SUMMARY • AGENCY

Agency Information	**1.** *By agreement*—Through express consent (oral or written) or implied by conduct. **2.** *By ratification*—The principal, either by act or agreement, ratifies the conduct of an agent who acted outside the scope of authority or the conduct of a person who is in fact not an agent. **3.** *By estoppel*—When the principal causes a third person to believe that another person is his or her agent, and the third person deals with the supposed agent, the principal is barred from denying the agency relationship. **4.** *By operation of law*—Based on a social duty (such as the need to support family members) or created in emergency situations when the agent is unable to contact the principal.
Duties of Agents and Principals	**1.** *Duties of the agent*— **a.** Performance—The agent must use reasonable diligence and skill in performing his or her duties. **b.** Notification—The agent is required to notify the principal of all matters that come to his or her attention concerning the subject matter of the agency. **c.** Loyalty—The agent has a duty to act solely for the benefit of his or her principal and not in the interest of the agent or a third party.

CHAPTER SUMMARY • *Continued*

Duties of Agents and Principals continued	**d.** Obedience—The agent must follow all lawful and clearly stated instructions of the principal. **e.** Accounting—The agent has a duty to make available to the principal records of all property and money received and paid out on behalf of the principal. **2.** *Duties of the principal*— **a.** Compensation—The principal must pay the agreed-on value (or reasonable value) for an agent's services. **b.** Reimbursement and indemnification—The principal must reimburse the agent for all sums of money disbursed at the request of the principal and for all sums of money the agent disburses for necessary expenses in the course of reasonable performance of his or her agency duties. **c.** Cooperation—A principal must cooperate with and assist an agent in performing the agent's duties.
Scope of Agent's Authority	**1.** *Express authority*—Can be oral or in writing. Authorization must be in writing if the agent is to execute a contract that must be in writing. **2.** *Implied authority*—Authority customarily associated with the position of the agent or authority that is deemed necessary for the agent to carry out expressly authorized tasks. **3.** *Apparent authority and agency by estoppel*—Exists when the principal, by word or action, causes a third party reasonably to believe that an agent has authority to act, even though the agent has no express or implied authority. **4.** *Ratification*—The affirmation by the principal of an agent's unauthorized action or promise. For the ratification to be effective, the principal must be aware of all material facts.
Liability for Contracts	**1.** *Disclosed principals*—The principal is liable to a third party for a contract made by the agent, if the agent acted within the scope of his or her authority. The agent is not liable. **2.** *Partially disclosed principals*—The principal is liable to a third party for a contract made by the agent, if the agent acted within the scope of his or her authority. The agent is also liable. **3.** *Undisclosed principals*—The agent is liable to a third party for a contract made by the agent. If the agent acted within the scope of authority, the principal is fully bound by the contract.
Liability for Agent's Torts	Under the doctrine of *respondeat superior,* the principal is liable for any harm caused to another through the agent's negligence if the agent was acting within the scope of his or her employment at the time the harmful act occurred.
Termination of an Agency	**1.** *By act of the parties*— **a.** Lapse of time (a definite time for the duration of the agency was agreed on when the agency was established). **b.** Purpose achieved. **c.** Occurrence of a specific event. **d.** Mutual agreement. **e.** Termination by act of either the principal (revocation) or the agent (renunciation). (A principal cannot revoke an agency coupled with an interest.) **2.** *By operation of law*— **a.** Death or mental incompetence of either the principal or the agent. **b.** Impossibility (when the purpose of the agency cannot be achieved because of an event beyond the parties' control). **c.** Changed circumstances (in which it would be inequitable to require that the agency be continued). **d.** Bankruptcy of the principal or the agent. **e.** War between the principal's and agent's countries. **3.** *Notification of termination*— **a.** When an agency is terminated by operation of law, no notice to third parties is required. **b.** When an agency is terminated by act of the parties, all third parties who have previously dealt with the agency must be directly notified. **c.** If an agent must be notified of the termination, the notice may come from the principal or through other means (unless the agency is in writing, in which situation it must be revoked in writing).

HYPOTHETICAL QUESTIONS

25–1. Agent's Duties to Principal. Iliana is a traveling sales agent. Iliana not only solicits orders but also delivers the goods and collects payments from her customers. Iliana places all payments in her private checking account and at the end of each month draws sufficient cash from her bank to cover the payments made. Giberson Corp., Iliana's employer, is totally unaware of this procedure. Because of a slowdown in the economy, Giberson tells all its sales personnel to offer 20 percent discounts on orders. Iliana solicits orders, but she offers only 15 percent discounts, pocketing the extra five percent paid by customers. Iliana has not lost any orders by this practice, and she is rated as one of Giberson's top salespersons. Giberson now learns of Iliana's actions. Discuss fully Giberson's rights in this matter.

25–2. Liability for Agent's Contracts. Michael Mosely works as a purchasing agent for Suharto Coal Supply, a partnership. Mosely has authority to purchase the coal needed by Suharto to satisfy the needs of its customers. While Mosely is leaving a coal mine from which he has just purchased a large quantity of coal, his car breaks down. He walks into a small roadside grocery store for help. While there, he runs into Wiley, who owns 360 acres back in the mountains with all mineral rights. Wiley, in need of money, offers to sell Mosely the property at $1,500 per acre. Upon inspection, Mosely concludes that the subsurface may contain valuable coal deposits. Mosely contracts to purchase the property for Suharto, signing the contract, "Suharto Coal Supply, Michael Mosely, agent." The closing date is set for August 1. Mosely takes the contract to the partnership. The managing partner is furious, as Suharto is not in the property business. Later, just before August 1, both Wiley and the partnership learn that the value of the land is at least $15,000 per acre. Discuss the rights of Suharto and Wiley concerning the land contract.

REAL WORLD CASE PROBLEM

25–3. Employee versus Independent Contractor. Stephen Hemmerling was a driver for the Happy Cab Co. Hemmerling paid certain fixed expenses and abided by a variety of rules relating to the use of the cab, the hours that could be worked, the solicitation of fares, and so on. Rates were set by the state. Happy Cab did not withhold taxes from Hemmerling's pay. While driving a cab, Hemmerling was injured in an accident and filed a claim against Happy Cab in a Nebraska state court for workers' compensation benefits. Such benefits are not available to independent contractors. On what basis might the court hold that Hemmerling is an employee? Explain. [*Hemmerling v. Happy Cab Co.,* 247 Neb. 919, 530 N.W.2d 916 (1995)]

For updated links to resources available on the Web, as well as a variety of other materials, visit this text's Web site at **http://blte.westbuslaw.com**.

An excellent source for information on agency law, including court cases involving agency concepts, is the Legal Information Institute (LII) at Cornell University. You can access the LII's Web page on this topic at

http://www.law.cornell.edu/topics/agency.html

The 'Lectric Law Library's Lawcopedia contains a summary of agency laws at

http://www.lectlaw.com/d-a.htm

Scroll down through the A's and select the link to Agent for useful information on this area of the law.

ONLINE LEGAL RESEARCH

Go to **http://blte.westbuslaw.com**, the Web site that accompanies this text. Select "Internet Applications," and then click on "Chapter 25." There you will find the following Internet research exercise that you can perform to learn more about agency law:

Activity 25–1: Liability in Agency Relationships

Activity 25–2: Employees or Independent Contractors?

Chapter 25 ■ WORK SET

TRUE-FALSE QUESTIONS

_____ **1.** An agent can perform legal acts that bind the principal.

_____ **2.** An agent must keep separate accounts for the principal's funds.

_____ **3.** Any information or knowledge obtained through an agency relationship is confidential.

_____ **4.** A disclosed principal is liable to a third party for a contract made by an agent acting within the scope of authority.

_____ **5.** Generally, a principal whose agent commits a tort in the scope of his or her employment is not liable to persons injured.

_____ **6.** An agent is always liable for a contract he or she enters into on behalf of an undisclosed principal.

_____ **7.** Both parties to an agency have the power and the right to terminate the agency at any time.

_____ **8.** The only way a principal can ratify a transaction is by a written statement.

MULTIPLE-CHOICE QUESTIONS

_____ **1.** National Supplies Company hires Linda and Brad as employees to deal with third-party purchasers and suppliers. Linda and Brad are

a. principals.
b. agents.
c. both a and b.
d. none of the above.

_____ **2.** Ann gives Bill the impression that Carol is Ann's agent, when in fact she is not. Bill deals with Carol as Ann's agent. Regarding any agency relationship, Ann

a. can deny it.
b. can deny it to the extent of any injury suffered by Bill.
c. can deny it to the extent of any liability that might be imposed on Ann.
d. cannot deny it.

_____ **3.** Dave is an accountant hired by Eagle Equipment Corporation to act as its agent. In acting as an agent for Eagle, Dave is expected to use

a. reasonable diligence and skill.
b. the degree of skill of a reasonable person under similar circumstances.
c. the special skills he has as an accountant.
d. none of the above.

_____ **4.** EZ Sales Company hired Jill as a sales representative for six months at a salary of $5,000 per month, plus a commission of 10 percent of sales. In matters concerning EZ's business, Jill must act

a. solely in EZ's interest.
b. solely in Jill's interest.
c. solely in the interest of the customers.
d. none of the above.

_____ **5.** Bass Corporation hires Ellen to manage one of its stores. Bass does not specify the extent, if any, of Ellen's authority to contract with third parties. The express authority that Bass gives Ellen to manage the store implies authority to do whatever

a. is customary to operate the business.
b. can be inferred from the manager's position.
c. both a and b.
d. none of the above.

_____ **6.** Ron orally engages Dian to act as his agent. During the agency, Ron knows that Dian deals with Mary. Ron also knows that Pete and Brad are aware of the agency but have not dealt with Dian. Ron decides to terminate the agency. Regarding notice of termination,

a. Dian need not be notified in writing.
b. Dian's actual authority terminates without notice to her of Ron's decision.
c. Dian's apparent authority terminates without notice to Mary.
d. Pete and Brad must be directly notified.

_____ **7.** Smith Petroleum, Inc., contracts to sell oil to Jones Petrochemicals, telling Jones that it is acting on behalf of "a rich Saudi Arabian who doesn't want his identity known." Smith signs the contract, "Smith, as agent only." In fact, Smith is acting on its own. If the contract is breached, Smith may

a. not be liable, because Smith signed the contract as an agent.
b. not be liable, unless Jones knew Smith did not have authority to act.
c. be liable, unless Jones knew Smith did not have authority to act.
d. be liable, because Smith signed the contract as an agent.

_____ **8.** Jill is employed by American Grocers to buy and install a computer system for American's distribution network. When the system is set up and running, the agency

a. terminates automatically.
b. terminates after fourteen days.
c. continues for one year.
d. continues indefinitely.

ISSUE SPOTTERS

1. Able Corporation wants to build a new mall on a specific tract of land. Able contracts with Sheila to buy the property. When Sheila learns of the difference between the price that Able is willing to pay and the price at which the owner is willing to sell, she wants to buy the land and sell it to Able herself. Can she do this?

2. Marie, owner of the Consumer Goods Company, employs Rachel as an administrative assistant. In Marie's absence, and without authority, Rachel represents herself as Marie and signs a promissory note in Marie's name. Under what circumstance is Marie liable on the note?

Employment Law

26

LEARNING OBJECTIVES

When you finish this chapter, you should be able to:

1. Identify limitations on an employer's monitoring of employees.
2. State exceptions to the employment-at-will doctrine.
3. Discuss the protection available to employees injured on the job.
4. Describe the overtime and minimum wage provisions of the Fair Labor Standards Act.

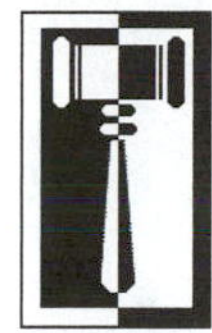

FACING A LEGAL PROBLEM

A U.S. Department of Transportation rule requires employees engaged in oil and gas pipeline operations to submit to random drug testing. The rule does not require that before being tested, the individual must be suspected of drug use. *If the employees challenge this rule in court, will the rule be upheld?*

At one time, employers and employees were on a nearly equal level in bargaining over the terms and conditions of employment. Most employer-employee relationships were considered to be "at will." Under the **employment-at-will doctrine,** either party can end an employment relationship at any time and for any reason.

EMPLOYMENT-AT-WILL DOCTRINE
A doctrine under which employer-employee contracts are considered to be "at will"—that is, either party may terminate an employment contract at any time and for any reason, unless the contract specifies otherwise. Exceptions are frequently made on the basis of a federal statute, an implied employment contract, or public policy.

As companies grew larger, there came to be less equality between employers and employees, and the government began to regulate employment relationships. At first, the law generally favored management. Since the 1930s, however, numerous statutes have been enacted to protect the rights of employees. In this chapter, we look at some of the significant laws that regulate employment relationships.

Privacy Issues

Lie-detector tests, drug tests, electronic monitoring of work, and other practices have been challenged as violations of employees' rights to privacy. Laws relating to these rights vary from state to state.

Lie-Detector Tests

In 1988, Congress passed the Employee Polygraph Protection Act. The act prohibits employers from (1) requiring or causing employees or job applicants to take lie-detector tests or suggesting or requesting that they do so; (2) using, accepting, referring to, or asking about the results of lie-detector tests taken by employees or applicants; and (3) taking or threatening negative employment-related action against employees or applicants based on results of lie-detector tests, or because they refused to take the tests.

Employers excepted from these prohibitions include federal, state, and local government employers; certain security service firms; and companies manufacturing and distributing controlled substances. Other employers may use polygraph tests when investigating losses due to theft—including the theft of trade secrets.

Drug Testing

Some state constitutions may apply to inhibit private employers' testing for drugs. State statutes also may restrict private drug testing in any number of ways. A collective bargaining agreement (a contract between a union and the management of a company) may also provide protection against drug testing.

Federal constitutional limitations apply to the testing of government employees. The Fourth Amendment provides that individuals have the right to be "secure in their persons" against "unreasonable searches and seizures" conducted by government agents. Drug tests have been held constitutional when there was a reasonable basis for suspecting a government employee's use of drugs. Also, when drug use in a particular government job could threaten public safety, testing has been upheld.

In the legal problem set out at the beginning of this chapter, a U.S. Department of Transportation rule requires employees engaged in oil and gas pipeline operations to submit to random drug testing. The rule does not require that before being tested, the individual must be suspected of drug use. *If the employees challenge this rule in court, will the rule be upheld?* Yes. The government's interest in promoting public safety in the pipeline industry outweighs the employees' privacy interests.

Electronic Monitoring and Other Practices

LEARNING OBJECTIVE NO. 1

Identifying Limitations on an Employer's Monitoring of Employees

Listening to employees' telephone conversations may violate the Electronic Communications Privacy Act (ECPA) of 1986, which updated federal wiretapping law to cover new forms of communication, such as cellular telephones and electronic mail (e-mail). The ECPA prohibits the intentional interception of any wire or electronic communication. Some courts have held, however, that an exception to the act—the "business-extension exception"—permits employers to monitor employee telephone *business* conversations (but not personal calls).

BUSINESS TIP

Develop a comprehensive policy statement stating how e-mail should and should not be used, why employees' e-mail messages are being monitored, and the methods used for monitoring.

Generally, there is little specific government regulation of monitoring activities, and an employer may be able to avoid what laws do exist by telling employees that they are subject to monitoring. Then, if employees challenge the monitoring, the employer can claim that the employees consented to it. Employers should be cautious, however, because an employee may bring an action for invasion of privacy. A court may then decide that the employee's reasonable expectation of privacy outweighs the employer's need for surveillance.

Similarly, an employer should consider alternatives before searching an employee's desk, filing cabinet, or office. If a search is conducted and the employee sues, a court may balance the purposes of the search against its intrusiveness and alternatives that would have accomplished the same purpose.

Employment at Will

LEARNING OBJECTIVE NO. 2

Stating Exceptions to the Employment-at-Will Doctrine

Federal statutes have modified the employment-at-will doctrine (discussed in this chapter's introduction) to protect some employees who report employer wrongdoing. Over the last thirty-five years, court rulings have also restricted the right of employers to fire workers, on the basis of an implied employment contract or on the ground that an employee's discharge cannot violate a fundamental public policy.

Statutory Limitations

To encourage workers to report employer wrongdoing, such as fraud, most of the states and the federal government have enacted **whistleblower** statutes. These statutes protect whistleblowers (those who report wrongdoing) from retaliation on the part of employers. They may also provide an incentive to disclose information by providing the whistleblower with a reward. For example, the False Claims Reform Act of 1986 requires that a whistleblower who has disclosed information relating to a fraud perpetrated against the U.S. government receive between 15 and 25 percent of the proceeds if the government sues the wrongdoer.

Whistleblower
An employee who tells the government or the press that his or her employer is engaged in some unsafe or illegal activity.

IN THE COURTROOM

Chester Walsh, an employee of the General Electric Corporation (GE), was assigned to manage a GE aircraft operation in Israel. Walsh learned that a substantial amount of the project money that had been provided by the U.S. government was being diverted to other projects and embezzled by Israeli officials and some other GE employees. Walsh smuggled evidence of the embezzlement out of Israel, into Switzerland, and then into the United States. He then delivered the information to the U.S. Department of Justice (DOJ). The DOJ proceeded with a lawsuit against the perpetrators of the fraud, including GE, and recovered a total of $59,500,000. *Was Walsh entitled to any of the proceeds?* Yes. Under the False Claims Reform Act, Walsh was awarded $13,387,500.

Exceptions Based on an Implied Contract

Some courts have held that an implied employment contract exists between the employer and the employee. If the employee is fired outside the terms of this implied contract, he or she may succeed in an action for breach of contract.

IN THE COURTROOM

Acme Corporation's employee handbook states that, as a matter of policy, workers will be dismissed only for good cause. The handbook also makes promises to employees regarding discharge procedures. Flo, an Acme employee, is aware of the promises and continues to work for Acme until she is suddenly discharged in a manner contrary to the handbook policy and procedures. *If Flo sues Acme, would a court rule in Flo's favor?* Yes, in most states. In any of those states, a court would hold that Acme's promises are part of an implied contract, which Acme violated. Acme would be liable for damages.

Public-Policy Exceptions

The most widespread common law exception to the employment-at-will doctrine is the public-policy exception. Under this rule, an employer may not fire a worker for reasons that violate a fundamental public policy of the jurisdiction. For example, an employer cannot fire a worker who serves on a jury and therefore cannot work scheduled hours. Similarly, if an employer fires an employee for refusing an order to do something illegal, in most states the firing would be held to violate public policy.

Injury, Compensation, and Safety

LEARNING OBJECTIVE NO. 3
Discussing the Protection Available to Employees Injured on the Job

Numerous state and federal statutes protect employees and their families from the risk of accidental injury, death, or disease resulting from their employment. This section discusses state workers' compensation acts and the Occupational Safety and Health Act of 1970.

State Workers' Compensation Acts

Workers' Compensation Laws
State statutes establishing an administrative procedure for compensating workers' injuries that arise on the job or in the course of their employment, regardless of fault. Instead of suing the employer, an injured worker files a claim with the administrative agency or board that administers the local workers' compensation claims.

State **workers' compensation laws** establish an administrative procedure through which employees can recover for employment-related injuries. Instead of suing, an injured worker files a claim with the administrative agency or board that administers the local workers' compensation claims.

The right to recover benefits is based on the fact that the injury was *accidental* and *occurred on the job or in the course of employment,* regardless of fault. Intentionally inflicted self-injury, for example, would not be considered accidental and hence would not be covered. If an injury occurred while an employee was commuting to or from work, it would not usually be considered to have occurred on the job or in the course of employment and hence would not be covered.

The Web site of the Occupational Safety and Health Administration (OSHA) offers information related to workplace health and safety at

http://www.osha.gov

Health and Safety Protection

At the federal level, the primary legislation for employee health and safety protection is the Occupational Safety and Health Act of 1970. The act requires that businesses be maintained free from recognized hazards.

Employees can file complaints of violations of the act with the Occupational Safety and Health Administration (OSHA), which is part of the Department of Labor. An employer cannot discharge an employee who files a complaint or who, in good faith, refuses to work in a high-risk area (if bodily harm or death might result).

Employers with eleven or more employees are required to keep occupational injury and illness records for each employee. Whenever a work-related injury or disease occurs, employers are required to make reports directly to OSHA. Whenever an employee is killed in a work-related accident, or if three or more employees are hospitalized in one accident, the Department of Labor must be notified within eight hours. Following the accident, a complete inspection of the premises is mandatory.

Retirement and Security Income

Federal and state governments participate in insurance programs to protect employees and their families by covering the financial impact of retirement, disability, death, hospitalization, and unemployment.

Old Age, Survivors, and Disability Insurance

The Social Security Act of 1935 provides for old age (retirement), survivors, and disability insurance. The act is therefore often referred to as the Old Age, Survivors, and Disability Insurance Act. Both employers and employees must "contribute" under the Federal Insurance Contributions Act (FICA) to help pay for the loss of income on retirement. The basis for the employee's contribution is the employee's annual wage base—the maximum amount of an employee's wages that are subject to the tax. Benefits are fixed by statute but increase automatically with increases in the cost of living.

Medicare

A health insurance program, Medicare is administered by the Social Security Administration for people sixty-five years of age and older and for some under age sixty-five who have disabilities. Medicare covers hospital costs and other medical expenses, such as visits to doctors' offices. Both employers and employees must "contribute" to help pay for the cost of Medicare.

PRIVATE RETIREMENT PLANS

There has been significant legislation to regulate retirement plans set up by employers to supplement Social Security benefits. The major federal act covering these retirement plans is the Employee Retirement Income Security Act (ERISA) of 1974. The Labor Management Services Administration of the Department of Labor enforces the ERISA provisions that cover individuals who operate employer-provided private pension funds.

UNEMPLOYMENT COMPENSATION

The United States has a system of unemployment insurance in which employers pay into a fund, the proceeds of which are paid out to qualified unemployed workers. The Federal Unemployment Tax Act of 1935 created a state system that provides unemployment compensation to eligible individuals. Employers that fall under the provisions of the act are taxed quarterly. Taxes are typically submitted by the employers to the states, which then deposit them with the federal government. The federal government maintains an Unemployment Insurance Fund, in which each state has an account.

Other Employment Laws

In this section, we examine important statutes governing such issues as health insurance for former employees, family and medical leave, child labor, overtime pay, minimum wages, and immigrant workers.

COBRA

The Consolidated Omnibus Budget Reconciliation Act (COBRA) of 1985 prohibits the elimination of a worker's medical, optical, or dental insurance coverage upon the voluntary or involuntary termination of the worker's employment. The ex-employees must pay the full cost of the premiums. The act includes most workers who have either lost their jobs or had their hours decreased such that they are no longer eligible for coverage under the employer's health plan. Only those workers fired for gross misconduct are excluded from protection. If the worker chooses to continue coverage, the employer is obligated to keep the policy active for up to eighteen months. If the worker is disabled, the employer must extend the coverage for up to twenty-nine months.

FAMILY AND MEDICAL LEAVE ACT

The Family and Medical Leave Act (FMLA) of 1993 requires qualifying employers to provide employees with up to twelve weeks of family or medical leave during any twelve-month period. During the employee's leave, the employer must continue the worker's health-care coverage and guarantee employment in the same position or a comparable position when the employee returns to work. An important exception to the FMLA, however, allows the employer to avoid reinstatement of a *key employee*—defined as an employee whose pay falls within the top 10 percent of the firm's work force.

The Bureau of Labor Statistics offers a wide variety of data on employment, including data on employment compensation, working conditions, and productivity. Go to

http://stats.bls.gov/blshome.html

FAIR LABOR STANDARDS ACT

The Fair Labor Standards Act (FLSA) of 1938 is concerned with child labor, maximum hours, and minimum wages.

The FLSA provides numerous restrictions on how many hours per day and per week, and in what occupations, children of different ages can work. For example, children of fourteen or fifteen years of age cannot work during school hours, for more than three hours on a school day (or eight hours on a nonschool day), for more than eighteen hours during a school week (or forty hours during a nonschool week), or before 7 A.M. or after 7 P.M. (9 P.M. during the summer).

LEARNING OBJECTIVE NO. 4
Describing the Overtime and Minimum Wage Provisions of the Fair Labor Standards Act

Any employee who works more than forty hours per week must be paid no less than one and a half times his or her regular pay for all hours over forty. Executives, administrative employees, professional employees, and outside salespersons are exempted.

A **minimum wage** of a specified amount (currently $5.15 per hour) must be paid to employees in covered industries. The term *wages* is meant to include the reasonable cost of the employer in furnishing employees with board, lodging, and other facilities if they are customarily furnished by that employer.

MINIMUM WAGE
The lowest hourly wage that an employer may legally pay an employee.

THE IMMIGRATION ACT OF 1990

The Immigration Act of 1990 limits the number of legal immigrants entering the United States by capping the number of visas (entry permits) that are issued each year. Employers recruiting workers from other countries must satisfy the Department of Labor that there is a shortage of qualified U.S. workers capable of performing the work. The employer must also establish that bringing foreign workers into this country will not adversely affect the existing labor market in the employer's particular area.

TERMS AND CONCEPTS FOR REVIEW

employment-at-will doctrine 325
minimum wage 330
whistleblower 327
workers' compensation law 328

CHAPTER SUMMARY • EMPLOYMENT LAW

Privacy Issues	The privacy rights of employees in the private sector are often established by state constitutions, legislation, or court decisions. Government employees are protected to some extent under the Fourth Amendment. Major privacy issues relate to lie-detector tests, drug testing, and electronic monitoring.
Employment at Will	Traditionally, the employment relationship has been at will—that is, the relationship could be terminated at any time for any reason by either the employer or the employee. Because of the harsh results of this doctrine for employees who are fired wrongfully, whistleblowing statutes and court decisions have limited the employment-at-will doctrine in certain circumstances.
Injury, Compensation, and Safety	**1.** *State workers' compensation acts*—Allow compensation to workers whose injuries occur on the job or in the course of their employment; regulated by a state agency or board. **2.** *Health and safety protection*—The Occupational Safety and Health Act of 1970 attempts to ensure safe and healthful working conditions for employees.
Retirement and Security Income	**1.** *Social Security*—Old age, survivors, and disability insurance provides retired or disabled employees or their families with income created by mandatory employer and employee contributions. Medicare is a health insurance program for people sixty-five years of age and older and for some under age sixty-five who are disabled. **2.** *Private retirement plans set up by employers*—These plans supplement Social Security income for retired individuals. Most plans are regulated by the Employee Retirement Income Security Act of 1974. **3.** *Unemployment compensation*—The Federal Unemployment Tax Act of 1935 created a state system that provides unemployment compensation to eligible individuals; funded by employer-paid taxes.

CHAPTER SUMMARY • *Continued*

Other Employment Laws	1. *Consolidated Omnibus Budget Reconciliation Act (COBRA) of 1985*—Prohibits the elimination of a worker's dental, medical, or optical insurance coverage on termination of the worker's employment. 2. *Family and Medical Leave Act (FMLA) of 1993*—Requires employers to provide employees with up to twelve weeks of family or medical leave during any twelve-month period. 3. *Fair Labor Standards Act (FLSA) of 1938*—Prohibits oppressive child labor, requires individuals working over forty hours a week to be paid overtime wages of no less than one and a half times the regular pay for hours worked beyond forty hours a week (with some exceptions), and provides that a minimum hourly wage rate be paid to covered employees. 4. *Immigration Act of 1990*—Limits legal immigration. Employers recruiting workers from other countries must show that (1) there is a shortage of such workers in the United States and (2) bringing the workers into this country will not affect the labor market in the employer's area.

HYPOTHETICAL QUESTIONS

26–1. Health and Safety Regulations. Denton and Carlo were employed at an appliance plant. Their job required them to do occasional maintenance work while standing on a wire mesh twenty feet above the plant floor. Other employees had fallen through the mesh, one of whom had been killed by the fall. When Denton and Carlo were asked by their supervisor to do work that would likely require them to walk on the mesh, they refused due to their fear of bodily harm or death. Because of their refusal to do the requested work, the two employees were fired from their jobs. Was their discharge wrongful? If so, under what federal employment law? To what federal agency or department should they turn for assistance?

26–2. Workers' Compensation. Galvin Strang worked for a tractor company in one of its factories. Near his work station there was a conveyor belt that ran through a large industrial oven. Sometimes, the workers would use the oven to heat their meals. Thirty-inch-high flasks containing molds were fixed at regular intervals on the conveyor and were transported into the oven. Strang had to walk between the flasks to get to his work station. One day, the conveyor was not moving, and Strang used the oven to cook a frozen pot pie. As he was removing the pot pie from the oven, the conveyor came on. One of the flasks struck Strang and seriously injured him. Strang sought recovery under the state workers' compensation law. Should he recover? Why or why not?

REAL WORLD CASE PROBLEM

26–3. Employment at Will. Robert Adams worked as a delivery truck driver for George W. Cochran & Co. Adams persistently refused to drive a truck that lacked a required inspection sticker and was subsequently fired as a result of his refusal. Adams was an at-will employee, and Cochran contended that because there was no written employment contract stating otherwise, Cochran was entitled to discharge Adams at will—that is, for cause or no cause. Adams sought to recover $7,094 in lost wages and $200,000 in damages for the "humiliation, mental anguish and emotional distress" that he had suffered as a result of being fired from his job. Under what legal doctrines discussed in this chapter—or exceptions to those doctrines—might Adams be able to recover damages from Cochran? Discuss fully. [*Adams v. George W. Cochran & Co.,* 597 A.2d 28 (D.C.App. 1991)]

For updated links to resources available on the Web, as well as a variety of other materials, visit this text's Web site at **http://blte.westbuslaw.com.**

An excellent Web site for information on employee benefits, including the full text of the FMLA, COBRA, other relevant statutes and case law, and current articles, is BenefitsLink. Go to

http://www.benefitslink.com/columns.shtml

The American Federation of Labor–Congress of Industrial Organizations (AFL–CIO) provides links to a broad variety of labor-related resources at

http://www.aflcio.org

The Occupational Safety and Health Administration (OSHA) offers information related to workplace health and safety at

http://www.osha.gov

The Bureau of Labor Statistics provides a wide variety of data on employment, including data on employment compensation, working conditions, and productivity. Go to

http://stats.bls.gov/blshome.html

The National Labor Relations Board is online at the following URL:

http://www.nlrb.gov

ONLINE LEGAL RESEARCH

Go to **http://blte.westbuslaw.com,** the Web site that accompanies this text. Select "Internet Applications," and then click on "Chapter 26." There you will find the following Internet research exercises that you can perform to learn more about employment laws and issues:

Activity 26–1: Workers' Compensation

Activity 26–2: Workplace Monitoring and Surveillance

Chapter 26 ■ WORK SET

TRUE-FALSE QUESTIONS

____ **1.** In some circumstances, the Constitution allows employers to test their employees for drugs.

____ **2.** Employment considered to be "at will" means that employers can fire employees only with good cause.

____ **3.** Employers are required by federal statute to establish health insurance and pension plans.

____ **4.** Under the FLSA, all nonexempt employees who work more than forty hours per week must be paid at least one and a half times their regular pay for all hours over forty.

____ **5.** Whistleblower statutes penalize those who report wrongdoing on the part of their employers.

____ **6.** In most states, an employer is justified in firing an employee who refuses to do something illegal.

____ **7.** Workers' compensation laws set up administrative procedures through which employees recover for work-related injuries.

____ **8.** Qualifying employers must provide employees with up to twelve weeks of family or medical leave during any twelve-month period.

____ **9.** Any employer can monitor any employee business or personal telephone conversation during working hours.

MULTIPLE-CHOICE QUESTIONS

____ **1.** Nationwide Distributors, Inc., is investigating warehouse inventory losses due to theft. Without violating employees' rights of privacy, Nationwide may

a. require warehouse employees to take polygraph tests.
b. search all employee desks and lockers without the employees' consent.
c. monitor all employee telephone conversations.
d. all of the above.

____ **2.** Fast Jack is a fast-food restaurant that employs minors. Fast Jack is subject to the federal child-labor, minimum-wage, and maximum-hour laws in

a. the Family and Medical Leave Act.
b. the Consolidated Omnibus Budget Reconciliation Act.
c. the Fair Labor Standards Act.
d. none of the above.

____ **3.** Erin, an employee of CamCorp, is injured. For Erin to receive *workers' compensation,* the injury must be

a. accidental and arise out of a preexisting disease or condition.
b. accidental and occur on the job or in the course of employment.
c. intentional and arise out of a preexisting disease or condition.
d. intentional and occur on the job or in the course of employment.

_____ **4.** U.S. Goods, Inc. (USG), recruits workers from other countries to work in its U.S. plant. To comply with the Immigration Act of 1990, USG must show that

a. there is a shortage of qualified U.S. workers to perform the work.
b. bringing aliens into the country will not adversely affect the existing labor market in that area.
c. both a and b.
d. none of the above.

_____ **5.** Ron is an employee of National Sales Company. Both Ron and National make contributions to the federal Social Security system under

a. the Federal Unemployment Tax Act.
b. the Federal Insurance Contributions Act.
c. the Employment Retirement Income Security Act.
d. none of the above.

_____ **6.** ABC Box Corporation provides health insurance for its 150 employees, including Diana. When Diana takes twelve weeks' leave to care for her new baby, she

a. can continue her heath insurance at her expense.
b. can continue her heath insurance at ABC's expense.
c. loses her heath insurance immediately on taking leave.
d. is entitled to "leave pay" equal to twelve weeks' of health insurance coverage.

_____ **7.** Mega Corporation provides health insurance for its employees. When Mega closes one of its offices and terminates the employees, the employees

a. can continue their heath insurance at their expense.
b. can continue their heath insurance at Mega's expense.
c. lose their heath insurance immediately on termination of employment.
d. are entitled to "severance pay" equal to twelve weeks' of health insurance coverage.

_____ **8.** Eagle Products, Inc., sets up a pension fund for its employees. Eagle's operation of the fund is regulated by

a. the Federal Unemployment Tax Act.
b. the Federal Insurance Contributions Act.
c. the Employment Retirement Income Security Act.
d. none of the above.

ISSUE SPOTTERS

1. American Manufacturing Company (AMC) issues an employee handbook that states employees will be discharged only for good cause. One day, Greg, an AMC supervisor, says to Larry, "I don't like your looks. You're fired." May AMC be held liable for breach of contract?

2. Workers' compensation laws establish a procedure for compensating workers who are injured on the job. Instead of suing, the worker files a claim with the appropriate state agency. Does the injury have to have been caused by the employer's negligence?

Discrimination and Labor Law

27

LEARNING OBJECTIVES

When you finish this chapter, you should be able to:

1. List the steps in a typical employment discrimination case.
2. Identify the steps in the process behind a union election.
3. Discuss issues that are appropriate for collective bargaining.
4. Describe unfair employer practices in labor-management relations.
5. List unfair union practices in labor-management relations.

FACING A LEGAL PROBLEM

Select Circuits, Inc., hires only applicants with high school diplomas. More members of minorities in the local labor market lack high school diplomas than do members of the majority. Thus, minorities are excluded from Select's work force at a substantially higher rate. Richard, a member of a minority who is refused a job because he does not have a high school diploma, charges the employer with discrimination. *What is Select's defense to the charge?*

Among the significant laws that regulate employment relationships are the statutes concerning *employment discrimination*. There are also a number of statutes that protect employees' rights to join unions and engage in collective bargaining with management to negotiate working conditions, salaries, and benefits. These rights are at the heart of all employment rights. In this chapter, we look at some of the significant laws that regulate employment discrimination and labor and management relationships.

Employment Discrimination

Employers are restricted in their ability to discriminate on the basis of race, color, religion, national origin, age, or gender. The most important statute relating to **employment discrimination** is Title VII of the Civil Rights Act of 1964.

Employment Discrimination Treating employees or job applicants unequally on the basis of race, color, gender, national origin, religion, or age; prohibited by Title VII of the Civil Rights Act of 1964 and other statutes.

Title VII of the Civil Rights Act of 1964

Title VII of the Civil Rights Act of 1964 eliminates job discrimination against employees, job applicants, and union members on the basis of race, color, national origin, religion, and sex at any stage of employment. A class of persons

PROTECTED CLASS
A class of persons with identifiable characteristics (age, color, gender, national origin, race, and religion) who historically have been discriminated against.

defined by one or more of these criteria is known as a **protected class.** Title VII applies to employers with fifteen or more employees, labor unions with fifteen or more members, labor unions that operate hiring halls (to which members go regularly to get jobs as they become available), employment agencies, and state and local governing units or agencies. A special section of Title VII forbids discrimination in most federal government employment.

Compliance with Title VII is monitored by the Equal Employment Opportunity Commission (EEOC). Before filing a lawsuit, a victim must file a claim with the EEOC, which investigates the facts and seeks to achieve a voluntary settlement between the employer and employee. If a settlement does not occur, the EEOC may sue the employer. If the EEOC chooses not to sue—for example, if it does not believe that the complaining individual was discriminated against—the victim may bring his or her own lawsuit.

Employer liability may be extensive. If the plaintiff proves that unlawful discrimination occurred, he or she may be awarded reinstatement, back pay, retroactive promotions (promotions that the plaintiff would have received but for the discrimination), and damages.

LEARNING OBJECTIVE NO. 1
Listing the Steps in a Typical Employment Discrimination Case

DISPARATE-TREATMENT DISCRIMINATION
In an employment context, intentional discrimination against individuals on the basis of color, gender, national origin, race, or religion.

***PRIMA FACIE* CASE**
A case in which the plaintiff has produced sufficient evidence to compel his or her conclusion if the defendant produces no evidence to rebut it.

DISPARATE-IMPACT DISCRIMINATION
In an employment context, discrimination that results from certain employer practices or procedures that, although not discriminatory on their face, have a discriminatory effect.

BUSINESS NECESSITY DEFENSE
A showing that an employment practice that discriminates against members of a protected class is related to job performance.

BONA FIDE OCCUPATIONAL QUALIFICATION (BFOQ)
Under Title VII of the Civil Rights Act of 1964, identifiable characteristics reasonably necessary to the normal operation of a particular business. These characteristics can include gender, national origin, and religion, but not race.

Intentional versus Unintentional Discrimination. Title VII prohibits both intentional and unintentional discrimination. Intentional discrimination by an employer against an employee is known as **disparate-treatment discrimination.** Suppose that a woman applies for employment with a construction firm and is rejected. If she sues on the basis of disparate-treatment discrimination in hiring, she must show that (1) she is a member of a protected class, (2) she applied and was qualified for the job in question, (3) she was rejected by the employer, and (4) the employer continued to seek applicants for the position or filled the position with a person not in a protected class. If she can meet these requirements, she makes out a ***prima facie* case** of illegal discrimination.

Disparate-impact discrimination occurs when, as a result of educational or other job requirements or hiring procedures, an employer's work force does not reflect the same percentage of nonwhites, women, or members of other protected classes that characterizes qualified individuals in the local labor market. If a person challenging an employment practice having a discriminatory effect can show a connection between the practice and the disparity, he or she makes out a *prima facie* case. No evidence of discriminatory intent is necessary. Disparate-impact discrimination can also occur when an educational or other job requirement or hiring procedure excludes members of a protected class from an employer's work force at a substantially higher rate than nonmembers.

Defenses. An employer may use certain defenses to justify a discriminatory practice. For example, an employer may offer a good business reason for a practice that has a discriminatory effect. This is the **business necessity defense.**

In the legal problem set out at the beginning of this chapter, Select Circuits, Inc., hires only applicants with high school diplomas, which, under conditions in the local labor market, has the effect of excluding minorities from Select's work force. Richard, a member of a minority who is refused a job at Select because he does not have a diploma, sues Select, charging discrimination. *What is Select's defense to the charge?* Select might argue that a high school education is required for workers to perform the job at a certain level of competence. Is this defense valid? If Select can prove that there exists a definite connection between a high school education and job performance, then Select may succeed.

Another defense applies when discrimination against a protected class is essential to a job—that is, when a particular trait is a **bona fide occupational qualification (BFOQ).** For example, a men's fashion magazine might legitimately hire only male models. Race can never be a BFOQ. The defense applies only to the traits of other protected classes.

A third defense protects **seniority systems.** If a present intent to discriminate is not shown, and promotions or other job benefits are distributed according to the length of time each employee has worked for the employer, the employer has a defense against a discrimination suit.

SENIORITY SYSTEM
In regard to employment relationships, a system in which those who have worked longest for the company are first in line for promotions, salary increases, and other benefits; they are also the last to be laid off if the work force must be reduced.

AGE DISCRIMINATION

Age discrimination is potentially the most widespread form of discrimination because anyone—regardless of race, color, national origin, or gender—could be a victim at some point in life. The Age Discrimination in Employment Act (ADEA) of 1967 prohibits employment discrimination on the basis of age against individuals forty years of age or older. An amendment to the act prohibits mandatory retirement for nonmanagerial workers. For the act to apply, an employer must have twenty or more employees. The ADEA is similar to Title VII in that it offers protection against both intentional (disparate-treatment) age discrimination and unintentional (disparate-impact) age discrimination.

To make out a *prima facie* case, a plaintiff must show that he or she was forty or older, that he or she was qualified for the job, and that he or she was discharged or otherwise rejected in circumstances that imply discrimination.

IN THE COURTROOM

A fifty-four-year-old manager of a plant who earned approximately $15.75 an hour was temporarily laid off when the plant was closed for the winter. When spring came, the manager was replaced by a forty-three-year-old worker who earned approximately $8.05 an hour. The older manager, who had worked for the firm for twenty-seven years, was given no opportunity to accept a lower wage rate or otherwise accommodate the firm's need to reduce costs. *Did this dismissal violate the ADEA?* Yes. In the older manager's suit against the employer, the court referred to the firm's dismissal of the manager as an exercise in "industrial capital punishment."

DISCRIMINATION BASED ON DISABILITY

The Americans with Disabilities Act (ADA) of 1990 was designed to eliminate discriminatory hiring and firing practices that prevent otherwise qualified persons with disabilities from fully participating in the national labor force. The ADA defines persons with disabilities as persons with a physical or mental impairment that "substantially limits" their everyday activities. Such disabilities include heart disease, cancer, muscular dystrophy, cerebral palsy, paraplegia, diabetes, and acquired immune-deficiency syndrome (AIDS). Excluded are such conditions as kleptomania.

Employers should make sure that the ways in which they advertise, word their job applications, and conduct job interviews meet the EEOC's guidelines.

An employer does not have to hire unqualified applicants who have disabilities. An applicant is not unqualified, however, simply because the employer may have to make some reasonable accommodations. Reasonable accommodations include installing ramps for a wheelchair, establishing more flexible working hours, creating new job assignments, and creating or improving training procedures. Such accommodations can be avoided only if they will cause "undue hardship."

Persons with disabilities who wish to file a claim under the ADA may sue for many of the same remedies available under Title VII. They may seek reinstatement, back pay, compensatory and punitive damages (for intentional discrimination), and other relief. Such actions may be commenced only after the plaintiff has pursued the claim through the Equal Employment Opportunity Commission.

State Laws Prohibiting Employment Discrimination

Most states prohibit employment discrimination. Generally, the kinds of discrimination prohibited under federal legislation are also prohibited by state laws. In addition, state statutes often provide protection for individuals who are not protected from discrimination under federal law (for example, gay men and lesbians who are not protected under federal law from discrimination on the basis of their sexual orientation).

Federal Labor Law

Most of the early legislation to protect employees focused on the rights of workers to join unions and to engage in collective bargaining.

Norris-LaGuardia Act

Congress protected peaceful strikes, picketing, and boycotts in 1932 with the Norris-LaGuardia Act. The act restricted federal courts in their power to issue injunctions against unions engaged in peaceful strikes. In effect, this act declared a national policy permitting employees to organize.

National Labor Relations Act

The National Labor Relations Act (NLRA) of 1935, also called the Wagner Act, established the rights of employees to form unions, to negotiate with employers over employment conditions, and to strike.

The act also created the National Labor Relations Board (NLRB) to oversee union elections and to prevent employers from engaging in unfair labor union activities and unfair labor practices. The NLRB has the power to investigate, issue, and serve complaints against employers in response to employee charges of unfair labor practices. The NLRB can issue cease-and-desist orders (which prohibit a firm from continuing the practice) when violations are found. These orders can be enforced by a federal court of appeals, if necessary.

Labor-Management Relations Act

The Labor-Management Relations Act (LMRA, or the Taft-Hartley Act) of 1947 was passed to proscribe certain union practices. The act contained provisions protecting employers as well as employees. It provided a detailed list of unfair labor activities that unions, as well as management, were forbidden to practice. In addition, the law gave the president the authority to intervene in labor disputes and to delay strikes that would "imperil the national health or safety."

An important provision outlawed the **closed shop**—a firm that requires union membership of its workers as a condition of obtaining employment. The act preserved the legality of the **union shop,** which does not require membership as a prerequisite for employment but can, and usually does, require that workers join the union after a specified amount of time on the job. The act also allowed individual states to pass their own **right-to-work laws**—laws making it illegal for union membership to be required for *continued* employment in any establishment. Thus, union shops are technically illegal in states with right-to-work laws.

Closed Shop
A firm that requires union membership by its workers as a condition of employment. The closed shop was made illegal by the Taft-Hartley Act of 1947.

Union Shop
A place of employment in which all workers, once employed, must become union members within a specified period of time as a condition of their continued employment.

Right-to-Work Law
State law generally providing that employees are not to be required to join a union as a condition of receiving or retaining employment.

Labor-Management Reporting and Disclosure Act

The Labor-Management Reporting and Disclosure Act of 1959 (the Landrum-Griffin Act) established an employee bill of rights and reporting requirements for union activities to prevent corruption. The act strictly regulated internal union business procedures, such as elections for union officers.

Union Organizing

LEARNING OBJECTIVE NO. 2

Identifying the Steps in the Process behind a Union Election

Nearly every union begins with a decision by some of the workers in a factory or office to form some sort of bargaining unit to negotiate with the employer over the terms and conditions of employment. A union representative must then determine the extent of support for a union.

Gauging Worker Support

The extent to which workers favor the establishment of a union to represent them is determined by how many of them sign **authorization cards.** These cards give an organizer some idea of the number of workers who desire union representation. The cards also indicate whether a union election can be won. If 30 percent of the workers sign the cards, they are presented to the NLRB with a petition for a vote.

Authorization Card
A card signed by an employee that gives a union permission to act on his or her behalf in negotiations with management once a majority of the employees have signed the cards.

IN THE COURTROOM

The International Order of Lumber Cutters (IOLC) union representative obtains authorization cards from a majority of the Northwest Lumber Yard employees. The IOLC asks Northwest to recognize the union, but Northwest refuses. *What should the IOLC do next?* The IOLC should submit the cards, with a petition calling for an election, to the nearest office of the National Labor Relations Board.

Determining the Appropriate Bargaining Unit

The NLRB determines whether an election will result in the formation of an **appropriate bargaining unit.** The NLRB considers whether the skills, tasks, and job classifications of the workers are sufficiently similar so that all of the members of the proposed bargaining unit can be adequately served by a single negotiating position. Also, the NLRB must verify that the proposed bargaining unit does not include persons who are part of management. If the NLRB decides that the proposed bargaining unit is appropriate, then it will order an election.

Appropriate Bargaining Unit
A group of employees defined by their job duties, skill levels, and other occupational characteristics and covered by a collective bargaining agreement.

Conducting a Union Election

The workers vote using secret ballots to ensure that the election accurately reflects their sentiments. The NLRB makes sure that the election is conducted in a lawful manner and that only those persons who are eligible to vote participate in the election. If these conditions are satisfied and a majority of the workers vote in favor of the union, then the NLRB will certify the union as the representative of the workers for purposes of collective bargaining. If the union does not win the election, the union will not be recognized.

Because management has a genuine interest in regulating employee conduct in the workplace, it may legally limit union activities, as long as the limitations can be justified by legitimate business considerations.

IN THE COURTROOM

A union believes that during its campaign to become the representative for the employees of Bogle Products, Inc., it needs to give the workers hour-long on-site pep talks every day during business hours to ensure maximum participation in the election. *Can Bogle lawfully refuse to permit the talks?* Yes. Such meetings would be too time consuming and would greatly disrupt production. Of course, the workers can meet with the union off-site on their own time as often as they wish.

NONDISCRIMINATION RULE
The requirement that an employer treat a union the same way it would treat any other entity with regard to on-site contact with workers.

The ability of employers to regulate union presence on the premises is restricted by the **nondiscrimination rule.** This rule requires that an employer treat a union the same way it would treat any other entity with regard to on-site contact with workers. The employer can lawfully prohibit on-site solicitations by any third party. It cannot discriminate against union organizers by refusing them access to workers while permitting other groups (such as charities) to solicit the same workers.

If the NLRB decides that the employer engaged in any unfair labor practices to influence the outcome of the election, then the NLRB may invalidate the outcome and certify the union as the appropriate representative, even if it does not obtain a majority vote.

Collective Bargaining

After the NLRB certifies the union, the union's local office will be authorized to negotiate with management on behalf of the workers in the bargaining unit. The process of **collective bargaining** (the process by which labor and management negotiate the terms and conditions of employment) is at the heart of the federal labor laws.

COLLECTIVE BARGAINING
The process by which labor and management negotiate the terms and conditions of employment, including such things as hours and workplace conditions.

LEARNING OBJECTIVE NO. 3
Discussing Issues That Are Appropriate for Collective Bargaining

NEGOTIATING TERMS AND CONDITIONS

Wages, hours of work, and certain other conditions of employment may be discussed during collective bargaining sessions. The subjects for negotiation include workplace safety, employee discounts, health-care plans, pension funds, and apprentice programs. Other subjects that may be raised include the establishment of college scholarship programs for the children of workers and the adoption of new technologies on the factory floor. The employer is not obligated to bargain over these issues. It may choose, however, to discuss some of these subjects to obtain concessions from the union on other subjects, such as overtime pay or pension-plan benefits.

Some demands are illegal in collective bargaining. Management need not bargain over a provision that would be illegal if it were included in a contract. Thus, if a union presents a demand for **featherbedding** (the hiring of unnecessary workers) or for an unlawful closed shop, management need not respond to these demands.

FEATHERBEDDING
Requiring the employment of more workers than necessary to do a particular job.

Management need not bargain over a decision to shut down certain facilities. It must bargain, however, over the economic consequences of this decision. Thus, issues such as **severance pay** (pay given to an employee on his or her termination) in the event of plant shutdown or rights of transfer to other plants are considered mandatory subjects of collective bargaining.

SEVERANCE PAY
Funds in excess of normal wages or salary paid to an employee on termination of his or her employment.

GOOD FAITH

The site of the American Federation of Labor–Congress of Industrial Organizations (AFL-CIO) provides links to a broad variety of labor-related resources. Go to

http://www.aflcio.org

Once an employer and the union sit down at the conference table, they must negotiate in good faith and make a reasonable effort to come to an agreement. They are not obligated to reach an agreement. Instead, they must approach the negotiations with the idea that an agreement is possible. Both parties may engage in hard bargaining with each other, but the bargaining process itself must be geared to reaching a compromise—not avoiding a compromise.

A party's actions may be used to evaluate the party's good or bad faith. Obviously, the employer must be willing to meet with union representatives. Excessive delaying tactics may be proof of bad faith, as is insistence on obviously unreasonable contract terms. The following additional actions constitute bad faith in bargaining:

- Rejecting a proposal without offering a counterproposal.
- Engaging in a campaign among workers to undermine the union.
- Unilaterally changing wages or terms and conditions of employment during the bargaining process.
- Constantly shifting positions on disputed contract terms.
- Sending bargainers who lack authority to commit the company to a contract.

Strikes

Sometimes a union and an employer may approach the bargaining table in good faith but simply be unable to reach an agreement because of genuine differences of opinion. If the parties are deadlocked, then the union may call a strike against the employer. Once the workers approve the plan to strike, then their services will no longer be available to the employer. Of course, an employer is not obligated to pay striking workers.

The right to strike is of fundamental importance to the collective bargaining process, because it is a threat that the union can use to offset the disparity in bargaining power between management and labor. Strikes are protected by the U.S. Constitution, under the commerce clause. Workers who are not involved in the strike also have the right to refuse to cross a **picket line** (strikers and other persons lined up outside the workplace protesting and attempting to discourage others from entering the workplace).

PICKET LINE
The presence at an employer's work site of employees or others to publicize a labor dispute and deter others from working for or doing business with the employer. Usually involves patrolling with signs.

ILLEGAL STRIKES

Violent strikes (including the threat of violence) are illegal. If the strikers form a massed barrier and deny management or other nonunion workers access to the plant, the strike is illegal. Similarly, "sitdown" strikes, in which employees simply stay in the plant without working, are illegal.

Secondary Boycotts. Strikers are not permitted to engage in **secondary boycotts** by picketing the suppliers and customers of the employer. These parties have no dispute with the striking workers and should not be penalized merely because they do business with the employer.

SECONDARY BOYCOTT
A union's refusal to work for, purchase from, or handle the products of a secondary employer, with whom the union has no dispute, with the object of forcing that employer to stop doing business with the primary employer, with whom the union has a labor dispute.

IN THE COURTROOM

The Association of Cannery Workers (ACW) is striking against the Nature Maid Company. *Can the ACW picket the farmers from whom Nature Maid buys the crops for its canned goods?* No. The union would be engaging in a secondary boycott if it picketed the farmers.

Common Situs Picketing. A union may picket a site occupied by both the primary employer (the object of the strike, such as a subcontractor) and a secondary employer (such as a general contractor), called **common situs picketing.** The strike can be directed against the primary employer only. A strike against a secondary employer is illegal.

COMMON SITUS PICKETING
A demonstration at a secondary employer's work site by workers involved in a labor dispute with a primary employer.

Hot-Cargo Agreements. Agreements in which employers voluntarily agree with unions not to handle, use, or deal in the non-union-produced goods of other employers—**hot-cargo agreements**—are illegal. Thus, unions and employees cannot coerce an employer's business customers into agreeing not to do business with the employer.

HOT-CARGO AGREEMENT
An illegal agreement in which employers voluntarily agree with unions not to handle, use, or deal in non-union-produced goods of other employers.

IN THE COURTROOM

The International Semiconductors Assembly Workers Union (ISAWU) is on strike against SemiCo, a leading manufacturer of semiconductors. The ISAWU wants to pressure computer manufacturers to stop buying SemiCo products. *If the manufacturers agree with the ISAWU not to buy SemiCo products, could the union be held liable to SemiCo?* Yes. The agreement between the union and the manufacturers would constitute a hot-cargo agreement. If SemiCo could no longer find outlets for its products, then it would be able to sue the union for any damages resulting from the boycott.

WILDCAT STRIKE
A strike that is not authorized by the union that represents the striking workers.

Wildcat Strikes. A **wildcat strike** occurs when a minority of union members, without the authorization of the union itself, go out on strike against an employer. Because the strike is not authorized, it is illegal. In general, a union is not liable for damages caused by wildcat strikes unless the union is contractually obligated in the collective bargaining agreement to pay for damages resulting from such strikes.

HIRING REPLACEMENT WORKERS

ECONOMIC STRIKE
A strike called by a union to pressure an employer to make concessions relating to hours, wages, or other terms of employment.

If a strike goes on for several weeks and management finds that it is unable to maintain the production schedules needed to fulfill existing orders, then it may decide to hire replacement workers to fill the positions vacated by the strikers. An employer may hire *permanent* replacement workers only if the dispute is an **economic strike** called by the union to pressure the employer to make concessions on wages, hours, or other terms of employment. An employer may hire *temporary* replacement workers during any strike.

LOCKOUTS

LOCKOUT
The closing of a workplace to employees by an employer to gain an advantage in collective bargaining negotiations.

Lockouts are the employer's counterpart to the worker's right to strike. A **lockout** occurs when the employer shuts down to prevent employees from working. Lockouts are usually used when the employer believes that a strike is imminent. Some lockouts are illegal. An employer may not use a lockout as a tool to pressure employees into quitting a union. Consequently, an employer must show some economic justification for instituting a lockout.

Employer Unfair Labor Practices

LEARNING OBJECTIVE NO. 4
Describing Unfair Employer Practices in Labor-Management Relations

The preceding sections have discussed unfair labor practices that take place during union elections, collective bargaining, and strikes. Many unfair labor practices may occur in other employment-related contexts. The most significant of these practices—an employer's refusal to recognize and negotiate with a union, an employer's interference in union activities, and an employer's discrimination against union members—are discussed here.

EMPLOYER'S REFUSAL TO RECOGNIZE AND NEGOTIATE

Failure of an employer to recognize and bargain in good faith with the union over issues affecting all employees in the bargaining unit is an unfair labor practice. If the union loses the majority support of those it represents, however, an employer is not obligated to continue recognition of the union.

Employer's Interference in Union Activities

It is an unfair labor practice for an employer to interfere with, restrain, or coerce employees in the exercise of their rights to form a union and bargain collectively. Unlawful employer interference may take a variety of forms.

It is an unfair practice for an employer to make threats that may interfere with an employee's decision to join a union. Even asking employees about their views on the union may be considered coercive. Employees responding to such questioning must be able to remain anonymous and must receive assurances against employer reprisals.

Employers also may not prohibit certain forms of union activity in the workplace. If an employee has a grievance with the company, for example, the employer cannot prevent the union's participation in support of the employee. If an employer has unlawfully interfered with the operation of a union, the NLRB or a court may issue a cease-and-desist order halting the practice.

BUSINESS TIP

One way to increase productivity and improve product quality is to ask employees for their input into the firm's decision-making process.

Discrimination

Employers cannot discriminate against workers because they are union officers or are otherwise associated with a union. When workers must be laid off, the company cannot consider union participation as a criterion for deciding whom to fire.

The decision to close a facility is generally within the discretion of management. Even this decision, however, cannot be made with a discriminatory motive. If a company has several facilities and only one is unionized, the company cannot shut down the union plant simply because of the union. The company could shut down the union plant if it were demonstrably less efficient than the other facilities, however.

Union Unfair Labor Practices

Certain union activities are unfair labor practices. Secondary boycotts, previously discussed, are one such union unfair labor practice. Others include those discussed here.

A significant union unfair labor practice is using coercion or restraint to influence an employee's decision to participate (or not participate) in union activities. Thus, it is unlawful for a union to threaten an employee or a family with violence, or with the loss of a job, for failure to join the union.

LEARNING OBJECTIVE NO. 5

Listing Unfair Union Practices in Labor-Management Relations

Unions have the authority to regulate their own internal affairs, which includes disciplining union members. This discipline, however, cannot be used to coerce workers to, for example, unanimously support a strike with which they do not all agree.

IN THE COURTROOM

A disaffected union member feels that the union is no longer providing proper representation for employees and starts a campaign to decertify the union. *What can the union do?* The union may expel the employee from membership but may not fine or otherwise discipline the worker.

Still another significant union unfair labor practice is discrimination. A union may not discriminate against workers because they refuse to join the union. Furthermore, a union may not use its influence to cause an employer to discriminate against workers who refuse to join the union. A union cannot force an employer to deny promotions to workers who fail to join the union.

TERMS AND CONCEPTS FOR REVIEW

CHAPTER SUMMARY • DISCRIMINATION AND LABOR LAW

Employment Discrimination	**1.** *Title VII of the Civil Rights Act (1964)*—Prohibits discrimination by most employers, labor unions, employment agencies, and state and local governments against employees, job applicants, and union members on the basis of race, color, national origin, religion, or gender. **a.** Both intentional (disparate-treatment) discrimination and unintentional (disparate-impact) discrimination are prohibited. **b.** As defenses, employers may assert that discrimination was required for reasons of business necessity, to meet a bona fide occupational qualification (BFOQ), or to maintain a legitimate seniority system. **2.** *Age Discrimination in Employment Act (1967)*—Prohibits discrimination on the basis of age against employees or job applicants aged forty or older. **3.** *Americans with Disabilities Act (1990)*—Prohibits discrimination on the basis of disability against individuals qualified for a given job. Employers must reasonably accommodate the needs of persons with disabilities. **4.** *State laws*—Most states have statutes or regulations prohibiting employment discrimination; often, in terms of the protections they offer, these laws are broader in scope than federal legislation.
Federal Labor Laws	**1.** *Norris-LaGuardia Act of 1932*—Permits employees to organize into unions and engage in peaceful strikes. **2.** *National Labor Relations Act of 1935*—Established the rights of employees to engage in collective bargaining and to strike. Created the National Labor Relations Board (NLRB). **3.** *Labor-Management Relations Act of 1947*—Listed unfair labor practices. **4.** *Labor Management Reporting and Disclosure Act of 1959*—Regulates internal union procedures and established reporting requirements for union activities.
Union Organizing	**1.** *Authorization cards*—Before beginning an organizing effort, a union will attempt to assess worker support for unionization by obtaining signed authorization cards from the employees. **2.** *Appropriate bargaining unit*—The National Labor Relations Board (NLRB) determines whether workers constitute an appropriate bargaining unit, so that they can be adequately served by a single negotiating position. **3.** *Union election campaign*—The NLRB monitors union elections. During an election campaign, the employer must treat the union in the same way it would treat any other entity having on-site contact with its workers. **4.** *Union certification*—Certification by the NLRB means that the union is the exclusive representative of a bargaining unit and that the employer must recognize the union.

CHAPTER SUMMARY • *Continued*

Collective Bargaining	Topics such as wages, hours of work, and other conditions of employment may be discussed during collective bargaining sessions. Some demands, such as a demand for featherbedding or for a closed shop, are illegal. The parties must bargain in good faith. If the parties reach an impasse, the union may call a strike against the employer.
Strikes	**1.** *Right to strike*—The right to strike is protected by the U.S. Constitution. **2.** *Secondary boycott*—Strikers are not permitted to engage in a secondary boycott by picketing the suppliers of an employer. Strikers are not permitted to coerce the employer's customers into agreeing not to do business with it. **3.** *Wildcat strike*—A wildcat strike occurs when a small group of union members engage in a strike against the employer without the permission of the union. **4.** *Replacement workers*—An employer may hire permanent replacement employees in the event of an economic strike. During other strikes, an employer may hire temporary replacement workers. **5.** *Lockouts*—Employers may respond to threatened employee strikes by shutting down the plant altogether to prevent employees from working.
Unfair Labor Practices	**1.** *Employer unfair labor practices*— **a.** Refusal to recognize and bargain with a union. **b.** Interference in union activities. **c.** Discrimination against union members. **2.** *Union unfair labor practices*— **a.** Secondary boycotts. **b.** Coercion or restraint to influence an employee's decision to participate (or not participate) in union activities. **c.** Discrimination against workers who refuse to join a union.

HYPOTHETICAL QUESTIONS

27–1. Disparate-Impact Discrimination. Chinawa, a major processor of cheese sold throughout the United States, employs one hundred workers at its principal processing plant. The plant is located in Heartland Corners, which has a population that is 50 percent white and 25 percent African American, with the balance Hispanic American, Asian American, and others. Chinawa requires a high school diploma as a condition of employment for its cleaning crew. Three-fourths of the white population complete high school, compared with only one-fourth of those in minority groups. Chinawa has an all-white cleaning crew. Has Chinawa violated Title VII of the Civil Rights Act of 1964? Explain.

27–2. Unfair Labor Practices. Suppose that Consolidated Stores is undergoing a unionization campaign. Prior to the union election, management says that the union is unnecessary to protect workers. Management also provides bonuses and wage increases to the workers during this period. The employees reject the union. Union organizers protest that the wage increases during the election campaign unfairly prejudiced the vote. Should these wage increases be regarded as an unfair labor practice? Discuss.

REAL WORLD CASE PROBLEM

27–3. Good Faith Bargaining. American Commercial Barge Line Co. was an affiliation made up of a number of barge and towing companies. The Seafarers International Union of North America (SIU) represented workers for Inland Tugs (IT), a separate corporate division of American Commercial Barge Line. When SIU and IT began negotiating a new collective bargaining agreement, SIU demanded that the bargaining unit include all the employees of American Commercial Barge Line. SIU also demanded that any contract include a pledge by other American Commercial Barge Line companies to continue their contributions to SIU funds, which provided for union activities. Unable to agree on these issues, the parties continued to meet for several years. Meanwhile, on the basis of an employee poll, IT changed its system of calculating wages. SIU filed a complaint with the NLRB, claiming that these changes were an unfair labor practice. IT responded that SIU was not bargaining in good faith. How should the NLRB rule? Explain. [*Inland Tugs, A Division of American Commercial Barge Line Co. v. NLRB,* 918 F.2d 1299 (7th Cir. 1990)]

For updated links to resources available on the Web, as well as a variety of other materials, visit this text's Web site at **http://blte.westbuslaw.com**.

The law firm of Arent Fox posts articles on current issues in the area of employment law, including sexual harassment, on its Web site at

http://www.arentfox.com

An abundance of helpful information on disability-based discrimination, including the text of the Americans with Disabilities Act of 1990, can be found at the following Web site:

http://janweb.icdi.wvu.edu/kinder

An excellent source for information on various forms of employment discrimination is the Equal Employment Opportunity Commission's Web site at

http://www.eeoc.gov

ONLINE LEGAL RESEARCH

Go to **http://blte.westbuslaw.com**, the Web site that accompanies this text. Select "Internet Applications," and then click on "Chapter 27." There you will find the following Internet research exercises that you can perform to learn more about laws prohibiting employment discrimination:

Activity 27–1: Americans with Disabilities

Activity 27–2: Equal Employment Opportunity

Chapter 27 ■ WORK SET

TRUE-FALSE QUESTIONS

_____ **1.** Employers can agree with unions not to handle, use, or deal in non-union-produced goods.

_____ **2.** Management serves as the representative of workers in bargaining with the union over the rights of employees.

_____ **3.** Peaceful strikes, picketing, and boycotts are protected under federal law.

_____ **4.** Employees have no right to engage in collective bargaining through elected representatives.

_____ **5.** Discrimination complaints under federal law must be filed with the Equal Opportunity Employment Commission.

_____ **6.** All employers are subject to Title VII of the Civil Rights Act of 1964 regardless of the number of their employees.

_____ **7.** Disparate-treatment discrimination occurs when an employer intentionally discriminates against an employee.

MULTIPLE-CHOICE QUESTIONS

_____ **1.** Don works for American Tools Company. Don and other employees designate the National Machinists Union (NMU) as their bargaining representative. Without violating federal labor law, American Tools can

a. refuse to bargain with NMU.
b. fire Don for "choosing the wrong side."
c. both a and b.
d. none of the above.

_____ **2.** Assembly Workers Union (AWU) represents the employees of National Manufacturing, Inc. When AWU calls an economic strike, National Manufacturing hires replacement workers. After the strike

a. the former strikers must be rehired.
b. the replacement workers must be fired.
c. both a and b.
d. none of the above.

_____ **3.** Tina believes that she has been discriminated against on the job because she is a woman. She attempts to resolve the dispute with her employer, who decides that her claim has no basis. Tina's next best step is to

a. file a lawsuit.
b. secretly sabotage company operations for revenge.
c. ask the Equal Opportunity Employment Commission whether a claim is justified.
d. forget about the matter.

_____ **4.** Janet, who is hearing impaired, applies for a position with Alpha Company. Janet is qualified but is refused the job because, she is told, "We can't afford to accommodate you with an interpreter." If Janet sues Alpha, she will

a. win, if Alpha has installed ramps for disabled persons.
b. win, if an interpreter would be a "reasonable accommodation."
c. lose, if she is not more than forty years old.
d. lose, if Alpha has never done anything to accommodate any disabled person.

_____ **5.** Digital Software, Inc., prefers to hire Asian Americans, because, according to its personnel director, "they're smarter and work harder" than other minorities. Showing a preference for one minority over another is prohibited by

a. Title VII of the Civil Rights Act of 1964.
b. the Age Discrimination in Employment Act of 1967.
c. the Americans with Disabilities Act of 1990.
d. none of the above.

_____ **6.** Eagle Sales, Inc., requires that all its secretaries be able to type. Alice, a member of a minority, applies to Eagle for a secretarial job. She cannot type but tells Eagle that she is willing to learn. When Eagle does not hire her, she sues. She will

a. win, if Eagle's work force does not reflect the same percentage of members of a protected class that characterizes qualified individuals in the local labor market.
b. win, because she was willing to learn and an employer is obligated to hire and train unqualified minority employees.
c. lose, because in this case being a member of the majority is a BFOQ.
d. lose, because Eagle has a valid business necessity defense.

_____ **7.** U.S. Tech, Inc., fires Mike. He believes that he was discriminated against because of his age. To bring a suit based on age discrimination, Mike must show that he

a. is forty or older and qualified for the job.
b. was discharged in circumstances that imply discrimination.
c. both a and b.
d. none of the above.

_____ **8.** National Mining Company requires job applicants to pass certain physical tests. Only a few women who apply to work for National can pass the tests, but if they pass, they are hired. National's best defense in a suit charging that the tests discriminate against women would be that

a. gender is a BFOQ.
b. some men cannot pass the tests.
c. any discrimination is not intentional.
d. passing the tests is a business necessity.

ISSUE SPOTTERS

1. Bob, an employee of Nationwide Products Company, is a vocal union advocate. When workers must be laid off, Nationwide fires Bob, using his union participation as a criterion. Is this legal?

2. Lani, a member of a minority, learns of a job opening at Alpha Engineering for which she is well-qualified. She applies for the job but is rejected. Alpha continues to seek applicants for the position and eventually fills the position with a person who is not a member of a minority. Could Lani succeed in a suit against Alpha for discrimination?

UNIT SIX
BUSINESS ORGANIZATIONS

UNIT OUTLINE

28 Sole Proprietorships, Partnerships, and Limited Liability Companies

LEARNING OBJECTIVES

When you finish this chapter, you should be able to:

1. State the advantages of doing business as a sole proprietorship.
2. Identify the essential elements of a partnership.
3. Discuss differences between general and limited partnerships.
4. Outline the advantages of limited liability companies.

FACING A LEGAL PROBLEM

West and Burke own a piece of rural land, which they lease to a farmer. West and Burke share the profits from the farming operation with the farmer, in lieu of rental payments, but only the farmer pays for the losses. *Are West, Burke, and the farmer partners?*

One of the questions faced by anyone who wishes to start up a business is what form of business organization to choose. The options include a sole proprietorship, a partnership, a limited liability company, and a corporation. In this chapter, we examine the features of sole proprietorships, partnerships, and limited liability companies. The corporation is discussed in detail in Chapters 29 and 30.

SOLE PROPRIETORSHIP
The simplest form of business, in which the owner is the business. A sole proprietor reports business income on his or her personal income tax return and is legally responsible for all debts of the business.

Sole Proprietorships

The simplest form of business is a **sole proprietorship.** In this form, the owner is the business. Anyone who does business without creating an organization has a sole proprietorship. Sole proprietorships constitute over two-thirds of all American businesses, from informal home offices to large construction firms.

LEARNING OBJECTIVE NO. 1
Stating the Advantages of Doing Business As a Sole Proprietorship

ADVANTAGES OF SOLE PROPRIETORSHIPS

A major advantage of the sole proprietorship is that the proprietor (owner) receives all the profits. In addition, it is often easier and less costly to start a sole proprietorship than to start any other kind of business, because few legal forms are involved. The sole proprietor is free to make any decision he or she wishes concerning the business—whom to hire, what kind of business to pursue, and so on. A sole proprietor pays only personal income taxes on profits. Sole proprietors can establish tax-exempt retirement accounts.

DISADVANTAGES OF SOLE PROPRIETORSHIPS

The major disadvantage of the sole proprietorship is that, as sole owner, the proprietor alone bears the burden of all liabilities incurred by the business. Another disadvantage is that the proprietor's opportunity to raise capital is limited to personal funds and the funds of those who are willing to make loans. A sole proprietorship also lacks the continuity of business on the death of the proprietor. When the owner dies, the business is automatically dissolved. If the business is transferred to family members or other heirs, a new sole proprietorship is created.

Partnerships

A **partnership** arises from an agreement, express or implied, between two or more persons to carry on a business for profit. A partnership is based on a voluntary contract between two or more competent persons who agree to place money, labor, and skill in a business with the understanding that profits and losses will be proportionately shared.

PARTNERSHIP
An association of two or more persons to carry on, as co-owners, a business for profit.

There are two basic types of partnerships: *general* partnerships and *limited* partnerships. In this section and in the following sections, we discuss general partnerships. We use the term *partnership* to refer to a general partnership. Limited partnerships are discussed later in this chapter.

Agency law (see Chapter 25) governs relationships arising in partnerships. In one important way, however, partnerships are distinct from agency relationships. In a nonpartnership agency relationship, the agent usually does not have an ownership interest in the business, nor is he or she obliged to bear a portion of the ordinary business losses.

The Uniform Partnership Act (UPA) governs the operation of partnerships *in the absence of a different agreement among the partners.* Except for Louisiana, the UPA has been adopted in all of the states and the District of Columbia.

ELEMENTS OF A PARTNERSHIP

LEARNING OBJECTIVE NO. 2
Identifying the Essential Elements of a Partnership

There are three essential elements to a partnership:

1. A sharing of profits and losses.
2. A joint ownership of the business.
3. An equal right in the management of the business.

The sharing of profits and losses from a business is considered *prima facie* (on the face of it) evidence that a partnership has been created. No such inference is made, however, if the profits were received as interest on a loan, as wages of an employee, as rent to a landlord, or from the sale of a business. Similarly, joint ownership of property does not in and of itself create a partnership.

In the legal problem set out at the beginning of this chapter, West and Burke own a piece of rural property, which they lease to a farmer. West, Burke, and the farmer share the profits from the farming operation, in lieu of set rental payments, but the farmer alone pays for the losses. *Are West, Burke, and the farmer partners?* No. West and Burke may be partners, but the farmer is not a partner with them. Only West and Burke jointly own the property and have an equal right to manage the business. Also, the three do not share losses. Sharing profits does not alone prove a partnership.

PARTNERSHIP CHARACTERISTICS

Sometimes the law of partnership recognizes a partnership as an *independent entity.* For example, a partnership can usually sue or be sued, collect judgments, and have all accounting procedures in the name of the partnership entity. Partnership property may be held in the name of the partnership rather than in the names of the individual partners.

When the partnership is not regarded as a separate legal entity, it is treated as an *aggregate of the individual partners.* For example, for federal income tax purposes, a partnership is not a tax-paying entity. The income or losses it incurs are "passed through" the partnership framework and attributed to the partners on their individual tax returns.

PARTNERSHIP FORMATION

A partnership is ordinarily formed by an agreement among the parties. The law, however, recognizes another form of partnership—*partnership by estoppel*—which arises when persons who are not partners represent themselves as partners when dealing with third parties. This section describes the requirements for the creation of a partnership.

Partnership by Agreement. Agreements to form a partnership can be oral, written, or implied by conduct. Some partnership agreements must be in writing to be enforceable under the Statute of Frauds (see Chapter 13). For example, a partnership agreement that, by its terms, is to continue for more than one year must be in writing. Similarly, a partnership that authorizes the partners to sell real estate must be in writing.

Practically speaking, the provisions of any partnership agreement should always be in writing. One disadvantage of an oral agreement is that its terms are difficult to prove, because a court must evaluate oral testimony given by persons with an interest in the eventual decision. In addition, potential problems that would have been detected in the course of drafting a written agreement may go unnoticed in an oral agreement.

IN THE COURTROOM

Terrence and Doug enter into a partnership to sell tires. They agree orally that Terrence will provide two-thirds of the capital to start up the business and receive two-thirds of the profits in return. The business does not turn a profit until the third year, at which time Doug insists on half of the profits. *Could Terrence succeed in a suit against Doug for two-thirds of the profits?* Possibly not. Without a writing, Terrence may have a hard time overcoming the presumption that he is entitled to only one-half of the profits of a two-person partnership. This problem could have been avoided by specifying in a written agreement how the profits would be shared.

ARTICLES OF PARTNERSHIP
A written agreement that sets forth each partner's rights in, and obligations to, the partnership.

A partnership agreement, called **articles of partnership,** usually specifies each partner's share of the profits. The agreement is binding regardless of how uneven the distribution appears to be. A sample partnership agreement is shown in Exhibit 28–1.

Partnership by Estoppel. Parties who are not partners sometimes represent themselves as such to third persons, who rely on the alleged partners' representations. This does not confer any partnership rights on these persons, but it may impose liability on them. The same is true when a partner represents that a

EXHIBIT 28–1
A Sample Partnership Agreement

PARTNERSHIP AGREEMENT

This agreement, made and entered into as of the __________, by and among __________ __________________ (hereinafter collectively sometimes referred to as "Partners").

WITNESSETH:

Whereas, the Parties hereto desire to form a General Partnership (hereinafter referred to as the "Partnership"), for the term and upon the conditions hereinafter set forth;

Now, therefore, in consideration of the mutual covenants hereinafter contained, it is agreed by and among the Parties hereto as follows:

Article I
BASIC STRUCTURE

Form. The Parties hereby form a General Partnership pursuant to the Laws of __________ __________.

Name. The business of the Partnership shall be conducted under the name of __________ __________.

Place of Business. The principal office and place of business of the Partnership shall be located at __________________, or such other place as the Partners may from time to time designate.

Term. The Partnership shall commence on ________, and shall continue for _____ years, unless earlier terminated in the following manner: (a) By the completion of the purpose intended, or (b) Pursuant to this Agreement, or (c) By applicable ____________ law, or (d) By death, insanity, bankruptcy, retirement, withdrawal, resignation, expulsion, or disability of all of the then Partners.

Purpose—General. The purpose for which the Partnership is organized is ____________ ____

Article II
FINANCIAL ARRANGEMENTS

Each Partner has contributed to the initial capital of the Partnership property in the amount and form indicated on Schedule A attached hereto and made a part hereof. Capital contributions to the Partnership shall not earn interest. An individual capital account shall be maintained for each Partner. If at any time during the existence of the Partnership it shall become necessary to increase the capital with which the said Partnership is doing business, then (upon the vote of the Managing Partner(s)): each party to this Agreement shall contribute to the capital of this Partnership within _ days notice of such need in an amount according to his then Percentage Share of Capital as called for by the Managing Partner(s).

The Percentage Share of Profits and Capital of each Partner shall be (unless otherwise modified by the terms of this Agreement) as follows:

Names	Initial Percentage Share of Profits and Capital

No interest shall be paid on any contribution to the capital of the Partnership. No Partner shall have the right to demand the return of his capital contributions except as herein provided. Except as herein provided, the individual Partners shall have no right to any priority over each other as to the return of capital contributions except as herein provided.

Distributions to the Partners of net operating profits of the Partnership, as hereinafter defined, shall be made at ____________________. Such contributions shall be made to the Partners simultaneously.

For the purpose of this Agreement, net operating profit for any accounting period shall mean the gross receipts of the Partnership for such period, less the sum of all cash expenses of operation of the Partnership, and such sums as may be necessary to establish a reserve for operating expenses. In determining net operating profit, deductions for depreciation, amortization, or other similar charges not requiring actual current expenditures of cash shall *not* be taken into account in accordance with generally accepted accounting principles.

EXHIBIT 28-1—Continued
A Sample Partnership Agreement

No partner shall be entitled to receive any compensation from the Partnership, nor shall any Partner receive any drawing account from the Partnership.

Article III
MANAGEMENT

The Managing Partner(s) shall be ______________________.

The Managing Partner(s) shall have the right to vote as to the management and conduct of the business of the Partnership as follows:

Names **Vote**

Article IV
DISSOLUTION

In the event that the Partnership shall hereafter be dissolved for any reason whatsoever, a full and general account of its assets, liabilities and transactions shall at once be taken. Such assets may be sold and turned into cash as soon as possible and all debts and other amounts due the Partnership collected. The proceeds thereof shall thereupon be applied as follows:

(a) To discharge the debts and liabilities of the Partnership and the expenses of liquidation.

(b) To pay each Partner or his legal representative any unpaid salary, drawing account, interest or profits to which he shall then be entitled and in addition, to repay to any Partner his capital contributions in excess of his original capital contribution.

(c) To divide the surplus, if any, among the Partners or their representatives as follows: (1) First (to the extent of each Partner's then capital account) in proportion to their then capital accounts. (2) Then according to each Partner's then Percentage Share of [*Capital/Income*].

No Partner shall have the right to demand and receive property in kind for his distribution.

Article V
MISCELLANEOUS

The Partnership's fiscal year shall commence on January 1st of each year and shall end on December 31st of each year. Full and accurate books of account shall be kept at such place as the Managing Partner(s) may from time to time designate, showing the condition of the business and finances of the Partnership; and each Partner shall have access to such books of account and shall be entitled to examine them at any time during ordinary business hours. At the end of each year, the Managing Partner(s) shall cause the Partnership's accountant to prepare a balance sheet setting forth the financial position of the Partnership as of the end of that year and a statement of operations (income and expenses) for that year. A copy of the balance sheet and statement of operations shall be delivered to each Partner as soon as it is available.

Each Partner shall be deemed to have waived all objections to any transaction or other facts about the operation of the Partnership disclosed in such balance sheet and/or statement of operations unless he shall have notified the Managing Partner(s) in writing of his objectives within thirty (30) days of the date on which statement is mailed.

The Partnership shall maintain a bank account or bank accounts in the Partnership's name in a national or state bank in the State of ______________. Checks and drafts shall be drawn on the Partnership's bank account for Partnership purposes only and shall be signed by the Managing Partner(s) or their designated agent.

Any controversy or claim arising out of or relating to this Agreement shall only be settled by arbitration in accordance with the rules of the American Arbitration Association, one Arbitrator, and shall be enforceable in any court having competent jurisdiction.

Witnesses	**Partners**
______________________	______________________
______________________	______________________

Date: __________

nonpartner is a member of the firm. When this occurs, the nonpartner is regarded as an agent whose acts are binding on the partnership.

If a third person has reasonably and detrimentally relied on the representation that the nonpartner was part of the partnership, *partnership by estoppel* exists. For the purpose of liability only, the partners (and the nonpartner) are prevented, or barred, from denying that the nonpartner is a partner.

RIGHTS AMONG PARTNERS

In the absence of provisions to the contrary in the partnership agreement, the law imposes on partners the rights and duties discussed below.

LEARNING OBJECTIVE NO. 3
Outlining the Rights of Partners to Manage the Firm

Management of the Partnership. All partners have equal rights in managing the partnership. Each partner in an ordinary partnership has one vote in management matters *regardless of the size of his or her interest in the firm.*

The majority rule controls decisions in ordinary matters connected with partnership business, unless otherwise specified in the agreement. Unanimous consent of the partners is required, however, to make basic changes in the nature of the business or the partnership agreement.

Interest in the Partnership. Each partner is entitled to the proportion of business profits and losses designated in the partnership agreement. If the agreement does not apportion profits or losses, profits are shared equally, and losses are shared in the same ratio as profits.

IN THE COURTROOM

A partnership agreement for a new chocolate cookie business between Ponce and Brent provides for capital contributions of $6,000 from Ponce and $4,000 from Brent. The agreement is silent as to how Ponce and Brent will share profits or losses. *In what proportion, then, would they share profits and losses?* Ponce and Brent would share profits and losses equally. If the agreement had provided for profits to be shared in the same ratio as capital contributions, the profits would be shared 60 percent for Ponce and 40 percent for Brent. If the agreement had been silent as to losses, they would be shared in the same ratio as profits (60/40).

Compensation from the Partnership. A partner has a duty to expend time, skill, and energy on behalf of the partnership business, and he or she is not generally paid for such services. Partners can, of course, agree otherwise. For example, the managing partner of a law firm often receives a salary in addition to his or her share of profits for performing special administrative duties in office and personnel management.

Inspection of Partnership Books. Each partner has the right to full and complete information concerning the conduct of all aspects of partnership business. Each firm keeps books in which to record such information. The books must be kept at the firm's principal business office and cannot be removed without the consent of all the partners.

Partner's Interest in the Firm. A partner's interest in the firm is a personal asset consisting of a proportionate share of the profits earned and a return of capital after the partnership is terminated. A partner's personal creditors can ask a court to order payments due to the partner from the partnership to be paid to them. Personal creditors may even ask a court to force the partner to sell his or her interest (but they cannot force the sale of specific partnership property).

Partnership Property. All property originally brought into the partnership or subsequently acquired on account of the partnership is partnership property. Every partner is a co-owner with all other partners of partnership property. Each partner has equal rights to possess partnership property for business purposes or in satisfaction of firm debts, but not for any other purpose without the consent of all the other partners.

Partners are *tenants in partnership* of all firm property. Thus, if a partner dies, the surviving partners retain all partnership property, including the deceased partner's share of specific assets. The surviving partners must account to the estate of the deceased partner, however, for the *value* of his or her interest in the property.

IN THE COURTROOM

Oxford, Walensa, and McKee are partners. Oxford dies. *In terms of the partnership, to what are Oxford's heirs entitled?* Oxford's heirs are entitled to the value of Oxford's interest in the firm. The heirs do not become partners with Walensa and McKee, nor are they entitled to specific assets of the firm. Walensa and McKee must account to the heirs, however, for the value of Oxford's interest by, for instance, hiring an accountant to determine how much the interest is worth and then paying the heirs that amount.

DUTIES AND POWERS OF PARTNERS

The duties and powers of partners basically consist of a *fiduciary* duty of each partner to the others and general agency powers.

FIDUCIARY
As a noun, a person having a duty created by his or her undertaking to act primarily for another's benefit in matters connected with the undertaking. As an adjective, a relationship founded upon trust and confidence.

Fiduciary Duties. Partners stand in a **fiduciary** relationship. A fiduciary relationship is one of extraordinary trust and loyalty. Each partner must act in good faith for the benefit of the partnership. Each partner must subordinate his or her personal interests, in the event of a conflict, to the mutual welfare of the partnership. Thus, a partner must account to the partnership for the personal profits or benefits derived without the consent of all of the partners in any partnership transaction.

IN THE COURTROOM

Hall, Banks, and Porter enter into a partnership. Porter undertakes independent consulting for an outside firm in competition with the partnership without the consent of Hall and Banks. *Has Porter breached the fiduciary duty that he owes to the partnership?* Yes. Even with a noncompetitive activity, a partner can breach his or her fiduciary duty if the partnership suffers a loss because of the time he or she spends on that activity. Of course, the partnership agreement or the unanimous consent of the partners can permit a partner to engage in any activity.

Agency Powers. Partnerships are governed by the principles of agency law. Each partner is an *agent* of every other partner and acts as both a principal and an agent in any business transaction within the scope of the partnership agreement. Each partner is a general agent of the partnership in carrying out the usual business of the firm. Every act of a partner concerning partnership business and every contract signed in the name of the partnership bind the firm.

JOINT LIABILITY
Shared liability. In partnership law, partners incur joint liability for partnership obligations and debts. For example, if a third party sues a partner on a partnership debt, the partner has the right to insist that the other partners be sued with him or her.

Joint Liability. In most states, partners are subject to unlimited, joint liability on partnership debts and contracts. **Joint liability** means that if a third party sues a partner on, for example, a partnership debt, the partner has the right to insist that the other partners be sued with him or her. Thus, to bring a successful claim against the partnership on a debt or contract, a plaintiff must name all the partners as defendants.

In some states, a partnership may be sued in its own name. A judgment will then bind the partnership's and the individual partners' property, even though not all the partners are named in the complaint.

In all states that impose joint liability, each partner is liable and may be required to pay the entire amount of a judgment. When one partner pays the entire amount, the partnership is required to repay that partner. If the partnership cannot do so, the obligation falls on the other partners.

Joint and Several Liability. In some states, partners are jointly and severally liable for partnership contracts. In all states, partners are jointly and severally liable for torts (wrongful interferences with others' rights). **Joint and several liability** means a third party may sue, at his or her option, any one or more of the partners without suing all of them or the partnership. The term *several* refers to the liability of each separate partner.

If the third party is successful, he or she may collect on the judgment only against the assets of those partners named as defendants. A judgment against only some of the partners does not extinguish the others' joint liability, however. For instance, Brian and Julie are partners. If Tom sues Brian for a debt on a partnership contract and wins, Tom can collect the amount of the judgment against Brian only. If Tom cannot collect enough from Brian, however, Tom can sue Julie for the difference. (Similarly, a release of one partner does not discharge the others' several liability.)

A partner who commits a tort that results in a judgment against the partnership is required to repay the firm for any damages it pays.

JOINT AND SEVERAL LIABILITY
A doctrine under which a plaintiff may sue, and collect a judgment from, any of several jointly liable defendants, regardless of that particular defendant's degree of fault. In partnership law, joint and several liability means a third party may sue one or more of the partners separately or all of them together, at his or her option. This is true even if the partner did not participate in, ratify, or know about whatever it was that gave rise to the cause of action.

PARTNERSHIP TERMINATION

The termination of a partnership has two stages, both of which must take place before termination is complete. The first stage, **dissolution,** occurs when any partner (or partners) indicates an intention to disassociate from the partnership. The second stage, **winding up,** is the actual process of collecting and distributing the partnership assets.

DISSOLUTION
The formal disbanding of a partnership or a corporation. It can take place by (1) agreement of the parties or the shareholders and board of directors, (2) the death of a partner, (3) the expiration of a time period stated in a partnership agreement or a certificate of incorporation, or (4) court order.

WINDING UP
The second of two stages involved in the dissolution of a partnership or corporation. Once the firm is dissolved, it continues to exist legally until the process of winding up all business affairs (collecting and distributing the firm's assets) is complete.

Dissolution. Dissolution of a partnership can be brought about by the acts of the partners, by the operation of law, and by judicial decree. Each of these methods is discussed here.

Dissolution by Acts of Partners. A partnership can be dissolved by the partners' agreement. For example, when a partnership agreement expresses a fixed term or a particular business objective to be accomplished, the passing of the date or the accomplishment of the objective dissolves the partnership.

A partner has the power to disassociate himself or herself from the partnership at any time and thus dissolve the partnership. Any change in the partnership, whether by the withdrawal of a partner or by the admission of a new partner, results in dissolution. In practice, this is modified by providing in the partnership agreement that the remaining or new partners may continue in the firm's business.

Dissolution by Operation of Law. If one of the partners dies, the partnership is dissolved by operation of law. Any change in the composition among partners results in a new partnership. The bankruptcy of a partner will also dissolve a partnership. Naturally, the bankruptcy of the firm itself will also result in dissolution.

Additionally, any event that makes it unlawful for the partnership to continue its business or for any partner to carry on in the partnership will result in dissolution. For example, suppose the state legislature passes a law making it illegal for judges to engage in the practice of law. If an attorney in a law firm is appointed a judge, the attorney must leave the law firm, and the partnership must be dissolved.

Dissolution by Judicial Decree. A court may order the dissolution of a partnership under any circumstances that render a decree of dissolution equitable. For example, a court can dissolve a partnership when a partner is determined to be mentally incompetent or appears incapable of performing his or her duties under the partnership agreement. In the latter situation, the incapacity must likely be permanent and affect substantially the partner's ability to discharge his or her duties to the firm.

A court may also order dissolution when it is impractical for the firm to continue—for example, if the business can only be operated at a loss for years to come. Additionally, a partner's impropriety involving partnership business (for example, fraud perpetrated upon the other partners) or improper behavior reflecting unfavorably on the firm may provide grounds for a decree of dissolution. Finally, if dissension between partners becomes so persistent and harmful as to undermine the confidence and cooperation necessary to carry on the firm's business, a court may grant a dissolution.

Winding Up. Once dissolution occurs and the partners have been notified, the partners cannot enter into new contracts on behalf of the partnership. Their only authority is to complete transactions begun but not finished at the time of dissolution and to wind up the business of the partnership. *Winding up* includes collecting and preserving partnership assets, discharging liabilities (paying debts), and accounting to each partner for the value of his or her interest in the partnership.

Creditors of the partnership and creditors of the individual partners can make claims on the partnership's assets. Creditors of the partnership have priority over creditors of individual partners in the distribution of partnership assets. In sum, the priorities to partnership assets on dissolution are as follows:

1. Payment of third party debts.
2. Refund of advances (loans) made to or for the firm by a partner.
3. Return of capital contribution to a partner.
4. Distribution of the balance, if any, to partners in accordance with their respective shares in the profits.

LIMITED PARTNERSHIP
A partnership consisting of one or more general partners (who manage the business and are liable to the full extent of their personal assets for debts of the partnership) and of one or more limited partners (who contribute only assets and are liable only up to the amount contributed by them).

GENERAL PARTNER
In a limited partnership, a partner who assumes responsibility for the management of the partnership and liability for all partnership debts.

LIMITED PARTNER
In a limited partnership, a partner who contributes capital to the partnership but has no right to participate in the management and operation of the business. The limited partner assumes no liability for partnership debts beyond the capital contributed.

LIMITED PARTNERSHIPS

A special and quite popular form of partnership is the **limited partnership,** which consists of at least one general partner and one or more limited partners. A **general partner** assumes responsibility for the management of the partnership and liability for all partnership debts. A **limited partner** has no right to participate in the management or operation of the partnership and assumes no liability for partnership debts beyond the amount of capital contributed. If limited partners participate in management, they risk having general-partner liability.

One of the major benefits of becoming a limited partner is this limitation on liability, both with respect to lawsuits brought against the partnership and with respect to money at risk. The maximum money at risk for each limited partner is defined by the limited-partnership agreement, which specifically states how much each limited partner must contribute to the partnership.

The limited partnership is created by an agreement. Unlike a general partnership, however, the limited partnership does not come into existence until a *certificate of partnership* is filed appropriately in a state. All states permit limited partnerships. Until 1976, all states except Louisiana had adopted the Uniform Limited Partnership Act to govern limited partnerships. Since 1976, most states and the District of Columbia have adopted its revision, the Revised Uniform Limited Partnership Act.

You can find the full text of the Internal Revenue Service rules concerning the taxation of limited liability partnerships by accessing the Treasure Chest of Important Documents at the following site:

http://www.LWeekly.com

LIMITED LIABILITY PARTNERSHIPS

The **limited liability partnership (LLP)** is designed for professionals who normally do business as partners in a partnership. LLPs must be formed and operated in compliance with state statutes. The appropriate form must be filled with a central state agency, usually the secretary of state's office, and the business's name must include either "Limited Liability Partnership" or "L.L.P."

The major advantage of the LLP is that it allows a partnership to limit the personal liability of the partners for partnership tort liability. For example, Delaware law protects each innocent partner from the "debts and obligations of the partnership arising from negligence, wrongful acts, or misconduct." In other states, the statutes protect innocent partners from obligations arising from "errors, omissions, negligence, incompetence, or malfeasance."

LIMITED LIABILITY PARTNERSHIP (LLP)
A form of partnership that allows professionals to enjoy the tax benefits of a partnership while limiting their personal liability for the malpractice of other partners.

In most states, it is relatively easy to convert a traditional partnership into an LLP because the firm's basic structure remains the same. Additionally, all of the law governing partnerships still applies (apart from that modified by the LLP statute).

Besides professional service firms, such as accounting firms and engineering firms, family businesses are expected, more than others, to use the LLP. A **family limited liability partnership (FLLP)** is a limited liability partnership in which the majority of the partners are persons related to each other, essentially as spouses, parents, grandparents, siblings, cousins, nephews, or nieces. A person acting in a fiduciary capacity for persons so related can also be a partner. All of the partners must be natural persons or persons acting in a fiduciary capacity for the benefit of natural persons.

FAMILY LIMITED LIABILITY PARTNERSHIP (FLLP)
A limited liability partnership (LLP) in which the majority of the partners are persons related to each other, essentially as spouses, parents, grandparents, siblings, cousins, nephews, or nieces. A person acting in a fiduciary capacity for persons so related could also be a partner.

Probably the most significant use of the FLLP form of business organization is in agriculture. Family-owned farms sometimes find this form to their benefit. The FLLP has the same advantages as other LLPs with some additional advantages, such as, an exemption from real estate transfer taxes when partnership real estate is transferred among partners.

LIMITED LIABILITY LIMITED PARTNERSHIPS

A **limited liability limited partnership (LLLP)** is a type of limited partnership. The difference between a limited partnership and an LLLP is that the liability of a general partner in an LLLP is the same as the liability of a partner in a limited liability partnership. That is, the liability of all partners is limited to the amount of their investments in the firm.

LIMITED LIABILITY LIMITED PARTNERSHIP (LLLP)
A type of limited partnership. The difference between a limited partnership and an LLLP is the liability of the general partner in an LLLP is the same as the liability of a partner in a limited liability partnership.

A few states provide expressly for LLLPs. In states that do not provide for LLLPs but do allow for limited partnerships and limited liability partnerships, a limited partnership should probably still be able to register with the state as an LLLP.

Limited Liability Companies

The **limited liability company (LLC)** is a relatively new form of business enterprise that offers the limited liability of a corporation and the tax advantages of a partnership.

LIMITED LIABILITY COMPANY (LLC)
A hybrid form of business enterprise that offers the limited liability of the corporation but the tax advantages of a partnership.

Like the limited partnership, an LLC must be formed and operated in compliance with state law. To form an LLC, *articles of organization* must be filed with a central state agency, such as the secretary of state's office. The business's name must include the words "Limited Liability Company" or the initials "L.L.C."

For information on limited liability companies, go to

http://www.mgovg.com

A major advantage of the LLC is that profits are "passed through" the LLC and taxes are paid personally by the owners of the company, who are called *members*.

LEARNING OBJECTIVE NO. 4
Outlining the Advantages of Limited Liability Companies

LLCs are much easier to establish and can operate with greater flexibility than regular corporations.

Another advantage is that the liability of the members is limited to the amount of their investments. In an LLC, members are allowed to participate fully in management activities, and under at least one state's statute, the firm's managers need not even be members of the LLC. Yet another advantage is that corporations and partnerships, as well as foreign investors, can be LLC members. Additionally, there is no limit on the number of shareholder-members of the LLC. Finally, part of the LLC's attractiveness to businesspersons is the flexibility it offers. The members can themselves decide how to operate the various aspects of the business through a simple operating agreement.

The disadvantages of the LLC are relatively few. One disadvantage of the LLC is that state statutes are not uniform. Until state LLC statutes are revised, as they probably will be in the near future, businesses must comply with existing requirements. Additionally, state laws may continue to vary with respect to state taxation.

TERMS AND CONCEPTS FOR REVIEW

articles of partnership 352
dissolution 357
family limited liability partnership (FLLP) 359
fiduciary 356
general partner 358
joint and several liability 357
joint liability 356
limited liability company (LLC) 359
limited liability limited partnership (LLLP) 359
limited liability partnership (LLP) 359
limited partner 358
limited partnership 358
partnership 351
sole proprietorship 350
winding up 357

CHAPTER SUMMARY • SOLE PROPRIETORSHIPS, PARTNERSHIPS, AND LIMITED LIABILITY COMPANIES

Sole Proprietorships	**1.** The simplest form of business, used by anyone who does business without creating an organization. The owner is the business. **2.** The owner pays personal income tax on all profits. **3.** The owner is personally liable for all business debts.
Partnerships	**1.** *General partnerships—* **a.** Created by agreement of the parties. **b.** Not treated as an entity except for limited purposes. **c.** Each partner has an equal voice in management unless otherwise provided for in the partnership agreement. **d.** Partners have unlimited liability for partnership debts. **e.** Terminated by agreement, action of partner (withdrawal), operation of law (death or bankruptcy), or court decree. **2.** *Limited partnerships—* **a.** Consists of one or more general partners and one or more limited partners. **b.** Only general partners can participate in management. If limited partners participate in management activities, they risk having general-partner liability. **c.** Must be formed in compliance with statutory requirements. **d.** General partners have unlimited liability for partnership losses. Limited partners are liable only to the extent of their contributions.
Limited Liability Companies	The limited liability company (LLC) offers the limited liability feature of corporations but the tax benefits of partnerships. LLC members participate in management. Members of LLCs may be corporations or partnerships, are not restricted in number, and may be residents of other countries.

HYPOTHETICAL QUESTIONS

28–1. Forms of Business Organization. In each of the following situations, determine whether Georgio's Fashions is a sole proprietorship, a partnership, or a limited partnership.

(a) Georgio's defaults on a payment to supplier Dee Creations. Dee sues Georgio's and each of the owners of Georgio's personally for payment of the debt.

(b) Georgio's is owned by three persons, two of whom are not allowed to participate in the firm's management.

28–2. Partnership Property. Schwartz and Zenov were partners in an accounting firm. Because business was booming and profits were better than ever, they decided to invest some of the firm's profits in Munificent Corp. stock. The investment turned out to be a good one, as the stock continued to increase in value. On Schwartz's death several years later, Zenov assumed full ownership of the business, including the Munificent Corp. stock, a partnership asset. Schwartz's daughter Rosalie, however, claimed a 50 percent ownership interest in the Munificent Corp. stock as Schwartz's sole heir. Can Rosalie enforce her claim? Explain.

REAL WORLD CASE PROBLEM

28–3. Rights among Partners. B&R Communications was a general partner in Amarillo CellTelco. Under the partnership agreement, each partner had the right to inspect partnership records "at reasonable times during business hours," as long as the inspection did not "unreasonably interfere with the operation of the partnership." B&R believed that the managers of the firm were using partnership money to engage in lawsuits that were too costly. B&R and other general partners filed a suit in a Texas state court against the managers. B&R wanted to inspect the firm's records to discover information about the lawsuits, but the court denied B&R's request. B&R asked the state appellate court to order the trial judge to grant the request. On what ground did the appellate court issue the order? [*B&R Communications v. Lopez,* 890 S.W.2d 224 (Tex.App.—Amarillo 1994)]

For updated links to resources available on the Web, as well as a variety of other materials, visit this text's Web site at **http://blte.westbuslaw.com**.

For information on the taxation of partnerships, see the article on this topic by Dennis D'Annunzio at

http://www.sunbeltnetwork.com/Journal/Current/D970804dsd.html

For some of the advantages and disadvantages of doing business as a partnership, go to the following page, which is part of the Small Business Administration's Web site:

http://www.sba.gov/starting/indexfaqs.html

You can find information on how to form an LLC, including the fees charged in each state for filing LLC articles of organization, at the Web site of BIZCORP International, Inc. Go to

http://www.bizcorp.com

Nolo Press provides information on LLCs and how they are operated at

http://www.nolo.com/chapter/RUNS/RUNS_toc.html

For an example of a state law (that of Florida) governing LLPs, go to the Internet Legal Resource Guide's Web page at

http://www.ilrg.com/whatsnews/statute.html

and scroll down the page to "Registered Limited Liability Partnerships."

The law firm of Wordes, Wilshin, Goren & Conner offers a comparison of the advantages and disadvantages of major business forms with respect to various factors, including ease of formation, management, and ability to raise capital. The firm's Web site can be accessed at

http://www.wwgc.com/wwgc-be1.htm

ONLINE LEGAL RESEARCH

Go to **http://blte.westbuslaw.com**, the Web site that accompanies this text. Select "Internet Applications," and then click on "Chapter 28." There you will find the following Internet research exercise that you can perform to learn more about partnerships:

Activity 28–1: Partnerships

Chapter 28 ■ WORK SET

TRUE-FALSE QUESTIONS

_____ **1.** In a sole proprietorship, the owner and the business are entirely separate.

_____ **2.** A partnership is an association of two or more persons to carry on, as co-owners, a business for profit.

_____ **3.** A general partnership cannot exist unless a certificate of partnership is filed appropriately in a state.

_____ **4.** The sharing of profits from joint ownership of property is usually enough to create a partnership.

_____ **5.** A writing is always necessary to form a partnership.

_____ **6.** Unless a partnership agreement specifies otherwise, each partner has one vote in management matters.

_____ **7.** A partner is co-owner with his or her partners of partnership property.

_____ **8.** A limited liability company offers the limited liability of a corporation and the tax advantages of a partnership.

MULTIPLE-CHOICE QUESTIONS

_____ **1.** Dave and Paul agree to go into business together. They do not formally declare that their business has a specific form of organization. Dave and Paul's business is

a. a proprietorship.
b. a partnership.
c. a limited liability company.
d. none of the above.

_____ **2.** Greg is a general partner, and Lee and Carol are limited partners in GLC Associates, a limited partnership. Lee and Carol

a. have less managerial powers than Greg.
b. cannot sue on behalf of the firm if Greg refuses to do so.
c. are personally liable only for the debts of the firm, unlike Greg.
d. risk nothing if they participate in the management of the partnership.

_____ **3.** To obtain a contract with Dick, Cindy misrepresents that she is a partner with Karl. Karl overhears Cindy's misrepresentation, but says nothing to Dick. Cindy breaches the contract. Who is liable to Dick?

a. Cindy only.
b. Karl only.
c. Cindy and Karl.
d. None of the above.

_____ **4.** Mark owns M Carpets, a home furnishings store. He hires Lois as a salesperson, agreeing to pay her $8.50 per hour plus 10 percent of her sales. Mark and Lois are

a. partners, because Lois receives a share of the store's profits.
b. partners, because Lois is responsible for some of the store's sales.
c. not partners, because Lois does not have an ownership interest or management right in the store.
d. not partners, because Lois does not receive an equal share of the store's profits.

_____ **5.** Greg, Kim, and Pete are partners in Northern Mines. Greg sells the ore extracted from the mines to Yukon Resources, Inc. Regarding the funds that Greg receives from Yukon for the ore, he

a. must account for the funds to Yukon only.
b. must account for the funds to Kim and Pete only.
c. must account for the funds to Yukon, Kim, and Pete.
d. is free to dispose of the funds in any manner.

_____ **6.** Don and Kim are partners in CompQuik, a computer store. Dissolution may be caused

a. only by Don and Kim expressly agreeing to dissolve their partnership.
b. only by Don selling his interest in the firm to Ted without Kim's consent.
c. only by Kim adding Lyle as a new partner without Don's consent.
d. by the partners agreeing to dissolve their firm, or by one partner, without the other's consent, selling his or her interest to a third party or adding another partner.

_____ **7.** Dr. Jones and Dr. Smith are partners in a medical clinic. Jones manages the clinic, which is organized as a limited liability partnership. A court holds Smith liable in a malpractice suit. Jones is

a. not liable.
b. liable only to the extent of her share of that year's profits.
c. liable only to the extent of her investment in the firm.
d. liable beyond her investment in the firm, because she managed the clinic.

_____ **8.** Nick and Laura are partners in Cafe Ole, a coffee shop. On the petition of one of the partners, a court could dissolve the partnership

a. only if Nick or Laura becomes mentally incompetent.
b. only if Nick or Laura engages in improper conduct.
c. only if Cafe Ole can be run at a loss.
d. under any circumstances that makes dissolution equitable.

ISSUE SPOTTERS

1. Sam plans to open a sporting goods store and to hire Gil and Art. Sam will invest only his own capital. He does not expect to make a profit for at least eighteen months and to make little profit for the first three years. He hopes to expand eventually. Which form of business organization would be most appropriate?

2. Hal and Gretchen are partners in a delivery business. When business is slow, without Gretchen's knowledge, Hal leases out the delivery vehicles as moving vans. Because the vehicles would otherwise be sitting idle in a parking lot, can Hal keep the lease money or does Hal have to account to Gretchen?

Formation and Termination of a Corporation

29

LEARNING OBJECTIVES

When you finish this chapter, you should be able to:

1 Define the differences among domestic, foreign, and alien corporations.

2 Summarize incorporation procedures.

3 Identify the basic steps involved in a corporate merger or consolidation.

4 Discuss the phases involved in the termination of a corporation.

FACING A LEGAL PROBLEM

Cynthia and Blake wish to go into business as Tints, Inc., a corporation to sell sunglasses at kiosks in shopping malls. In taking steps to form and promote their business, Cynthia and Blake enter into a contract with Mira-Lenses to buy inventory for Tints. They tell Mira-Lenses that they are acting on behalf of a business that is not yet incorporated. Due to circumstances beyond their control, Tints is never incorporated. Mira-Lenses sues Cynthia and Blake to pay for the merchandise they contracted for on behalf of Tints. *Will a court grant the supplier's request?*

A corporation is an artificial being, existing in law only and neither tangible nor visible. Its existence depends generally on state law. Of course, each state has its own body of corporate law, and these laws are not entirely uniform.

Corporations consist of shareholders, who are the owners of the business. A board of directors, elected by the shareholders, manages the business. The board of directors normally employs officers to oversee day-to-day operations. One of the key advantages of the corporate form of business is that the liability of its owners (shareholders) is limited to their investments. They are not otherwise liable for the debts of the corporation.

In this chapter, we examine various classifications of corporations. We then discuss the formation and financing of a corporation. Finally, we look at four types of corporate expansion, and the reasons and methods for terminating a corporation.

Classification of Corporations

The classification of a corporation depends on its location, purpose, or ownership characteristics.

LEARNING OBJECTIVE NO. 1

Defining the Differences among Domestic, Foreign, and Alien Corporations

Domestic, Foreign, and Alien Corporations

A corporation is referred to as a **domestic corporation** by its home state (the state in which it incorporates). A corporation formed in one state but doing business in another is referred to in that other state as a **foreign corporation.** A corporation formed in another country (say, Mexico) but doing business within the United States is referred to in the United States as an **alien corporation.**

Domestic Corporation
In a given state, a corporation that does business in, and is organized under the laws of, that state.

Foreign Corporation
In a given state, a corporation that does business in the state without being incorporated therein.

Alien Corporation
A designation in the United States for a corporation formed in another country but doing business in the United States.

A foreign corporation does not have an automatic right to do business in a state other than its state of incorporation. It normally must obtain a *certificate of authority* in any state in which it plans to do business. Once the certificate is issued, the powers conferred upon a corporation by its home state can be exercised in the other state.

Public and Private Corporations

A public corporation is one formed by the government to meet some political or governmental purpose. Cities and towns that incorporate are common examples. In addition, many federal government organizations, such as the U.S. Postal Service, the Tennessee Valley Authority, and AMTRAK, are public corporations.

Private corporations, however, are created either wholly or in part for private benefit. Most corporations are private. Although they may serve a public purpose, such as a public utility does, private corporations are owned by private persons rather than by the government.

Close Corporation
A corporation whose shareholders are limited to a small group of persons, often including only family members. The rights of shareholders of a close corporation usually are restricted regarding the transfer of shares to others.

Stock
In corporation law, an equity or ownership interest in a corporation, measured in units of shares.

A private corporation with a small number of shareholders is a **close corporation.** Shareholders are those who own **stock** in a corporation and thereby own the corporation. *Stock* is an ownership interest, measured in units of shares. Close corporations are often managed by their shareholders, who are therefore subject to restrictions in the transfer of their shares to others.

Nonprofit Corporations

Corporations formed without a profit-making purpose are called *nonprofit* or *not-for-profit* corporations. Usually private corporations, they can be used in conjunction with an ordinary (for-profit) corporation to facilitate making contracts with the government. Private hospitals, educational institutions, charities, religious organizations, and the like are often organized as nonprofit corporations. The nonprofit corporation is a convenient form of organization that allows various groups to own property and to form contracts without exposing the individual members to personal liability.

S Corporations

S Corporation
A business corporation that has met certain requirements as set out by the Internal Revenue Code and thus qualifies for special income-tax treatment. Essentially, an S corporation is taxed the same as a partnership, but its owners enjoy the privilege of limited liability.

The Subchapter S Revision Act of 1982 divided corporations into two groups: **S corporations,** which have elected Subchapter S treatment, and *C corporations,* which are all other corporations. Certain corporations can choose to qualify under Subchapter S of the Internal Revenue Code to avoid the imposition of income taxes at the corporate level while retaining many of the advantages of a corporation, particularly limited liability.

Qualification Requirements for S Corporations. Among the requirements for S corporation status, the following are the most important:

1. The corporation must be a domestic corporation.
2. The corporation must not be a member of an affiliated group of corporations.
3. The shareholders of the corporation must be individuals, estates, or certain trusts. Partnerships and nonqualifying trusts cannot be shareholders. Corporations can be shareholders under certain circumstances.

4. The corporation must have seventy-five or fewer shareholders.
5. The corporation must have only one class of stock, although not all shareholders need have the same voting rights.
6. No shareholder of the corporation may be a nonresident alien.

Benefits of S Corporations. At times, it is beneficial for a regular corporation to elect S corporation status. Benefits include the following:

1. When the corporation has losses, the S election allows the shareholders to use the losses to offset other income.
2. When the shareholder's tax bracket is lower than the corporation's tax bracket, the S election causes the corporation's pass-through net income to be taxed in the shareholder's bracket. This is particularly attractive when the corporation wants to accumulate earnings for some future business purpose.
3. A single tax on corporate income is imposed at individual income tax rates at the shareholder level. (The income is taxable to shareholders whether or not it is actually distributed.)

Corporate Formation

The formation of a corporation involves two steps: (1) preliminary organizational and promotional undertakings—particularly, obtaining capital (money) for the future corporation—and (2) the legal process of incorporation.

If you believe that the business in which you are going to engage has growth potential and may require significant financing in the future, you should contact an attorney to take you through the necessary steps in incorporating your business.

Promotional Activities

Before a corporation becomes a reality, people invest in the proposed corporation as subscribers. In addition, contracts are frequently made by *promoters* on behalf of the future corporation.

Promoters. Those who, for themselves or others, take the preliminary steps in organizing a corporation are called **promoters.** A promoter may enter into contracts with attorneys, accountants, architects, or other professionals whose services are needed in planning the corporation.

Promoter
An entrepreneur who participates in the organization of a corporation in its formative stage, usually by issuing a prospectus, procuring subscriptions to the stock, making contract purchases, securing a charter, and the like.

As a general rule, a promoter is personally liable on these contracts, even if the promoter enters into the contracts in the name of the proposed corporation. The personal liability of the promoter continues after incorporation unless the party with whom the promoter contracted releases the promoter or the corporation assumes the preincorporation contract by *novation* (see Chapter 15). Novation releases the promoter and obligates the corporation to perform the contract.

In the legal problem set out at the beginning of this chapter, Cynthia and Blake take preliminary steps to organize Tints, Inc., a corporation to sell sunglasses at kiosks in shopping malls. As promoters, they enter into a contract with Mira-Lenses to buy inventory for Tints, telling Mira-Lenses that their business is not yet incorporated. Due to circumstances beyond their control, Tints never comes into existence. Mira-Lenses sues Cynthia and Blake to pay for the merchandise that they ordered. *Will a court grant the request?* Probably. Generally, promoters are personally liable on contracts entered into in the name of a proposed corporation. This liability exists even if the corporation is never formed.

Subscribers and Subscriptions. Before the actual formation of a corporation, a promoter can contact potential individual investors, and they can agree to buy stock in the future corporation. This agreement is a *subscription agreement,* and the potential investor is a *subscriber.*

Most courts view preincorporation subscriptions as continuing offers to purchase corporate stock. On or after its formation, the corporation can choose to accept the offer to purchase stock. Some courts allow a subscriber to revoke the offer before the corporation accepts. Many other courts treat a subscription as a contract between the subscribers, making it irrevocable except with the consent of all of the subscribers. In many of those states, a subscription is irrevocable for a period of six months unless otherwise provided in the subscription agreement or unless all the subscribers agree to the revocation of the subscription.

Incorporation Procedures

LEARNING OBJECTIVE NO. 2
Summarizing Incorporation Procedures

Exact procedures for incorporation differ among states. The basic requirements are similar, however. They include selecting the state in which to incorporate, drafting and filing the articles of incorporation, receiving the certificate of incorporation, and holding the first organizational meeting. These steps are discussed below.

State Chartering. The first step in the incorporation procedure is to select a state in which to incorporate. Because state incorporation laws differ, individuals have found some advantage in looking for the states that offer the most advantageous tax or incorporation provisions. Delaware has historically had the least restrictive laws. Consequently, many corporations, including some of the largest, are incorporated there.

Articles of Incorporation The document filed with the appropriate governmental agency, usually the secretary of state, when a business is incorporated; state statutes usually prescribe what kind of information must be contained in the articles of incorporation.

Articles of Incorporation. The primary document needed to begin the incorporation process is called the **articles of incorporation** (see Exhibit 29–1). The articles include basic information about the corporation and serve as a primary source of authority for its future organization and business functions. Generally, the articles of incorporation include the corporation's name, its nature and purpose, its duration, its capital structure, and its registered office and agent, as well as the names of the incorporators.

Corporate Name. All states require a corporation name to include the word *Corporation, Incorporated, Company,* or *Limited,* or abbreviations of these terms. A corporate name is prohibited from being the same as, or deceptively similar to, the name of an existing corporation doing business within the state.

Nature and Purpose. The intended business activities of the corporation must be specified in the articles. The charter can state generally that the corporation is organized to conduct "any lawful business." Alternatively, it may state more specifically that the corporation is organized, for example, to "engage in the production and sale of agricultural products."

To learn how the U.S. Small Business Administration assists in forming, financing, and operating businesses, go to

http://www.sbaonline.sba.gov

Duration. A corporation can have perpetual existence under most state corporate statutes. A few states, however, prescribe a maximum duration, after which the corporation must formally renew its existence.

Capital Structure. Some states have no minimum capital requirement. A few states require a small capital investment (for example, $1,000) for ordinary business corporations. Some states require a greater investment for those engaged in insurance or banking. In all states, the number of shares of stock authorized for issuance, their valuation, the various types or classes of stock authorized for issuance, and other relevant information concerning the financing of the corporation must be outlined in the articles.

Registered Office and Agent. The corporation must identify a specific person as an agent to receive legal documents on behalf of the corporation. The agent

EXHIBIT 29–1
Articles of Incorporation

ARTICLE ONE

The name of the corporation is ______________________________.

ARTICLE TWO

The period of its duration is perpetual (may be a number of years or until a certain date).

ARTICLE THREE

The purpose (or purposes) for which the corporation is organized is (are) ______________________________
______________________________.

ARTICLE FOUR

The aggregate number of shares that the corporation shall have authority to issue is ________ of the par value of ________ dollar(s) each (or without par value).

ARTICLE FIVE

The corporation will not commence business until it has received for the issuance of its shares consideration of the value of $1,000 (can be any sum not less that $1,000).

ARTICLE SIX

The address of the corporation's registered office is ______________________________,
New Pacum, and the name of its registered agent at such address is ______________________________
______________________________.
(Use the street or building or rural address of the registered office, not a post office box number.)

ARTICLE SEVEN

The number of initial directors is ________________, and the names and addresses of the directors are
____
______________________________.

ARTICLE EIGHT

The name and address of the incorporator is ______________________________
______________________________.

(signed) ______________________________
Incorporator

Sworn to on ________________ by the above-named incorporator.
(date)

____
Notary Public ________ County, New Pacum

(Notary Seal)

receives, for example, service of process (the delivery of a court order requiring an appearance in court).

Incorporators. An incorporator is a person who applies to the state on behalf of the corporation to obtain its *certificate of incorporation,* or corporate charter. This document is issued by a state to grant a corporation legal existence and the right to function. The incorporator need not have any interest in the corporation. Many states do not impose residency or age requirements on incorporators. States vary on the required number of incorporators. It can be as few as one or as many as three. Incorporators must sign the articles of incorporation. In some states, they participate at the first organizational meeting of the corporation.

Certificate of Incorporation. Once the articles of incorporation have been prepared, signed, and authenticated by the incorporators, they are sent to the appropriate state official (usually the secretary of state) along with the appropriate filing fee. In many states, the secretary of state then issues a **certificate of incorporation** representing the state's authorization for the corporation to conduct business. The certificate and a copy of the articles are returned to the incorporators. The incorporators then hold the initial organizational meeting, which completes the details of incorporation.

Certificate of Incorporation
The primary document that evidences corporate existence (referred to as articles of incorporation in some states).

First Organizational Meeting. The first organizational meeting is held after the charter is granted. At this meeting, the incorporators may elect the first board of directors and complete the routine business of incorporation. Sometimes, the meeting is held after the election of the board of directors. Other business conducted at the meeting depends on the requirements of the state's incorporation statute and the provisions made in the articles.

Adoption of **bylaws**—the internal rules of management for the corporation—is probably the most important function of the first organizational meeting. The shareholders, directors, and officers must abide by the bylaws in conducting corporate business. Typical bylaw provisions describe the process for the election of the board of directors, the methods of replacing directors, and the manner and time of scheduling shareholder and board meetings.

Bylaws
A set of governing rules or regulations adopted by a corporation or other association.

Corporate Powers

A corporation can engage in all acts and enter into any contract to accomplish the purposes for which it was created. When a corporation is created, the express and implied powers necessary to achieve its purpose also come into existence.

Express and Implied Powers

The express powers of a corporation are found in its articles of incorporation, in the law of the state of incorporation, and in the state and federal constitutions. Corporate bylaws and the resolutions of the corporation's board of directors also grant or restrict certain powers.

The following order of priority is used when conflicts arise among documents involving corporations:

1. The U.S. Constitution.
2. State constitutions.
3. State statutes.
4. The articles of incorporation.
5. Bylaws.
6. Resolutions of the board of directors.

Access to the Internet

The Center for Corporate Law at the University of Cincinnati College of Law is a good source of information on corporate law. Go to

http://www.law.uc.edu/CCL

When a corporation is created, it has certain implied powers. To accomplish its purposes, a corporation has the implied power to borrow money within certain limits, to lend money or extend credit to those with whom it has a legal or contractual relationship, and to make charitable contributions.

Ultra Vires Doctrine

The term ***ultra vires*** means "beyond the powers." Acts of a corporation that are beyond the authority given to it under its charter or under the statutes by which it was incorporated are *ultra vires* acts. Such acts may be held to be illegal.

Ultra Vires
A Latin term meaning "beyond the powers." Activities of a corporation's managers that are outside the scope of the power granted them by the corporation's charter or the laws of the state of incorporation are *ultra vires* acts.

IN THE COURTROOM

The stated purpose of the First Rate Plumbing Corporation is to provide plumbing installation and services. Officers of the company enter into a contract for First Rate to buy six thousand cases of vodka. Yusef, a First Rate shareholder, objects to the contract and asks a court to declare it *ultra vires. Will the court grant Yusef's request?* Probably. It is difficult to see how a contract made by a plumbing company for the purchase of six thousand cases of vodka is reasonably related to the conduct and furtherance of the corporation's stated purpose of providing plumbing installation and services.

Because of the *ultra vires* doctrine, corporations often adopt a very broad statement of purpose in their articles of incorporation to include virtually all conceivable activities. Statutes generally permit the expression "any lawful purpose" to be a legally sufficient stated purpose in the articles of incorporation. Also, courts have held that any legal action that a corporation undertakes to profit its shareholders is allowable and proper.

Corporate Financing

To obtain financing, corporations issue **securities**—evidence of the obligation to pay money or of the right to participate in earnings and the distribution of corporate trusts and other property. Securities consist of *stocks* and *bonds,* both of which are sold to investors. Stocks represent the purchase of ownership in the business firm. **Bonds** (debentures) represent the long-term borrowing of money by a firm.

SECURITIES
Stock certificates, bonds, notes, debentures, warrants, or other documents given as evidence of an ownership interest in the corporation or as a promise of repayment by the corporation.

BOND
A certificate that evidences a corporate debt. It is a security that involves no ownership interest in the issuing corporation.

STOCKS

The most important characteristics of stocks are as follows:

1. They need not be paid back.
2. Stockholders receive dividends (corporate earnings) only when so voted by the directors.
3. Stockholders are the last investors to be paid off on dissolution.
4. Stockholders vote for directors and on major issues.

Exhibit 29–2 on the next page lists the types of stocks issued by corporations. The two major types are *common stock* and *preferred stock.*

Common Stock. **Common stock** represents the true ownership of a corporation. It provides a proportionate interest in the corporation with regard to (1) control, (2) earning capacity, and (3) net assets. A shareholder's interest is generally in proportion to the number of shares owned out of the total number of shares issued.

Control is exercised by shareholders in the form of voting rights. Shareholders vote in elections for a firm's board of directors and for any proposed changes in the ownership structure of a firm (such as a merger with another firm).

In terms of receiving payment for their investment, holders of common stock are last in line. The earnings to which they are entitled also depend on all the other groups—suppliers, employees, managers, bankers, governments, bondholders, and holders of preferred stock—being paid what is due them first.

COMMON STOCK
Shares of ownership in a corporation that are lowest in priority with respect to payment of dividends and distribution of the corporation's assets upon dissolution.

Preferred Stock. Stock with *preferences* is **preferred stock.** This means that holders of preferred stock have priority over holders of common stock as to

PREFERRED STOCK
Classes of stock that have priority over common stock both as to payment of dividends and distribution of assets upon the corporation's dissolution.

EXHIBIT 29–2
Types of Stocks

TYPES	DEFINITIONS
Common Stock	Voting shares that represent ownership interest in a corporation. Common stock has the lowest priority with respect to payment of dividends.
Preferred Stock	Shares of stock that have priority over common-stock shares as to payment of dividends and distribution of assets upon dissolution. Dividend payments are usually a fixed percentage of the face value of the share.
Cumulative Preferred Stock	Required dividends not paid in a given year must be paid in a subsequent year before any common-stock dividends are paid.
Participating Preferred Stock	The owner is entitled to receive the preferred-stock dividend and additional dividends after payment of dividends on common stock.
Convertible Preferred Stock	Preferred shareholders with the option to convert their shares into a specified number of common shares either in the issuing corporation or, sometimes, in another corporation.
Redeemable, or Callable, Preferred Stock	Preferred shares issued with the express condition that the issuing corporation has the right to repurchase the shares as specified.

dividends and to payment upon dissolution of the corporation. Preferred-stock shareholders may or may not have the right to vote.

From an investment standpoint, preferred stock is more similar to bonds (discussed below) than to common stock. Preferred shareholders receive periodic dividend payments, usually established as a fixed percentage of the face amount of each preferred share. A 6 percent preferred share with a face amount of $100 would pay its owner a $6 dividend each year. This is not a legal obligation on the part of the firm, however, and preferred shares have no fixed maturity date. A sample certificate of a share of preferred stock is shown in Exhibit 29–3.

BONDS

When bonds are issued, they almost always have a designated *maturity date*—the date when the principal or face amount of the bond is returned to the investor. The features and terms of a particular bond issue are specified in a lending agreement called a **bond indenture.** A corporate trustee, often a commercial bank trust department, represents the collective well-being of all bondholders in ensuring that the corporation meets the terms of the bond issue.

BOND INDENTURE
A contract between the issuer of a bond and the bondholder.

Merger and Consolidation

LEARNING OBJECTIVE NO. 3
Identifying the Basic Steps Involved in a Corporate Merger or Consolidation

A corporation often extends its operations by combining with another corporation through a merger or a consolidation. The terms *merger* and *consolidation* are often used interchangeably, but they refer to two legally distinct proceedings. The effect of either proceeding on the rights and liabilities of the corporation, its shareholders, and its creditors are the same, however.

MERGER

A **merger** involves the legal combination of two or more corporations in such a way that only one of the corporations continues to exist. For example, Corporation A and Corporation B decide to merge. It is agreed that A will absorb B. On merger, then, B ceases to exist as a separate entity, and A continues as the *surviving corporation.* This process is illustrated graphically in Exhibit 29–4 on page 374.

MERGER
A process by which one corporation (the surviving corporation) acquires all the assets and liabilities of another corporation (the merged corporation). The shareholders of the merged corporation receive either payment for their shares or shares in the surviving corporation.

EXHIBIT 29–3
Preferred Stock Certificate

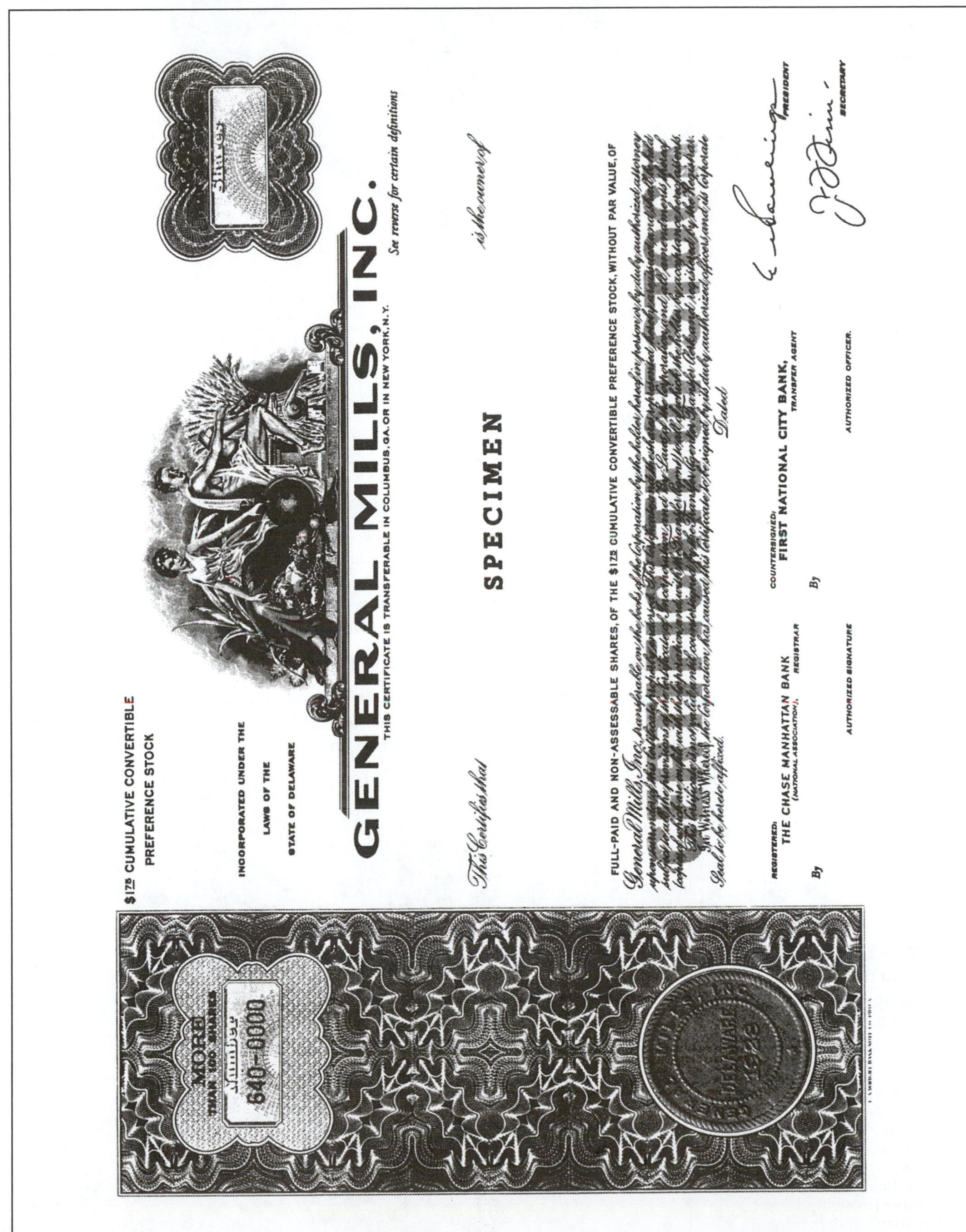

$1.75 CUMULATIVE CONVERTIBLE PREFERENCE STOCK

INCORPORATED UNDER THE LAWS OF THE STATE OF DELAWARE

GENERAL MILLS, INC.

THIS CERTIFICATE IS TRANSFERABLE IN COLUMBUS, GA. OR IN NEW YORK, N.Y.

See reverse for certain definitions

MORE THAN 100 SHARES

Number 640-0000

SPECIMEN

This Certifies that is the owner of

FULL-PAID AND NON-ASSESSABLE SHARES, OF THE $1.75 CUMULATIVE CONVERTIBLE PREFERENCE STOCK, WITHOUT PAR VALUE, OF

General Mills, Inc. transferable on the books of the Corporation by the holder hereof in person or by duly authorized attorney ...

In Witness Whereof, the Corporation has caused this Certificate to be signed by its duly authorized officers and its Corporate Seal to be hereto affixed.

Dated

PRESIDENT

SECRETARY

REGISTERED: THE CHASE MANHATTAN BANK (NATIONAL ASSOCIATION), REGISTRAR

By AUTHORIZED SIGNATURE

COUNTERSIGNED: FIRST NATIONAL CITY BANK, TRANSFER AGENT

By AUTHORIZED OFFICER.

GENERAL MILLS, INC. DELAWARE 1928

EXHIBIT 29–4
Merger

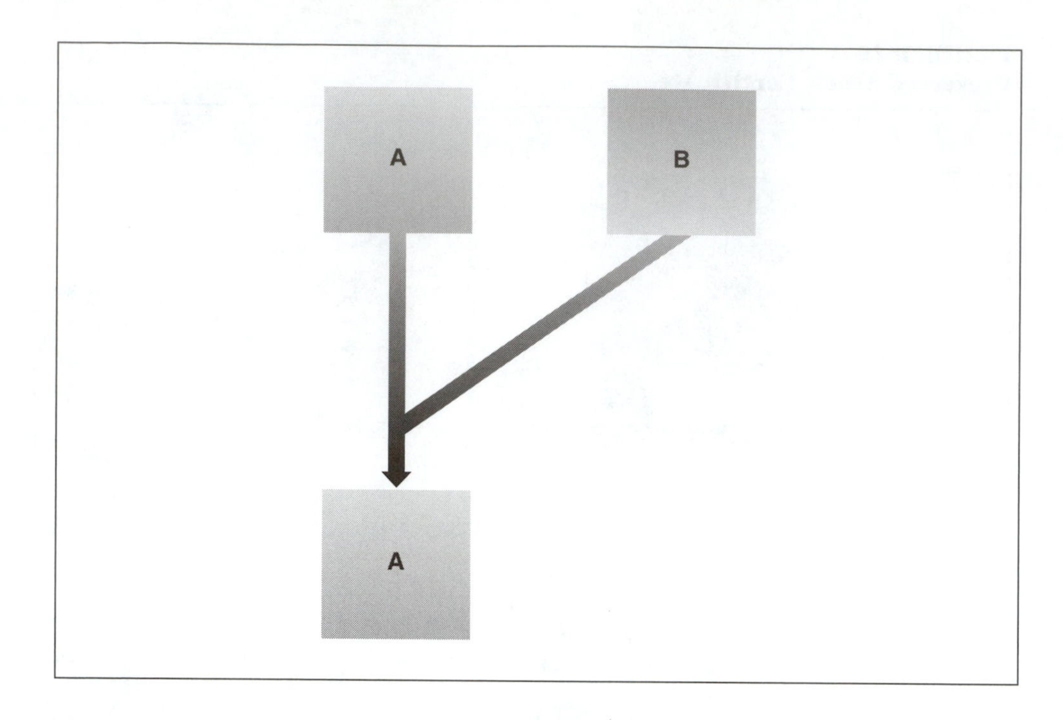

CONSOLIDATION

CONSOLIDATION
A process whereby two or more corporations join to become a completely new corporation. The original corporations cease to exist, and the new corporation acquires all their assets and liabilities.

In the case of a **consolidation,** two or more corporations combine in such a way that each corporation ceases to exist, and a new one emerges. For example, Corporation A and Corporation B consolidate to form an entirely new organization, Corporation C. In the process, A and B both terminate, and C comes into existence as an entirely new entity. This process is illustrated graphically in Exhibit 29–5.

RESULTS OF MERGER OR CONSOLIDATION

The results of a merger are similar to the results of a consolidation. In a merger, the surviving corporation assumes all of the assets and liabilities of the disappearing corporation. The articles of merger (the agreement between the merging

EXHIBIT 29–5
Consolidation

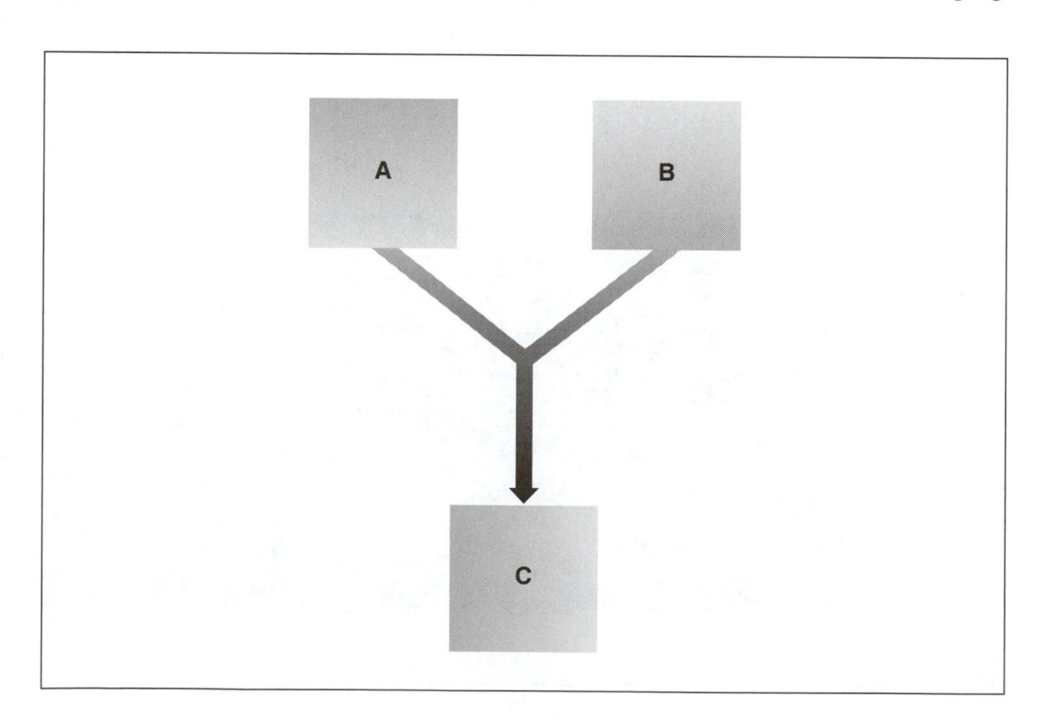

corporations, which sets out the surviving corporation's name, capital structure, and so forth) are deemed to amend the articles of the surviving corporation.

After a consolidation, the new corporation acquires all of the assets and liabilities of the corporations that were consolidated. The articles of consolidation (the agreement between the consolidating corporations, which sets out the new corporation's name, capital structure, and so forth) take the place of the disappearing corporations' original corporate articles and are thereafter regarded as the new corporation's corporate articles.

IN THE COURTROOM

McCarty Music Corporation and Rosen Instruments, Inc., decide to consolidate to form MCR, Inc., an entirely new corporation. After the consolidation, McCarty and Rosen will cease to exist. *What happens to McCarty's assets? Who pays Rosen's creditors?* After the consolidation, MCR will be recognized as a new corporation and a single entity. MCR will assume all the rights, privileges, and powers previously held by McCarty and Rosen. Title to any assets owned by McCarty and Rosen passes to MCR without formal transfer. MCR assumes liability for all debts owed by McCarty and Rosen.

In a merger or consolidation, the surviving corporation is vested with the pre-existing legal rights and obligations of the disappearing corporation (or corporations).

When a merger or a consolidation takes place, the surviving corporation or newly formed corporation issues shares to pay some fair consideration to the shareholders of the corporation that ceases to exist.

PROCEDURE FOR MERGER OR CONSOLIDATION

All states have statutes authorizing mergers and consolidations for domestic corporations. Most states also allow the combination of domestic (in-state) and foreign (out-of-state) corporations. Although the procedures vary somewhat among jurisdictions, in each situation the basic requirements are as follows:

1. The board of directors of each corporation involved must approve a merger or consolidation plan.
2. The shareholders of each corporation must vote approval of the plan at a shareholders' meeting. Most state statutes require the approval of two-thirds of the outstanding shares of voting stock, although some states require only a simple majority and others require a four-fifths vote. Frequently, statutes require that each class of stock approve the merger. Thus, the holders of nonvoting stock (such as preferred stock) must also approve. A corporation's bylaws can dictate a stricter requirement.
3. Once approved by all the directors and the shareholders, the plan (articles of merger or consolidation) is filed, usually with the secretary of state.
4. When state formalities are satisfied, the state issues a certificate of merger to the surviving corporation or a certificate of consolidation to the newly consolidated corporation.

Hoover's Online has an extensive collection of data on U.S. corporations. To access this site, go to

http://www.hoovers.com

SHORT-FORM MERGER
A merger between a subsidiary corporation and a parent corporation that owns at least 90 percent of the outstanding shares of each class of stock issued by the subsidiary corporation. Short-form mergers can be accomplished without the approval of the shareholders of either corporation.

Some states provide a simplified procedure for the merger of a subsidiary corporation into its parent corporation. Under these provisions, a **short-form merger** can be accomplished if the parent owns substantially all of the stock of the subsidiary *without the approval of the other shareholders* of either corporation.

Generally, the short-form merger can be utilized only when the parent corporation owns at least 90 percent of the outstanding shares of each class of stock of the subsidiary corporation. The simplified procedure requires that a plan for the merger be approved by the board of directors of the parent corporation before it is filed with the state. A copy of the merger plan must be sent to each shareholder of record of the subsidiary corporation.

Appraisal Rights

What if a shareholder disapproves of the merger or consolidation but is outvoted by the other shareholders? The law recognizes that a dissenting shareholder should not be forced to become an unwilling shareholder in a corporation that is new or different from the one in which the shareholder originally invested. The shareholder has the right to dissent and may be entitled to be paid the *fair value* for the number of shares held on the date of the merger or consolidation. This right is referred to as the shareholder's **appraisal right.**

Appraisal Right
A dissenting shareholder's right, if he or she objects to an extraordinary transaction of the corporation (such as a merger or consolidation), to have his or her shares appraised and to be paid the fair market value of his or her shares by the corporation.

An appraisal right is available only when a state statute specifically provides for it. It is normally extended to regular mergers; consolidations; short-form mergers; sales of substantially all of the corporate assets not in the ordinary course of business; and in certain states, amendments to the articles of incorporation. The appraisal right may be lost if the statutory procedures are not followed precisely. Whenever the right is lost, the dissenting shareholder must go along with the transaction despite his or her objections.

Shareholder Approval

Actions taken on extraordinary matters must be authorized by the board of directors and the shareholders. Often, modern statutes require that certain types of extraordinary matters—such as the sale, lease, or exchange of all or substantially all corporate assets outside of the corporation's regular course of business—be approved by a prescribed voter consent of the shareholders. Hence, when any extraordinary matter arises, the corporation must proceed as authorized by law to obtain the approval of the shareholders and the board of directors.

Purchase of Assets

When a corporation acquires all or substantially all of the assets of another corporation by direct purchase, the purchasing, or *acquiring,* corporation simply extends its ownership and control over more physical assets. Because no change in the legal entity occurs, the acquiring corporation is not required to obtain shareholder approval for the purchase.

For daily news on the world of business, including corporate activities, you can access Money Online at

http://www.money.com

Although the acquiring corporation may not be required to obtain shareholder approval for such an acquisition, the U.S. Department of Justice has issued guidelines that significantly constrain, and often prohibit, mergers that could result from a purchase of assets. These guidelines are part of the federal antitrust laws (see Chapter 40).

Note that the corporation that is selling all its assets is substantially changing its business position and perhaps its ability to carry out its corporate purposes. For that reason, the corporation whose assets are acquired must obtain the approval of both the board of directors and the shareholders. In most states, a dissenting shareholder of the selling corporation can demand appraisal rights.

Generally, a corporation that purchases the assets of another corporation is not responsible for the liabilities of the selling corporation. Exceptions to this rule are made in the following circumstances:

1. When the purchasing corporation assumes the seller's liabilities (or a court imposes the seller's liabilities on the purchasing corporation).
2. When the sale amounts to what in fact is a merger or consolidation.

3. When the purchaser continues the seller's business and retains the same personnel (same shareholders, directors, and officers).
4. When the sale is fraudulently executed to escape liability.

Purchase of Stock

An alternative to the purchase of another corporation's assets is the purchase of a substantial number of the voting shares of its stock. This enables the acquiring corporation to control the acquired corporation. The acquiring corporation deals directly with the shareholders in seeking to purchase the shares they hold.

When the acquiring corporation makes a public offer to all shareholders of the **target corporation** (the corporation that the acquiring corporation seeks to take over), it is called a **tender offer** (an offer that is publicly advertised and addressed to all shareholders of the target company). The price of the stock in the tender offer is generally higher than the market price of the target stock prior to the announcement of the tender offer. The higher price induces shareholders to sell their shares to the acquiring firm.

TARGET CORPORATION
The acquired corporation in a corporate takeover; a corporation to whose shareholders a tender offer is submitted.

TENDER OFFER
An offer by one company to buy shares in another company made directly to the shareholders.

Termination

Termination of a corporate life has two phases. **Dissolution** is the legal death of the artificial "person" of the corporation. **Liquidation** is the process by which corporate assets are converted into cash and distributed among creditors and shareholders according to specific rules of preference.

LEARNING OBJECTIVE NO. 4
Discussing the Phases Involved in the Termination of a Corporation

DISSOLUTION

Dissolution of a corporation can be brought about in any of the following ways:

1. An act of the legislature in the state of incorporation.
2. Expiration of the time provided in the certificate of incorporation.
3. Voluntary approval of the shareholders and the board of directors.
4. Unanimous action by all shareholders.
5. Court decree.

When buying or selling a corporation, consult an attorney before taking any irrevocable steps.

IN THE COURTROOM

Dee and Jim form Home Remodeling, Inc. They are Home Corporation's only shareholders and directors. After three years, they decide to cease business, dissolve the corporation, and go their separate ways. *Can they simply dissolve Home at will?* Yes. Shareholders acting unanimously can dissolve a corporation. Also, close corporations (corporations with a small number of shareholders) may be dissolved by a single shareholder if the articles of incorporation provide for it.

DISSOLUTION
The formal disbanding of a partnership or a corporation. A corporation can be dissolved by (1) the legislature in the state of incorporation, (2) the expiration of time stated in the certificate of incorporation, (3) agreement of the shareholders and board of directors, (4) unanimous act by all shareholders, or (5) court order.

LIQUIDATION
The sale of the assets of a business or an individual for cash and the distribution of the cash received to creditors, with the balance going to the owner(s).

Sometimes an *involuntary* dissolution of a corporation is necessary. For example, the board of directors may be deadlocked. A shareholder may petition a court to dissolve a corporation. Courts hesitate to order involuntary dissolution in such circumstances unless there is specific statutory authorization to do so. If the deadlock cannot be resolved by the shareholders, however, and if it will irreparably injure the corporation, the court will proceed with an involuntary dissolution. Courts can also dissolve a corporation for mismanagement.

The attorney general of the state of incorporation may ask a court to dissolve a corporation for any of the following reasons: (a) the failure to comply with administrative requirements (for example, failure to pay annual franchise taxes, to submit an annual report, or to have a designated registered agent), (b) the procurement of a corporation charter through fraud or misrepresentation on the state, (c) the abuse of corporate powers (*ultra vires* acts), (d) the violation of the state criminal code after the demand to discontinue has been made by the secretary of state, (e) the failure to commence business operations, or (f) the abandonment of operations before starting up.

LIQUIDATION

When dissolution takes place by voluntary action, the members of the board of directors act as trustees of the corporate assets. As trustees, they are responsible for winding up the affairs of the corporation for the benefit of corporate creditors and shareholders. This makes the board members personally liable for any breach of their fiduciary trustee duties.

RECEIVER
A court-appointed person who receives, preserves, and manages a business or other property that is involved in the dissolution of a corporation.

Liquidation can be accomplished without court supervision unless the members of the board do not wish to act in this capacity, or unless shareholders or creditors can show cause to the court why the board should not be permitted to assume the trustee function. In either case, the court will appoint a **receiver** to wind up the corporate affairs and liquidate corporate assets. A receiver is always appointed by the court if the dissolution is involuntary.

TERMS AND CONCEPTS FOR REVIEW

alien corporation 366
appraisal right 376
articles of incorporation 368
bond 371
bond indenture 372
bylaws 370
certificate of incorporation 370
close corporation 366
common stock 371
consolidation 374
dissolution 377
domestic corporation 366
foreign corporation 366
liquidation 377
merger 372
preferred stock 371
promoter 367
receiver 378
S corporation 366
securities 371
short-form merger 375
stock 366
target corporation 377
tender offer 377
***ultra vires* 370**

CHAPTER SUMMARY • FORMATION AND TERMINATION OF A CORPORATION

Classification of Corporations	1. *Domestic, foreign, and alien corporations*—A corporation is referred to as a *domestic corporation* within its home state (the state in which it incorporates). A corporation is referred to as a *foreign corporation* by any state that is not its home state. A corporation is referred to as an *alien corporation* if it originates in another country but does business in the United States. 2. *Public and private corporations*—A public corporation is one formed by government (for example, cities, towns, and public projects). A private corporation is one formed wholly or in part for private benefit. Most corporations are private. A private corporation with a small number of shareholders is a *close corporation.* 3. *Nonprofit corporations*—Corporations formed without a profit-making purpose (for example, charitable, educational, and religious organizations and hospitals). 4. *S corporations*—Small domestic corporations that, under Subchapter S of the Internal Revenue Code, are given special tax treatment. These corporations allow shareholders to enjoy limited legal liability but avoid double taxation (taxes are paid by shareholders as personal income, and the S corporation is not taxed separately).

CHAPTER SUMMARY • *Continued*

Corporate Formation	**1.** *Promoter*—One who takes the preliminary steps in organizing a corporation. **2.** *Incorporation procedures*— **a.** Selection of a state in which to incorporate. **b.** Preparation and filing of the articles of incorporation. The articles generally should include the following information concerning the corporation: name, nature and purpose, duration, capital structure, registered office and agent, and incorporators. **c.** Certificate of incorporation—Charter received from the appropriate state office (usually the secretary of state) after the articles of incorporation have been filed. Authorizes the corporation to conduct business. **d.** First organizational meeting—Provided for in the articles of incorporation but held after the charter is granted. The board of directors is elected and other business is completed.
Corporate Powers	**1.** *Express powers*—The express powers of a corporation are granted by the following laws and documents (listed according to their priority): U.S. Constitution, state constitutions, state statutes, articles of incorporation, bylaws, and resolutions of the board of directors. **2.** *Implied powers*—A corporation has the implied power to do all acts reasonably appropriate and necessary to accomplish its corporate purposes. **3.** Ultra vires *doctrine*—Any act of a corporation that is beyond the authority given to it under its charter or under the statutes by which it was incorporated is an *ultra vires* act. *Ultra vires* contracts may or may not be enforced by the courts.
Corporate Financing	**1.** *Stocks*—Stocks are securities issued by a corporation that represent the purchase of ownership in the firm. The most important characteristics of stock include: they need not be paid back, stockholders receive dividends only when so voted by the directors, stockholders are the last investors to be paid on dissolution, and stockholders vote for directors and on other issues. **2.** *Bonds*—Corporate bonds are securities representing corporate debt (money borrowed by a corporation).
Merger and Consolidation	**1.** *Merger*—The combination of two or more corporations, the result of which is that the surviving corporation acquires all the assets and obligations of the other corporation, which then ceases to exist. **2.** *Consolidation*—The combination of two or more corporations, the result of which is that each corporation ceases to exist and a new one emerges. The new corporation assumes all the assets and obligations of the former corporations. **3.** *Procedure*—Determined by state statutes. Basic requirements are: **a.** The board of directors of each corporation involved must approve the merger or consolidation plan. **b.** The shareholders of each corporation must approve the merger or consolidation plan at a shareholders' meeting. **c.** Articles of merger or consolidation (the plan) must be filed, usually with the secretary of state. **d.** The state issues a certificate of merger (or consolidation) to the surviving (or newly consolidated) corporation. **4.** *Short-form merger (parent-subsidiary merger)*—Possible when the parent corporation owns at least 90 percent of the outstanding shares of each class of stock of the subsidiary corporation. **a.** Shareholder approval is not required. **b.** The merger must be approved only by the board of directors of the parent corporation. **c.** A copy of the merger plan must be sent to each shareholder. **d.** The merger plan must be filed with the state. **5.** *Appraisal rights*—Rights of shareholders (given by state statute) to receive the *fair value* for their shares when a merger or consolidation takes place.
Purchase of Assets	The acquisition by a corporation of all or substantially all of the assets of another corporation. The acquiring corporation is not required to obtain shareholder approval (the corporation is merely increasing its assets, and no fundamental business change occurs). The acquired corporation must obtain the approval of both its directors and its shareholders, because the sale creates a substantial change in the corporation's business position.

CHAPTER SUMMARY • *Continued*

Purchase of Stock	The acquisition by a corporation of a substantial number of the voting shares of another (target) corporation may involve a public offer to all shareholders of the target corporation to purchase its stock at a price generally higher than the market price of the target stock prior to the offer.
Termination	The termination of a corporation involves the following two phases: **1.** *Dissolution*—The legal death of the corporation. Dissolution can be brought about in any of the following ways: **a.** An act of the legislature in the state of incorporation. **b.** Expiration of the time provided in the corporate charter. **c.** Voluntary approval of the shareholders and the board of directors. **d.** Unanimous action by all shareholders. **e.** Court decree. **2.** *Liquidation*—The process by which corporate assets are converted into cash and distributed to creditors and shareholders according to specified rules of preference. Liquidation may be supervised by members of the board of directors (when dissolution is voluntary) or by a receiver appointed by the court to wind up corporate affairs.

HYPOTHETICAL QUESTIONS

29–1. Liability for Preincorporation Contracts. Christy, Briggs, and Dobbs are recent college graduates who want to form a corporation to manufacture and sell personal computers. Perez tells them that he will set in motion the formation of their corporation. Perez first makes a contract with Oliver for the purchase of a parcel of land for $25,000. Oliver does not know of the prospective corporate formation at the time the contract is signed. Perez then makes a contract with Kovac to build a small plant on the property being purchased. Kovac's contract is conditional on the corporation's formation. Perez secures all necessary subscription agreements and capitalization, and he files the articles of incorporation. A charter is issued.

(a) Discuss whether the newly formed corporation or Perez (or both) is liable on the contracts with Oliver and Kovac.

(b) Discuss whether the corporation, on coming into legal existence, is automatically liable to Kovac.

29–2. Corporate Powers. Kora Nayenga and two business associates formed a corporation called Nayenga Corp. for the purpose of selling computer services. Kora, who owned 50 percent of the corporate shares, served as the corporation's president. Kora wished to obtain a personal loan from his bank for $250,000, but the bank required the note to be cosigned by a third party. Kora cosigned the note in the name of the corporation. Later, Kora defaulted on the note, and the bank sued the corporation for payment. The corporation asserted, as a defense, that Kora had exceeded his authority when he cosigned the note. Had he? Explain.

REAL WORLD CASE PROBLEM

29–3. Appraisal Rights. Travelers Corp. announced that it would merge with Primerica Corp. At a special shareholders meeting, a vote of the Travelers shareholders revealed that 95 percent approved of the merger. Robert Brandt and other shareholders who did not approve of the merger sued Travelers and others, complaining that the defendants had not obtained "the highest possible price for shareholders." Travelers asked the court to dismiss the suit, contending that Brandt and the others had, as a remedy for their complaint, their statutory appraisal rights. On what basis might the court dismiss the suit? Discuss. [*Brandt v. Travelers Corp.*, 44 Conn.Supp. 12, 665 A.2d 616 (1995)]

For updated links to resources available on the Web, as well as a variety of other materials, visit this text's Web site at **http://blte.westbuslaw.com.**

Cornell University's Legal Information Institute has links to state corporation statutes at

http://fatty.law.cornell.edu/topics/state_statutes.html

For an example of one state's (Florida's) statute governing corporations, go to

http://www.ilrg.com/whatsnews/statute.html

and scroll down the page to "Corporations."

For information on incorporation, including a list of "frequently asked questions" on this topic, go to

http://www.bizfilings.com

You may be able to find your state's statutory requirements for merger and consolidation procedures at

http://wwwsecure.law.cornell.edu/topics/state_statutes.html

The court opinions of Delaware's Court of Chancery, which is widely considered to be the nation's premier trial court for corporate law, are now available on the Web in a searchable database offered by the Delaware Corporate Law Clearinghouse. The site also offers valuable links to other sites dealing with corporate law and litigation. Go to

http://corporate-law.widener.edu

ONLINE LEGAL RESEARCH

Go to **http://blte.westbuslaw.com**, the Web site that accompanies this text. Select "Internet Applications," and then click on "Chapter 29." There you will find the following Internet research exercise that you can perform to learn more about the law governing corporations:

Activity 29–1: Corporate Law

Chapter 29 ■ WORK SET

TRUE-FALSE QUESTIONS

_____ **1.** A corporation is an artificial being.

_____ **2.** A corporation that is formed in a country other than the United States, but which does business in the United States, is a foreign corporation.

_____ **3.** Generally, a promoter is personally liable on a preincorporation contract until the corporation assumes it by novation or adopts it by performance.

_____ **4.** When conflicts arise among documents involving corporations, resolutions of the board of directors have the highest priority.

_____ **5.** Stocks are certificates that evidence corporate ownership.

_____ **6.** During the liquidation of a corporation, corporate assets are converted to cash and distributed to creditors and shareholders.

_____ **7.** Shareholders who disapprove of a merger or a consolidation may be entitled to be paid the fair value of their shares.

_____ **8.** A corporation that purchases the assets of another corporation always assumes the selling corporation's liabilities.

MULTIPLE-CHOICE QUESTIONS

_____ **1.** Adam, Terry, and Victor want to form ATV Corporation. Which of the following is NOT a step in forming the corporation?

a. The promoters make preincorporation contracts.
b. The incorporators execute the articles of incorporation.
c. The shareholders approve or disapprove of corporate business matters at a shareholders' meeting.
d. The incorporators (or the board of directors) hold an organizational meeting to complete details of incorporation.

_____ **2.** Mike, Nora, and Paula are shareholders in National Business, Inc. All of the shareholders are National's

a. owners.
b. directors.
c. incorporators.
d. promoters.

_____ **3.** Responsibility for the overall management of Standard Products, Inc., a corporation, rests with its

a. owners.
b. directors.
c. incorporators.
d. promoters.

_____ **4.** U.S. Digital Corporation incorporated in Ohio, its only place of business. Its stock is owned by ten shareholders. Two are resident aliens. Three of the others are the directors and officers. The stock has never been sold to the public. If a shareholder wants to sell his or her shares, the other shareholders must be given the opportunity to buy them first. U.S. Digital is

a. a close corporation.
b. a foreign corporation.
c. an alien corporation.
d. none of the above.

_____ **5.** General Manufacturing, Inc. (GMI), issues bonds to finance the purchase of a factory. Regarding those bonds, which of the following is TRUE?

a. The bonds must be repaid.
b. The bondholders will receive interest payments only when voted by GMI directors.
c. The bonds are identical to preferred stock from an investment standpoint.
d. The bondholders will be the last investors paid on GMI's dissolution.

_____ **6.** Nationwide Investments, Inc., incorporates in Delaware. Delaware's state attorney general may seek a court decree to dissolve Nationwide if the firm

a. does not file an annual report.
b. does not commence business operations.
c. attempts to take over another corporation through stock acquisition.
d. both a and b.

_____ **7.** Sugar Corporation and Spice Products, Inc., decide to combine. Afterwards, Sugar will cease to exist—only Spice will function, as the surviving corporation. The combination of Sugar and Spice is

a. a consolidation.
b. a merger.
c. both a and b.
d. none of the above.

_____ **8.** Mary and Adam are the directors and majority shareholders of U.S. Imports, Inc., and Overseas Corporation. U.S. Imports owes $5,000 to International Transport, Inc. To avoid the debt, Mary and Adam vote to sell all of U.S. Imports' assets to Overseas. If International sues Overseas on the debt, International will

a. win, because an acquiring firm always assumes a selling corporation's liabilities.
b. win, because the sale was fraudulently executed to avoid liability.
c. lose, because Overseas refused to assume U.S. Imports' debt.
d. lose, because U.S. Imports has ceased to exist.

ISSUE SPOTTERS

1. Northwest Brands, Inc., is a small business. Incorporated in Minnesota, its one class of stock is owned by twelve members of a single family. Ordinarily, corporate income is taxed at the corporate and shareholder levels. Is there a way for Northwest Brands to avoid this double income taxation?

2. The incorporators of Consumer Investments, Inc., want their new corporation to have the authority to transact virtually all types of conceivable business. Can they grant this authority to their firm? How?

Ownership and Management of a Corporation

30

LEARNING OBJECTIVES

When you finish this chapter, you should be able to:

1 List corporate directors' management responsibilities.

2 State the effect of the business judgment rule on directors' liability for poor business decisions.

3 Discuss the purpose and effect of cumulative voting.

4 Identify shareholders' liability for corporate debts.

FACING A LEGAL PROBLEM

Tim Rodale, one of the directors of the First National Bank, fails to attend any board of directors' meetings in five and a half years, never inspects any of the bank's books or records, and generally fails to supervise the efforts of the bank president and the loan committee. Meanwhile, the bank president makes various improper loans and permits large overdrafts. *Can Rodale be held liable to the bank for losses resulting from the unsupervised actions of the bank president and the loan committee?*

A corporation joins the efforts and resources of a large number of individuals for the purpose of producing greater returns than those persons could have obtained individually. This chapter focuses on corporate directors, managers, and shareholders (those who own stock in the corporation) and ways in which conflicts among them can be resolved.

Corporate Management—Directors and Officers

Every corporation is governed by a board of directors. The number of directors is set forth in the corporation's articles of incorporation or bylaws. Some states set the minimum number of directors at three, but many states permit fewer. Some states permit corporations with fewer than fifty shareholders to eliminate the board of directors.

Election of Directors

The first board of directors is normally appointed by the incorporators upon the creation of the corporation, or directors are named by the corporation itself in

At last count, the corporation statutes of about one-fourth of the states were online. Cornell University Legal Information Institute has links to these statutes at

http://fatty.law.cornell.edu/topics/ state_statutes.html

the articles. The first board serves until the first annual shareholders' meeting. Subsequent directors are elected by a majority vote of the shareholders.

The term of office for a director is usually one year—from annual meeting to annual meeting. Longer and staggered terms are permissible under most state statutes. A common practice is to elect one-third of the board members each year for a three-year term. In this way, there is greater management continuity.

A director can be removed *for cause* (breach of duty or other misconduct), either as specified in the articles or bylaws or by shareholder action. Even the board of directors itself may be given power to remove a director for cause, subject to shareholder review. In most states, unless the shareholders have reserved the right at the time of election, a director cannot be removed without cause.

Sometimes, vacancies occur on the board of directors due to death or resignation. New positions may be created through amendment of the articles or bylaws. When a vacancy exists, either the shareholders or the board itself can fill the position, depending on state law or on the provisions of the bylaws.

Directors' Qualifications

Few legal qualifications exist for directors. Only a handful of states have minimum age and residency requirements. A director is sometimes a shareholder, but this is not a necessary qualification unless, of course, statutory provisions or corporate articles or bylaws require ownership.

Board of Directors' Forum

The board of directors conducts business by holding formal meetings with recorded minutes. The date at which regular meetings are held is usually established in the articles and bylaws or by board resolution. No further notice is customarily required. Special meetings can be called with notice sent to all directors.

Quorum
The number of members of a decision-making body that must be present before business may be transacted.

Quorum requirements vary among jurisdictions. (A **quorum** is the minimum number of members of a body of officials or other group that must be present before business can validly be transacted.) Many states leave the decision to the corporate articles or bylaws. If the articles or bylaws do not state quorum requirements, most states provide that a quorum is a majority of the number of directors authorized in the articles or bylaws.

Voting is done in person. The rule is one vote per director. Ordinary matters generally require a majority vote. Certain extraordinary issues may require a greater-than-majority vote.

Directors' Responsibilities

LEARNING OBJECTIVE NO. 1
Listing Corporate Directors' Management Responsibilities

Directors have responsibility for all policymaking decisions necessary to the management of all corporate affairs. The directors must act as a body in carrying out routine corporate business.

The general areas of responsibility of the board of directors include the following:

1. Authorization for major corporate policy decisions (for example, the determination of new product lines and the overseeing of major contract negotiations and major management-labor negotiations).
2. Appointment, supervision, and removal of corporate officers and other managerial employees and the determination of their compensation.
3. Financial decisions, such as the declaration and payment of dividends to shareholders or the issuance of authorized shares (stocks) or bonds.

The board of directors can delegate some of its functions to an executive committee or to corporate officers. In doing so, the board is not relieved of its overall responsibility for directing the affairs of the corporation. Corporate officers and managerial personnel, however, are then empowered to make decisions relating to ordinary, daily corporate affairs within well-defined guidelines.

In the legal problem set out at the beginning of this chapter, Tim Rodale, one of the directors of the First National Bank, fails to attend any board meetings in five and a half years, never inspects any of the bank's books or records, and fails to supervise the bank president and the loan committee. Meanwhile, the bank president makes improper loans and permits large overdrafts. *Can Rodale be held liable to the bank for losses resulting from the actions of the president and the loan committee?* Yes. As explained below, the director has breached his duty of care. In this situation, the director may be held liable to the bank for the losses.

Role of Corporate Officers

The officers and other executive employees are hired by the board of directors or, in rare instances, by the shareholders. Corporate officers carry out the duties articulated in the bylaws. They also act as agents of the corporation. The ordinary rules of agency (see Chapter 25) apply.

Qualifications are determined at the discretion of the corporation and are included in the articles or bylaws. In most states, a person can hold more than one office and can be both an officer and a director of the corporation.

The rights of corporate officers and other high-level managers are defined by employment contracts, because officers and managers are employees of the company. Corporate officers, however, normally can be removed by the board of directors at any time with or without cause and regardless of the terms of the employment contract, although it is possible for the corporation to be held liable for breach of contract.

You can find an online newsletter dealing with corporate officers' and employees' personal liability for business taxes at

http://www.integritax.com

Duties of Directors and Officers

Directors and officers are deemed fiduciaries of the corporation. A *fiduciary* is a person with a duty to act primarily for another's benefit. A fiduciary relationship involves trust and confidence. The relationship of directors and officers with the corporation and its shareholders is one of trust and confidence. The fiduciary duties of the directors and officers include the duty of care and the duty of loyalty.

Duty of Care. Directors are obligated to be honest and to use prudent business judgment in the conduct of corporate affairs. Directors must exercise the same degree of care that reasonably prudent people use in the conduct of their own personal affairs. Directors must carry out their responsibilities in an informed, businesslike manner and act in accordance with their own knowledge and training.

Directors can be held answerable to the corporation and to the shareholders for breach of their duty of care. When directors delegate work to corporate officers and employees, they are expected to use a reasonable amount of supervision. Otherwise, they will be held liable for *negligence* or *mismanagement* of corporate personnel.

Before discarding old files, find out which documents must be retained under the Code of Federal Regulations and under other government agency regulations to which your corporation is subject.

Duty of Loyalty. *Loyalty* can be defined as faithfulness to one's obligations and duties. The essence of the duty of loyalty is the subordination of self-interest to the interest of the entity to which the duty is owed. The duty presumes constant loyalty to the corporation on the part of the directors and officers. In general, the duty of loyalty prohibits directors from using corporate funds or confidential corporate information for their personal advantage.

Sometimes a corporation enters into a contract or engages in a transaction in which an officer or director has a material interest. The director or officer must make a *full disclosure* of that interest and must abstain from voting on the proposed transaction.

IN THE COURTROOM

Sunwood Corporation needs office space. Lambert Alden, one of its five directors, owns the building adjoining the corporate headquarters. He negotiates a lease with Sunwood for the space, making a full disclosure to Sunwood and the other four board directors. The lease arrangement is fair, and it is unanimously approved by Sunwood's board of directors. *Has Alden breached the duty of loyalty simply because he personally benefited from the lease?* No. In evaluating such situations, the rule is one of reason: Is the deal reasonable? Otherwise, directors would be prevented from ever giving financial assistance to the corporations they serve.

LEARNING OBJECTIVE NO. 2

Stating the Effect of the Business Judgment Rule on Directors' Liability for Poor Business Decisions

The Business Judgment Rule. Directors are not insurers of business success. Honest mistakes of judgment and poor business decisions on their part do not make them liable to the corporation for resulting damages. This is the **business judgment rule.** The rule immunizes directors and officers from liability when a decision is within managerial authority, as long as the decision complies with management's fiduciary duties and as long as acting on the decision is within the powers of the corporation. Consequently, if there is a reasonable basis for a business decision, it is unlikely that a court will interfere with that decision, even if the corporation suffers thereby. For instance, if the directors of the American Cola Corporation decide to change the taste of American Cola (the principal product of the company) and the public rejects the new product, the directors are not liable for the lost sales.

BUSINESS JUDGMENT RULE
A rule that immunizes corporate management from liability for actions that are undertaken in good faith, when the actions are within both the power of the corporation and the authority of management to make.

Corporate Ownership—Shareholders

The acquisition of a share of stock makes a person an owner and shareholder in a corporation. Shareholders thus own the corporation. As a general rule, shareholders have no responsibility for the daily management of the corporation. They are, however, ultimately responsible for choosing the board of directors, which does have that control. Here, we look at the powers and rights of shareholders, which are generally established in the articles of incorporation and under each state's general incorporation laws.

SHAREHOLDERS' POWERS

Shareholders must approve fundamental changes affecting the corporation before the changes can be effected. Hence, shareholders must approve amendments to the articles of incorporation and bylaws, they must approve a merger or the dissolution of the corporation (see Chapter 29), and they must approve the sale of all or substantially all of the corporation's assets. Some of these actions are subject to prior board approval.

Election and removal of directors are accomplished by a vote of the shareholders. As explained earlier, the first board of directors is either named in the articles of incorporation or chosen by the incorporators to serve until the first shareholders' meeting. From that time on, selection and retention of directors are exclusively shareholder functions.

Shareholders have the inherent power to remove a director from office *for cause* by a majority vote. Some state statutes even permit removal of directors *without cause* by the vote of a majority of the holders of outstanding shares entitled to vote. Some corporate charters expressly provide that shareholders, by majority vote, can remove a director at any time *without cause.*

SHAREHOLDERS' FORUM

Shareholders' meetings must occur at least annually. Additionally, special meetings can be called to take care of urgent matters. Because it is usually not practical for owners of only a few shares of stock of publicly traded corporations to attend shareholders' meetings, such stockholders normally give third parties a written authorization to vote their shares at the meeting. This authorization is called a **proxy.**

PROXY
In corporation law, a written agreement between a stockholder and another under which the stockholder authorizes the other to vote the stockholder's shares in a certain manner.

Shareholder Voting. Shareholders exercise ownership control through the power of their votes. Each shareholder is entitled to one vote per share. The articles of incorporation can exclude or limit voting rights, particularly to certain classes of shares. For example, owners of preferred stock (see Chapter 29) are usually denied the right to vote.

For shareholders to act, a quorum (a minimum number of shareholders, in terms of the number of shares held) must be present at a meeting. Generally, a quorum is more than 50 percent. Corporate business matters are presented in the form of resolutions, which shareholders vote to approve or disapprove. Some state statutes set forth voting limits. Corporations' articles or bylaws must remain within these statutory limitations. Some states provide that the unanimous written consent of shareholders is a permissible alternative to holding a shareholders' meeting.

Once a quorum is present, a majority vote of the shares represented at the meeting is usually required to pass resolutions. At times, a larger-than-majority vote will be required either by statute or by corporate charter. Extraordinary corporate matters, such as a merger, consolidation, or dissolution of the corporation (see Chapter 29), require a higher percentage of the representatives of all corporate shares entitled to vote, not just a majority of those present at that particular meeting.

IN THE COURTROOM

Novo Pictures, Inc., has 10,000 outstanding shares of voting stock. Its articles of incorporation set the quorum for shareholders' meetings at 50 percent of outstanding shares and provide that a majority vote of the shares present is necessary to pass on ordinary matters. *How many outstanding shares must be represented at a shareholders' meeting to conduct business?* A quorum of shareholders representing 5,000 of the outstanding shares must be present to conduct business. *A vote of how many of those shares is required to pass an ordinary resolution?* If 5,000 shares are represented, a vote of at least 2,501 of those shares is needed to pass a resolution. If more than 5,000 shares are represented, a larger vote will be required.

LEARNING OBJECTIVE NO. 3
Discussing the Purpose and Effect of Cumulative Voting

Cumulative Voting. Most states permit or require shareholders to elect directors by *cumulative voting,* a method of voting designed to allow minority shareholders to obtain representation on the board of directors. When cumulative voting is allowed or required, the number of members of the board to be elected is multiplied by the total number of voting shares held. The result equals the number of votes a shareholder has. The shareholder can cast this total number of votes for one or more nominees for director. All nominees stand for election at the same time. When cumulative voting is not required either by statute or under the articles, the entire board can be elected by a majority of shares at a shareholders' meeting.

IN THE COURTROOM

Tam Corporation has 10,000 outstanding shares. Three members of the board are to be elected. A majority of the shareholders (holding 7,000 shares) favor Acevedo, Barkley, and Craycik. The other shareholders (3,000 shares) favor Drake. *Can Drake be elected by the minority shareholders?* If cumulative voting is allowed, the answer is yes. The minority shareholders have 9,000 votes among them (the number of directors to be elected times the number of shares is 3 times 3,000, which equals 9,000 votes). All of these votes can be cast to elect Drake. The majority shareholders have 21,000 votes (3 times 7,000 equals 21,000 votes), but these votes have to be distributed among their three choices. No matter how the majority shareholders cast their votes, they cannot elect all three directors if the minority shareholders cast all of their votes for Drake. See Exhibit 30–1.

SHAREHOLDERS' RIGHTS

Shareholders possess numerous rights. In addition to voting rights (discussed above), a shareholder has the rights discussed below.

STOCK CERTIFICATE
A certificate issued by a corporation evidencing the ownership of a specified number of shares at a specified value.

Stock Certificates. A **stock certificate** is a certificate issued by a corporation that evidences ownership of a specified number of shares in the corporation. In jurisdictions that require the issuance of stock certificates, shareholders have the right to demand that the corporation issue a certificate and record their names and addresses in the corporate stock record books. In most states, boards of directors may provide that shares of stock be uncertificated (that is, that actual, physical stock certificates need not be issued). In that circumstance, the corporation may be required to send the holders of uncertificated shares letters or some other form of notice containing the same information required to be included on the face of stock certificates.

Stock is intangible personal property. The ownership right exists independently of the certificate itself. A stock certificate may be lost or destroyed, but ownership is not destroyed with it. A new certificate can be issued to replace one that has been lost or destroyed. Notice of shareholder meetings, dividends, and operational and financial reports are all distributed according to the recorded ownership listed in the corporation's books, not on the basis of possession of the certificate.

PREEMPTIVE RIGHTS
Rights held by shareholders that entitle them to purchase newly issued shares of a corporation's stock, equal in percentage to shares presently held, before the stock is offered to any outside buyers. Preemptive rights enable shareholders to maintain their proportionate ownership and voice in the corporation.

Preemptive Rights. A **preemptive right** is a preference given to a shareholder over all other purchasers to subscribe to or purchase a prorated share of a new issue of stock. This allows the shareholder to maintain his or her portion of control, voting power, or financial interest in the corporation. For example, a

EXHIBIT 30–1
Results of Cumulative Voting

This exhibit illustrates how cumulative voting gives minority shareholders a greater chance of electing a director of their choice. By casting all of their 9,000 votes for one candidate (Drake), the minority shareholders will succeed in electing Drake to the board of directors.

BALLOT	MAJORITY SHAREHOLDERS' VOTES			MINORITY SHAREHOLDERS' VOTES	DIRECTORS ELECTED
	Acevedo	Barkley	Craycik	Drake	
1	10,000	10,000	1,000	9,000	Acevedo/Barkley/Drake
2	9,001	9,000	2,999	9,000	Acevedo/Barkley/Drake
3	6,000	7,000	8,000	9,000	Barkley/Craycik/Drake

shareholder who owns 10 percent of a company and who has preemptive rights can buy 10 percent of any new issue (to maintain his or her 10 percent position). Thus, if the shareholder owns 100 shares of 1,000 outstanding shares, and the corporation issues 1,000 more shares, the shareholder can buy 100 of the new shares.

The articles of incorporation determine the existence and scope of preemptive rights. Generally, preemptive rights apply only to additional, newly issued stock sold for cash and must be exercised within a specified time period (usually thirty days).

Dividends. A **dividend** is a distribution of corporate profits or income *ordered by the directors* and paid to the shareholders in proportion to their respective shares in the corporation. Dividends can be paid in cash, property, stock of the corporation that is paying the dividends, or stock of other corporations.

DIVIDEND
A distribution to shareholders, disbursed in proportion to the number of shares held.

State laws vary, but every state determines the general circumstances and legal requirements under which dividends are paid. Generally, dividends are allowed so long as the corporation can continue to pay its debts as they come due or the amount of the dividends does not exceed the corporation's *net worth* (the corporation's total assets minus its total liabilities). Once declared, a cash dividend becomes a corporate debt enforceable at law like any other debt.

Inspection Rights. The shareholder's right of inspection is limited to the inspection and copying of corporate books and records for a *proper purpose,* provided the request is made in advance. Either the shareholder can inspect in person, or an attorney, agent, accountant, or other type of assistant can do so. In some states, the corporation must maintain an alphabetical voting list of shareholders with addresses and number of shares owned; this list must be kept open at the annual meeting for inspection by any shareholder of record.

Transfer of Shares. Corporate stock represents an ownership right in intangible personal property. The law generally recognizes the right of an owner to transfer property to another person unless there are valid restrictions on its transferability.

Sometimes corporations or their shareholders restrict transferability by reserving the option to purchase any shares offered for resale by a shareholder. This **right of first refusal** remains with the corporation or the shareholders for only a specified time or a reasonable time. Variations on the purchase option are possible. For example, a shareholder might be required to offer the shares to other shareholders or to the corporation first.

RIGHT OF FIRST REFUSAL
The right to purchase personal or real property—such as corporate shares or real estate—before the property is offered for sale to others.

When shares are transferred, a new entry is made in the corporate books to indicate the new owner. Until the corporation is notified and the entry is complete, the right to vote, the right to receive notice of shareholders' meetings, the right to receive dividends, and so forth, are all held by the current record owner.

Shareholder's Derivative Suit. When those in control of a corporation—the corporate directors—fail to sue in the corporate name to redress a wrong suffered by the corporation, shareholders are permitted to do so "derivatively" in what is known as a **shareholder's derivative suit.** Some wrong must have been done to the corporation, and any damages recovered by the suit usually go into the corporation's treasury. The right of shareholders to bring a derivative action is especially important when the wrong suffered by the corporation results from the actions of corporate directors or officers, because in such cases the directors and officers would probably want to prevent any action against themselves.

SHAREHOLDER'S DERIVATIVE SUIT
A suit brought by a shareholder to enforce a corporate cause of action against a third person.

LIABILITY OF SHAREHOLDERS

LEARNING OBJECTIVE NO. 4
Identifying Shareholders' Liability for Corporate Debts

One of the hallmarks of the corporate organization is that shareholders are not personally liable for the debts of the corporation. If the corporation fails, shareholders can lose their investments, but that is generally the limit of their liability. In certain instances of fraud, undercapitalization, or careless observance of corporate formalities, a court will pierce the corporate veil (disregard the corporate entity) and hold the shareholders individually liable. But these situations are the exception, not the rule.

TERMS AND CONCEPTS FOR REVIEW

business judgment rule 388
dividend 391
preemptive rights 390
proxy 389
quorum 386
right of first refusal 391
shareholder's derivative suit 391
stock certificate 390

CHAPTER SUMMARY • OWNERSHIP AND MANAGEMENT OF A CORPORATION

Directors and Officers	**1.** *Election of directors*—The first board of directors is usually appointed by the incorporators. Thereafter, directors are elected by the shareholders. **2.** *Directors' qualifications*—Few qualifications are required. A director can be a shareholder but is not required to be. **3.** *Board of directors' forum*—The board of directors conducts business by holding formal meetings with recorded minutes. Quorum requirements vary. Usually, a quorum is a majority of directors. In ordinary matters, a majority vote of the directors present is required. **4.** *Directors' management responsibilities*— **a.** Directors' management responsibilities include the following: **1)** Corporate policymaking decisions. **2)** Appointment, supervision, compensation, and removal of corporate officers and other managerial employees. **3)** Declaration and payment of corporate dividends to shareholders; issuance of authorized shares or bonds. **b.** Directors may delegate some of their responsibilities to executive committees or corporate officers and executives. **5.** *Directors' and officers' fiduciary duties*—Directors and officers must use care in conducting corporate business and must subordinate their own interests to those of the corporation in corporate matters. There must be full disclosure of any potential conflicts of interest between personal interests and those of the corporation.
Shareholders	**1.** *Shareholders' powers*—Shareholders' powers include approval of all fundamental changes affecting the corporation and election of the board of directors. **2.** *Shareholders' forum*—Shareholders' meetings must occur at least annually. Special meetings can be called when necessary. Voting requirements and procedures are as follows: **a.** A shareholder may appoint a proxy to vote his or her shares. **b.** A minimum number of shareholders (a quorum—generally, more than 50 percent of shares held) must be present at a meeting; resolutions are passed (usually) by majority vote. **c.** Cumulative voting may be required or permitted so as to give minority shareholders a better chance to be represented on the board of directors. **3.** *Rights of shareholders*—Shareholders have numerous rights, including voting rights, the right to a stock certificate, preemptive rights, the right to obtain a dividend (at the discretion of the directors), the right to inspect the corporate records, the right to transfer their shares (this right may be restricted), and the right to sue on behalf of the corporation (bring a shareholder's derivative suit) when the directors fail to do so.

HYPOTHETICAL QUESTIONS

30–1. Rights of Shareholders. Dmitri has acquired one share of common stock of a multimillion-dollar corporation with over 500,000 shareholders. Dmitri's ownership is so small that he is questioning what his rights are as a shareholder. For example, he wants to know whether this one share entitles him to attend and vote at shareholders' meetings, inspect the corporate books, and receive periodic dividends. Discuss Dmitri's rights in these matters.

30–2. Duties of Directors. Starboard, Inc., has a board of directors consisting of three members (Ellsworth, Green, and Morino) and approximately five hundred shareholders. At a regular meeting of the board, the board selects Tyson as president of the corporation by a two-to-one vote, with Ellsworth dissenting. The minutes of the meeting do not register Ellsworth's dissenting vote. Later, during an audit, it is discovered that Tyson is a former convict and has openly embezzled $500,000 from Starboard. This loss is not covered by insurance. The corporation wants to hold directors Ellsworth, Green, and Morino liable. Ellsworth claims no liability. Discuss the personal liability of the directors to the corporation.

REAL WORLD CASE PROBLEM

30–3. Business Judgment Rule. William Bear was the president of the William R. Bear Agency, Inc. (Bear Agency). Timothy Schirmer was a shareholder. In 1990, the YMCA was an important client of Bear Agency, and Bear spent company funds for family memberships in the YMCA. The same year, Bear put his wife on the payroll because, at the time, she was the only one in the office with computer experience. He decided not to declare a bonus for the employees in 1990, in part to invest the money in computers for the firm. The next April, Bear bought a BMW with company funds to use as a company car. Disapproving these actions, Schirmer filed a suit against Bear, Bear Agency, and others in an Illinois state court, asking the court to dissolve the corporation, among other things. Discuss how the decision not to dissolve Bear Agency might be supported by the business judgment rule. [*Schirmer v. Bear,* 271 Ill.App.3d 778, 648 N.E.2d 1131, Ill.Dec. 209 (1994)]

For updated links to resources available on the Web, as well as a variety of other materials, visit this text's Web site at **http://blte.westbuslaw.com.**

One of the best sources on the Web for information on corporations, including their directors, is the EDGAR database of the Securities and Exchange Commission (SEC) at

http://www.sec.gov/edgarhp.htm

ONLINE LEGAL RESEARCH

Go to **http://blte.westbuslaw.com,** the Web site that accompanies this text. Select "Internet Applications," and then click on "Chapter 30." There you will find the following Internet research exercise that you can perform to learn more about the liability of corporate directors and officers:

Activity 30–1: Liability of Directors and Officers

Chapter 30 ■ WORK SET

TRUE-FALSE QUESTIONS

_____ **1.** Both directors and officers may be immunized from liability for poor business decisions under the business judgment rule.

_____ **2.** Officers have the same fiduciary duties as directors.

_____ **3.** The rights of shareholders are established only in the articles of incorporation.

_____ **4.** Dividends can be paid in cash or property.

_____ **5.** Damages recovered in a shareholder's derivative suit are normally paid to the shareholder who brought the suit.

_____ **6.** As a general rule, shareholders are not personally responsible for the debts of the corporation.

_____ **7.** Officers, but not directors, owe a duty of loyalty to the corporation.

_____ **8.** The business judgment rule makes a director liable for losses to the firm that result from the director's authorized, good faith business decisions.

_____ **9.** Shareholders may vote to elect directors, and they may vote to remove directors.

MULTIPLE-CHOICE QUESTIONS

_____ **1.** Jill is a shareholder of United Manufacturing Company. As a shareholder, Jill's rights include all of the following EXCEPT a right to

a. one vote per share.
b. access to corporate books and records.
c. transfer shares.
d. sell corporate property when directors are mishandling corporate assets.

_____ **2.** The board of directors of U.S. Goods Corporation announces that the corporation will pay a cash dividend to its shareholders. Once declared, a cash dividend is

a. a corporate debt.
b. a personal debt of the directors.
c. a personal debt of the shareholders.
d. an illusory promise.

_____ **3.** Julio and Gloria are officers of World Export Corporation. As corporate officers, their rights are set out in

a. state corporation statutes.
b. World Export's certificate of authority.
c. their employment contracts with World Export.
d. international agreements with non-resident shareholders.

_____ **4.** The board of Consumer Sales Corporation delegates work to corporate officers and employees. If the directors do not use a reasonable amount of supervision, they could be held liable for

a. negligence only.
b. mismanagement of corporate personnel only.
c. negligence or mismanagement of corporate personnel.
d. none of the above.

_____ **5.** The management of National Brands, Inc., is at odds with the shareholders over some recent decisions. To redress a wrong suffered by National from the actions of management, the shareholders may

a. exercise their preemptive rights.
b. exercise their rights of first refusal.
c. file a shareholder's derivative suit.
d. issue a proxy.

_____ **6.** Federated Products Corporation uses cumulative voting in its elections of directors. Mary owns 3,000 Federated shares. At an annual meeting at which three directors are to be elected, how many votes may Mary cast for any one candidate?

a. 1,000.
b. 3,000.
c. 9,000.
d. 2,700.

_____ **7.** Bob is a director and shareholder of Eagle Corporation and of American Goods, Inc. If a resolution comes before the Eagle board to enter into a contract with American, Bob

a. must resign the directorship with Eagle.
b. must resign the directorship with American.
c. must disclose the potential conflict of interest.
d. need not disclose the potential conflict of interest.

_____ **8.** Nationwide Company's chief financial officer resigns. After a personnel search, an investigation, and an interview, the board of directors hires Ed. Ed turns out to be dishonest. Nationwide's shareholders sue the board. The board's best defense is

a. the business judgment rule.
b. the directors' duty of care.
c. the directors' duty of loyalty.
d. a shareholder's derivative suit.

ISSUE SPOTTERS

1. Glen is a director and shareholder of Diamond Corporation and of Emerald, Inc. If a resolution comes before the Emerald board to compete with Diamond, what is Glen's responsibility?

2. Joe is a director and officer of United Products, Inc. Joe makes a decision about the marketing of United products that results in a dramatic decrease in profits for United and its shareholders. The shareholders accuse Joe of breaching his fiduciary duty to the corporation. What is Joe's best defense?

UNIT SEVEN
CREDIT AND RISK

UNIT OUTLINE

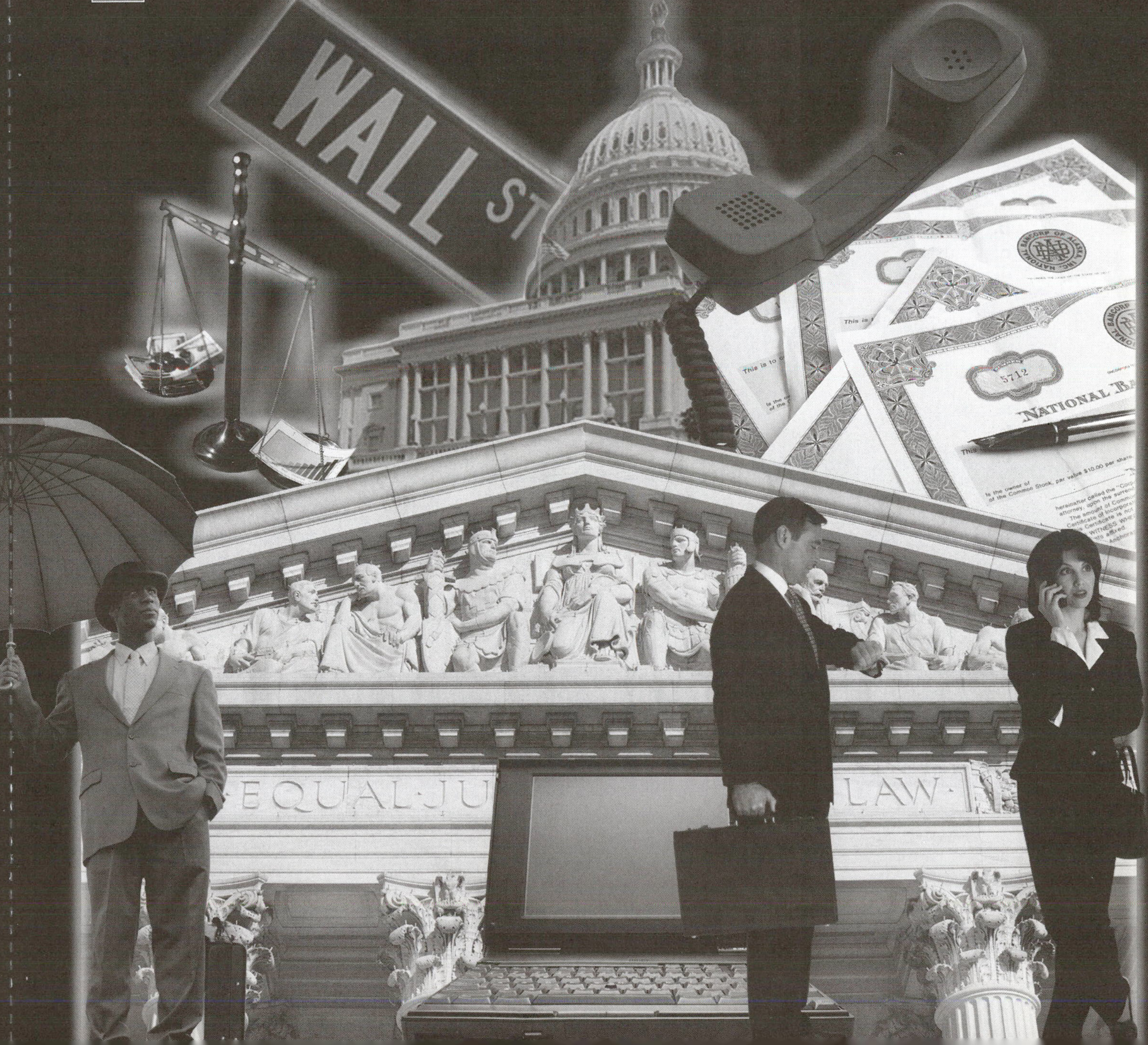

31 Secured Transactions

LEARNING OBJECTIVES

When you finish this chapter, you should be able to:

1. State the requirements of an enforceable security interest.
2. Identify what must be included in a financing statement.
3. Discuss the scope of a security interest.
4. Pinpoint the priorities among perfected security interests.
5. List the secured party's options on a debtor's default.

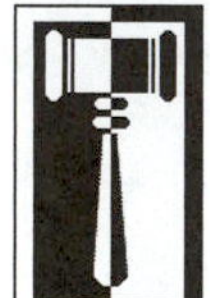

FACING A LEGAL PROBLEM

Home State Bank lends money to Moran Manufacturing, Inc. As part of the deal, Moran gives Home State the right to take possession of Moran Manufacturing's equipment if the loan is not repaid. The agreement between Home State and Moran describes the equipment in detail, including each item's serial number. To inform other creditors of the interest that Home State has in the equipment, the bank files a statement in a certain state office that exists for that purpose. *In this statement, can the bank use the same description of the equipment that it used in the loan agreement?*

SECURED TRANSACTION
Any transaction in which the payment of a debt is guaranteed by personal property or fixtures.

SECURITY INTEREST
Every interest in personal property or fixtures that secures payment or performance of an obligation.

SECURED PARTY
A lender, seller, or any other person in whose favor there is a security interest.

DEBTOR
A person who owes payment or performance of a secured obligation.

Whenever the payment of a debt is guaranteed by personal property owned by the debtor or in which the debtor has a legal interest, the transaction is known as a **secured transaction.** The creditors in such transactions are generally not hampered by state laws favorable to debtors. They also have a favored position should the debtor become bankrupt.

The Terminology of Secured Transactions

The Uniform Commercial Code (UCC) provides the law covering secured transactions. A brief summary of the UCC's definition of terms relating to secured transactions follows.

1. A **security interest** is every interest in personal property or fixtures that secures (guarantees) the payment or performance of an obligation.
2. A **secured party** is a lender, a seller, or any person in whose favor there is a security interest. The terms *secured party* and *secured creditor* are used interchangeably.
3. A **debtor** is the party who owes payment or performance of the secured obligation.

4. A **security agreement** is the agreement that creates or provides for a security interest between the debtor and a secured party.
5. **Collateral** is the property subject to a security interest (the property that secures the payment or performance of the obligation).

These definitions form the concept under which a debtor-creditor relationship becomes a secured transaction (see Exhibit 31–1).

SECURITY AGREEMENT
The agreement that creates or provides for a security interest between the debtor and a secured party.

COLLATERAL
In a broad sense, any property used as security for a loan. Under the UCC, property of a debtor in which a creditor has an interest or a right.

Creating a Security Interest

Before a creditor can become a secured party, the creditor must have a security interest in the collateral of the debtor. Three requirements must be met for a creditor to have an enforceable security interest:

LEARNING OBJECTIVE NO. 1
Stating the Requirements of an Enforceable Security Interest

1. The collateral must either (a) be in the possession of the secured party or (b) there must be a written security agreement describing the collateral and signed by the debtor.
2. The secured party must give value to the debtor. Normally, the value is in the form of a direct loan or a commitment to sell goods on credit.
3. The debtor must have rights in the collateral.

In most situations, a written security agreement is used to create a security interest. To be effective, the agreement must (1) be signed by the debtor, (2) contain a description of the collateral; and (3) the description must reasonably identify the collateral. See Exhibit 31–2 for a sample security agreement.

Once these requirements are met, the creditor's rights *attach* to the collateral. This means that the creditor has a security interest against the debtor that is enforceable. **Attachment** ensures that the security interest between the debtor and the secured party is effective.

ATTACHMENT
In a secured transaction, the process by which a security interest in the property of another becomes enforceable.

For instance, assume that you apply for a credit card at a local department store. The application likely contains a clause under which the store retains a security interest in the goods that you buy with the card until you have paid for the goods in full. This application meets the requirement for a written security agreement (the first requirement for an enforceable security interest). The store's commitment to sell goods to you on credit constitutes *value* (the second requirement for an enforceable security interest). The goods that you buy with the card are the collateral, and the right that you have in those goods is your ownership interest in them (the third requirement). Thus, the requirements for an enforceable security interest are met. When you buy something with the card, the store's rights attach to it.

Perfecting a Security Interest

Even though a security interest has attached, the secured party must take steps to protect its claim to the collateral in the event that the debtor **defaults** (fails to

DEFAULT
The failure to observe a promise or discharge an obligation. The term is commonly used to mean the failure to pay a debt when it is due.

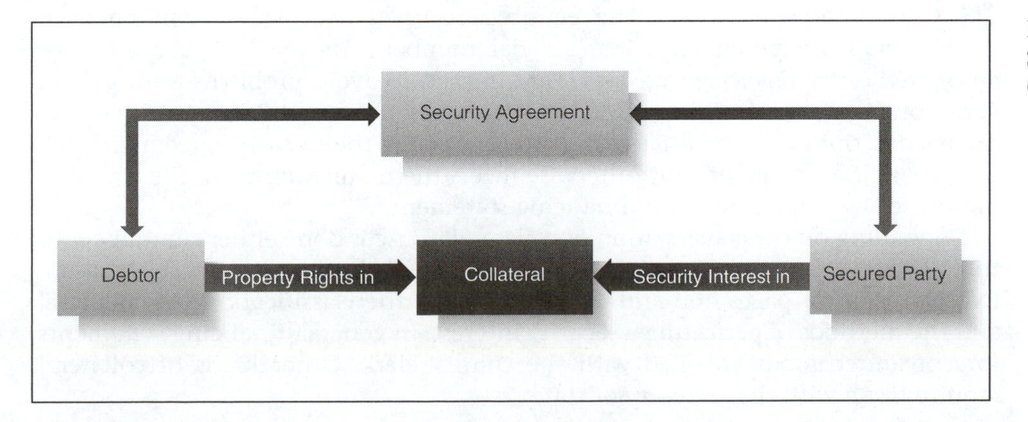

EXHIBIT 31–1
Secured Transactions—Concepts and Terminology

EXHIBIT 31–2
A Sample Security Agreement

____
Date

____
Name No. and Street City County State

(hereinafter called "Debtor") hereby grants to ______________________________
Name

____
No. and Street City County State

(hereinafter called "Secured Party") a security interest in the following property (hereinafter called the "Collateral"): _______________________________________

to secure payment and performance of obligations identified or set out as follows (hereinafter called the "Obligations"): _______________________________________

Default in payment or performance of any of the Obligations or default under any agreement evidencing any of the Obligations is a default under this agreement. Upon such default Secured Party may declare all Obligations immediately due and payable and shall have the remedies of a secured party under the ________ Uniform Commercial Code.

Signed in (duplicate) triplicate.

____________________	____________________
Debtor	Secured Party
By____________________	By____________________

LEARNING OBJECTIVE NO. 2
Identifying What Must Be Included in a Financing Statement

PERFECTION
The method by which a secured party obtains a priority by notice that his or her security interest in the debtor's collateral is effective against the debtor's subsequent creditors. Usually accomplished by filing a financing statement at a location set out in the state statute.

FINANCING STATEMENT
A document prepared by a secured creditor, and filed with the appropriate state or local official, to give notice to the public that the creditor claims an interest in collateral belonging to a certain named debtor. The financing statement must be signed by the debtor, contain the addresses of both the debtor and creditor, and describe the collateral by type or item.

pay the debt as promised). **Perfection** is the legal process by which secured parties protect themselves against the claims of third parties who may wish to have their debts satisfied out of the same collateral.

In most situations, perfection is accomplished by filing a **financing statement** with the appropriate state or local official. A sample financing statement is shown in Exhibit 31–3. A financing statement must contain (1) the signature of the debtor, (2) the addresses of the debtor and the creditor, and (3) a description of the collateral by type or item.

In the legal problem set out at the beginning of this chapter, Home State Bank lent money to Moran Manufacturing, Inc., taking a security interest in Moran's equipment. The security agreement described the equipment in detail, including each item's serial number. *Can the bank use the same description in the financing statement?* Yes. In fact, to avoid problems arising from variations in descriptions, a secured party may repeat exactly the security agreement's description in the financing statement or file the security agreement itself as a financing statement (if it otherwise meets the requirements) or file a combination security agreement and financing statement.

Depending on the classification of collateral, filing is done either centrally with the secretary of state or locally with the county clerk or other official, or both. Exhibit 31–4 on pages 402 and 403 summarizes the classifications of collateral and the methods of perfecting a security interest. In general, financing statements for consumer goods are filed with the county clerk. Other kinds of collateral require filing with the secretary of state.

EXHIBIT 31–3
A Sample Financing Statement

This FINANCING STATEMENT is presented for filing pursuant to the California Uniform Commercial Code.

1. DEBTOR (LAST NAME FIRST—IF AN INDIVIDUAL)		**1A.** SOCIAL SECURITY OR FEDERAL TAX NO.
1B. MAILING ADDRESS	**1C.** CITY, STATE	**1D.** ZIP CODE
2. ADDITIONAL DEBTOR (IF ANY) (LAST NAME FIRST—IF AN INDIVIDUAL)		**2A.** SOCIAL SECURITY OR FEDERAL TAX NO.
2B. MAILING ADDRESS	**2C.** CITY, STATE	**2D.** ZIP CODE
3. DEBTOR'S TRADE NAMES OR STYLES (IF ANY)		**3A.** FEDERAL TAX NUMBER
4. SECURED PARTY NAME MAILING ADDRESS CITY STATE ZIP CODE		**4A.** SOCIAL SECURITY NO., FEDERAL TAX NO. OR BANK TRANSIT AND A.B.A. NO.
5. ASSIGNEE OF SECURED PARTY (IF ANY) NAME MAILING ADDRESS CITY STATE ZIP CODE		**5A.** SOCIAL SECURITY NO., FEDERAL TAX NO. OR BANK TRANSIT AND A.B.A. NO.

6. This FINANCING STATEMENT covers the following types or items of property **(include description of real property on which located and owner of record when required by instruction 4).**
As security for and in consideration of all present and any future advances or other obligations debtor hereby grants United California Bank a security interest in all of the following types or items of property ("Collateral" herein) in which the debtor now has or hereafter acquires any right, title, or interest, or rights present and future, wheresoever located and whether in the possession of the debtor, a warehouseman, bailee, trustee or any other person, and all increases, therein and replacements, products, and proceeds thereof. Proceeds include but are not limited to inventory, returned merchandise, accounts, chattel paper, general intangibles, insurance proceeds, documents, money, goods, equipment, instruments, and any other tangible or intangible property arising under the sale, lease or other disposition of collateral:

7. CHECK IF APPLICABLE ☒	**7A.** ☐ PRODUCTS OF COLLATERAL ARE ALSO COVERED	**7B.** DEBTOR(S) SIGNATURE NOT REQUIRED IN ACCORDANCE WITH INSTRUCTION 5(c) ITEM: ☐ (1) ☐ (2) ☐ (3) ☐ (4)
8. CHECK IF APPLICABLE ☒	☐ DEBTOR IS A "TRANSMITTING UTILITY" IN ACCORDANCE WITH UCC § 9105 (1) (n)	

9. DATE: ▶ SIGNATURE(S) of DEBTOR(S)	C O D E	**10.** THIS SPACE FOR USE OF FILING OFFICER (DATE, TIME, FILE NUMBER AND FILING OFFICER)
TYPE OR PRINT NAME(S) OF DEBTOR(S)	1	
▶ SIGNATURE(S) OF SECURED PARTY(IES)	2 3	
TYPE OR PRINT NAME(S) OF SECURED PARTY(IES)	4 5	
11. *Return copy to:* NAME ADDRESS CITY STATE ZIP CODE	6 7 8 9 0	
(1) FILING OFFICER COPY FORM UCC-1—FILING FEE $3.00 ***Approved by the Secretary of State***		

MS-336 10-78

EXHIBIT 31–4
Types of Collateral and Methods of Perfection

TYPE OF COLLATERAL	DEFINITIONS	PERFECTION METHOD
TANGIBLE	All things that are *movable* at the time the security interest attaches or that are *fixtures*. This includes timber to be cut, growing crops, and unborn animals.	
1. Consumer Goods	Goods used or bought primarily for personal, family, or household purposes—for example, household furniture.	For most consumer goods, security interests are perfected as soon as they attach (filing by the secured party is not necessary); for boats, motor vehicles, and trailers, filing is not necessary when security interests are noted on certificates of title; for other consumer goods, filing is necessary (unless the collateral is in the secured party's possession).
2. Equipment	Goods bought for or used primarily in business—for example, a delivery truck.	Filing by the secured party (unless the collateral is in the secured party's possession).
3. Farm Products	Crops, livestock, and supplies used or produced in a farming operation in the possession of a farmer debtor. This includes products of crops or livestock—for example, milk, eggs, maple syrup, and ginned cotton.	Filing or possession.
4. Inventory	Goods held for sale or lease and materials used or consumed in the course of business—for example, raw materials or floor stock of a retailer.	Filing or possession.
5. Fixtures	Goods that become so affixed to realty that an interest in them arises under real estate law—for example, a central air-conditioning unit.	Filing only.

CONTINUATION STATEMENT
A statement that, if filed within six months prior to the expiration date of the original financing statement, continues the effectiveness of the original statement for another five years. The effectiveness of a financing statement can be continued in the same manner indefinitely.

A financing statement is effective for five years from the date of filing. If a **continuation statement** is filed *within six months* prior to the expiration date, the effectiveness of the original statement is continued for another five years, starting with the expiration date of the first five-year period. The effectiveness of the statement can be continued in the same manner indefinitely.

The Scope of a Security Interest

A security agreement can cover various types of property in addition to collateral already in the debtor's possession—the proceeds of the sale of collateral, after-acquired property, and future advances.

PROCEEDS
In secured-transactions law, whatever is received when the collateral is sold, exchanged, collected, or otherwise disposed of, such as insurance payments for destroyed or lost collateral.

PROCEEDS

Proceeds include whatever is received when collateral is sold, exchanged, collected, or disposed of. A secured party has an interest in the proceeds of the sale of collateral.

EXHIBIT 31-4—Continued
Types of Collateral and Methods of Perfection

TYPE OF COLLATERAL	DEFINITIONS	PERFECTION METHOD
INTANGIBLE	Nonphysical property that exists only in connection with something else.	
1. Chattel Paper	Any writing that evidences both a *monetary obligation and a security interest*—for example, a thirty-six-month-payment retail security agreement signed by a buyer to purchase a car.	Filing by the secured party (unless the collateral is in the secured party's possession).
2. Documents of Title	Papers that entitle the person in possession to hold, receive, or dispose of the paper or goods the documents cover—for example, bills of lading, warehouse receipts, and dock warrants.	Filing or possession.
3. Instruments	Any writing that evidences a right to payment of money that is not a security agreement or lease, and any negotiable instrument or certificated security that in the ordinary course of business is transferred by delivery with any necessary indorsement or assignment—for example, stock certificates, promissory notes, and certificates of deposit.	Except for temporary perfected status, security interests in instruments can be perfected only by the secured party's taking possession.
4. Accounts	Any right to payment for goods sold or leased or services *rendered* that is not evidenced by an instrument or chattel paper—for example, accounts receivable and contract right payments.	Filing (with exceptions).
5. General Intangibles	Any personal property other than that defined above—for example, a patent, a copyright, goodwill, or a trademark.	Filing only.

IN THE COURTROOM

A bank has a perfected security interest in the inventory of a retail seller of heavy farm machinery. The retailer sells a tractor out of this inventory to a farmer, a buyer in the ordinary course of business. The farmer agrees, in a retail security agreement, to make monthly payments for a period of twenty-four months. *If, two months later, the retailer should go into default on the loan from the bank, is the bank entitled to the remaining payments the farmer owes to the retailer?* Yes. These payments are proceeds. They are what the retailer was to receive for the collateral. The bank, as a secured party, has an interest in such proceeds.

LEARNING OBJECTIVE NO. 3
Discussing the Scope of a Security Interest

After-Acquired Property

After-acquired property of the debtor is property acquired after the execution of the security agreement. To cover after-acquired property, the security agreement must provide for the coverage. This provision often accompanies security agreements covering a debtor's inventory.

After-Acquired Property Property of the debtor that is acquired after a secured creditor's interest in the debtor's property has been created.

IN THE COURTROOM

Amato buys factory equipment from Bronson on credit, giving as security an interest in all of her equipment—both what she is buying and what she already owns. The security agreement with Bronson contains an after-acquired property clause. Six months later, Amato pays cash to another seller for other equipment. Six months after that, Amato goes out of business before she has paid off her debt to Bronson. *Does Bronson's security interest cover the equipment bought from the other seller?* Yes. Under the after-acquired property clause, Bronson has a security interest in all of Amato's equipment, even the equipment bought from the other seller.

Future Advances

Often, a debtor will arrange with a bank to have a continuing *line of credit* under which the debtor can borrow funds intermittently. Advances against lines of credit can be subject to a perfected security interest in certain collateral. The security agreement may provide that any future advances made against that line of credit are also subject to the security interest in the same collateral.

IN THE COURTROOM

Stroh is the owner of a small manufacturing plant with equipment valued at $1 million. He has an immediate need for $50,000 of working capital, so he secures a loan from Midwestern Bank and signs a security agreement, putting up all his equipment as security. The security agreement provides that Stroh can borrow up to $500,000 in the future, using the same equipment as collateral for any future advances. *Is it necessary to execute a new security agreement and perfect a security interest in the collateral each time an advance is made to Stroh?* No. Stroh has a line of credit with the bank, which has an express security interest in advances made against that line of credit.

The Floating-Lien Concept

Floating Lien
A security interest retained in collateral even when the collateral changes in character, classification, or location.

When a security agreement provides for the creation of a security interest in proceeds of the sale of the after-acquired property or future advances, or both, it is referred to as a **floating lien** (see Chapter 32 for a further discussion of liens). Floating liens commonly arise in the financing of inventories. A creditor is not interested in specific pieces of inventory, because they are constantly changing. Thus, the lien "floats" from one item to another, as the inventory changes.

IN THE COURTROOM

Cascade Sports, Inc., a cross-country ski dealer, has a line of credit with Portland First Bank to finance an inventory of cross-country skis. Cascade and Portland First enter into a security agreement that provides for coverage of proceeds, after-acquired inventory, present inventory, and future advances. The security interest is perfected by filing centrally (with the secretary of state). One day, Cascade sells a new pair of cross-country skis, for which it receives a used pair in trade. The same day, it buys two new pairs of skis from a local manufacturer with a new advance of money from Portland First. *Does Portland First have a perfected security interest in the used skis, the new skis, and the advance?* Yes. All of this is accomplished under the original perfected security interest. The bank has a perfected security interest in the used skis under the proceeds clause, in the new skis under the after-acquired property clause, and in the advance under the future-advance clause. Hence, Portland First has a floating lien.

Priorities among Security Interests

Whether a creditor's security interest is perfected or unperfected may have serious consequences for the creditor if the debtor defaults on the debt or files for bankruptcy. Generally, the following rules apply when more than one party, or creditor, claims rights in the same collateral:

LEARNING OBJECTIVE NO. 4

Pinpointing the Priorities among Perfected Security Interests

1. *Conflicting unperfected security interests.* When two conflicting security interests are unperfected, the first to attach has priority.
2. *Perfected security interests versus unperfected interests.* When a security interest is perfected, it has priority over any unperfected interests.
3. *Conflicting perfected security interests.* When two or more creditors have perfected security interests in the same collateral, the interest that was the first to perfect generally has priority.
4. *Conflicting perfected security interests in commingled or processed goods.* Goods, to which two or more perfected security interests attach, may be so manufactured or commingled that they lose their separate identities into a single product or mass. For example, the wheat harvested on different farms may be so mixed for storage in a single grain bin that one farm's wheat cannot be distinguished from another's. When the wheat is processed and made into bread, the identity of each farm's crop is further lost. In such a situation, the perfected parties' security interests attach to the product or mass (the bread) in the proportion that the cost of goods to which each interest originally attached (each farm's wheat) bears to the total cost of the product or mass (the bread).

For updated information on Article 9 of the Uniform Commercial Code, go to

http://www.law.cornell.edu/disk_titles.html

One exception to these rules concerns a *buyer in the ordinary course of business.* A buyer in the ordinary course of business is any person who in good faith, and without knowledge that a sale is in violation of the ownership rights or security interest of a third party in the goods, buys in the normal course of business from a person in the business of selling goods of that kind. Such a buyer takes goods free of any security interest in a merchant's inventory. In other words, the buyer's interest takes priority over any other security interest in the merchant's inventory. This is so even if the security interest is perfected and even if the buyer knows of its existence.

Most of the customers of any business are buyers in the ordinary course of business. For instance, when you buy clothes at a store in your local mall, you take those items free of any security interest that a creditor (a bank or the store's supplier) has in them, even if you know that the store borrowed the money to buy its inventory and used that inventory (including the clothes you bought) to guarantee repayment of the loan.

Rights and Duties of Debtor and Creditor

The security agreement determines most of the rights and duties of the debtor and creditor. Rights and duties that apply in the absence of a security agreement to the contrary include the following.

Reasonable Care of Collateral

If a secured party is in possession of the collateral, he or she must use reasonable care in preserving it. If the collateral increases in value, the secured party can hold this increased value or profit as additional security unless it is in the form of money, which must be paid to the debtor or applied toward reducing the debt. The debtor must pay for all reasonable charges incurred by the secured party in caring for the collateral.

In a financing statement, describe the collateral well—it is better to err by giving too much detail than by giving too little detail.

Termination Statement

When a secured debt is paid, the secured party may send a termination statement to the debtor or file such a statement with the filing officer to whom the original financing statement was given. In situations involving most types of goods, a termination statement must be filed or sent within ten days after the debt is paid. If it is not, the secured party is liable to the debtor for $100, plus any loss to the debtor.

Default

LEARNING OBJECTIVE NO. 5

Listing the Secured Party's Options on a Debtor's Default

Although any breach of the terms of a security agreement can constitute default, default occurs most commonly when the debtor fails to meet the scheduled payments that the parties have agreed on or when the debtor becomes bankrupt.

On the debtor's default, a secured party can take possession of the collateral covered by the security agreement. On taking possession, the secured party can retain the collateral covered by the security agreement for satisfaction of the debt or can resell the goods and apply the proceeds toward the debt. These rights and remedies are *cumulative*. That is, if a creditor is unsuccessful in enforcing rights by one method, another method can be pursued.

For instance, Gillian loans money to Blum to buy a car, using the car as collateral. Blum fails to repay the loan. Gillian can sue Blum for the money. If that proves unsuccessful, Gillian can repossess the car. In other words, Gillian's attempt to sue Blum for the money does not prevent Gillian from repossessing the car if the suit does not result in satisfaction of the debt.

Taking Possession of the Collateral

In taking possession, a secured party may proceed without going to court if this can be done without a breach of the peace. It is not always easy to predict what will or will not constitute a breach of the peace. Generally, the creditor or the creditor's agent cannot enter a debtor's home, garage, or place of business without permission.

IN THE COURTROOM

Rollo's automobile is collateral for a loan from the Kato Loan Company. When Rollo fails to make the payments, Kato decides to repossess the car. Kato's agent walks onto Rollo's property, enters the vehicle without entering the garage, and drives off. *Is this a breach of the peace?* Probably not. If the agent had entered the garage, however, in some states such an action of wrongful trespass could constitute a breach of the peace.

Retaining or Disposing of the Collateral

Once default has occurred and the secured party has obtained possession of the collateral, the secured party may retain the collateral. It also may sell, lease, or otherwise dispose of the collateral in any commercially reasonable manner.

Retention of the Collateral by the Secured Party. A secured party can retain the collateral, subject to several conditions. Written notice must be sent to the debtor if the debtor has not signed a statement renouncing or modifying his or her rights after default. In the case of consumer goods, no other notice need be given. In all other cases, notice must be sent to any other secured creditor from whom the secured party has received written notice of a claim to the collateral. If, within twenty-one days, the debtor or other secured creditor objects to the retention of the collateral, the secured party must sell or otherwise dispose of it.

Disposition of the Collateral by the Secured Party. A secured party who does not choose to retain the collateral must dispose of it in a commercially reasonable manner. If the secured party sells the collateral using the same method that dealers in that type of property use, the secured party has sold it in a commercially reasonable manner. For instance, if the collateral is livestock of a type that is usually sold at auction, the secured party who sells the livestock at an auction sells it in a commercially reasonable manner. The sale can be public or private. It can be conducted in any manner, place, and time, and according to any terms, as long as it is commercially reasonable and in good faith.

Notice of the sale must be sent to the debtor (unless the debtor has signed a statement renouncing or modifying the right to notice). For consumer goods, no other notice need be sent. If the debtor has paid 60 percent or more of the cash price or loan, the secured party must sell or otherwise dispose of the collateral within ninety days. In all other cases, notice must be sent to any other secured creditor from whom the secured party has received written notice of a claim to the collateral. No notice is necessary if the collateral is perishable, threatens to decline speedily in value, or is of a type customarily sold on a recognized market.

Proceeds from Disposition. Proceeds from the disposition must be applied in the following order:

1. Reasonable expenses stemming from the retaking, holding, or preparing for sale.
2. Satisfaction of the balance of the debt owed to the secured party.
3. Subordinate security interests of creditors whose written demands are received prior to the completion of distribution of the proceeds.
4. Any surplus to the debtor.

Often, after proper disposition of the collateral, the secured party does not collect all that is still owed by the debtor. Unless otherwise agreed, the debtor is liable for any deficiency.

Redemption Rights. Any time before the secured party disposes of the collateral or enters into a contract for its disposition, or before the debtor's obligation has been discharged through the secured party's retention of the collateral, the debtor (or any other secured party, if there is one) can exercise the right of *redemption.* This is done by tendering performance of all obligations secured by the collateral, by paying the expenses reasonably incurred by the secured party (including, if provided in the security agreement, reasonable attorneys' fees and legal expenses), and by retaking the collateral and maintaining its care and custody.

For example, suppose that you borrow the money to buy a car and give the car as security for the loan but fail to make the payments. The lender repossesses the car and plans to sell it to get back some of the money that you borrowed. Before the car is sold (or before the lender has contracted to sell it), you can exercise your right of redemption—that is, you can pay the lender what you owe, plus his or her expenses, and take the car back.

TERMS AND CONCEPTS FOR REVIEW

after-acquired property 403
attachment 399
collateral 399
continuation statement 402
debtor 398
default 399
financing statement 400
floating lien 404
perfection 400
proceeds 402
secured party 398
secured transaction 398
security agreement 399
security interest 398

CHAPTER SUMMARY • SECURED TRANSACTIONS

Creating a Security Interest	**1.** The creditor must possess the collateral, or there must be an agreement in writing, signed by the debtor, describing and reasonably identifying the collateral. **2.** The secured party must give value to the debtor. **3.** The debtor must have rights in the collateral.
Perfecting a Security Interest	The most common method of perfection is filing a financing statement that contains the names and addresses of the secured party and the debtor, describes the collateral, and is signed by the debtor.
The Scope of a Security Interest	**1.** *Collateral* in the possession of the debtor. **2.** *Proceeds* from a sale, exchange, or disposition of secured collateral. **3.** *After-acquired property*—A security agreement may provide that property acquired after the execution of the security agreement will also be secured by the agreement. **4.** *Future advances*—A security agreement may provide that any future advances made against a line of credit will be subject to the security interest in the same collateral.
Rights and Duties of Debtors and Creditors	**1.** *Reasonable care of collateral*—If a secured party is in possession of the collateral, he or she must use reasonable care in preserving it. **2.** *Termination statement*—When a debt is paid, the secured party generally must send a termination statement to the debtor or file one with the filing officer to whom the original financing statement was given.
Priorities and Remedies on the Debtor's Default	**1.** *Priorities*—When several creditors claim the same collateral, the following general rules apply: **a.** A creditor whose interest has attached has priority over a creditor whose interest has not attached. **b.** A secured creditor has priority over an unsecured creditor. **c.** A secured creditor has priority over a secured creditor whose interest was perfected later. **d.** A secured creditor has an interest in processed or commingled goods in the proportion that the cost of the item to which his or her interest originally attached bears to the cost of the processed or commingled goods. **e.** A secured creditor does not prevail against a buyer in the ordinary course of business. **2.** *Remedies*—A creditor who lawfully takes possession of the collateral covered by a security agreement can pursue one of two alternatives: **a.** *Retain the collateral*—The creditor must notify (1) the debtor (if the debtor has not signed a statement renouncing or modifying his or her rights) and (2) except in sales of consumer goods, any other secured party with an interest in the same collateral. If the debtor or a secured party objects, the creditor must sell or otherwise dispose of the collateral. **b.** *Sell the collateral*—The creditor must notify (1) the debtor and (2) except in sales of consumer goods, other secured parties having claims to the collateral of the sale (unless the collateral is perishable or will decline rapidly in value). The creditor must sell the goods in a commercially reasonable manner. Proceeds are applied to the expenses of the sale, the debt owed to the secured party, and debts owed to other secured parties. Any surplus is returned to the debtor.

HYPOTHETICAL QUESTIONS

31–1. Priority Disputes. Redford is a seller of electric generators. He purchases a large quantity of generators from a manufacturer, Mallon Corp., by making a down payment and signing an agreement to make the balance of payments over a period of time. The agreement gives Mallon Corp. a security interest in the generators and the proceeds. Mallon Corp. files a financing statement on its security interest centrally. Redford receives the generators and immediately sells one of them to Garfield on an installment contract, with payment to be made in twelve equal installments. At the time of sale, Garfield knows of Mallon's security interest. Two months later, Redford goes into default on his payments to Mallon. Discuss Mallon's rights against purchaser Garfield in this situation.

31–2. The Scope of Security Interest. Edward owned a retail sporting goods shop. A new ski resort was being created in his area, and to take advantage of the potential business, Edward decided to expand his operations. He borrowed a large sum of money from his bank, which took a security interest in his present inventory and any after-acquired inventory as collateral for the loan. The bank properly perfected the security interest by filing a financing statement. A year later, just a few months after the ski resort had opened, an avalanche destroyed the ski slope and lodge. Edward's business consequently took a turn for the worse, and he defaulted on his debt to the bank. The bank sought possession of his entire inventory, even though the inventory was now twice as large as it had been when the loan was made. Edward claimed that the bank only had rights to half his inventory. Is Edward correct? Explain.

REAL WORLD CASE PROBLEM

31–3. Sale of Collateral. To pay for the purchases of several aircraft, Robert Wall borrowed money from the Cessna Finance Corp., using the aircraft as collateral. Wall defaulted on the loans. Cessna took possession of the collateral (the aircraft) and sold it. Cessna filed a suit in a federal district court against Wall for the difference between the amount due on the loans and the amount received from the sale of the aircraft. Wall claimed that he could have obtained a higher price for the aircraft if he had sold it himself. What effect does the issue concerning whether a better price could have been obtained have on whether the sale was commercially reasonable? Discuss. [*Cessna Finance Corp. v. Wall*, 876 F.Supp. 273 (M.D.Ga. 1994)]

For updated links to resources available on the Web, as well as a variety of other materials, visit this text's Web site at **http://blte.westbuslaw.com.**

The National Conference of Commissioners on Uniform State Laws, in association with the University of Pennsylvania Law School, now offers an official site for UCC articles. To keep abreast of changes in the UCC, including the revisions to Article 9, go to

http://www.law.upenn.edu/bll/ulc/ulc.htm

The Web site of Cornell University's Legal Information Institute offers an overview and menu of sources on legal materials relating to secured transactions at

http://www.law.cornell.edu/topics/secured_transactions.html

ONLINE LEGAL RESEARCH

Go to **http://blte.westbuslaw.com**, the Web site that accompanies this text. Select "Internet Applications," and then click on "Chapter 31." There you will find the following Internet research exercise that you can perform to learn more about repossession of collateral under Article 9:

Activity 31–1: Repossession

Chapter 31 ■ WORK SET

TRUE-FALSE QUESTIONS

____ **1.** Perfection is the process through which a debt is satisfied by disposing of collateral in any commercially reasonable manner.

____ **2.** A secured party needs to file copies of a financing statement only in his or her own office to protect all of his or her rights.

____ **3.** Generally, a security interest in collateral terminates when the debt is paid.

____ **4.** A security agreement provides for a security interest between a debtor and a secured party.

____ **5.** When a debt is paid, the secured party can send a termination statement to the debtor or file one with the officer to whom the financing statement was given.

____ **6.** Default occurs most commonly when a debtor fails to repay the loan for which his or her property served as collateral.

____ **7.** After a debtor has defaulted and the secured party has taken possession of the property that was the collateral, the debtor can never get it back.

____ **8.** When several secured parties claim a security interest in the same collateral of a debtor, the last to have been perfected takes priority.

MULTIPLE-CHOICE QUESTIONS

____ **1.** A document reads, "Debtor (Consumer Goods, Inc., 711 Fifth Avenue, Seattle, WA) grants to secured party (Ace Finance Company, 115 First Street, Seattle, WA) a security interest in debtor's inventory." For this document to qualify as a financing statement, which of the following is NOT necessary?

a. The debtor's signature.
b. The creditor 's signature.
c. Both parties' addresses.
d. The description of the collateral ("debtor's inventory").

____ **2.** Friendly Loan Company loans $5,000 to A&B Warehouse to buy a new forklift. The agreement provides that A&B will repay the loan over a three-year period and that default occurs if a single payment is missed. When A&B misses two payments, Friendly declares default. Friendly may take possession of the forklift and

a. keep it.
b. sell it to anyone after giving A&B an opportunity to comply with the security agreement.
c. sell it to A&B on A&B's full compliance with the security agreement.
d. any of the above.

_____ **3.** Paul owns a restaurant, Paul's Diner. He wants to borrow $60,000 from First National Bank to open another Paul's Diner, using the first restaurant as collateral. The bank asks him to sign a *security agreement.* Besides his signature, to be effective the agreement must

a. contain a description that reasonably identifies the collateral.
b. include the addresses of the debtor and the creditor.
c. both a and b.
d. none of the above.

_____ **4.** Chris defaults on a loan from EZ Loan Company. EZ takes possession of the collateral and would like to keep it. Ace Capital, which also has an interest in the collateral, sends EZ notice of its claim. EZ may

a. not retain the collateral because it would violate Ace's interest.
b. retain the collateral if it sends notice to Ace.
c. be forced to sell the collateral if Ace objects to the retention.
d. be forced to sell the collateral and be forced to pay Ace.

_____ **5.** Eve and Jay sign an agreement that states, "Debtor (Eve) grants to secured party (Jay) a security interest in debtor's 1997 Miata." Jay gives Eve a check for $5,000. For an enforceable security interest, which of the following is NOT necessary?

a. Eve's giving of rights in her car.
b. A written agreement.
c. Jay's signature on the agreement.
d. All of the above.

_____ **6.** Business Credit, Inc., loans $10,000 to Al's Hardware. The loan is secured by Al's inventory, which includes tools that Al sells to customers on installment payment plans. Eventually, Al defaults on the loan. Business Credit is entitled to

a. all of the inventory sold to customers.
b. any remaining installment payments.
c. both a and b.
d. none of the above.

_____ **7.** On May 1, First State Bank lends $10,000 to Diane. On May 10, the bank files a financing statement. Before that statement is filed, however, Diane uses the same collateral to borrow $5,000 from City Bank, which files a statement on May 4. In a dispute between the banks over the collateral

a. First State Bank wins because it lent money first.
b. First State Bank wins because its interest attached first.
c. City Bank wins because it perfected first.
d. City Bank wins because its interest attached first.

ISSUE SPOTTERS

1. Stan needs $300 to buy textbooks, notebooks, and other supplies. Duane says, "I'll lend you $300 if you'll agree that if you don't pay it back, I get your laptop." Stan agrees, they put their agreement in writing, and Duane gives Stan $300. How does Duane let other creditors know of his interest in the laptop?

2. Avco Finance loans $3,000 to Brad to buy a computer. The loan is secured by the computer. Brad defaults on the loan. Avco can repossess and keep the computer, but Avco does not want it. What are the alternatives?

Creditors' Rights and Remedies

32

LEARNING OBJECTIVES

When you finish this chapter, you should be able to:

1 Identify a mechanic's lien.

2 Explain what a judicial lien is.

3 Distinguish between a suretyship contract and a guaranty contract.

4 State what a homestead exemption is.

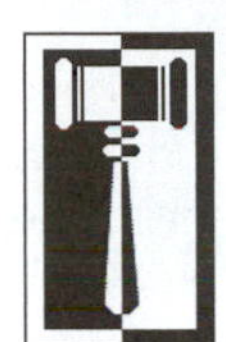

FACING A LEGAL PROBLEM

Adrian, a painter, agrees to paint a house for the Swensens, the homeowners, for a certain price to cover labor and materials. *If the Swensens cannot pay or they pay only a portion of the charges, can Adrian get the rest of what he is owed?*

The remedies available to secured creditors under the Uniform Commercial Code are examined in Chapter 31. In this chapter, we focus on rights and remedies available under other statutory laws, the common law, and contract law to assist the debtor and creditor in resolving their disputes without the debtor's having to resort to bankruptcy.

Laws Assisting Creditors

Numerous laws create rights and remedies for creditors. We discuss some of them in this section.

Mechanic's Lien

LEARNING OBJECTIVE NO. 1
Identifying a Mechanic's Lien

When a person contracts for labor, services, or material to be furnished for the purpose of making improvements on real property but does not immediately pay for the improvements, a creditor can place a **mechanic's lien** on the property. This creates a special type of debtor-creditor relationship in which the real estate itself becomes security for the debt (that is, the property can be taken and held to guarantee payment of the debt or it can be sold to effect actual payment).

Mechanic's Lien
A statutory lien on the real property of another, created to ensure priority of payment for work performed and materials furnished in erecting or repairing a building or other structure.

In the legal problem set out at the beginning of this chapter, Adrian agreed to paint the Swensens' house for a certain price to cover labor and materials. *If the Swensens cannot pay or they pay only a portion of the charges, can Adrian get the rest of what he is owed?* Yes. A mechanic's lien against the property can be created. Adrian would be the lienholder. The property would be subject to the mechanic's lien for the amount owed. If the Swensens do not pay the lien, the property can be sold to satisfy the debt.

State law governs mechanic's liens. The time period within which a mechanic's lien must be filed is usually 60 to 120 days from the last date labor or materials were provided.

ARTISAN'S LIEN

ARTISAN'S LIEN
A possessory lien given to a person who has made improvements and added value to another person's personal property as security for payment for services performed.

An **artisan's lien** is a security device created at common law through which a creditor can recover payment from a debtor for labor and materials furnished in the repair of personal property. In contrast to a mechanic's lien, an artisan's lien is *possessory*—requiring possession. The lienholder ordinarily must have retained possession of the property and have expressly or impliedly (implicitly) agreed to provide the services on a cash, not a credit, basis. The artisan's lien exists as long as the lienholder maintains possession. The lien terminates when possession is voluntarily surrendered.

Modern statutes permit the holder of an artisan's lien to foreclose and sell the property subject to the lien to satisfy payment of the debt. As with the mechanic's lien, the lienholder is required to give notice to the owner of the property prior to foreclosure and selling. The sale proceeds are used to pay the debt and the costs of the legal proceedings. The surplus, if any, is paid to the former owner.

IN THE COURTROOM

Rosa leaves her diamond ring at Dana's Jewelry to be repaired and to have her initials engraved on the band. *Does Dana have any recourse if she does the work, but Rosa fails to pay?* Yes. In the absence of an agreement to the contrary, Dana can keep the ring until Rosa pays for the services that Dana provides. Should Rosa fail to pay, Dana has a lien on Rosa's ring for the amount of the bill and can sell the ring in satisfaction of the lien.

INNKEEPER'S LIEN

INNKEEPER'S LIEN
A common law lien allowing the innkeeper to take the personal property of a guest, brought into the hotel, as security for nonpayment of the guest's bill (debt).

An **innkeeper's lien** is another security device created at common law. An innkeeper's lien is placed on the baggage of guests for the agreed-on hotel charges that remain unpaid. If no express agreement is made on those charges, then the lien will be the reasonable value of the accommodations furnished. The innkeeper's lien is terminated either by the guest's payment of the hotel charges, by surrender of the baggage to the guest (unless such surrender is temporary), or by a public sale of the guest's baggage by the innkeeper.

JUDICIAL LIENS

LEARNING OBJECTIVE NO. 2
Explaining What a Judicial Lien Is

A debt must be past due before a creditor can begin legal action against a debtor. Once legal action is brought, the debtor's property may be seized to satisfy the debt. If the property is seized before a trial, the seizure is referred to as an *attachment* of the property (explained below). If the seizure occurs following a court judgment in the creditor's favor, the court's order to seize the property is referred to as a *writ of execution.*

ATTACHMENT
The legal process of seizing another's property under a court order to secure satisfaction of a judgment yet to be rendered.

Attachment. **Attachment** is a court-ordered seizure and taking into custody of property prior to the securing of a judgment for a past-due debt. (Note that attachment has a different meaning under the Uniform Commercial Code—see Chapter 31.) Normally a *prejudgment* remedy, attachment occurs either at the time of or immediately after the commencement of a lawsuit and before the entry of a final judgment.

To use attachment as a remedy, the creditor must have an enforceable right to payment of the debt under law, and the creditor must follow certain procedures. He or she must file with the court an **affidavit** (a written or printed statement, made under oath or sworn to) stating that the debtor is in default and stating the statutory grounds under which attachment is sought. A bond must be posted by the creditor to cover at least court costs, the value of the loss of use of the good suffered by the debtor, and the value of the property attached. When the court is satisfied that all the requirements have been met, it issues a **writ of attachment,** which directs the sheriff or other officer to seize the debtor's property. If the creditor prevails at trial, the seized property can be sold to satisfy the judgment.

AFFIDAVIT
A written or printed voluntary statement of facts, confirmed by the oath or affirmation of the party making it and made before a person having the authority to administer the oath or affirmation.

WRIT OF ATTACHMENT
A writ employed to enforce obedience to an order or judgment of the court. The writ may take the form of taking or seizing property to bring it under the control of the court.

Writ of Execution. If a creditor is successful in a legal action against a debtor, the court awards the creditor a judgment against the debtor (usually for the amount of the debt plus any interest and legal costs). Frequently, however, the creditor fails to collect the awarded amount.

If the debtor will not or cannot pay the judgment, the creditor is entitled to go back to the court and obtain a **writ of execution.** This order, usually issued by the clerk of the court, directs the sheriff to seize and sell the debtor's property that is within the court's geographical jurisdiction (usually the county in which the courthouse is located). The proceeds of the sale are used to pay off the judgment and the costs of the sale. Any excess is paid to the debtor. The debtor can pay the judgment and redeem the property any time before the sale takes place. Because of exemption laws (discussed below) and bankruptcy laws (see Chapter 33), however, many judgments are virtually uncollectible.

WRIT OF EXECUTION
A writ that puts in force a court's decree or judgment.

GARNISHMENT

Garnishment occurs when a creditor is permitted to collect a debt by seizing property of the debtor (such as wages or money in a bank account) that is being held by a third party (such as an employer or a bank). As a result of a garnishment proceeding, the debtor's employer may be ordered by the court to turn over a portion of the debtor's wages to pay the debt.

GARNISHMENT
A legal process whereby a creditor appropriates the debtor's property or wages that are in the hands of a third party.

Garnishment operates differently from state to state. According to the laws in some states, the judgment creditor (the creditor who obtains the garnishment order) needs to obtain only one order of garnishment, which will then continuously apply to the weekly wages of the judgment debtor (the debtor whose wages will be garnished) until the entire debt is paid. In other states, the judgment creditor must go back to court for a separate order of garnishment for each pay period.

The Legal Information Institute at Cornell University offers a collection of law materials concerning debtor-creditor relationships, including federal statutes and recent Supreme Court decisions on this topic, at

http://www.law.cornell.edu/topics/debtor_creditor.html

Both federal laws and state laws limit the amount of money that can be garnished from a debtor's weekly take-home pay. Federal law provides a minimal framework to protect debtors from losing all their income in order to pay judgment debts. State laws also provide dollar exemptions, and these amounts are often larger than those provided by federal law. State and federal statutes can be applied together to help create a pool of funds sufficient to enable a debtor to continue to provide for family needs while also reducing the amount of the judgment debt in a reasonable way.

Under federal law, garnishment of an employee's wages for any one indebtedness cannot be grounds for dismissal of an employee.

CREDITORS' COMPOSITION AGREEMENTS

Creditors may contract with the debtor for discharge of the debtor's liquidated debts (debts that are definite, or fixed, in amount) upon payment of a sum less than that owed. These agreements are called **creditors' composition agreements** and are usually held to be enforceable.

CREDITORS' COMPOSITION AGREEMENT
An agreement formed between a debtor and his or her creditors in which the creditors agree to accept a lesser sum than that owed by the debtor in full satisfaction of the debt.

MORTGAGE FORECLOSURE

A *mortgage* is a pledge of real property as security for the payment of a debt. Mortgage holders have the right to *foreclose* on the mortgaged property if the debtor does not make the payments. That is, the creditor can prevent the debtor from obtaining ownership of the property and force a sale of the property to pay the debt.

The usual method of foreclosure is by a judicial sale of the property, although the statutory methods of foreclosure vary from state to state. If the proceeds of the foreclosure sale are sufficient to cover both the costs of the foreclosure and the mortgaged debt, any surplus is received by the debtor.

MORTGAGEE
The creditor who takes the security interest under the mortgage agreement.

MORTGAGOR
The debtor who pledges collateral in a mortgage agreement.

If the sale proceeds are insufficient to cover the foreclosure costs and the mortgaged debt, however, the **mortgagee** (the creditor/lender) can seek to recover the difference from the **mortgagor** (the debtor) by obtaining a *deficiency judgment* representing the difference between the mortgaged debt and the amount actually received from the proceeds of the foreclosure sale. A deficiency judgment is obtained in a separate legal action that is pursued after the foreclosure action. It entitles the creditor to recover from other nonexempt property owned by the debtor.

SURETYSHIP AND GUARANTY

When a third person promises to pay a debt owed by another in the event the debtor does not pay, either a *suretyship* or *guaranty* relationship is created. Exhibit 32–1 illustrates these relationships. The third person's credit becomes the security for the debt owed.

SURETYSHIP
A contract in which a third party to a debtor-creditor relationship (the surety) promises that the third party will be primarily responsible for the debtor's obligation.

SURETY
One who agrees to be primarily responsible for the debt of another, such as a cosigner on a note.

Surety. A contract of strict **suretyship** is a promise made by a third person to be responsible for a debtor's obligation. It is an express contract between the **surety** (the party, other than the debtor, who agrees to assume the debt) and the creditor. The surety is *primarily* liable for the debt of the principal. That is, the creditor can demand payment from the surety from the moment that the debt is due. The creditor need not exhaust all legal remedies against the principal debtor before holding the surety responsible for payment. A surety agreement does not have to be in writing to be enforceable, although it usually is.

EXHIBIT 32–1
Suretyship and Guaranty Parties

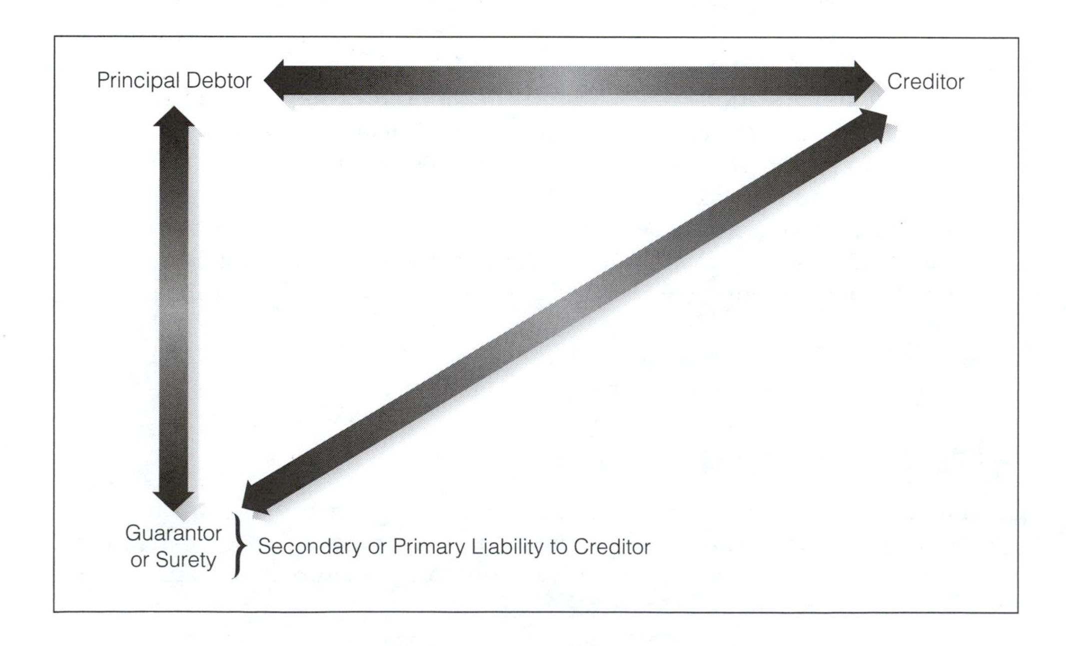

IN THE COURTROOM

Robert Delmar wants to borrow money from the bank to buy a used car. Because Robert is still in college, the bank will not lend him the money unless his father, Joseph Delmar, who has dealt with the bank before, will cosign (add his signature to) the note, thereby becoming jointly liable for payment of debt. *When Mr. Delmar cosigns the note, is he primarily liable to the bank?* Yes. Once he signs the note, Mr. Delmar is a surety. On the note's due date, the bank can seek payment from Robert or his father, or both jointly.

LEARNING OBJECTIVE NO. 3

Distinguishing between a Suretyship Contract and a Guaranty Contract

Guaranty. A **guaranty contract** is similar to a suretyship contract in that it includes a promise to answer for the debt or default of another. With a suretyship arrangement, however, the surety is primarily liable for the debtor's obligation. With a guaranty arrangement, the **guarantor**—the third person making the guaranty—is *secondarily* liable. The guarantor can be required to pay the obligation only after the debtor defaults, and then usually only after the creditor has made an attempt to collect from the principal debtor.

GUARANTY CONTRACT
An agreement in which a guarantor agrees to pay the debt of another only if and when the debtor fails to pay.

GUARANTOR
One who agrees to satisfy the debt of another (the debtor) only if and when the debtor fails to pay the debt. A guarantor's liability is thus secondary.

IN THE COURTROOM

BX Enterprises needs to borrow money to meet its payroll. The bank is skeptical about the creditworthiness of BX and requires Dawson, its president, who is a wealthy businessperson and owner of 70 percent of BX Enterprises, to sign an agreement making himself personally liable for payment if BX does not pay off the loan. *Is Dawson a guarantor of the loan?* Yes. As a guarantor of the loan, however, Dawson cannot be held liable until BX Enterprises is in default.

A guaranty contract between the guarantor and creditor must be in writing to be enforceable unless the *main purpose* exception applies. Briefly, this exception provides that if the main purpose of the guaranty agreement is to benefit the guarantor, then the contract need not be in writing to be enforceable. (See Chapter 13 for a more detailed discussion of this exception.)

Defenses of the Surety and Guarantor. The defenses of the surety and guarantor are basically the same. Therefore, this discussion applies to both. Their defenses include the following:

1. *Modification of the contract between the debtor and creditor.* Any material change made in the terms of the original contract between the principal debtor and the creditor, including the awarding of a binding extension of time for making payment without first obtaining the consent of the surety, will discharge the surety either completely or to the extent that the surety suffers a loss.
2. *Payment of the obligation or tender of payment.* If the principal obligation is paid by the debtor or by another person on behalf of the debtor, the surety is discharged from the obligation. Similarly, if valid tender of payment is made, and the creditor for some reason rejects it with knowledge of the surety's existence, then the surety is released from any obligation on the debt.
3. *Principal debtor's defenses.* Generally, any defenses available to a principal debtor can be used by the surety to avoid liability on the obligation to the creditor. The ability of the surety to assert any defenses the debtor may have against the creditor is the most important concept in suretyship because most of the defenses available to the surety are also those of the debtor.

4. *Surety's own defenses.* A surety may have his or her own defenses. For example, if the creditor fraudulently induced the surety to guarantee the debt of the debtor, the surety can assert fraud as a defense. In most states, the creditor has a legal duty to inform the surety, prior to the formation of the suretyship contract, of material facts known by the creditor that would substantially increase the surety's risk. Failure to so inform is fraud and makes the suretyship obligation voidable.
5. *Creditor's surrender or impairment of the collateral.* If a creditor surrenders the collateral to the debtor or impairs it (that is, does something that reduces its value in terms of paying the debt) while knowing of the surety and without the surety's consent, the surety is released to the extent of any loss that would be suffered from the creditor's actions.

Rights of the Surety and Guarantor. The rights of the surety and guarantor are basically the same. Therefore, this discussion applies to both. When the surety pays the debt owed to the creditor, the surety is entitled to the following rights:

RIGHT OF SUBROGATION
The right of a person to stand in the place of (be substituted for) another, giving the substituted party the same legal rights that the original party had.

RIGHT OF REIMBURSEMENT
The legal right of a person to be restored, repaid, or indemnified for costs, expenses, or losses incurred or expended on behalf of another.

CO-SURETY
A joint surety. One who assumes liability jointly with another surety for the payment of an obligation.

RIGHT OF CONTRIBUTION
The right of a co-surety who pays more than his or her proportionate share upon a debtor's default to recover the excess paid from other co-sureties.

1. *Right of subrogation.* The surety has the **right of subrogation.** Simply stated, this means that any right the creditor had against the debtor becomes the right of the surety. Included are creditor rights in bankruptcy, rights to collateral possessed by the creditor, and rights to judgments secured by the creditor. In short, the surety stands in the shoes of the creditor and may pursue any remedies that were available to the creditor against the debtor.
2. *Right of reimbursement.* The surety has a **right of reimbursement** from the debtor. Basically, the surety is entitled to receive from the debtor all outlays made on behalf of the suretyship arrangement. Such outlays can include expenses incurred as well as the actual amount of the debt paid to the creditor.
3. *Co-sureties' right of contribution.* In the case of **co-sureties** (two or more sureties on the same obligation owed by the debtor), a surety who pays more than his or her proportionate share on a debtor's default is entitled to recover from the co-sureties the amount paid above the surety's obligation. This is the **right of contribution.** Generally, a co-surety's liability either is determined by agreement or, in the absence of agreement, is set at the maximum liability under the suretyship contract.

IN THE COURTROOM

Two co-sureties—Yasser and Itzhak—are obligated under a suretyship contract to guarantee the debt of Jules. Itzhak's maximum liability is $15,000, and Yasser's is $10,000. Jules owes $10,000 and is in default. Itzhak pays the creditor the entire $10,000. *Can Itzhak recover anything from Yasser?* Yes. *How much?* In the absence of an agreement to the contrary, Itzhak can recover $4,000 from Yasser. The amount of the debt that Yasser agreed to cover is divided by the total amount that Itzhak and Yasser together agreed to cover. The quotient is multiplied by the amount of the default. The result is the amount that Yasser owes ($10,000 ÷ $25,000 × $10,000 = $4,000). Because Itzhak paid the entire amount of the default, Yasser owes this sum to Itzhak.

Protection for Debtors

The law protects debtors as well as creditors. Certain property of the debtor, for example, is exempt from creditors' actions. Consumer protection statutes also protect debtors' rights. Of course, bankruptcy laws, which are discussed in Chapter 33, are designed specifically to assist debtors in need of help.

EXEMPTIONS

LEARNING OBJECTIVE NO. 4

Stating What a Homestead Exemption Is

In most states, certain types of property are exempt from writs of attachment or execution. Probably the most familiar of these exemptions is the **homestead exemption.** Each state permits the debtor to retain the family home, either in its entirety or up to a specified dollar amount, free from the claims of unsecured creditors or trustees in bankruptcy.

HOMESTEAD EXEMPTION A law allowing an owner to designate his or her house and adjoining land as a homestead and thus exempt it from liability for his or her general debt.

IN THE COURTROOM

Van Cleave owes Acosta $40,000. The debt is the subject of a lawsuit, and the court awards Acosta a judgment of $40,000 against Van Cleave. The homestead of Van Cleave is valued at around $50,000. There are no outstanding mortgages or other liens. To satisfy the judgment debt, Van Cleave's family home is sold at public auction for $45,000. Assume that the homestead exemption is $25,000. *How are the proceeds of the sale distributed?* First, Van Cleave is given $25,000 as his homestead exemption. Second, Acosta is paid $20,000 toward the judgment debt, leaving a $20,000 deficiency that can be paid from any other non-exempt property that Van Cleave may have, if allowed by state law.

Other property that is most often exempt from satisfaction of judgment debts includes the following:

1. Household furniture up to a specified dollar amount.
2. Clothing and certain personal possessions, such as family pictures or a Bible.
3. A vehicle (or vehicles) for transportation (at least up to a specified dollar amount).
4. Certain classified animals, usually livestock but including pets.
5. Equipment that the debtor uses in a business or trade, such as tools or professional instruments, up to a specified dollar amount.

SPECIAL PROTECTION FOR CONSUMER DEBTORS

Numerous consumer protection statutes and rules apply to the debtor-creditor relationship. The Federal Trade Commission's rule limiting the rights of a holder in due course (HDC) when the debtor-buyer executes a negotiable promissory note as part of a consumer transaction is discussed in Chapter 23. This rule provides that any personal defenses the buyer can assert against the seller can also be asserted against an HDC. The seller must disclose this information clearly on the sales agreement.

Other laws regulating debtor-creditor relationships include the Truth-in-Lending Act, which protects consumers by requiring creditors to disclose specific types of information when making loans to consumers. This act, along with other consumer protection statutes, is discussed in Chapter 20.

As a creditor, before hiring a professional debt collector or taking any other steps, you could contact your debtor—he or she may have a good reason for not paying on time.

TERMS AND CONCEPTS FOR REVIEW

affidavit 415
artisan's lien 414
attachment 414
co-surety 418
creditors' composition agreement 415
garnishment 415
guarantor 417
guaranty contract 417
homestead exemption 419
innkeeper's lien 414
mechanic's lien 413
mortgagee 416
mortgagor 416
right of contribution 418
right of reimbursement 418
right of subrogation 418
surety 416
suretyship 416
writ of attachment 415
writ of execution 415

CHAPTER SUMMARY • CREDITORS' RIGHTS AND REMEDIES

Mechanic's Lien	A nonpossessory, filed lien on an owner's real estate for labor, services, or materials furnished to or made on the property.
Artisan's Lien	A possessory lien on an owner's personal property for labor performed or value added.
Innkeeper's Lien	A possessory lien on a hotel guest's baggage for hotel charges that remain unpaid.
Judicial Liens	**1.** *Attachment*—A court-ordered seizure of property prior to a court's final determination of the creditor's rights to the property. **2.** *Writ of execution*—A court order directing the sheriff to seize and sell a debtor's nonexempt property to satisfy a court judgment in the creditor's favor.
Garnishment	A collection remedy that allows the creditor to attach a debtor's property (such as wages owed or bank accounts) held by a third person.
Creditors' Composition Agreement	A contract between a debtor and his or her creditors under which the debtor's debts are discharged by payment of a sum less than that owed in the original debt.
Mortgage Foreclosure	A creditor who holds a mortgage has a right to foreclose on the mortgaged property if the debtor defaults. The creditor can prevent the debtor from obtaining ownership of the property, and the creditor can sell the property to pay the debt.
Suretyship or Guaranty	Under contract, a third person agrees to be primarily or secondarily liable for the debt owed by the principal debtor. A creditor can turn to this third person for satisfaction of the debt.
Exemptions	State laws exempt some property from execution or attachment. **1.** A debtor can retain the family home, either in its entirety or up to a specified dollar amount, free from the claims of unsecured creditors or trustees in bankruptcy (homestead exemption). **2.** Most often exempt from satisfaction of judgment debts are certain items, up to a specified dollar amount, such as household furniture, clothing, personal possessions, vehicles, certain animals (livestock and pets), and equipment that a debtor uses in a business or trade.

HYPOTHETICAL QUESTIONS

32–1. Creditor's Remedies. In what circumstances would a creditor resort to each of the following remedies when trying to collect on a debt?

(a) Mechanic's lien.
(b) Artisan's lien.
(c) Innkeeper's lien.
(d) Writ of attachment.
(e) Writ of execution.
(f) Garnishment.

32–2. Creditor's Remedies. Orkin owns a relatively old home valued at $45,000. He notices that the bathtubs and fixtures in both bathrooms are leaking and need to be replaced. He contracts with Pike to replace the bathtubs and fixtures. Pike replaces them and submits her bill of $4,000 to Orkin. Because of financial difficulties, Orkin does not pay the bill. Orkin's only asset is his home, which under state law is exempt up to $40,000 as a homestead. Discuss fully Pike's remedies in this situation.

REAL WORLD CASE PROBLEM

32–3. Writ of Attachment. Topjian Plumbing and Heating, Inc., the plaintiff, sought prejudgment writs of attachment to satisfy an anticipated judgment in a contract action against Bruce Topjian, Inc., the defendant. The plaintiff did not petition the court for permission to effect the attachments but merely completed the forms, served them on the defendant and on the Fencers (the owners of a parcel of land that had previously belonged to the defendant), and recorded them at the registry of deeds. On what grounds might the court invalidate the attachments? [*Topjian Plumbing and Heating, Inc. v. Bruce Topjian, Inc.,* 129 N.H. 481, 529 A.2d 391 (1987)]

For updated links to resources available on the Web, as well as a variety of other materials, visit this text's Web site at **http://blte.westbuslaw.com.**

The Legal Information Institute at Cornell University offers a collection of law materials concerning debtor-creditor relationships at

http://www.law.cornell.edu/topics/debtor_creditor.html

For an example of one state's (South Dakota's) laws on garnishment, go to

http://legis.state.sd.us/statutes/index.cfm

When the page opens, conduct a "text search" for "garnishment."

ONLINE LEGAL RESEARCH

Go to **http://blte.westbuslaw.com,** the Web site that accompanies this text. Select "Internet Applications," and then click on "Chapter 32." There you will find the following Internet research exercise that you can perform to learn more about debtor-creditor relations:

Activity 32–1: Debtor-Creditor Relations

Chapter 32 ■ WORK SET

TRUE-FALSE QUESTIONS

____ **1.** A mechanic's lien always involves real property, and an artisan's lien always involves personal property.

____ **2.** Federal and state laws limit the amount that can be garnished from wages, but they cannot be applied together to determine how much is exempt.

____ **3.** An innkeeper's lien is placed on the baggage of guests for agreed-on hotel charges that remain unpaid.

____ **4.** Generally, to avoid liability, a surety or a guarantor cannot use any defenses available to the principal debtor.

____ **5.** If a creditor obtains a judgment against a debtor and the debtor does not willingly pay, there is nothing that the creditor can do.

____ **6.** A surety or guarantor is discharged from his or her obligation when the principal debtor pays the debt.

____ **7.** A writ of execution is issued before the entry of a final judgment.

MULTIPLE-CHOICE QUESTIONS

____ **1.** Jan leaves her necklace with Gold Jewelers to be repaired. When Jan returns to pick up the necklace, she says, "I don't have the money now, but I'll pay you for the repairs later." Gold

a. can keep the necklace until Jan pays for the repairs.
b. can keep the necklace for a reasonable time but must then return it to Jan even if she does not pay for the repairs.
c. cannot keep the necklace.
d. none of the above.

____ **2.** Don owes Barb $500 but refuses to pay. To collect, Barb files a suit against Don and wins. Don still refuses to pay. To collect the amount of the judgment, Barb can use

a. an artisan's lien.
b. a creditor's composition agreement.
c. a foreclosure.
d. a writ of execution.

____ **3.** John owes First State Bank $40,000, secured by a mortgage on his warehouse. He fails to pay off the loan. To obtain the amount that is owed, the bank can use

a. an artisan's lien.
b. a creditor's composition agreement.
c. a foreclosure.
d. a writ of execution.

_____ **4.** Dian's $6,000 debt to Ace Credit Company is past due, and Ace files suit. Before the judge hears the case, Ace learns that Dian has hidden some of her property from Ace. Ace believes that Dian is about to hide the rest of her property. To ensure there will be some assets to satisfy the debt if Ace wins the suit, Ace can use

a. garnishment.
b. a mechanic's lien.
c. an artisan's lien.
d. attachment.

_____ **5.** Ed's $2,500 debt to Owen is past due. Ed does not own a house and has very little personal property, but he has a checking account, a savings account, and a job. To reach these assets to satisfy the debt, Owen can use

a. garnishment.
b. a mechanic's lien.
c. an artisan's lien.
d. attachment.

_____ **6.** Bob obtains a judgment for $30,000 and a writ of execution against Mary. To enforce the writ, Mary's home is sold for $60,000. The homestead exemption is $35,000. All of Mary's personal property is exempt, except two motorcycles that are sold for $5,000. After applying the appropriate amounts to payment of the debt, how much of the debt will be unpaid?

a. $25,000
b. $10,000
c. $5,000
d. $0

_____ **7.** L&R Computers, Inc., wants to borrow money from First National Bank. The bank refuses to lend L&R the money unless Lee, the sole stockholder, agrees to assume liability if L&R does not pay off the loan. Lee agrees. When the first payment is due, the bank can seek payment from L&R

a. but not Lee, because Lee is a guarantor.
b. but not Lee, because Lee is a surety.
c. or Lee, because Lee is a surety.
d. or Lee, because Lee is a guarantor.

_____ **8.** Glen agrees to act, without compensation, as a surety for Tina's loan from Ace Credit. Later, without Glen's knowledge, Tina and Ace agree to extend the time for repayment and to increase the interest rate. Tina's obligation

a. remains the same.
b. changes to match Tina's obligation.
c. is discharged to the extent of any loss caused by the extension of time.
d. is discharged completely.

ISSUE SPOTTERS

1. Joe contracts with Larry of Midwest Roofing to fix Joe's roof. Joe pays half of the contract price in advance. Larry and Midwest complete the job, but Joe refuses to pay the rest of the price. What can Larry and Midwest do?

2. Al owes Don $5,000 and refuses to pay. Don obtains a garnishment order and serves it on Al's employer. If the employer complies with the order and Al stays on the job, is one order enough to garnish all of Al's wages for each pay period until the debt is paid?

Bankruptcy

33

LEARNING OBJECTIVES

When you finish this chapter, you should be able to:

1. Explain what an ordinary, or straight, bankruptcy is.
2. Identify the property of a debtor's estate.
3. Define reorganization in the context of a bankruptcy.
4. List debts that may be discharged under a Chapter 13 plan.

FACING A LEGAL PROBLEM

G&M Trucking borrows money from Middleton Bank to buy two trucks, giving the bank a security interest in the trucks. G&M fails to make its monthly payments for two months and files a petition in bankruptcy. Under bankruptcy law, the bank is prevented from repossessing the trucks. The trucks are depreciating at a rate of several hundred dollars a month, however, and will soon be worth much less than the balance due on the loan. *Is there anything that the bank can do to protect its investment?*

Bankruptcy law in the United States has two goals: (1) to protect a debtor by giving him or her a fresh start, free from creditors' claims, and (2) to ensure equitable treatment to creditors who are competing for a debtor's remaining assets. There are different types of bankruptcy plans for different individuals and businesses. This chapter deals with the most frequently used plans.

The Bankruptcy Code

The federal bankruptcy law is known as the Bankruptcy Code (or simply as the Code). The most frequently used bankruptcy plans are contained in specific chapters of the Code: Chapter 7, liquidations; Chapter 11, reorganizations; and Chapter 13, adjustments of debt. As you read about these bankruptcy plans, be sure to keep in mind that references to Chapter 7, Chapter 11, and Chapter 13 are references to chapters in the Code, not references to chapters within this textbook.

Bankruptcy proceedings are held in federal bankruptcy courts. Bankruptcy courts are under the authority of U.S. district courts (see the exhibit on the federal court system in Chapter 3). Rulings from bankruptcy courts can be appealed to the district courts.

LIQUIDATION
The sale of the assets of a business or an individual for cash and the distribution of the cash received to creditors, with the balance going to the owner(s).

LEARNING OBJECTIVE NO. 1
Explaining What an Ordinary, or Straight, Bankruptcy Is

Chapter 7 Liquidations

Liquidation under Chapter 7 is the most familiar type of bankruptcy proceeding and is often referred to as an *ordinary,* or *straight, bankruptcy.* Put simply, debtors in straight bankruptcies state their debts and turn their assets over to trustees. The trustees sell the assets and distribute the proceeds to creditors. With certain exceptions, the remaining debts are then discharged (extinguished), and the debtors are relieved of their obligation to pay the debts. This gives the debtor an opportunity for a fresh start.

Any "person"—defined as including individuals, partnerships, and corporations—may be a debtor under Chapter 7. Railroads, insurance companies, banks, savings and loan associations, credit unions, and investment companies licensed by the Small Business Administration cannot be Chapter 7 debtors. Rather, other chapters of the Bankruptcy Code or other federal or state statutes apply to them.

The U.S. Bankruptcy Code is online at

http://www4.law.cornell.edu/uscode/11

FILING THE PETITION

A straight bankruptcy may be commenced by the filing of either a voluntary or an involuntary petition.

Voluntary Bankruptcy. A voluntary petition is brought by the debtor, who files official forms designated for that purpose in the bankruptcy court. A debtor does not have to be **insolvent** (insolvency exists when debts exceed the fair market value of assets exclusive of exempt property) to file a petition. A husband and wife can file jointly for bankruptcy under a single petition.

INSOLVENT
When a person's liabilities exceed the value of his or her assets.

The official forms must be completed accurately, sworn to under oath, and signed by the debtor. To conceal assets or knowingly supply false information is a crime. If the petition for bankruptcy is found to be proper, the filing of the petition will itself constitute an **order for relief.** (This order relieves the debtor of having to pay the debts listed in the petition.)

ORDER FOR RELIEF
A court's grant of assistance to a complainant. In the context of bankruptcy, relief consists of discharging a complainant's debts.

Involuntary Bankruptcy. An involuntary bankruptcy occurs when the debtor's creditors force the debtor into bankruptcy proceedings. Such a case cannot be commenced against a farmer or a charitable institution, however. Nor can it be filed unless one of the following two requirements are met: (1) if the debtor has twelve or more creditors, three or more of those having unsecured claims aggregating at least $11,625 must join in the petition; or (2) if a debtor has fewer than twelve creditors, one or more creditors having an unsecured claim of $11,625 may file.

Sometimes, a debtor challenges the involuntary petition. The court will listen to the debtor's arguments, but it will go ahead with the bankruptcy proceeding if it finds either of the following:

1. That the debtor is generally not paying debts as they become due.
2. That a custodian was appointed to take charge, or took possession, of substantially all of the debtor's property within 120 days before the filing of the petition.

AUTOMATIC STAY

The filing of a petition, either voluntary or involuntary, operates as an **automatic stay** on (suspension of) virtually all litigation and other action by creditors against the debtor or the debtor's property. In other words, once a petition is filed, creditors cannot commence or continue most legal actions against the debtor to recover claims. Nor can creditors take any action to repossess property in the hands of the debtor. A secured creditor, however, may petition the bankruptcy court for relief from the automatic stay in certain circumstances. Also, the automatic stay does not apply to paternity, alimony, spousal maintenance, and child-support debts.

AUTOMATIC STAY
A suspension of all judicial proceedings upon the occurrence of an independent event. Under the Bankruptcy Code, the moment a petition to commence bankruptcy proceedings is filed, all litigation by creditors against a debtor and the debtor's property is suspended.

In the legal problem set out at the beginning of this chapter, G&M Trucking borrows money from Middleton Bank to buy two trucks, giving the bank a security interest in the trucks. G&M fails to make its payments for two months and files a petition in bankruptcy. Under bankruptcy law, Middleton is prevented from repossessing the trucks. This is the automatic stay.

The trucks are rapidly depreciating, however, and will soon be worth much less than the balance due on the loan. *Is there anything that Middleton can do to protect its investment?* Yes. The bank can ask the court to require G&M to make a one-time cash payment or periodic cash payments (or to provide additional collateral) to the extent that the trucks are depreciating. If G&M cannot provide adequate protection, the court may vacate (cancel) the automatic stay and allow the bank to repossess the trucks.

Creditors' Meeting

Within a reasonable time after the order for relief is granted (not less than ten days or more than thirty days), the court must call a meeting of creditors. At this meeting, a trustee is elected to take over the assets of the debtor. The debtor is required to attend this meeting (unless excused by the court) and to submit to an examination under oath by the creditors and the trustee. Failure to appear when required or making false statements under oath may result in the debtor's being denied a discharge of his or her debts in the bankruptcy proceeding.

At the meeting, the trustee ensures that the debtor is aware of the potential consequences of bankruptcy and of his or her ability to file for bankruptcy under a different chapter. Proof of claims by creditors must normally be filed within ninety days of this meeting.

Property of the Estate

On the commencement of a Chapter 7 proceeding, an **estate in property** is created. The estate consists of all the debtor's property, together with certain jointly owned property, property transferred in a transaction voidable by the trustee (discussed below), and proceeds and profits from the property of the estate. Interests in certain property—such as gifts, inheritances, property settlements (divorce), or life insurance death proceeds—to which the debtor becomes entitled *within 180 days after filing* may also become part of the estate.

LEARNING OBJECTIVE NO. 2

Identifying the Property of a Debtor's Estate

Estate in Property
All of the property owned by a person, including real estate and personal property. In bankruptcy law, an estate in property may include property transferred within 180 days of the filing of a petition to declare bankruptcy.

Exemptions

A debtor is entitled to exempt certain property from the property of the estate. Under the Code, the following property (among other property) is exempt:

1. Up to $17,425 in equity in the debtor's residence and burial plot.
2. Interest in a motor vehicle up to $2,775.
3. Interest, up to $450 for any particular item or $9,300 for all items together, in household goods and furnishings, wearing apparel, appliances, books, animals, crops, or musical instruments.
4. Interest in any tools of the debtor's trade, up to $1,750.
5. The right to receive Social Security and certain welfare benefits, alimony and support payments, and certain pension benefits.

The states can pass legislation to preclude the use of the federal exemptions by debtors in their states. A majority of the states have done this. In those states, debtors may use only state (not federal) exemptions. In the rest of the states, a debtor can choose between the exemptions provided under the applicable state law or the federal exemptions.

Trustee's Powers

The basic duty of the trustee is to collect the debtor's property and reduce it to money for distribution, preserving the interests of both the debtor and the unsecured creditors. In other words, the trustee is accountable for administering the debtor's estate. To enable the trustee to accomplish this duty, the Code gives him or her certain powers.

These powers enable the trustee to exercise, in some situations, the same rights as creditors. For example, a trustee can ask the court for a writ of execution. (This is an order directing the sheriff to seize and sell the debtor's property that is within the court's geographic jurisdiction. Proceeds of the sale are used to pay off creditors. See Chapter 32 for more details about writs of execution.) This power means that a trustee has priority over an unsecured creditor (a creditor whose debt is not backed by any collateral).

In addition, the trustee has the power to avoid (cancel) certain types of transactions, including fraudulent transfers by the debtor and **preferences** (a debtor's transfer of property or money, generally within ninety days of filing the petition in bankruptcy, favoring one creditor over others). A trustee can also cancel transactions that the debtor could rightfully cancel (such as those involving fraud on the part of someone other than the debtor) and obtain the return of the debtor's property.

PREFERENCE
In bankruptcy proceedings, the debtor's favoring of one creditor over others by making payments or transferring property to that creditor at the expense of the rights of other creditors in the bankruptcy estate. The bankruptcy trustee is allowed to recover payments made both voluntarily and involuntarily to one creditor in preference over another.

IN THE COURTROOM

Rob sells his boat to Inga. Inga gives Rob a check, knowing that there are insufficient funds in her bank account to cover the check. Inga has committed fraud. Within a month, Rob files a bankruptcy petition. *Can Rob cancel the transfer of the boat to Inga?* Yes. Rob has the right to avoid that transfer and recover the boat from Inga, because she committed fraud. *Could the trustee of Rob's estate cancel the transfer of the boat?* Yes. Once an order for relief has been entered for Rob, the trustee can exercise the same right to recover the boat from Inga.

PROPERTY DISTRIBUTION

The right of a creditor to be paid from the property of the debtor's estate depends on whether the creditor is secured or unsecured.

Secured Creditors. A secured creditor has a security interest in collateral that secures the debt. (The rights of secured creditors are discussed in Chapter 31.) If the value of the secured collateral exceeds the secured party's claim, the secured party has priority to the proceeds from the sale of the debtor's property in an amount that will cover reasonable fees and costs incurred because of the debtor's default. Any excess over this amount is used to satisfy the claims of unsecured creditors. If the secured collateral is insufficient to cover the secured debt owed, the secured creditor becomes an unsecured creditor for the difference.

Unsecured Creditors. Unsecured creditors (creditors who do not have security interests in collateral) are paid in a certain order of priority. Each class of debt must be fully paid before the next class is entitled to any of the proceeds. If there are insufficient funds to pay the entire class, the proceeds are distributed *proportionately* to each creditor in a class, and all classes lower in priority on the list receive nothing. The order of priority among the most important classes of unsecured creditors is as follows:

1. All costs and expenses for preserving and administering the estate, including such items as bankruptcy costs, court costs, and trustee and attorneys' fees.
2. Unsecured claims in an involuntary bankruptcy proceeding after commencement of the case, but before the appointment of a trustee or issuance of an order for relief.

3. Claims for wages, salaries, and commissions up to $4,650 per claimant, provided that they were earned within ninety days of the filing of the petition in bankruptcy.
4. Unsecured claims for contributions to employee-benefit plans arising under services rendered within 180 days before the petition and limited to the number of employees covered by the plan multiplied by $4,650.
5. Unsecured claims for money deposited (up to $2,100) with the debtor before the filing of the petition in connection with the purchase, lease, or rental of property or services that were not delivered or provided.
6. Paternity, alimony, spousal maintenance, and child-support debts.
7. Certain taxes and penalties owed to the government.

DISCHARGE

A discharge voids any judgment on a discharged debt and prevents any action to collect it. (A discharge does not affect the liability of a co-debtor.) In some circumstances, however, a claim will not be discharged.

The American Bankruptcy Institute (ABI) is a good resource for bankruptcy information. You can access the site at

http://www.abiworld.org

Exceptions to Discharge. The most important claims that are not dischargeable under Chapter 7 include the following:

1. Claims for back taxes accruing within three years prior to bankruptcy.
2. Claims for amounts borrowed by the debtor to pay federal taxes.
3. Claims against property or money obtained by the debtor under false pretenses or by false representations.
4. Claims based on fraud or misuse of funds by the debtor or claims involving the debtor's embezzlement (taking the property of others who entrusted the debtor with the property) or larceny (theft).
5. Alimony, child support, and property settlements.
6. Certain government fines and penalties.
7. Certain student loans.

Objections to Discharge. In addition to the exceptions to discharge previously listed, the following circumstances (relating to the debtor's *conduct* and not to the debt) will cause a discharge to be denied:

1. The debtor's concealment or destruction of property with the intent to hinder, delay, or defraud a creditor.
2. The debtor's fraudulent concealment or destruction of records, or failure to keep adequate records, of his or her financial condition.
3. The granting of a discharge to the debtor within six years of the filing of the petition.
4. The debtor's written waiver of discharge, approved by the court.

When a discharge is denied under these circumstances, the assets of the debtor are still distributed to the creditors. After the bankruptcy proceeding, however, the debtor remains liable for the unpaid portions of all claims.

A discharge may be revoked (taken back) within one year if it is discovered that the debtor acted fraudulently or dishonestly during the bankruptcy proceeding. In that situation, a creditor whose claim was not satisfied in the distribution of the debtor's property can proceed with his or her claim against the debtor.

IN THE COURTROOM

Alicia files a voluntary petition for bankruptcy. Uri is one of Alicia's unsecured creditors. In listing her assets, Alicia intentionally does not include her collection of rare comic books, which is of considerable value. Alicia is granted a discharge, which includes Uri's claim. Six months after the discharge, Uri learns of the comic books and of Alicia's concealment. *Is there*

anything Uri can do now—after Alicia's discharge—to enforce his claim? Yes. Uri can enforce his claim against Alicia on the ground that she fraudulently concealed an important asset. Alicia will be held liable for the unpaid portion of Uri's claim.

Chapter 11 Reorganizations

LEARNING OBJECTIVE NO. 3

Defining Reorganization in the Context of a Bankruptcy

REORGANIZATION
In bankruptcy law, a plan for the readjustment of a corporation and its debt, the submission of the plan to a bankruptcy court, and the court's approval or rejection of the plan based on a determination of the feasibility of the plan.

In a Chapter 11 **reorganization,** the creditors and the debtor formulate a plan under which the debtor pays a portion of his or her debts and is discharged of the remainder. Then the debtor is allowed to continue in business. Although this type of bankruptcy is commonly a corporate reorganization, any debtor who is eligible for Chapter 7 relief is eligible for Chapter 11 relief. In addition, railroads are also eligible.

The same principles that govern the filing of a Chapter 7 petition apply to Chapter 11 proceedings. The petition may be filed either voluntarily or involuntarily. The same principles govern the entry of the order for relief. The automatic-stay provision also applies.

CREDITORS' COMMITTEES

Soon after the entry of the order for relief, a creditors' committee of unsecured creditors is appointed to consult with the trustee or the debtor concerning the administration of the case or the formulation of the plan.

Orders affecting the debtor's property generally will not be entered without either the consent of the committee or a hearing by the judge on the position of the committee. In cases involving small businesses (those with debts of less than $2 million that do not own or manage real estate), orders can be entered without the committee's consent.

THE CHAPTER 11 PLAN

Consult with creditors in advance, and have an acceptable Chapter 11 plan prepared before filing in order to expedite bankruptcy proceedings and save on costs.

A Chapter 11 plan is a plan to conserve and administer the debtor's assets in the hope of an eventual return to successful operation and solvency. The plan must do the following:

1. Designate classes of creditors under the plan.
2. Specify the treatment to be afforded the classes of creditors. Also, the plan must provide the same treatment for each claim in a particular class.
3. Provide an adequate means for the plan's execution.

Filing the Plan. Only the debtor may file a plan within the first 120 days after the date of the order for relief. If the debtor does not meet the deadline or fails to obtain the required creditor consent (within 180 days), any party with a sufficient interest in the proceeding may propose a plan. If a small-business debtor chooses to avoid creditors' committees, the time for the debtor's filing is shortened to 100 days, and any other party's plan must be filed within 160 days.

Confirming the Plan. The classes of creditors vote on the plan, and the court confirms it. A plan is binding upon confirmation, and the debtor is discharged from all claims not protected under the plan. This discharge, however, does not apply to any claims denied discharge under Chapter 7.

A court may refuse to confirm a plan if it is not "in the best interests of the creditors." A spouse or child of the debtor can block a plan if it does not provide for payment of their claims in cash.

Even if only one class of creditors accepts a plan, the court may confirm it under the Code's *cram-down* provision, if it is "fair and equitable." In other words, the court may confirm the plan over the objections of creditors.

Chapter 13 Adjustments

Individuals (not partnerships or corporations) with regular income who owe fixed, unsecured debts of less than $290,525 or fixed, secured debts of less than $871,550 may take advantage of Chapter 13. Sole proprietors and individuals on welfare, Social Security, fixed pensions, or investment income are included.

Filing a Chapter 13 plan is less expensive and less complicated than a Chapter 11 proceeding or a Chapter 7 liquidation. Also, the debtor in a Chapter 13 bankruptcy continues in business or in possession of most of his or her assets. Most debts are discharged within three years.

Filing the Petition

A Chapter 13 case can be initiated only by the filing of a voluntary petition by the debtor. A trustee must be appointed.

The Chapter 13 Plan

Only the debtor may file a plan under Chapter 13. This plan may provide for the payment of all obligations in full or for payment of an amount less than 100 percent. The plan must provide for the following:

1. The turnover of such future earnings or income of the debtor to the trustee as is necessary for execution of the plan.
2. Full payment in deferred cash payments of all claims entitled to priority. Payments must be completed within three years, unless an extension is granted (which cannot be longer than two years).
3. The same treatment of each claim within a particular class of claims.

Confirming the Plan. The court will confirm a plan with respect to each claim of a secured creditor under any of the following circumstances:

1. If the secured creditors have accepted the plan.
2. If the value of the property to be distributed to the creditors under the plan is not less than the secured portion of their claims.
3. If the debtor surrenders the collateral to the creditors.

Objecting to the Plan. Unsecured creditors do not have a vote to confirm a Chapter 13 plan. The court can approve a plan over the objection of the trustee or any unsecured creditor in one of the following situations:

1. The value of the property to be distributed under the plan is at least equal to the amount of the claims.
2. All of the debtor's projected disposable income to be received during the three-year period will be applied to making payments. Disposable income is all income received less amounts needed to support the debtor and dependents or amounts needed to meet ordinary expenses to continue the operation of a business.

Discharge

After the completion of all payments under the plan, the court grants a discharge of all debts provided for by the plan. Except for allowed claims not provided for by the plan, certain long-term debts provided for by the plan, and claims for alimony and child support, all other debts are dischargeable, including fraudulently incurred debts and claims resulting from malicious or willful injury.

LEARNING OBJECTIVE NO. 4

Listing Debts That May Be Discharged under a Chapter 13 Plan

TERMS AND CONCEPTS FOR REVIEW

automatic stay 426
estate in property 427
insolvent 426
liquidation 425
order for relief 426
preference 428
reorganization 430

CHAPTER SUMMARY • BANKRUPTCY

Issue	Chapter 7	Chapter 11	Chapter 13
Purpose	Liquidation.	Reorganization.	Adjustment.
Who Can Petition	Debtor (voluntary) or creditors (involuntary).	Debtor (voluntary) or creditors (involuntary).	Debtor (voluntary) only.
Who Can Be a Debtor	Any "person" (including partnerships and corporations) except railroads, insurance companies, banks, savings and loan institutions, credit unions, and investment companies licensed by the Small Business Administration. Farmers and charitable institutions cannot be involuntarily petitioned.	Any debtor eligible for Chapter 7 relief. Railroads are also eligible.	Any individual (not partnerships or corporations) with regular income who owes fixed, unsecured debts of less than $290,525 or fixed, secured debts of less than $871,550.
Procedure Leading to Discharge	Nonexempt property is sold with proceeds distributed (in order) to prioritized groups. Dischargeable debts are terminated.	Plan is submitted, and if it is approved and followed, debts are discharged.	Plan is submitted, and if it is approved and followed, all debts are discharged.
Advantages	On liquidation and distribution, most debts are discharged, and debtor has opportunity for fresh start.	Debtor continues in business. Plan allows for reorganization and liquidation of debts.	Debtor continues in business or possession of assets. Most debts are discharged after a three-year period.

HYPOTHETICAL QUESTIONS

33–1. Distribution of Property. Runyan voluntarily petitions for bankruptcy. He has three major claims against his estate. One is by Calvin, a friend who holds Runyan's negotiable promissory note for $2,500; one is by Kohak, an employee who is owed three months' back wages of $4,500; and one is by First Bank of Sunny Acres on an unsecured loan of $5,000. In addition, Martinez, an accountant retained by the trustee, is owed $500, and property taxes of $1,000 are owed to Micanopa County. Runyan's nonexempt property has been liquidated, with the proceeds totaling $7,500. Discuss fully what amount each party will receive, and why.

33–2. Debts under Chapter 7. Darin is experiencing personal financial problems. The amount of income he receives from the corporation is barely sufficient to cover his living expenses, the payments due on his mortgage, various credit-card debts, and some loans that he took out to pay for his son's college tuition. He would like to file for Chapter 7 liquidation just to be rid

HYPOTHETICAL QUESTIONS (*Continued*)

of the debts entirely, but he knows that he could probably pay them off over a four-year period if he really scrimped and used every cent available to pay his creditors. Darin decides to file for bankruptcy relief under Chapter 7. Are all of Darin's debts dischargeable under Chapter 7, including the debts incurred for his son's education? Given the fact that Darin could foreseeably pay off his debts over a four-year period, will the court allow Darin to obtain relief under Chapter 7? Why or why not?

REAL WORLD CASE PROBLEM

33–3. Dismissal of Chapter 7 Case. Ellis and Bonnie Jarrell filed a Chapter 7 petition. The petition was not filed due to a calamity, sudden illness, disability, or unemployment—both Jarrells were employed. Their petition was full of inaccuracies that understated their income and overstated their obligations. For example, they declared as an expense a monthly contribution to an investment plan. The truth was that they had monthly income of $3,197.45 and expenses of $2,159.44. They were attempting to discharge a total of $15,391.64 in unsecured debts. Most of these were credit-card debts, at least half of which had been taken as cash advances. Should the court dismiss the petition? If so, why? Discuss. [*In re Jarrell,* 189 Bankr. 374 (M.D.N.C. 1995)]

For updated links to resources available on the Web, as well as a variety of other materials, visit this text's Web site at **http://blte.westbuslaw.com**.

You can find links to an extensive number of bankruptcy resources on the Internet by accessing the Bankruptcy Lawfinder at

http://www.agin.com/lawfind

ONLINE LEGAL RESEARCH

Go to **http://blte.westbuslaw.com**, the Web site that accompanies this text. Select "Internet Applications," and then click on "Chapter 33." There you will find the following Internet research exercises that you can perform to learn more about bankruptcy and its alternatives:

Activity 33–1: Bankruptcy

Activity 33–2: Bankruptcy Alternatives

Chapter 33 ■ WORK SET

TRUE-FALSE QUESTIONS

_____ **1.** A debtor must be insolvent to file a voluntary petition under Chapter 7.

_____ **2.** Debtors are protected from losing the value of their property as a result of the automatic stay.

_____ **3.** The same principles cover the filing of a Chapter 7 petition and a Chapter 11 proceeding.

_____ **4.** A bankruptcy may be commenced by involuntary petition under Chapter 13.

_____ **5.** Under Chapter 13, a discharge obtained by fraud can be revoked within one year.

_____ **6.** Filing for bankruptcy under Chapter 13 is less expensive and less complicated than other bankruptcy proceedings.

_____ **7.** No small business can avoid creditors' committees under Chapter 11.

_____ **8.** Bankruptcy proceedings are held in federal bankruptcy courts.

MULTIPLE-CHOICE QUESTIONS

_____ **1.** Jill's monthly income is $2,000, her monthly expenses are $2,800, and her debts are nearly $40,000. To obtain a fresh start, Jill could file for bankruptcy under

a. Chapter 7.
b. Chapter 11.
c. Chapter 13.
d. none of the above.

_____ **2.** Pat files a Chapter 7 petition for a discharge in bankruptcy. Pat may be denied a discharge on which of the following grounds?

a. Concealing property with the intent to defraud a creditor.
b. Paying for services received in the ordinary course of business.
c. Having obtained a bankruptcy discharge twelve years earlier.
d. Both a and c.

_____ **3.** Ted is the sole proprietor of Ted's Restaurant, which owes secured debts of $225,000 and unsecured debts of $75,000. The amount is more than Ted believes he and the restaurant can reasonably repay Most of the creditors agree that liquidating Ted and the restaurant would not be in their best interests. To stay in business, Ted could file for bankruptcy under

a. an artisan's lien.
b. a creditors' composition agreement.
c. a foreclosure.
d. a writ of execution.

_____ **4.** Jerry's monthly income is $2,500, his monthly expenses are $2,100, and his debts are nearly $15,000. If he applied the difference between his income and expenses to pay off the debts, they could be eliminated within three years. The provision in the Bankruptcy Code that covers this plan is

a. Chapter 7.
b. Chapter 11.
c. Chapter 12.
d. Chapter 13.

_____ **5.** General Supplies Corporation (GSC) has not paid any of its fifteen creditors, six of whom have unsecured claims of more than $8,000. Under which chapter of the Bankruptcy Code can they force GSC into bankruptcy?

a. Chapter 7 only.
b. Chapter 11 only.
c. Chapter 13 only.
d. Chapter 7 or Chapter 11.

_____ **6.** Dick pays for college by taking out student loans. After graduation, he marries, has a child, and works briefly before divorcing and filing for Chapter 7 bankruptcy. Dick's only debts are student loans, taxes accruing within the three previous years, alimony, and child support. The debts that can be discharged in the bankruptcy are

a. the student loans.
b. the taxes.
c. the alimony and child support.
d. none of the above.

_____ **7.** Donna makes a down payment on goods to be received from Ace Furniture Store. Before the goods are delivered, Ace files for bankruptcy. Besides consumers like Donna, Ace owes wages to its employees and taxes to the government. In what order will these debts be paid?

a. Unpaid wages, consumer deposits, taxes.
b. Taxes, consumer deposits, unpaid wages.
c. Consumer deposits, unpaid wages, taxes.
d. Unpaid wages, taxes, consumer deposits.

_____ **8.** National Stores, Inc., decides to file for bankruptcy. Under which chapter of the Bankruptcy Code can a corporation file a petition for bankruptcy?

a. Chapter 7 only.
b. Chapter 11 only.
c. Chapter 13 only.
d. Chapter 7 or Chapter 11.

ISSUE SPOTTERS

1. Al's Retail Store is a sole proprietorship. Smith & Jones is an advertising partnership. Roth & Associates, Inc., is a professional corporation. First State Savings & Loan is a savings and loan corporation. Which of these is not eligible for reorganization under Chapter 11?

2. After graduating from college, Tina works briefly as a salesperson before filing for bankruptcy. As part of her petition, Tina reveals her only debts as student loans, taxes accruing within the last year, and a claim against her based on misuse of customers' funds during her employment. Are these debts dischargeable in bankruptcy?

Insurance

LEARNING OBJECTIVES

When you finish this chapter, you should be able to:

1. Discuss the concept of insurable interest.
2. State the impact of false statements in an application for insurance.
3. Explain how courts interpret insurance provisions.
4. Identify defenses an insurance company may have against payment on a policy.

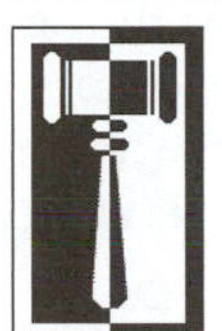

FACING A LEGAL PROBLEM

Brigit and Elias are married and have two children. When they divorce, Brigit gives her interest in their house to Elias and moves out. Elias dies, leaving the house to the children. Because the children are minors, Brigit moves back into the house with them. She keeps the house in good repair and takes out an insurance policy on the property. When the house is destroyed in a fire, the insurance company refuses to pay, arguing that Brigit could not legally take out insurance on the house because she did not own it—her children did. *Is Brigit entitled to payment under the policy?*

People often take precautions to protect against the hazards of life. For example, an individual may wear a seat belt to protect against automobile injuries or install smoke detectors to guard against injury from fire. Of course, no one can predict whether an accident or a fire will ever occur, but individuals and businesses must establish plans to protect their personal and financial interests should some event threaten to undermine their security. By insuring their property, they protect themselves against damage and loss. Most individuals insure both real and personal property (as well as their lives). Businesses almost always insure their real and personal property, too. Insurance is the subject we discuss in this chapter.

Insurance Concepts and Terminology

Insurance has its own concepts and terminology, a knowledge of which is essential to understanding insurance law.

INSURANCE
A contract in which, for a stipulated consideration, one party agrees to compensate the other for loss on a specific subject by a specified peril.

Risk Management

Insurance is a contract by which the insurance company promises to pay a sum of money or give something of value to another in the event that the insured is injured

RISK MANAGEMENT
Planning that is undertaken to protect one's interest should some event threaten to undermine its security. In the context of insurance, transferring certain risks from the insured to the insurance company.

RISK
A specified contingency or peril.

or sustains damage as a result of particular, stated contingencies. Basically, insurance is an arrangement for *transferring and allocating risk.* This concept is known as **risk management. Risk** can be described as a prediction concerning potential loss based on known and unknown factors. The most common method of risk management is the transfer of certain risks from the individual to the insurance company.

RISK POOLING

All types of insurance companies use the principle of risk pooling. They spread the risk among a large number of people—the pool—to make the premiums small compared with the coverage offered. Life insurance companies, for example, know that only a small proportion of the individuals in any particular age group will die in any one year. If a large percentage of this age group pays premiums to the company in exchange for a benefit payment in case of death, there will be a sufficient amount of money to pay the beneficiaries of the policyholders who die.

Through the extensive correlation of data over a period of time, insurers can estimate fairly accurately the total amount they will have to pay if they insure a particular group. With this estimate, insurers can determine the rates they will have to charge each member of the group so they can make the necessary payments and still show a profit.

CLASSIFICATIONS OF INSURANCE

Insurance is classified according to the nature of the risk involved. For example, fire insurance, casualty insurance, life insurance, and title insurance apply to different types of risk. Furthermore, policies of these types differ in relation to the persons and interests that they protect. This is reasonable because the types of losses that are expected and the types that are foreseeable or unforeseeable vary with the nature of the activity. See Exhibit 34–1 for a list of various insurance classifications.

POLICY
In insurance law, the contract of indemnity against a contingent loss between the insurer and the insured.

PREMIUM
In insurance law, the price for insurance protection for a specified period of time.

UNDERWRITER
In insurance law, the one assuming a risk in return for the payment of a premium; the insurer.

INSURABLE INTEREST
An interest either in a person's life or well-being or in property that is sufficiently substantial that insuring against injury to the person or damage to the property does not amount to a mere wagering (betting) contract.

INSURANCE TERMINOLOGY

An insurance contract is called a **policy.** The consideration paid to the insurer is called a **premium.** The insurance company is sometimes called an **underwriter.**

The parties to an insurance policy are the *insurer* (the insurance company) and the *insured* (the person covered by the policy's provisions or the holder of the policy). Insurance contracts are usually obtained through an *agent,* who ordinarily works for the insurance company, or through a *broker,* who is ordinarily an *independent contractor.*

When a broker deals with an applicant for insurance, the broker is, in effect, the applicant's agent. By contrast, an insurance agent is an agent of the insurance company, not of the applicant. As a general rule, the insurance company is bound by the acts of its agents when they act within the agency relationship (see Chapter 25). A broker, however, has no relationship with the insurance company and is an agent of the insurance applicant.

LEARNING OBJECTIVE NO. 1
Discussing the Concept of Insurable Interest

INSURABLE INTEREST

A person can insure anything in which he or she has an **insurable interest.** Without this insurable interest, there is no enforceable contract, and a transaction to insure would have to be treated as a wager.

In the case of real and personal property, an insurable interest exists when the insured derives a pecuniary (consisting of or relating to money) benefit from the preservation and continued existence of the property. Put another way, one has an insurable interest in property when one would sustain a pecuniary loss from its destruction.

EXHIBIT 34–1
Insurance Classifications

TYPE OF INSURANCE	COVERAGE
Accident	Covers expenses, losses, and suffering incurred by the insured because of accidents causing physical injury and any consequent disability; sometimes includes a specified payment to heirs of the insured if death results from an accident.
All-risk	Covers all losses that the insured may incur except those resulting from fraud on the part of the insured.
Automobile	May cover damage to automobiles resulting from specified hazards or occurrences (such as fire, vandalism, theft, or collision); normally provides protection against liability for personal injuries and property damage resulting from the operation of the vehicle.
Casualty	Protects against losses that may be incurred by the insured as a result of being held liable for personal injuries or property damage sustained by others.
Credit	Pays to a creditor the balance of a debt upon the disability, death, insolvency, or bankruptcy of the debtor; often offered by lending institutions.
Employer's liability	Insures employers against liability for injuries or losses sustained by employees during the course of their employment; covers claims not covered under workers' compensation insurance.
Fidelity or guaranty	Provides indemnity against losses in trade or losses caused by the dishonesty of employees, the insolvency of debtors, or breaches of contract.
Fire	Covers losses caused to the insured as a result of fire.
Floater	Covers movable property, as long as the property is within the territorial boundaries specified in the contract.
Group	Provides individual life, medical, or disability insurance coverage; obtainable by persons who are members of certain groups; when the group is employees, the policy premium is paid either entirely by the employer or partially by the employer and partially by the employees.
Health	Covers expenses incurred by the insured resulting from physical injury or illness and other expenses relating to health and life maintenance.
Homeowners'	Protects homeowners against some or all risks of loss to their residences and the residences' contents or liability related to such property.
Key-person	Protects a business in the event of the death or disability of a key employee.
Liability	Protects against liability imposed on the insured resulting from injuries to the person or property of another.
Life	Covers the death of the policyholder. Upon the death of the insured, an amount specified in the policy is paid by the insurer to the insured's beneficiary.
Major medical	Protects the insured against major hospital, medical, or surgical expenses.
Malpractice	Protects professionals (doctors, lawyers, and others) against malpractice claims brought against them by their patients or clients; a form of liability insurance.
Marine	Covers movable property (ships, freight, or cargo) against certain perils or navigation risks during a specific voyage or time period.
Mortgage	Covers a mortgage loan; the insurer pays the balance of the mortgage to the creditor upon the death or disability of the debtor.
No-fault auto	Covers personal injury and (sometimes) property damage resulting from automobile accidents. The insured submits his or her claims to his or her own insurance company, regardless of who was at fault. A person may sue the party at fault or that party's insurer only in cases involving serious medical injury and consequent high medical costs. Governed by state "no fault" statutes.
Title	Protects against any defects in title to real property and any losses incurred as a result of existing claims against or liens on the property at the time of purchase.

In the legal problem set out at the beginning of this chapter, Brigit and Elias are married and have two children. When they divorce, Brigit gives her interest in their house to Elias and moves out. Elias dies, leaving the house to the children. Because the children are minors, Brigit moves back into the house with them. She keeps the house in good repair and takes out an insurance policy on the property. When the house is destroyed in a fire, the insurance company refuses to pay, arguing that Brigit could not legally take out insurance on the house because she did not own it—her children did. *Is Brigit entitled to payment under the policy?* Yes. Brigit had an insurable interest in the house. The money she spent to keep the house in repair, the loss she suffered by having to obtain other housing, and the loss she suffered as guardian of the children indicate that Brigit had an insurable interest in the house, even if she did not own it.

If anyone in your partnership or close corporation can be considered a key person, then you should probably buy key-person life insurance on that individual.

In the case of life insurance, a person must have a reasonable expectation of benefit from the continued life of another in order to have an insurable interest in that person's life. The benefit may be pecuniary (such as so-called *key-person insurance,* insuring the lives of important corporate officers, usually in small companies), or it may be founded upon the relationship between the parties (by blood or affinity). Also, the insurable interest in life insurance must exist at the time the policy is obtained. This is exactly the opposite of property insurance, for which the insurable interest must exist at the time the loss occurs and not necessarily when the policy is purchased. The existence of an insurable interest is a primary concern when determining liability under an insurance policy.

The Insurance Contract

An insurance contract is governed by the general principles of contract law, although the insurance industry is heavily regulated by each state.

The Application

LEARNING OBJECTIVE NO. 2
Stating the Impact of False Statements in an Application for Insurance

The filled-in application form for insurance is usually attached to the policy and made a part of the insurance contract. Thus, an insurance applicant is bound by any false statements that appear in the application (subject to certain exceptions). Because the insurance company evaluates the risk factors based on the information included in the insurance application, misstatements or misrepresentations can void a policy, especially if the insurance company can show that it would not have extended insurance if it had known the facts.

The Effective Date

The effective date of an insurance contract is important. In some instances, the insurance applicant is not protected until a formal written policy is issued. In other situations, the applicant is protected between the time an application is received and the time the insurance company either accepts or rejects it. Four facts should be kept in mind:

BINDER
A written, temporary insurance policy.

1. A broker is merely the agent of an applicant. Therefore, until the broker obtains a policy, the applicant normally is not insured.
2. A person who seeks insurance from an insurance company's agent will usually be protected from the moment the application is made, provided—in the case of life insurance—that some form of premium has been paid. Between the time the application is received and either rejected or accepted, the applicant is covered (possibly subject to a medical examination). Usually, the agent will write a memorandum, or **binder,** indicating that a policy is pending and stating its essential terms.
3. If the parties agree that the policy will be issued and delivered at a later time, the contract is not effective until the policy is issued and delivered or sent to

the applicant, depending on the agreement. Thus, any loss sustained between the time of application and the delivery of the policy is not covered.

4. Parties may agree that a life insurance policy will be binding at the time the insured pays the first premium. Alternatively, the policy may be expressly contingent upon the applicant's passing a physical examination.

IN THE COURTROOM

McNeal pays a premium to CPB Insurance Company for a life insurance policy that is expressly contingent on McNeal's passing a physical examination. If McNeal passes the examination, the policy coverage will date from the payment of the premium. McNeal dies before having the physical examination. *Can McNeal's beneficiary collect on the policy?* Yes. To collect, however, the beneficiary must show that McNeal would have passed the examination had he not died.

Coverage on an insurance policy can begin when a binder is written, when the policy is issued, or, depending on the terms of the contract, after a certain period of time has elapsed.

Provisions and Clauses

LEARNING OBJECTIVE NO. 3
Explaining How Courts Interpret Insurance Provisions

Some of the important provisions and clauses contained in insurance contracts are listed and defined in Exhibit 34–2 on the next page. The courts are increasingly cognizant of the fact that most people do not have the special training necessary to understand the intricate terminology used in insurance policies. Courts interpret the words used in an insurance contract according to their ordinary meaning and in light of the nature of the coverage involved. When there is an ambiguity in the policy, the provision is interpreted against the insurance company. When it is unclear whether an insurance contract actually exists because the written policy has not been delivered, the uncertainty will be determined against the insurance company. The court will presume that the policy is in effect unless the company can show otherwise.

Cancellation

When an insurance company can cancel its insurance contract, the policy or a state statute usually requires that the insurer give advance written notice of the cancellation to the insured.

IN THE COURTROOM

As part of an employee-benefits package, the Bobcat Company pays for a group life insurance plan. To cut back on the amount of its financial risk, however, the insurance company cancels the policy. A state statute requires written notice of the cancellation, but an insurance company employee merely telephones Bobcat to tell the company of the cancellation. No written notice is sent to Bobcat or Bobcat's employees. When Meade, a Bobcat employee, dies, the insurance company refuses to pay on the policy. *Can the company be required to pay?* Yes. The state statute requires written notice. A telephone call is not sufficient.

Cancellation of an insurance policy can occur for various reasons, depending on the type of insurance. For example, automobile insurance can be canceled for

EXHIBIT 34–2
Insurance Contract Provisions and Clauses

PROVISION	DEFINITION
Incontestability clause	An incontestability clause provides that after a policy has been in force for a specified length of time—usually two or three years—the insurer cannot contest statements made in the application.
Coinsurance clause	A coinsurance clause provides that if the owner insures his or her property up to a specified percentage—usually 80 percent—of its value, she or he will recover any loss up to the face amount of the policy. If the insurance is for less than the fixed percentage, the owner is responsible for a proportionate share of the loss.
Appraisal clause and arbitration clause	Insurance policies frequently provide that if the parties cannot agree on the amount of a loss covered under the policy or the value of the property lost, an appraisal, or estimate, by an impartial and qualified third party can be demanded. Similarly, many insurance policies include clauses that call for arbitration of disputes that may arise between the insurer and the insured concerning the settlement of claims.
Antilapse clause	An antilapse clause provides that the policy will not automatically lapse if no payment is made on the date due. Ordinarily, under such a provision, the insured has a *grace period* of thirty or thirty-one days within which to pay an overdue premium before the policy is canceled.
Cancellation	Cancellation of an insurance policy can occur for various reasons, depending on the type of insurance. When an insurance company can cancel its insurance contract, the policy or a state statute usually requires that the insurer give advance written notice of the cancellation. An insurer cannot cancel—or refuse to renew—a policy because of the national origin or race of an applicant or because the insured has appeared as a witness in a case against the company.

nonpayment of premiums or suspension of the insured's driver's license. Property insurance can be canceled for nonpayment of premiums or for other reasons, including the insured's fraud or misrepresentation, conviction for a crime that increases the hazard covered by the insurance, or gross negligence that increases the hazard covered by the insurance. Life and health policies can be canceled due to false statements made by the insured in the application. An insurer cannot cancel—or refuse to renew—a policy for discriminatory or other reasons that violate public policy or because the insured has appeared as a witness in a case against the company.

DEFENSES AGAINST PAYMENT

LEARNING OBJECTIVE NO. 4
Identifying Defenses an Insurance Company May Have against Payment on a Policy

An insurance company can raise any of the defenses that would be valid in any ordinary action on a contract, as well as some defenses that do not apply in ordinary contract actions. If the insurance company can show that the policy was procured by fraud, misrepresentation, or violation of warranties, it may have a valid defense for not paying on a claim. Improper actions, such as those that are against public policy or that are otherwise illegal, can also give the insurance company a defense against the payment of a claim or allow it to rescind the contract.

IN THE COURTROOM

Stuart applies for life insurance. On the application, Stuart states that he never smokes cigarettes. In fact, Stuart smokes half a pack a day and has smoked the same quantity for at least twelve years. The insurance company grants the policy. A year later, Stuart dies for reasons unrelated to smoking. During its investigation, the insurance company discovers that Stuart lied on the application and refuses to pay on the policy. *Is the beneficiary enti-*

tled to payment? No. The policy is void. Because smoking is linked so closely to premature death, it is material to the risk that a life insurance company assumes. Because Stuart lied on the application, the company could not fully assess the risk. The beneficiary is entitled only to a refund of the premiums that Stuart paid.

An insurance company can be prevented from asserting some defenses that are normally available. For example, if a company tells an insured that information requested on a form is optional and the insured provides it anyway, the company cannot use the information to avoid its contractual obligation under the insurance contract. Similarly, incorrect statements as to the age of the insured normally do not provide the company with a way to escape payment on the death of the insured.

TERMS AND CONCEPTS FOR REVIEW

binder 440
insurable interest 438
insurance 437
policy 438
premium 438
risk 438
risk management 438
underwriter 438

CHAPTER SUMMARY • INSURANCE

Risk Management	Insurance is an arrangement for transferring and allocating certain risks from individuals to insurance companies. Insurance is based on the principle of pooling risks—spreading the risk among a large number of people to make the premiums small compared with the coverage offered.
Terminology	**1.** *Policy*—The insurance contract. **2.** *Premium*—The consideration paid to the insurer for a policy. **3.** *Underwriter*—The insurance company. **4.** *Parties*—Include the insurer (the insurance company), the insured (the person covered by insurance), and an agent (representative of the insurance company) or a broker (ordinarily an independent contractor). **5.** *Insurable interest*—Exists whenever an individual or entity benefits from the preservation of the health or life of the insured or the property to be insured.
The Insurance Contract	**1.** *Laws governing*—The general principles of contract law apply, subject to state statutes and regulations. **2.** *Timing of coverage*—Coverage on an insurance policy can begin when the binder (a written memorandum indicating that a formal policy is pending and stating its essential terms) is written, when the policy is issued, or, depending on the terms of the contract, when a certain period of time has elapsed. **3.** *Provisions and clauses*—Words will be given their ordinary meaning, and any ambiguity in the policy will be interpreted against the insurance company. When the written policy has not been delivered and it is unclear whether an insurance contract actually exists, the uncertainty will be determined against the insurance company. The court will presume that the policy is in effect unless the company can show otherwise. **4.** *Defenses against payment to the insured*—Misrepresentation, fraud, or violation of warranties by the applicant.

HYPOTHETICAL QUESTIONS

34–1. Timing of Insurance Coverage. On October 10, Joleen Vora applied for a $50,000 life insurance policy with Magnum Life Insurance Co.; she named her husband, Jay, as the beneficiary. Joleen paid the insurance company the first year's policy premium upon making the application. Two days later, before she had a chance to take the physical examination required by the insurance company and before the policy was issued, Joleen was killed in an automobile accident. Jay submitted a claim to the insurance company for the $50,000. Can Jay collect? Explain.

34–2. Types of Insurance Policies. Joel and Marsha Cummings operate a consulting business out of their home. Most of their work consists of creating and maintaining "home pages" on the Internet for various clients. Marsha and Joel are concerned about the potential liability they will incur if a customer is injured on their business premises. They also want to protect against the loss of income that they would suffer if one of them were disabled or died. What types of insurance policies would best meet each of these needs? Why?

REAL WORLD CASE PROBLEM

34–3. Insurer's Defenses. Kirk Johnson applied for life insurance with New York Life Insurance Co. on October 7, 1986. In answer to a question about smoking habits, Johnson stated that he had not smoked in the past twelve months and that he had never smoked cigarettes. In fact, Johnson had smoked for thirteen years, and during the month prior to the insurance application, he was smoking approximately ten cigarettes per day. Johnson died on July 17, 1988, for reasons unrelated to smoking. Johnson's father, Lawrence Johnson, who was the beneficiary of the policy, filed a claim for the insurance proceeds. While investigating the claim, New York Life discovered Kirk Johnson's misrepresentation and denied the claim. The company canceled the policy and sent Lawrence Johnson a check for the premiums that had been paid. Lawrence Johnson refused to accept the check and New York Life brought an action for a declaratory judgment (a court determination of a plaintiff's rights). What should the court decide? Discuss fully. [*New York Life Insurance Co. v. Johnson,* 923 F.2d 279 (3d Cir. 1991)]

For updated links to resources available on the Web, as well as a variety of other materials, visit this text's Web site at **http://blte.westbuslaw.com**.

For a summary of the law governing insurance contracts in the United States, including rules of interpretation, go to

http://www.consumerlawpage.com/article/insureds.shtml

The law firm of Anderson Kill & Olick usually includes a number of articles relating to insurance on its Web site. Go to the following URL and click on "What's New":

http://www.andersonkill.com/index.asp

ONLINE LEGAL RESEARCH

Go to **http://blte.westbuslaw.com**, the Web site that accompanies this text. Select "Internet Applications," and then click on "Chapter 34." There you will find the following Internet research exercises that you can perform to learn more about new types of insurance coverage and some of the consequences of settlements in insurance cases:

Activity 34–1: Technoinsurance

Activity 34–2: Disappearing Decisions

Chapter 34 ■ WORK SET

TRUE-FALSE QUESTIONS

_____ **1.** Risk management involves the transfer of certain risks from an individual or a business to an insurance company.

_____ **2.** Insurance is classified by the nature of the person or interest protected.

_____ **3.** An insurance broker is an agent of an insurance company.

_____ **4.** An insurance applicant is usually protected from the time an application is made, if a premium has been paid, possibly subject to certain conditions.

_____ **5.** A person can insure anything in which he or she has an insurable interest.

_____ **6.** An application for insurance is not part of the insurance contract.

_____ **7.** The insurable interest in life insurance must exist at the time the policy is obtained.

_____ **8.** An antilapse clause provides that an insurance policy lapses if the insured does not pay a premium exactly on time.

MULTIPLE-CHOICE QUESTIONS

_____ **1.** Satellite Communications, Inc., takes out an insurance policy on its plant. For which of the following reasons could the insurer cancel the policy?

a. Satellite's president appears as a witness in a case against the company.
b. Satellite begins using grossly careless manufacturing practices.
c. Two of Satellite's drivers have their driver's licenses suspended.
d. All of the above.

_____ **2.** Sue applies for an A&I Insurance Company fire insurance policy for her warehouse. To obtain a lower premium, she misrepresents the age of the property. The policy is granted. After the warehouse is destroyed by fire, A&I learns the truth. A&I can

a. refuse to pay on the ground of fraud in the application.
b. refuse to pay on the ground that the warehouse has been destroyed by fire.
c. not refuse to pay, because an application is not part of an insurance contract.
d. not refuse to pay, because the warehouse has been destroyed by fire.

_____ **3.** Technon Corporation manufactures computers. To insure its products to cover injuries to consumers if the products prove defective, Technon should buy

a. group insurance.
b. liability insurance.
c. major medical insurance.
d. life insurance.

_____ **4.** Jim is an executive with E-Tech Corporation. Because his death would cause a financial loss to E-Tech, the firm insures his life. Later, Jim resigns to work for MayCom, Inc., one of E-Tech's competitors. Six months later, Jim dies. Regarding payment for the loss, E-Tech can

a. collect, because its insurable interest existed when the policy was obtained.
b. not collect, because its insurable interest did not exist when a loss occurred.
c. not collect, because it suffered no financial loss from the death of Jim, who resigned to work for one of its competitors.
d. none of the above.

_____ **5.** Tom takes out a mortgage with First National Bank to buy a house. Tom obtains a fire insurance policy, partially payable to the bank. After Tom makes the last mortgage payment, the house is destroyed by fire. Regarding payment for the loss, the bank can

a. collect, because its insurable interest existed when the policy was obtained.
b. collect, because its mortgage required Tom to take out the policy.
c. not collect, because its insurable interest did not exist when a loss occurred.
d. not collect, because its mortgage required Tom to take out the policy.

_____ **6.** Ace Manufacturing, Inc., has property insurance with National Insurer, Inc. When Ace suffers a loss in a burglary, Ace and National cannot agree on the amount of recovery. Under an appraisal and arbitration clause

a. only Ace can demand an appraisal by a third party.
b. only National can demand an appraisal by a third party.
c. either party can demand an appraisal by a third party.
d. the government sets the value of the loss which both parties must accept.

_____ **7.** Lee buys BizNet, a company that provides Internet access, and takes out property insurance with InsCo to cover a loss of the equipment. Two years later, Lee sells BizNet. Six months after the sale, BizNet's equipment is stolen. Under InsCo's policy, Lee can recover

a. the total amount of the insurance.
b. the total amount of the loss.
c. InsCo's proportionate share of the loss to the total amount of insurance.
d. nothing.

_____ **8.** Insurance premiums are small relative to the coverage offered because

a. the risks are spread among a large number of people.
b. agents and brokers receive only a small percentage of the premiums.
c. insurance companies rarely have to pay any claims.
d. the government guarantees insurance payments up to a certain amount.

ISSUE SPOTTERS

1. Neal applies to Farm Insurance Company for a life insurance policy. On the application, Neal understates his age. Neal obtains the policy, but for a lower premium than he would have had to pay had he disclosed his actual age. The policy includes an incontestability clause. Six years later, Neal dies. Can the insurer refuse payment?

2. Al is divorced and owns a house. Al has no reasonable expectation of benefit from the life of Bea, his ex-spouse, but applies for insurance on her life anyway. Al obtains a fire insurance policy on the house, then sells the house. Ten years later, Bea dies and the house is destroyed by fire. Can Al obtain payment for these events?

UNIT EIGHT
PROPERTY

UNIT OUTLINE

35 Personal Property and Bailments

LEARNING OBJECTIVES

When you finish this chapter, you should be able to:

1. Explain the difference between real and personal property.
2. Identify different types of property ownership.
3. List the requirements for an effective gift.
4. Discuss who gets title to lost property.
5. List the elements of a bailment.

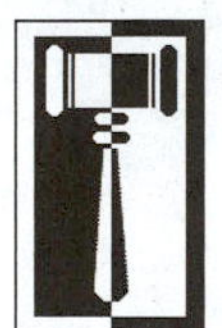

FACING A LEGAL PROBLEM

Claxton has a cable-ready television set and would like to watch cable broadcasts without paying for them. Claxton lives in an apartment building in which many of the tenants subscribe to Apollo Cable Communications, a local cable service. Claxton carefully splices into one of Apollo's cable lines that runs into the other tenants' apartments so that he can connect his set to the line without Apollo's knowledge. *Has Claxton committed a theft of personal property?*

Property consists of the legally protected rights and interests a person has in anything with an ascertainable value that is subject to ownership. The law defines the right to use property, to sell or dispose of it, and to prevent trespassing on it. In this chapter, we look at the nature of personal property, the methods of acquiring ownership of personal property and issues relating to mislaid, lost, and abandoned personal property. We also look at bailments.

The Nature of Personal Property

LEARNING OBJECTIVE NO. 1
Explaining the Difference between Real and Personal Property

Property is divided into two categories. *Real property* consists of the land and everything permanently attached to the land. When structures are permanently attached to the land, then everything attached permanently to the structures is also real property, or realty. All other property is **personal property,** or *personalty.*

PERSONAL PROPERTY Property that is movable; any property that is not real property.

Personal property can be tangible or intangible. *Tangible* personal property, such as a TV set or a car, has physical substance. *Intangible* personal property represents some set of rights and interests but has no real physical existence. Stocks and bonds, patents, and copyrights are examples of intangible personal property.

In a dynamic society, the concept of personal property must expand to take account of new types of ownership rights. For example, gas, water, and telephone services are now considered to be personal property for the purpose of criminal prosecution when they are stolen or used without authorization. Federal and state statutes protect against the copying of musical compositions. It is a crime to engage in the "bootlegging" (illegal copying for resale) of records and tapes. The theft of computer programs is usually considered a theft of personal property.

In the legal problem set out at the beginning of this chapter, Claxton has a cable-ready television set and wants to watch cable programs without paying for them. Claxton lives in an apartment building in which many of the tenants subscribe to Apollo Cable Communications, a local cable service. Claxton splices into one of Apollo's lines that runs into the other tenants' apartments so that he can connect his set without Apollo's knowledge. *Is this a theft of personal property?* Yes. Although Apollo and Claxton's neighbors may not know what Claxton has done, and Apollo subscribers can continue to watch cable programs, cable services are personal property for the purpose of criminal prosecution when they are used without permission.

Property Ownership

Property ownership can be viewed as a bundle of rights, including the right to possession of the property. The rights of possession discussed below apply to both personal property and real property. Rights of possession that apply only to real property are discussed in Chapter 36.

Another property right is the right to dispose of it—by sale, gift, rental, lease, or other means. Disposition of personal property and disposition of real property are examined later in this chapter and in Chapter 36, respectively.

Fee Simple

A person who holds the entire bundle of rights to property is said to be the owner in **fee simple.** The owner in fee simple is entitled to use, possess, or dispose of the property as he or she chooses during his or her lifetime. On death, the interests in the property descend to his or her heirs. We will return to this form of property ownership in Chapter 36, in the context of ownership rights in real property.

FEE SIMPLE
A form of property ownership entitling the property owner to use, possess, or dispose of the property as he or she chooses during his or her lifetime. Upon death, the interest in the property descends to the owner's heirs.

Concurrent Ownership

Persons who share ownership rights simultaneously in a particular parcel of property are said to be *concurrent* owners. There are two principal types of *concurrent ownership:* tenancy in common and joint tenancy. Other types of concurrent ownership include tenancy by the entirety and community property.

LEARNING OBJECTIVE NO. 2
Identifying Different Types of Ownership

Tenancy in Common. Co-ownership in which each of two or more persons owns an undivided fractional interest in the property is a **tenancy in common.** Those fractional interests do not need to be equal. Upon one tenant's death, that interest passes to his or her heirs.

TENANCY IN COMMON
Co-ownership of property in which each party owns an undivided interest that passes to his or her heirs at death.

IN THE COURTROOM

Rosalind and Chad each own one-half of a rare stamp collection as tenants in common. If Rosalind sells her interest to Fred, Fred and Chad would be co-owners of the stamp collection as tenants in common. *If Rosalind dies before selling her interest to Fred, however, do her heirs become tenants in common with Chad?* Yes. On Rosalind's death, one-half of the stamp collection would become the property of Rosalind's heirs. If she completes the sale to

Fred before she dies, however, and then Fred dies, his interest in the collection would pass to his heirs. They in turn would own the property with Chad as tenants in common.

Joint Tenancy. Co-ownership in which each of two or more persons owns an undivided interest in the property, and a deceased co-owner's interest passes to the surviving co-owner or co-owners, is **joint tenancy.** A joint tenancy can be terminated at any time by gift or by sale before a joint tenant's death. If termination occurs, the co-owners become tenants in common. If no termination occurs, then on the death of a joint tenant, his or her interest transfers to the remaining joint tenants, not to the heirs of the deceased joint tenant. This "right of survivorship" is the main feature distinguishing a joint tenancy from a tenancy in common.

JOINT TENANCY
The ownership interest of two or more co-owners of property whereby each owns an undivided portion of the property. Upon the death of one of the joint tenants, his or her interest automatically passes to the others and cannot be transferred by the will of the deceased.

In most states, it is presumed that a tenancy is a tenancy in common unless it is clear that the parties intended to establish a joint tenancy. In those states, specific language is necessary to create a joint tenancy.

IN THE COURTROOM

Through hard work, Dion establishes and runs Blackwater's, a successful restaurant. After many years, Dion decides to retire. Guerra and Piper wish to buy Dion's business. They wish to own and run it as joint tenants, so that if one or the other dies, Blackwater's will become the entire property of the other. On the deed transferring ownership of land that includes the restaurant, and in the other documents relating to transfer of the business, Dion indicates that everything is being conveyed to Guerra and Piper as "joint tenants with right of survivorship, and not as tenants in common." *Is this language sufficient to create a joint tenancy?* Yes. This language makes it clear that the parties intended to establish a joint tenancy.

Tenancy by the Entirety. Concurrent ownership of property can also take the form of a **tenancy by the entirety.** This form of co-ownership between a husband and wife is similar to a joint tenancy, except that a spouse cannot transfer separately his or her interest during his or her lifetime. This distinguishes a tenancy by the entirety from a joint tenancy.

TENANCY BY THE ENTIRETY
The joint ownership of property by husband and wife. Neither party can alienate or encumber the property without the consent of the other.

Typically, a tenancy by the entirety is created by a conveyance (transfer) of real property to a husband and wife. In states in which statutes give the wife the ability to separately convey her interest, this tenancy has been effectively eliminated. A tenancy by the entirety is terminated if the spouses divorce, either spouse dies, or the spouses agree to terminate it.

Community Property. Property can also be held as **community property**—in which each spouse technically owns an undivided one-half interest in property acquired during the marriage. This type of ownership occurs in only a few states. In those states, it applies to most property acquired by the husband or the wife during the course of their marriage. It does not apply to most property acquired before their marriage or to property acquired by gift or inheritance during their marriage. (Other methods by which property can be acquired are discussed in Chapter 36.) After divorce, community property is divided equally in some states and according to the discretion of a court in other states.

COMMUNITY PROPERTY
A form of concurrent ownership of property in which each spouse owns an undivided one-half interest in most property acquired by the husband or wife during the course of marriage.

Acquiring Ownership of Personal Property

The ownership of personal property can be acquired by possession, purchase, production, gift, will or inheritance, and accession. Each of these is discussed here.

Possession

A particularly interesting example of acquiring ownership by possession is the capture of wild animals. Wild animals belong to no one in their natural state, and the first person to take possession of a wild animal normally owns it. The killing of a wild animal amounts to assuming ownership of it. Merely being in hot pursuit does not give title, however. There are two exceptions to this basic rule. First, any wild animals captured by a trespasser are the property of the landowner, not the trespasser. Second, if wild animals are captured or killed in violation of wild game statutes, the capturer does not obtain title to the animals; rather, the state does. Other illustrations of acquiring ownership of personal property by possession are presented later in this chapter (see the discussion of mislaid, lost, and abandoned property).

Access to the Internet

For an index of legal sites that is simple to use, go to the Law Engine site at

http://www.thelawengine.com

Purchase

Purchase is one of the most common means of acquiring and transferring ownership of personal property. The purchase or sale of personal property (called *goods*) falls under the Uniform Commercial Code and was discussed in detail in Chapters 16 through 19.

Production

Production—the fruits of labor—is another means of acquiring ownership of personal property. For example, writers, inventors, and manufacturers all produce personal property and thereby acquire title to it. (In some situations—for example, when researchers are hired for that purpose—the producer does not own what is produced, however.)

Gifts

A **gift** is another fairly common means of both acquiring and transferring ownership of real and personal property. A gift is essentially a voluntary transfer of property ownership. It is not supported by legally sufficient consideration (the value—such as money—given in return for a promise) because the very essence of a gift is transferring without consideration. (Consideration is discussed more fully in Chapter 9.) A gift must be transferred or delivered in the present rather than in the future. In other words, a *promise* to make a gift tomorrow is not a gift.

GIFT
Any voluntary transfer of property made without consideration, past or present.

IN THE COURTROOM

Gayla, a successful account executive with Business Marketing, Inc., tells Paul, her personal assistant, that she is going to give him a new Mercedes-Benz for his next birthday. She explains to Paul that although he works hard, the car is not in appreciation for his efforts or for his contribution to the company. Instead, it is a personal gift from her because she generously wants to share the results of her own success. At this point, Gayla's expression of intent is a promise, not a gift. *When does the promise become a gift?* It becomes a gift when the Mercedes-Benz is delivered to Paul, the donee (recipient of the gift), and Paul accepts it.

The Elements of an Effective Gift. Three elements determine whether an effective gift exists—donative intent, delivery, and acceptance.

LEARNING OBJECTIVE NO. 3
Listing the Requirements for an Effective Gift

1. *Donative intent.* There must be evidence of the donor's intent to give the donee the gift. Such donative intent is determined from the language of the donor

and the surrounding circumstances. Thus, when a gift is challenged in court, the court may look at the relationship between the parties and the size of the gift in relation to the donor's other assets. A gift to a mortal enemy is viewed with suspicion. Likewise, when a gift represents a large portion of a person's assets, the courts scrutinize the transaction closely to determine the mental capacity of the donor and whether there is any element of fraud or duress (pressure brought to bear on a person through threats of serious bodily harm or death) present.

2. *Delivery.* An effective delivery requires giving up complete control of, and **dominion** (ownership rights) over, the subject matter of the gift. Delivery is obvious in most situations. In some circumstances, however, when the physical object cannot be delivered, a symbolic, or constructive, delivery will be sufficient. **Constructive delivery** is a general term for all those acts that the law holds to be equivalent to acts of real delivery. The delivery of intangible property—such as stocks, bonds, insurance policies, contracts, and so on—is always accomplished by symbolic, or constructive, delivery. This is because the documents represent rights and are not, by themselves, the true property.

   Delivery may be accomplished by means of a third party. If the third party is the agent of the donor, the delivery is effective when the agent delivers the gift to the donee. If the third party is the agent of the donee, then the gift is effectively delivered when the donor delivers the property to the donee's agent. Naturally, no delivery is necessary if the gift is already in the hands of the donee.

3. *Acceptance.* The final requirement of a valid gift is acceptance by the donee. This rarely presents any problems, as most donees readily accept their gifts. The courts generally assume acceptance unless shown otherwise.

Dominion
The rights to own, use, and possess property.

Constructive Delivery
An act equivalent to the physical delivery of property that cannot be physically delivered because of difficulty or impossibility.

Gifts *Inter Vivos* and Gifts *Causa Mortis*. Gifts made during one's lifetime are **gifts *inter vivos*.** **Gifts *causa mortis*** (so-called *deathbed gifts*) are made in contemplation of imminent death. A gift *causa mortis* does not become absolute until the donor dies from the illness and is automatically revoked if the donor recovers from the illness. Moreover, the donee must survive to take the gift.

A gift *causa mortis* is revocable at any time up to the death of the donor. To be effective, however, the gift must meet the three requirements discussed earlier—donative intent, delivery, and acceptance by the donee.

Gift *Inter Vivos*
A gift made during one's lifetime and not in contemplation of imminent death, in contrast to a gift *causa mortis*.

Gift *Causa Mortis*
A gift made in contemplation of death. If the donor does not die of that ailment, the gift is revoked.

Will or Inheritance

Ownership of personal property may be transferred by will or by inheritance under state statutes. These transfers will be discussed in detail in Chapter 38.

Accession

Accession means "adding on" to something. It occurs when someone adds value to a piece of personal property by either labor or materials. For instance, adding an extra diamond to a ring, restoring an antique cabinet, or putting new spark plugs in a car adds value to those items. Generally, there is no dispute about who owns the property after accession has occurred, especially when the accession is accomplished with the owner's consent.

Accession
Increasing the value of property by adding something (such as adding a diamond to a ring).

If accession occurred without the permission of the owner, the courts will tend to favor the owner over the improver—the one who improved the property—provided the accession was caused wrongfully and in bad faith. In addition, many courts would deny the improver (wrongdoer) any compensation for the value added. For example, a car thief who put new tires on the stolen car would obviously not be compensated for the value of the new tires.

If the accession is performed in good faith, however, even without the owner's consent, ownership of the improved item most often depends on whether the accession increased the value of the property or changed its identity. The greater the increase in value, the more likely it is that ownership will pass to the improver. If ownership so passes, the improver obviously must compensate the original owner for the value of the property prior to the accession. If the increase in value is not sufficient to pass ownership to the improver, most courts will require the owner to compensate the improver for the value added.

Confusion

Confusion is defined as the commingling (mixing together) of goods such that one person's personal property cannot be distinguished from another's. Confusion frequently occurs when the goods are *fungible,* meaning that each particle is identical to every other particle, such as with grain and oil. For example, if two farmers were to put their Number 2–grade winter wheat into the same storage bin, confusion would occur.

Confusion
The mixing together of goods belonging to two or more owners so that the independent goods cannot be identified.

If confusion of goods is caused by a person who wrongfully and willfully mixes them for the purpose of rendering them indistinguishable, the innocent party acquires title to the whole. If confusion occurs as a result of agreement, an honest mistake, or the act of some third party, the owners share ownership as *tenants in common* and will share any loss in proportion to their shares of ownership of the property.

Mislaid, Lost, and Abandoned Property

If you find another's property, it is important to learn whether the owner mislaid, lost, or simply abandoned the property. This is because the legal effect differs in each case. We define and discuss each of these three categories in the next sections.

Mislaid Property

Property that has been placed somewhere by the owner voluntarily and then inadvertently forgotten is **mislaid property.** Suppose you go to the theater and leave your gloves on the concession stand. The gloves are mislaid property, and the theater owner is entrusted with the duty of taking reasonable care of the gloves (that is, taking the same care of the gloves as would any reasonable person in similar circumstances). Because it is highly likely that the true owner will return for property that is mislaid, the finder does not obtain title to the goods. Instead, the finder is obligated to return the property to the true owner. (In this situation, the finder is an *involuntary bailee.* Bailments are discussed in more detail later in this chapter.)

Mislaid Property
Property with which the owner has voluntarily parted and then cannot find or recover.

Lost Property

Property that is involuntarily left and forgotten is **lost property.** A finder of the property can claim title to the property against the whole world, *except the true owner.* If the true owner demands that the lost property be returned, the finder must return it. If a third party attempts to take possession of lost property from a finder, the third party cannot assert a better title than the finder. Whenever a finder knows who the true owners of property are and fails to return the property to them, that finder is guilty of *conversion* (an unauthorized act that deprives an owner of his or her property permanently or for an indefinite time). Finally, many states require the finder to make a reasonably diligent search to locate the true owner of lost property.

LEARNING OBJECTIVE NO. 4
Discussing Who Gets Title to Lost Property

Lost Property
Property with which the owner has involuntarily parted and then cannot find or recover.

IN THE COURTROOM

Kormian works in a hotel. On her way home one evening, she finds a piece of gold jewelry in the courtyard of the hotel. Covered with dust and dirt, the piece appears to have been lost. The piece also looks like it has several precious stones in it. Kormian takes it to Marx Jewelry to have it appraised. While pretending to weigh the jewelry, a Marx employee removes several of the stones. When Kormian discovers that the stones are missing, she sues Marx. *Will she win?* Yes. Kormian will win, because she found lost property and holds valid title against everyone *except the true owner.* Because the property was lost, rather than mislaid, the owner of the hotel is not the caretaker of the jewelry. Instead, Kormian acquires title good against the whole world (except the true owner).

ABANDONED PROPERTY

ABANDONED PROPERTY
Property with which the owner has voluntarily parted, with no intention of recovering it.

Property that has been discarded by the true owner with no intention of reclaiming title to it is **abandoned property.** Someone who finds abandoned property acquires title to it, and such title is good against the whole world, *including the original owner.* The owner of lost property who eventually gives up any further attempt to find the lost property is frequently held to have abandoned the property. When a finder is trespassing on the property of another and finds abandoned property, the owner of the land, not the finder, gets title to the property.

TREASURE TROVE

TREASURE TROVE
Money or coin, gold, silver, or bullion found hidden in the earth or other private place, the owner of which is unknown; literally, treasure found.

Treasure trove is treasure (money, gold, silver, or bullion) that is found. Unless there is a statute that provides otherwise, a finder has title to treasure trove against all but the true owner. Generally, to constitute treasure trove, property need not have been buried. It could have been hidden in some other private place, such as behind loose bricks in an old chimney. Its owner, however, must be unknown, and its finder must not have been trespassing.

LOST-PROPERTY STATUTES

Many states have enacted lost-property statutes. The statutes differ significantly from state to state. Typically, however, they eliminate the distinction between lost property, mislaid property, abandoned property, and treasure trove. Also, many statutes require the finder to deposit found property with local authorities, with a penalty imposed for failure to do so. (In Illinois, for example, a finder who fails to comply with the requirements of that state's lost-property statute may be fined $10.) Lost-property statutes also typically require the police to attempt to find the true owner—by calling the owner or person in charge of the premises on which the property was found, for example. Sometimes, the finder must advertise, at the county court, the property and its discovery.

Generally, if the true owner cannot be located within a certain period of time—which varies depending on the value of the property and whether the property is perishable—the finder gets the property. If the finder does not appear after the period of time lapses, the property may be sold and the proceeds disposed of as specified by the statute. In California, for instance, the proceeds from such a sale go into a state abandoned-property fund (if the state police had custody of the lost property) or become the property of the city, county, town, or village (if police other than the state police had custody).

Every statute has exceptions, of course. In some situations, an employer may have rights to property found by an employee. Property found in a safe-deposit area in a bank may also be subject to different rules.

Bailments

Virtually every business is affected by the law of bailments at one time or another (and sometimes even on a daily basis). When individuals deal with bailments, whether they realize it or not, they are subject to the obligations and duties that arise from the bailment relationship. A **bailment** is formed by the delivery of personal property, without transfer of title, by one person (called a **bailor**) to another (called a **bailee**), usually under an agreement for a particular purpose (for example, for storage, repair, or transportation). Upon completion of the purpose, the bailee is obligated to return the bailed property to the bailor or to a third person, or to dispose of it as directed.

BAILMENT
An agreement in which the personal property of one person (a bailor) is entrusted to another (a bailee), who is obligated to return the bailed property to the bailor or dispose of it as directed.

BAILOR
One who entrusts goods to a bailee.

BAILEE
One to whom goods are entrusted by a bailor.

THE CREATION OF A BAILMENT

Most bailments are created by agreement, but not necessarily by contract, because many bailments do not include all of the elements of a contract (such as mutual assent or consideration). (The basic elements of a contract are listed in Chapter 7.) For example, if you loan your bicycle to a friend, a bailment is created, but not by contract because there is no consideration. Many commercial bailments, such as the delivery of your suit or dress to the cleaners for dry cleaning, are based on contract, however.

THE ELEMENTS OF A BAILMENT

LEARNING OBJECTIVE NO. 5
Listing the Elements of a Bailment

Not all transactions involving the delivery of property from one person to another create a bailment. For such a transfer to become a bailment, the following three conditions must be met: (1) the property involved must be personal property, (2) the property must be delivered to the bailee, and (3) there must be an agreement for the return or disposal of the property. These conditions are discussed below.

Personal Property. A bailment involves only personal property. A bailment of persons is not possible. Although a bailment of your luggage is created when it is transported by an airline, as a passenger you are not the subject of a bailment. Also, you cannot bail real property. Thus, leasing your house to a tenant is not a bailment.

Delivery of Possession. Possession of the property must be transferred to the bailee in such a way that (1) the bailee is given both exclusive possession of the property and control over it, and (2) the bailee *knowingly* accepts the personal property. If either of these conditions for effective *delivery of possession* is lacking, there is no bailment relationship.

IN THE COURTROOM

Brice takes Joyce, a friend, out to dinner at an expensive restaurant. On arrival, Brice turns his car over to the parking attendant. When Brice and Joyce enter the restaurant, Joyce checks her coat. In the pocket of the coat is a $20,000 diamond necklace. *Has a bailment of any of these items—Brice's car, Joyce's coat, or the diamond necklace—been created?* Yes. There is a bailment of the car and the coat, but not of the necklace. As a general rule, valet parking constitutes a bailment, but self-parking does not. The difference is found in the control of the car keys. If Brice parked the car himself, locked it, and kept the keys, this would be considered a lease of space from the owner of the parking space. The owner would be a *lessor,* and Brice would be a *lessee* of the space. With respect to the coat and the necklace, by accepting the coat, the bailee does not *knowingly* also accept the necklace. Thus, a bailment of the coat exists—the restaurant has exclusive possession of the coat, control over it, and knowingly accepted it—but a bailment of the necklace does not exist.

Two types of delivery—*physical* and *constructive*—will result in the bailee's exclusive possession of the property and control over it. As discussed in the context of gifts, constructive delivery is a substitute, or symbolic, delivery. What is delivered to the bailee is not the actual property bailed, but something so related to the property that the requirement of delivery is satisfied.

In certain unique situations, a bailment is found despite the apparent lack of the requisite elements of control and knowledge. In particular, rental of safe-deposit boxes is usually held to constitute a bailor-bailee relationship between the bank and its customer, despite the bank's lack of knowledge of the contents and its inability to have exclusive control of the property. Another example of such a situation is when the bailee acquires the property accidentally or by mistake—such as in finding someone else's lost or mislaid property. A bailment is created even though the bailor did not voluntarily deliver the property to the bailee. These are called *constructive* or *involuntary* bailments.

Common carriers, such as trucking companies and warehousing companies, are special bailees subject to different standards than ordinary bailees.

The Bailment Agreement. A bailment agreement can be *express* or *implied*. Although a written agreement is not required for bailments of less than one year (that is, the Statute of Frauds does not apply—see Chapter 13), it is a good idea to have one, especially when valuable property is involved.

The bailment agreement expressly or impliedly provides for the return of the bailed property to the bailor or to a third person, or it provides for disposal by the bailee. The agreement presupposes that the bailee will return the identical goods originally given by the bailor. In certain types of bailments, however, such as bailments of *fungible goods* (uniformly identical goods), only equivalent property must be returned.

TERMS AND CONCEPTS FOR REVIEW

CHAPTER SUMMARY • PERSONAL PROPERTY AND BAILMENTS

Nature of Personal Property	Personal property (personalty) is considered to include all property not classified as real property (realty). It can be tangible (such as a TV set or a car) or intangible (such as stocks or bonds).
Property Ownership	**1.** *Fee simple*—Exists when an individual has the right to possess, use, or dispose of the property as he or she chooses during his or her lifetime and to pass on the property to his or her heirs at death. **2.** *Concurrent ownership*— **a.** Tenancy in common—Co-ownership in which each of two or more persons owns an undivided fractional interest in the property. On one tenant's death, the property interest passes to his or her heirs.

CHAPTER SUMMARY • *Continued*

Property Ownership Continued	**b.** Joint tenancy—Exists when each of two or more persons owns an undivided interest in property. On the death of a joint tenant, the property interest transfers to the remaining joint tenant(s), not to the heirs of the deceased. **c.** Tenancy by the entirety—A form of co-ownership between a husband and wife that is similar to a joint tenancy, except that a spouse cannot transfer separately his or her interest during his or her lifetime. **d.** Community property—A form of co-ownership in which each spouse technically owns an undivided one-half interest in property acquired during the marriage. This type of ownership occurs in only a few states.
How Ownership of Personal Property Is Acquired	**1.** *Possession*—Ownership may be acquired by possession if no other person has ownership (for example, wild animals or abandoned property). **2.** *Purchase*—One of the most common means of acquiring and transferring ownership of personal property. **3.** *Production*—Any product or item produced by an individual (with minor exceptions) becomes the property of that individual. **4.** *Gift*—An effective gift exists when: **a.** There is evidence of *intent* to make a gift. **b.** The gift is delivered (physically or constructively) to the donee or the donee's agent. **c.** The gift is accepted by the donee or the donee's agent. **5.** *Will or inheritance*—On death, the property of the deceased passes to family members or others by will or inheritance laws. **6.** *Accession*—When someone adds value to a piece of property by labor or materials, the added value generally becomes the property of the owner of the original property (includes accessions made in bad faith or wrongfully). Good faith accessions that substantially increase the property's value or change the identity of the property may cause ownership to pass to the improver. **7.** *Confusion*—In the case of fungible goods, if a person wrongfully and willfully commingles goods with those of another in order to render them indistinguishable, the innocent party acquires title to the whole. Otherwise, the owners become tenants in common of the intermingled goods.
Mislaid, Lost, and Abandoned Property and Treasure Trove	**1.** *Mislaid property*—Property that is placed somewhere *voluntarily* by the owner and then inadvertently forgotten. A finder of mislaid property will not acquire title to the goods. The owner of the place where the property was mislaid becomes a caretaker of the mislaid property. **2.** *Lost property*—Property that is *involuntarily* left and forgotten. A finder of lost property can claim title to the property against the whole world *except the true owner.* **3.** *Abandoned property*—Property that has been discarded by the true owner, who has no intention of claiming title to the property in the future. A finder of abandoned property can claim title to it against the whole world, *including the original owner.* **4.** *Treasure trove*—Money, gold, silver, or bullion that is found. Unless there is a statute that provides otherwise, a finder can claim title to treasure trove against all but the true owner.
Elements of a Bailment	**1.** *Personal property*—Bailments involve only personal property. **2.** *Delivery of possession*—The bailee (the one receiving the property) must be given exclusive possession and control over the property. In a voluntary bailment, the bailee must knowingly accept the personal property. **3.** *Bailment agreement*—Provides for the return of the property to the bailor or a third party or for the disposal of the property by the bailee.

HYPOTHETICAL QUESTIONS

35–1. Gifts. In 1968, Armando was about to be shipped to Vietnam for active duty with the U.S. Marines. Shortly before he left, he gave an expensive stereo set and other personal belongings to his girlfriend, Sara, saying, "I'll probably not return from this war, so I'm giving these to you." Armando returned eighteen months later and requested that Sara return the property. Sara said that because Armando had given her these items to keep, she was not required to return them. Was a gift made in this instance, and can Armando recover his property? Discuss fully.

35–2. Requirements of a Bailment. Calvin is an executive on a business trip to the West Coast. He has driven his car on this trip and checks into the Hotel Ritz. The hotel has a guarded underground parking lot. Calvin gives his car keys to the parking-lot attendant but fails to notify the attendant that his wife's $10,000 diamond necklace is in a box in the trunk. The next day, upon checking out, he discovers that his car has been stolen. Calvin wants to hold the hotel liable for both the car and the necklace. Discuss the probable success of his claim.

REAL WORLD CASE PROBLEM

35–3. Concurrent Ownership. A. B. Paul was the owner of real estate located in Putnam County, Florida. In 1982, while Paul was living with Lucille Foucart, he executed a deed conveying the property to himself and Foucart as joint tenants with right of survivorship. In 1985, Paul and Foucart stopped living together, and three months later, Foucart conveyed her interest in the property to her daughter, Sandra Foucart. What type of interest does Sandra possess in the property, and why? [*Foucart v. Paul,* 516 So.2d 1035 (Fla.App. 1987)]

For updated links to resources available on the Web, as well as a variety of other materials, visit this text's Web site at **http://blte.westbuslaw.com**.

To learn about whether a married person has ownership rights in a gift received by his or her spouse, go to Scott Law Firm's Web page at

http://www.scottlawfirm.com/property.htm

For a discussion of the origins of the term *bailment* and how bailment relationships have been defined, go to

http://www.lectlaw.com/def/b005.htm

ONLINE LEGAL RESEARCH

To go **http://blte.westbuslaw.com**, the Web site that accompanies this text. Select "Internet Applications," and then click on "Chapter 35." There you will find the following Internet research exercise that you can perform to learn more about bailment relationships:

Activity 35–1: Bailments

Chapter 35 ■ WORK SET

TRUE-FALSE QUESTIONS

_____ **1.** Generally, those who produce personal property have title to it.

_____ **2.** If goods are confused due to a wrongful act and the innocent party cannot prove what percentage is his or hers, all of the goods belong to the wrongdoer.

_____ **3.** To constitute a gift, a voluntary transfer of property must be supported by consideration.

_____ **4.** One who finds abandoned property acquires good title to the property against the whole world, except the true owner.

_____ **5.** Co-ownership in which of each of two or more persons owns an undivided fractional interest in the property is a tenancy in common.

_____ **6.** Gas, water, and other utility services are considered personal property.

_____ **7.** If an object cannot be physically delivered, it cannot be a gift.

_____ **8.** Any delivery of personal property from one person to another creates a bailment.

MULTIPLE-CHOICE QUESTIONS

_____ **1.** Eve designs an Internet home page to advertise her services as a designer of home pages. Tim hires her to design a home page for his business. Eve has title to

a. her home page only.
b. Tim's home page only.
c. her home page, Tim's home page, and any other home page she creates.
d. none of the above.

_____ **2.** Dan sells his multimedia system to Paul and Amy, who each take a one-half interest in it. Paul and Amy are not married. Nothing is said about the form of the buyers' ownership. They own the system as

a. tenants in common.
b. joint tenants.
c. tenants by the entirety.
d. community property.

_____ **3.** Nancy sells her boat to Chris and Nora. Chris and Nora are not married. The contract of sale says that the buyers each have a right of survivorship in the boat. Chris and Nora own the boat as

a. tenants in common.
b. joint tenants.
c. tenants by the entirety.
d. community property.

_____ **4.** Meg wants to give Lori a pair of diamond earrings that Meg has in her safe-deposit box at First National Bank. Meg gives Lori the key to the box and tells her to go to the bank and take the earrings from the box. Lori does so. Two days later, Meg dies. Who do the earrings belong to?

a. Lori.
b. Meg's heirs.
c. First National Bank.
d. The state government.

_____ **5.** John is employed in remodeling homes bought and sold by Best Sale Realty. In one of the homes, John finds an item of jewelry and takes it to Hall Gems, Inc., to be appraised. The appraiser removes some of the jewels. Who has the best title to the jewels that were removed?

a. John.
b. Hall Gems, Inc.
c. Best Sale Realty.
d. John's employer.

_____ **6.** Jane, Mark, and Guy are farmers who store their grain in three silos. Jane contributes half of the grain, Mark a third, and Guy a sixth. A tornado hits two of the silos and scatters the grain. If each farmer can prove how much he or she deposited in the silos, how much of what is left belongs to each?

a. Jane owns half, Mark a third, and Guy a sixth.
b. Because only a third is left, Mark owns it all.
c. Because Jane and Mark lost the most, they split what is left equally.
d. Jane, Mark, and Guy share what is left equally.

_____ **7.** Doug wants to give Kim a laptop computer in a locker at the airport. Doug gives Kim the key to the locker and tells her to take the laptop from the locker. Kim says that she doesn't want the computer and leaves the key on Doug's desk. The next day, Doug dies. Who gets the computer?

a. Kim.
b. Doug's heirs.
c. The airport.
d. The state government.

_____ **8.** Eve parks her car in an unattended lot behind Bob's store, which is closed. Eve locks the car and takes the keys. This is NOT a bailment because

a. no money is involved.
b. no personal property is involved.
c. there is no transfer of possession.
d. neither party signed a contract.

ISSUE SPOTTERS

1. Dave and Paul share ownership rights in a multimedia computer. When they acquired the computer, they agreed in writing that if one dies, the other inherits his interest. Are Dave and Paul tenants in common or joint tenants?

2. Mac wants to give Rita a pearl necklace that Mac has in his safe deposit box at First State Bank. The bank is closed for a holiday. Mac gives Rita a key to the box and tells her to go to the bank after the holiday and take the necklace. Rita does so. The next day, Mac dies. Mac's heirs want the necklace. Can Rita keep it?

Real Property

LEARNING OBJECTIVES

When you finish this chapter, you should be able to:

1. Define fixtures.
2. Identify the most common type of property ownership.
3. Explain the function of a deed.
4. List the elements for acquiring property by adverse possession.
5. Define the government's right of eminent domain.

FACING A LEGAL PROBLEM

Garza Construction Company erects a silo (a grain-storage facility) on Reeve's ranch. Garza also lends Reeve the money to pay for the silo under an agreement providing that the silo is not to become part of the land until it is fully paid for. Before the silo is paid for, Metropolitan State Bank, the mortgage holder on Reeve's land, forecloses on the property. Metropolitan contends that the silo is a fixture to the realty and that therefore the bank is entitled to the proceeds from its sale. Garza argues that the silo is personal property, and that therefore the proceeds should go to Garza. *Is the silo personal property?*

From earliest times, property has provided a means for survival. Primitive peoples lived off the fruits of the land, eating the vegetation and wildlife. Later, as the wildlife was domesticated and the vegetation cultivated, property provided pasturage and farmland. The protection of an individual's right to his or her property became, and remains, one of the most important rights of citizenship.

In this chapter, we look at real property and the various ways in which real property can be owned. We also examine how ownership rights in real property are transferred from one person to another.

The Nature of Real Property

Whereas personal property is generally movable, *real property*—also called *real estate* or *realty*—is generally immovable. **Real property** consists of land and the buildings, plants, and trees that it contains. It also includes subsurface and air rights. Personal property that has become permanently attached to real property (such as a mobile home that is connected to utilities and otherwise so anchored to the land as to become part of it) is also considered part of the land.

REAL PROPERTY
Immovable property consisting of land and buildings there on. Includes things growing on the land before they are severed (such as timber), as well as fixtures.

LAND

Land includes the soil on the surface of the earth and the natural or artificial structures that are attached to the land. It further includes all the waters contained on or under the surface and much, but not necessarily all, of the airspace above it. The exterior boundaries of land extend straight down to the center of the earth and straight up to the furthest reaches of the atmosphere (subject to certain qualifications).

AIR RIGHTS AND SUBSURFACE RIGHTS

The owner of real property has relatively exclusive rights to the airspace above the land, as well as to the soil and minerals underneath it. Significant limits on air or subsurface rights normally must be indicated on the deed or other document transferring title to the land.

Air Rights. Early cases involving air rights dealt with matters such as the right to run a telephone wire across a person's property when the wire did not touch any of the property and whether a bullet shot over a person's land constituted trespass.

Today, air rights cases involve the right of commercial and private planes to fly over property and the right of individuals and governments to seed clouds and produce artificial rain. Flights over private land do not normally violate the property owners' rights unless the flights are low and frequent, causing a direct interference with the enjoyment and the use of the land.

Subsurface Rights. Subsurface rights can be extremely valuable, as these rights include the ownership of minerals and, in most states, oil and natural gas. In many states, the owner of the surface of a parcel of land is not the owner of the subsurface, and hence the land ownership may be separated. When the ownership is separated into surface and subsurface rights, each owner can pass title to what he or she owns without the consent of the other. In some cases, a conflict will arise between a surface owner's use and the subsurface owner's need to extract minerals, oil, or natural gas. An owner of subsurface rights has a right to go onto the surface of the land to, for example, find and remove minerals. The owner of the surface, however, has a right to have the land supported in its natural condition. The subsurface owner cannot excavate in a way that causes the surface to collapse. In many states, a subsurface owner who excavates is also responsible for any damage that the excavation causes to buildings on the surface. State statutes typically provide exact guidelines as to the requirements for excavations of various depths.

PLANT LIFE AND VEGETATION

Plant life, both natural and cultivated, is also considered to be real property. In many instances, the natural vegetation, such as trees, adds greatly to the value of the realty. When a parcel of land is sold and the land has growing crops on it, the sale includes the crops, unless otherwise specified in the sales contract. When crops are sold by themselves, however, they are considered to be personal property. Consequently, the sale of crops is a sale of goods. It is governed by the Uniform Commercial Code rather than by real property law.

FIXTURES

LEARNING OBJECTIVE NO. 1
Defining Fixtures

Certain personal property can become so closely associated with the real property to which it is attached that the law views it as real property. Such property is known as a **fixture**—a thing *affixed* to realty, meaning it is attached to it by roots; embedded in it; or permanently attached by means of cement, plaster, bolts, nails, or screws. The fixture can be physically attached to real property, be attached to another fixture, or even be without any actual physical attachment to the land. As long as the owner *intends* the property to be a fixture, it will be a fixture.

FIXTURE
A thing that was once personal property but that has become attached to real property in such a way that it takes on the characteristics of real property and becomes part of that real property.

Certain items can only be attached to property permanently. Such items are fixtures. It is assumed that the owner intended for them to be fixtures, because they had to be permanently attached to the property. A tile floor, cabinets, and carpeting are examples. Also, when an item of property is custom made for installation on real property, such as storm windows, the property is usually classified as a fixture. Again, it is assumed that the owner intended the item of property to become part of the real property.

Fixtures are included in the sale of land if the sales contract does not provide otherwise. The sale of a house includes the land and the house and garage on it, as well as the cabinets, plumbing, and windows. Because these are permanently affixed to the property, they are considered to be a part of it. Unless otherwise agreed, however, the curtains and throw rugs are not included. Items such as drapes and window-unit air conditioners are difficult to classify. Thus, a contract for the sale of a house or commercial realty should indicate which items of this sort are included in the sale.

In the legal problem set out at the beginning of this chapter, Garza Construction Company erects a silo (a grain-storage facility) on Reeve's ranch. Garza also lends Reeve the money to pay for the silo under an agreement providing that the silo is not to become part of the land until it is fully paid for. Before the silo is paid for, Metropolitan State Bank, the mortgage holder on Reeve's land, forecloses on the property. Metropolitan contends that the silo is a fixture to the realty and that therefore the bank is entitled to the proceeds from its sale. Garza argues that the silo is personal property, and that therefore the proceeds should go to Garza. *Is the silo personal property?* Yes. Under the provisions of the parties' agreement, they had not intended the silo to become a part of the real property until full payment had been made. Because full payment had not been made, the silo had not become a fixture. Garza is entitled to the proceeds.

Ownership of Real Property

Ownership of property is an abstract concept that cannot exist independently of the legal system. No one can actually possess or *hold* a piece of land, the air above, the earth below, and all the water contained on it. The legal system therefore recognizes certain rights and duties that constitute ownership interests in real property.

The Internet Law Library of the House of Representatives offers extensive links to sources of law relating to real estate. Go to

http://www.priweb.com/internetlawlib/1.htm

Recall from Chapter 35 that property ownership is often viewed as a bundle of rights. One who possesses the entire bundle of rights is said to hold the property in *fee simple,* which is the most complete form of ownership. When some of the rights in the bundle are transferred to another person, the effect is to limit the ownership rights of both the one transferring the rights and the one receiving them.

We look first at ownership rights held in fee simple. Then we examine how these rights can be limited through certain types of real property transfers.

OWNERSHIP IN FEE SIMPLE

FEE SIMPLE ABSOLUTE
An estate or interest in land with no time, disposition, or descendibility limitations.

LEARNING OBJECTIVE NO. 2
Identifying the Most Common Type of Property Ownership

The most common type of property ownership today is the fee simple. Generally, the term *fee simple* is used to designate a **fee simple absolute,** in which the owner has the greatest possible aggregation of rights, privileges, and power. The fee simple is owned absolutely by a person and his or her heirs and is assigned forever without limitation or condition. The rights that accompany a fee simple include the right to use the land for whatever purpose the owner sees fit, subject to the limitation of such laws as those that prevent the owner from unreasonably interfering with another person's land.

A fee simple is potentially infinite in duration. It can be disposed of by deed or by will (by selling or giving it away). When there is no will, the fee simple passes to the owner's legal heirs. The owner of a fee simple absolute also has the rights of *exclusive possession* and *use* of the property.

FEE SIMPLE DEFEASIBLE
An estate that can be taken away (by the prior grantor) upon the occurrence or nonoccurrence of a specified event.

Ownership in fee simple may become limited whenever the property is transferred to another *conditionally.* When this occurs, the fee simple is known as a **fee simple defeasible** (*defeasible* means "capable of being terminated"). The original owner retains a *partial* ownership interest, because if the specified condition occurs (or, depending on how the condition is worded, does not occur), the land reverts, or returns, to the original owner. If the original owner is not living at the time, the land passes to his or her heirs.

IN THE COURTROOM

Avril conveys (transfers) a plot of land "to Yolanda Iverson and her heirs as long as the land is used for charitable purposes." For thirty years, Yolanda uses the land to generate income that is donated to various charities. After both Avril and Yolanda die, however, Yolanda's son Irwin begins to keep the income from the property for himself. *Now that the property is no longer being used for "charitable purposes," does ownership of it return to Avril's heirs?* Yes. The original conveyance (transfer) of the land creates a fee simple defeasible, because ownership of the property is conditioned on the land's being used for charitable purposes. Avril retains a partial ownership interest, because if the condition does not occur (if the land is not used for charitable purposes), then the land reverts to her. Because Avril is not living at the time, the land passes to her heirs.

LIFE ESTATES

LIFE ESTATE
An interest in land that exists only for the duration of the life of some person, usually the holder of the estate.

A **life estate** is an estate that lasts for the life of a specified individual. A conveyance "to Alvin Mueller for his life" creates a life estate. In a life estate, the life tenant (the holder of the life estate) has fewer rights of ownership than the holder of a fee simple defeasible, because the rights necessarily cease to exist on the life tenant's death. The life tenant has the right to use the land, provided no waste (injury to the land) is committed. In other words, the life tenant cannot injure the land in a manner that would adversely affect its value to its future owner. The life tenant can use the land to harvest crops. If mines and oil wells are already on the land, he or she can extract minerals and oil from it. The life tenant, however, cannot further exploit the land by creating new wells or mines.

The life tenant has the right to mortgage the life estate and create leases and other interests. A mortgage or other interest, however, cannot extend beyond the life of the tenant. Also, with few exceptions, the owner of a life estate has an exclusive right to possession during his or her life.

Along with these rights, the life tenant also has some duties—to keep the property in repair and to pay property taxes. In short, the owner of the life estate has the same rights as a fee simple owner except that the life tenant must maintain the value of the property during his or her tenancy, less the decrease in value resulting from normal use of the property allowed by the life tenancy.

FUTURE INTERESTS

When an owner in fee simple absolute conveys (transfers) the estate conditionally to another (such as with a fee simple defeasible) or for a limited period of time (such as with a life estate), the original owner still retains an interest in the land. The owner retains the right to repossess ownership of the land if the conditions of the fee simple defeasible are not met or when the life of the life-estate holder ends. The residuary (or "leftover") interest in the property that the owner retains is called a **future interest,** because if it arises, it will only arise in the future.

FUTURE INTEREST
An interest in real property that is not at present possessory but will or may be possessory in the future.

If the owner retains ownership of the future interest, then the future interest is a **reversionary interest,** because the property will *revert* to the original owner if the condition specified in a fee simple defeasible fails or when a life tenant dies. If, however, the owner of the future interest transfers ownership rights in that future interest to another, the future interest is a **remainder.** For example, a conveyance "to Case Morgan for life, then to Ruby Gomez" creates a life estate for Morgan and a remainder (future interest) for Gomez.

REVERSIONARY INTEREST
A future residuary interest retained in property by the grantor. For example, a landowner who conveys property to another for life retains a future interest in the property. When the person holding the life estate dies, the property will revert to the grantor (unless the grantor has transferred the future interest to another party).

An **executory interest** is a type of future interest very similar to a remainder. The difference is that an executory interest does not take effect immediately on the expiration of another interest, such as a life estate. For example, a conveyance "to Hal Delaney for life and one year after Delaney's death to Bob Butterworth" creates an executory interest in the property for Butterworth.

REMAINDER
A future interest in property, held by a person other than the grantor, that occurs at the natural termination of the preceding estate.

EXECUTORY INTEREST
A future interest, held by a person other than the grantor, that either cuts short or begins some time after the natural termination of the preceding estate.

NONPOSSESSORY INTERESTS

Some interests in land do not include any rights to possess the property. These interests, known as *nonpossessory interests,* include easements, profits, and licenses. Easements and profits are similar, and the same rules apply to both.

Easements and Profits. An **easement** is the right of a person to make limited use of another person's real property without taking anything from the property. An easement, for example, can be the right to walk across another's property. In contrast, a **profit** (which in this context does not mean a gain or a return on an investment) is the right to go onto land in possession of another and take away some part of the land itself or some product of the land.

EASEMENT
A nonpossessory right to use another's property.

PROFIT
In real property law, the right to enter upon and remove things from the property of another (for example, the right to enter onto a person's land and remove sand).

IN THE COURTROOM

Akhmed, the owner of Sandy View, gives Carmen the right to go there and remove all the sand and gravel that she needs for her cement business. *Is Carmen's interest an easement or a profit?* A profit. An easement merely allows a person to use land without taking anything from it (such as allowing the person to walk across it). A profit allows a person to take something (such as sand and gravel) from the land.

Licenses. Like an easement, a **license** involves the right of a person to come onto another person's land. Unlike an easement, however, a license is a personal privilege that arises from the consent of the owner of the land and that can be withdrawn or recalled by the owner.

LICENSE
A revocable privilege to enter onto another's real property.

IN THE COURTROOM

Carlotta buys a ticket to attend a movie at a Cineplex Sixteen theater. When she tries to enter the theater, Glenn, the manager, refuses to admit Carlotta because she is improperly dressed. Carlotta argues that she has a ticket, which guarantees her the same right as an owner to come onto the property. Glenn explains that a ticket is a right that he, as the representative of the owner, can take back. *Is Glenn correct?* Yes. A movie ticket is only a license, not a conveyance of an interest in property. A ticket holder has no right to force his or her way into a theater.

LEARNING OBJECTIVE NO. 3

Explaining the Function of a Deed

Transfer of Ownership

Ownership of real property can pass from one person to another in a number of ways. Commonly, ownership interests in land are transferred by sale, in which case the terms of the transfer are specified in a real estate sales contract. Whenever real property is sold or transferred as a gift, title to the property is conveyed by means of a **deed**—the instrument of conveyance of real property. We look here at transfers of real property by deed, as well as at some other ways in which ownership rights in real property can be transferred.

DEED
A document by which title to property is passed.

When you are entering into business, leasing rather than buying property has advantages, because it reduces your liability in the event that your business is unsuccessful.

DEEDS

A valid deed must contain the following elements:

1. The names of the buyer (grantee) and seller (grantor).
2. Words indicating an intent to convey the property (for example, "I hereby bargain, sell, grant, or give").
3. A legally sufficient description of the land.
4. The grantor's (and usually the spouse's) signature.

Additionally, to be valid, a deed must be delivered to the person to whom the property is being conveyed or to his or her agent.

Warranty Deeds. Different types of deeds provide different degrees of protection against defects of title. A defect of title would exist, for example, if an undisclosed third person had an ownership interest in the property. A **warranty deed** warrants the greatest number of things and thus provides the greatest protection for the buyer, or grantee. In most states, special language is required to make a general warranty deed. Generally, the deed must include a written promise to protect the buyer against all claims of ownership of the property. A sample warranty deed is shown in Exhibit 36–1.

WARRANTY DEED
A deed under which the grantor guarantees to the grantee that, among other things, the grantee will enjoy quiet possession.

Warranty deeds commonly include a number of *covenants,* or promises, that the grantor makes to the grantee. One of these promises, the **covenant of quiet enjoyment,** guarantees that the buyer will not be disturbed in his or her possession of the land by the seller or any third persons.

COVENANT OF QUIET ENJOYMENT
A promise by the grantor of real property that the grantee will not be disturbed in his or her possession of the property by the grantor or anyone having a lien against the property or superior title to it.

IN THE COURTROOM

Julio sells a two-acre lot and office building by warranty deed to the Lynn Company. Subsequently, Perkins shows that he, not Julio, actually owned the property and proceeds to evict Lynn. Lynn sues Julio on the ground that he breached the covenant of quiet enjoyment. *Will Lynn succeed in its suit?* Yes. The covenant of quiet enjoyment has been breached. Thus, the buyer can recover the purchase price of the lot and building, plus any other damages incurred as a result of the eviction.

QUITCLAIM DEED
A deed intended to pass any title, interest, or claim that the grantor may have in the premises but not professing that such title is valid and not containing any warranty.

Quitclaim Deeds. A **quitclaim deed** offers the least amount of protection against defects in the title. Basically, a quitclaim deed conveys to the grantee whatever interest the grantor had. Therefore, if the grantor had no interest, then the grantee receives no interest. Quitclaim deeds are often used when the seller, or grantor, is uncertain as to the extent of his or her rights in the property.

EXHIBIT 36–1
A Sample Warranty Deed

Date: May 31, 2002

Grantor: GAYLORD A. JENTZ AND WIFE, JOANN H. JENTZ

Grantor's Mailing Address (including county):
4106 North Loop Drive
Austin, Travis County, Texas

Grantee: DAVID F. FRIEND AND WIFE, JOAN E. FRIEND AS JOINT TENANTS WITH RIGHT OF SURVIVORSHIP

Grantee's Mailing Address (including county):
5929 Fuller Drive
Austin, Travis County, Texas

Consideration:
For and in consideration of the sum of Ten and No/100 Dollars ($10.00) and other valuable consideration to the undersigned paid by the grantees herein named, the receipt of which is hereby acknowledged, and for which no lien is retained, either express or implied.

Property (including any improvements):
Lot 23, Block "A", Northwest Hills, Green Acres Addition, Phase 4, Travis County, Texas, according to the map or plat of record in volume 22, pages 331-336 of the Plat Records of Travis County, Texas.

Reservations from and Exceptions to Conveyance and Warranty:

This conveyance with its warranty is expressly made subject to the following:

Easements and restrictions of record in Volume 7863, Page 53, Volume 8430, Page 35, Volume 8133, Page 152 of the Real Property Record of Travis County, Texas; Volume 22, Pages 335-339, of the Plat Records of Travis County, Texas; and to any other restrictions and easements affecting said property which are of record in Travis County, Texas.

Grantor, for the consideration and subject to the reservations from and exceptions to conveyance and warranty, grants, sells, and conveys to Grantee the property, together with all and singular the rights and appurtenances thereto in any wise belonging, to have and hold it to Grantee, Grantee's heirs, executors, administrators, successors, or assigns forever. Grantor binds Grantor and Grantor's heirs, executors, administrators, and successors to warrant and forever defend all and singular the property to Grantee and Grantee's heirs, executors, administrators, successors, and assigns against every person whomsoever lawfully claiming or to claim the same or any part thereof, except as to the reservations from and exceptions to conveyance and warranty.

When the context requires, singular nouns and pronouns include the plural.

BY: Gaylord A. Jentz
Gaylord A. Jentz

BY: JoAnn H. Jentz
JoAnn H. Jentz

(Acknowledgment)

STATE OF TEXAS
COUNTY OF TRAVIS

This instrument was acknowledged before me on the 31st day of May, 2002 by Gaylord A. and JoAnn H. Jentz

Rosemary Potter
Notary Public,State of Texas
Notary's name (printed): Rosemary Potter

Notary Seal

Notary's commission expires: 1/31/2005

Transfer by Will or Inheritance

Property that is transferred on an owner's death is passed either by will or by state inheritance laws. If the owner of land dies with a will, the property that the owner had prior to death passes in accordance with the terms of the will. If the owner dies without a will, state inheritance statutes prescribe how and to whom the property will pass. Transfers of property by will or inheritance laws are examined in detail in Chapter 38.

Adverse Possession

Adverse Possession
The acquisition of title to real property by occupying it openly, without the consent of the owner, for a period of time specified by state statutes. The occupation must be actual, open, notorious, exclusive, and in opposition to all others, including the owner.

LEARNING OBJECTIVE NO. 4
Listing the Elements for Acquiring Property by Adverse Possession

Adverse possession is a means of obtaining title to land without delivery of a deed. Essentially, when one person possesses the property of another for a certain statutory period of time (three to thirty years, with ten years being most common), that person, called the adverse possessor, acquires title to the land and cannot be removed from it by the original owner. The adverse possessor is vested with title to the property, just as if there had been a conveyance by deed.

For property to be held adversely, four elements must be satisfied:

1. Possession must be actual and exclusive. That is, the possessor must take sole physical occupancy of the property.
2. The possession must be open, visible, and notorious (that is, having such notoriety that the owner may be presumed to know of it, such as if it were so conspicuous that people in the neighborhood talked about it)—not secret or clandestine. The possessor must occupy the land for all the world to see.
3. Possession must be continuous and peaceable for the required period of time. This requirement means that the possessor must not be interrupted in the occupancy by the true owner or by the courts.
4. Possession must be hostile and adverse. In other words, the possessor must claim the property as against the whole world. He or she cannot be living on the property with the permission of the owner.

There are a number of public-policy reasons for the adverse possession doctrine. First, society has an interest in resolving boundary disputes and determining ownership rights when title to property is in question. Second, society also has an interest in ensuring that real property remains in the stream of commerce. Other policies behind the doctrine include punishing owners who sit on their rights too long and rewarding possessors for putting land to productive use.

Eminent Domain

Eminent Domain
The power of a government to take land for public use from private citizens for just compensation.

Even if ownership in real property is in fee simple absolute, there is still a superior ownership that limits the fee simple absolute. The government has an ultimate ownership right in all land. This right is known as **eminent domain,** and it is sometimes referred to as the condemnation power of the government to take land for public use. It gives a right to the government to acquire possession of real property in the manner directed by the Constitution and the laws of the state whenever the public interest requires it. Property may be taken only for public use.

Taking
Government interference with an owner's use and enjoyment of his or her property. Requires the payment of just compensation to the owner.

LEARNING OBJECTIVE NO. 5
Defining the Government's Right of Eminent Domain

Whenever the government takes land owned by a private party for public use, it is referred to as a **taking.** The government must compensate the private party. Under the so-called *takings clause* of the Fifth Amendment to the Constitution, private property may not be taken for public use without "just compensation."

The power of eminent domain is generally invoked through condemnation proceedings. For example, when a new public highway is to be built, the government must decide where to build it and how much land to condemn. After the government determines that a particular parcel of land is necessary for public use, it brings a judicial proceeding to obtain title to the land. Then, in another proceeding, the court determines the *fair value* of the land, which is usually approximately equal to its market value.

TERMS AND CONCEPTS FOR REVIEW

CHAPTER SUMMARY • REAL PROPERTY

Nature of Real Property	*Real property*—also called real estate or realty—is generally immovable. It includes land, subsurface and air rights, plant life and vegetation, and fixtures.
Ownership	**1.** *Fee simple absolute*—The most complete form of ownership. **2.** *Fee simple defeasible*—Ownership in fee simple that can end if a specified event or condition occurs. **3.** *Life estate*—An estate that lasts for the life of a specified individual. These rights are subject to the rights of the future-interest holder. **4.** *Future interest*—An interest that follows a life estate (or any estate limited by time) or an estate that exists only on the condition that a specific event does or does not occur. The grantor may retain the future interest (which is then called a reversionary interest) or transfer ownership rights in the future interest to another (in which case the interest is referred to as a remainder). **5.** *Nonpossessory interest*—An interest that involves the right to use real property but not to possess it. Easements, profits, and licenses are nonpossessory interests.
Transfer of Ownership Rights	**1.** *By deed*—Whenever real property is sold or transferred as a gift, title to the property is conveyed by means of a deed. A *warranty deed* warrants the most extensive protection against defects of title. A *quitclaim deed* conveys to the grantee whatever interest the grantor had. It warrants less than any other deed. **2.** *By will or inheritance*—If the owner dies after having made a valid will, the land passes as specified in the will. If the owner dies without having made a will, the heirs inherit according to state inheritance statutes. **3.** *By adverse possession*—When a person possesses the property of another for a statutory period of time (three to thirty years, with ten years being the most common), that person acquires title to the property, provided the possession is actual and exclusive, open and visible, continuous and peaceable, and hostile and adverse (without the permission of the owner). **4.** *By eminent domain*—The taking of private land by the government for public use and for just compensation, when the public interest requires the taking.

HYPOTHETICAL QUESTIONS

36–1. Property Ownership. Antonio is the owner of a lakeside house and lot. He deeds the house and lot "to my wife, Angela, for life, then to my son, Charles." Given these facts, answer the following questions:

(a) Does Antonio have any ownership interest in the lakeside house after making these transfers? Explain.

(b) What is Angela's interest called? Is there any limitation on her rights to use the property as she wishes?

(c) What is Charles's interest called? Why?

36–2. Deeds. Wiley and Gemma are neighbors. Wiley's lot is extremely large, and his present and future use of it will not involve the entire area. Gemma wants to build a single-car garage and driveway along the present lot boundary. Because of ordinances requiring buildings to be set back fifteen feet from an adjoining property line, and because of the placement of her existing structures, Gemma cannot build the garage. Gemma contracts to purchase ten feet of Wiley's property along their boundary line for $3,000. Wiley is willing to sell but will give Gemma only a quitclaim deed, whereas Gemma wants a warranty deed. Discuss the differences between these deeds as they would affect the rights of the parties if the title to this ten feet of land later proved to be defective.

REAL WORLD CASE PROBLEM

36–3. Easements. Merton Peterson owned a golf course, a supper club, and the parking lot between them. Both golfers and club patrons always parked in the lot. Peterson sold the club and the lot to the American Legion, which sold them to VBC, Inc. (owned by Richard Beck and others). When VBC demanded rent from Peterson for the use of the lot, Peterson filed a suit in a South Dakota state court to determine title. On what basis might the court hold that Peterson has an easement for the use of the lot? Does Peterson have an easement? [*Peterson v. Beck,* 537 N.W.2d 375 (S.Dak. 1995)]

For updated links to resources available on the Web, as well as a variety of other materials, visit this text's Web site at **http://blte.westbuslaw.com**.

Homes and Communities is a Web site offered by the U.S. Department of Housing and Urban Development. Information of interest to both consumers and businesses is available at this site, which can be accessed at

http://www.hud.gov

Information on the buying and financing of homes, as well as the full text of the Real Estate Settlement of Disputes Act, is online at

http://www.hud.gov/offices/hsg/index.cfm

For answers to frequently asked questions on Veterans Administration home loans, go to

http://www.va.gov/vas/loan/index.htm

ONLINE LEGAL RESEARCH

Go to **http://blte.westbuslaw.com**, the Web site that accompanies this text. Select "Internet Applications," and then click on "Chapter 36." There you will find the following Internet research exercises that you can use to learn more about laws governing real property:

Activity 36–1: Real Estate Law

Activity 36–2: Fair Housing

Chapter 36 ■ WORK SET

TRUE-FALSE QUESTIONS

_____ **1.** A fee simple absolute is potentially infinite in duration and can be disposed of by deed or by will.

_____ **2.** The owner of a life estate has the same rights as a fee simple owner.

_____ **3.** An easement allows a person to use land and take something from it, but a profit allows a person only to use land.

_____ **4.** Deeds offer different degrees of protection against defects of title.

_____ **5.** The government can take private property for *public* use without just compensation.

_____ **6.** The government can take private property for *private* uses only.

_____ **7.** A license is a revocable right of a person to come onto another person's land.

_____ **8.** When real property is sold, the title to the property is conveyed by a deed.

MULTIPLE-CHOICE QUESTIONS

_____ **1.** Lou owns two hundred acres next to Brook's lumber mill. Lou sells to Brook the privilege of removing timber from his land to refine into lumber. The privilege of removing the timber is

a. an easement.
b. a profit.
c. a license.
d. none of the above.

_____ **2.** Evan owns an apartment building in fee simple. Evan can

a. give the building away.
b. sell the building for a price or transfer it by a will.
c. both a and b.
d. none of the above.

_____ **3.** Gina conveys her warehouse to Sam under a warranty deed. Later, Rosa appears, holding a better title to the warehouse than Sam's. Rosa proceeds to evict Sam. Sam can recover from Gina

a. the purchase price of the property.
b. damages from being evicted.
c. both a and b.
d. none of the above.

_____ **4.** Dan owns a half acre of land that fronts on Blue Lake. Rod owns the property behind Dan's land. No road runs to Dan's land, but Rod's driveway runs between a road and Dan's property, so Dan uses Rod's driveway. The right-of-way that Dan has across Rod's property is

a. an easement.
b. a profit.
c. a license.
d. none of the above.

_____ **5.** Dave owns an office building. Dave sells the building to P&I Corporation. To be valid, the deed that conveys the property from Dave to P&I must include a description of the property and

a. only Dave's name and P&I's name.
b. only words evidencing Dave's intent to convey.
c. only Dave's signature (witnessed and acknowledged).
d. words evidencing Dave's intent to convey, Dave's name, P&I's name, and Dave's signature (witnessed and acknowledged).

_____ **6.** Lana owns a cabin on Long Lake. Bob takes possession of the cabin without Lana's permission and puts up a sign that reads "No Trespassing by Order of Bob, the Owner." The statutory period for adverse possession is ten years. Bob is in the cabin for eleven years. Lana sues to remove Bob. She will

a. win, because she sued Bob after the statutory period for adverse possession.
b. win, because Bob did not have permission to take possession of the cabin.
c. lose, because the no-trespassing sign misrepresented ownership of the cabin.
d. lose, because Bob acquired the cabin by adverse possession.

_____ **7.** Ron sells his house and yard to Jill. When Jill arrives to take possession, she learns that Ron has removed the kitchen cabinets from the house and the plastic lawn furniture from the yard. Jill is entitled to the return of

a. the lawn furniture only.
b. the cabinets only.
c. the lawn furniture and the cabinets.
d. none of the above.

_____ **8.** Betty owns real property on which is situated a farm. On the land are a barn and other farm buildings. Under the surface of the land are valuable minerals. Betty's deed does not indicate any significant limits on her rights to the realty. Betty owns

a. only the surface of the land.
b. only the surface of the land and the buildings on it.
c. the surface of the land, the buildings on it, and the minerals beneath the surface.
d. none of the above.

ISSUE SPOTTERS

1. Rob owns a commercial building in fee simple. Rob transfers temporary possession of the building to the Alliance Corporation. Can Alliance transfer possession for even less time to American Manufacturing, Inc.?

2. Charles sells his house to Diane under a warranty deed. Later, Carol appears, holding a better title to the house than Diane. Carol wants Diane off the property. What can Diane do?

Landlord and Tenant

37

LEARNING OBJECTIVES

When you finish this chapter, you should be able to:

1 Identify a tenancy for years.

2 Describe what a lease agreement should do.

3 Define the landlord's duties regarding the use and maintenance of the leased premises.

4 State the obligations of a tenant with respect to rent.

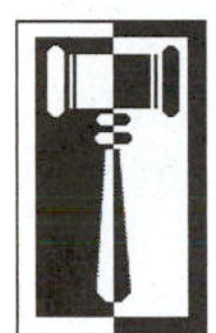

FACING A LEGAL PROBLEM

Darryl Katz signs a one-year lease to occupy an apartment. The lease does not contain a renewal clause. Eleven months and two weeks later, the landlord tells Katz that the apartment has been rented to someone else, and he must move out at the end of the month. Katz argues that the landlord did not give him enough notice. *Does Katz have to move out at the end of the month?*

Much real property is used by those who do not own it. A **lease** is a contract by which the owner (the landlord) grants someone else (the tenant) an exclusive right to use and possess the land, usually for a specified period of time, in return for rent or some other form of payment. In this chapter, we discuss leased property and landlord-tenant relationships.

LEASE
A transfer by the landlord of real property to the tenant for a period of time for consideration (usually the payment of rent). Upon termination of the lease, the property reverts to the lessor.

Types of Tenancies

A tenancy, or **leasehold estate,** is created when a real property owner or lessor (landlord) agrees to convey the right to possess and use the property to a lessee (tenant) for a certain period of time. In every leasehold estate, the tenant has a *qualified* right to exclusive possession (qualified by the right of the landlord to enter on the premises to ensure that no waste is being committed). The tenant can use the land—for example, by harvesting crops—but cannot injure the land by such activities as cutting down timber for sale or extracting oil. Here we look at the types of leasehold estates, or tenancies, that can be created when real property is leased.

LEASEHOLD ESTATE
An estate held by a tenant under a lease. The tenant has a qualified right to possess and use the land.

TENANCY FOR YEARS

TENANCY FOR YEARS
A lease for a specified period of time, after which the interest reverts to the grantor.

A **tenancy for years** is created by an express contract (a contract that is oral or written, as opposed to a contract that is implied) by which property is leased for

LEARNING OBJECTIVE NO. 1
Identifying a Tenancy for Years

a specified period of time, such as a month, a year, or a period of years. At the end of the period specified in the lease, the lease ends (without notice), and possession of the property returns to the lessor. If the tenant dies during the period of the lease, the lease interest passes to the tenant's heirs as personal property. Often, leases include renewal or extension provisions.

In the legal problem set out at the beginning of this chapter, Darryl Katz signs a one-year lease to occupy an apartment. The lease does not contain a renewal clause. Eleven months and two weeks later, the landlord tells Katz that the apartment has been rented to someone else, and he must move out at the end of the month. Katz argues that the landlord did not give him enough notice. *Does Katz have to move out at the end of the month?* Yes. The lease signed by Katz and the landlord creates a tenancy for years. At the end of the period specified in the lease, the lease ends (without notice), and possession of the property returns to the landlord. Although leases often include renewal provisions, this lease did not.

Periodic Tenancy

Periodic Tenancy
A lease interest in land for an indefinite period involving payment of rent at fixed intervals, such as week to week, month to month, or year to year.

A **periodic tenancy** is created by a lease that does not specify how long it is to last but does specify that rent is to be paid at certain intervals. This type of tenancy is automatically renewed for another rental period unless properly terminated. For example, a periodic tenancy is created by a lease that states, "Rent is due on the tenth day of every month." This provision creates a tenancy from month to month. A periodic tenancy can also be from week to week or from year to year. A periodic tenancy sometimes arises when a landlord allows a tenant under a tenancy for years to hold over and continue paying monthly or weekly rent.

To terminate a periodic tenancy, the landlord or tenant must give at least one period's notice to the other party. If the tenancy is month to month, for example, at least one month's notice must be given. If the tenancy is week to week, at least one week's notice must be given.

Tenancy at Will

Tenancy at Will
The right of a tenant to remain in possession of land with permission of the landlord until either the tenant or the landlord chooses to terminate the tenancy.

Suppose a landlord rents an apartment to a tenant "for as long as both agree." In such a case, the tenant receives a leasehold estate known as a **tenancy at will.** Either party can terminate the tenancy without notice (that is, "at will").

This type of leasehold estate usually arises when a tenant who has been under a tenancy for years retains possession after the termination date of that tenancy with the landlord's consent. A tenancy at will may be terminated by converting it into a periodic tenancy (by the periodic payment of rent) or into a tenancy for years (by creating a new express contract). The death of either party or the voluntary commission of waste (such as failing to take proper care of the premises) by the tenant will also terminate a tenancy at will.

Tenancy at Sufferance

Tenancy at Sufferance
Tenancy by one who, after rightfully being in possession of leased premises, continues (wrongfully) to occupy the property after the lease has been terminated. The tenant has no estate in the land and occupies it only because the person entitled to evict has not done so.

The mere possession of land without right is called a **tenancy at sufferance.** It is not a true tenancy. A tenancy at sufferance is not a leasehold estate, because it is created by a tenant's *wrongfully* retaining possession of property. Whenever a life estate (an estate for the life of a named individual), tenancy for years, periodic tenancy, or tenancy at will ends and the tenant continues to retain possession of the premises without the owner's permission, a tenancy at sufferance is created.

The Landlord-Tenant Relationship

In the past century—and particularly in the past two decades—landlord-tenant relationships have become much more complex than they were before, as has the law governing them. Generally, the law has come to apply contract doctrines, such as those providing for implied warranties (see Chapter 19), to the landlord-tenant relationship. Increasingly, landlord-tenant relationships have become subject to specific state and local statutes and ordinances as well. We look here at how a landlord-tenant relationship is created and at the respective rights and duties of landlords and tenants.

Creating the Landlord-Tenant Relationship

A landlord-tenant relationship is established by a lease agreement, which may be oral or written. An oral lease may be valid, but as is the case with most oral agreements, a party who seeks to enforce an oral lease may have difficulty proving its existence. In most states, leases must be in writing for some tenancies (such as those exceeding one year). To ensure the validity of a lease agreement, it should therefore be in writing and do the following:

LEARNING OBJECTIVE NO. 2
Describing What a Lease Agreement Should Do

1. Express an intent to establish the relationship.
2. Provide for the transfer of the property's possession to the tenant at the beginning of the term.
3. Provide for the landlord's *reversionary* (future) interest, which entitles the property owner to retake possession at the end of the term.
4. Describe the property—for example, give its street address.
5. Indicate the length of the term, the amount of the rent, and how and when the rent is to be paid.

When entering into a lease, to protect yourself in the event your business is unsuccessful, start with a short-term initial lease, perhaps with an option to renew the lease in the future.

State or local law often dictates permissible lease terms. For example, a statute or ordinance might prohibit leasing a structure that is in a certain physical condition or is not in compliance with local building codes. Similarly, a statute might prohibit the leasing of property for a particular purpose. For instance, a state law might prohibit gambling houses. Thus, if a landlord and tenant intend that the leased premises be used only to house an illegal betting operation, their lease is unenforceable.

The *unconscionability* concept is one of the most important of the contract doctrines applied to leases. Under this doctrine, a court may declare an entire contract or any of its clauses unenforceable and thus illegal when one party, as a result of his or her disproportionate bargaining power, is forced to accept terms that unfairly benefit the other party.

IN THE COURTROOM

Waterbury Properties, Inc., owns a number of residential buildings in which it leases space. Waterbury provides each tenant with a lease that contains a clause claiming to absolve Waterbury from responsibility for interruptions in such essential services as central heating or air conditioning. *If the systems break down, will the tenants be able to hold Waterbury liable?* Yes. The clause in Waterbury's lease will not shield it from liability if the systems break down when they are needed the most. Under the unconscionability doctrine, a court can declare the clause unenforceable, on the ground of the unequal bargaining power between Waterbury, which is a corporation that can refuse to lease to those who do not accept its terms, and its tenants, who are separate individuals with sometimes more limited power to bargain over the terms of their individual leases.

A property owner cannot legally discriminate against prospective tenants on the basis of race, color, religion, national origin, or sex. Often, rental properties are leased by agents of the landowner. Recall from Chapter 25 that under the theory of *respondeat superior,* a principal (a landlord, with respect to leases) is liable for the wrongful actions of his or her agent if the actions occurred within the scope of employment. Thus, a landlord can be held liable for his or her agent's discrimination on the basis of race, color, religion, national origin, or sex against potential tenants. Similarly, a tenant cannot legally promise to do something counter to laws prohibiting discrimination. A tenant, for example, cannot legally promise to do business only with members of a particular race. The public policy underlying these prohibitions is to treat all people equally.

RIGHTS AND DUTIES

The rights and duties of landlords and tenants generally pertain to four broad areas of concern—the possession, use, and maintenance of leased property and, of course, rent.

Possession. Possession involves the obligation of the landlord to deliver possession to the tenant at the beginning of the lease term and the right of the tenant to obtain possession and retain it until the lease expires.

The *covenant of quiet enjoyment* mentioned in Chapter 36 also applies to leased premises. Under this covenant, the landlord promises that during the lease term, neither the landlord nor any third party with an unlawful claim will interfere with the tenant's use and enjoyment of the property. This covenant forms the essence of the landlord-tenant relationship. If it is breached, the tenant can terminate the lease and sue for damages.

If the landlord deprives the tenant of the tenant's possession of the leased property or interferes with the tenant's use or enjoyment of it, an **eviction** occurs. This is the case, for example, when the landlord changes the lock and refuses to give the tenant a new key.

EVICTION
Depriving a person of the possession of property that he or she leases.

CONSTRUCTIVE EVICTION
Depriving a person of the possession of rental property that he or she leases by rendering the premises unfit or unsuitable for occupancy.

A **constructive eviction** occurs when the landlord wrongfully performs or fails to perform any of the undertakings the lease requires, thereby making the tenant's further use and enjoyment of the property exceedingly difficult or impossible. Examples of constructive eviction include a landlord's failure to provide heat in the winter, light, or other essential utilities.

Use and Maintenance of the Premises. If the parties do not limit by agreement the uses to which the property may be put, the tenant may make any use of it, as long as the use is legal. The use also must reasonably relate to the purpose for which the property is adapted or ordinarily used and must not injure the landlord's interest.

The tenant is responsible for all damage that he or she causes, intentionally or negligently. The tenant may be held liable for the cost of returning the property to the physical condition it was in at the lease's inception. Unless the parties have agreed otherwise, the tenant is not responsible for ordinary wear and tear or for the property's consequent depreciation in value.

Make sure that a lease contract clearly indicates whether the landlord or tenant is to be responsible for taxes on the property, costs relating to necessary maintenance and repairs, and utility costs.

IN THE COURTROOM

BRB Restaurants, Inc., leases property from Dahl Enterprises, Inc. The lease provides for lower payments of rent than normal but requires BRB to return the property in the condition in which BRB received it. On the property, BRB operates a restaurant. When the lease expires, BRB moves off the property, leaving it in a state of disrepair. Dahl replaces the roof, the air-conditioning unit, and the restroom fixtures. Dahl also repaves the parking lot. *Is BRB liable for the cost of these repairs?* Yes. Except for ordinary wear and tear, a tenant is responsible for all damage that he or she causes, intentionally or negligently. In addition, BRB and Dahl—parties of "equal bargaining power"—signed a lease in which BRB agreed to pay the cost of returning the property to the physical condition it was in at the beginning of the lease.

Usually, the landlord must comply with state statutes and city ordinances that delineate specific standards for the construction and maintenance of buildings. Typically, these codes contain structural requirements common to the construction, wiring, and plumbing of residential and commercial buildings. In some jurisdictions, landlords of residential property are required by statute to maintain the premises in good repair.

LEARNING OBJECTIVE NO. 3
Defining the Landlord's Duties Regarding Use and Maintenance of the Leased Premises

The **implied warranty of habitability** requires a landlord who leases residential property to furnish the premises in a habitable condition—that is, in a condition that is safe and suitable for people to live in—at the beginning of a lease term and to maintain the premises in that condition for the lease's duration. Some state legislatures have enacted this warranty into law. In other jurisdictions, courts have based this warranty on the existence of a landlord's statutory duty to keep leased premises in good repair, or they have simply applied it as a matter of public policy.

IMPLIED WARRANTY OF HABITABILITY
A presumed promise by the landlord that rented residential premises are fit for human habitation—that is, free of violations of building and sanitary codes.

Generally, this warranty applies to major—or *substantial*—physical defects that the landlord knows or should know about and has had a reasonable time to repair—for example, a large hole in the roof. An unattractive or annoying feature, such as a crack in the wall, may be unpleasant, but unless the crack is a structural defect or affects the residence's heating capabilities, it is probably not sufficiently substantial to make the place uninhabitable.

LEARNING OBJECTIVE NO. 4
Stating the Obligations of a Tenant with Respect to Rent

Rent. *Rent* is the tenant's payment to the landlord for the tenant's occupancy or use of the landlord's real property. Generally, the tenant must pay the rent even if the tenant refuses to occupy the property or moves out, as long as the lease is in force and the refusal or the move is unjustifiable (that is, if the property is still habitable, and the landlord has done nothing to evict the tenant).

In some situations, such as when a landlord breaches the implied warranty of habitability, a tenant is allowed to withhold rent as a remedy. When rent withholding is authorized under a statute (sometimes referred to as a "rent strike" statute), the tenant must usually put the amount withheld into an *escrow account.* This account is held in the name of the depositor (in this case, the tenant) and an *escrow agent* (in this case, usually the court or a government agency). The funds are returnable to the depositor if the third person (in this case, the landlord) fails to fulfill the escrow condition (such as making the premises habitable).

Generally, the tenant may withhold an amount equal to the amount by which the defect rendering the premises unlivable reduces the property's rental value. How much that is may be determined in different ways. The tenant who withholds more than is legally permissible is liable to the landlord for the excessive amount withheld.

TRANSFERRING RIGHTS TO LEASED PROPERTY

Either the landlord or the tenant may wish to transfer his or her rights to the leased property during the term of the lease.

Transferring the Landlord's Interest. Just as any other real property owner can sell, give away, or otherwise transfer his or her property, so can a landlord—who is, of course, the leased property's owner. If complete title to the leased property is transferred, the tenant becomes the tenant of the new owner. The new owner may collect subsequent rent and normally must also abide by the terms of the existing lease.

Homes and Communities is a Web site offered by the U.S. Department of Housing and Urban Development. Information of interest to both consumers and businesses is available at this site, which can be accessed at

http://www.hud.gov

Transferring the Tenant's Interest. The tenant's transfer of his or her entire interest in the leased property to a third person is an *assignment of the lease.* A lease assignment is an agreement to transfer all rights, title, and interest in the lease to the assignee. It is a complete transfer. Many leases require that the assignment have the landlord's written consent. An assignment that lacks consent can be avoided by the landlord. A landlord who knowingly accepts rent from the assignee, however, will be held to have waived the requirement.

A tenant does not end his or her liabilities on a lease on assignment, because the tenant may assign rights but not duties. Thus, even though the assignee of the lease is required to pay rent, the original tenant is not released from the contractual obligation to pay the rent if the assignee fails to do so.

SUBLEASE
A lease executed by the lessee of real estate to a third person, conveying the same interest that the lessee enjoys, but for a shorter term than that held by the lessee.

The tenant's transfer of all or part of the premises for a period shorter than the lease term is a **sublease.** The same restrictions that apply to an assignment of the tenant's interest in leased property apply to a sublease.

IN THE COURTROOM

Derek gets a new job and leases an apartment for a two-year period. Six months later, Derek is offered a short-term transfer and accepts. Because he does not wish to pay rent for an unoccupied apartment, Derek subleases the apartment to Pamela, a co-worker (the sublessee). (Derek may have to obtain his landlord's consent for this sublease if the lease requires it.) The sublessee is bound by the same terms of the lease as the tenant. Thus, Pamela is bound to pay the rent. *If Pamela does not pay the rent, can the landlord hold Derek liable?* Yes. As in a lease assignment, the tenant remains liable for the obligations under the lease if the sublessee fails to fulfill them.

TERMS AND CONCEPTS FOR REVIEW

constructive eviction 476
eviction 476
implied warranty of habitability 477
lease 473
leasehold estate 473
periodic tenancy 474
sublease 478
tenancy at sufferance 474
tenancy at will 474
tenancy for years 473

CHAPTER SUMMARY • LANDLORD AND TENANT

Types of Tenancies	Types of tenancies (leasehold estates) relating to leased property include the following: **1.** *Tenancy for years*—Tenancy for a period of time stated by express contract. **2.** *Periodic tenancy*—Tenancy for a period determined by the frequency of rent payments. It is automatically renewed unless proper notice is given. **3.** *Tenancy at will*—Tenancy for as long as both parties agree. No notice of termination is required. **4.** *Tenancy at sufferance*—Possession of land without legal right.
The Landlord-Tenant Relationship	**1.** *Lease agreement*—The landlord-tenant relationship is created by a lease agreement. State or local law may dictate whether the lease must be in writing and what lease terms are permissible. **2.** *Rights and duties*—The rights and duties that arise under a lease agreement generally pertain to the following areas: **a.** Possession—The tenant has an exclusive right to possess the leased premises, which must be available to the tenant at the agreed-on time. Under the covenant of quiet enjoyment, the landlord promises that during the lease term, neither the landlord nor anyone with an unlawful claim will disturb the tenant's use and enjoyment of the property.

CHAPTER SUMMARY • *Continued*

The Landlord-Tenant Relationship Continued	**b.** Use and maintenance of the premises—Unless the parties agree otherwise, the tenant may make any legal use of the property. The tenant is responsible for any damage that he or she causes. The landlord must comply with laws that set specific standards for the maintenance of real property. The implied warranty of habitability requires that a landlord furnish and maintain residential premises in a habitable condition (that is, in a condition safe and suitable for human life). **3.** *Rent*—The tenant must pay the rent as long as the lease is in force, unless the tenant justifiably refuses to occupy the property or withholds the rent because of the landlord's failure to maintain the premises properly. **4.** *Transferring rights to leased property*— **a.** If the landlord transfers complete title to the leased property, the tenant becomes the tenant of the new owner. The new owner may then collect the rent but also must abide by the existing lease. **b.** Unless prohibited (and, if required, the landlord gives his or her consent), tenants may assign their rights (but not their duties) under a lease contract to a third person. **c.** Unless prohibited (and, if required, the landlord gives his or her consent), tenants may sublease leased property to a third person. The original tenant, however, is not relieved of any obligations to the landlord under the lease.

HYPOTHETICAL QUESTIONS

37–1. Tenant's Rights and Responsibilities. You are a student in college and plan to attend classes for nine months. You sign a twelve-month lease for an apartment. Discuss fully each of the following situations:

(a) You have a summer job in another town and wish to assign the balance of your lease (three months) to a fellow student who will be attending summer school. Can you do so?

(b) You are graduating in May. The lease will have three months remaining. Can you terminate the lease without liability by giving a thirty-day notice to the landlord?

37–2. Landlord's Responsibilities. Sarah has rented a house from Franks. The house is only two years old. Sarah's roof leaks every time it rains. The water that has accumulated in the attic has caused plaster to fall off ceilings in the upstairs bedrooms, and one ceiling has started to sag. Sarah has complained to Franks and asked him to have the roof repaired. Franks says he has caulked the roof, but the roof still leaks. Franks claims that because Sarah has sole control of the leased premises, she has the duty to repair the roof. Sarah insists that the repair of the roof is Franks's responsibility. Discuss fully who is responsible for repairing the roof and, if the responsibility belongs to Franks, what remedies are available to Sarah.

REAL WORLD CASE PROBLEM

37–3. The Lease Contract. Christine Callis formed a lease agreement with Colonial Properties, Inc., to lease property in a shopping center in Montgomery, Alabama. Callis later alleged that before signing the lease agreement, she had told a representative of Colonial that she wanted to locate in a shopping center that would attract a wealthy clientele, and the representative had assured her that no discount stores would be allowed to lease space in the shopping center. The written lease agreement, which Callis signed, contained a clause stating that "[n]o representation, inducement, understanding or anything of any nature whatsoever made, stated, or represented on Landlord's behalf, either orally or in writing (except this Lease), has induced Tenant to enter into this lease." The lease also stipulated that Callis would not conduct any type of business commonly called a discount store, surplus store, or other similar business. Later, Colonial did, in fact, lease space to discount stores, and Callis sued Colonial for breach of the lease contract. Will Callis succeed in her claim? Discuss fully. [*Callis v. Colonial Properties, Inc.*, 597 So.2d 660 (Ala. 1991)]

For updated links to resources available on the Web, as well as a variety of other materials, visit this text's Web site at **http://blte.westbuslaw.com**.

You can find online links to most uniform laws, including the URLTA, at

http://www.lawsource.com/also

Many Web sites now provide information on laws and other information relating to landlord-tenant relationships. One of them is TenantNet at

http://tenant.net

Online Legal Research

Go to **http://blte.westbuslaw.com**, the Web site that accompanies this text. Select "Internet Applications," and then click on "Chapter 37." There you will find the following Internet research exercise that you can perform to learn more about landlord-tenant relationships:

Activity 37–1: The Rights of Tenants

Chapter 37 ■ WORK SET

TRUE-FALSE QUESTIONS

_____ **1.** A covenant of quiet enjoyment guarantees that a tenant will not be disturbed in his or her possession of leased property by the landlord or any third person.

_____ **2.** If the covenant of quiet enjoyment is breached, the tenant can sue the landlord for damages.

_____ **3.** Generally, a tenant must pay rent even if he or she moves out, if the move is unjustifiable.

_____ **4.** A tenant does not have to pay rent if there is anything wrong with leased property, no matter how slight the defect.

_____ **5.** In most states, a tenant can make an alteration to leased premises without the landlord's consent.

_____ **6.** When a landlord sells leased premises to a third party, any existing leases terminate automatically.

_____ **7.** When a tenant assigns a lease to a third party, the tenant's obligations under the lease terminate automatically.

_____ **8.** A landlord who leases residential property must furnish the premises in a condition that is safe and suitable for people to live in.

MULTIPLE-CHOICE QUESTIONS

_____ **1.** Jim leases an apartment from Maria. With Maria's consent, Jim assigns the lease to Nell for the last two months of the term, after which Nell exercises an option under the original lease to renew for three months. One month later, Nell moves out. Regarding the rent for the rest of the term

a. no one is liable.
b. Jim can be held liable.
c. only Nell is liable.
d. Maria is liable.

_____ **2.** Dian leases an apartment from Tom. The lease provides that Tom is not liable for any injury if the heating system fails to function. In midwinter, the system breaks down. Dian becomes seriously ill. If Dian sues Tom, she will

a. win, because Dian is the tenant.
b. win, because the clause absolving Tom of liability is unconscionable.
c. lose, because the lease absolves Tom of responsibility.
d. lose, because Tom is the landlord.

_____ **3.** Jill reports housing code violations in her apartment to local authorities. In retaliation, her landlord Ken changes the lock on her door, refuses to give her a new key, and starts eviction proceedings. If Jill sues Ken, she will

a. win, because Jill is the tenant.
b. win, because Ken is attempting a retaliatory eviction.
c. lose, because Ken is attempting a retaliatory eviction.
d. lose, because Tom is the landlord.

_____ **4.** Paul rents an office from John for an eighteen-month term. Their lease

a. must be oral to be enforceable.
b. must be in writing to be enforceable.
c. is enforceable whether or not it is in writing.
d. is not enforceable whether or not it is in writing.

_____ **5.** Ron signs a one-year lease for an apartment. Kim is the landlord. Six months later, Ron moves out of the apartment with no intent of returning. Ron has no more obligation to pay rent if Kim

a. moves into the apartment.
b. enters the apartment to make a repair.
c. does not ask for the rent.
d. does nothing.

_____ **6.** Dick rents an apartment from Sue. Two months later, Dick moves out, and arranges with Lee to move in and pay the rent to Sue for the rest of the term. This is

a. an assignment.
b. a sublease.
c. both a and b.
d. none of the above.

_____ **7.** Ray operates the Family Restaurant in space that he leases in Village Mall. Village Mall is owned by VM Associates. VM Associates sells the mall to BB Properties. For the rest of the lease term, Ray owes rent to

a. VM Associates.
b. BB Properties.
c. the Family Restaurant.
d. none of the above.

_____ **8.** Susan signs a lease for an apartment, agreeing to make rental payments before the fifth of each month. The lease does not specify a termination date. This tenancy is

a. a periodic tenancy.
b. a tenancy for years.
c. a tenancy at will.
d. a tenancy at sufferance.

ISSUE SPOTTERS

1. Ann leases an office in Ted's building for a one-year term. At the end of the period specified in the lease, the lease ends without notice, and possession of the office returns to Ted. If Ann dies during the period of the lease, what happens to the leased property?

2. Eve orally agrees to rent an apartment to Nancy for a six-month term. Is this lease enforceable if it is not in writing?

Wills and Trusts

LEARNING OBJECTIVES

When you finish this chapter, you should be able to:

1. List the requirements of a will.
2. Discuss how a will can be revoked in writing.
3. Describe the distribution of the property of a party who dies without a will.
4. List the essential elements of a trust.

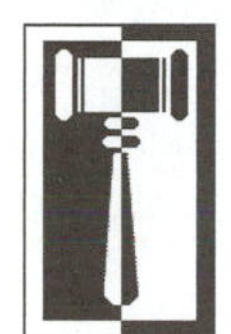

FACING A LEGAL PROBLEM

Fran's will provides that a certain sum of money is to be divided among a group of charities named in a written memorandum that Fran gives to her lawyer the same day the will is signed. *Is this list a valid part of Fran's will?*

In this chapter, we examine how property is passed on the death of its owner. Our laws require that on death, the rights to ownership of the property of the decedent (the one who has died) must be delivered in full somewhere. This can be done by will, through state laws prescribing distribution of property among heirs or next of kin, or through trusts.

Wills

A **will** is the final declaration of how a person desires to have his or her property disposed of after death. A will is a formal instrument that must follow exactly the requirements of state law to be effective. The reasoning behind such a strict requirement is obvious. A will becomes effective only *after* death. No attempts to modify it after death are allowed because the court cannot ask the deceased to confirm the attempted modifications.

Parties

A person who makes out a will is known as a **testator.** After the testator dies, his or her will is subject to *probate*. To probate a will means to establish its validity and to carry the administration of the estate through a court process. The court that oversees this process is called a **probate court.**

A *personal representative* of the decedent's estate often becomes involved in probate. The personal representative settles the affairs of the deceased. An **executor** is a personal representative named in a will. An **administrator** is a personal

Will
An instrument directing what is to be done with the testator's property upon his or her death, made by the testator.

Testator
One who makes and executes a will.

Probate Court
A court having jurisdiction over proceedings concerning the settlement of a person's estate.

Executor
A person appointed by a testator to see that his or her will is administered appropriately.

Administrator
One who is appointed by a court to handle the probate (disposition) of a person's estate if that person dies intestate (without a will).

representative appointed by a court for a decedent who dies without a will, who fails to name an executor in the will, who names an executor lacking the capacity to serve, or who writes a will that the court refuses to accept.

Gifts

Devise
To make a gift of real property by will.

Bequest
A gift by will of personal property.

Legacy
A gift of personal property under a will.

Legatee
A person who inherits personal property under a will.

A gift of real estate by will is generally called a **devise.** A gift of personal property by will is called a **bequest** or **legacy.** Gifts by will can be specific, general, or residuary. A *specific* devise or bequest (legacy) describes particular property (for example, a specific devise may consist of a particular piece of real estate) that can be distinguished from all the rest of the testator's property.

A *general* devise or bequest (legacy) does not single out any particular item of property to be transferred by will but usually specifies the property's value in monetary terms (such as "shares of stock worth $1,000") or simply states a sum of money ("$1,000"). If the assets of an estate are insufficient to pay in full all general bequests provided for in the will, an *abatement* takes place. In an abatement, the **legatees** (those who inherit legacies) receive reduced benefits.

Sometimes a will provides that any assets remaining after gifts are made and debts are paid are to be distributed through a *residuary* clause. This is necessary when the exact amount to be distributed cannot be determined until all other gifts and payouts are made.

Requirements of Wills

A will must comply with statutory formalities designed to ensure that the testator understood his or her actions at the time the will was made. These formalities are intended to help prevent fraud. Unless they are followed, the will is declared void and the decedent's property is distributed according to the state laws. In all states, the testator must have capacity. In most states, a will must be in writing, signed by the testator, witnessed, and published.

LEARNING OBJECTIVE NO. 1
Listing the Requirements of a Will

1. *The testator must have capacity.* That is, a testator must be of legal age and sound mind *at the time a will is made.* The legal age for executing a will varies. In most states, the minimum age is eighteen years. The concept of "sound mind" refers to the testator's ability to formulate and understand a personal plan for the disposition of property. Further, a testator must intend the document to be his or her will.
2. *A will must be in writing.* The writing can be informal (in some states a will can be handwritten in crayon). It can be written on a scrap of paper, a paper bag, or a piece of cloth. A will that is completely in the handwriting of the testator is called a **holographic** (or olographic) **will.** A will also can refer to a written memorandum that itself is not in the will but that contains information necessary to carry out the will and is in existence when the will is signed.

Holographic Will
A will written entirely in the signer's handwriting and usually not witnessed.

In the legal problem set out at the beginning of this chapter, Fran's will provides that a certain sum of money is to be divided among a group of charities named in a written memorandum that Fran gives to her lawyer the same day the will is signed. *Is this list a valid part of Fran's will?* Yes. The written list of charities will be "incorporated by reference" into the will. It is in existence when the will is signed, and it is sufficiently described in the will so that it can be identified.

3. *A formal (nonholographic) will must be signed by the testator.* The testator's signature must appear in the will, generally at the end. Each jurisdiction dictates by statute and court decision what constitutes a signature. Initials, an "X" or other mark, and words like "Mom" have all been upheld as valid when the testator intended them to be a signature.
4. *A formal (nonholographic) will must be witnessed.* A will must be attested (affirmed to be genuine) by two, and sometimes three, witnesses. The number

of witnesses, their qualifications, and the manner in which the witnessing must be done are generally set out in a statute. Some states require a witness to be disinterested—that is, not a beneficiary under the will. There are no age requirements. Witnesses must be mentally competent, however.
5. *Sometimes a will must be published.* A will is *published* by an oral declaration of the testator to the witnesses that the document they are about to sign is his or her will.

Undue Influence

A valid will is one that represents the testator's intention to transfer and distribute his or her property. When it can be shown that the decedent's plan of distribution was the result of improper pressure brought by another person, the will is declared invalid.

Undue influence may be inferred if the testator ignores blood relatives and names as a beneficiary a nonrelative who is in constant close contact and in a position to influence the making of the will. For example, if a nurse caring for the deceased at the time of death is named as beneficiary to the exclusion of all family members, the validity of the will might well be challenged on the basis of undue influence.

Some state statutes provide that title to cars, savings and checking accounts, and certain other property can be passed after a person's death merely by filling out forms.

Revocation of Wills

An executed will is revocable by the testator at any time during his or her life. Wills can also be revoked by operation of law. Revocation can be partial or complete. It must follow certain strict formalities.

To learn about some estate-planning software available from a Web site, access

http://www.atlaw.com

Revocation by Act of the Testator. Revocation of a will by an *act of the testator* can be effected by a physical act, such as burning the will. It can also be effected by a writing that revokes the will.

Physical Acts. The physical acts by which a testator may revoke a will may include, in addition to intentionally burning it, intentionally tearing, canceling, obliterating, or destroying it, or having someone else do so in the presence of the testator and at the testator's direction. In some states, partial revocation by physical act is recognized. Thus, those portions of a will lined out or torn away are dropped, and the remaining parts of the will are valid. In no case, however, can a provision be crossed out and an additional or substitute provision written in. To add new provisions, the testator and witnesses must sign the will again.

LEARNING OBJECTIVE NO. 2
Discussing How a Will Can Be Revoked in Writing

Writings. A will may also be wholly or partially revoked by a **codicil,** a written instrument separate from the will that amends or revokes provisions in the will. A codicil eliminates the necessity of redrafting an entire will merely to add to it or amend it. It can also be used to revoke an entire will. The codicil must be executed with the same formalities required for a will, and it must refer expressly to the will.

A second will, or new will, can be executed that may revoke a prior will. The second will must use specific language, such as "This will hereby revokes all prior wills." If such an express *declaration of revocation* is missing, then both wills are read together. If any of the dispositions made in the second will are inconsistent with the prior will, the second will controls.

Codicil
A written supplement or modification to a will. Codicils must be executed with the same formalities as a will.

Revocation by Operation of Law. Revocation by *operation of law* occurs when marriage, divorce or annulment, or the birth of children takes place after a will has been made.

Marriage. In most states, when a testator marries after making a will that does not include the new spouse, the spouse can still receive the amount the spouse

INTESTATE
As a noun, one who has died without having created a valid will; as an adjective, the state of having died without a will.

would have taken had the testator died **intestate** (without a valid will). In effect, this revokes the will to the point of providing the spouse with a share of the estate. The rest of the estate is distributed according to the terms of the will. If, however, the omission of a future spouse is intentional in the existing will, or the spouse is otherwise provided for in the will (or by transfer of property outside the will), the omitted spouse will not be given a share.

Divorce. Divorce does not necessarily revoke an entire will. A divorce or an annulment occurring after a will has been written revokes those dispositions of property made under the will to the former spouse.

Children. If a child is born after a will has been executed and if it appears that the testator would have made a provision for the child, then the child is entitled to receive whatever portion of the estate he or she is allowed under state intestacy laws (discussed below). Most states allow a child to receive some portion of the estate if no provision is made in a will, unless it appears from the terms of the will that the testator intended that the child receive nothing.

Intestacy Laws

INTESTACY LAWS
State laws determining the division and descent of the property of one who dies intestate (without a will).

Statutes of descent and distribution regulate how property is distributed when a person dies without a will. These statutes—called **intestacy laws**—attempt to carry out the likely intent and wishes of the decedent.

ORDER OF DISTRIBUTION

LEARNING OBJECTIVE NO. 3
Describing the Distribution of the Property of a Party Who Dies without a Will

Intestacy laws specify the order in which the heirs of an intestate (one who dies without a will) share in the estate. First, the debts of the decedent must be satisfied out of his or her estate. Then the remaining assets pass to the surviving spouse and to the decedent's children. When there is no surviving spouse or child, then grandchildren, brothers and sisters, and in some states, parents of the decedent are the next in line. These relatives are usually called *lineal descendants*. If there are no lineal descendants, then *collateral heirs*—nieces, nephews, aunts, and uncles of the decedent—are the next group.

If there are no survivors in any of those groups of people related to the decedent, most statutes provide that the property shall be distributed among the next of kin of any of the collateral heirs. Stepchildren are not considered kin. Legally adopted children, however, are recognized as lawful heirs of their adoptive parents. If no heirs exist, then the property **escheats,** or reverts to the state (that is, the state assumes ownership of the property).

ESCHEAT
The transfer of property to the state when the owner of the property dies without heirs.

SURVIVING SPOUSE AND CHILDREN

A surviving spouse usually receives the homestead (the family home) and a share of the estate—one-half if there is also a surviving child, and one-third if there are two or more children. Only if no children or grandchildren survive the decedent will a surviving spouse succeed to the entire estate.

IN THE COURTROOM

Mario dies intestate and is survived by his wife, Delia, and his children, Francisco and Tara. Mario's property passes according to intestacy laws. *Do Delia and the children receive any of Mario's property?* Yes. After Mario's outstanding debts are paid, Delia will receive the homestead and one-third of all other property. The remaining real and personal property will pass to Francisco and Tara in equal portions.

Grandchildren

When an intestate is survived by descendants of deceased children, a question arises as to what share the descendants (that is, grandchildren of the intestate) will receive. ***Per stirpes*** is a method of dividing an intestate share by which a class or group of distributees (for example, grandchildren) take the share that their deceased parent *would have been* entitled to inherit had that parent lived. Exhibit 38–1 illustrates the *per stirpes* method of distribution.

Per Stirpes
A Latin term meaning "by the roots." In the law governing estate distribution, a method of distributing an intestate's estate in which a class or group of distributees take the share to which their deceased ancestor would have been entitled.

IN THE COURTROOM

Michael, a widower, has two children, Scott and Jonathan. Scott has two children (Becky and Holly), and Jonathan has one child (Paul). At the time of Michael's death, Scott and Jonathan have predeceased their father (died before he did). *If Michael's estate is distributed* per stirpes, *what share will each grandchild inherit?* The following distribution will take place: Becky and Holly will receive one-fourth each, sharing Scott's one-half share, and Paul will receive one-half, taking Jonathan's share.

An estate may also be distributed on a ***per capita*** basis. This means that each person takes an equal share of the estate. Exhibit 38–2 on the next page illustrates the *per capita* method of distribution.

Per Capita
A Latin term meaning "per person." In the law governing estate distribution, a method of distributing the property of an intestate's estate by which all the heirs receive equal shares.

IN THE COURTROOM

Michael, a widower, has two children, Scott and Jonathan. Scott has two children (Becky and Holly), and Jonathan has one child (Paul). At the time of Michael's death, Scott and Jonathan have predeceased their father (died before he did). *If Michael's estate is distributed* per capita, *what share will each grandchild inherit?* Each of them will receive a one-third share.

EXHIBIT 38–1
***Per Stirpes* Distribution**

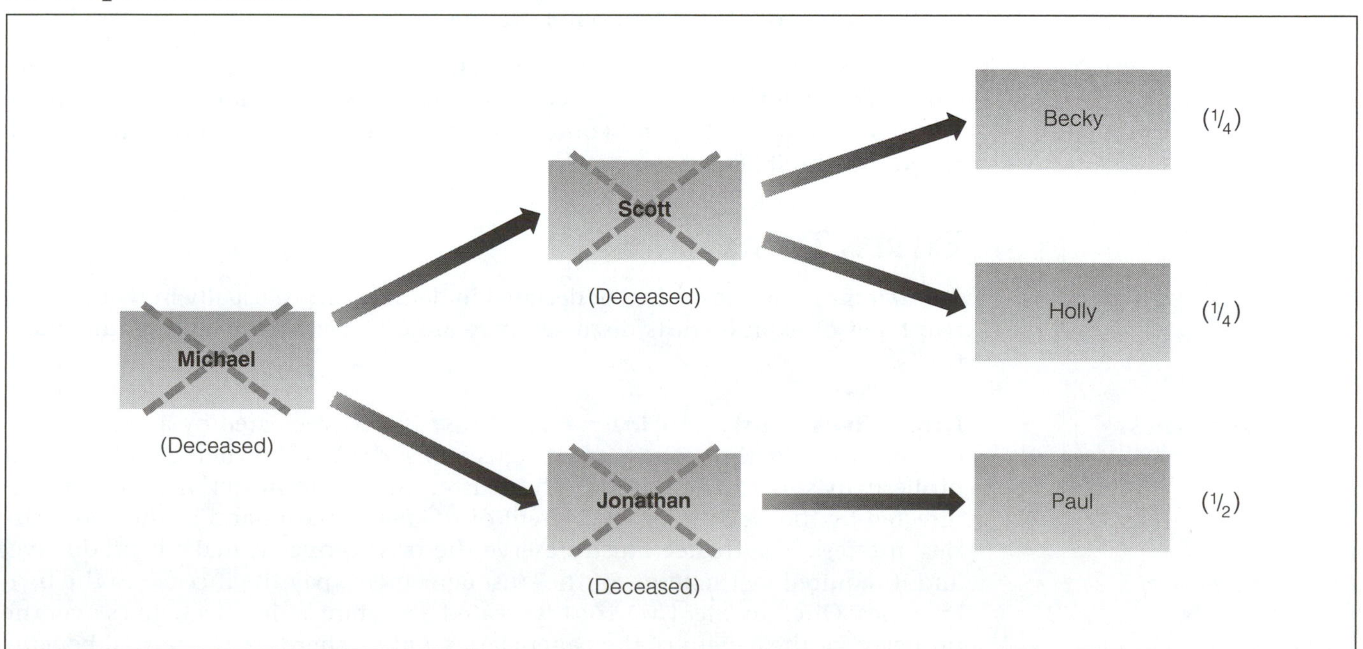

EXHIBIT 38–2
***Per Capita* Distribution**

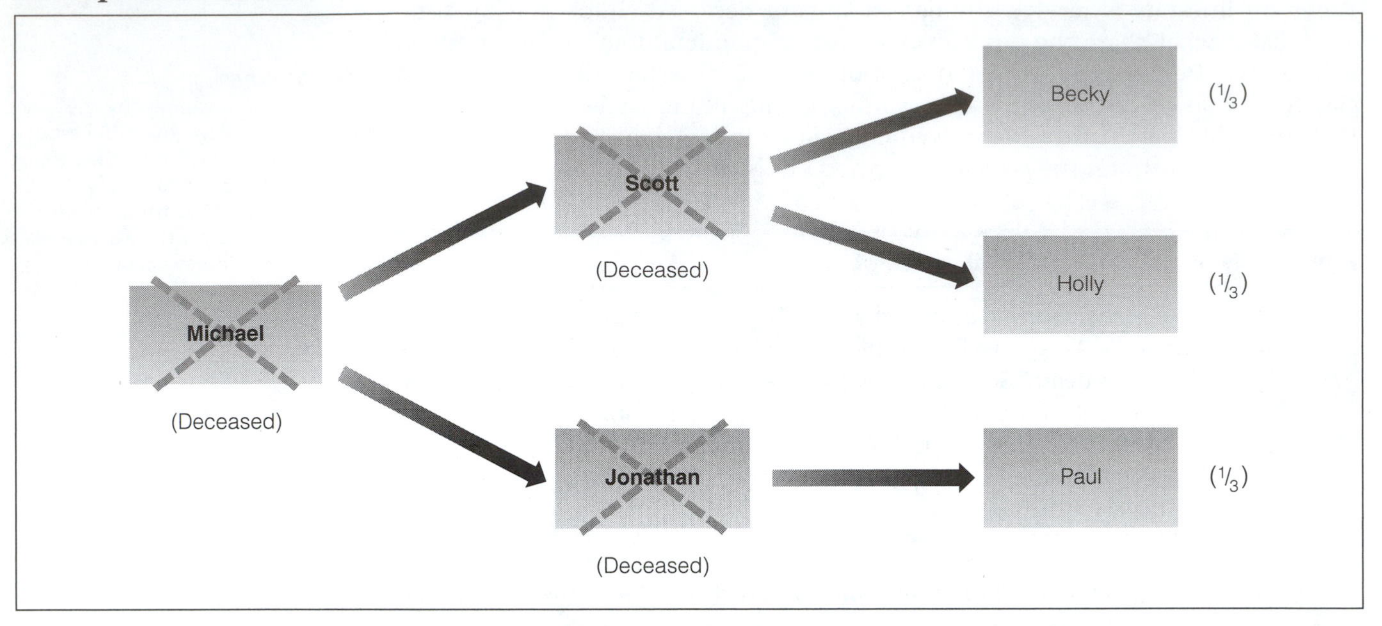

Trusts

TRUST
An arrangement in which title to property is held by one person (a trustee) for the benefit of another (a beneficiary).

A **trust** involves any arrangement through which property is transferred from one person to a trustee to be administered for the first person's or another party's benefit. A trust can also be defined as a right or property held by one party for the benefit of another.

The essential elements of a trust are as follows:

LEARNING OBJECTIVE NO. 4
Listing the Essential Elements of a Trust

1. A designated beneficiary.
2. A designated trustee.
3. A fund sufficiently identified to enable title to pass to the trustee.
4. Actual delivery by the settlor or grantor (the person who creates the trust) to the trustee with the intention of passing title.

If James conveys his farm to the First Bank of Minnesota to be held for the benefit of his daughters, he has created a trust. James is the settlor, the First Bank of Minnesota is the trustee, and James's daughters are the beneficiaries. This is illustrated in Exhibit 38–3.

EXPRESS TRUSTS

An *express trust* is one created or declared in definite terms, usually in writing. The two types of express trusts discussed here are *inter vivos* trusts and testamentary trusts.

***INTER VIVOS* TRUST**
A trust created by the grantor (settlor) and effective during the grantor's lifetime (that is, a trust not established by a will).

***Inter Vivos* Trust.** An ***inter vivos* trust** is a trust created by a grantor during his or her lifetime. The grantor signs a *trust deed,* and ownership of the trust property passes to the trustee. The trustee must administer the property as directed by the grantor for the benefit of the beneficiaries and in the beneficiaries' interest. The trustee must preserve the trust property, make it productive, and if required by the terms of the trust agreement, pay the income to the beneficiaries. Once an *inter vivos* trust is created, the grantor, in effect, gives over the property for the benefit of the beneficiaries. Often, there are tax-related benefits with this type of trust.

EXHIBIT 38–3
Trust Arrangement

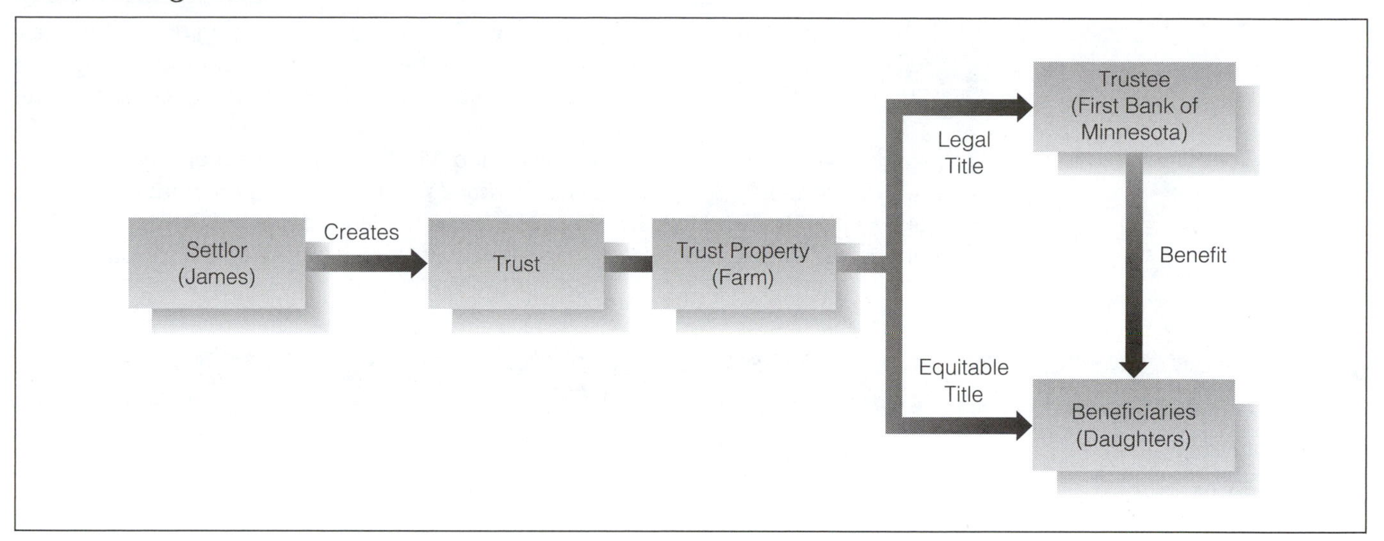

Testamentary Trust. A **testamentary trust** is a trust created by a will to come into existence on the settlor's death. After the death, a trustee takes title to the trust property, but his or her actions are subject to judicial approval. The legal responsibilities of this trustee are the same as those of the trustee of an *inter vivos* trust, however. The trustee of a testamentary trust can be named in the will or be appointed by the court.

TESTAMENTARY TRUST A trust that is created by will and therefore does not take effect until the death of the testator.

If the will setting up a testamentary trust is invalid, then the trust will also be invalid. The property that was supposed to be in the trust will then pass according to intestacy laws, not according to the terms of the trust.

IMPLIED TRUSTS

Sometimes a trust will be imposed by law, even in the absence of an express trust. Customarily, these *implied trusts* are divided into constructive and resulting trusts.

Constructive Trust. A **constructive trust** differs from an express trust in that it arises by operation of law. Whenever a transaction takes place in which the person who takes the rights of the ownership of property cannot also enjoy the benefits of that ownership without violating the law, the court will create a constructive trust. In effect, the owner becomes a trustee for the parties who are entitled to the benefit of the property.

CONSTRUCTIVE TRUST A trust created by operation of law against one who wrongfully has obtained or holds a legal right to property that the person should not, in equity and good conscience, hold and enjoy.

IN THE COURTROOM

Dino and Benito are partners in buying, developing, and selling real estate. Dino learns through the staff of the partnership that two hundred acres of land will soon come on the market. Dino secretly buys the land in his own name, violating his duties to the partnership. *Does Dino hold the property in constructive trust for the partnership?* Yes. A court would determine that because of Dino's wrongful action, Dino holds the land in constructive trust for the partnership. Any income from the property or profits from its sale belong to the partnership.

Resulting Trust. A **resulting trust** arises from the conduct of the parties. The trust results from, or is created by, the *apparent intention* of the parties. The conduct of the parties evidencing the intent to create a trust relationship is carefully scrutinized.

RESULTING TRUST A trust implied in law from the intentions of the parties to a given transaction.

IN THE COURTROOM

Garrison buys one acre of land from Villard. Garrison is going out of the country for a period of two years and will be unable to attend the closing. She therefore asks Villard to deed the property to Garrison's friend, Oswald, at the closing. Garrison and Oswald agree that Oswald will deed the land back to Garrison on her return. At the closing, Villard conveys the property to Oswald. *Does Oswald hold the property in trust for Garrison?* Yes. The intent of the transaction is not to make a gift of the land to Oswald but to transfer the land to him only temporarily. The property is held in a resulting trust, with Oswald as trustee for the benefit of Garrison.

TERMS AND CONCEPTS FOR REVIEW

CHAPTER SUMMARY • WILLS AND TRUSTS

<table>
<tr><td>Wills</td><td>
1. Formal requirements of a will—
a. The testator must have capacity (legal age and sound mind).
b. A will must be in writing.
c. A will must be signed by the testator.
d. A nonholographic will must be witnessed.
e. A will may have to be published (that is, the testator may be required to announce to witnesses that it is his or her will).
2. Methods of revoking or modifying a will—
a. By acts of the testator—
1) Physical act—Burning, tearing up, canceling, obliterating, or deliberately destroying part or all of a will.
2) Codicil—A formal, separate document amending or revoking an existing will.
3) New will—A new will expressly revoking an existing will.
b. By operation of law—
1) Marriage—Revokes part of a will written before the marriage.
2) Divorce or annulment—Revokes dispositions made under a will to a former spouse.
3) Child—It is implied that a child born after a will is written is entitled to receive the portion of the estate granted under intestacy laws.
3. Intestacy laws (statutes of descent and distribution)—
a. Vary from state to state. Usually, the surviving spouse and children inherit the property of the decedent (after the decedent's debts are paid).
b. If there is no surviving spouse or child, then, in order, lineal descendants (grandchildren, brothers and sisters, and parents of the decedent) inherit. If there are no lineal descendants, then collateral heirs (nieces, nephews, aunts, and uncles of the decedent) inherit.
</td></tr>
<tr><td>Trusts</td><td>The essential elements of a trust are (1) a beneficiary, (2) a trustee, (3) a fund sufficiently identified to enable ownership to pass to the trustee, and (4) delivery to the trustee with the intention of passing ownership. The types of trusts include:</td></tr>
</table>

CHAPTER SUMMARY • *Continued*

Trusts—Continued	**1.** *Express trusts*—Created by express terms, usually in writing. **a.** *Inter vivos* trust—*Executed by a grantor during his or her life.* **b.** Testamentary trust—Created by will and coming into existence on the death of the grantor. **2.** *Implied trusts*—Imposed by law. **a.** Constructive trust—Arises by operation of law whenever a transaction occurs in which the person who takes ownership of the property is not legally entitled to enjoy its benefit. **b.** Resulting trust—Arises from the conduct of the parties when an *apparent intention* to create a trust is present.

HYPOTHETICAL QUESTIONS

38–1. Validity of Wills. Merlin Winters had three sons. Merlin and his youngest son, Abraham, had a falling out in 1994 and had not spoken to each other since. Merlin made a formal will in 1996, leaving all his property to the two older children and deliberately excluding Abraham. Merlin's health began to deteriorate, and by 1997 he was under the full-time care of a nurse, Julia. In 1998, he made a new will expressly revoking the 1996 will and leaving all his property to Julia. On Merlin's death, the two older children contested the 1998 will, claiming that Julia had exercised undue influence over their father. Abraham claimed that both wills were invalid, because the first one had been revoked by the second will, and the second will was invalid on the ground of undue influence. Is Abraham's contention correct? Explain.

38–2. Estate Distribution. Benjamin is a widower who has two married children, Edward and Patricia. Patricia has two children, Perry and Paul. Edward has no children. Benjamin dies, and his typewritten will leaves all his property equally to his children, Edward and Patricia, and provides that should a child predecease him, the grandchildren are to take *per stirpes*. The will was witnessed by Patricia and by Benjamin's lawyer and was signed by Benjamin in their presence. Patricia has predeceased Benjamin. Edward claims the will is invalid.

(a) Discuss whether the will is valid.
(b) Discuss the distribution of Benjamin's estate if the will is invalid.
(c) Discuss the distribution of Benjamin's estate if the will is valid.

REAL WORLD CASE PROBLEM

38–3. Validity of Wills. In the last fourteen years of Evelyn Mahera's life, William Cook, a Baptist pastor, became her spiritual adviser and close personal friend. Cook—and no one else—actively participated in helping Mahera's draft her will. He gave Mahera's a church-sponsored booklet on will drafting, recommended an attorney (a church member) to do the drafting, and reviewed the terms of the will with Mahera's. When Mahera's died, she left most of her estate to Cook's church. Cook personally received nothing under the will. Maheras's nephew and only heir, Richard Suagee, filed a suit against Cook in an Oklahoma state court to contest the will, arguing that Cook unduly influenced Mahera's. Can a party who receives nothing under a will be regarded as having exercised undue influence over the testator? What should the court in Maheras's case do? [*Estate of Maheras's,* 897 P.2d 268 (Okla. 1995)]

For updated links to resources available on the Web, as well as a variety of other materials, visit this text's Web site at **http://blte.westbuslaw.com**.

The wills of various historical figures and celebrities, including Elvis Presley, Jacqueline Kennedy Onassis, and Richard Nixon, are online at

http://www.ca-probate.com/wills.htm

The Senior Law Web site offers information on a variety of topics, including elder law, estate planning, and trusts. The URL for this site is

http://www.seniorlaw.com

You can find the Uniform Probate Code, as well as links to various state probate statutes, at Cornell Law University's Legal Information Institute. Go to

http://www.law.cornell.edu/uniform/probate.html

Online Legal Research

Go to **http://blte.westbuslaw.com**, the Web site that accompanies this text. Select "Internet Applications," and then click on "Chapter 38." There you will find the following Internet research exercise that you can perform to learn more about wills and trusts:

Activity 38–1: Wills and Trusts

Chapter 38 ■ WORK SET

TRUE-FALSE QUESTIONS

_____ **1.** A will is revocable only after the testator's death.

_____ **2.** The testator generally must sign a will.

_____ **3.** If a person dies without a will, all of his or her property automatically passes to the state in which that person lived most of his or her life.

_____ **4.** An *inter vivos* trust is a trust created by a grantor during his or her lifetime.

_____ **5.** A testamentary trust is created by will to begin on the settlor's death.

_____ **6.** If a person marries after executing a will that does not include the spouse, the spouse gets nothing on the person's death.

_____ **7.** If a will setting up a trust is invalid, the trust is also invalid.

_____ **8.** A constructive trust does not differ from an express trust.

MULTIPLE-CHOICE QUESTIONS

_____ **1.** Joe's will provides for specific items of property to be given to certain individuals, including employees of Joe's business. The will also provides for certain sums of money to be given to Joe's daughters, Gail and Laura. Because Joe's assets are insufficient to pay in full all of the bequests

a. all of the property must be sold and the proceeds distributed to the heirs.
b. the employees, who are not in a blood relationship with Joe, get nothing.
c. Gail and Laura get nothing.
d. the gifts to Gail and Laura will be reduced proportionately.

_____ **2.** Donna dies without a will, but with many relatives—a spouse, children, adopted children, sisters, brothers, uncles, aunts, cousins, nephews, and nieces. Who gets what is determined by the state's

a. intestacy law.
b. statute of frauds.
c. trustee, who is appointed by Donna's executor.
d. personal representative, who is appointed by a probate court.

_____ **3.** Paul executes a will that leaves all his property to Dave. Two years later, Paul executes a will that leaves all his property to Nora. The second will does not expressly revoke the first will. Paul dies. Who gets his property?

a. Dave, because he was given the property in the first will.
b. Dave, because the second will did not expressly revoke the first will.
c. Nora, because the first will was revoked by the second will.
d. Nora, because two years separated the execution of the wills.

_____ **4.** Tony dies intestate, survived by Lisa, his mother; Grace, his wife; Abby and Selena, their two daughters; and Brock, the son of Cliff, their son, who predeceased his father. Under intestacy laws,

a. Grace receives one-third of Tony's estate, and Abby, Selena, and Brock receive equal portions of the rest.
b. Abby and Selena receive half of Tony's estate, and Grace receives the rest.
c. Lisa and Grace receive equal portions of Tony's estate.
d. Grace receives all of Tony's estate.

_____ **5.** Kate wants Bev and Nina, her daughters, to get the benefit of Kate's farm when she dies. She believes that her daughters cannot manage the farm effectively, because they live in other states. She can provide for them to get the farm's income, under another party's management, by setting up

a. a constructive trust.
b. a resulting trust.
c. a testamentary trust.
d. none of the above.

_____ **6.** Al's will provides, "I, Al, leave all my computer equipment to my good friend, Ray." When Al dies, the personal representative gives Ray the computer equipment. Ray is

a. a devisee.
b. a legatee.
c. a residuary.
d. none of the above.

_____ **7.** Joan, a nurse, cares for Ted for one year before Ted's death. Joan is named the sole beneficiary under Ted's will, to the exclusion of Ted's family members. Ted's family may challenge the will on the basis of

a. the state's intestacy laws.
b. undue influence.
c. both a and b.
d. none of the above.

_____ **8.** Bob's will provides that each of his lineal descendants who are living at the time of his death are to take an equal share of his estate. This means that Bob intends for his estate to be distributed on

a. a *per capita* basis.
b. a *per stirpes* basis.
c. a residuary basis.
d. none of the above.

ISSUE SPOTTERS

1. Sheila makes out a will, leaving her property in equal thirds to Mark and Paula, her children, and Carol, her niece. Two years later, Sheila is adjudged mentally incompetent, and that same year, she dies. Can Mark and Paula have Sheila's will revoked, on grounds that she did not have the capacity to make a will?

2. Lee's will provides for a distribution of Lee's property. First, the assets need to be collected and inventoried, however. They may also need to be appraised. Creditors' claims must be sorted out. Federal and state income taxes must be paid. Finally, the assets must be distributed. Who does these things?

UNIT NINE
GOVERNMENT REGULATION

UNIT OUTLINE

39 Administrative Law

LEARNING OBJECTIVES

When you finish this chapter, you should be able to:

1. Explain the rulemaking function of administrative agencies.
2. Describe the investigation function of agencies.
3. Identify how agency authority is held in check.
4. State what the Freedom of Information Act requires.
5. Discuss the relation between state and federal agencies.

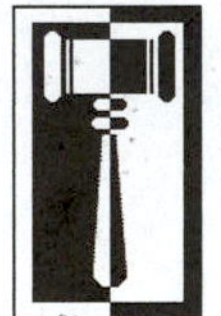

FACING A LEGAL PROBLEM

The Occupational Safety and Health Administration (OSHA) issues a rule to protect health-care workers from viruses that can be transmitted in the blood of patients. Before issuing the rule, OSHA asks whether the restrictions materially reduce a significant workplace risk to human health without imperiling the existence of, or threatening massive dislocation to, the health care industry. The American Dental Association objects to the rule on the ground that OSHA did not prove that dental workers are sufficiently at risk to benefit from the rule. *Can the rule be set aside for this reason?*

ADMINISTRATIVE AGENCY A federal or state government agency established to perform a specific function.

Administrative law consists of the rules, orders, and decisions of **administrative agencies** (government bodies, such as the Federal Trade Commission, charged by the legislature with carrying out the terms of particular laws).

Administrative agencies have a tremendous impact on the day-to-day operation of the government and the economy. Their rules cover virtually every aspect of a business's operation. For example, at the federal level, the Environmental Protection Agency and the Occupational Safety and Health Administration affect the way products are made, and the Federal Trade Commission affects the way products are marketed. State agencies may cover many of the same activities. Agencies at the county or municipal level also affect certain types of business activities. We discuss in this chapter how these agencies exercise their authority.

Agency Creation and Powers

Congress creates federal administrative agencies. Because Congress cannot possibly oversee the actual implementation of all the laws it enacts, it must delegate such tasks to others, particularly when the issues relate to highly technical areas, such as air and water pollution.

ENABLING LEGISLATION

To create an administrative agency, Congress passes **enabling legislation,** which specifies the name, purposes, functions, and powers of the agency being created. Through similar enabling acts, state legislatures create state administrative agencies.

ENABLING LEGISLATION
Statutes enacted by Congress that authorize the creation of an administrative agency and specify the name, composition, and powers of the agency being created.

TYPES OF AGENCIES

There are two basic types of administrative agencies, executive agencies and independent regulatory agencies. Federal **executive agencies** include the cabinet departments of the executive branch, which were formed to assist the president in carrying out executive functions, and the subagencies within the cabinet departments. The Occupational Safety and Health Administration, for example, is a subagency within the Department of Labor.

All administrative agencies are part of the executive branch of government, but **independent regulatory agencies** are outside the major executive departments. The Federal Trade Commission and the Securities and Exchange Commission are examples of independent regulatory agencies.

The significant difference between the two types of agencies lies in the accountability of the regulators. Agencies that are part of the executive branch are subject to the authority of the president, who has the power to appoint and remove federal officers. The president has less power over independent agencies, whose officers serve for fixed terms and cannot be removed without just cause.

EXECUTIVE AGENCY
A type of administrative agency that is under the authority of the president, who has the power to appoint and remove federal officers.

INDEPENDENT REGULATORY AGENCY
A type of administrative agency that is not subject to the authority of the president and whose officials cannot be removed without cause.

Administrative Process

The basic functions of an administrative agency include making rules, investigating activities regulated by the agency, enforcing the agency's rules, and adjudicating disputes between the agency and those who may be subject to its rules. These functions make up what is called the **administrative process** (the administration of law by administrative agencies, in contrast to judicial process, which involves the administration of law by the courts).

The Administrative Procedure Act (APA) of 1946 imposes requirements that all federal agencies must follow. The APA is an integral part of the administrative process.

ADMINISTRATIVE PROCESS
The procedure used by administrative agencies in the administration of law.

RULEMAKING
The actions undertaken by administrative agencies when formally adopting new regulations or amending old ones.

LEARNING OBJECTIVE NO. 1
Explaining the Rulemaking Function of Administrative Agencies

RULEMAKING

An agency's formulation of new regulations is known as **rulemaking.** In an agency's enabling legislation, Congress confers the agency's power to make rules. For example, the Occupational Safety and Health Act of 1970 authorized the Occupational Health and Safety Administration (OSHA) to develop and issue rules governing safety in the workplace. In 1991, OSHA issued a new rule regulating the health-care industry to prevent the spread of such diseases as acquired immune-deficiency syndrome (AIDS). In this rule, OSHA specified various standards—on how contaminated instruments should be handled, for example—with which employers in that industry must comply.

In formulating its rule, OSHA followed one of the rulemaking procedures required by the APA. We look here at the most common rulemaking procedure, called **notice-and-comment rulemaking.** This procedure involves three basic steps: notice of the proposed rulemaking, a comment period, and the final rule.

NOTICE-AND-COMMENT RULEMAKING
A procedure in agency rulemaking that requires (1) notice, (2) opportunity for comment, and (3) a published draft of the final rule.

The Web site of the U.S. Government Printing Office offers access to the Federal Register at

http://www.access.gpo.gov/su_docs

Notice of the Proposed Rulemaking. When a federal agency decides to create a new rule, the agency publishes a notice of the proposed rulemaking proceedings in the *Federal Register,* a daily publication of the executive branch that prints government orders, rules, and regulations. The notice states where and when the proceedings will be held, the agency's authority for making the rule (usually its enabling legislation), and the terms or subject matter of the proposed rule.

Comment Period. Following the publication of the notice, the agency allows time for persons to comment in writing on the proposed rule. The comments may be in writing or, if a hearing is held, may be given orally. The agency need not respond to all comments, but it must respond to any significant comments that bear directly on the proposed rule. The agency responds by either modifying its final rule or explaining, in a statement accompanying the final rule, why it did not make any changes.

The Final Rule. After the agency reviews the comments, it drafts the final rule and publishes it in the *Federal Register.* The final rule is later compiled with the rules and regulations of other federal agencies in the *Code of Federal Regulations* (CFR). Final rules have binding legal effect unless the courts later overturn them.

In the legal problem set out at the beginning of this chapter, the Occupational Safety and Health Administration (OSHA) issues a rule to protect health-care workers from viruses that can be transmitted in the blood of patients. Before issuing the rule, OSHA asks whether the restrictions materially reduce a significant workplace risk to human health without imperiling the existence of, or threatening massive dislocation to, the health care industry. The American Dental Association objects to the rule on the ground that OSHA did not prove that dental workers are sufficiently at risk to benefit from the rule. *Can the rule be set aside for this reason?* No. OSHA cannot impose onerous requirements on an industry that does not pose substantial hazards to the safety or health of its workers. The agency is not required, however, to issue separate rules for each workplace. If an agency provides a rational explanation for its rules, the rules will not be set aside.

INVESTIGATION

LEARNING OBJECTIVE NO. 2

Describing the Investigation Function of Agencies

Administrative agencies conduct investigations of the entities that they regulate. A typical investigation occurs during the rulemaking process to obtain information about a certain industry. The purpose of such an investigation is to issue a rule that is based on a consideration of relevant factors. After final rules are issued, agencies conduct investigations to monitor compliance with those rules.

Inspections and Tests. Many agencies gather information through on-site inspections. Sometimes, inspecting an office, a factory, or some other business facility is the only way to obtain the evidence to prove a regulatory violation. At other times, an inspection or test is used in place of a formal hearing to correct or prevent an undesirable condition. Administrative inspections and tests cover a wide range of activities, including safety inspections of mines, safety tests of equipment, and environmental monitoring of factory emissions. An agency may also ask a firm or individual to submit certain documents or records to the agency for examination.

If a business firm refuses to comply with an agency request to inspect facilities or business records, the agency may resort to the use of a subpoena or a search warrant.

Subpoenas. There are two basic types of subpoenas. The subpoena *ad testificandum* ("to testify") is the technical term for an ordinary subpoena. It is a writ, or order, compelling a witness to appear at an agency hearing. The subpoena *duces tecum* ("bring it with you") compels an individual or organization to hand over books, papers, records, or documents to the agency.

There are limits on what an agency can demand. To determine whether an agency is abusing its discretion in its pursuit of information, a court may consider such factors as the following:

- The purpose of the investigation. An investigation must have a legitimate purpose. An improper purpose is, for example, harassment.
- The relevancy of the information. Information is relevant if it reveals that the law is being violated or if it assures the agency that the law is not being violated.
- The specificity of the demand for testimony or documents. A subpoena must, for example, adequately describe what is being sought.
- The burden of the demand on the party from whom the information is sought. In responding to a request for information, a party is protected, for example, from revealing trade secrets.

IN THE COURTROOM

Natalie is a director of the First National Bank when it is declared insolvent. As part of an investigation into the bank's finances, the Federal Deposit Insurance Corporation (FDIC) issues a subpoena to Natalie for her personal financial records relating to gains and losses in her assets. She objects that the subpoena intrudes on her privacy. The FDIC says that it needs to determine whether she used bank funds for her personal benefit and asks a court to enforce the subpoena. *Will the court enforce the subpoena?* Yes. When personal documents of individuals are the subject of an administrative subpoena, privacy concerns must be considered. But there is a significant public interest in promptly resolving the affairs of insolvent banks on behalf of their creditors and depositors. The FDIC has a reasonable need to gain access to some of Natalie's records to determine whether she improperly used bank funds for her personal benefit.

Search Warrants. The Fourth Amendment protects against unreasonable searches and seizures by requiring that in most instances a physical search for evidence must be conducted under the authority of a search warrant. An agency's search warrant is an order directing law-enforcement officials to search a specific place for a specific item and present it to the agency.

Agencies can conduct warrantless searches in several situations. Warrants are not required to conduct searches in highly regulated industries. Firms that sell firearms or liquor, for example, are automatically subject to inspections without warrants. Sometimes, a statute permits warrantless searches of certain types of hazardous operations, such as coal mines. Also, a warrantless inspection in an emergency situation is normally considered reasonable.

If a person who claims to be an OSHA inspector attempts to collect a penalty or sell a product, he or she is NOT an official OSHA inspector.

ADJUDICATION

After conducting an investigation of a suspected rule violation, an agency may begin to take administrative action against an individual or organization. Most administrative actions are resolved through negotiated settlements at their initial stages.

Negotiated Settlements. Depending on the agency, negotiations may take the form of a simple conversation or a series of informal conferences. The purpose is to correct the problem to the agency's satisfaction and eliminate the need for additional proceedings.

Formal Complaints. If a settlement cannot be reached, the agency may issue a formal *complaint* against the suspected violator. If the Environmental Protection Agency (EPA), for example, finds that a factory is polluting groundwater in violation of federal pollution laws, the EPA will issue a complaint against the violator in an effort to bring the plant into compliance with federal regulations. The factory charged in the complaint will respond by filing an *answer* to the EPA's allegations. If the factory and the EPA cannot agree on a settlement, the case is

EXHIBIT 39–1 The Process of Administrative Adjudication

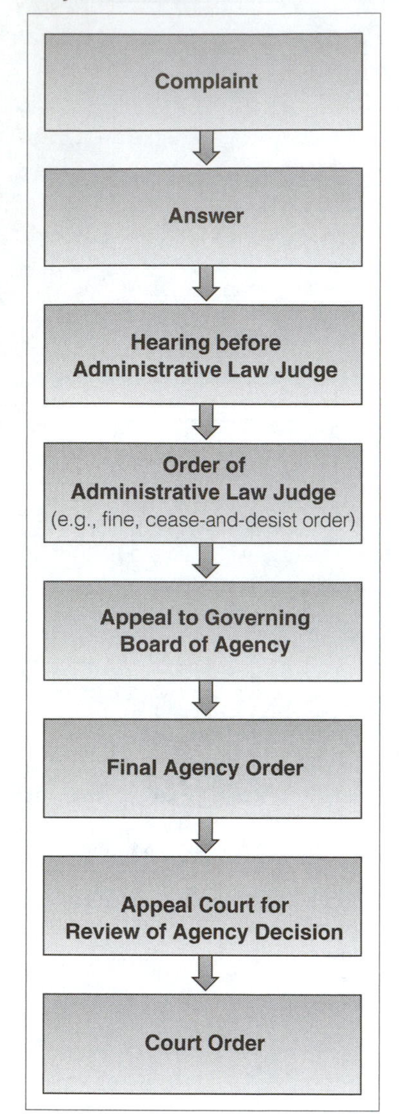

heard in a trial-like setting before an **administrative law judge (ALJ).** The adjudication process is described below and illustrated in Exhibit 39–1.

The Role of an Administrative Law Judge. The ALJ presides over the hearing and has the power to administer oaths, take testimony, rule on questions of evidence, and make determinations of fact. The law requires an ALJ to be an unbiased adjudicator (judge).

Certain safeguards prevent bias on the part of the ALJ and promote fairness in the proceedings. For example, the Administrative Procedure Act requires that the ALJ be separate from the agency's investigative and prosecutorial staff. The APA prohibits private communications between the ALJ and any party to a proceeding, such as the EPA or the factory in our example. The APA also protects the ALJ from agency disciplinary actions unless there is good cause.

Hearing Procedures. Hearing procedures vary widely from agency to agency. Often, disputes are resolved through informal proceedings. For example, the parties, their lawyers, and the ALJ may simply meet at a table in a conference room to settle a dispute.

A formal hearing, in contrast, resembles a trial. Before the hearing, the parties are permitted to undertake extensive discovery (as described in Chapter 3). During the hearing, the parties may give testimony, present other evidence, and cross-examine witnesses.

A difference between a trial and an agency hearing is that normally, much more information, including hearsay (secondhand information offered for its truth), can be introduced as evidence during an administrative hearing.

Agency Orders. Following a hearing, the ALJ renders an **initial order,** or decision. Either party may appeal the ALJ's decision to the board or commission that governs the agency. In our example, if the factory is dissatisfied with the ALJ's decision, it may appeal the decision to the commission that governs the EPA. If the factory is dissatisfied with the commission's decision, it may appeal the decision to a federal court of appeals. If no party appeals the case, the ALJ's decision becomes the **final order** of the agency. If a party does appeal the case, the final order comes from the commission's decision or that of the reviewing court. If a party appeals and the commission and the court decline to review the case, the ALJ's decision also becomes final.

ADMINISTRATIVE LAW JUDGE
One who presides over an administrative agency hearing and has the power to administer oaths, take testimony, rule on questions of evidence, and make determinations of fact.

INITIAL ORDER
In the context of administrative law, an agency's disposition in a matter other than a rulemaking. An administrative law judge's initial order becomes final unless it is appealed.

FINAL ORDER
The final decision of an administrative agency on an issue.

IN THE COURTROOM

American Mining, Inc. (AMI), operates a coal mine. When Greg Rich, an inspector for the Mine Safety and Health Administration (MSHA), inspects the mine, he notes an accumulation of coal dust in the feeder area, where mined coal is transferred from mine shuttle cars to conveyor belts. Rich issues a citation, charging AMI with violating a regulation that requires mine operators to keep feeder areas clean. After hearing evidence from both sides, an ALJ fines AMI $2,000. AMI asks the MSHA to review the case. It declines. *Does the ALJ's order become final?* Yes, unless a party appeals to a court, and the court agrees to review the order. Even if a court does agree to a review, however, it may decide to uphold the agency's order.

Limitations on Agency Powers

Administrative agencies have considerable power. One of the major objectives of the government is to control the abuse of this power without hindering the effective use of it to deal with particular problem areas.

The judicial branch of the government exercises control over agency powers through the courts' review of agency actions. The executive and legislative branches of government also exercise control over agency authority.

LEARNING OBJECTIVE NO. 3

Identifying How Agency Authority is Held in Check

Judicial Controls

The APA provides for judicial review of most agency decisions. If the factory in the above example is dissatisfied with the agency's order, it can appeal the decision to a federal appeals court. Agency actions are not automatically subject to judicial review, however. Parties seeking review must meet certain requirements, including those listed here:

- The action must be *reviewable* by the court. The APA provides that unless proven otherwise, agency actions are reviewable, making this requirement easy to satisfy.
- The party must have *standing* to sue the agency (the party must have a direct stake in the outcome).
- The party must have *exhausted* all possible administrative remedies. Each agency has its "chain of review," and the party must follow agency appeal procedures before a court will review the case.

Appellate courts normally defer to the decisions of administrative agencies on questions of fact. When reviewing an agency decision, a court considers the following types of issues:

- Whether the agency exceeded its authority under its enabling legislation.
- Whether the agency properly interpreted the laws that apply to the action under review.
- Whether the agency violated any constitutional provisions.
- Whether the agency followed the procedural requirements of the law.
- Whether the agency's actions were arbitrary, capricious, or an abuse of discretion.
- Whether any conclusions drawn by the agency are not supported by substantial evidence.

IN THE COURTROOM

National Message Centers (NMC) buys telephone service from International Communications, Inc. (ICI). ICI's tariff (a public document setting out rates and rules relating to ICI's services) states that the "subscriber shall be responsible for the payment of all charges for service." Computer hackers obtain the access code for NMC's lines and make $10,000 in long distance calls. NMC asks ICI to absorb the cost. ICI refuses. NMC complains to the Federal Communications Commission (FCC), claiming that ICI's tariff is too vague. The FCC rejects the complaint. NMC asks a court to review the case. *Is the FCC's decision in this case arbitrary and capricious?* No. ICI's tariff sets out its customer's obligation to pay "all charges for service." This is clear and definite. If ICI provides the service, the customer must pay.

Executive Controls

The executive branch of government exercises control over agencies through the president's powers to appoint federal officers and through the president's veto powers. The president may veto enabling legislation presented by Congress or congressional attempts to modify an existing agency's authority.

Legislative Controls

Congress exercises authority over agency powers. Through enabling legislation, Congress gives power to an agency. An agency may not exceed the power that Congress gives to it. Through later legislation, Congress can take away that power or even abolish an agency altogether. Congressional authority is required to fund an agency, and enabling legislation usually sets time and monetary limits relating to particular programs. Congress can always change these limits. In addition, Congress can investigate the agencies that it creates.

Other legislative checks on agency actions include the Administrative Procedure Act, discussed earlier in this chapter, and the laws discussed in the next section.

Public Accountability

There are several laws that make agencies more accountable through public scrutiny. We discuss here the most significant of these laws.

Freedom of Information Act

LEARNING OBJECTIVE NO. 4

Stating What the Freedom of Information Act Requires

Enacted in 1966, the Freedom of Information Act (FOIA) requires the federal government to disclose certain "records" to "any person" on request, even without any reason being given for the request. Some records are exempt. For most records, a request need only include a reasonable description of the information sought. An agency's failure to comply with a request may be challenged in a federal district court. The media, public interest groups, and even companies seeking information about competitors may obtain information from government agencies under this law.

Government-in-the-Sunshine Act

Congress passed the Government-in-the-Sunshine Act in 1976. It requires that "every portion of every meeting of an agency" be open to "public observation." The act also requires that the public be given advance notice of the agency's scheduled meeting and agenda. Closed meetings are permitted, however, when (1) the subject of the meeting concerns accusing any person of a crime, (2) open meetings would frustrate implementation of future agency actions, or (3) the meeting involves matters relating to future litigation or rulemaking. Courts interpret these exceptions to allow open access whenever possible.

Regulatory Flexibility Act

Congress passed the Regulatory Flexibility Act in 1980. Under this act, whenever a new regulation will have a "significant impact upon a substantial number" of small businesses, the agency must conduct a regulatory flexibility analysis. The analysis must measure the cost that the rule would impose on small businesses and must consider less burdensome alternatives. The act also contains provisions to alert small businesses about forthcoming regulations.

Small Business Regulatory Enforcement Fairness Act

The Small Business Regulatory Enforcement Fairness Act (SBREFA) of 1996 allows Congress to review new federal regulations for at least sixty days before they take effect. This period gives opponents of the rules time to present their arguments to Congress.

The SBREFA also requires federal agencies to prepare guides that explain in "plain English" how small businesses can comply with regulations. The act set up the National Enforcement Ombudsman at the Small Business Administration to receive comments from small businesses about their dealings with federal agencies. Based on these comments, Regional Small Business Fairness Boards rate the agencies and publicize their findings.

State Administrative Agencies

LEARNING OBJECTIVE NO. 5
Discussing the Relation Between State and Federal Agencies

State agencies play a significant role in regulating activities within the states. A state often creates an agency as a parallel to a federal agency to provide similar services on a more localized basis. Such parallel agencies include the federal Social Security Administration and the state welfare agency, and the Environmental Protection Agency and the state pollution-control agency.

If the actions of parallel state and federal agencies conflict, the actions of the federal agency prevail. For example, if the Federal Aviation Administration specifies the hours during which airplanes may land at and depart from airports, a state agency cannot issue inconsistent regulations governing the same activities. The priority of federal law over conflicting state laws is based on the supremacy clause of the U.S. Constitution.

TERMS AND CONCEPTS FOR REVIEW

administrative agency 496
administrative law judge (ALJ) 500
administrative process 497
enabling legislation 497
executive agency 497
final order 500
independent regulatory agency 497
initial order 500
notice-and-comment rulemaking 497
rulemaking 497

CHAPTER SUMMARY • ADMINISTRATIVE LAW

Creation and Powers of Administrative Agencies	**1.** Administrative agencies are created by enabling legislation, which usually specifies the name, composition, and powers of the agency. **2.** Administrative agencies exercise enforcement, rulemaking, and adjudicatory powers.
Administrative Process—Rulemaking	**1.** Agencies are authorized to create new regulations. This power is conferred on an agency in the enabling legislation. **2.** *Notice-and-comment rulemaking*—The most common rulemaking procedure. Begins with the publication of the proposed regulation in the *Federal Register.* Publication of the notice is followed by a comment period to allow comments on the proposed rule.
Administrative Process—Investigation	**1.** Administrative agencies investigate the entities that they regulate. Investigations are conducted during the rulemaking process to obtain information and after rules are issued to monitor compliance. **2.** The most important investigative tools available to an agency are the following: **a.** *Inspections and tests*—Used to gather information and to correct or prevent undesirable conditions. **b.** *Subpoenas*—Orders that direct individuals to appear at a hearing or to hand over specified documents. **3.** Limits on administrative investigations include the following: **a.** The investigation must be for a legitimate purpose. **b.** The information sought must be relevant, and the investigative demands must be specific and not unreasonably burdensome. **c.** Search warrants are required in most instances.
Administrative Process—Adjudication	**1.** After a preliminary investigation, an agency may initiate an administrative action against an individual or organization by filing a complaint. Most such actions are resolved at this stage before they go through the formal adjudicatory process. **2.** If there is no settlement, the case is presented to an administrative law judge (ALJ) in a proceeding similar to a trial. **3.** After a case is concluded, the ALJ renders an order that may be appealed by either party in federal appeals court. If no appeal is taken or the case is not reviewed, the order becomes final.

CHAPTER SUMMARY • *Continued*

Limitations on Agency Powers	**1.** *Judicial controls*—Administrative agencies are subject to the judicial review of the courts. A court may review whether— **a.** An agency has exceeded the scope of its enabling legislation. **b.** An agency has properly interpreted the laws. **c.** An agency has violated the U.S. Constitution. **d.** An agency has complied with all applicable procedural requirements. **e.** An agency's actions are arbitrary or capricious, or an abuse of discretion. **f.** An agency's conclusions are not supported by substantial evidence. **2.** *Executive controls*—The president can control administrative agencies through appointments of federal officers and through vetoes of legislation creating or affecting agency powers. **3.** *Legislative controls*—Congress can give power to an agency, take it away, increase or decrease the agency's finances, or abolish the agency. The Administrative Procedure Act of 1946 also limits agencies.
Public Accountability	**1.** *Freedom of Information Act of 1966*—Requires the government to disclose records to "any person" on request. **2.** *Government-in-the-Sunshine Act of 1976*—Requires the following: **a.** Every meeting of an agency must be open to "public observation." **b.** The public must be given advance notice of the agency's scheduled meeting and agenda. **3.** *Regulatory Flexibility Act of 1980*—Requires an analysis whenever a new regulation will have a "significant impact upon a substantial number" of small businesses. **4.** *The Small Business Regulatory Enforcement Fairness Act of 1996*—Allows Congress sixty days to review new regulations. Requires federal agencies to explain in "plain English" how to comply wih regulations. Empowered the Small Business Adminsitration to rate federal agencies based on comments from small businesses.
State Administrative Agencies	States create agencies that parallel federal agencies to provide similar services on a localized basis. If the actions of parallel state and federal agencies conflict, the actions of the federal agency prevail.

HYPOTHETICAL QUESTIONS

39–1. Rulemaking Procedures. Assume that the Food and Drug Administration (FDA), using proper procedures, adopts a rule describing its future investigations. This new rule covers all future cases in which the FDA wants to regulate food additives. Under the new rule, the FDA says that it will not regulate food additives without giving food companies an opportunity to cross-examine witnesses. Some time later, the FDA wants to regulate methylisocyanate, a food additive. In doing so, the FDA undertakes an informal rulemaking procedure, without cross-examination, and regulates methylisocyanate. Producers protest, saying that the FDA promised cross-examination. The FDA responds that the Administrative Procedure Act does not require such cross-examination and that it could freely withdraw the promise made in its new rule. If the producers challenge the FDA in a court, on what basis would the court rule in their favor?

39–2. Rulemaking and Adjudication Powers. For decades, the Federal Trade Commission (FTC) resolved fair trade and advertising disputes through individual adjudications. In the 1960s, the FTC began promulgating rules that defined fair and unfair trade practices. In cases involving violations of these rules, the due process rights of participants were more limited and did not include cross-examination. This was because, although anyone found violating a rule would receive a full adjudication, the legitimacy of the rule itself could not be challenged in the adjudication. Any party charged with violating a rule was almost certain to lose the adjudication. Affected parties complained to a court, arguing that their rights before the FTC were unduly limited by the new rules. What will the court examine to determine whether to uphold the new rules?

REAL WORLD CASE PROBLEM

39–3. Executive Controls. In 1982, the president of the United States appointed Matthew Chabal, Jr., to the position of U.S. marshal. U.S. marshals are assigned to the federal courts. In the fall of 1985, Chabal received an unsatisfactory annual performance rating, and he was fired shortly thereafter by the president. Given that U.S. marshals are assigned to the federal courts, are these appointees members of the executive branch? Did the president have the right to fire Chabal without consulting Congress about the decision? [*Chabal v. Reagan*, 841 F.2d 1216 (3d Cir. 1988)]

For updated links to resources available on the Web, as well as a variety of other materials, visit this text's Web site at **http://blte.westbuslaw.com**.

The Federal Web Locator permits searches for the names of federal administrative agencies and provides links to agency-related information. Go to

http://www.infoctr.edu/fwl

ONLINE LEGAL RESEARCH

Go to **http://blte.westbuslaw.com**, the Web site that accompanies this text. Select "Internet Applications," and then click on "Chapter 39." There you will find the following Internet research exercise that you can perform to learn more about how to obtain information from government agencies:

Activity 39–1: The Freedom of Information Act

Chapter 39 ■ WORK SET

TRUE-FALSE QUESTIONS

_____ **1.** Enabling legislation specifies the powers of an agency.

_____ **2.** Most federal agencies are part of the executive branch of government.

_____ **3.** To create an agency, Congress enacts enabling legislation.

_____ **4.** After an agency adjudication, the administrative law judge's order must be appealed to become final.

_____ **5.** The Administrative Procedure Act provides for judicial review of most agency actions.

_____ **6.** When a new regulation will have a significant impact on a substantial number of small entities, an analysis must be conducted to measure the cost imposed on small businesses.

_____ **7.** State administrative agency operations prevail over federal agency actions.

_____ **8.** An agency cannot conduct a search without a warrant.

MULTIPLE-CHOICE QUESTIONS

_____ **1.** Congress has the power to establish administrative agencies to perform which of the following functions?

a. Make administrative rules.
b. Adjudicate disputes arising from administrative rules.
c. Investigate violations of administrative rules.
d. All of the above.

_____ **2.** An agency may obtain information concerning activities and organizations that it oversees through

a. a subpoena only.
b. a search only.
c. a subpoena and a search.
d. neither a subpoena nor a search.

_____ **3.** The Occupational Safety and Health Administration (OSHA) issues a subpoena for Triplex Corporation to hand over all of its files. Triplex's possible defenses against the subpoena include

a. OSHA is a federal agency, but Triplex only does business locally.
b. an administrative agency cannot issue a subpoena.
c. the demand is not specific enough.
d. none of the above.

_____ **4.** In making rules, an agency's procedure normally includes

a. notice.
b. opportunity for comments by interested parties.
c. publication of the final draft of the rule.
d. all of the above.

_____ **5.** The National Oceanic and Atmospheric Administration (NOAA) is a federal agency. To limit the authority of NOAA, the president can

a. abolish the agency.
b. take away the agency's power.
c. veto legislative modifications to the agency's authority.
d. refuse to appropriate funds to the agency.

_____ **6.** The Bureau of Indian Affairs (BIA) wants to close a series of its meetings to the public. To open the meetings, a citizen would sue the BIA under

a. the Freedom of Information Act.
b. the Government-in-the-Sunshine Act.
c. the Regulatory Flexibility Act.
d. the Administrative Procedure Act.

_____ **7.** The United States Fish and Wildlife Service orders Bill to stop using a certain type of fishing net from his fishing boat. Before a court will hear Bill's appeal of the order, Bill must

a. exhaust all administrative remedies.
b. bypass all administrative remedies and appeal directly to the court.
c. appeal simultaneously to the agency and the court.
d. ignore the agency and continue using the net.

_____ **8.** The Federal Trade Commission (FTC) issues an order relating to the advertising of Midtron Corporation. Midtron appeals the order to a court. The court may review whether the FTC has

a. exceeded its authority.
b. taken an action that is arbitrary, capricious, or an abuse of discretion.
c. violated any constitutional provisions.
d. any of the above.

_____ **9.** The Environmental Protection Agency (EPA) publishes notice of a proposed rule. When comments are received about the rule, the EPA must respond to

a. all of the comments.
b. any significant comments that bear directly on the proposed rule.
c. only comments by businesses engaged in interstate commerce.
d. none of the comments.

ISSUE SPOTTERS

1. The Securities and Exchange Commission (SEC) makes rules regarding what must be in a stock prospectus, prosecutes and adjudicates alleged violations, and prescribes punishment. This gives the SEC considerable power. What checks are there against this power?

2. Itex Corporation would like to know what information federal agencies have about Itex's business operations, so that Itex will know what its competitors may be able to learn about it. Under what federal law can Itex require the agencies to disclose whatever information they may have concerning it?

Antitrust and Environmental Law

40

LEARNING OBJECTIVES

When you finish this chapter, you should be able to:

1. List anticompetitive activities prohibited by the antitrust laws.
2. State who can enforce the antitrust laws.
3. Identify exemptions from antitrust laws.
4. Discuss the regulation of hazardous waste disposal sites.

FACING A LEGAL PROBLEM

A group of independent oil producers in Texas and Louisiana were caught between falling demand due to bad economic times and increasing supply from newly discovered oil fields in the region. In response to these conditions, a group of the major refining companies agreed to buy excess supplies from the independents so as to dispose of the excess supplies in an "orderly manner." It was clear that the purpose was to limit the supply of gasoline on the market and thereby raise prices. In a lawsuit challenging the agreement, the producers claimed that under the circumstances, the agreement was reasonable. *Did the agreement violate the law?*

Important areas of business regulations include antitrust legislation and environmental laws. Antitrust legislation is based on the desire to foster competition. Antitrust legislation was initially created—and continues to be enforced—because of our belief that competition leads to lower prices, more product information, and a better distribution of wealth between consumers and producers. Environmental protection is an even more recent form of government regulation. In the last three decades, a growing body of environmental law has been created. In the last part of this chapter, we examine some of the major statutes that seek to protect our environment.

ANTITRUST LAW
The body of federal and state laws and statutes protecting trade and commerce from unlawful restraints, price discrimination, price fixing, and monopolies. The principal federal antitrust statutes are the Sherman Act (1890), the Clayton Act (1914), and the Federal Trade Commission Act (1914).

RESTRAINT OF TRADE
Any conspiracy or combination that unlawfully eliminates competition or facilitates the creation of a monopoly or monopoly pricing.

Antitrust Law

LEARNING OBJECTIVE NO. 1
Listing Anticompetitive Activities Prohibited by the Antitrust Laws

Laws that regulate economic competition are referred to as **antitrust laws.** Today's antitrust laws are the direct descendants of common law actions intended to limit **restraints of trade** (agreements between firms that have the effect of reducing competition in the marketplace). Concern arose following the Civil War over the growth of large corporate enterprises and their attempts to reduce or eliminate competition. At the national level, the government recognized the problem and passed the Sherman Act in 1890. In 1914, Congress passed the

Clayton Act, as well as the Federal Trade Commission Act, to further curb anticompetitive business practices.

THE SHERMAN ACT

The Sherman Act of 1890 is the most important antitrust law. It provides:

> 1: Every contract, combination in the form of trust or otherwise, or conspiracy, in restraint of trade or commerce among the several States, or with foreign nations, is hereby declared to be illegal [and is a crime punishable by fine and/or imprisonment].
>
> 2: Every person who shall monopolize [*monopolize* is defined later in this chapter], or attempt to monopolize, or combine or conspire with any other person or persons, to monopolize any part of the trade or commerce among the several States, or with foreign nations, shall be deemed guilty of a felony [and is similarly punishable].

Jurisdictional Requirements. Any activity that substantially affects interstate commerce (trade between two or more states) falls under the Sherman Act. The Sherman Act also extends to U.S. nationals abroad who are engaged in activities that affect U.S. foreign commerce.

The Rule of Reason. The underlying assumption of Section 1 of the Sherman Act is that society's welfare is harmed if rival firms are permitted to join in an agreement that consolidates their market power or otherwise restrains competition. Not all agreements between rivals, however, result in enhanced market power or *unreasonably* restrain trade. Under what is called the **rule of reason,** anticompetitive agreements that supposedly violate Section 1 of the Sherman Act are analyzed with the view that they may, in fact, constitute reasonable restraints of trade. When applying this rule, the court considers the purpose of the arrangement, the powers of the parties, and the effect of their actions in restraining trade. If the court deems that legitimate competitive benefits outweigh the anticompetitive effects of the agreement, it will be held lawful.

RULE OF REASON
A test by which a court balances the reasons (such as economic efficiency) for an agreement against its potentially anticompetitive effects. In antitrust litigation, many practices are analyzed under the rule of reason.

For example, an agreement between a manufacturer and a distributor or retailer in which the manufacturer specifies what the retail prices of its products must be is subject to the rule of reason. Such an agreement is referred to as a **resale price maintenance agreement.**

RESALE PRICE MAINTENANCE AGREEMENT
An agreement between a manufacturer and a retailer in which the manufacturer specifies the minimum retail price of its products.

***Per Se* Violations.** Some agreements are so blatantly and substantially anticompetitive that they are deemed illegal *per se* (on their face, or inherently) under Section 1. If an agreement is found to be of a type that is deemed a ***per se* violation,** a court is prevented from determining whether the agreement's benefits outweigh its anticompetitive effects.

***PER SE* VIOLATION**
A type of anticompetitive agreement—such as a price-fixing agreement—that is considered to be so injurious to the public that there is no need to determine whether it actually injures market competition; rather, it is in itself *(per se)* a violation of the Sherman Act.

Price-Fixing Agreements. One *per se* violation of Section 1 is a **price-fixing agreement** (an agreement among competitors to set prices).

PRICE-FIXING AGREEMENT
Fixing—by means of an anticompetitive agreement between competitors—the prices of products or services.

In the legal problem set out at the beginning of this chapter, a group of independent oil producers in Texas and Louisiana were caught between falling demand due to bad economic times and increasing supply from newly discovered oil fields in the region. In response to these conditions, a group of the major refining companies agreed to buy excess supplies from the independents so as to dispose of the excess supplies in an "orderly manner." It was clear that the purpose was to limit the supply of gasoline on the market and thereby raise prices. In a lawsuit challenging the agreement, the producers claimed that under the circumstances, the agreement was reasonable. *Did the agreement violate the law?* Yes. Any agreement among competitors to restrict output or fix prices constitutes a *per se* violation of Section 1 of the Sherman Act. The "reasonableness" of a price-fixing agreement is never a defense.

Group Boycotts. Another *per se* violation of Section 1 of the Sherman Act is a group boycott. A **group boycott** is an agreement by two or more sellers to boycott, or refuse to deal with, a particular person or firm. Section 1 will be violated if it can be demonstrated that the boycott or joint refusal to deal was undertaken with the intention of eliminating competition or preventing entry into a given market.

GROUP BOYCOTT
The boycott of a particular person or firm by a group of competitors; prohibited under the Sherman Act.

Market Divisions. It is a *per se* violation of Section 1 of the Sherman Act for competitors to divide up territories or customers.

IN THE COURTROOM

Manufacturers A, B, and C compete against one another in the states of Kansas, Nebraska, and Iowa. By agreement, A sells products only in Kansas; B sells only in Nebraska; and C sells only in Iowa. This concerted action reduces costs and allows all three (assuming there is no other competition) to raise the price of the goods sold in their respective states. *Is this a violation of Section 1 of the Sherman Act?* Yes. Any agreement to divide up territories is a *per se* violation. *Would the same violation take place if A, B, and C had simply agreed that A would sell only to institutional purchasers (school districts, universities, state agencies and departments, cities, and so on) in the three states, B only to wholesalers, and C only to retailers?* Yes.

Monopolies. Two distinct types of behavior are subject to sanction under Section 2 of the Sherman Act: *monopolization* and *attempts to monopolize.* Monopolization cases deal with the structure of a **monopoly.** The term *monopoly* is generally used to describe a market in which there is a single seller. Section 2 looks at the misuse of **monopoly power** in the marketplace. Monopoly power exists when a firm has an extreme amount of **market power**—the power to affect the market price of its product. To be a violation of the Sherman Act, the power must have been acquired or maintained willfully.

Cases involving attempts to monopolize are concerned with actions that (1) are intended to exclude competitors and garner monopoly power and (2) have a dangerous probability of success.

MONOPOLY
A term generally used to describe a market for which there is a single seller.

MONOPOLY POWER
An extreme amount of market power.

MARKET POWER
The power of a firm to control the market for its product. A monopoly has the greatest degree of market power.

THE CLAYTON ACT

In 1914, Congress attempted to strengthen federal antitrust laws by enacting the Clayton Act. The Clayton Act was aimed at four specific anticompetitive or monopolistic practices that were not covered by the Sherman Act. The Clayton Act makes these practices illegal only if they substantially lessen competition or tend to create monopoly power.

Price Discrimination. When a seller charges different prices to different buyers for identical goods, it is **price discrimination.** As amended by the Robinson-Patman Act in 1936, the Clayton Act prohibits certain classes of price discrimination that cannot be justified by differences in production or transportation costs. Under the act, sellers are prohibited from reducing prices to levels substantially below those charged by their competitors unless the reduction can be justified by demonstrating that the lower price was charged "in good faith to meet an equally low price of a competitor."

PRICE DISCRIMINATION
Setting prices in such a way that two competing buyers pay two different prices for an identical product or service.

Exclusionary Practices. Under the Clayton Act, sellers or lessors (those who lease goods) cannot sell or lease on the condition that the buyer or lessee will not use or deal in the goods of the seller's competitors. This effectively prohibits two types of agreements: exclusive-dealing contracts and tying arrangements.

Exclusive-Dealing Contract
An agreement under which a producer of goods agrees to sell its goods exclusively through one distributor.

Exclusive-Dealing Contracts. A contract under which a seller forbids a buyer to purchase products from the seller's competitors is called an **exclusive-dealing contract.** An exclusive-dealing contract is prohibited if the effect of the contract is to substantially lessen competition or to tend to create a monopoly.

IN THE COURTROOM

The largest gasoline seller in the nation made exclusive-dealing contracts with independent gasoline stations in seven western states. The contracts involved 16 percent of all retail outlets, whose sales were approximately 7 percent of all retail sales in that market. At the time, the next six largest gasoline suppliers all used exclusive-dealing contracts with their independent retailers. Together, these seven suppliers controlled 65 percent of the market. *Did these contracts violate the Clayton Act?* Yes. Because the seven largest gasoline suppliers used exclusive-dealing contracts with their independent retailers and together controlled 65 percent of the market, the effect was to substantially lessen competition. Any new competitor's attempt to enter into that market would be effectively blocked.

Tying Arrangement
An agreement between a buyer and a seller under which the buyer of a specific product or service is obligated to purchase additional products or services from the seller.

Tying Arrangements. When a seller conditions the sale of a product (the tying product) on the buyer's agreement to purchase another product (the tied product) produced or distributed by the same seller, a **tying arrangement,** or *tie-in sales agreement,* results. The legality of such an agreement depends on many factors, particularly the purpose of the agreement and the agreement's likely effect on competition in the relevant markets.

IN THE COURTROOM

Alpha, Inc., manufactures computer hardware and provides repair service for the hardware. Alpha also makes and markets software and support for those who use the software, but the company refuses to provide software support to those who do not buy its hardware service. *Is Alpha's practice a tying arrangement?* Yes. When a seller conditions the sale of its product on the purchase of another product produced or distributed by the same seller, a tying arrangement results. Depending on the purpose of the agreement and the effect of the agreement on competition in the market for the two products, the agreement may be illegal.

Market Concentration
A situation that exists when a small number of firms share the market for a particular good or service. For example, if the four largest grocery stores in Chicago accounted for 80 percent of all retail food sales, the market clearly would be concentrated in those four firms.

Mergers. A *merger* occurs when one business firm absorbs the assets and liabilities of another, so that the other ceases to exist. A business organization cannot merge with another if the effect may be to substantially lessen competition. A crucial consideration is **market concentration,** which refers to the market shares among the various firms in a market. For example, if the four largest grocery stores in Chicago accounted for 80 percent of all retail food sales, that market clearly would be concentrated in those four firms. If one of these stores absorbed the assets and liabilities of another, so that the other ceased to exist, the result would be a merger that would more clearly concentrate the market and thereby possibly diminish competition. Competition, however, is not necessarily diminished solely as a result of market concentration. Other factors will be considered in determining whether a merger violates the Clayton Act, including whether the merger will make it more difficult for potential competitors to enter the market.

Interlocking Directorates. The Clayton Act deals with *interlocking directorates*—that is, the practice of having individuals serve as directors on the boards of two or more competing companies simultaneously. No person may be a director in two or more corporations at the same time if either of the corporations has capital, surplus, or undivided profits aggregating more than $16,732,000 or if the competitive sales of the company are $1,673,200 or more. The FTC adjusts the threshold amounts each year. (The amounts given here are those announced by the FTC in 2000.)

THE FEDERAL TRADE COMMISSION ACT

The Federal Trade Commission Act was enacted in 1914. It provides, in part, that "unfair methods of competition in or affecting commerce, and unfair or deceptive acts or practices in or affecting commerce are hereby declared illegal." The act condemns all forms of anticompetitive behavior that are not covered under other federal antitrust laws. The act also created the Federal Trade Commission, an administrative agency with functions that include antitrust enforcement and other duties relating to consumer protection (see Chapter 20).

Exercise caution when communicating and dealing with competitors.

ENFORCEMENT OF ANTITRUST LAWS

LEARNING OBJECTIVE NO. 2
Stating Who Can Enforce the Antitrust Laws

The federal agencies that enforce the federal antitrust laws are the U.S. Department of Justice (DOJ) and the Federal Trade Commission (FTC). The DOJ can prosecute violations of the Sherman Act as either criminal or civil violations. Violations of the Clayton Act are not crimes, and the DOJ can enforce that statute only through civil proceedings. The various remedies that the DOJ has asked the courts to impose include **divestiture** (making a company give up one or more of its operating functions) and dissolution. The DOJ might force a group of meat packers, for example, to divest itself of control or ownership of butcher shops. The FTC also enforces the Clayton Act (but not the Sherman Act) and has sole authority to enforce violations of the Federal Trade Commission Act.

DIVESTITURE
The act of selling one or more of a company's parts, such as a subsidiary or plant; often mandated by the courts in merger or monopolization cases.

A private party can sue for treble (triple) damages and attorneys' fees under the Clayton Act if the party is injured as a result of a violation of any of the federal antitrust laws, except of the Federal Trade Commission Act. A person wishing to sue under the Sherman Act must prove (1) that the antitrust violation either caused or was a substantial factor in causing the injury that was suffered and (2) that the unlawful actions of the accused party affected business activities of the plaintiff that were protected by the antitrust laws.

EXEMPTIONS FROM ANTITRUST LAWS

LEARNING OBJECTIVE NO. 3
Identifying Exemptions from Antitrust Laws

There are many limitations on antitrust enforcement. Most exemptions to the antitrust laws apply to the following areas or activities:

1. *Labor.* The Clayton Act generally permits labor unions to organize and bargain without violating antitrust laws and specifies that strikes and other labor activities are not violations of any law of the United States.
2. *Agricultural associations and fisheries.* Agricultural cooperatives are exempt from the antitrust laws. Individuals in the fishing industry who collectively catch, produce, and prepare for market their products are also exempt. Members of such co-ops may combine and set prices for a particular product, but they cannot engage in exclusionary practices or restraints of trade directed at competitors.
3. *Insurance.* The insurance business is exempt from the antitrust laws whenever state regulation exists. This exemption does not cover boycotts, coercion, or intimidation on the part of insurance companies.
4. *Foreign trade.* American exporters may engage in cooperative activity to compete with similar foreign associations. This type of cooperative activity may not, however, restrain trade within the United States or injure other American exporters.

5. *Professional baseball.* In 1922, the United States Supreme Court held that professional baseball is not within the reach of federal antitrust laws.
6. *Oil marketing.* States may set quotas on oil that will be marketed in interstate commerce.
7. *Cooperative research and production.* Cooperative research among small business firms is exempt. Research or production of a product, process, or service by joint ventures consisting of competitors is exempt.
8. *Joint efforts by businesspersons to obtain legislative or executive action.* For example, video producers might jointly lobby Congress to change the copyright laws, or a video-rental company might sue another video-rental firm, without being held liable for attempting to restrain trade. An action will not be protected, however, if it is clear that the action is "objectively baseless in the sense that no reasonable [person] could reasonably expect success on the merits" and it is an attempt to make anticompetitive use of government processes.
9. *Other exemptions.* Other activities exempt from antitrust laws include activities approved by the president in furtherance of the defense of our nation, state actions, when the state policy is clearly articulated and the policy is actively supervised by the state; and activities of regulated industries (such as the communication and banking industries) when federal commissions, boards, or agencies (such as the Federal Communications Commission) have primary regulatory authority.

Environmental Law

We now turn to a discussion of the various ways in which businesses are regulated by government in the interest of protecting the environment. Concern over the destruction of the environment has increased over time in response to the environmental effects of population growth, urbanization, and industrialization.

State and Local Regulation

Many states regulate the degree to which the environment may be polluted. State laws may restrict a business's discharge of chemicals into the air or water or regulate its disposal of toxic wastes. States may also regulate the disposal or recycling of other wastes, including glass, metal, plastic containers, and paper. Additionally, states may restrict the emissions from motor vehicles.

City, county, and other local governments control some aspects of the environment. For instance, local zoning laws may be designed to direct the growth of cities and suburbs. Other aspects of the environment may be subject to local regulation. Methods of waste and garbage removal and disposal, for example, can have a substantial impact on a community. The appearance of buildings and other structures, including advertising signs and billboards, may affect traffic safety, property values, or local aesthetics.

Federal Regulation

Congress has passed a number of statutes to control the impact of human activities on the environment. Some of these have been passed in an attempt to improve the quality of air and water. Some of them regulate toxic chemicals specifically.

Environmental Impact Statement (EIS)
A statement required by the National Environmental Policy Act for any major federal action that will significantly affect the quality of the environment. The statement must analyze the action's impact on the environment and alternative actions that might be taken.

Environmental Responsibilities. The National Environmental Policy Act (NEPA) of 1969 imposes environmental responsibilities on all agencies of the federal government. NEPA requires that all agencies consider environmental factors when making significant decisions. For every major federal action that significantly affects the quality of the environment, an **environmental impact statement (EIS)** must be prepared. An EIS analyzes the effect of the action and its alternatives on the environment.

In 1970, the Environmental Protection Agency (EPA) was created to coordinate federal environmental responsibilities. The EPA administers most federal environmental policies and statutes. Other federal agencies that regulate specific environmental matters include the Department of the Interior, the Department of Defense, the Department of Labor, the Food and Drug Administration, and the Nuclear Regulatory Commission.

Air Pollution. In 1963, the federal government passed the Clean Air Act, which focused on multistate air pollution. Various amendments, particularly in 1970, 1977, and 1990, strengthened the government's authority to regulate the quality of air.

For information on the standards, guidelines, and regulations of the Environmental Protection Agency, go to

http://www.epa.gov

These laws provide the basis for issuing regulations to control pollution coming primarily from stationary sources (such as electric utilities and industrial plants) and motor vehicles. The EPA sets air quality standards for major pollutants. General guidelines set out requirements for protecting vegetation, climate, visibility, and certain economic conditions.

Mobile Sources. Regulations governing air pollution from automobiles and other mobile sources specify pollution standards and time schedules for meeting the standards.

For example, under the 1990 amendments, automobile manufacturers were required to cut new automobiles' exhaust emissions of nitrogen oxide by 60 percent and emission of other pollutants by 35 percent. To ensure compliance, the EPA certifies the prototype of a new automobile whose emission controls are effective up to 50,000 miles. The EPA may also inspect production models. If a vehicle does not meet the standards in actual driving, the EPA can order a recall and the repair or replacement of pollution-control equipment at the manufacturer's expense.

The EPA attempts to update pollution-control standards when new scientific information becomes available. In light of purported evidence that very small particles (2.5 microns, or millionths of a meter) of soot affect our health as significantly as larger particles, the EPA issued new particulate standards for motor vehicle exhaust systems and other sources of pollution. The EPA also decreased the acceptable standard for ozone, which is formed when sunlight combines with pollutants from cars and other sources. Ozone is the basic ingredient of smog.

Stationary Sources. The primary responsibility for preventing and controlling air pollution rests with state and local governments. The EPA sets primary and secondary levels of ambient standards—that is, the maximum levels of certain pollutants—and the states formulate plans to achieve those standards.

Different standards apply to sources of pollution in clean areas and sources in polluted areas. Different standards also apply to existing sources of pollution and major new sources. Major new sources include existing sources modified by a change in a method of operation that increases emissions. Performance standards for major sources require use of the *maximum achievable control technology,* or MACT, to reduce emissions from the combustion of fossil fuels (coal and oil). The EPA issues guidelines as to what equipment meets this standard.

Under the 1990 amendments to the Clean Air Act, 110 of the oldest coal-burning power plants in the United States must cut their emissions by 40 percent to reduce acid rain. Utilities were granted "credits" to emit certain amounts of sulfur dioxide, and those that emit less than the allowed amounts can sell their credits to other polluters. Controls on other factories and businesses are intended to reduce ground-level ozone pollution in ninety-six cities to healthful levels by 2005 (except Los Angeles, which has until 2010). Industrial emissions of 189 hazardous air pollutants must be reduced by 90 percent. By 2002, the production of chlorofluorocarbons (such as Freon), carbon tetrachloride, and methyl chloroform—used in air conditioning, refrigeration, and insulation and linked to depletion of the ozone layer—must stop.

Water Pollution. Federal regulations governing the pollution of water include coverage of navigable waters and drinking water.

Navigable Waters. The term *navigable waters* includes coastal and freshwater wetlands, as well as lakes and streams used by interstate travelers and industries. In 1948, Congress passed the Federal Water Pollution Control Act (FWPCA). In 1972, amendments to the FWPCA—known as the Clean Water Act—established goals to (1) make waters safe for swimming, (2) protect fish and wildlife, and (3) eliminate the discharge of pollutants into the water. The amendments set forth specific time schedules to reach these goals. The time schedules were extended by amendment in 1977 and by the Water Quality Act of 1987.

Regulations for the most part specify that the *best available control technology,* or BACT, be installed. The EPA issues guidelines as to what equipment meets this standard, which essentially requires the most effective pollution-control equipment available. New sources must install BACT equipment before beginning operations. Existing sources are subject to timetables for installation of BACT equipment. These sources must immediately install equipment that utilizes the *best practical control technology,* or BPCT. The EPA also issues guidelines as to what equipment meets this standard.

The 1972 amendments also require municipal and industrial polluters to apply for permits before discharging wastes into navigable waters. A polluting party can be required to clean up the pollution or pay for the cost of doing so. The party may also be further penalized.

Drinking Water. Another statute governing water pollution is the Safe Drinking Water Act. Passed in 1974, this act requires the EPA to set maximum levels for pollutants in public water systems. Public water system operators must come as close as possible to meeting the EPA's standards by using the best available technology that is economically feasible. The EPA is particularly concerned with contamination from underground sources.

Under amendments passed in 1996, each supplier of drinking water must send to every household it supplies with water an annual statement describing the source of its water, the level of any contaminants contained in the water, and any possible health concerns associated with the contaminants.

Toxic Chemicals. Control of toxic chemicals is an important part of environmental law.

Pesticides and Herbicides. The federal statute regulating pesticides and herbicides is the Federal Insecticide, Fungicide, and Rodenticide Act (FIFRA) of 1947. Under FIFRA, pesticides and herbicides must be (1) registered before they can be sold, (2) certifed and used only for approved applications, and (3) used in limited quantities when applied to food crops.

Under 1996 amendments to the Federal Food, Drug, and Cosmetic Act, for a pesticide to remain on the market, there must be no more than a one-in-a-million risk to people of developing cancer from exposure in any way, including eating food that contains residues from the pesticide. The EPA must distribute to grocery stores brochures on high-risk pesticides that are in food, and the stores must display these brochures for consumers.

Toxic Substances. The first comprehensive law covering toxic substances was the Toxic Substances Control Act, which was passed in 1976. This act regulates chemicals and chemical compounds that are known to be toxic and institutes investigation of any possible harmful effects from chemical compounds, such as polychlorinated biphenyls (PCBs). The regulations authorize the EPA to require that manufacturers, processors, and other organizations planning to use chemicals first determine their effects on human health and the environment. The EPA can regulate substances that potentially pose an imminent hazard or an unreasonable risk of injury to health or the environment.

Hazardous Waste Disposal Sites. In 1980, Congress passed the Comprehensive Environmental Response, Compensation, and Liability Act (CERCLA), also known as Superfund. Basically, CERCLA provides for the clean-up of hazardous waste disposal sites that threaten environmental safety. When a release or threatened release of hazardous waste from a site (into the soil or ground water, for example) occurs, the EPA can clean up the site and recover the cost of the clean-up from (1) any person who generated the wastes disposed of at the site, (2) any person who transported hazardous wastes to the site, (3) any person who owned or operated the site at the time of the disposal, or (4) the current owner or operator of the site. A person who generated only a fraction of the hazardous waste disposed of at the site may be liable for all of the clean-up costs.

LEARNING OBJECTIVE NO. 4
Discussing the Regulation of Hazardous Waste Disposal Sites

IN THE COURTROOM

Standard Landfill, Inc., owns and operates a landfill site at which hazardous wastes are disposed. National Chemical Corporation generates waste disposed of at the site. When the EPA discovers that waste at Standard's site is being disposed of improperly and has contaminated the soil, the EPA cleans up the site and files suit in a federal district court to recover the costs from Standard and National. *Who may be held liable for the cost of the cleanup?* Standard, National, or any other party who falls into any of the categories of potentially responsible parties. Any of these parties may be liable for the entire cost, even if the party generated only a fraction of the waste.

Radiation. Nuclear power plants are built and operated by private industry. The Nuclear Regulatory Commission (NRC) is the federal agency responsible for regulating the private nuclear industry. The NRC review the plans for each proposed nuclear plant and issues a construction permit only after preparing an environmental impact statement that considers the impact of an accidental release of radiation.

The Environmental Protection Agency sets standards for radioactivity in the overall environment and for the disposal of some radioactive waste. Low-level radioactive waste generated by private facilities is the responsibility of each state. The NRC regulates the use and disposal of other nuclear materials and radioactive waste. Currently, most of it is stored at the plants in which it is produced.

TERMS AND CONCEPTS FOR REVIEW

antitrust law 509
divestiture 513
environmental impact statement (EIS) 514
exclusive-dealing contract 512
group boycott 511
market concentration 512
market power 511
monopoly 511
monopoly power 511
***per se* violation 510**
price discrimination 511
price-fixing agreement 510
resale price maintenance agreement 510
restraint of trade 509
rule of reason 510
tying arrangement 512

CHAPTER SUMMARY • ANTITRUST AND ENVIRONMENTAL LAW

Antitrust Law	**1.** *Sherman Act of 1890*—Prohibits contracts, combinations, and conspiracies in restraint of trade; monopolies; and attempts or conspiracies to monopolize. Applies only to activities that have a significant impact on interstate commerce. **a.** Rule of reason—Applied when an anticompetitive agreement may be justified by legitimate benefits. **b.** *Per se* rule—Applied to restraints of trade that are so anticompetitive they are deemed illegal as a matter of law. These include price-fixing agreements, group boycotts, and market divisions. **2.** *Clayton Act of 1914*—Prohibits price discrimination (charging different prices to different buyers for identical goods), exclusionary practices (exclusive-dealing contracts and tying arrangements), mergers that may substantially lessen competition, and interlocking directorates. **3.** *Federal Trade Commission Act of 1914*—Prohibits unfair methods of competition; established the Federal Trade Commission.
Environmental Law	**1.** *State and local regulation*—Activities affecting the environment are controlled at the local and state levels through regulation of land use, garbage and waste, and pollution-causing activities in general. **2.** *Federal regulation*— **a.** National Environmental Policy Act (1969)—Imposes environmental responsibilities on all federal agencies and requires for every major federal action the preparation of an environmental impact statement. **b.** Environmental Protection Agency—Created in 1970 to administer most federal environmental policies and statutes. **3.** *Air pollution*—Regulated under the Clean Air Act of 1963 and its amendments, particularly those of 1970, 1977, and 1990. **4.** *Water pollution*—Regulated under the Federal Water Pollution Control Act of 1948, as amended by the Clean Water Act of 1972. **5.** *Toxic chemicals*—Pesticides and herbicides, toxic substances, and hazardous waste are regulated under the Toxic Substances Control Act of 1976 and the Comprehensive Environmental Response, Compensation, and Liability Act (CERCLA) of 1980.

HYPOTHETICAL QUESTIONS

40–1. Antitrust Laws. Allitron, Inc., and Donovan, Ltd., are interstate competitors selling similar appliances, principally in the states of Indiana, Kentucky, Illinois, and Ohio. Allitron and Donovan agree that Allitron will no longer sell in Ohio and Indiana and that Donovan will no longer sell in Kentucky and Illinois. Have Allitron and Donovan violated any antitrust laws? If so, which law or laws? Explain.

40–2. Environmental Laws. Fruitade, Inc., is a processor of a soft drink called Freshen Up. Fruitade uses returnable bottles and uses a special acid to clean its bottles for further beverage processing. The acid is diluted with water and then allowed to pass into a navigable stream. Fruitade crushes its broken bottles and also throws the crushed glass into the stream. Discuss *fully* any environmental laws that Fruitade had violated.

REAL WORLD CASE PROBLEM

40–3. Antitrust Laws. Great Western Directories, Inc. (GW), is an independent publisher of telephone directory Yellow Pages. GW buys information for its listings from Southwestern Bell Telephone Co. (SBT). Southwestern Bell Corp. owns SBT and Southwestern Bell Yellow Pages (SBYP), which publishes a directory in competition with GW. In June 1988, in some markets, SBT raised the price for its listing information, and SBYP lowered the price for advertising in its Yellow Pages. GW feared that these companies would do the same thing in other local markets, and it would then be too expensive to compete in those markets. Because of this fear, GW left one market and declined to compete in another. Consequently, SBYP had a monopoly in those markets. GW and another independent publisher filed a suit in a federal district court against Southwestern Bell Corp. What antitrust law, if any, did Southwestern Bell Corp. violate? Should the independent companies be entitled to damages? [*Great Western Directories, Inc. v. Southwestern Bell Telephone Co.*, 74 F.3d 613 (5th Cir. 1996)]

For updated links to resources available on the Web, as well as a variety of other materials, visit this text's Web site at **http://blte.westbuslaw.com**.

You can access the Antitrust Division of the U.S. Department of Justice online at

http://www.usdoj.gov

To see the American Bar Association's Web page on antitrust law, go to

http://www.abanet.org/antitrust

The Federal Trade Commission offers an abundance of information on antitrust law, including "An English Guide to Antitrust Laws," at

http://www.ftc.gov/ftc/antitrust.htm

ONLINE LEGAL RESEARCH

Go to **http://blte.westbuslaw.com**, the Web site that accompanies this text. Select "Internet Applications," and then click on "Chapter 40." There you will find the following Internet research exercises that you can perform to learn more about antitrust law and environmental law:

Activity 40–1: Vertical Restraints and the Rule of Reason

Activity 40–2: Nuisance Law

Chapter 40 ■ WORK SET

TRUE-FALSE QUESTIONS

_____ **1.** Monopoly power is market power sufficient to control prices and exclude competition.

_____ **2.** An exclusive dealing contract is a contract under which competitors agree to divide up territories or customers.

_____ **3.** Price discrimination occurs when a seller forbids a buyer from buying products from the seller's competitors.

_____ **4.** An agreement between competitors to fix prices is a per se violation of antitrust law.

_____ **5.** Local governments can control some aspects of the environment through zoning laws.

_____ **6.** Under federal environmental laws, there is a single standard for all polluters and all pollutants.

_____ **7.** The Toxic Substances Control Act of 1976 regulates the clean-up of leaking hazardous waste disposal sites.

_____ **8.** If a release of hazardous waste occurs at a hazardous waste disposal site, the Environmental Protection Agency (EPA) can clean it up and recover the entire cost from a potentially responsible party.

MULTIPLE-CHOICE QUESTIONS

_____ **1.** The National Coal Association (NCA) is a group of independent coal mining companies. Demand for coal falls and so the price drops. The Coal Refiners Association, a group of coal refining companies, agrees to buy NCA's coal and sell it according to a schedule that will increase the price. This agreement is

a. exempt from the antitrust laws.
b. subject to evaluation under the rule of reason.
c. a *per se* violation of the Sherman Act.
d. none of the above.

_____ **2.** A&B Software Corporation and Tech Products, Inc., are competitors. They form a joint venture to research, develop, and produce new software for a particular line of computers. This joint venture is

a. exempt from the antitrust laws.
b. subject to evaluation under the rule of reason.
c. a *per se* violation of the Sherman Act.
d. none of the above.

_____ **3.** Federated Tools, Inc., charges Jack's Hardware five cents per item and Eve's Home Store ten cents per item for the same product. Jack's Hardware and Eve's Home Store are competitors. If this substantially lessens competition, it constitutes

a. a market division.
b. an exclusionary practice.
c. price discrimination.
d. none of the above.

_____ **4.** American Goods, Inc., and Consumer Products Corporation are competitors. They merge, and after the merger, Consumer Products is the surviving firm. To assess whether the merger is in violation of the Clayton Act requires a look at

a. market division.
b. market concentration.
c. market power.
d. none of the above.

_____ **5.** The U.S. Department of the Interior's approval of oil drilling operations in several western states requires an environmental impact statement

a. only because it affects the quality of the environment.
b. only because it is major.
c. only because it is federal.
d. because it affects the quality of the environment, is major, and is federal.

_____ **6.** National Motors Corporation (NMC) does not manufacture its cars to comply with current EPA standards for automobile exhaust emissions. The EPA can

a. order NMC's lender to pay any clean-up costs.
b. order NMC to recall its cars and repair or replace exhaust controls.
c. order NMC's customers to fix their cars at the customers' expense.
d. do nothing.

_____ **7.** Eagle Industries, Inc., fails to obtain a permit before discharging waste into navigable waters. Under the Clean Water Act, Eagle can be required

a. only to clean up the pollution.
b. only to pay for the cost of cleaning up the pollution.
c. to clean up the pollution or pay for the cost of doing so.
d. none of the above.

ISSUE SPOTTERS

1. Alpha, Inc., Beta Corporation, and Omega Company compete against each other in Illinois, Indiana, and Ohio. To reduce marketing costs, they agree that Alpha will sell products only in Illinois, Beta only in Indiana, and Omega only in Ohio. This allows each firm to raise the price of the goods in its state and increase profits. Is this a violation of antitrust law? If so, is it a *per se* violation, or is it subject to evaluation under the rule of reason?

2. ChemCorp generates hazardous wastes from its operations. Central Trucking Company transports those wastes to Intrastate Disposal, Inc., which owns a hazardous waste disposal site. Intrastate sells the property on which the disposal site is located to ABC Properties, Inc., If the EPA cleans up the site, from which party can it recover the cost?

The Constitution of the United States

A

Preamble

We the People of the United States, in Order to form a more perfect Union, establish Justice, insure domestic Tranquility, provide for the common defence, promote the general Welfare, and secure the Blessings of Liberty to ourselves and our Posterity, do ordain and establish this Constitution for the United States of America.

Article I

Section 1. All legislative Powers herein granted shall be vested in a Congress of the United States, which shall consist of a Senate and House of Representatives.

Section 2. The House of Representatives shall be composed of Members chosen every second Year by the People of the several States, and the Electors in each State shall have the Qualifications requisite for Electors of the most numerous Branch of the State Legislature.

No Person shall be a Representative who shall not have attained to the Age of twenty five Years, and been seven Years a Citizen of the United States, and who shall not, when elected, be an Inhabitant of that State in which he shall be chosen.

Representatives and direct Taxes shall be apportioned among the several States which may be included within this Union, according to their respective Numbers, which shall be determined by adding to the whole Number of free Persons, including those bound to Service for a Term of Years, and excluding Indians not taxed, three fifths of all other Persons. The actual Enumeration shall be made within three Years after the first Meeting of the Congress of the United States, and within every subsequent Term of ten Years, in such Manner as they shall by Law direct. The Number of Representatives shall not exceed one for every thirty Thousand, but each State shall have at Least one Representative; and until such enumeration shall be made, the State of New Hampshire shall be entitled to chuse three, Massachusetts eight, Rhode Island and Providence Plantations one, Connecticut five, New York six, New Jersey four, Pennsylvania eight, Delaware one, Maryland six, Virginia ten, North Carolina five, South Carolina five, and Georgia three.

When vacancies happen in the Representation from any State, the Executive Authority thereof shall issue Writs of Election to fill such Vacancies.

The House of Representatives shall chuse their Speaker and other Officers; and shall have the sole Power of Impeachment.

Section 3. The Senate of the United States shall be composed of two Senators from each State, chosen by the Legislature thereof, for six Years; and each Senator shall have one Vote.

Immediately after they shall be assembled in Consequence of the first Election, they shall be divided as equally as may be into three Classes. The Seats of the Senators of the first Class shall be vacated at the Expiration of the second Year, of the second Class at the Expiration of the fourth Year, and of the third Class at the Expiration of the sixth Year, so that one third may be chosen every second Year; and if Vacancies happen by Resignation, or otherwise, during the Recess of the Legislature of any State, the Executive thereof may make temporary Appointments until the next Meeting of the Legislature, which shall then fill such Vacancies.

No Person shall be a Senator who shall not have attained to the Age of thirty Years, and been nine Years a Citizen of the United States, and who shall not, when elected, be an Inhabitant of that State for which he shall be chosen.

The Vice President of the United States shall be President of the Senate, but shall have no Vote, unless they be equally divided.

The Senate shall chuse their other Officers, and also a President pro tempore, in the Absence of the Vice President, or when he shall exercise the Office of President of the United States.

The Senate shall have the sole Power to try all Impeachments. When sitting for that Purpose, they shall be on Oath or Affirmation. When the President of the United States is tried, the Chief Justice shall preside: And no Person shall be convicted without the Concurrence of two thirds of the Members present.

Judgment in Cases of Impeachment shall not extend further than to removal from Office, and disqualification to hold and enjoy any Office of honor, Trust, or Profit under the United States: but the Party convicted shall nevertheless be liable and subject to Indictment, Trial, Judgment, and Punishment, according to Law.

Section 4. The Times, Places and Manner of holding Elections for Senators and Representatives, shall be prescribed in each State by the Legislature thereof; but the Congress may at any time by Law make or alter such Regulations, except as to the Places of chusing Senators.

The Congress shall assemble at least once in every Year, and such Meeting shall be on the first Monday in December, unless they shall by Law appoint a different Day.

Section 5. Each House shall be the Judge of the Elections, Returns, and Qualifications of its own Members, and a Majority of each shall constitute a Quorum to do Business; but a smaller Number may adjourn from day to day, and may be authorized to compel the Attendance of absent Members, in such Manner, and under such Penalties as each House may provide.

Each House may determine the Rules of its Proceedings, punish its Members for disorderly Behavior, and, with the Concurrence of two thirds, expel a Member.

Each House shall keep a Journal of its Proceedings, and from time to time publish the same, excepting such Parts as may in their Judgment require Secrecy; and the Yeas and Nays of the Members of either House on any question shall, at the Desire of one fifth of those Present, be entered on the Journal.

Neither House, during the Session of Congress, shall, without the Consent of the other, adjourn for more than three days, nor to any other Place than that in which the two Houses shall be sitting.

Section 6. The Senators and Representatives shall receive a Compensation for their Services, to be ascertained by Law, and paid out of the Treasury of the United States. They shall in all Cases, except Treason, Felony and Breach of the Peace, be privileged from Arrest during their Attendance at the Session of their respective Houses, and in going to and returning from the same; and for any Speech or Debate in either House, they shall not be questioned in any other Place.

No Senator or Representative shall, during the Time for which he was elected, be appointed to any civil Office under the Authority of the United States, which shall have been created, or the Emoluments whereof shall have been increased during such time; and no Person holding any Office under the United States, shall be a Member of either House during his Continuance in Office.

Section 7. All Bills for raising Revenue shall originate in the House of Representatives; but the Senate may propose or concur with Amendments as on other Bills.

Every Bill which shall have passed the House of Representatives and the Senate, shall, before it become a Law, be presented to the President of the United States; If he approve he shall sign it, but if not he shall return it, with his Objections to the House in which it shall have originated, who shall enter the Objections at large on their Journal, and proceed to reconsider it. If after such Reconsideration two thirds of that House shall agree to pass the Bill, it shall be sent together with the Objections, to the other House, by which it shall likewise be reconsidered, and if approved by two thirds of that House, it shall become a Law. But in all such Cases the Votes of both Houses shall be determined by Yeas and Nays, and the Names of the Persons voting for and against the Bill shall be entered on the Journal of each House respectively. If any Bill shall not be returned by the President within ten Days (Sundays excepted) after it shall have been presented to him, the Same shall be a Law, in like Manner as if he had signed it, unless the Congress by their Adjournment prevent its Return in which Case it shall not be a Law.

Every Order, Resolution, or Vote, to which the Concurrence of the Senate and House of Representatives may be necessary (except on a question of Adjournment) shall be presented to the President of the United States; and before the Same shall take Effect, shall be approved by him, or being disapproved by him, shall be repassed by two thirds of the Senate and House of Representatives, according to the Rules and Limitations prescribed in the Case of a Bill.

Section 8. The Congress shall have Power To lay and collect Taxes, Duties, Imposts and Excises, to pay the Debts and provide for the common Defence and general Welfare of the United States; but all Duties, Imposts and Excises shall be uniform throughout the United States;

To borrow Money on the credit of the United States;

To regulate Commerce with foreign Nations, and among the several States, and with the Indian Tribes;

To establish an uniform Rule of Naturalization, and uniform Laws on the subject of Bankruptcies throughout the United States;

To coin Money, regulate the Value thereof, and of foreign Coin, and fix the Standard of Weights and Measures;

To provide for the Punishment of counterfeiting the Securities and current Coin of the United States;

To establish Post Offices and post Roads;

To promote the Progress of Science and useful Arts, by securing for limited Times to Authors and Inventors the exclusive Right to their respective Writings and Discoveries;

To constitute Tribunals inferior to the supreme Court;

To define and punish Piracies and Felonies committed on the high Seas, and Offenses against the Law of Nations;

To declare War, grant Letters of Marque and Reprisal, and make Rules concerning Captures on Land and Water;

To raise and support Armies, but no Appropriation of Money to that Use shall be for a longer Term than two Years;

To provide and maintain a Navy;

To make Rules for the Government and Regulation of the land and naval Forces;

To provide for calling forth the Militia to execute the Laws of the Union, suppress Insurrections and repel Invasions;

To provide for organizing, arming, and disciplining, the Militia, and for governing such Part of them as may be employed in the Service of the United States, reserving to the States respectively, the Appointment of the

Officers, and the Authority of training the Militia according to the discipline prescribed by Congress;

To exercise exclusive Legislation in all Cases whatsoever, over such District (not exceeding ten Miles square) as may, by Cession of particular States, and the Acceptance of Congress, become the Seat of the Government of the United States, and to exercise like Authority over all Places purchased by the Consent of the Legislature of the State in which the Same shall be, for the Erection of Forts, Magazines, Arsenals, dock-Yards, and other needful Buildings;—And

To make all Laws which shall be necessary and proper for carrying into Execution the foregoing Powers, and all other Powers vested by this Constitution in the Government of the United States, or in any Department or Officer thereof.

Section 9. The Migration or Importation of such Persons as any of the States now existing shall think proper to admit, shall not be prohibited by the Congress prior to the Year one thousand eight hundred and eight, but a Tax or duty may be imposed on such Importation, not exceeding ten dollars for each Person.

The privilege of the Writ of Habeas Corpus shall not be suspended, unless when in Cases of Rebellion or Invasion the public Safety may require it.

No Bill of Attainder or ex post facto Law shall be passed.

No Capitation, or other direct, Tax shall be laid, unless in Proportion to the Census or Enumeration herein before directed to be taken.

No Tax or Duty shall be laid on Articles exported from any State.

No Preference shall be given by any Regulation of Commerce or Revenue to the Ports of one State over those of another: nor shall Vessels bound to, or from, one State be obliged to enter, clear, or pay Duties in another.

No Money shall be drawn from the Treasury, but in Consequence of Appropriations made by Law; and a regular Statement and Account of the Receipts and Expenditures of all public Money shall be published from time to time.

No Title of Nobility shall be granted by the United States: And no Person holding any Office of Profit or Trust under them, shall, without the Consent of the Congress, accept of any present, Emolument, Office, or Title, of any kind whatever, from any King, Prince, or foreign State.

Section 10. No State shall enter into any Treaty, Alliance, or Confederation; grant Letters of Marque and Reprisal; coin Money; emit Bills of Credit; make any Thing but gold and silver Coin a Tender in Payment of Debts; pass any Bill of Attainder, ex post facto Law, or Law impairing the Obligation of Contracts, or grant any Title of Nobility.

No State shall, without the Consent of the Congress, lay any Imposts or Duties on Imports or Exports, except what may be absolutely necessary for executing its inspection Laws: and the net Produce of all Duties and Imposts, laid by any State on Imports or Exports, shall be for the Use of the Treasury of the United States; and all such Laws shall be subject to the Revision and Controul of the Congress.

No State shall, without the Consent of Congress, lay any Duty of Tonnage, keep Troops, or Ships of War in time of Peace, enter into any Agreement or Compact with another State, or with a foreign Power, or engage in War, unless actually invaded, or in such imminent Danger as will not admit of delay.

Article II

Section 1. The executive Power shall be vested in a President of the United States of America. He shall hold his Office during the Term of four Years, and, together with the Vice President, chosen for the same Term, be elected, as follows:

Each State shall appoint, in such Manner as the Legislature thereof may direct, a Number of Electors, equal to the whole Number of Senators and Representatives to which the State may be entitled in the Congress; but no Senator or Representative, or Person holding an Office of Trust or Profit under the United States, shall be appointed an Elector.

The Electors shall meet in their respective States, and vote by Ballot for two Persons, of whom one at least shall not be an Inhabitant of the same State with themselves. And they shall make a List of all the Persons voted for, and of the Number of Votes for each; which List they shall sign and certify, and transmit sealed to the Seat of the Government of the United States, directed to the President of the Senate. The President of the Senate shall, in the Presence of the Senate and House of Representatives, open all the Certificates, and the Votes shall then be counted. The Person having the greatest Number of Votes shall be the President, if such Number be a Majority of the whole Number of Electors appointed; and if there be more than one who have such Majority, and have an equal Number of Votes, then the House of Representatives shall immediately chuse by Ballot one of them for President; and if no Person have a Majority, then from the five highest on the List the said House shall in like Manner chuse the President. But in chusing the President, the Votes shall be taken by States, the Representation from each State having one Vote; A quorum for this Purpose shall consist of a Member or Members from two thirds of the States, and a Majority of all the States shall be necessary to a Choice. In every Case, after the Choice of the President, the Person having the greater Number of Votes of the Electors shall be the Vice President. But if there should remain two or more who have equal Votes, the Senate shall chuse from them by Ballot the Vice President.

The Congress may determine the Time of chusing the Electors, and the Day on which they shall give their Votes; which Day shall be the same throughout the United States.

No person except a natural born Citizen, or a Citizen of the United States, at the time of the Adoption of this Constitution, shall be eligible to the Office of President; neither shall any Person be eligible to that Office who shall not have attained to the Age of thirty five Years, and been fourteen Years a Resident within the United States.

In Case of the Removal of the President from Office, or of his Death, Resignation or Inability to discharge the Powers and Duties of the said Office, the same shall devolve on the Vice President, and the Congress may by Law provide for the Case of Removal, Death, Resignation or Inability, both of the President and Vice President, declaring what Officer shall then act as President, and such Officer shall act accordingly, until the Disability be removed, or a President shall be elected.

The President shall, at stated Times, receive for his Services, a Compensation, which shall neither be increased nor diminished during the Period for which he shall have been elected, and he shall not receive within that Period any other Emolument from the United States, or any of them.

Before he enter on the Execution of his Office, he shall take the following Oath or Affirmation: "I do solemnly swear (or affirm) that I will faithfully execute the Office of President of the United States, and will to the best of my Ability, preserve, protect and defend the Constitution of the United States."

Section 2. The President shall be Commander in Chief of the Army and Navy of the United States, and of the Militia of the several States, when called into the actual Service of the United States; he may require the Opinion, in writing, of the principal Officer in each of the executive Departments, upon any Subject relating to the Duties of their respective Offices, and he shall have Power to grant Reprieves and Pardons for Offenses against the United States, except in Cases of Impeachment.

He shall have Power, by and with the Advice and Consent of the Senate to make Treaties, provided two thirds of the Senators present concur; and he shall nominate, and by and with the Advice and Consent of the Senate, shall appoint Ambassadors, other public Ministers and Consuls, Judges of the supreme Court, and all other Officers of the United States, whose Appointments are not herein otherwise provided for, and which shall be established by Law; but the Congress may by Law vest the Appointment of such inferior Officers, as they think proper, in the President alone, in the Courts of Law, or in the Heads of Departments.

The President shall have Power to fill up all Vacancies that may happen during the Recess of the Senate, by granting Commissions which shall expire at the End of their next Session.

Section 3. He shall from time to time give to the Congress Information of the State of the Union, and recommend to their Consideration such Measures as he shall judge necessary and expedient; he may, on extraordinary Occasions, convene both Houses, or either of them, and in Case of Disagreement between them, with Respect to the Time of Adjournment, he may adjourn them to such Time as he shall think proper; he shall receive Ambassadors and other public Ministers; he shall take Care that the Laws be faithfully executed, and shall Commission all the Officers of the United States.

Section 4. The President, Vice President and all civil Officers of the United States, shall be removed from Office on Impeachment for, and Conviction of, Treason, Bribery, or other high Crimes and Misdemeanors.

Article III

Section 1. The judicial Power of the United States, shall be vested in one supreme Court, and in such inferior Courts as the Congress may from time to time ordain and establish. The Judges, both of the supreme and inferior Courts, shall hold their Offices during good Behaviour, and shall, at stated Times, receive for their Services a Compensation, which shall not be diminished during their Continuance in Office.

Section 2. The judicial Power shall extend to all Cases, in Law and Equity, arising under this Constitution, the Laws of the United States, and Treaties made, or which shall be made, under their Authority;—to all Cases affecting Ambassadors, other public Ministers and Consuls;—to all Cases of admiralty and maritime Jurisdiction;—to Controversies to which the United States shall be a Party;—to Controversies between two or more States;—between a State and Citizens of another State;—between Citizens of different States;—between Citizens of the same State claiming Lands under Grants of different States, and between a State, or the Citizens thereof, and foreign States, Citizens or Subjects.

In all Cases affecting Ambassadors, other public Ministers and Consuls, and those in which a State shall be a Party, the supreme Court shall have original Jurisdiction. In all the other Cases before mentioned, the supreme Court shall have appellate Jurisdiction, both as to Law and Fact, with such Exceptions, and under such Regulations as the Congress shall make.

The Trial of all Crimes, except in Cases of Impeachment, shall be by Jury; and such Trial shall be held in the State where the said Crimes shall have been committed; but when not committed within any State, the Trial shall be at such Place or Places as the Congress may by Law have directed.

Section 3. Treason against the United States, shall consist only in levying War against them, or, in adhering to their Enemies, giving them Aid and Comfort. No Person shall be convicted of Treason unless on the Testimony of two Witnesses to the same overt Act, or on Confession in open Court.

The Congress shall have Power to declare the Punishment of Treason, but no Attainder of Treason shall work Corruption of Blood, or Forfeiture except during the Life of the Person attainted.

Article IV

Section 1. Full Faith and Credit shall be given in each State to the public Acts, Records, and judicial Proceedings of every other State. And the Congress may by general Laws prescribe the Manner in which such Acts, Records and Proceedings shall be proved, and the Effect thereof.

Section 2. The Citizens of each State shall be entitled to all Privileges and Immunities of Citizens in the several States.

A Person charged in any State with Treason, Felony, or other Crime, who shall flee from Justice, and be found in another State, shall on Demand of the executive Authority of the State from which he fled, be delivered up, to be removed to the State having Jurisdiction of the Crime.

No Person held to Service or Labour in one State, under the Laws thereof, escaping into another, shall, in Consequence of any Law or Regulation therein, be discharged from such Service or Labour, but shall be delivered up on Claim of the Party to whom such Service or Labour may be due.

Section 3. New States may be admitted by the Congress into this Union; but no new State shall be formed or erected within the Jurisdiction of any other State; nor any State be formed by the Junction of two or more States, or Parts of States, without the Consent of the Legislatures of the States concerned as well as of the Congress.

The Congress shall have Power to dispose of and make all needful Rules and Regulations respecting the Territory or other Property belonging to the United States; and nothing in this Constitution shall be so construed as to Prejudice any Claims of the United States, or of any particular State.

Section 4. The United States shall guarantee to every State in this Union a Republican Form of Government, and shall protect each of them against Invasion; and on Application of the Legislature, or of the Executive (when the Legislature cannot be convened) against domestic Violence.

Article V

The Congress, whenever two thirds of both Houses shall deem it necessary, shall propose Amendments to this Constitution, or, on the Application of the Legislatures of two thirds of the several States, shall call a Convention for proposing Amendments, which, in either Case, shall be valid to all Intents and Purposes, as part of this Constitution, when ratified by the Legislatures of three fourths of the several States, or by Conventions in three fourths thereof, as the one or the other Mode of Ratification may be proposed by the Congress; Provided that no Amendment which may be made prior to the Year One thousand eight hundred and eight shall in any Manner affect the first and fourth Clauses in the Ninth Section of the first Article; and that no State, without its Consent, shall be deprived of its equal Suffrage in the Senate.

Article VI

All Debts contracted and Engagements entered into, before the Adoption of this Constitution shall be as valid against the United States under this Constitution, as under the Confederation.

This Constitution, and the Laws of the United States which shall be made in Pursuance thereof; and all Treaties made, or which shall be made, under the Authority of the United States, shall be the supreme Law of the Land; and the Judges in every State shall be bound thereby, any Thing in the Constitution or Laws of any State to the Contrary notwithstanding.

The Senators and Representatives before mentioned, and the Members of the several State Legislatures, and all executive and judicial Officers, both of the United States and of the several States, shall be bound by Oath or Affirmation, to support this Constitution; but no religious Test shall ever be required as a Qualification to any Office or public Trust under the United States.

Article VII

The Ratification of the Conventions of nine States shall be sufficient for the Establishment of this Constitution between the States so ratifying the Same.

Amendment I [1791]

Congress shall make no law respecting an establishment of religion, or prohibiting the free exercise thereof; or abridging the freedom of speech, or of the press; or the right of the people peaceably to assembly, and to petition the Government for a redress of grievances.

Amendment II [1791]

A well regulated Militia, being necessary to the security of a free State, the right of the people to keep and bear Arms, shall not be infringed.

Amendment III [1791]

No Soldier shall, in time of peace be quartered in any house, without the consent of the Owner, nor in time of war, but in a manner to be prescribed by law.

Amendment IV [1791]

The right of the people to be secure in their persons, houses, papers, and effects, against unreasonable searches and seizures, shall not be violated, and no Warrants shall issue, but upon probable cause, supported by Oath or affirmation, and particularly describing the place to be searched, and the persons or things to be seized.

Amendment V [1791]

No person shall be held to answer for a capital, or otherwise infamous crime, unless on a presentment or indictment of a Grand Jury, except in cases arising in the land or naval forces, or in the Militia, when in actual service in time of War or public danger; nor shall any person be subject for the same offence to be twice put in jeopardy of life or limb; nor shall be compelled in any criminal case to be a witness against himself, nor be deprived of life, liberty, or property, without due process of law; nor shall private property be taken for public use, without just compensation.

Amendment VI [1791]

In all criminal prosecutions, the accused shall enjoy the right to a speedy and public trial, by an impartial jury of the State and district wherein the crime shall have been committed, which district shall have been previously ascertained by law, and to be informed of the nature and cause of the accusation; to be confronted with the witnesses against him; to have compulsory process for obtaining witnesses in his favor, and to have the Assistance of Counsel for his defence.

Amendment VII [1791]

In Suits at common law, where the value in controversy shall exceed twenty dollars, the right of trial by jury shall be preserved, and no fact tried by jury, shall be otherwise reexamined in any Court of the United States, than according to the rules of the common law.

Amendment VIII [1791]

Excessive bail shall not be required, nor excessive fines imposed, nor cruel and unusual punishments inflicted.

Amendment IX [1791]

The enumeration in the Constitution, of certain rights, shall not be construed to deny or disparage others retained by the people.

Amendment X [1791]

The powers not delegated to the United States by the Constitution, nor prohibited by it to the States, are reserved to the States respectively, or to the people.

Amendment XI [1798]

The Judicial power of the United States shall not be construed to extend to any suit in law or equity, commenced or prosecuted against one of the United States by Citizens of another State, or by Citizens or Subjects of any Foreign State.

Amendment XII [1804]

The Electors shall meet in their respective states, and vote by ballot for President and Vice-President, one of whom, at least, shall not be an inhabitant of the same state with themselves; they shall name in their ballots the person voted for as President, and in distinct ballots the person voted for as Vice-President, and they shall make distinct lists of all persons voted for as President, and of all persons voted for as Vice-President, and of the number of votes for each, which lists they shall sign and certify, and transmit sealed to the seat of the government of the United States, directed to the President of the Senate;—The President of the Senate shall, in the presence of the Senate and House of Representatives, open all the certificates and the votes shall then be counted;—The person having the greatest number of votes for President, shall be the President, if such number be a majority of the whole number of Electors appointed; and if no person have such majority, then from the persons having the highest numbers not exceeding three on the list of those voted for as President, the House of Representatives shall choose immediately, by ballot, the President. But in choosing the President, the votes shall be taken by states, the representation from each state having one vote; a quorum for this purpose shall consist of a member or members from two-thirds of the states, and a majority of all states shall be necessary to a choice. And if the House of Representatives shall not choose a President whenever the right of choice shall devolve upon them, before the fourth day of March next following, then the Vice-President shall act as President, as in the case of the death or other constitutional disability of the President.—The person having the greatest number of votes as Vice-President, shall be the Vice-President, if such number be a majority of the whole number of Electors appointed, and if no person have a majority, then from the two highest numbers on the list, the Senate shall choose the Vice-President; a quorum for the purpose shall consist of two-thirds of the whole number of Senators, and a majority of the whole number shall be necessary to a choice. But no person constitutionally ineligible to the office of President shall be eligible to that of Vice-President of the United States.

Amendment XIII [1865]

Section 1. Neither slavery nor involuntary servitude, except as a punishment for crime whereof the party shall have been duly convicted, shall exist within the United States, or any place subject to their jurisdiction.

Section 2. Congress shall have power to enforce this article by appropriate legislation.

Amendment XIV [1868]

Section 1. All persons born or naturalized in the United States, and subject to the jurisdiction thereof, are citizens of the United States and of the State wherein they reside. No State shall make or enforce any law which shall abridge the privileges or immunities of citizens of the United States; nor shall any State deprive any person of life, liberty, or property, without due process of law; nor deny to any person within its jurisdiction the equal protection of the laws.

Section 2. Representatives shall be apportioned among the several States according to their respective numbers, counting the whole number of persons in each State, excluding Indians not taxed. But when the right to vote at any election for the choice of electors for President and Vice President of the United States, Representatives in Congress, the Executive and Judicial officers of a State, or the members of the Legislature thereof, is denied to any of the male inhabitants of such State, being twenty-one years of age, and citizens of the United States, or in any way abridged, except for participation in rebellion, or other crime, the basis of representation therein shall be reduced in the proportion which the number of such male citizens shall bear to the whole number of male citizens twenty-one years of age in such State.

Section 3. No person shall be a Senator or Representative in Congress, or elector of President and Vice President, or hold any office, civil or military, under the United States, or under any State, who having previously taken an oath, as a member of Congress, or as an officer of the United States, or as a member of any State legislature, or as an executive or judicial officer of any State, to support the Constitution of the United States, shall have engaged in insurrection or rebellion against the same, or given aid or comfort to the enemies thereof. But Congress may by a vote of two-thirds of each House, remove such disability.

Section 4. The validity of the public debt of the United States, authorized by law, including debts incurred for payment of pensions and bounties for services in suppressing insurrection or rebellion, shall not be questioned. But neither the United States nor any State shall assume or pay any debt or obligation incurred in aid of insurrection or rebellion against the United States, or any claim for the loss or emancipation of any slave; but all such debts, obligations and claims shall be held illegal and void.

Section 5. The Congress shall have power to enforce, by appropriate legislation, the provisions of this article.

AMENDMENT XV [1870]

Section 1. The right of citizens of the United States to vote shall not be denied or abridged by the United States or by any State on account of race, color, or previous condition of servitude.

Section 2. The Congress shall have power to enforce this article by appropriate legislation.

AMENDMENT XVI [1913]

The Congress shall have power to lay and collect taxes on incomes, from whatever source derived, without apportionment among the several States, and without regard to any census or enumeration.

AMENDMENT XVII [1913]

Section 1. The Senate of the United States shall be composed of two Senators from each State, elected by the people thereof, for six years; and each Senator shall have one vote. The electors in each State shall have the qualifications requisite for electors of the most numerous branch of the State legislatures.

Section 2. When vacancies happen in the representation of any State in the Senate, the executive authority of such State shall issue writs of election to fill such vacancies: *Provided,* That the legislature of any State may empower the executive thereof to make temporary appointments until the people fill the vacancies by election as the legislature may direct.

Section 3. This amendment shall not be so construed as to affect the election or term of any Senator chosen before it becomes valid as part of the Constitution.

AMENDMENT XVIII [1919]

Section 1. After one year from the ratification of this article the manufacture, sale, or transportation of intoxicating liquors within, the importation thereof into, or the exportation thereof from the United States and all territory subject to the jurisdiction thereof for beverage purposes is hereby prohibited.

Section 2. The Congress and the several States shall have concurrent power to enforce this article by appropriate legislation.

Section 3. This article shall be inoperative unless it shall have been ratified as an amendment to the Constitution by the legislatures of the several States, as provided in the Constitution, within seven years from the date of the submission hereof to the States by the Congress.

AMENDMENT XIX [1920]

Section 1. The right of citizens of the United States to vote shall not be denied or abridged by the United States or by any State on account of sex.

Section 2. Congress shall have power to enforce this article by appropriate legislation.

AMENDMENT XX [1933]

Section 1. The terms of the President and Vice President shall end at noon on the 20th day of January, and the terms of Senators and Representatives at noon on the 3d day of January, of the years in which such terms would have ended if this article had not been ratified; and the terms of their successors shall then begin.

Section 2. The Congress shall assemble at least once in every year, and such meeting shall begin at noon on the 3d day of January, unless they shall by law appoint a different day.

Section 3. If, at the time fixed for the beginning of the term of the President, the President elect shall have died, the Vice President elect shall become President. If the President shall not have been chosen before the time fixed for the beginning of his term, or if the President elect shall have failed to qualify, then the Vice President elect shall act as President until a President shall have qualified; and the Congress may by law provide for the case wherein neither a President elect nor a Vice President elect shall have qualified, declaring who shall then act as President, or the manner in which one who is to act shall be selected, and such person shall act accordingly until a President or Vice President shall have qualified.

Section 4. The Congress may by law provide for the case of the death of any of the persons from whom the House of Representatives may choose a President whenever the right of choice shall have devolved upon them, and for the case of the death of any of the persons from whom the Senate may choose a Vice President whenever the right of choice shall have devolved upon them.

Section 5. Sections 1 and 2 shall take effect on the 15th day of October following the ratification of this article.

Section 6. This article shall be inoperative unless it shall have been ratified as an amendment to the Constitution by the legislatures of three-fourths of the several States within seven years from the date of its submission.

AMENDMENT XXI [1933]

Section 1. The eighteenth article of amendment to the Constitution of the United States is hereby repealed.

Section 2. The transportation or importation into any State, Territory, or possession of the United States for delivery or use therein of intoxicating liquors, in violation of the laws thereof, is hereby prohibited.

Section 3. This article shall be inoperative unless it shall have been ratified as an amendment to the Constitution by conventions in the several States, as provided in the Constitution, within seven years from the date of the submission hereof to the States by the Congress.

Amendment XXII [1951]

Section 1. No person shall be elected to the office of the President more than twice, and no person who has held the office of President, or acted as President, for more than two years of a term to which some other person was elected President shall be elected to the office of President more than once. But this Article shall not apply to any person holding the office of President when this Article was proposed by the Congress, and shall not prevent any person who may be holding the office of President, or acting as President, during the term within which this Article becomes operative from holding the office of President or acting as President during the remainder of such term.

Section 2. This article shall be inoperative unless it shall have been ratified as an amendment to the Constitution by the legislatures of three-fourths of the several States within seven years from the date of its submission to the States by the Congress.

Amendment XXIII [1961]

Section 1. The District constituting the seat of Government of the United States shall appoint in such manner as the Congress may direct:

A number of electors of President and Vice President equal to the whole number of Senators and Representatives in Congress to which the District would be entitled if it were a State, but in no event more than the least populous state; they shall be in addition to those appointed by the states, but they shall be considered, for the purposes of the election of President and Vice President, to be electors appointed by a state; and they shall meet in the District and perform such duties as provided by the twelfth article of amendment.

Section 2. The Congress shall have power to enforce this article by appropriate legislation.

Amendment XXIV [1964]

Section 1. The right of citizens of the United States to vote in any primary or other election for President or Vice President, for electors for President or Vice President, or for Senator or Representative in Congress, shall not be denied or abridged by the United States, or any State by reason of failure to pay any poll tax or other tax.

Section 2. The Congress shall have power to enforce this article by appropriate legislation.

Amendment XXV [1967]

Section 1. In case of the removal of the President from office or of his death or resignation, the Vice President shall become President.

Section 2. Whenever there is a vacancy in the office of the Vice President, the President shall nominate a Vice President who shall take office upon confirmation by a majority vote of both Houses of Congress.

Section 3. Whenever the President transmits to the President pro tempore of the Senate and the Speaker of the House of Representatives his written declaration that he is unable to discharge the powers and duties of his office, and until he transmits to them a written declaration to the contrary, such powers and duties shall be discharged by the Vice President as Acting President.

Section 4. Whenever the Vice President and a majority of either the principal officers of the executive departments or of such other body as Congress may by law provide, transmit to the President pro tempore of the Senate and the Speaker of the House of Representatives their written declaration that the President is unable to discharge the powers and duties of his office, the Vice President shall immediately assume the powers and duties of the office as Acting President.

Thereafter, when the President transmits to the President pro tempore of the Senate and the Speaker of the House of Representatives his written declaration that no inability exists, he shall resume the powers and duties of his office unless the Vice President and a majority of either the principal officers of the executive department or of such other body as Congress may by law provide, transmit within four days to the President pro tempore of the Senate and the Speaker of the House of Representatives their written declaration that the President is unable to discharge the powers and duties of his office. Thereupon Congress shall decide the issue, assembling within forty-eight hours for that purpose if not in session. If the Congress, within twenty-one days after receipt of the latter written declaration, or, if Congress is not in session, within twenty-one days after Congress is required to assemble, determines by two-thirds vote of both Houses that the President is unable to discharge the powers and duties of his office, the Vice President shall continue to discharge the same as Acting President; otherwise, the President shall resume the powers and duties of his office.

Amendment XXVI [1971]

Section 1. The right of citizens of the United States, who are eighteen years of age or older, to vote shall not be denied or abridged by the United States or by any State on account of age.

Section 2. The Congress shall have power to enforce this article by appropriate legislation.

Amendment XXVII [1992]

No law, varying the compensation for the services of the Senators and Representatives, shall take effect, until an election of Representatives shall have intervened.

Article 2 of the Uniform Commercial Code

B

ARTICLE 2
SALES

Part 1 Short Title, General Construction and Subject Matter

§ 2—101. Short Title.

This Article shall be known and may be cited as Uniform Commercial Code—Sales.

§ 2—102. Scope; Certain Security and Other Transactions Excluded From This Article.

Unless the context otherwise requires, this Article applies to transactions in goods; it does not apply to any transaction which although in the form of an unconditional contract to sell or present sale is intended to operate only as a security transaction nor does this Article impair or repeal any statute regulating sales to consumers, farmers or other specified classes of buyers.

§ 2—103. Definitions and Index of Definitions.

(1) In this Article unless the context otherwise requires

(a) "Buyer" means a person who buys or contracts to buy goods.

(b) "Good faith" in the case of a merchant means honesty in fact and the observance of reasonable commercial standards of fair dealing in the trade.

(c) "Receipt" of goods means taking physical possession of them.

(d) "Seller" means a person who sells or contracts to sell goods.

(2) Other definitions applying to this Article or to specified Parts thereof, and the sections in which they appear are:

"Acceptance". Section 2—606.

"Banker's credit". Section 2—325.

"Between merchants". Section 2—104.

"Cancellation". Section 2—106(4).

"Commercial unit". Section 2—105.

"Confirmed credit". Section 2—325.

"Conforming to contract". Section 2—106.

"Contract for sale". Section 2—106.

"Cover". Section 2—712.

"Entrusting". Section 2—403.

"Financing agency". Section 2—104.

"Future goods". Section 2—105.

"Goods". Section 2—105.

"Identification". Section 2—501.

"Installment contract". Section 2—612.

"Letter of Credit". Section 2—325.

"Lot". Section 2—105.

"Merchant". Section 2—104.

"Overseas". Section 2—323.

"Person in position of seller". Section 2—707.

"Present sale". Section 2—106.

"Sale". Section 2—106.

"Sale on approval". Section 2—326.

"Sale or return". Section 2—326.

"Termination". Section 2—106.

(3) The following definitions in other Articles apply to this Article:

"Check". Section 3—104.

"Consignee". Section 7—102.

"Consignor". Section 7—102.

"Consumer goods". Section 9—109.

"Dishonor". Section 3—507.

"Draft". Section 3—104.

(4) In addition Article 1 contains general definitions and principles of construction and interpretation applicable throughout this Article.

§ 2—104. Definitions: "Merchant"; "Between Merchants"; "Financing Agency".

(1) "Merchant" means a person who deals in goods of the kind or otherwise by his occupation holds himself out as having knowledge or skill peculiar to the practices or goods involved in the transaction or to whom such knowledge or

skill may be attributed by his employment of an agent or broker or other intermediary who by his occupation holds himself out as having such knowledge or skill.

(2) "Financing agency" means a bank, finance company or other person who in the ordinary course of business makes advances against goods or documents of title or who by arrangement with either the seller or the buyer intervenes in ordinary course to make or collect payment due or claimed under the contract for sale, as by purchasing or paying the seller's draft or making advances against it or by merely taking it for collection whether or not documents of title accompany the draft. "Financing agency" includes also a bank or other person who similarly intervenes between persons who are in the position of seller and buyer in respect to the goods (Section 2—707).

(3) "Between merchants" means in any transaction with respect to which both parties are chargeable with the knowledge or skill of merchants.

§ 2—105. Definitions: Transferability; "Goods"; "Future" Goods; "Lot"; "Commercial Unit".

(1) "Goods" means all things (including specially manufactured goods) which are movable at the time of identification to the contract for sale other than the money in which the price is to be paid, investment securities (Article 8) and things in action. "Goods" also includes the unborn young of animals and growing crops and other identified things attached to realty as described in the section on goods to be severed from realty (Section 2—107).

(2) Goods must be both existing and identified before any interest in them can pass. Goods which are not both existing and identified are "future" goods. A purported present sale of future goods or of any interest therein operates as a contract to sell.

(3) There may be a sale of a part interest in existing identified goods.

(4) An undivided share in an identified bulk of fungible goods is sufficiently identified to be sold although the quantity of the bulk is not determined. Any agreed proportion of such a bulk or any quantity thereof agreed upon by number, weight or other measure may to the extent of the seller's interest in the bulk be sold to the buyer who then becomes an owner in common.

(5) "Lot" means a parcel or a single article which is the subject matter of a separate sale or delivery, whether or not it is sufficient to perform the contract.

(6) "Commercial unit" means such a unit of goods as by commercial usage is a single whole for purposes of sale and division of which materially impairs its character or value on the market or in use. A commercial unit may be a single article (as a machine) or a set of articles (as a suite of furniture or an assortment of sizes) or a quantity (as a bale, gross, or carload) or any other unit treated in use or in the relevant market as a single whole.

§ 2—106. Definitions: "Contract"; "Agreement"; "Contract for Sale"; "Sale"; "Present Sale"; "Conforming" to Contract; "Termination"; "Cancellation".

(1) In this Article unless the context otherwise requires "contract" and "agreement" are limited to those relating to the present or future sale of goods. "Contract for sale" includes both a present sale of goods and a contract to sell goods at a future time. A "sale" consists in the passing of title from the seller to the buyer for a price (Section 2—401). A "present sale" means a sale which is accomplished by the making of the contract.

(2) Goods or conduct including any part of a performance are "conforming" or conform to the contract when they are in accordance with the obligations under the contract.

(3) "Termination" occurs when either party pursuant to a power created by agreement or law puts an end to the contract otherwise than for its breach. On "termination" all obligations which are still executory on both sides are discharged but any right based on prior breach or performance survives.

(4) "Cancellation" occurs when either party puts an end to the contract for breach by the other and its effect is the same as that of "termination" except that the cancelling party also retains any remedy for breach of the whole contract or any unperformed balance.

§ 2—107. Goods to Be Severed From Realty: Recording.

(1) A contract for the sale of minerals or the like (including oil and gas) or a structure or its materials to be removed from realty is a contract for the sale of goods within this Article if they are to be severed by the seller but until severance a purported present sale thereof which is not effective as a transfer of an interest in land is effective only as a contract to sell.

(2) A contract for the sale apart from the land of growing crops or other things attached to realty and capable of severance without material harm thereto but not described in subsection (1) or of timber to be cut is a contract for the sale of goods within this Article whether the subject matter is to be severed by the buyer or by the seller even though it forms part of the realty at the time of contracting, and the parties can by identification effect a present sale before severance.

(3) The provisions of this section are subject to any third party rights provided by the law relating to realty records, and the contract for sale may be executed and recorded as a document transferring an interest in land and shall then constitute notice to third parties of the buyer's rights under the contract for sale.

Part 2 Form, Formation and Readjustment of Contract

§ 2—201. Formal Requirements; Statute of Frauds.

(1) Except as otherwise provided in this section a contract for the sale of goods for the price of $500 or more is not enforceable by way of action or defense unless there is some writing sufficient to indicate that a contract for sale has been made between the parties and signed by the party against whom enforcement is sought or by his authorized agent or broker. A writing is not insufficient because it omits or incorrectly states a term agreed upon but the contract is not enforceable under this paragraph beyond the quantity of goods shown in such writing.

(2) Between merchants if within a reasonable time a writing in confirmation of the contract and sufficient against the sender is received and the party receiving it has reason to know its contents, it satisfies the requirements of subsection (1) against such party unless written notice of objection to its contents is given within ten days after it is received.

(3) A contract which does not satisfy the requirements of subsection (1) but which is valid in other respects is enforceable

(a) if the goods are to be specially manufactured for the buyer and are not suitable for sale to others in the ordinary course of the seller's business and the seller, before notice of repudiation is received and under circumstances which reasonably indicate that the goods are for the buyer, has made either a substantial beginning of their manufacture or commitments for their procurement; or

(b) if the party against whom enforcement is sought admits in his pleading, testimony or otherwise in court that a contract for sale was made, but the contract is not enforceable under this provision beyond the quantity of goods admitted; or

(c) with respect to goods for which payment has been made and accepted or which have been received and accepted
(Sec. 2—606).

§ 2—202. Final Written Expression: Parol or Extrinsic Evidence.

Terms with respect to which the confirmatory memoranda of the parties agree or which are otherwise set forth in a writing intended by the parties as a final expression of their agreement with respect to such terms as are included therein may not be contradicted by evidence of any prior agreement or of a contemporaneous oral agreement but may be explained or supplemented

(a) by course of dealing or usage of trade (Section 1—205) or by course of performance (Section 2—208); and

(b) by evidence of consistent additional terms unless the court finds the writing to have been intended also as a complete and exclusive statement of the terms of the agreement.

§ 2—203. Seals Inoperative.

The affixing of a seal to a writing evidencing a contract for sale or an offer to buy or sell goods does not constitute the writing a sealed instrument and the law with respect to sealed instruments does not apply to such a contract or offer.

§ 2—204. Formation in General.

(1) A contract for sale of goods may be made in any manner sufficient to show agreement, including conduct by both parties which recognizes the existence of such a contract.

(2) An agreement sufficient to constitute a contract for sale may be found even though the moment of its making is undetermined.

(3) Even though one or more terms are left open a contract for sale does not fail for indefiniteness if the parties have intended to make a contract and there is a reasonably certain basis for giving an appropriate remedy.

§ 2—205. Firm Offers.

An offer by a merchant to buy or sell goods in a signed writing which by its terms gives assurance that it will be held open is not revocable, for lack of consideration, during the time stated or if no time is stated for a reasonable time, but in no event may such period of irrevocability exceed three months; but any such term of assurance on a form supplied by the offeree must be separately signed by the offeror.

§ 2—206. Offer and Acceptance in Formation of Contract.

(1) Unless otherwise unambiguously indicated by the language or circumstances

(a) an offer to make a contract shall be construed as inviting acceptance in any manner and by any medium reasonable in the circumstances;

(b) an order or other offer to buy goods for prompt or current shipment shall be construed as inviting acceptance either by a prompt promise to ship or by the prompt or current shipment of conforming or non-conforming goods, but such a shipment of non-conforming goods does not constitute an acceptance if the seller seasonably notifies the buyer that the shipment is offered only as an accommodation to the buyer.

(2) Where the beginning of a requested performance is a reasonable mode of acceptance an offeror who is not notified of acceptance within a reasonable time may treat the offer as having lapsed before acceptance.

§ 2—207. Additional Terms in Acceptance or Confirmation.

(1) A definite and seasonable expression of acceptance or a written confirmation which is sent within a reasonable time operates as an acceptance even though it states terms additional to or different from those offered or agreed upon, unless acceptance is expressly made conditional on assent to the additional or different terms.

(2) The additional terms are to be construed as proposals for addition to the contract. Between merchants such terms become part of the contract unless:

(a) the offer expressly limits acceptance to the terms of the offer;

(b) they materially alter it; or

(c) notification of objection to them has already been given or is given within a reasonable time after notice of them is received.

(3) Conduct by both parties which recognizes the existence of a contract is sufficient to establish a contract for sale although the writings of the parties do not otherwise establish a contract. In such case the terms of the particular contract consist of those terms on which the writings of the parties agree, together with any supplementary terms incorporated under any other provisions of this Act.

§ 2—208. Course of Performance or Practical Construction.

(1) Where the contract for sale involves repeated occasions for performance by either party with knowledge of

the nature of the performance and opportunity for objection to it by the other, any course of performance accepted or acquiesced in without objection shall be relevant to determine the meaning of the agreement.

(2) The express terms of the agreement and any such course of performance, as well as any course of dealing and usage of trade, shall be construed whenever reasonable as consistent with each other; but when such construction is unreasonable, express terms shall control course of performance and course of performance shall control both course of dealing and usage of trade (Section 1—205).

(3) Subject to the provisions of the next section on modification and waiver, such course of performance shall be relevant to show a waiver or modification of any term inconsistent with such course of performance.

§ 2—209. Modification, Rescission and Waiver.

(1) An agreement modifying a contract within this Article needs no consideration to be binding.

(2) A signed agreement which excludes modification or rescission except by a signed writing cannot be otherwise modified or rescinded, but except as between merchants such a requirement on a form supplied by the merchant must be separately signed by the other party.

(3) The requirements of the statute of frauds section of this Article (Section 2—201) must be satisfied if the contract as modified is within its provisions.

(4) Although an attempt at modification or rescission does not satisfy the requirements of subsection (2) or (3) it can operate as a waiver.

(5) A party who has made a waiver affecting an executory portion of the contract may retract the waiver by reasonable notification received by the other party that strict performance will be required of any term waived, unless the retraction would be unjust in view of a material change of position in reliance on the waiver.

§ 2—210. Delegation of Performance; Assignment of Rights.

(1) A party may perform his duty through a delegate unless otherwise agreed or unless the other party has a substantial interest in having his original promisor perform or control the acts required by the contract. No delegation of performance relieves the party delegating of any duty to perform or any liability for breach.

(2) Unless otherwise agreed all rights of either seller or buyer can be assigned except where the assignment would materially change the duty of the other party, or increase materially the burden or risk imposed on him by his contract, or impair materially his chance of obtaining return performance. A right to damages for breach of the whole contract or a right arising out of the assignor's due performance of his entire obligation can be assigned despite agreement otherwise.

(3) Unless the circumstances indicate the contrary a prohibition of assignment of "the contract" is to be construed as barring only the delegation to the assignee of the assignor's performance.

(4) An assignment of "the contract" or of "all my rights under the contract" or an assignment in similar general terms is an assignment of rights and unless the language or the circumstances (as in an assignment for security) indicate the contrary, it is a delegation of performance of the duties of the assignor and its acceptance by the assignee constitutes a promise by him to perform those duties. This promise is enforceable by either the assignor or the other party to the original contract.

(5) The other party may treat any assignment which delegates performance as creating reasonable grounds for insecurity and may without prejudice to his rights against the assignor demand assurances from the assignee (Section 2—609).

Part 3 General Obligation and Construction of Contract

§ 2—301. General Obligations of Parties.

The obligation of the seller is to transfer and deliver and that of the buyer is to accept and pay in accordance with the contract.

§ 2—302. Unconscionable Contract or Clause.

(1) If the court as a matter of law finds the contract or any clause of the contract to have been unconscionable at the time it was made the court may refuse to enforce the contract, or it may enforce the remainder of the contract without the unconscionable clause, or it may so limit the application of any unconscionable clause as to avoid any unconscionable result.

(2) When it is claimed or appears to the court that the contract or any clause thereof may be unconscionable the parties shall be afforded a reasonable opportunity to present evidence as to its commercial setting, purpose and effect to aid the court in making the determination.

§ 2—303. Allocations or Division of Risks.

Where this Article allocates a risk or a burden as between the parties "unless otherwise agreed", the agreement may not only shift the allocation but may also divide the risk or burden.

§ 2—304. Price Payable in Money, Goods, Realty, or Otherwise.

(1) The price can be made payable in money or otherwise. If it is payable in whole or in part in goods each party is a seller of the goods which he is to transfer.

(2) Even though all or part of the price is payable in an interest in realty the transfer of the goods and the seller's obligations with reference to them are subject to this Article, but not the transfer of the interest in realty or the transferor's obligations in connection therewith.

§ 2—305. Open Price Term.

(1) The parties if they so intend can conclude a contract for sale even though the price is not settled. In such a case the price is a reasonable price at the time for delivery if

(a) nothing is said as to price; or

(b) the price is left to be agreed by the parties and they fail to agree; or

(c) the price is to be fixed in terms of some agreed market or other standard as set or recorded by a third person or agency and it is not so set or recorded.

(2) A price to be fixed by the seller or by the buyer means a price for him to fix in good faith.

(3) When a price left to be fixed otherwise than by agreement of the parties fails to be fixed through fault of one party the other may at his option treat the contract as cancelled or himself fix a reasonable price.

(4) Where, however, the parties intend not to be bound unless the price be fixed or agreed and it is not fixed or agreed there is no contract. In such a case the buyer must return any goods already received or if unable so to do must pay their reasonable value at the time of delivery and the seller must return any portion of the price paid on account.

§ 2—306. Output, Requirements and Exclusive Dealings.

(1) A term which measures the quantity by the output of the seller or the requirements of the buyer means such actual output or requirements as may occur in good faith, except that no quantity unreasonably disproportionate to any stated estimate or in the absence of a stated estimate to any normal or otherwise comparable prior output or requirements may be tendered or demanded.

(2) A lawful agreement by either the seller or the buyer for exclusive dealing in the kind of goods concerned imposes unless otherwise agreed an obligation by the seller to use best efforts to supply the goods and by the buyer to use best efforts to promote their sale.

§ 2—307. Delivery in Single Lot or Several Lots.

Unless otherwise agreed all goods called for by a contract for sale must be tendered in a single delivery and payment is due only on such tender but where the circumstances give either party the right to make or demand delivery in lots the price if it can be apportioned may be demanded for each lot.

§ 2—308. Absence of Specified Place for Delivery.

Unless otherwise agreed

(a) the place for delivery of goods is the seller's place of business or if he has none his residence; but

(b) in a contract for sale of identified goods which to the knowledge of the parties at the time of contracting are in some other place, that place is the place for their delivery; and

(c) documents of title may be delivered through customary banking channels.

§ 2—309. Absence of Specific Time Provisions; Notice of Termination.

(1) The time for shipment or delivery or any other action under a contract if not provided in this Article or agreed upon shall be a reasonable time.

(2) Where the contract provides for successive performances but is indefinite in duration it is valid for a reasonable time but unless otherwise agreed may be terminated at any time by either party.

(3) Termination of a contract by one party except on the happening of an agreed event requires that reasonable notification be received by the other party and an agreement dispensing with notification is invalid if its operation would be unconscionable.

§ 2—310. Open Time for Payment or Running of Credit; Authority to Ship Under Reservation.

Unless otherwise agreed

(a) payment is due at the time and place at which the buyer is to receive the goods even though the place of shipment is the place of delivery; and

(b) if the seller is authorized to send the goods he may ship them under reservation, and may tender the documents of title, but the buyer may inspect the goods after their arrival before payment is due unless such inspection is inconsistent with the terms of the contract (Section 2—513); and

(c) if delivery is authorized and made by way of documents of title otherwise than by subsection (b) then payment is due at the time and place at which the buyer is to receive the documents regardless of where the goods are to be received; and

(d) where the seller is required or authorized to ship the goods on credit the credit period runs from the time of shipment but post-dating the invoice or delaying its dispatch will correspondingly delay the starting of the credit period.

§ 2—311. Options and Cooperation Respecting Performance.

(1) An agreement for sale which is otherwise sufficiently definite (subsection (3) of Section 2—204) to be a contract is not made invalid by the fact that it leaves particulars of performance to be specified by one of the parties. Any such specification must be made in good faith and within limits set by commercial reasonableness.

(2) Unless otherwise agreed specifications relating to assortment of the goods are at the buyer's option and except as otherwise provided in subsections (1)(c) and (3) of Section 2—319 specifications or arrangements relating to shipment are at the seller's option.

(3) Where such specification would materially affect the other party's performance but is not seasonably made or where one party's cooperation is necessary to the agreed performance of the other but is not seasonably forthcoming, the other party in addition to all other remedies

(a) is excused for any resulting delay in his own performance; and

(b) may also either proceed to perform in any reasonable manner or after the time for a material part of his own performance treat the failure to specify or to cooperate as a breach by failure to deliver or accept the goods.

§ 2—312. Warranty of Title and Against Infringement; Buyer's Obligation Against Infringement.

(1) Subject to subsection (2) there is in a contract for sale a warranty by the seller that

(a) the title conveyed shall be good, and its transfer rightful; and

(b) the goods shall be delivered free from any security interest or other lien or encumbrance of which the buyer at the time of contracting has no knowledge.

(2) A warranty under subsection (1) will be excluded or modified only by specific language or by circumstances

which give the buyer reason to know that the person selling does not claim title in himself or that he is purporting to sell only such right or title as he or a third person may have.

(3) Unless otherwise agreed a seller who is a merchant regularly dealing in goods of the kind warrants that the goods shall be delivered free of the rightful claim of any third person by way of infringement or the like but a buyer who furnishes specifications to the seller must hold the seller harmless against any such claim which arises out of compliance with the specifications.

§ 2—313. Express Warranties by Affirmation, Promise, Description, Sample.

(1) Express warranties by the seller are created as follows:

(a) Any affirmation of fact or promise made by the seller to the buyer which relates to the goods and becomes part of the basis of the bargain creates an express warranty that the goods shall conform to the affirmation or promise.

(b) Any description of the goods which is made part of the basis of the bargain creates an express warranty that the goods shall conform to the description.

(c) Any sample or model which is made part of the basis of the bargain creates an express warranty that the whole of the goods shall conform to the sample or model.

(2) It is not necessary to the creation of an express warranty that the seller use formal words such as "warrant" or "guarantee" or that he have a specific intention to make a warranty, but an affirmation merely of the value of the goods or a statement purporting to be merely the seller's opinion or commendation of the goods does not create a warranty.

§ 2—314. Implied Warranty: Merchantability; Usage of Trade.

(1) Unless excluded or modified (Section 2—316), a warranty that the goods shall be merchantable is implied in a contract for their sale if the seller is a merchant with respect to goods of that kind. Under this section the serving for value of food or drink to be consumed either on the premises or elsewhere is a sale.

(2) Goods to be merchantable must be at least such as

(a) pass without objection in the trade under the contract description; and

(b) in the case of fungible goods, are of fair average quality within the description; and

(c) are fit for the ordinary purposes for which such goods are used; and

(d) run, within the variations permitted by the agreement, of even kind, quality and quantity within each unit and among all units involved; and

(e) are adequately contained, packaged, and labeled as the agreement may require; and

(f) conform to the promises or affirmations of fact made on the container or label if any.

(3) Unless excluded or modified (Section 2—316) other implied warranties may arise from course of dealing or usage of trade.

§ 2—315. Implied Warranty: Fitness for Particular Purpose.

Where the seller at the time of contracting has reason to know any particular purpose for which the goods are required and that the buyer is relying on the seller's skill or judgment to select or furnish suitable goods, there is unless excluded or modified under the next section an implied warranty that the goods shall be fit for such purpose.

§ 2—316. Exclusion or Modification of Warranties.

(1) Words or conduct relevant to the creation of an express warranty and words or conduct tending to negate or limit warranty shall be construed wherever reasonable as consistent with each other; but subject to the provisions of this Article on parol or extrinsic evidence (Section 2—202) negation or limitation is inoperative to the extent that such construction is unreasonable.

(2) Subject to subsection (3), to exclude or modify the implied warranty of merchantability or any part of it the language must mention merchantability and in case of a writing must be conspicuous, and to exclude or modify any implied warranty of fitness the exclusion must be by a writing and conspicuous. Language to exclude all implied warranties of fitness is sufficient if it states, for example, that "There are no warranties which extend beyond the description on the face hereof."

(3) Notwithstanding subsection (2)

(a) unless the circumstances indicate otherwise, all implied warranties are excluded by expressions like "as is", "with all faults" or other language which in common understanding calls the buyer's attention to the exclusion of warranties and makes plain that there is no implied warranty; and

(b) when the buyer before entering into the contract has examined the goods or the sample or model as fully as he desired or has refused to examine the goods there is no implied warranty with regard to defects which an examination ought in the circumstances to have revealed to him; and

(c) an implied warranty can also be excluded or modified by course of dealing or course of performance or usage of trade.

(4) Remedies for breach of warranty can be limited in accordance with the provisions of this Article on liquidation or limitation of damages and on contractual modification of remedy (Sections 2—718 and 2—719).

§ 2—317. Cumulation and Conflict of Warranties Express or Implied.

Warranties whether express or implied shall be construed as consistent with each other and as cumulative, but if such construction is unreasonable the intention of the parties shall determine which warranty is dominant. In ascertaining that intention the following rules apply:

(a) Exact or technical specifications displace an inconsistent sample or model or general language of description.

(b) A sample from an existing bulk displaces inconsistent general language of description.

(c) Express warranties displace inconsistent implied warranties other than an implied warranty of fitness for a particular purpose.

§ 2—318. Third Party Beneficiaries of Warranties Express or Implied.

Note: If this Act is introduced in the Congress of the United States this section should be omitted. (States to select one alternative.)

Alternative A

A seller's warranty whether express or implied extends to any natural person who is in the family or household of his buyer or who is a guest in his home if it is reasonable to expect that such person may use, consume or be affected by the goods and who is injured in person by breach of the warranty. A seller may not exclude or limit the operation of this section.

Alternative B

A seller's warranty whether express or implied extends to any natural person who may reasonably be expected to use, consume or be affected by the goods and who is injured in person by breach of the warranty. A seller may not exclude or limit the operation of this section.

Alternative C

A seller's warranty whether express or implied extends to any person who may reasonably be expected to use, consume or be affected by the goods and who is injured by breach of the warranty. A seller may not exclude or limit the operation of this section with respect to injury to the person of an individual to whom the warranty extends. As amended 1966.

§ 2—319. F.O.B. and F.A.S. Terms.

(1) Unless otherwise agreed the term F.O.B. (which means "free on board") at a named place, even though used only in connection with the stated price, is a delivery term under which

(a) when the term is F.O.B. the place of shipment, the seller must at that place ship the goods in the manner provided in this Article (Section 2—504) and bear the expense and risk of putting them into the possession of the carrier; or

(b) when the term is F.O.B. the place of destination, the seller must at his own expense and risk transport the goods to that place and there tender delivery of them in the manner provided in this Article (Section 2—503);

(c) when under either (a) or (b) the term is also F.O.B. vessel, car or other vehicle, the seller must in addition at his own expense and risk load the goods on board. If the term is F.O.B. vessel the buyer must name the vessel and in an appropriate case the seller must comply with the provisions of this Article on the form of bill of lading (Section 2—323).

(2) Unless otherwise agreed the term F.A.S. vessel (which means "free alongside") at a named port, even though used only in connection with the stated price, is a delivery term under which the seller must

(a) at his own expense and risk deliver the goods alongside the vessel in the manner usual in that port or on a dock designated and provided by the buyer; and

(b) obtain and tender a receipt for the goods in exchange for which the carrier is under a duty to issue a bill of lading.

(3) Unless otherwise agreed in any case falling within subsection (1)(a) or (c) or subsection (2) the buyer must seasonably give any needed instructions for making delivery, including when the term is F.A.S. or F.O.B. the loading berth of the vessel and in an appropriate case its name and sailing date. The seller may treat the failure of needed instructions as a failure of cooperation under this Article (Section 2—311). He may also at his option move the goods in any reasonable manner preparatory to delivery or shipment.

(4) Under the term F.O.B. vessel or F.A.S. unless otherwise agreed the buyer must make payment against tender of the required documents and the seller may not tender nor the buyer demand delivery of the goods in substitution for the documents.

§ 2—320. C.I.F. and C. & F. Terms.

(1) The term C.I.F. means that the price includes in a lump sum the cost of the goods and the insurance and freight to the named destination. The term C. & F. or C.F. means that the price so includes cost and freight to the named destination.

(2) Unless otherwise agreed and even though used only in connection with the stated price and destination, the term C.I.F. destination or its equivalent requires the seller at his own expense and risk to

(a) put the goods into the possession of a carrier at the port for shipment and obtain a negotiable bill or bills of lading covering the entire transportation to the named destination; and

(b) load the goods and obtain a receipt from the carrier (which may be contained in the bill of lading) showing that the freight has been paid or provided for; and

(c) obtain a policy or certificate of insurance, including any war risk insurance, of a kind and on terms then current at the port of shipment in the usual amount, in the currency of the contract, shown to cover the same goods covered by the bill of lading and providing for payment of loss to the order of the buyer or for the account of whom it may concern; but the seller may add to the price the amount of the premium for any such war risk insurance; and

(d) prepare an invoice of the goods and procure any other documents required to effect shipment or to comply with the contract; and

(e) forward and tender with commercial promptness all the documents in due form and with any indorsement necessary to perfect the buyer's rights.

(3) Unless otherwise agreed the term C. & F. or its equivalent has the same effect and imposes upon the seller the same obligations and risks as a C.I.F. term except the obligation as to insurance.

(4) Under the term C.I.F. or C. & F. unless otherwise agreed the buyer must make payment against tender of the required documents and the seller may not tender nor the buyer demand delivery of the goods in substitution for the documents.

§ 2—321. C.I.F. or C. & F.: "Net Landed Weights"; "Payment on Arrival"; Warranty of Condition on Arrival.

Under a contract containing a term C.I.F. or C. & F.

(1) Where the price is based on or is to be adjusted according to "net landed weights", "delivered weights", "out turn" quantity or quality or the like, unless otherwise agreed the seller must reasonably estimate the price. The payment due on tender of the documents called for by the contract is the amount so estimated, but after final adjustment of the price a settlement must be made with commercial promptness.

(2) An agreement described in subsection (1) or any warranty of quality or condition of the goods on arrival places upon the seller the risk of ordinary deterioration, shrinkage and the like in transportation but has no effect on the place or time of identification to the contract for sale or delivery or on the passing of the risk of loss.

(3) Unless otherwise agreed where the contract provides for payment on or after arrival of the goods the seller must before payment allow such preliminary inspection as is feasible; but if the goods are lost delivery of the documents and payment are due when the goods should have arrived.

§ 2—322. Delivery "Ex-Ship".

(1) Unless otherwise agreed a term for delivery of goods "ex-ship" (which means from the carrying vessel) or in equivalent language is not restricted to a particular ship and requires delivery from a ship which has reached a place at the named port of destination where goods of the kind are usually discharged.

(2) Under such a term unless otherwise agreed

(a) the seller must discharge all liens arising out of the carriage and furnish the buyer with a direction which puts the carrier under a duty to deliver the goods; and

(b) the risk of loss does not pass to the buyer until the goods leave the ship's tackle or are otherwise properly unloaded.

§ 2—323. Form of Bill of Lading Required in Overseas Shipment; "Overseas".

(1) Where the contract contemplates overseas shipment and contains a term C.I.F. or C. & F. or F.O.B. vessel, the seller unless otherwise agreed must obtain a negotiable bill of lading stating that the goods have been loaded on board or, in the case of a term C.I.F. or C. & F., received for shipment.

(2) Where in a case within subsection (1) a bill of lading has been issued in a set of parts, unless otherwise agreed if the documents are not to be sent from abroad the buyer may demand tender of the full set; otherwise only one part of the bill of lading need be tendered. Even if the agreement expressly requires a full set

(a) due tender of a single part is acceptable within the provisions of this Article on cure of improper delivery (subsection (1) of Section 2—508); and

(b) even though the full set is demanded, if the documents are sent from abroad the person tendering an incomplete set may nevertheless require payment upon furnishing an indemnity which the buyer in good faith deems adequate.

(3) A shipment by water or by air or a contract contemplating such shipment is "overseas" insofar as by usage of trade or agreement it is subject to the commercial, financing or shipping practices characteristic of international deep water commerce.

§ 2—324. "No Arrival, No Sale" Term.

Under a term "no arrival, no sale" or terms of like meaning, unless otherwise agreed,

(a) the seller must properly ship conforming goods and if they arrive by any means he must tender them on arrival but he assumes no obligation that the goods will arrive unless he has caused the non-arrival; and

(b) where without fault of the seller the goods are in part lost or have so deteriorated as no longer to conform to the contract or arrive after the contract time, the buyer may proceed as if there had been casualty to identified goods (Section 2—613).

§ 2—325. "Letter of Credit" Term; "Confirmed Credit".

(1) Failure of the buyer seasonably to furnish an agreed letter of credit is a breach of the contract for sale.

(2) The delivery to seller of a proper letter of credit suspends the buyer's obligation to pay. If the letter of credit is dishonored, the seller may on seasonable notification to the buyer require payment directly from him.

(3) Unless otherwise agreed the term "letter of credit" or "banker's credit" in a contract for sale means an irrevocable credit issued by a financing agency of good repute and, where the shipment is overseas, of good international repute. The term "confirmed credit" means that the credit must also carry the direct obligation of such an agency which does business in the seller's financial market.

§ 2—326. Sale on Approval and Sale or Return; Consignment Sales and Rights of Creditors.

(1) Unless otherwise agreed, if delivered goods may be returned by the buyer even though they conform to the contract, the transaction is

(a) a "sale on approval" if the goods are delivered primarily for use, and

(b) a "sale or return" if the goods are delivered primarily for resale.

(2) Except as provided in subsection (3), goods held on approval are not subject to the claims of the buyer's creditors until acceptance; goods held on sale or return are subject to such claims while in the buyer's possession.

(3) Where goods are delivered to a person for sale and such person maintains a place of business at which he deals in goods of the kind involved, under a name other than the name of the person making delivery, then with respect to claims of creditors of the person conducting the business the goods are deemed to be on sale or return. The provisions of this subsection are applicable even though an agreement purports to reserve title to the person making delivery until payment or resale or uses such words as "on consignment" or "on memorandum". However, this subsection is not applicable if the person making delivery

(a) complies with an applicable law providing for a consignor's interest or the like to be evidenced by a sign, or

(b) establishes that the person conducting the business is generally known by his creditors to be substantially engaged in selling the goods of others, or

(c) complies with the filing provisions of the Article on Secured Transactions (Article 9).

(4) Any "or return" term of a contract for sale is to be treated as a separate contract for sale within the statute of frauds section of this Article (Section 2—201) and as contradicting the sale aspect of the contract within the provisions of this Article on parol or extrinsic evidence (Section 2—202).

§ 2—327. Special Incidents of Sale on Approval and Sale or Return.

(1) Under a sale on approval unless otherwise agreed

(a) although the goods are identified to the contract the risk of loss and the title do not pass to the buyer until acceptance; and

(b) use of the goods consistent with the purpose of trial is not acceptance but failure seasonably to notify the seller of election to return the goods is acceptance, and if the goods conform to the contract acceptance of any part is acceptance of the whole; and

(c) after due notification of election to return, the return is at the seller's risk and expense but a merchant buyer must follow any reasonable instructions.

(2) Under a sale or return unless otherwise agreed

(a) the option to return extends to the whole or any commercial unit of the goods while in substantially their original condition, but must be exercised seasonably; and

(b) the return is at the buyer's risk and expense.

§ 2—328. Sale by Auction.

(1) In a sale by auction if goods are put up in lots each lot is the subject of a separate sale.

(2) A sale by auction is complete when the auctioneer so announces by the fall of the hammer or in other customary manner. Where a bid is made while the hammer is falling in acceptance of a prior bid the auctioneer may in his discretion reopen the bidding or declare the goods sold under the bid on which the hammer was falling.

(3) Such a sale is with reserve unless the goods are in explicit terms put up without reserve. In an auction with reserve the auctioneer may withdraw the goods at any time until he announces completion of the sale. In an auction without reserve, after the auctioneer calls for bids on an article or lot, that article or lot cannot be withdrawn unless no bid is made within a reasonable time. In either case a bidder may retract his bid until the auctioneer's announcement of completion of the sale, but a bidder's retraction does not revive any previous bid.

(4) If the auctioneer knowingly receives a bid on the seller's behalf or the seller makes or procures such a bid, and notice has not been given that liberty for such bidding is reserved, the buyer may at his option avoid the sale or take the goods at the price of the last good faith bid prior to the completion of the sale. This subsection shall not apply to any bid at a forced sale.

Part 4 Title, Creditors and Good Faith Purchasers

§ 2—401. Passing of Title; Reservation for Security; Limited Application of This Section.

Each provision of this Article with regard to the rights, obligations and remedies of the seller, the buyer, purchasers or other third parties applies irrespective of title to the goods except where the provision refers to such title. Insofar as situations are not covered by the other provisions of this Article and matters concerning title become material the following rules apply:

(1) Title to goods cannot pass under a contract for sale prior to their identification to the contract (Section 2—501), and unless otherwise explicitly agreed the buyer acquires by their identification a special property as limited by this Act. Any retention or reservation by the seller of the title (property) in goods shipped or delivered to the buyer is limited in effect to a reservation of a security interest. Subject to these provisions and to the provisions of the Article on Secured Transactions (Article 9), title to goods passes from the seller to the buyer in any manner and on any conditions explicitly agreed on by the parties.

(2) Unless otherwise explicitly agreed title passes to the buyer at the time and place at which the seller completes his performance with reference to the physical delivery of the goods, despite any reservation of a security interest and even though a document of title is to be delivered at a different time or place; and in particular and despite any reservation of a security interest by the bill of lading

(a) if the contract requires or authorizes the seller to send the goods to the buyer but does not require him to deliver them at destination, title passes to the buyer at the time and place of shipment; but

(b) if the contract requires delivery at destination, title passes on tender there.

(3) Unless otherwise explicitly agreed where delivery is to be made without moving the goods,

(a) if the seller is to deliver a document of title, title passes at the time when and the place where he delivers such documents; or

(b) if the goods are at the time of contracting already identified and no documents are to be delivered, title passes at the time and place of contracting.

(4) A rejection or other refusal by the buyer to receive or retain the goods, whether or not justified, or a justified revocation of acceptance revests title to the goods in the seller. Such revesting occurs by operation of law and is not a "sale".

§ 2—402. Rights of Seller's Creditors Against Sold Goods.

(1) Except as provided in subsections (2) and (3), rights of unsecured creditors of the seller with respect to goods which have been identified to a contract for sale are subject to the buyer's rights to recover the goods under this Article (Sections 2—502 and 2—716).

(2) A creditor of the seller may treat a sale or an identification of goods to a contract for sale as void if as against him a retention of possession by the seller is fraudulent under any rule of law of the state where the goods are situated, except that retention of possession in good faith and current course of trade by a merchant-seller for a commercially reasonable time after a sale or identification is not fraudulent.

(3) Nothing in this Article shall be deemed to impair the rights of creditors of the seller

(a) under the provisions of the Article on Secured Transactions (Article 9); or

(b) where identification to the contract or delivery is made not in current course of trade but in satisfaction of or as security for a pre-existing claim for money, security or the like and is made under circumstances which under any rule of law of the state where the goods are situated would apart from this Article constitute the transaction a fraudulent transfer or voidable preference.

§ 2—403. Power to Transfer; Good Faith Purchase of Goods; "Entrusting".

(1) A purchaser of goods acquires all title which his transferor had or had power to transfer except that a purchaser of a limited interest acquires rights only to the extent of the interest purchased. A person with voidable title has power to transfer a good title to a good faith purchaser for value. When goods have been delivered under a transaction of purchase the purchaser has such power even though

(a) the transferor was deceived as to the identity of the purchaser, or

(b) the delivery was in exchange for a check which is later dishonored, or

(c) it was agreed that the transaction was to be a "cash sale", or

(d) the delivery was procured through fraud punishable as larcenous under the criminal law.

(2) Any entrusting of possession of goods to a merchant who deals in goods of that kind gives him power to transfer all rights of the entruster to a buyer in ordinary course of business.

(3) "Entrusting" includes any delivery and any acquiescence in retention of possession regardless of any condition expressed between the parties to the delivery or acquiescence and regardless of whether the procurement of the entrusting or the possessor's disposition of the goods have been such as to be larcenous under the criminal law.

(4) The rights of other purchasers of goods and of lien creditors are governed by the Articles on Secured Transactions (Article 9), Bulk Transfers (Article 6) and Documents of Title (Article 7).

Part 5 Performance

§ 2—501. Insurable Interest in Goods; Manner of Identification of Goods.

(1) The buyer obtains a special property and an insurable interest in goods by identification of existing goods as goods to which the contract refers even though the goods so identified are non-conforming and he has an option to return or reject them. Such identification can be made at any time and in any manner explicitly agreed to by the parties. In the absence of explicit agreement identification occurs

(a) when the contract is made if it is for the sale of goods already existing and identified;

(b) if the contract is for the sale of future goods other than those described in paragraph (c), when goods are shipped, marked or otherwise designated by the seller as goods to which the contract refers;

(c) when the crops are planted or otherwise become growing crops or the young are conceived if the contract is for the sale of unborn young to be born within twelve months after contracting or for the sale of crops to be harvested within twelve months or the next normal harvest season after contracting whichever is longer.

(2) The seller retains an insurable interest in goods so long as title to or any security interest in the goods remains in him and where the identification is by the seller alone he may until default or insolvency or notification to the buyer that the identification is final substitute other goods for those identified.

(3) Nothing in this section impairs any insurable interest recognized under any other statute or rule of law.

§ 2—502. Buyer's Right to Goods on Seller's Insolvency.

(1) Subject to subsection (2) and even though the goods have not been shipped a buyer who has paid a part or all of the price of goods in which he has a special property under the provisions of the immediately preceding section may on making and keeping good a tender of any unpaid portion of their price recover them from the seller if the seller becomes insolvent within ten days after receipt of the first installment on their price.

(2) If the identification creating his special property has been made by the buyer he acquires the right to recover the goods only if they conform to the contract for sale.

§ 2—503. Manner of Seller's Tender of Delivery.

(1) Tender of delivery requires that the seller put and hold conforming goods at the buyer's disposition and give the buyer any notification reasonably necessary to enable him to take delivery. The manner, time and place for tender are determined by the agreement and this Article, and in particular

(a) tender must be at a reasonable hour, and if it is of goods they must be kept available for the period reasonably necessary to enable the buyer to take possession; but

(b) unless otherwise agreed the buyer must furnish facilities reasonably suited to the receipt of the goods.

(2) Where the case is within the next section respecting shipment tender requires that the seller comply with its provisions.

(3) Where the seller is required to deliver at a particular destination tender requires that he comply with subsec-

tion (1) and also in any appropriate case tender documents as described in subsections (4) and (5) of this section.

(4) Where goods are in the possession of a bailee and are to be delivered without being moved

(a) tender requires that the seller either tender a negotiable document of title covering such goods or procure acknowledgment by the bailee of the buyer's right to possession of the goods; but

(b) tender to the buyer of a non-negotiable document of title or of a written direction to the bailee to deliver is sufficient tender unless the buyer seasonably objects, and receipt by the bailee of notification of the buyer's rights fixes those rights as against the bailee and all third persons; but risk of loss of the goods and of any failure by the bailee to honor the non-negotiable document of title or to obey the direction remains on the seller until the buyer has had a reasonable time to present the document or direction, and a refusal by the bailee to honor the document or to obey the direction defeats the tender.

(5) Where the contract requires the seller to deliver documents

(a) he must tender all such documents in correct form, except as provided in this Article with respect to bills of lading in a set (subsection (2) of Section 2—323); and

(b) tender through customary banking channels is sufficient and dishonor of a draft accompanying the documents constitutes non-acceptance or rejection.

§ 2—504. Shipment by Seller.

Where the seller is required or authorized to send the goods to the buyer and the contract does not require him to deliver them at a particular destination, then unless otherwise agreed he must

(a) put the goods in the possession of such a carrier and make such a contract for their transportation as may be reasonable having regard to the nature of the goods and other circumstances of the case; and

(b) obtain and promptly deliver or tender in due form any document necessary to enable the buyer to obtain possession of the goods or otherwise required by the agreement or by usage of trade; and

(c) promptly notify the buyer of the shipment.

Failure to notify the buyer under paragraph (c) or to make a proper contract under paragraph (a) is a ground for rejection only if material delay or loss ensues.

§ 2—505. Seller's Shipment under Reservation.

(1) Where the seller has identified goods to the contract by or before shipment:

(a) his procurement of a negotiable bill of lading to his own order or otherwise reserves in him a security interest in the goods. His procurement of the bill to the order of a financing agency or of the buyer indicates in addition only the seller's expectation of transferring that interest to the person named.

(b) a non-negotiable bill of lading to himself or his nominee reserves possession of the goods as security but except in a case of conditional delivery (subsection (2) of Section 2—507) a non-negotiable bill of lading naming the buyer as consignee reserves no security interest even though the seller retains possession of the bill of lading.

(2) When shipment by the seller with reservation of a security interest is in violation of the contract for sale it constitutes an improper contract for transportation within the preceding section but impairs neither the rights given to the buyer by shipment and identification of the goods to the contract nor the seller's powers as a holder of a negotiable document.

§ 2—506. Rights of Financing Agency.

(1) A financing agency by paying or purchasing for value a draft which relates to a shipment of goods acquires to the extent of the payment or purchase and in addition to its own rights under the draft and any document of title securing it any rights of the shipper in the goods including the right to stop delivery and the shipper's right to have the draft honored by the buyer.

(2) The right to reimbursement of a financing agency which has in good faith honored or purchased the draft under commitment to or authority from the buyer is not impaired by subsequent discovery of defects with reference to any relevant document which was apparently regular on its face.

§ 2—507. Effect of Seller's Tender; Delivery on Condition.

(1) Tender of delivery is a condition to the buyer's duty to accept the goods and, unless otherwise agreed, to his duty to pay for them. Tender entitles the seller to acceptance of the goods and to payment according to the contract.

(2) Where payment is due and demanded on the delivery to the buyer of goods or documents of title, his right as against the seller to retain or dispose of them is conditional upon his making the payment due.

§ 2—508. Cure by Seller of Improper Tender or Delivery; Replacement.

(1) Where any tender or delivery by the seller is rejected because non-conforming and the time for performance has not yet expired, the seller may seasonably notify the buyer of his intention to cure and may then within the contract time make a conforming delivery.

(2) Where the buyer rejects a non-conforming tender which the seller had reasonable grounds to believe would be acceptable with or without money allowance the seller may if he seasonably notifies the buyer have a further reasonable time to substitute a conforming tender.

§ 2—509. Risk of Loss in the Absence of Breach.

(1) Where the contract requires or authorizes the seller to ship the goods by carrier

(a) if it does not require him to deliver them at a particular destination, the risk of loss passes to the buyer when the goods are duly delivered to the carrier even though the shipment is under reservation (Section 2—505); but

(b) if it does require him to deliver them at a particular destination and the goods are there duly tendered while in the possession of the carrier, the risk of loss passes to the buyer when the goods are there duly so tendered as to enable the buyer to take delivery.

(2) Where the goods are held by a bailee to be delivered without being moved, the risk of loss passes to the buyer

(a) on his receipt of a negotiable document of title covering the goods; or

(b) on acknowledgment by the bailee of the buyer's right to possession of the goods; or

(c) after his receipt of a non-negotiable document of title or other written direction to deliver, as provided in subsection (4)(b) of Section 2—503.

(3) In any case not within subsection (1) or (2), the risk of loss passes to the buyer on his receipt of the goods if the seller is a merchant; otherwise the risk passes to the buyer on tender of delivery.

(4) The provisions of this section are subject to contrary agreement of the parties and to the provisions of this Article on sale on approval (Section 2—327) and on effect of breach on risk of loss (Section 2—510).

§ 2—510. Effect of Breach on Risk of Loss.

(1) Where a tender or delivery of goods so fails to conform to the contract as to give a right of rejection the risk of their loss remains on the seller until cure or acceptance.

(2) Where the buyer rightfully revokes acceptance he may to the extent of any deficiency in his effective insurance coverage treat the risk of loss as having rested on the seller from the beginning.

(3) Where the buyer as to conforming goods already identified to the contract for sale repudiates or is otherwise in breach before risk of their loss has passed to him, the seller may to the extent of any deficiency in his effective insurance coverage treat the risk of loss as resting on the buyer for a commercially reasonable time.

§ 2—511. Tender of Payment by Buyer; Payment by Check.

(1) Unless otherwise agreed tender of payment is a condition to the seller's duty to tender and complete any delivery.

(2) Tender of payment is sufficient when made by any means or in any manner current in the ordinary course of business unless the seller demands payment in legal tender and gives any extension of time reasonably necessary to procure it.

(3) Subject to the provisions of this Act on the effect of an instrument on an obligation (Section 3—802), payment by check is conditional and is defeated as between the parties by dishonor of the check on due presentment.

§ 2—512. Payment by Buyer Before Inspection.

(1) Where the contract requires payment before inspection non-conformity of the goods does not excuse the buyer from so making payment unless

(a) the non-conformity appears without inspection; or

(b) despite tender of the required documents the circumstances would justify injunction against honor under the provisions of this Act (Section 5—114).

(2) Payment pursuant to subsection (1) does not constitute an acceptance of goods or impair the buyer's right to inspect or any of his remedies.

§ 2—513. Buyer's Right to Inspection of Goods.

(1) Unless otherwise agreed and subject to subsection (3), where goods are tendered or delivered or identified to the contract for sale, the buyer has a right before payment or acceptance to inspect them at any reasonable place and time and in any reasonable manner. When the seller is required or authorized to send the goods to the buyer, the inspection may be after their arrival.

(2) Expenses of inspection must be borne by the buyer but may be recovered from the seller if the goods do not conform and are rejected.

(3) Unless otherwise agreed and subject to the provisions of this Article on C.I.F. contracts (subsection (3) of Section 2—321), the buyer is not entitled to inspect the goods before payment of the price when the contract provides

(a) for delivery "C.O.D." or on other like terms; or

(b) for payment against documents of title, except where such payment is due only after the goods are to become available for inspection.

(4) A place or method of inspection fixed by the parties is presumed to be exclusive but unless otherwise expressly agreed it does not postpone identification or shift the place for delivery or for passing the risk of loss. If compliance becomes impossible, inspection shall be as provided in this section unless the place or method fixed was clearly intended as an indispensable condition failure of which avoids the contract.

§ 2—514. When Documents Deliverable on Acceptance; When on Payment.

Unless otherwise agreed documents against which a draft is drawn are to be delivered to the drawee on acceptance of the draft if it is payable more than three days after presentment; otherwise, only on payment.

§ 2—515. Preserving Evidence of Goods in Dispute.

In furtherance of the adjustment of any claim or dispute

(a) either party on reasonable notification to the other and for the purpose of ascertaining the facts and preserving evidence has the right to inspect, test and sample the goods including such of them as may be in the possession or control of the other; and

(b) the parties may agree to a third party inspection or survey to determine the conformity or condition of the goods and may agree that the findings shall be binding upon them in any subsequent litigation or adjustment.

Part 6 Breach, Repudiation and Excuse

§ 2—601. Buyer's Rights on Improper Delivery.

Subject to the provisions of this Article on breach in installment contracts (Section 2—612) and unless otherwise agreed under the sections on contractual limitations of remedy (Sections 2—718 and 2—719), if the goods or the tender of delivery fail in any respect to conform to the contract, the buyer may

(a) reject the whole; or

(b) accept the whole; or

(c) accept any commercial unit or units and reject the rest.

§ 2—602. Manner and Effect of Rightful Rejection.

(1) Rejection of goods must be within a reasonable time after their delivery or tender. It is ineffective unless the buyer seasonably notifies the seller.

(2) Subject to the provisions of the two following sections on rejected goods (Sections 2—603 and 2—604),

(a) after rejection any exercise of ownership by the buyer with respect to any commercial unit is wrongful as against the seller; and

(b) if the buyer has before rejection taken physical possession of goods in which he does not have a security interest under the provisions of this Article (subsection (3) of Section 2—711), he is under a duty after rejection to hold them with reasonable care at the seller's disposition for a time sufficient to permit the seller to remove them; but

(c) the buyer has no further obligations with regard to goods rightfully rejected.

(3) The seller's rights with respect to goods wrongfully rejected are governed by the provisions of this Article on Seller's remedies in general (Section 2—703).

§ 2—603. Merchant Buyer's Duties as to Rightfully Rejected Goods.

(1) Subject to any security interest in the buyer (subsection (3) of Section 2—711), when the seller has no agent or place of business at the market of rejection a merchant buyer is under a duty after rejection of goods in his possession or control to follow any reasonable instructions received from the seller with respect to the goods and in the absence of such instructions to make reasonable efforts to sell them for the seller's account if they are perishable or threaten to decline in value speedily. Instructions are not reasonable if on demand indemnity for expenses is not forthcoming.

(2) When the buyer sells goods under subsection (1), he is entitled to reimbursement from the seller or out of the proceeds for reasonable expenses of caring for and selling them, and if the expenses include no selling commission then to such commission as is usual in the trade or if there is none to a reasonable sum not exceeding ten per cent on the gross proceeds.

(3) In complying with this section the buyer is held only to good faith and good faith conduct hereunder is neither acceptance nor conversion nor the basis of an action for damages.

§ 2—604. Buyer's Options as to Salvage of Rightfully Rejected Goods.

Subject to the provisions of the immediately preceding section on perishables if the seller gives no instructions within a reasonable time after notification of rejection the buyer may store the rejected goods for the seller's account or reship them to him or resell them for the seller's account with reimbursement as provided in the preceding section. Such action is not acceptance or conversion.

§ 2—605. Waiver of Buyer's Objections by Failure to Particularize.

(1) The buyer's failure to state in connection with rejection a particular defect which is ascertainable by reasonable inspection precludes him from relying on the unstated defect to justify rejection or to establish breach

(a) where the seller could have cured it if stated seasonably; or

(b) between merchants when the seller has after rejection made a request in writing for a full and final written statement of all defects on which the buyer proposes to rely.

(2) Payment against documents made without reservation of rights precludes recovery of the payment for defects apparent on the face of the documents.

§ 2—606. What Constitutes Acceptance of Goods.

(1) Acceptance of goods occurs when the buyer

(a) after a reasonable opportunity to inspect the goods signifies to the seller that the goods are conforming or that he will take or retain them in spite of their nonconformity; or

(b) fails to make an effective rejection (subsection (1) of Section 2—602), but such acceptance does not occur until the buyer has had a reasonable opportunity to inspect them; or

(c) does any act inconsistent with the seller's ownership; but if such act is wrongful as against the seller it is an acceptance only if ratified by him.

(2) Acceptance of a part of any commercial unit is acceptance of that entire unit.

§ 2—607. Effect of Acceptance; Notice of Breach; Burden of Establishing Breach After Acceptance; Notice of Claim or Litigation to Person Answerable Over.

(1) The buyer must pay at the contract rate for any goods accepted.

(2) Acceptance of goods by the buyer precludes rejection of the goods accepted and if made with knowledge of a non-conformity cannot be revoked because of it unless the acceptance was on the reasonable assumption that the non-conformity would be seasonably cured but acceptance does not of itself impair any other remedy provided by this Article for non-conformity.

(3) Where a tender has been accepted

(a) the buyer must within a reasonable time after he discovers or should have discovered any breach notify the seller of breach or be barred from any remedy; and

(b) if the claim is one for infringement or the like (subsection (3) of Section 2—312) and the buyer is sued as a result of such a breach he must so notify the seller within a reasonable time after he receives notice of the litigation or be barred from any remedy over for liability established by the litigation.

(4) The burden is on the buyer to establish any breach with respect to the goods accepted.

(5) Where the buyer is sued for breach of a warranty or other obligation for which his seller is answerable over

(a) he may give his seller written notice of the litigation. If the notice states that the seller may come in and defend and that if the seller does not do so he will be bound in any action against him by his buyer by any determination of fact common to the two litigations, then unless the seller after seasonable receipt of the notice does come in and defend he is so bound.

(b) if the claim is one for infringement or the like (subsection (3) of Section 2—312) the original seller may demand in writing that his buyer turn over to him control of the litigation including settlement or else be barred from any remedy over and if he also agrees to bear all expense and to satisfy any adverse judgment, then unless the buyer after seasonable receipt of the demand does turn over control the buyer is so barred.

(6) The provisions of subsections (3), (4) and (5) apply to any obligation of a buyer to hold the seller harmless against infringement or the like (subsection (3) of Section 2—312).

§ 2—608. Revocation of Acceptance in Whole or in Part.

(1) The buyer may revoke his acceptance of a lot or commercial unit whose non-conformity substantially impairs its value to him if he has accepted it

(a) on the reasonable assumption that its nonconformity would be cured and it has not been seasonably cured; or

(b) without discovery of such non-conformity if his acceptance was reasonably induced either by the difficulty of discovery before acceptance or by the seller's assurances.

(2) Revocation of acceptance must occur within a reasonable time after the buyer discovers or should have discovered the ground for it and before any substantial change in condition of the goods which is not caused by their own defects. It is not effective until the buyer notifies the seller of it.

(3) A buyer who so revokes has the same rights and duties with regard to the goods involved as if he had rejected them.

§ 2—609. Right to Adequate Assurance of Performance.

(1) A contract for sale imposes an obligation on each party that the other's expectation of receiving due performance will not be impaired. When reasonable grounds for insecurity arise with respect to the performance of either party the other may in writing demand adequate assurance of due performance and until he receives such assurance may if commercially reasonable suspend any performance for which he has not already received the agreed return.

(2) Between merchants the reasonableness of grounds for insecurity and the adequacy of any assurance offered shall be determined according to commercial standards.

(3) Acceptance of any improper delivery or payment does not prejudice the party's right to demand adequate assurance of future performance.

(4) After receipt of a justified demand failure to provide within a reasonable time not exceeding thirty days such assurance of due performance as is adequate under the circumstances of the particular case is a repudiation of the contract.

§ 2—610. Anticipatory Repudiation.

When either party repudiates the contract with respect to a performance not yet due the loss of which will substantially impair the value of the contract to the other, the aggrieved party may

(a) for a commercially reasonable time await performance by the repudiating party; or

(b) resort to any remedy for breach (Section 2—703 or Section 2—711), even though he has notified the repudiating party that he would await the latter's performance and has urged retraction; and

(c) in either case suspend his own performance or proceed in accordance with the provisions of this Article on the seller's right to identify goods to the contract notwithstanding breach or to salvage unfinished goods (Section 2—704).

§ 2—611. Retraction of Anticipatory Repudiation.

(1) Until the repudiating party's next performance is due he can retract his repudiation unless the aggrieved party has since the repudiation cancelled or materially changed his position or otherwise indicated that he considers the repudiation final.

(2) Retraction may be by any method which clearly indicates to the aggrieved party that the repudiating party intends to perform, but must include any assurance justifiably demanded under the provisions of this Article (Section 2—609).

(3) Retraction reinstates the repudiating party's rights under the contract with due excuse and allowance to the aggrieved party for any delay occasioned by the repudiation.

§ 2—612. "Installment Contract"; Breach.

(1) An "installment contract" is one which requires or authorizes the delivery of goods in separate lots to be separately accepted, even though the contract contains a clause "each delivery is a separate contract" or its equivalent.

(2) The buyer may reject any installment which is non-conforming if the non-conformity substantially impairs the value of that installment and cannot be cured or if the non-conformity is a defect in the required documents; but if the non-conformity does not fall within subsection (3) and the seller gives adequate assurance of its cure the buyer must accept that installment.

(3) Whenever non-conformity or default with respect to one or more installments substantially impairs the value of the whole contract there is a breach of the whole. But the aggrieved party reinstates the contract if he accepts a non-conforming installment without seasonably notifying of cancellation or if he brings an action with respect only to past installments or demands performance as to future installments.

§ 2—613. Casualty to Identified Goods.

Where the contract requires for its performance goods identified when the contract is made, and the goods suffer casualty without fault of either party before the risk of loss passes to the buyer, or in a proper case under a "no arrival, no sale" term (Section 2—324) then

(a) if the loss is total the contract is avoided; and

(b) if the loss is partial or the goods have so deteriorated as no longer to conform to the contract the buyer may nevertheless demand inspection and at his option either treat the contract as voided or accept the goods with due allowance from the contract price for the deterioration or the deficiency in quantity but without further right against the seller.

§ 2—614. Substituted Performance.

(1) Where without fault of either party the agreed berthing, loading, or unloading facilities fail or an agreed type of carrier becomes unavailable or the agreed manner of delivery otherwise becomes commercially impracticable but a commercially reasonable substitute is available, such substitute performance must be tendered and accepted.

(2) If the agreed means or manner of payment fails because of domestic or foreign governmental regulation, the seller may withhold or stop delivery unless the buyer provides a means or manner of payment which is commercially a substantial equivalent. If delivery has already been taken, payment by the means or in the manner provided by the regulation discharges the buyer's obligation unless the regulation is discriminatory, oppressive or predatory.

§ 2—615. Excuse by Failure of Presupposed Conditions.

Except so far as a seller may have assumed a greater obligation and subject to the preceding section on substituted performance:

(a) Delay in delivery or non-delivery in whole or in part by a seller who complies with paragraphs (b) and (c) is not a breach of his duty under a contract for sale if performance as agreed has been made impracticable by the occurrence of a contingency the nonoccurrence of which was a basic assumption on which the contract was made or by compliance in good faith with any applicable foreign or domestic governmental regulation or order whether or not it later proves to be invalid.

(b) Where the causes mentioned in paragraph (a) affect only a part of the seller's capacity to perform, he must allocate production and deliveries among his customers but may at his option include regular customers not then under contract as well as his own requirements for further manufacture. He may so allocate in any manner which is fair and reasonable.

(c) The seller must notify the buyer seasonably that there will be delay or non-delivery and, when allocation is required under paragraph (b), of the estimated quota thus made available for the buyer.

§ 2—616. Procedure on Notice Claiming Excuse.

(1) Where the buyer receives notification of a material or indefinite delay or an allocation justified under the preceding section he may by written notification to the seller as to any delivery concerned, and where the prospective deficiency substantially impairs the value of the whole contract under the provisions of this Article relating to breach of installment contracts (Section 2—612), then also as to the whole,

(a) terminate and thereby discharge any unexecuted portion of the contract; or

(b) modify the contract by agreeing to take his available quota in substitution.

(2) If after receipt of such notification from the seller the buyer fails so to modify the contract within a reasonable time not exceeding thirty days the contract lapses with respect to any deliveries affected.

(3) The provisions of this section may not be negated by agreement except in so far as the seller has assumed a greater obligation under the preceding section.

Part 7 Remedies

§ 2—701. Remedies for Breach of Collateral Contracts Not Impaired.

Remedies for breach of any obligation or promise collateral or ancillary to a contract for sale are not impaired by the provisions of this Article.

§ 2—702. Seller's Remedies on Discovery of Buyer's Insolvency.

(1) Where the seller discovers the buyer to be insolvent he may refuse delivery except for cash including payment for all goods theretofore delivered under the contract, and stop delivery under this Article (Section 2—705).

(2) Where the seller discovers that the buyer has received goods on credit while insolvent he may reclaim the goods upon demand made within ten days after the receipt, but if misrepresentation of solvency has been made to the particular seller in writing within three months before delivery the ten day limitation does not apply. Except as provided in this subsection the seller may not base a right to reclaim goods on the buyer's fraudulent or innocent misrepresentation of solvency or of intent to pay.

(3) The seller's right to reclaim under subsection (2) is subject to the rights of a buyer in ordinary course or other good faith purchaser under this Article (Section 2—403). Successful reclamation of goods excludes all other remedies with respect to them.

§ 2—703. Seller's Remedies in General.

Where the buyer wrongfully rejects or revokes acceptance of goods or fails to make a payment due on or before delivery or repudiates with respect to a part or the whole, then with respect to any goods directly affected and, if the breach is of the whole contract (Section 2—612), then also with respect to the whole undelivered balance, the aggrieved seller may

(a) withhold delivery of such goods;

(b) stop delivery by any bailee as hereafter provided (Section 2—705);

(c) proceed under the next section respecting goods still unidentified to the contract;

(d) resell and recover damages as hereafter provided (Section 2—706);

(e) recover damages for non-acceptance (Section 2—708) or in a proper case the price (Section 2—709);

(f) cancel.

§ 2—704. Seller's Right to Identify Goods to the Contract Notwithstanding Breach or to Salvage Unfinished Goods.

(1) An aggrieved seller under the preceding section may

(a) identify to the contract conforming goods not already identified if at the time he learned of the breach they are in his possession or control;

(b) treat as the subject of resale goods which have demonstrably been intended for the particular contract even though those goods are unfinished.

(2) Where the goods are unfinished an aggrieved seller may in the exercise of reasonable commercial judgment for the purposes of avoiding loss and of effective realization either complete the manufacture and wholly identify the goods to the contract or cease manufacture and resell for scrap or salvage value or proceed in any other reasonable manner.

§ 2—705. Seller's Stoppage of Delivery in Transit or Otherwise.

(1) The seller may stop delivery of goods in the possession of a carrier or other bailee when he discovers the buyer to be insolvent (Section 2—702) and may stop delivery of carload, truckload, planeload or larger shipments of express or freight when the buyer repudiates or fails to make a payment due before delivery or if for any other reason the seller has a right to withhold or reclaim the goods.

(2) As against such buyer the seller may stop delivery until

(a) receipt of the goods by the buyer; or

(b) acknowledgment to the buyer by any bailee of the goods except a carrier that the bailee holds the goods for the buyer; or

(c) such acknowledgment to the buyer by a carrier by reshipment or as warehouseman; or

(d) negotiation to the buyer of any negotiable document of title covering the goods.

(3) (a) To stop delivery the seller must so notify as to enable the bailee by reasonable diligence to prevent delivery of the goods.

(b) After such notification the bailee must hold and deliver the goods according to the directions of the seller but the seller is liable to the bailee for any ensuing charges or damages.

(c) If a negotiable document of title has been issued for goods the bailee is not obliged to obey a notification to stop until surrender of the document.

(d) A carrier who has issued a non-negotiable bill of lading is not obliged to obey a notification to stop received from a person other than the consignor.

§ 2—706. Seller's Resale Including Contract for Resale.

(1) Under the conditions stated in Section 2—703 on seller's remedies, the seller may resell the goods concerned or the undelivered balance thereof. Where the resale is made in good faith and in a commercially reasonable manner the seller may recover the difference between the resale price and the contract price together with any incidental damages allowed under the provisions of this Article (Section 2—710), but less expenses saved in consequence of the buyer's breach.

(2) Except as otherwise provided in subsection (3) or unless otherwise agreed resale may be at public or private sale including sale by way of one or more contracts to sell or of identification to an existing contract of the seller. Sale may be as a unit or in parcels and at any time and place and on any terms but every aspect of the sale including the method, manner, time, place and terms must be commercially reasonable. The resale must be reasonably identified as referring to the broken contract, but it is not necessary that the goods be in existence or that any or all of them have been identified to the contract before the breach.

(3) Where the resale is at private sale the seller must give the buyer reasonable notification of his intention to resell.

(4) Where the resale is at public sale

(a) only identified goods can be sold except where there is a recognized market for a public sale of futures in goods of the kind; and

(b) it must be made at a usual place or market for public sale if one is reasonably available and except in the case of goods which are perishable or threaten to decline in value speedily the seller must give the buyer reasonable notice of the time and place of the resale; and

(c) if the goods are not to be within the view of those attending the sale the notification of sale must state the place where the goods are located and provide for their reasonable inspection by prospective bidders; and

(d) the seller may buy.

(5) A purchaser who buys in good faith at a resale takes the goods free of any rights of the original buyer even though the seller fails to comply with one or more of the requirements of this section.

(6) The seller is not accountable to the buyer for any profit made on any resale. A person in the position of a seller (Section 2—707) or a buyer who has rightfully rejected or justifiably revoked acceptance must account for any excess over the amount of his security interest, as hereinafter defined (subsection (3) of Section 2—711).

§ 2—707. "Person in the Position of a Seller".

(1) A "person in the position of a seller" includes as against a principal an agent who has paid or become responsible for the price of goods on behalf of his principal or anyone who otherwise holds a security interest or other right in goods similar to that of a seller.

(2) A person in the position of a seller may as provided in this Article withhold or stop delivery (Section 2—705) and resell (Section 2—706) and recover incidental damages (Section 2—710).

§ 2—708. Seller's Damages for Non-Acceptance or Repudiation.

(1) Subject to subsection (2) and to the provisions of this Article with respect to proof of market price (Section 2—

723), the measure of damages for non-acceptance or repudiation by the buyer is the difference between the market price at the time and place for tender and the unpaid contract price together with any incidental damages provided in this Article (Section 2—710), but less expenses saved in consequence of the buyer's breach.

(2) If the measure of damages provided in subsection (1) is inadequate to put the seller in as good a position as performance would have done then the measure of damages is the profit (including reasonable overhead) which the seller would have made from full performance by the buyer, together with any incidental damages provided in this Article (Section 2—710), due allowance for costs reasonably incurred and due credit for payments or proceeds of resale.

§ 2—709. Action for the Price.

(1) When the buyer fails to pay the price as it becomes due the seller may recover, together with any incidental damages under the next section, the price

(a) of goods accepted or of conforming goods lost or damaged within a commercially reasonable time after risk of their loss has passed to the buyer; and

(b) of goods identified to the contract if the seller is unable after reasonable effort to resell them at a reasonable price or the circumstances reasonably indicate that such effort will be unavailing.

(2) Where the seller sues for the price he must hold for the buyer any goods which have been identified to the contract and are still in his control except that if resale becomes possible he may resell them at any time prior to the collection of the judgment. The net proceeds of any such resale must be credited to the buyer and payment of the judgment entitles him to any goods not resold.

(3) After the buyer has wrongfully rejected or revoked acceptance of the goods or has failed to make a payment due or has repudiated (Section 2—610), a seller who is held not entitled to the price under this section shall nevertheless be awarded damages for non-acceptance under the preceding section.

§ 2—710. Seller's Incidental Damages.

Incidental damages to an aggrieved seller include any commercially reasonable charges, expenses or commissions incurred in stopping delivery, in the transportation, care and custody of goods after the buyer's breach, in connection with return or resale of the goods or otherwise resulting from the breach.

§ 2—711. Buyer's Remedies in General; Buyer's Security Interest in Rejected Goods.

(1) Where the seller fails to make delivery or repudiates or the buyer rightfully rejects or justifiably revokes acceptance then with respect to any goods involved, and with respect to the whole if the breach goes to the whole contract (Section 2—612), the buyer may cancel and whether or not he has done so may in addition to recovering so much of the price as has been paid

(a) "cover" and have damages under the next section as to all the goods affected whether or not they have been identified to the contract; or

(b) recover damages for non-delivery as provided in this Article (Section 2—713).

(2) Where the seller fails to deliver or repudiates the buyer may also

(a) if the goods have been identified recover them as provided in this Article (Section 2—502); or

(b) in a proper case obtain specific performance or replevy the goods as provided in this Article (Section 2—716).

(3) On rightful rejection or justifiable revocation of acceptance a buyer has a security interest in goods in his possession or control for any payments made on their price and any expenses reasonably incurred in their inspection, receipt, transportation, care and custody and may hold such goods and resell them in like manner as an aggrieved seller (Section 2—706).

§ 2—712. "Cover"; Buyer's Procurement of Substitute Goods.

(1) After a breach within the preceding section the buyer may "cover" by making in good faith and without unreasonable delay any reasonable purchase of or contract to purchase goods in substitution for those due from the seller.

(2) The buyer may recover from the seller as damages the difference between the cost of cover and the contract price together with any incidental or consequential damages as hereinafter defined (Section 2—715), but less expenses saved in consequence of the seller's breach.

(3) Failure of the buyer to effect cover within this section does not bar him from any other remedy.

§ 2—713. Buyer's Damages for Non-Delivery or Repudiation.

(1) Subject to the provisions of this Article with respect to proof of market price (Section 2—723), the measure of damages for non-delivery or repudiation by the seller is the difference between the market price at the time when the buyer learned of the breach and the contract price together with any incidental and consequential damages provided in this Article (Section 2—715), but less expenses saved in consequence of the seller's breach.

(2) Market price is to be determined as of the place for tender or, in cases of rejection after arrival or revocation of acceptance, as of the place of arrival.

§ 2—714. Buyer's Damages for Breach in Regard to Accepted Goods.

(1) Where the buyer has accepted goods and given notification (subsection (3) of Section 2—607) he may recover as damages for any non-conformity of tender the loss resulting in the ordinary course of events from the seller's breach as determined in any manner which is reasonable.

(2) The measure of damages for breach of warranty is the difference at the time and place of acceptance between the value of the goods accepted and the value they would have had if they had been as warranted, unless special circumstances show proximate damages of a different amount.

(3) In a proper case any incidental and consequential damages under the next section may also be recovered.

§ 2—715. Buyer's Incidental and Consequential Damages.

(1) Incidental damages resulting from the seller's breach include expenses reasonably incurred in inspection, receipt, transportation and care and custody of goods rightfully rejected, any commercially reasonable charges, expenses or commissions in connection with effecting cover and any other reasonable expense incident to the delay or other breach.

(2) Consequential damages resulting from the seller's breach include

(a) any loss resulting from general or particular requirements and needs of which the seller at the time of contracting had reason to know and which could not reasonably be prevented by cover or otherwise; and

(b) injury to person or property proximately resulting from any breach of warranty.

§ 2—716. Buyer's Right to Specific Performance or Replevin.

(1) Specific performance may be decreed where the goods are unique or in other proper circumstances.

(2) The decree for specific performance may include such terms and conditions as to payment of the price, damages, or other relief as the court may deem just.

(3) The buyer has a right of replevin for goods identified to the contract if after reasonable effort he is unable to effect cover for such goods or the circumstances reasonably indicate that such effort will be unavailing or if the goods have been shipped under reservation and satisfaction of the security interest in them has been made or tendered.

§ 2—717. Deduction of Damages From the Price.

The buyer on notifying the seller of his intention to do so may deduct all or any part of the damages resulting from any breach of the contract from any part of the price still due under the same contract.

§ 2—718. Liquidation or Limitation of Damages; Deposits.

(1) Damages for breach by either party may be liquidated in the agreement but only at an amount which is reasonable in the light of the anticipated or actual harm caused by the breach, the difficulties of proof of loss, and the inconvenience or nonfeasibility of otherwise obtaining an adequate remedy. A term fixing unreasonably large liquidated damages is void as a penalty.

(2) Where the seller justifiably withholds delivery of goods because of the buyer's breach, the buyer is entitled to restitution of any amount by which the sum of his payments exceeds

(a) the amount to which the seller is entitled by virtue of terms liquidating the seller's damages in accordance with subsection (1), or

(b) in the absence of such terms, twenty per cent of the value of the total performance for which the buyer is obligated under the contract or $500, whichever is smaller.

(3) The buyer's right to restitution under subsection (2) is subject to offset to the extent that the seller establishes

(a) a right to recover damages under the provisions of this Article other than subsection (1), and

(b) the amount or value of any benefits received by the buyer directly or indirectly by reason of the contract.

(4) Where a seller has received payment in goods their reasonable value or the proceeds of their resale shall be treated as payments for the purposes of subsection (2); but if the seller has notice of the buyer's breach before reselling goods received in part performance, his resale is subject to the conditions laid down in this Article on resale by an aggrieved seller (Section 2—706).

§ 2—719. Contractual Modification or Limitation of Remedy.

(1) Subject to the provisions of subsections (2) and (3) of this section and of the preceding section on liquidation and limitation of damages,

(a) the agreement may provide for remedies in addition to or in substitution for those provided in this Article and may limit or alter the measure of damages recoverable under this Article, as by limiting the buyer's remedies to return of the goods and repayment of the price or to repair and replacement of non-conforming goods or parts; and

(b) resort to a remedy as provided is optional unless the remedy is expressly agreed to be exclusive, in which case it is the sole remedy.

(2) Where circumstances cause an exclusive or limited remedy to fail of its essential purpose, remedy may be had as provided in this Act.

(3) Consequential damages may be limited or excluded unless the limitation or exclusion is unconscionable. Limitation of consequential damages for injury to the person in the case of consumer goods is prima facie unconscionable but limitation of damages where the loss is commercial is not.

§ 2—720. Effect of "Cancellation" or "Rescission" on Claims for Antecedent Breach.

Unless the contrary intention clearly appears, expressions of "cancellation" or "rescission" of the contract or the like shall not be construed as a renunciation or discharge of any claim in damages for an antecedent breach.

§ 2—721. Remedies for Fraud.

Remedies for material misrepresentation or fraud include all remedies available under this Article for non-fraudulent breach. Neither rescission or a claim for rescission of the contract for sale nor rejection or return of the goods shall bar or be deemed inconsistent with a claim for damages or other remedy.

§ 2—722. Who Can Sue Third Parties for Injury to Goods.

Where a third party so deals with goods which have been identified to a contract for sale as to cause actionable injury to a party to that contract

(a) a right of action against the third party is in either party to the contract for sale who has title to or a security interest or a special property or an insurable interest in the goods; and if the goods have been destroyed or converted a right of action is also in the party who either bore the risk of loss under the contract for sale or has since the injury assumed that risk as against the other;

(b) if at the time of the injury the party plaintiff did not bear the risk of loss as against the other party to the contract for sale and there is no arrangement between them for disposition of the recovery, his suit or settlement is, subject to his own interest, as a fiduciary for the other party to the contract;

(c) either party may with the consent of the other sue for the benefit of whom it may concern.

§ 2—723. Proof of Market Price: Time and Place.

(1) If an action based on anticipatory repudiation comes to trial before the time for performance with respect to some or all of the goods, any damages based on market price (Section 2—708 or Section 2—713) shall be determined according to the price of such goods prevailing at the time when the aggrieved party learned of the repudiation.

(2) If evidence of a price prevailing at the times or places described in this Article is not readily available the price prevailing within any reasonable time before or after the time described or at any other place which in commercial judgment or under usage of trade would serve as a reasonable substitute for the one described may be used, making any proper allowance for the cost of transporting the goods to or from such other place.

(3) Evidence of a relevant price prevailing at a time or place other than the one described in this Article offered by one party is not admissible unless and until he has given the other party such notice as the court finds sufficient to prevent unfair surprise.

§ 2—724. Admissibility of Market Quotations.

Whenever the prevailing price or value of any goods regularly bought and sold in any established commodity market is in issue, reports in official publications or trade journals or in newspapers or periodicals of general circulation published as the reports of such market shall be admissible in evidence. The circumstances of the preparation of such a report may be shown to affect its weight but not its admissibility.

§ 2—725. Statute of Limitations in Contracts for Sale.

(1) An action for breach of any contract for sale must be commenced within four years after the cause of action has accrued. By the original agreement the parties may reduce the period of limitation to not less than one year but may not extend it.

(2) A cause of action accrues when the breach occurs, regardless of the aggrieved party's lack of knowledge of the breach. A breach of warranty occurs when tender of delivery is made, except that where a warranty explicitly extends to future performance of the goods and discovery of the breach must await the time of such performance the cause of action accrues when the breach is or should have been discovered.

(3) Where an action commenced within the time limited by subsection (1) is so terminated as to leave available a remedy by another action for the same breach such other action may be commenced after the expiration of the time limited and within six months after the termination of the first action unless the termination resulted from voluntary discontinuance or from dismissal for failure or neglect to prosecute.

(4) This section does not alter the law on tolling of the statute of limitations nor does it apply to causes of action which have accrued before this Act becomes effective.

C Spanish Equivalents for Important Legal Terms in English

Abandoned property: bienes abandonados
Acceptance: aceptación; consentimiento; acuerdo
Acceptor: aceptante
Accession: toma de posesión; aumento; accesión
Accommodation indorser: avalista de favor
Accommodation party: firmante de favor
Accord: acuerdo; convenio; arregio
Accord and satisfaction: transacción ejecutada
Act of state doctrine: doctrina de acto de gobierno
Administrative law: derecho administrativo
Administrative process: procedimiento o metódo administrativo
Administrator: administrador (-a)
Adverse possession: posesión de hecho susceptible de proscripción adquisitiva
Affirmative action: acción afirmativa
Affirmative defense: defensa afirmativa
After-acquired property: bienes adquiridos con posterioridad a un hecho dado
Agency: mandato; agencia
Agent: mandatorio; agente; representante
Agreement: convenio; acuerdo; contrato
Alien corporation: empresa extranjera
Allonge: hojas adicionales de endosos
Answer: contestación de la demande; alegato
Anticipatory repudiation: anuncio previo de las partes de su imposibilidad de cumplir con el contrato
Appeal: apelación; recurso de apelación
Appellate jurisdiction: jurisdicción de apelaciones
Appraisal right: derecho de valuación
Arbitration: arbitraje
Arson: incendio intencional
Articles of partnership: contrato social
Artisan's lien: derecho de retención que ejerce al artesano
Assault: asalto; ataque; agresión
Assignment of rights: transmisión; transferencia; cesión
Assumption of risk: no resarcimiento por exposición voluntaria al peligro
Attachment: auto judicial que autoriza el embargo; embargo

Bailee: depositario
Bailment: depósito; constitución en depósito
Bailor: depositante
Bankruptcy trustee: síndico de la quiebra
Battery: agresón; física
Bearer: portador; tenedor
Bearer instrument: documento al portador
Bequest or legacy: legado (de bienes muebles)
Bilateral contract: contrato bilateral
Bill of lading: conocimiento de embarque; carta de porte
Bill of Rights: declaración de derechos
Binder: póliza de seguro provisoria; recibo de pago a cuenta del precio
Blank indorsement: endoso en blanco
Blue sky laws: leyes reguladoras del comercio bursátil
Bond: título de crédito; garantía; cación
Bond indenture: contrato de emisión de bonos; contrato del ampréstito
Breach of contract: incumplimiento de contrato
Brief: escrito; resumen; informe
Burglary: violación de domicilio
Business judgment rule: regla de juicio comercial
Business tort: agravio comercial

Case law: ley de casos; derecho casuístico
Cashier's check: cheque de caja
Causation in fact: causalidad en realdad
Cease-and-desist order: orden para cesar y desistir
Certificate of deposit: certificado de depósito
Certified check: cheque certificado
Charitable trust: fideicomiso para fines benéficos
Chattel: bien mueble
Check: cheque
Chose in action: derecho inmaterial; derecho de acción
Civil law: derecho civil
Close corporation: sociedad de un solo accionista o de un grupo restringido de accionistas
Closed shop: taller agremiado (emplea solamente a miembros de un gremio)

Closing argument: argumento al final
Codicil: codicilo
Collateral: guarantía; bien objeto de la guarantía real
Comity: cortesía; cortesía entre naciones
Commercial paper: instrumentos negociables; documentos a valores commerciales
Common law: derecho consuetudinario; derecho común; ley común
Common stock: acción ordinaria
Comparative negligence: negligencia comparada
Compensatory damages: daños y perjuicios reales o compensatorios
Concurrent conditions: condiciones concurrentes
Concurrent jurisdiction: competencia concurrente de varios tribunales para entender en una misma causa
Concurring opinion: opinión concurrente
Condition: condición
Condition precedent: condición suspensiva
Condition subsequent: condición resolutoria
Confiscation: confiscación
Confusion: confusión; fusión
Conglomerate merger: fusión de firmas que operan en distintos mercados
Consent decree: acuerdo entre las partes aprobado por un tribunal
Consequential damages: daños y perjuicios indirectos
Consideration: consideración; motivo; contraprestación
Consolidation: consolidación
Constructive delivery: entrega simbólica
Constructive trust: fideicomiso creado por aplicación de la ley
Consumer protection law: ley para proteger el consumidor
Contract: contrato
Contract under seal: contrato formal o sellado
Contributory negligence: negligencia de la parte actora
Conversion: usurpación; conversión de valores
Copyright: derecho de autor
Corporation: sociedad anómina; corporación; persona juridica
Co-sureties: cogarantes
Counterclaim: reconvención; contrademanda
Counteroffer: contraoferta
Course of dealing: curso de transacciones
Course of performance: curso de cumplimiento
Covenant: pacto; garantía; contrato
Covenant not to sue: pacto or contrato a no demandar
Covenant of quiet enjoyment: garantía; del uso y goce pacífico del inmueble
Creditors' composition agreement: concordato preventivo
Crime: crimen; delito; contravención
Criminal law: derecho penal
Cross-examination: contrainterrogatorio
Cure: cura; cuidado; derecho de remediar un vicio contractual
Customs receipts: recibos de derechos aduaneros

Damages: daños; indemnización por daños y perjuicios
Debit card: tarjeta de dé bito
Debtor: deudor
Debt securities: seguridades de deuda
Deceptive advertising: publicidad engañosa
Deed: escritura; título; acta translativa de domino
Defamation: difamación
Delegation of duties: delegación de obligaciones
Demand deposit: depósito a la vista
Depositions: declaración de un testigo fuera del tribunal
Devise: legado; deposición testamentaria (bienes inmuebles)
Directed verdict: veredicto según orden del juez y sin participación activa del jurado
Direct examination: interrogatorio directo; primer interrogatorio
Disaffirmance: repudiación; renuncia; anulación
Discharge: descargo; liberación; cumplimiento
Disclosed principal: mandante revelado
Discovery: descubrimiento; producción de la prueba
Dissenting opinion: opinión disidente
Dissolution: disolución; terminación
Diversity of citizenship: competencia de los tribunales federales para entender en causas cuyas partes intervinientes son cuidadanos de distintos estados
Divestiture: extinción premature de derechos reales
Dividend: dividendo
Docket: orden del día; lista de causas pendientes
Domestic corporation: sociedad local
Draft: orden de pago; letrade cambio
Drawee: girado; beneficiario
Drawer: librador
Duress: coacción; violencia

Easement: servidumbre
Embezzlement: desfalco; malversación
Eminent domain: poder de expropiación
Employment discrimination: discriminación en el empleo
Entrepreneur: empresario
Environmental law: ley ambiental
Equal dignity rule: regla de dignidad egual
Equity security: tipo de participación en una sociedad
Estate: propiedad; patrimonio; derecho
Estop: impedir; prevenir
Ethical issue: cuestión ética
Exclusive jurisdiction: competencia exclusiva
Exculpatory clause: cláusula eximente
Executed contract: contrato ejecutado
Execution: ejecución; cumplimiento
Executor: albacea
Executory contract: contrato aún no completamente consumado
Executory interest: derecho futuro
Express contract: contrato expreso
Expropriation: expropriación

Federal question: caso federal
Fee simple: pleno dominio; dominio absoluto
Fee simple absolute: dominio absoluto
Fee simple defeasible: dominio sujeta a una condición resolutoria
Felony: crimen; delito grave
Fictitious payee: beneficiario ficticio
Fiduciary: fiduciaro

Firm offer: oferta en firme
Fixture: inmueble por destino, incorporación a anexación
Floating lien: gravamen continuado
Foreign corporation: sociedad extranjera; U.S. sociedad constituída en otro estado
Forgery: falso; falsificación
Formal contract: contrato formal
Franchise: privilegio; franquicia; concesión
Franchisee: persona que recibe una concesión
Franchisor: persona que vende una concesión
Fraud: fraude; dolo; engaño
Future interest: bien futuro

Garnishment: embargo de derechos
General partner: socio comanditario
General warranty deed: escritura translativa de domino con garantía de título
Gift: donación
Gift *causa mortis*: donación por causa de muerte
Gift *inter vivos*: donación entre vivos
Good faith: buena fe
Good faith purchaser: comprador de buena fe

Holder: tenedor por contraprestación
Holder in due course: tenedor legítimo
Holographic will: testamento olográfico
Homestead exemption laws: leyes que exceptúan las casas de familia de ejecución por duedas generales
Horizontal merger: fusión horizontal

Identification: identificación
Implied-in-fact contract: contrato implícito en realidad
Implied warranty: guarantía implícita
Implied warranty of merchantability: garantía implícita de vendibilidad
Impossibility of performance: imposibilidad de cumplir un contrato
Imposter: imposter
Incidental beneficiary: beneficiario incidental; beneficiario secundario
Incidental damages: daños incidentales
Indictment: auto de acusación; acusación
Indorsee: endorsatario
Indorsement: endoso
Indorser: endosante
Informal contract: contrato no formal; contrato verbal
Information: acusación hecha por el ministerio público
Injunction: mandamiento; orden de no innovar
Innkeeper's lien: derecho de retención que ejerce el posadero
Installment contract: contrato de pago en cuotas
Insurable interest: interés asegurable
Intended beneficiary: beneficiario destinado
Intentional tort: agravio; cuasi-delito intencíónal
International law: derecho internacinal
Interrogatories: preguntas escritas sometidas por una parte a la otra o a un testigo
***Inter vivos* trust:** fideicomiso entre vivos
Intestacy laws: leyes de la condición de morir intestado
Intestate: intestado
Investment company: compañia de inversiones
Issue: emisión

Joint tenancy: derechos conjuntos en un bien inmueble en favor del beneficiario sobreviviente
Judgment *n.o.v.*: juicio no obstante veredicto
Judgment rate of interest: interés de juicio
Judicial process: acto de procedimiento; proceso jurídico
Judicial review: revisión judicial
Jurisdiction: jurisdicción

Larceny: robo; hurto
Law: derecho; ley; jurisprudencia
Lease: contrato de locación; contrato de alquiler
Leasehold estate: bienes forales
Legal rate of interest: interés legal
Legatee: legatario
Letter of credit: carta de crédito
Levy: embargo; comiso
Libel: libelo; difamación escrita
Life estate: usufructo
Limited partner: comanditario
Limited partnership: sociedad en comandita
Liquidation: liquidación; realización
Lost property: objetos perdidos

Majority opinion: opinión de la mayoría
Maker: persona que realiza u ordena; librador
Mechanic's lien: gravamen de constructor
Mediation: mediación; intervención
Merger: fusión
Mirror image rule: fallo de reflejo
Misdemeanor: infracción; contravención
Mislaid property: bienes extraviados
Mitigation of damages: reducción de daños
Mortgage: hypoteca
Motion to dismiss: excepción parentoria
Mutual fund: fondo mutual

Negotiable instrument: instrumento negociable
Negotiation: negociación
Nominal damages: daños y perjuicios nominales
Novation: novación
Nuncupative will: testamento nuncupativo

Objective theory of contracts: teoria objetiva de contratos
Offer: oferta
Offeree: persona que recibe una oferta
Offeror: oferente
Order instrument: instrumento o documento a la orden
Original jurisdiction: jurisdicción de primera instancia
Output contract: contrato de producción

Parol evidence rule: regla relativa a la prueba oral
Partially disclosed principal: mandante revelado en parte
Partnership: sociedad colectiva; asociación; asociación de participación
Past consideration: causa o contraprestación anterior
Patent: patente; privilegio
Pattern or practice: muestra o práctica

Payee: beneficiario de un pago
Penalty: pena; penalidad
Per capita: por cabeza
Perfection: perfeción
Performance: cumplimiento; ejecución
Personal defenses: excepciones personales
Personal property: bienes muebles
Per stirpes: por estirpe
Plea bargaining: regateo por un alegato
Pleadings: alegatos
Pledge: prenda
Police powers: poderes de policia y de prevención del crimen
Policy: póliza
Positive law: derecho positivo; ley positiva
Possibility of reverter: posibilidad de reversión
Precedent: precedente
Preemptive right: derecho de prelación
Preferred stock: acciones preferidas
Premium: recompensa; prima
Presentment warranty: garantía de presentación
Price discrimination: discriminación en los precios
Principal: mandante; principal
Privity: nexo jurídico
Privity of contract: relación contractual
Probable cause: causa probable
Probate: verificación; verificación del testamento
Probate court: tribunal de sucesiones y tutelas
Proceeds: resultados; ingresos
Profit: beneficio; utilidad; lucro
Promise: promesa
Promisee: beneficiario de una promesa
Promisor: promtente
Promissory estoppel: impedimento promisorio
Promissory note: pagaré; nota de pago
Promoter: promotor; fundador
Proximate cause: causa inmediata o próxima
Proxy: apoderado; poder
Punitive, or exemplary, damages: daños y perjuicios punitivos o ejemplares

Qualified indorsement: endoso con reservas
Quasi contract: contrato tácito o implícito
Quitclaim deed: acto de transferencia de una propiedad por finiquito, pero sin ninguna garantía sobre la validez del título transferido

Ratification: ratificación
Real property: bienes inmuebles
Reasonable doubt: duda razonable
Rebuttal: refutación
Recognizance: promesa; compromiso; reconocimiento
Recording statutes: leyes estatales sobre registros oficiales
Redress: reporacíon
Reformation: rectificación; reforma; corrección
Rejoinder: dúplica; contrarréplica
Release: liberación; renuncia a un derecho
Remainder: substitución; reversión
Remedy: recurso; remedio; reparación
Replevin: acción reivindicatoria; reivindicación
Reply: réplica
Requirements contract: contrato de suministro
Rescission: rescisión
Res judicata: cosa juzgada; res judicata
Respondeat superior: responsabilidad del mandante o del maestro
Restitution: restitución
Restrictive indorsement: endoso restrictivo
Resulting trust: fideicomiso implícito
Reversion: reversión; sustitución
Revocation: revocación; derogación
Right of contribution: derecho de contribución
Right of reimbursement: derecho de reembolso
Right of subrogation: derecho de subrogación
Right-to-work law: ley de libertad de trabajo
Robbery: robo
Rule 10b-5: Regla 10b-5

Sale: venta; contrato de compreventa
Sale on approval: venta a ensayo; venta sujeta a la aprobación del comprador
Sale or return: venta con derecho de devolución
Sales contract: contrato de compraventa; boleto de compraventa
Satisfaction: satisfacción; pago
Scienter: a sabiendas
S corporation: S corporación
Secured party: acreedor garantizado
Secured transaction: transacción garantizada
Securities: volares; titulos; seguridades
Security agreement: convenio de seguridad
Security interest: interés en un bien dado en garantía que permite a quien lo detenta venderlo en caso de incumplimiento
Service mark: marca de identificación de servicios
Shareholder's derivative suit: acción judicial entablada por un accionista en nombre de la sociedad
Signature: firma; rúbrica
Slander: difamación oral; calumnia
Sovereign immunity: immunidad soberana
Special indorsement: endoso especial; endoso a la orden de una person en particular
Specific performance: ejecución precisa, según los términos del contrato
Spendthrift trust: fideicomiso para pródigos
Stale check: cheque vencido
***Stare decisis*:** acatar las decisiones, observar los precedentes
Statutory law: derecho estatutario; derecho legislado; derecho escrito
Stock: acciones
Stock warrant: certificado para la compra de acciones
Stop-payment order: orden de suspensión del pago de un cheque dada por el librador del mismo
Strict liability: responsabilidad uncondicional
Summary judgment: fallo sumario

Tangible property: bienes corpóreos
Tenancy at will: inguilino por tiempo indeterminado (según la voluntad del propietario)
Tenancy by sufferance: posesión por tolerancia
Tenancy by the entirety: locación conyugal conjunta
Tenancy for years: inguilino por un término fijo
Tenancy in common: specie de copropiedad indivisa

Tender: oferta de pago; oferta de ejecución
Testamentary trust: fideicomiso testamentario
Testator: testador (-a)
Third party beneficiary contract: contrato para el beneficio del tercero-beneficiario
Tort: agravio; cuasi-delito
Totten trust: fideicomiso creado por un depósito bancario
Trade acceptance: letra de cambio aceptada
Trademark: marca registrada
Trade name: nombre comercial; razón social
Traveler's check: cheque del viajero
Trespass to land: ingreso no authorizado a las tierras de otro
Trespass to personal property: violación de los derechos posesorios de un tercero con respecto a bienes muebles
Trust: fideicomiso; trust

Ultra vires: ultra vires; fuera de la facultad (de una sociedad anónima)
Unanimous opinion: opinión unámine
Unconscionable contract or clause: contrato leonino; cláusula leonino
Underwriter: subscriptor; asegurador
Unenforceable contract: contrato que no se puede hacer cumplir
Unilateral contract: contrato unilateral
Union shop: taller agremiado; empresa en la que todos los empleados son miembros del gremio o sindicato
Universal defenses: defensas legitimas o legales
Usage of trade: uso comercial
Usury: usura

Valid contract: contrato válido
Venue: lugar; sede del proceso
Vertical merger: fusión vertical de empresas
Voidable contract: contrato anulable
Void contract: contrato nulo; contrato inválido, sin fuerza legal
Voir dire: examen preliminar de un testigo a jurado por el tribunal para determinar su competencia
Voting trust: fideicomiso para ejercer el derecho de voto

Waiver: renuncia; abandono
Warranty of habitability: garantía de habitabilidad
Watered stock: acciones diluídos; capital inflado
White-collar crime: crimen administrativo
Writ of attachment: mandamiento de ejecución; mandamiento de embargo
Writ of *certiorari*: auto de avocación; auto de certiorari
Writ of execution: auto ejecutivo; mandamiento de ejecutión
Writ of mandamus: auto de mandamus; mandamiento; orden judicial

Glossary

A

Abandoned property Property with which the owner has voluntarily parted, with no intention of recovering it.

Acceleration clause A clause in an installment contract that provides for all future payments to become due immediately upon the failure to tender timely payments or upon the occurrence of a specified event.

Acceptance (1) In contract law, the offeree's notification to the offeror that the offeree agrees to be bound by the terms of the offeror's proposal. Although historically the terms of acceptance had to be the mirror image of the terms of the offer, the UCC provides that even modified terms of the offer in a definite expression of acceptance constitute a contract. (2) In commercial paper law, the drawee's signed agreement to pay a draft when presented.

Acceptor The person (the drawee) who accepts a draft and who engages to be primarily responsible for its payment.

Accession Increasing the value of property by adding something (such as adding a diamond to a ring).

Accord and satisfaction An agreement and payment (or other performance) between two parties, one of whom has a right of action against the other. After the agreement has been made and payment or other performance has been tendered, the "accord and satisfaction" is complete.

Actual malice Real and demonstrable evil intent. In a defamation suit, a statement made about a public figure normally must be made with actual malice (with either knowledge of its falsity or a reckless disregard of the truth) for liability to be incurred.

Adhesion contract A "standard form" contract, such as that between a large retailer and a consumer, in which the stronger party dictates the terms.

Adjudication Rendering a judicial decision. In the administrative process, the proceeding in which an administrative law judge hears and decides on issues that arise when an administrative agency charges a person or a firm with violating a law or regulation enforced by the agency.

Administrative agency A federal or state government agency established to perform a specific function. Administrative agencies are authorized by legislative acts to make and enforce rules relating to the purpose for which they were established.

Administrative law A body of law created by administrative agencies—such as the Securities and Exchange Commission and the Federal Trade Commission—in the form of rules, regulations, orders, and decisions in order to carry out their duties and responsibilities. This law can initially be enforced by these agencies outside the judicial process.

Administrative law judge One who presides over an administrative agency hearing and who has the power to administer oaths, take testimony, rule on questions of evidence, and make determinations of fact.

Administrative process The procedure used by administrative agencies in the administration of law.

Administrator One who is appointed by a court to handle the probate (disposition) of a person's estate if that person dies intestate (without a will).

Adverse possession The acquisition of title to real property by occupying it openly, without the consent of the owner, for a period of time specified by state statutes. The occupation must be actual, open, notorious, exclusive, and in opposition to all others, including the owner.

Affidavit A written or printed voluntary statement of facts, confirmed by the oath or affirmation of the party making it and made before a person having the authority to administer the oath or affirmation.

After-acquired property Property of the debtor that is acquired after a secured creditor's interest in the debtor's property has been created.

Agency A relationship between two persons in which, by agreement or otherwise, one is bound by the words and acts of the other. The former is a principal; the latter is an agent.

Agent A person authorized by another to act for or in place of him or her.

Agreement A meeting of two or more minds. Often used as a synonym for contract.

Alien corporation A designation in the United States for a corporation formed in another country but doing business in the United States.

Alienation The process of transferring land.

Answer Procedurally, a defendant's response to the complaint.

Antitrust law The body of federal and state laws and statutes protecting trade and commerce from unlawful restraints, price discrimination, price fixing, and monopolies. The principal federal antitrust statutes are

the Sherman Act (1890), the Clayton Act (1914), and the Federal Trade Commission Act (1914).
Appellant The party who takes an appeal from one court to another; sometimes referred to as the petitioner.
Appellee The party against whom an appeal is taken—that is, the party who opposes setting aside or reversing the judgment; sometimes referred to as the respondent.
Appraisal right A dissenting shareholder's right, if he or she objects to an extraordinary transaction of the corporation (such as a merger or consolidation), to have his or her shares appraised and to be paid the fair market value of his or her shares by the corporation.
Appropriate bargaining unit A group of employees defined by their job duties, skill levels, and other occupational characteristics and covered by a collective bargaining agreement.
Articles of incorporation The document filed with the appropriate governmental agency, usually the secretary of state, when a business is incorporated; state statutes usually prescribe what kind of information must be contained in the articles of incorporation.
Articles of partnership A written agreement that sets forth each partner's rights in, and obligations to, the partnership.
Artisan's lien A possessory lien given to a person who has made improvements and added value to another person's personal property as security for payment for services performed.
Assault Any word or action intended to make another person fearful of immediate physical harm; a reasonably believable threat.
Assignment The act of transferring to another all or part of one's rights arising under a contract.
Assumption of risk A doctrine whereby a plaintiff may not recover for injuries or damages suffered from risks he or she knows of and assents to. A defense against negligence that can be used when the plaintiff has knowledge of and appreciates a danger and voluntarily exposes himself or herself to the danger.
Attachment (1) In a secured transaction, the process by which a security interest in the property of another becomes enforceable. (2) The legal process of seizing another's property under a court order to secure satisfaction of a judgment yet to be rendered.
Authenticate To sign a record, or with the intent to sign a record, to execute, or to adopt an electronic sound, symbol, or the like to link with the record. See *record*.
Authorization card A card signed by an employee that gives a union permission to act on his or her behalf in negotiations with management once a majority of the employees have signed the cards.
Automatic stay A suspension of all judicial proceedings upon the occurrence of an independent event. Under the Bankruptcy Code, the moment a petition to commence bankruptcy proceedings is filed, all litigation by creditors against a debtor and the debtor's property is suspended.

B

Bailee One to whom goods are entrusted by a bailor.
Bailment An agreement in which goods or personal property of one person (a bailor) are entrusted to another (a bailee), who is obligated to return the bailed property to the bailor or dispose of it as directed.
Bailor One who entrusts goods to a bailee.
Bait-and-switch advertising Advertising a product at a very attractive price (the "bait") and then informing the consumer, once he or she is in the store, that the advertised product is either not available or is of poor quality; the customer is then urged to purchase ("switched" to) a more expensive item.
Battery The unprivileged, intentional touching of another.
Bearer A person in the possession of an instrument payable to bearer or indorsed in blank.
Bearer instrument A negotiable instrument that is payable to the bearer, including instruments payable to "cash."
Bequest A gift by will of personal property.
Bilateral contract A contract that includes the exchange of a promise for a promise.
Binder A written, temporary insurance policy.
Blue laws State or local laws that make the performance of commercial activities on Sunday illegal.
Blue sky law State law that regulates the offer and sale of securities.
Bona fide occupational qualification (BFOQ) Under Title VII of the Civil Rights Act of 1964, identifiable characteristics reasonably necessary to the normal operation of a particular business. These characteristics can include gender, national origin, and religion, but not race.
Bond A certificate that evidences a corporate debt. It is a security that involves no ownership interest in the issuing corporation.
Bond indenture A contract between the issuer of a bond and the bondholder.
Breach of contract Failure, without legal excuse, of a promisor to perform the obligations of a contract.
Brief A written summary or statement prepared by one side in a lawsuit to explain its case to the judge; a typical brief has a facts summary, a law summary, and an argument about how the law applies to the facts.
Business ethics Ethics in a business context; a consensus of what constitutes right or wrong behavior in the world of business and the application of moral principles to situations that arise in a business setting.
Business invitees Those people, such as customers or clients, who are invited onto business premises by the owner of those premises for business purposes.
Business judgment rule A rule that immunizes corporate management from liability for actions that are undertaken in good faith, when the actions are within both the power of the corporation and the authority of management to make.
Business necessity defense A showing that an employment practice that discriminates against members of a protected class is related to job performance.
Business tort A tort occurring within the business context; typical business torts are wrongful interference with the business or contractual relationships of others and unfair competition.
Bylaws A set of governing rules or regulations adopted by a corporation or other association.

C

Case law Rules of law announced in court decisions. Case law includes the cases that interpret judicial precedents, statutes, regulations, and constitutional provisions.

Categorical imperative A concept developed by the philosopher Immanuel Kant as an ethical guideline for behavior. In deciding whether an action is right or wrong, or desirable or undesirable, a person should evaluate the action in terms of what would happen if everybody else in the same situation, or category, acted the same way.

Causation in fact An act or omission without which an event would not have occurred.

Cease-and-desist order An administrative or judicial order prohibiting a person or business firm from conducting activities that an agency or court has deemed illegal.

Certificate of deposit (CD) An instrument evidencing a promissory acknowledgment by a bank of a receipt of money with an engagement to repay it.

Certificate of incorporation The primary document that evidences corporate existence (referred to as articles of incorporation in some states).

Check A draft drawn by a drawer ordering the drawee bank or financial institution to pay a certain amount of money to the holder on demand.

Civil law The branch of law dealing with the definition and enforcement of all private or public rights, as opposed to criminal matters.

Civil law system A system of law derived from that of the Roman Empire and based on a code rather than case law; the predominant system of law in the nations of continental Europe and the nations that were once their colonies. In the United States, Louisiana is the only state that has a civil law system.

Click-on agreement This occurs when a buyer, completing a transaction on a computer, is required to indicate his or her assent to be bound by the terms of an offer by clicking on a button that says, for example, "I agree." Sometimes referred to as a *click-on license* or a *click-wrap agreement.*

Close corporation A corporation whose shareholders are limited to a small group of persons, often including only family members. The rights of shareholders of a close corporation usually are restricted regarding the transfer of shares to others.

Closed shop A firm that requires union membership by its workers as a condition of employment. The closed shop was made illegal by the Taft-Hartley Act of 1947.

Closing argument An argument made after the plaintiff and defendant have rested their cases.

Codicil A written supplement or modification to a will. Codicils must be executed with the same formalities as a will.

Collateral In a broad sense, any property used as security for a loan. Under the UCC, property of a debtor in which a creditor has an interest or a right.

Collateral promise A secondary promise that is ancillary to a principal transaction or primary contractual relationship, such as a promise made by one person to pay the debts or discharge the duties of another if the latter fails to perform. A collateral promise normally must be in writing to be enforceable.

Collecting bank Any bank handling an item for collection, except the payor bank.

Collective bargaining The process by which labor and management negotiate the terms and conditions of employment, including such things as hours and workplace conditions.

Commercial impracticability A doctrine under which a seller may be excused from performing a contract when (1) a contingency occurs, (2) the contingency's occurrence makes performance impracticable, and (3) the nonoccurrence of the contingency was a basic assumption on which the contract was made.

Common carrier An individual or firm offering transportation services (via truck, railroad, ship, and so on) to the public.

Common law That body of law developed from custom or judicial decisions in English and U.S. courts, not attributable to a legislature.

Common situs picketing A demonstration at a secondary employer's work site by workers involved in a labor dispute with a primary employer.

Common stock Shares of ownership in a corporation that are lowest in priority with respect to payment of dividends and distribution of the corporation's assets upon dissolution.

Community property A form of concurrent ownership of property in which each spouse owns an undivided one-half interest in most property acquired by the husband or wife during the course of marriage.

Comparative negligence A theory under which the liability for injuries resulting from negligent acts is shared by all persons who were guilty of negligence (including the injured party), on the basis of each person's proportionate carelessness.

Compensatory damages A money award equivalent to the actual value of injuries or damages sustained by the aggrieved party.

Complaint The pleading made by a plaintiff or a charge made by the state alleging wrongdoing on the part of the defendant.

Computer crime Any wrongful act that is directed against computers and computer parts, or wrongful use or abuse of computers or software.

Computer information Information in electronic form obtained from or through use of a computer, or that is in digital or an equivalent form capable of being processed by a computer.

Consent Voluntary agreement to a proposition or an act of another. A concurrence of wills.

Consequential damages Special damages that compensate for a loss that is not direct or immediate (for example, lost profits). The special damages must have been reasonably foreseeable at the time the breach or injury occurred.

Consideration That which motivates the exchange of promises or performance in a contractual agreement. The consideration, which must be present to make the contract legally binding, must result in a detriment to the promisee (something of legal value, legally sufficient, and bargained for) or a benefit to the promisor.

Consignment A transaction in which an owner of goods (the consignor) delivers the goods to another (the

consignee) for the consignee to sell. The consignee pays the consignor for the goods when the consignee sells the goods.
Consolidation A process whereby two or more corporations join to become a completely new corporation. The original corporations cease to exist, and the new corporation acquires all their assets and liabilities.
Constructive delivery An act equivalent to the physical delivery of property that cannot be physically delivered because of difficulty or impossibility.
Constructive eviction Depriving a person of the possession of rental property that he or she leases by rendering the premises unfit or unsuitable for occupancy.
Constructive trust A trust created by operation of law against one who wrongfully has obtained or holds a legal right to property that the person should not, in equity and good conscience, hold and enjoy.
Continuation statement A statement that, if filed within six months prior to the expiration date of the original financing statement, continues the effectiveness of the original statement for another five years. The effectiveness of a financing statement can be continued in the same manner indefinitely.
Contract A set of promises constituting an agreement between parties, giving each a legal duty to the other and also the right to seek a remedy for the breach of the promises/duties owed to each. The elements of an enforceable contract are competent parties, a proper or legal purpose, consideration (an exchange of promises/duties), and mutuality of agreement and of obligation.
Contractual capacity The capacity required by the law for a party who enters into a contract to be bound by that contract.
Conversion The wrongful taking, using, or retaining possession of personal property that belongs to another.
"Cooling off" law A law that allows a buyer a period of time (typically three days) in which to cancel a door-to-door sales contract.
Copyright The exclusive right of "authors" to publish, print, or sell an intellectual production for a statutory period of time. A copyright has the same monopolistic nature as a patent or trademark, but it differs in that it applies exclusively to works of art, literature, and other works of authorship (including computer programs).
Cost-benefit analysis A decision-making technique that involves weighing the costs of a given action against the benefits of the action.
Co-surety A joint surety. One who assumes liability jointly with another surety for the payment of an obligation.
Counteradvertising New advertising that is undertaken pursuant to a Federal Trade Commission order for the purpose of correcting earlier false claims that were made about a product.
Counteroffer An offeree's response to an offer in which the offeree rejects the original offer and at the same time makes a new offer.
Course of dealing A sequence of previous conduct between the parties to a particular transaction that establishes a common basis for their understanding.
Course of performance The conduct that occurs under the terms of a particular agreement; such conduct indicates what the parties to an agreement intended it to mean.
Covenant not to sue An agreement to substitute a contractual obligation for some other type of action.
Covenant of quiet enjoyment A promise by the grantor of real property that the grantee will not be disturbed in his or her possession of the property by the grantor or anyone having a lien against the property or superior title to it.
Cover Under the UCC, a remedy of the buyer that allows the buyer, on the seller's breach, to purchase the goods from another seller and substitute them for the goods due under the contract. If the cost of cover exceeds the cost of the contract goods, the breaching seller will be liable to the buyer for the difference.
Creditors' composition agreement An agreement formed between a debtor and his or her creditors in which the creditors agree to accept a lesser sum than that owed by the debtor in full satisfaction of the debt.
Crime A wrong against society proclaimed in a statute and, if committed, punishable by society through fines and/or imprisonment—and, in some cases, death.
Criminal law Law that governs and defines those actions that are crimes and that subject the convicted offender to punishment imposed by the government.
Cross-examination The questioning of an opposing witness during the trial.
Cure The right of a party who tenders nonconforming performance to correct his or her performance within the contract period.
Cybernotary A legally recognized certification authority that issues the keys for digital signatures, identifies their owners, certifies their validity, and serves as a repository for public keys.

D

Damages Money sought as a remedy for a harm suffered.
Debtor A person who owes payment or performance of a secured obligation.
Deceptive advertising Advertising that misleads consumers.
Deed A document by which title to property is passed.
Defamation Anything published or publicly spoken that causes injury to another's good name, reputation, or character.
Default The failure to observe a promise or discharge an obligation. The term is commonly used to mean the failure to pay a debt when it is due.
Default judgment A judgment entered by a clerk or court against a party who has failed to appear in court to answer or defend against a claim that has been brought against him or her by another party.
Default Rules Under the Uniform Computer Information Transaction Act, rules that apply only in the absence of an agreement between contracting parties to the contrary.
Defendant One against whom a lawsuit is brought; the accused person in a criminal proceeding.
Defense That which a defendant offers and alleges in an action or suit as a reason why the plaintiff should not recover or establish what he or she seeks.

Delegation The transfer of a contractual duty to a third party. The party delegating the duty (the delegator) to the third party (the delegatee) is still obliged to perform on the contract if the delegatee fails to perform.
Demand deposit Funds (accepted by a bank) subject to immediate withdrawal, in contrast to a time deposit, which requires that a depositor wait a specific time before withdrawing or pay a penalty for early withdrawal.
Depositary bank The first bank to which an item is transferred for collection, even though it may also be the payor bank.
Deposition A generic term that refers to any evidence verified by oath. As a legal term, it is often limited to the testimony of a witness taken under oath before a trial, with the opportunity of cross-examination.
Destination contract A contract for the sale of goods in which the seller assumes liability for any losses or damage to the goods until they are tendered at the destination specified in the contract.
Devise To make a gift of real property by will.
Direct examination The examination of a witness by the attorney who calls the witness to the stand to testify on behalf of the attorney's client.
Disaffirmance The repudiation of an obligation.
Discharge The termination of one's obligation. In contract law, discharge occurs when the parties have fully performed their contractual obligations or when events, conduct of the parties, or operation of the law releases the parties from further performance.
Disclosed principal A principal whose identity and existence as a principal is known by a third person at the time a transaction is conducted by an agent.
Discovery A method by which opposing parties may obtain information from each other to prepare for trial. Generally governed by rules of procedure, but may be controlled by the court.
Disparagement of property Economically injurious falsehoods made about another's product or property. A general term for torts that are more specifically referred to as slander of quality or slander of title.
Disparate-impact discrimination In an employment context, discrimination that results from certain employer practices or procedures that, although not discriminatory on their face, have a discriminatory effect.
Disparate-treatment discrimination In an employment context, intentional discrimination against individuals on the basis of color, gender, national origin, race, or religion.
Dissolution The formal disbanding of a partnership or a corporation. A corporation can be dissolved by (1) the legislature in the state of incorporation, (2) the expiration of time stated in the certificate of incorporation, (3) agreement of the shareholders and the board of directors, (4) unanimous act by all shareholders, or (5) court order.
Diversity of citizenship Under Article III, Section 2, of the Constitution, a basis for federal court jurisdiction over a lawsuit between citizens of different states.
Dividend A distribution to shareholders, disbursed in proportion to the number of shares held.
Document of title Paper exchanged in the regular course of business that evidences the right to possession of goods (for example, a bill of lading or warehouse receipt).
Domestic corporation In a given state, a corporation that does business in, and is organized under the laws of, that state.
Dominion The rights to own, use, and possess property.
Double jeopardy A situation occurring when a person is tried twice for the same criminal offense; prohibited by the Fifth Amendment to the Constitution.
Draft Any instrument drawn on a drawee (such as a bank) that orders the drawee to pay a certain sum of money.
Drawee The person who is ordered to pay a draft or check. With a check, a financial institution is always the drawee.
Drawer A person who initiates a draft (including a check), thereby ordering the drawee to pay.
Duress Unlawful pressure brought to bear on a person, overcoming that person's free will and causing him or her to do (or refrain from doing) what he or she otherwise would not (or would) have done.
Duty of care The duty of all persons, as established by tort law, to exercise a reasonable amount of care in their dealings with others. Failure to exercise due care, which is normally determined by the "reasonable person standard," constitutes the tort of negligence.

E

E-Agent A computer program, or electronic or other automated means used to independently initiate an action or to respond to electronic messages or performances without review by an individual, according to the Uniform Computer Information Transactions Act.
Easement A nonpossessory right to use another's property.
Eighty-day cooling-off period A provision of the Taft-Hartley Act that allows federal courts to issue injunctions against strikes that might create a national emergency.
E-Commerce Business transacted in cyberspace.
Economic strike A strike called by a union to pressure an employer to make concessions relating to hours, wages, or other terms of employment.
Emancipation In regard to minors, the act of being freed from parental control. The parents renounce parental duties and surrender the right to the custody and earnings of the minor.
Embezzlement The fraudulent appropriation of money or other property by a person to whom the money or property has been entrusted.
Eminent domain The power of a government to take land for public use from private citizens for just compensation.
Employment-at-will doctrine A common law doctrine under which employer-employee contracts are considered to be "at will"—that is, either party may terminate an employment contract at any time and for any reason, unless the contract specifies otherwise. Exceptions are frequently made on the basis of a federal statute, an implied employment contract, or public policy.
Employment discrimination Treating employees or job applicants unequally on the basis of race, color,

gender, national origin, religion, or age; prohibited by Title VII of the Civil Rights Act of 1964 and other statutes.

Enabling legislation Statutes enacted by Congress that authorize the creation of an administrative agency and specify the name, composition, and powers of the agency being created.

Entrapment In criminal law, a defense in which the defendant claims that he or she was induced by a public official—usually an undercover agent or police officer—to commit a crime that he or she would otherwise not have committed.

Environmental impact statement (EIS) A statement required by the National Environmental Policy Act for any major federal action that will significantly affect the quality of the environment. The statement must analyze the action's impact on the environment and alternative actions that might be taken.

Equal dignity rule In most states, a rule stating that express authority given to an agent must be in writing if the contract to be made on behalf of the principal is required to be in writing.

Escheat The transfer of property to the state when the owner of the property dies without heirs.

E-Signature An electronic sound, symbol, or process attached to or logically associated with a record and executed or adopted by a person with the intent to sign the record, according to the Uniform Electronic Transactions Act.

Estate in property All of the property owned by a person, including real estate and personal property. In bankruptcy law, an estate in property may include property transferred within 180 days of the filing of a petition to declare bankruptcy.

Estop To bar, impede, or preclude.

Estray statutes Statutes dealing with finders' rights in property when the true owners are unknown.

Ethics Moral principles and values applied to social behavior.

Eviction Depriving a person of the possession of property that he or she leases.

Exclusionary rule In criminal procedure, a rule under which any evidence that is obtained in violation of the accused's constitutional rights guaranteed by the Fourth, Fifth, and Sixth Amendments, as well as any evidence derived from illegally obtained evidence, will not be admissible in court.

Exclusive-dealing contract An agreement under which a producer of goods agrees to sell its goods exclusively through one distributor.

Exculpatory clause A clause that releases a party (to a contract) from liability for his or her wrongful acts.

Executed contract A contract that has been completely performed by both parties.

Executive agency An administrative agency within the executive branch of government. At the federal level, executive agencies are those within the cabinet departments.

Executor A person appointed by a testator to see that his or her will is administered appropriately.

Executory contract A contract that has not as yet been fully performed.

Executory interest A future interest, held by a person other than the grantor, that either cuts short or begins some time after the natural termination of the preceding estate.

Express contract A contract that is oral and/or written (as opposed to an implied contract).

Express warranty A promise, ancillary to an underlying sales agreement, that is included in the written or oral terms of the sales agreement under which the promisor assures the quality, description, or performance of the goods.

Extension clause A clause in a time instrument extending the instrument's date of maturity. An extension clause is the reverse of an acceleration clause.

F

Featherbedding Requiring the employment of more workers than necessary to do a particular job.

Federal Reserve System A network of twelve central banks headed by a board of governors, with the advice of the Federal Advisory Council and the Federal Open Market Committee, to give the United States an elastic currency, supervise and regulate banking activities, and facilitate the flow and discounting of commercial paper. All national banks and state-chartered banks that voluntarily join the system are members.

Federal question A question that pertains to the U.S. Constitution, acts of Congress, or treaties. A federal question provides jurisdiction for federal courts. This jurisdiction arises from Article III, Section 2, of the Constitution.

Fee simple A form of property ownership entitling the property owner to use, possess, or dispose of the property as he or she chooses during his or her lifetime. Upon death, the interest in the property descends to the owner's heirs.

Fee simple absolute An estate or interest in land with no time, disposition, or descendibility limitations.

Fee simple defeasible An estate that can be taken away (by the prior grantor) upon the occurrence or nonoccurrence of a specified event.

Felony A crime—such as arson, murder, rape, or robbery—that carries the most severe sanctions, usually ranging from one year in a state or federal prison to the forfeiture of one's life.

Fictitious payee A payee on a negotiable instrument whom the maker or drawer does not intend to have an interest in the instrument. Indorsements by fictitious payees are not forgeries under negotiable instruments law.

Fiduciary As a noun, a person having a duty created by his or her undertaking to act primarily for another's benefit in matters connected with the undertaking. As an adjective, a relationship founded upon trust and confidence.

Final order The final decision of an administrative agency on an issue. If no appeal is taken, or if the cas is not reviewed or considered anew by the agency commission, the administrative law judge's initial order becomes the final order of the agency.

Financing statement A document prepared by a secured creditor, and filed with the appropriate state or local official, to give notice to the public that the creditor claims an interest in collateral belonging to a certain named debtor. The financing statement must be signed by the debtor, contain the addresses of both the debtor and creditor, and describe the collateral by type or item.

Firm offer An offer (by a merchant) that is irrevocable without consideration for a period of time (not longer than three months). A firm offer by a merchant must be in writing and must be signed by the offeror.

Fixture A thing that was once personal property but that has become attached to real property in such a way that it takes on the characteristics of real property and becomes part of that real property.

Floating lien A security interest retained in collateral even when the collateral changes in character, classification, or location.

Foreign corporation In a given state, a corporation that does business in the state without being incorporated therein.

Forgery The fraudulent making or altering of any writing in a way that changes the legal rights and liabilities of another.

Form The manner observed in creating a legal agreement, as opposed to the substance of the agreement.

Formal contract An agreement or contract that by law requires for its validity a specific form, such as executed under seal.

Fraudulent misrepresentation (fraud) Any misrepresentation, either by misstatement or omission of a material fact, knowingly made with the intention of deceiving another and on which a reasonable person would and does rely to his or her detriment.

Fungible goods Goods that are alike by physical nature, by agreement, or by trade usage. Examples of fungible goods are wheat, oil, and wine that are identical in type and quality.

Future interest An interest in real property that is not at present possessory but will or may be possessory in the future.

G

Garnishment A legal process whereby a creditor appropriates the debtor's property or wages that are in the hands of a third party.

General partner In a limited partnership, a partner who assumes responsibility for the management of the partnership and liability for all partnership debts.

Gift Any voluntary transfer of property made without consideration, past or present.

Gift *causa mortis* A gift made in contemplation of death. If the donor does not die of that ailment, the gift is revoked.

Gift *inter vivos* A gift made during one's lifetime and not in contemplation of imminent death, in contrast to a gift *causa mortis*.

Good faith purchaser A purchaser who buys without notice of any circumstance that would put a person of ordinary prudence on inquiry as to whether the seller has valid title to the goods being sold.

Group boycott The boycott of a particular person or firm by a group of competitors; prohibited under the Sherman Act.

Guarantor One who agrees to satisfy the debt of another (the debtor) only if and when the debtor fails to pay the debt. A guarantor's liability is thus secondary.

Guaranty contract An agreement in which a guarantor agrees to pay the debt of another only if and when the debtor fails to pay.

H

Holder The person who, by the terms of a negotiable instrument, is legally entitled to payment on it.

Holder in due course (HDC) Any holder who acquires a negotiable instrument for value; in good faith; and without notice that the instrument is overdue, that it has been dishonored, or that any defense or claim to it exists on the part of any person.

Holographic will A will written entirely in the signer's handwriting and usually not witnessed.

Homestead exemption A law allowing an owner to designate his or her house and adjoining land as a homestead and thus exempt it from liability for his or her general debt.

Hot-cargo agreement An illegal agreement in which employers voluntarily agree with unions not to handle, use, or deal in non–union-produced goods of other employers.

I

Identification In the sale of goods, the express designation of the goods provided for in the contract.

Implied warranty A warranty that the law implies through either the situation of the parties or the nature of the transaction.

Implied warranty of habitability A presumed promise by the landlord that rented residential premises are fit for human habitation—that is, free of violations of building and sanitary codes.

Implied warranty of merchantability A presumed promise by a merchant seller of goods that the goods are reasonably fit for the general purpose for which they are sold, are properly packaged and labeled, and are of proper quality.

Implied-in-fact contract A contract formed in whole or in part from the conduct of the parties (as opposed to an express contract).

Impossibility of performance A doctrine under which a party to a contract is relieved of his or her duty to perform when performance becomes impossible or totally impracticable (through no fault of either party).

Imposter One who, with the intent to deceive, pretends to be somebody else.

Incidental beneficiary A third party who incidentally benefits from a contract but whose benefit was not the reason the contract was formed; an incidental beneficiary has no rights in a contract and cannot sue the promisor if the contract is breached.

Incidental damages Damages resulting from a breach of contract, including all reasonable expenses incurred because of the breach.

Independent contractor One who works for, and receives payment from, an employer but whose working conditions and methods are not controlled by the employer. An independent contractor is not an employee but may be an agent.

Independent regulatory agency An administrative agency that is not considered part of the government's executive branch and is not subject to the authority of the president. Independent agency officials cannot be removed without cause.

Indorsement A signature placed on an instrument or a document of title for the purpose of transferring one's ownership in the instrument or document of title.

Informal contract A contract that does not require a specified form or formality for its validity.

Initial order In the context of administrative law, an agency's disposition in a matter other than a rulemaking. An administrative law judge's initial order becomes final unless is is appealed.

Innkeeper's lien A common law lien allowing the innkeeper to take the personal property of a guest, brought into the hotel, as security for nonpayment of the guest's bill (debt).

Insolvent When a person's liabilities exceed the value of his or her assets.

Installment contract A contract in which payments due are made periodically. Also may allow for delivery of goods in separate lots with payment made for each.

Insurable interest An interest either in a person's life or well-being or in property that is sufficiently substantial that insuring against injury to the person or damage to the property does not amount to a mere wagering (betting) contract.

Insurance A contract in which, for a stipulated consideration, one party agrees to compensate the other for loss on a specific subject by a specified peril.

Integrated contract A written contract that constitutes the final expression of the parties' agreement. If a contract is integrated, evidence extraneous to the contract that contradicts or alters the meaning of the contract in any way is inadmissible.

Intended beneficiary A third party for whose benefit a contract is formed; intended beneficiaries can sue the promisor if such a contract is breached.

Intentional tort A wrongful act knowingly committed.

***Inter vivos* trust** A trust created by the grantor (settlor) and effective during the grantor's lifetime (that is, a trust not established by a will).

Intermediary bank Any bank to which an item is transferred in the course of collection, except the depositary or payor bank.

International law The law that governs relations among nations. International customs and treaties are generally considered to be two of the most important sources of international law.

Interrogatory A series of written questions for which written answers are prepared and then signed under oath by a party to a lawsuit (the plaintiff or the defendant).

Intestacy laws State laws determining the division and descent of the property of one who dies intestate (without a will).

Intestate As a noun, one who has died without having created a valid will. As an adjective, the state of having died without a will.

Issue The first transfer, or delivery, of an instrument to a holder.

J

Joint and several liability A doctrine under which a plaintiff may sue, and collect a judgment from, any of several jointly liable defendants, regardless of that particular defendant's degree of fault. In partnership law, joint and several liability means a third party may sue one or more of the partners separately or all of them together, at his or her option. This is true even if the partner did not participate in, ratify, or know about whatever it was that gave rise to the cause of action.

Joint liability Shared liability. In partnership law, partners incur joint liability for partnership obligations and debts. For example, if a third party sues a partner on a partnership debt, the partner has the right to insist that the other partners be sued with him or her.

Joint tenancy The ownership interest of two or more co-owners of property whereby each owns an undivided portion of the property. Upon the death of one of the joint tenants, his or her interest automatically passes to the others and cannot be transferred by the will of the deceased.

Judgment *n.o.v.* A judgment notwithstanding the verdict; may be entered by the court for the plaintiff (or the defendant) after there has been a jury verdict for the defendant (or the plaintiff).

Jurisdiction The authority of a court to hear and decide a specific action.

L

Larceny The wrongful taking and carrying away of another person's personal property with the intent to permanently deprive the owner of the property. Some states classify larceny as either grand or petit, depending on the property's value.

Law A body of rules of conduct with legal force and effect, prescribed by the controlling authority (the government) of a society.

Lease A transfer by the landlord of real property to the tenant for a period of time for consideration (usually the payment of rent). Upon termination of the lease, the property reverts to the lessor.

Lease agreement In regard to the lease of goods, an agreement in which one person (the lessor) agrees to transfer the right to the possession and use of property to another person (the lessee) in exchange for rental payments.

Leasehold estate An estate held by a tenant under a lease. The tenant has a qualified right to possess and use the land.

Legacy A gift of personal property under a will.

Legatee A person who inherits personal property under a will.

Lessee A person who acquires the right to the possession and use of another's property in exchange for rental payments.

Lessor A person who sells the right to the possession and use of property to another in exchange for rental payments.

Libel Defamation in written form.

License A revocable privilege to enter onto another's real property.

Lien An encumbrance upon a property to satisfy or protect a claim for payment of a debt.

Life estate An interest in land that exists only for the duration of the life of some person, usually the holder of the estate.

Limited liability company (LLC) A hybrid form of business enterprise that offers the limited liability of the coporation but the tax advantages of a partnership.

Limited liability limited partnership (LLLP) A type of limited partnership. The difference between a limited partnership and an LLLP is that the liability of the general partner in an LLLP is the same as the liability of the limited partner. That is, the liability of all partners is limited to the amount of their investments in the firm.

Limited liability partnership A form of partnership that allows professionals to enjoy the tax benefits of a partnership while avoiding personal liability for the malpractice of other partners.

Limited partner In a limited partnership, a partner who contributes capital to the partnership but has no right to participate in the management and operation of the business. The limited partner assumes no liability for partnership debts beyond the capital contributed.

Limited partnership A partnership consisting of one or more general partners (who manage the business and are liable to the full extent of their personal assets for debts of the partnership) and of one or more limited partners (who contribute only assets and are liable only up to the amount contributed by them).

Liquidated damages An amount, stipulated in the contract, that the parties to a contract believe to be a reasonable estimation of the damages that will occur in the event of a breach.

Liquidation The sale of the assets of a business or an individual for cash and the distribution of the cash received to creditors, with the balance going to the owner(s).

Lockout The closing of a workplace to employees by an employer to gain an advantage in collective bargaining negotiations.

Lost property Property with which the owner has involuntarily parted and then cannot find or recover.

M

Mailbox rule A rule providing that an acceptance of an offer becomes effective upon dispatch (upon being placed in a mailbox), if mail is, expressly or impliedly, an authorized means of communication of acceptance to the offeror.

Maker One who issues a promissory note or certificate of deposit (that is, one who promises to pay a certain sum to the holder of the note or CD).

Market concentration A situation that exists when a small number of firms share the market for a particular good or service. For example, if the four largest grocery stores in Chicago accounted for 80 percent of all retail food sales, the market clearly would be concentrated in those four firms.

Market power The power of a firm to control the market for its product. A monopoly has the greatest degree of market power.

Mass-market license An e-contract that is presented with a package of computer information in the form of a *click-on license* or a *shrink-wrap license.*

Mechanic's lien A statutory lien on the real property of another, created to ensure priority of payment for work performed and materials furnished in erecting or repairing a building or other structure.

Merchant Under the UCC, a person who deals in goods of the kind involved (see UCC 2–104).

Merger A process by which one corporation (the surviving corporation) acquires all the assets and liabilities of another corporation (the merged corporation). The shareholders of the merged corporation receive either payment for their shares or shares in the surviving corporation.

Minimum wage The lowest hourly wage that an employer may legally pay an employee.

Mirror image rule A common law rule that requires, for a valid contractual agreement, that the terms of the offeree's acceptance adhere exactly to the terms of the offeror's offer.

Misdemeanor A lesser crime than a felony, punishable by a fine or imprisonment for up to one year in other than a state or federal penitentiary.

Mislaid property Property with which the owner has voluntarily parted and then cannot find or recover.

Monopoly A term generally used to describe a market for which there is a single seller.

Monopoly power An extreme amount of market power.

Mortgage A written instrument giving a creditor (the mortgagee) an interest (lien) in the debtor's (mortgagor's) property as security for a debt.

Mortgagee The creditor who takes the security interest under the mortgage agreement.

Mortgagor The debtor who pledges collateral in a mortgage agreement.

Motion for a directed verdict A motion for the judge to direct a verdict for the moving party on the grounds that the other party has not produced sufficient evidence to support his or her claim.

Motion to dismiss A pleading in which a defendant admits the facts as alleged by the plaintiff but asserts that the plaintiff's claim fails to state a cause of action (that is, has no basis in law) or that there are other grounds on which a suit should be dismissed. Also called a demurrer.

N

Necessaries Necessities required for life, such as food, shelter, clothing, and medical attention; normally, necessaries are also considered to include items or services appropriate to an individual's circumstances and condition in life.

Negligence The failure to exercise the standard of care that a reasonable person would exercise in similar circumstances.

Negotiable instrument A written and signed unconditional promise or order to pay a specified sum of money on demand or at a definite time to order (to a specific person or entity) or to bearer.

Negotiation The transferring of a negotiable instrument to another in such form that the transferee becomes a holder.

Nondiscrimination rule The requirement that an employer treat a union the same way it would treat any other entity with regard to on-site contact with workers.

Notice-and-comment rulemaking An administrative rulemaking procedure that involves the publication of a notice of proposed rulemaking in the *Federal Register,* a comment period for interested parties to express their views on the proposed rule, and the publication of the agency's final rule of the *Federal Register.*

Novation The substitution, by agreement, of a new contract for an old one, with the rights under the old one being terminated. Typically, there is a substitution of a new person who is responsible for the contract and the removal of the original party's rights and duties under the contract.

O

Objective theory of contracts The view taken by American law that contracting parties shall only be bound by terms that can actually be inferred from promises made. Contract law does not examine a contracting party's subjective intent or underlying motive.

Offer An offeror's proposal to do something, which creates in the offeree accepting the offer a legal power to bind the offeror to the terms of the proposal by accepting the offer.

Offeree A person to whom an offer is made.

Offeror A person who makes an offer.

Option contract A contract under which the offeror cannot revoke his or her offer for a stipulated time period, and the offeree can accept or reject the offer during this period without fear of the offer's being made to another person. The offeree must give consideration for the option (the irrevocable offer) to be enforceable.

Order for relief A court's grant of assistance to a complainant. In the context of bankruptcy, relief consists of discharging a complainant's debts.

Order instrument A negotiable instrument that is payable to the order of a specified person.

Overdraft A check written on a checking account in which there are insufficient funds to cover the check.

P

Parol evidence rule A rule of contracts under which a court will not receive into evidence prior statements or contemporaneous oral statements that contradict a written agreement when the court finds that the written agreement was intended by the parties to be a final, complete, and unambiguous expression of their agreement.

Partially disclosed principal A principal whose identity is unknown by a third person, but the third person knows that the agent is or may be acting for a principal at the time the contract is made.

Partnership An association of two or more persons to carry on, as co-owners, a business for profit.

Past consideration An act done before the contract is made, which ordinarily, by itself, cannot be consideration for a later promise to pay for the act.

Patent A government grant that gives an inventor the exclusive right or privilege to make, use, or sell his or her invention for a limited time period. The word patent usually refers to some invention and designates either the instrument by which patent rights are evidenced or the patent itself.

Payee A person to whom an instrument is made payable.

Payor bank A bank on which an item is payable as drawn (or is payable as accepted).

Penalty A sum inserted into a contract, not as a measure of compensation for its breach but rather as punishment for a default. The agreement as to the amount will not be enforced, and recovery will be limited to actual damages.

Per capita A Latin term meaning "per person." In the law governing estate distribution, a method of distributing the property of an intestate's estate by which all the heirs receive equal shares.

***Per se* violation** A type of anticompetitive agreement—such as a price-fixing agreement—that is considered to be so injurious to the public that there is no need to determine whether it actually injures market competition; rather, it is in itself (*per se*) a violation of the Sherman Act.

Per stirpes A Latin term meaning "by the roots." In the law governing estate distribution, a method of distributing an intestate's estate in which a class or group of distributees take the share to which their deceased ancestor would have been entitled.

Perfection The method by which a secured party obtains a priority by notice that his or her security interest in the debtor's collateral is effective against the debtor's subsequent creditors. Usually accomplished by filing a financing statement at a location set out in the state statute.

Performance In contract law, the fulfillment of one's duties arising under a contract with another; the normal way of discharging one's contractual obligations.

Periodic tenancy A lease interest in land for an indefinite period involving payment of rent at fixed intervals, such as week to week, month to month, or year to year.

Personal defenses Defenses that can be used to avoid payment to an ordinary holder of a negotiable instrument. Personal defenses cannot be used to avoid payment to a holder in due course (HDC) or (under the shelter principle) to a holder through an HDC.

Personal property Property that is movable; any property that is not real property.

Petty offense In criminal law, the least serious kind of criminal offense, such as a traffic or building-code violation.

Picket line The presence at an employer's work site of employees or others to publicize a labor dispute and deter others from working for or doing business with the employer. Usually involves patrolling with signs.

Plaintiff One who initiates a lawsuit.

Pleadings Statements by the plaintiff and the defendant that detail the facts, charges, and defenses.

Policy In insurance law, the contract of indemnity against a contingent loss between the insurer and the insured.

Power of attorney A document or instrument authorizing another to act as one's agent or attorney.

Precedent A court decision that furnishes an example or authority for deciding subsequent cases in which identical or similar facts are presented.

Preemptive right Right held by shareholders that entitles them to purchase newly issued shares of a corporation's stock, equal in percentage to shares presently held, before the stock is offered to any outside buyers. Preemptive rights enable shareholders to maintain their proportionate ownership and voice in the corporation.

Preference In bankruptcy proceedings, the debtor's favoring of one creditor over others by making payments or transferring property to that creditor at the expense of the rights of other creditors in the bankruptcy estate. The bankruptcy trustee is allowed to recover payments made both voluntarily and involuntarily to one creditor in preference over another.

Preferred stock Classes of stock that have priority over common stock both as to payment of dividends and distribution of assets upon the corporation's dissolution.

Premium In insurance law, the price for insurance protection for a specified period of time.

Prenuptial agreement An agreement entered into in contemplation of marriage, specifying the rights and ownership of the parties' property.

Presentment warranties Warranties made by any person who obtains payment or acceptance of an instrument to any person who in good faith pays or accepts the instrument that (1) the party obtaining payment or acceptance is entitled to enforce the instrument, or is entitled to obtain payment or acceptance on behalf of one who is entitled to enforce it; (2) the instrument has not been altered; and (3) the person obtaining payment or acceptance has no knowledge that the signature of the drawer or maker is unauthorized.

Price discrimination Setting prices in such a way that two competing buyers pay two different prices for an identical product or service.

Price-fixing agreement Fixing—by means of an anticompetitive agreement between competitors—the prices of products or services.

***Prima facie* case** A case in which the plaintiff has produced sufficient evidence to compel his or her conclusion if the defendant produces no evidence to rebut it.

Principal In agency law, a person who, by agreement or otherwise, authorizes an agent to act on his or her behalf in such a way that the acts of the agent become binding on the principal.

Privilege In tort law, the ability to act contrary to another person's right without that person's having legal redress for such acts. Privilege may be raised as a defense to defamation.

Privity of contract The relationship that exists between the promisor and the promisee of a contract.

Probate court A court having jurisdiction over proceedings concerning the settlement of a person's estate.

Proceeds In secured-transactions law, whatever is received when the collateral is sold, exchanged, collected, or otherwise disposed of, such as insurance payments for destroyed or lost collateral.

Product liability The legal liability of manufacturers and sellers to buyers, users, and sometimes bystanders for injuries or damages suffered because of defects in goods purchased.

Profit In real property law, the right to enter upon and remove things from the property of another (for example, the right to enter onto a person's land and remove sand).

Promise A declaration that binds the person who makes it (promisor) to do or not to do a certain act. The person to whom the promise is made (promisee) has a right to expect or demand the performance of some particular thing.

Promisee A person to whom a promise is made.

Promisor A person who makes a promise.

Promissory estoppel When a promisor reasonably expects a promise to induce definite and substantial action or forbearance by the promisee, and it does induce such action or forbearance in reliance thereon, the promise is binding if injustice can be avoided only by enforcing it.

Promissory note A written instrument signed by a maker unconditionally promising to pay a certain sum in money to a payee or a holder on demand or on a specified date.

Promoter An entrepreneur who participates in the organization of a corporation in its formative stage, usually by issuing a prospectus, procuring subscriptions to the stock, making contract purchases, securing a charter, and the like.

Protected class A class of persons with identifiable characteristics (age, color, gender, national origin, race, and religion) who historically have been discriminated against.

Proximate cause Legal cause; exists when the connection between an act and an injury is strong enough to justify imposing liability.

Proxy In corporation law, a written agreement between a stockholder and another under which the stockholder authorizes the other to vote the stockholder's shares in a certain manner.

Puffery A salesperson's often exaggerated claims concerning the quality of property offered for sale. Such claims involve opinions rather than facts and are not considered to be legally binding promises or warranties.

Punitive damages Compensation in excess of actual or consequential damages. They are awarded in order to punish the wrongdoer and usually will be awarded only in cases involving willful or malicious misconduct.

Q

Quasi contract An obligation or contract imposed by law, in the absence of agreement, to prevent unjust enrichment. Sometimes referred to as an implied-in-law contract (a legal fiction) to distinguish it from an implied-in-fact contract.

Quitclaim deed A deed intended to pass any title, interest, or claim that the grantor may have in the premises but not professing that such title is valid and not containing any warranty.

Quorum The number of members of a decision-making body that must be present before business may be transacted.

R

Ratification The approval or validation of a previous action. In contract law, the confirmation of a voidable act (that is, an act that without ratification would not be an enforceable contractual obligation). In agency law, the confirmation by one person of an act or contract performed or entered into on his or her behalf by another, who assumed, without authority, to act as his or her agent.

Real property Immovable property consisting of land and buildings thereon. Includes things growing on the land before they are severed (such as timber), as well as fixtures.

Rebuttal The refutation of evidence introduced by an adverse party's attorney.

Receiver A court-appointed person who receives, preserves, and manages a business or other property that is involved in bankruptcy proceedings.

Record Information that is inscribed in either a tangible medium or stored in an electronic or other medium and that is retrievable, according to the Uniform Electronic Transactions Act. The Uniform Computer Information Transaction Act uses *record* instead of *writing*.

Redress Satisfaction for damage caused by the wrongdoing of another.

Reformation A court-ordered correction of a written contract so that it reflects the true intentions of the parties.

Regulation Z A set of rules promulgated by the Federal Reserve System's board of governors to implement the provisions of the Truth-in-Lending Act.

Rejoinder The defendant's answer to the plaintiff's rebuttal.

Release The relinquishment, concession, or giving up of a right, claim, or privilege, by the person in whom it exists or to whom it accrues, to the person against whom it might have been enforced or demanded.

Remainder A future interest in property, held by a person other than the grantor, that occurs at the natural termination of the preceding estate.

Remedy The relief given to innocent parties, by law or by contract, to enforce a right or to prevent or compensate for the violation of a right.

Reorganization In bankruptcy law, a plan for the readjustment of a corporation and its debt, the submission of the plan to a bankruptcy court, and the court's approval or rejection of the plan based on a determination of the feasibility of the plan.

Resale price maintenance agreement An agreement between a manufacturer and a retailer in which the manufacturer specifies the minimum retail price of its products. Resale price maintenance agreements are illegal *per se* under the Sherman Act.

Rescission A remedy whereby a contract is terminated and the parties are returned to the positions they occupied before the contract was made; may be effected through the mutual consent of the parties, by their conduct, or by the decree of a court of equity.

Respondeat superior In Latin, "Let the master respond." A principle of law whereby a principal or an employer is held liable for the wrongful acts committed by agents or employees while acting within the scope of their agency or employment.

Restitution A remedy under which a person is restored to his or her original position prior to a contract.

Restraint of trade Any conspiracy or combination that unlawfully eliminates competition or facilitates the creation of a monopoly or monopoly pricing.

Resulting trust A trust implied in law from the intentions of the parties to a given transaction.

Reversionary interest A future residuary interest retained in property by the grantor. For example, a landowner who conveys property to another for life retains a future interest in the property. When the person holding the life estate dies, the property will revert to the grantor (unless the grantor has transferred the future interest to another party).

Revocation In contract law, the withdrawal of an offer by an offeror; unless the offer is irrevocable, it can be revoked at any time prior to acceptance without liability.

Right of contribution The right of a co-surety who pays more than his or her proportionate share upon a debtor's default to recover the excess paid from other co-sureties.

Right of first refusal The right to purchase personal or real property—such as corporate shares or real estate—before the property is offered for sale to others.

Right of reimbursement The legal right of a person to be restored, repaid, or indemnified for costs, expenses, or losses incurred or expended on behalf of another.

Right of subrogation The right of a person to stand in the place of (be substituted for) another, giving the substituted party the same legal rights that the original party had.

Right-to-work law State law generally providing that employees are not to be required to join a union as a condition of receiving or retaining employment.

Risk A specified contingency or peril.

Risk management Planning that is undertaken to protect one's interest should some event threaten to undermine its security. In the context of insurance, transferring certain risks from the insured to the insurance company.

Robbery The act of forcefully and unlawfully taking personal property of any value from another; force or intimidation is usually necessary for an act of theft to be considered a robbery.

Rule of reason A test by which a court balances the reasons (such as economic efficiency) for an agreement against its potentially anticompetitive effects. In antitrust litigation, many practices are analyzed under the rule of reason.

Rulemaking The actions undertaken by administrative agencies when formally adopting new regulations or amending old ones. Rulemaking includes notifying the public of proposed rules or changes and receiving and considering the public's comments.

S

S corporation A close business corporation that has met certain requirements as set out by the Internal Revenue Code and thus qualifies for special income-tax treatment. Essentially, an S corporation is taxed the same as a partnership, but its owners enjoy the privilege of limited liability.

Sale The passing of title to property from the seller to the buyer for a price.

Sale on approval A type of conditional sale that becomes absolute only when the buyer approves, or is satisfied with, the good(s) sold. Besides express approval of goods, approval may be inferred if the buyer keeps the goods beyond a reasonable time or uses the goods in any way that is inconsistent with the seller's ownership.

Sale or return A type of conditional sale wherein title and possession pass from the seller to the buyer; however, the buyer retains the option to rescind or return the goods during a specified period even though the goods conform to the contract.

Sales contract A contract to sell goods.

Scienter Knowledge by the misrepresenting party that material facts have been falsely represented or omitted with an intent to deceive.

Seasonably Within a specified time period, or if no time is specified, within a reasonable time.

Secondary boycott A union's refusal to work for, purchase from, or handle the products of a secondary employer, with whom the union has no dispute, with the object of forcing that employer to stop doing business with the primary employer, with whom the union has a labor dispute.

Secured party A lender, seller, or any other person in whose favor there is a security interest.

Secured transaction Any transaction in which the payment of a debt is guaranteed by personal property or fixtures.

Securities Stock certificates, bonds, notes, debentures, warrants, or other documents given as evidence of an ownership interest in the corporation or as a promise of repayment by the corporation.

Security agreement The agreement that creates or provides for a security interest between the debtor and a secured party.

Security interest Every interest in personal property or fixtures that secures payment or performance of an obligation.

Seniority system In regard to employment relationships, a system in which those who have worked longest for the company are first in line for promotions, salary increases, and other benefits; they are also the last to be laid off if the work force must be reduced.

Service mark A mark used in the sale or the advertising of services, such as to distinguish the services of one person from the services of others. Titles, character names, and other distinctive features of radio and television programs may be registered as service marks.

Severance pay Funds in excess of normal wages or salary paid to an employee on termination of his or her employment.

Shareholder's derivative suit A suit brought by a shareholder to enforce a corporate cause of action against a third person.

Shelter principle The principle that the holder of a negotiable instrument who cannot qualify as a holder in due course (HDC), but who derives his or her title through an HDC, acquires the rights of an HDC.

Shipment contract A contract for the sale of goods in which the buyer assumes liability for any losses or damage to the goods on the seller's delivery of the goods to a carrier.

Short-form merger A merger between a subsidiary corporation and a parent corporation that owns at least 90 percent of the outstanding shares of each class of stock issued by the subsidiary corporation. Short-form mergers can be accomplished without the approval of the shareholders of either corporation.

Shrink-Wrap Agreement An agreement whose terms are expressed inside a box in which goods are packaged. Sometimes called a *shrink-wrap license*.

Signature The name or mark of a person, written by that person or at his or her direction. In commercial law, any name, word, or mark used with the intention to authenticate a writing constitutes a signature.

Slander Defamation in oral form.

Slander of quality Publication of false information about another's product, alleging it is not what its seller claims; also referred to as trade libel.

Slander of title The publication of a statement that denies or casts doubt upon another's legal ownership of any property, causing financial loss to that property's owner.

Small claims courts Special courts in which parties may litigate small claims (usually, claims involving $2,500 or less). Attorneys are not required in small claims courts, and in many states, attorneys are not allowed to represent the parties.

Sole proprietorship The simplest form of business, in which the owner is the business. A sole proprietor reports business income on his or her personal income tax return and is legally responsible for all debts and obligations of the business.

Specific performance An equitable remedy requiring exactly the performance that was specified in a contract. Usually granted only when money damages would be an inadequate remedy and the subject matter of the contract is unique (for example, real property).

Stale check A check, other than a certified check, that is presented for payment more than six months after its date.

Stare decisis A flexible doctrine of the courts, recognizing the value of following prior decisions (precedents) in cases similar to the one before the court; the courts' practice of being consistent with prior decisions based on similar facts.

Statute of Frauds A state statute under which certain types of contracts must be in writing to be enforceable.

Statutory law Laws enacted by a legislative body (as opposed to constitutional law, administrative law, or case law).

Stock In corporation law, an equity or ownership interest in a corporation, measured in units of shares.

Stock certificate A certificate issued by a corporation evidencing the ownership of a specified number of shares at a specified value.

Stop-payment order An order by the drawer of a draft or check directing the drawer's bank not to pay the check.

Strict liability Liability regardless of fault. In tort law, strict liability may be imposed on defendants in cases involving abnormally dangerous activities, dangerous animals, or defective products.

Sublease A lease executed by the lessee of real estate to a third person, conveying the same interest that the lessee enjoys, but for a shorter term than that held by the lessee.

Summary judgment A judgment entered by a trial court prior to trial that is based on the valid assertion by one of the parties that there are no disputed issues of fact that would necessitate a trial.
Surety One who agrees to be primarily responsible for the debt of another, such as a cosigner on a note.
Suretyship A contract in which a third party to a debtor-creditor relationship (the surety) promises that the third party will be primarily responsible for the debtor's obligation.

T

Taking Government interference with an owner's use and enjoyment of his or her property. Requires the payment of just compensation to the owner.
Tangible property Property that has physical existence (such as a car).
Target corporation The acquired corporation in a corporate takeover; a corporation to whose shareholders a tender offer is submitted.
Tenancy at sufferance Tenancy by one who, after rightfully being in possession of leased premises, continues (wrongfully) to occupy the property after the lease has been terminated. The tenant has no estate in the land and occupies it only because the person entitled to evict has not done so.
Tenancy at will The right of a tenant to remain in possession of land with permission of the landlord until either the tenant or the landlord chooses to terminate the tenancy.
Tenancy by the entirety The joint ownership of property by husband and wife. Neither party can alienate or encumber the property without the consent of the other.
Tenancy for years A lease for a specified period of time, after which the interest reverts to the grantor.
Tenancy in common Co-ownership of property in which each party owns an undivided interest that passes to his or her heirs at death.
Tender A timely offer or expression of willingness to pay a debt or perform an obligation.
Tender offer An offer by one company to buy shares in another company made directly to the shareholders.
Testamentary trust A trust that is created by will and therefore does not take effect until the death of the testator.
Testator One who makes and executes a will.
Third party beneficiary One who is not a party to a contract but for whose benefit a promise is made in the contract.
Tort Civil (as opposed to criminal) wrong not arising from a breach of contract. A breach of a legal duty owed by the defendant to the plaintiff; the breach must be the proximate cause of harm to the plaintiff.
Tortfeasor One who commits a tort.
Trade acceptance A draft drawn by the seller of goods on the purchaser and accepted by the purchaser's written promise to pay the draft. Once accepted, the purchaser becomes primarily liable to pay the draft.
Trade name A name used in commercial activity to designate a particular business, a place at which a business is located, or a class of goods. Trade names can be exclusive or nonexclusive. Examples of trade names are Sears, Safeway, and Firestone.
Trade secrets Information or processes that give a business an advantage over competitors who do not know the information or processes.
Trademark A word or symbol that has become sufficiently associated with a good (at common law) or has been registered with a government agency. Once a trademark is established, the owner has exclusive use of it and has the right to bring a legal action against those who infringe upon the protection given the trademark.
Transfer warranties Guaranties made by the indorser and transferor of a negotiable instrument to all subsequent transferees and holders who take the instrument in good faith that (1) the transferor is entitled to enforce the instrument; (2) all signatures are authentic or authorized; (3) the instrument has not been materially altered; (4) no defense or claim of any party is good against the transferor; and (5) the transferor has no knowledge of any insolvency proceedings against the maker, the acceptor, or the drawer of an unaccepted instrument.
Treasure trove Money or coin, gold, silver, or bullion found hidden in the earth or other private place, the owner of which is unknown; literally, treasure found.
Trespass to land The entry onto, above, or below the surface of land owned by another without the owner's permission or legal authorization.
Trespass to personal property The unlawful taking or harming of another's personal property; interference with another's right to the exclusive possession of his or her personal property.
Trust (1) A form of business organization somewhat similar to a corporation. Originally, the trust was a device by which several corporations that were engaged in the same general line of business combined for their mutual advantage to eliminate competition and control the market for their products. The term trust derived from the transfer of the voting power of the corporations' shareholders to the committee or board that controlled the organization. (2) An arrangement in which title to property is held by one person (a trustee) for the benefit of another (a beneficiary).
Tying arrangement An agreement between a buyer and a seller under which the buyer of a specific product or service is obligated to purchase additional products or services from the seller.

U

Ultra vires A Latin term meaning "beyond the powers." Activities of a corporation's managers that are outside the scope of the power granted them by the corporation's charter or the laws of the state of incorporation are *ultra vires* acts.
Unconscionable contract or clause A contract or clause that is void on the basis of public policy because one party, as a result of his or her disproportionate bargaining power, is forced to accept terms that are unfairly burdensome and that unfairly benefit the dominating party.
Underwriter In insurance law, the one assuming a risk in return for the payment of a premium; the insurer.

Undisclosed principal A principal whose identity is unknown by a third person, and the third person has no knowledge that the agent is acting in an agency capacity at the time the contract is made.
Undue influence Persuasion that is less than actual force but more than advice and that induces a person to act according to the will or purposes of the dominating party.
Unenforceable contract A valid contract having no legal effect or force in a court action.
Unilateral contract A contract that includes the exchange of a promise for an act.
Union shop A place of employment in which all workers, once employed, must become union members within a specified period of time as a condition of their continued employment.
Universal defenses Defenses that can be used to avoid payment to all holders of a negotiable instrument, including a holder in due course (HDC) or (under the shelter principle) a holder through an HDC. Also called real defenses.
Unreasonably dangerous In product liability, defective to the point of threatening a consumer's health or safety, dangerous beyond the expectation of the ordinary consumer, or when a less dangerous alternative is economically feasible for a manufacturer but the manufacturer fails to use it.
Usage of trade Any practice or method of dealing having such regularity of observance in a place, vocation, or trade as to justify an expectation that it will be observed with respect to the transaction in question.
Usury Charging an illegal rate of interest.
Utilitarianism An approach to ethical reasoning in which ethically correct behavior is not related to any absolute ethical or moral values but to an evaluation of the consequences of a given action on those who will be affected by it. In utilitarian reasoning, a "good" decision is one that results in the greatest good for the greatest number of people affected by the decision.

V

Valid contract A properly constituted contract having legal strength or force.
Void contract A contract having no legal force or binding effect.
Voidable contract A contract that may be legally annulled at the option of one of the parties.

W

Warranty deed A deed under which the grantor guarantees to the grantee that, among other things, the grantee will enjoy quiet possession.
Whistleblower An employee who tells the government or the press that one's employer is engaged in some unsafe or illegal activity.
White-collar crime Nonviolent crime committed by corporations and individuals. Embezzlement and commercial bribery are two examples of white-collar crime.
Wildcat strike A strike that is not authorized by the union that represents the striking workers.
Will An instrument directing what is to be done with the testator's property upon his or her death, made by the testator.
Winding up The second of two stages involved in the dissolution of a partnership or corporation. Once the firm is dissolved, it continues to exist legally until the process of winding up all business affairs (collecting and distributing the firm's assets) is complete.
Workers' compensation laws State statutes establishing an administrative procedure for compensating workers' injuries that arise on the job or in the course of employment, regardless of fault. Instead of suing the employer, an injured worker files a claim with the administrative agency or board that administers the local workers' compensation claims.
Writ of attachment A writ employed to enforce obedience to an order or judgment of the court. The writ may take the form of taking or seizing property to bring it under the control of the court.
Writ of *certiorari* A writ from a higher court asking the lower court for the record of a case.
Writ of execution A writ that puts in force a court's decree or judgment.

INDEX

E

N

O

Q

R

V

W

Y